Pro SharePoint 2013 Branding and Responsive Web Development

x

Eric Overfield

Rita Zhang

Oscar Medina

Kanwal Khipple

Apress

Pro SharePoint 2013 Branding and Responsive Web Development

ISBN-13 (pbk): 978-1-4302-5028-9

ISBN-13 (electronic): 978-1-4302-5029-6

President and Publisher: Paul Manning
Lead Editor: Chris Nelson
Technical Reviewer: Sahil Malik
Editorial Board: Steve Anglin, Mark Beckner, Ewan Buckingham, Gary Cornell, Louise Corrigan, Morgan Ertel, Jonathan Gennick, Jonathan Hassell, Robert Hutchinson, Michelle Lowman, James Markham, Matthew Moodie, Jeff Olson, Jeffrey Pepper, Douglas Pundick, Ben Renow-Clarke, Dominic Shakeshaft, Gwenan Spearing, Matt Wade, Tom Welsh
Coordinating Editor: Mark Powers
Copy Editor: Teresa Horton
Compositor: SPi Global
Indexer: SPi Global
Artist: SPi Global
Cover Designer: Anna Ishchenko

Distributed to the book trade worldwide by Springer Science+Business Media New York, 233 Spring Street, 6th Floor, New York, NY 10013. Phone 1-800-SPRINGER, fax (201) 348-4505, e-mail orders-ny@springer-sbm.com, or visit www.springeronline.com. Apress Media, LLC is a California LLC and the sole member (owner) is Springer Science + Business Media Finance Inc (SSBM Finance Inc). SSBM Finance Inc is a Delaware corporation.

For information on translations, please e-mail rights@apress.com, or visit www.apress.com.

Apress and friends of ED books may be purchased in bulk for academic, corporate, or promotional use. eBook versions and licenses are also available for most titles. For more information, reference our Special Bulk Sales–eBook Licensing web page at www.apress.com/bulk-sales.

Any source code or other supplementary materials referenced by the author in this text is available to readers at www.apress.com/9781430250289. For detailed information about how to locate your book's source code, go to www.apress.com/source-code/.

I would like to dedicate this book to Robin and my parents. Robin, thank you for your unwavering support even after all of the lost days, nights and weekends. Mom and Dad, thank you for your endless advice and encouragement.

—Eric Overfield

To my boyfriend and my parents, thank you for inspiring me to always challenge myself to be better.

—Rita Zhang

I dedicate this book to my lovely wife and daughter, who put up with my lack of "being there" during my writing experience. Every day that went by, I felt both a bit of guilt and sense of accomplishment. Without their support, understanding, and love, I wouldn't have been able to spend time contributing to this wonderful book.

—Oscar Medina

I'd like to dedicate this book to my wife, Hardip, who has provided me unwavering support and continues to push me to be a better man. Also, my two bundles of joy, Paras and Harsimran, for giving me another reason to smile every day.

—Kanwal Khipple

Contents at a Glance

Contents

About the Authors

Eric Overfield is a leading expert in SharePoint branding and user interface design. Eric, President and co-founder of PixelMill, has over 13 years of experience with web design best practices and techniques, and over 8 years of experience with SharePoint branding. Besides his in-depth knowledge of SharePoint's branding capabilities, his expertise includes general SharePoint technology, design, and architecture along with custom-coded web parts, solutions, JavaScript, HTML5, and CSS3. An active speaker and organizer of User Groups and SharePoint events as well as an active blogger (ericoverfield.com), he discusses all things SharePoint branding and UI design at @ericoverfield as well.

Rita Zhang is a Senior Consultant with Microsoft Consulting Services in Northern California. She specializes in Information Worker Solutions and Custom Application Development Technologies. She has extensive experience in working with enterprise customers to deliver end-to-end SharePoint solutions and custom-developed applications from architecture, design, and development, to deployment and production. Rita has acted as an extension to the Microsoft product group to provide proactive help to large customers to unblock deployment issues and ensure fast and smooth implementation of SharePoint technologies. Rita is the Founder and Senior Architect of SP.me, the first mobile social app for SharePoint that allows companies to enable their employees to stay connected with their team on the go. You can learn more at spmobile.me and facebook.com/spmobile.me. Rita has an active blog at http://blogs.msdn.com/b/ritazh/.

Oscar Medina is a seasoned technology consultant with over 17 years of software development experience. He runs SharePointAce Consulting Group, a boutique SharePoint consulting firm based in Northern California. His SharePoint specific experience dates back to the SharePoint Portal Server 2001. Oscar was previously at Microsoft Consulting Services, helping Fortune 1000 companies reap the benefits of the entire platform and related technologies. He has a diverse technical expertise on multiple platforms, including web development and design, n-tier app development and mobile app development on Windows Phone and the iPhone platforms. Oscar is the Founder, Senior Architect, and Creative Director of SP.me, the first mobile social app for SharePoint that allows companies to enable their employees to stay connected with their team on the go (spmobile.me). You can stay in touch with him via his blog sharepointoscar.com and @SharePointOscar.

Kanwal Khipple is a leading user experience expert within the SharePoint industry, with experience in building solutions for large intranets, extranets, and Internets all based on the Microsoft SharePoint platform. As Vice President of Consulting for BrightStarr, a digital design agency, he continues to push for user experience innovation when redesigning intranets for some of the largest brands in the world. He continues to preach about the importance of designing with usability as the primary focus. Because of his passion and his involvement in many community-driven events, including launching successful user groups in Canada and the United States, Kanwal has been recognized as a SharePoint MVP by Microsoft for the past four years (2009–2013). He also manages @sharepointbuzz, a popular SharePoint-focused Twitter account.

About the Contributing Author

Benjamin Niaulin is a geek and SharePoint MVP. He has been around the globe helping people reach their goals by simplifying SharePoint. As a Certified Trainer for well over 6 years, he has become very comfortable training and sharing his experiences.

But first of all, Benjamin is just a geek in love with SharePoint since the beginning of the 2007 version up to now, amidst the cool new features of SharePoint 2013. He has written a branding series on nothingbutsharepoint.com to help power users and designers alike get started with SharePoint branding. He has also written many other articles on multiple blogs over the Internet, including his own at bniaulin.wordpress.com.

Benjamin's focus has, and always will be, to help simplify SharePoint solutions and make it accessible for everyone. Follow him at bniaulin.wordpress.com or @bniaulin.

About the Technical Reviewer

Sahil Malik, the founder and principal of Winsmarts.com, has been a Microsoft trainer and consultant for many years. Having authored more than 10 books, trained and spoken at conferences all across the world, and delivered solutions for many high-profile clients across four continents, he brings with him invaluable practical experience. For his community contributions, Sahil has been awarded the Microsoft MVP award for the past several years. You will find his interactions devoid of marketing, and deeply rooted in solid knowledge and expertise that is easy to grasp and understand.

Acknowledgments

There are so many people to thank as this book was definitively a group project. Thanks first to Chris Beckett for helping get this book off the ground. Without Chris's and Oscar's original conversations, this book would never have been. Chris's design and technical knowledge was utilized throughout the writing process. Thanks also to Benjamin Niaulin, who stepped in as a contributing author and really pulled through. We are not sure how we could have finished without him.

We have so many thanks to give to Apress for giving us the opportunity to write this book and for their constant support and guidance. This book would not have been completed without them. In particular we would like to thank our editors Chris Nelson and Jonathan Hassell, our coordinating editor Mark Powers who had the job of herding us, our copyeditor Teresa Horton, Anna Ishchenko, and SPi Global. We would also like to thank our technical editor, Sahil Malik, who provided such excellent technical feedback and witty comments that made every chapter, every section, and every paragraph that much clearer.

A special thanks is in order to Cloudshare (`www.cloudshare.com`). We wanted to offer a fully functional demonstration site that incorporates the material in this book to our readers. Cloudshare offered to provide a free trial of their services that includes a snapshot of our development environment for you to use. We greatly appreciate Cloudshare's offer to help make the material in this book more accessible and ready to use to our readers.

Finally, we would like to thank our families, sponsors, significant others, coworkers, and friends for all of their support. We all sacrificed a lot to make this book what it is, but it was worth it. Thank you.

Foreword

In just a few short years, we have seen some seismic shifts in how people create and consume content over the Internet. Two fundamental shifts include the meteoric rise of social networking, and the great migration from the dominance of desktop computers to mobile smart phones and tablets. Users now have high expectations for web sites and content to be personalized, interactive, and easily available from any device and form factor. These changes have fundamentally changed the nature of web design and development. As the "Internet of Everything" continues to evolve rapidly, as web designers and developers, we must evolve with it.

With the explosion in browsers, devices, and form factors, we have seen a strong preference across the technology industry for more open and accessible standards for web-based computing. HTML5 has become a rallying point in this movement, both a ubiquitous and continuously evolving set of technologies and standards that will both enable and define the next generation of web sites and applications. It is no surprise that technology vendors, driven by the success of so many open source communities and the demands of customers, have heeded this call. Microsoft is helping lead the way, driving new open standards, and incorporating these standards into the next generation of their servers, applications, development tools, and frameworks.

The release of SharePoint 2013 marks what might be its most important milestone. It is clear that Microsoft has listened to the needs of customers. SharePoint 2013 has introduced must-have features for web content management including improvements in search engine optimization (SEO), multilingual sites, and mobile device support. One of the most significant new changes has been to embrace HTML5 templates as the basis for site designs, rather than the proprietary and SharePoint-specific site design templates that were required in previous versions. All of these new features are covered in-depth through the chapters of this book, but it also provides much more.

Great web sites are not the product of technology alone. SharePoint does provide a robust platform for web sites, but it requires a blend of design and technology carefully crafted by designers to create great user experiences. The authors of this book are recognized SharePoint community leaders, and experts in SharePoint web design and development. In each chapter they walk you through the process of designing web sites using the latest techniques in responsive web design, and demonstrate how to build web sites incorporating essential features of HTML5 and SharePoint 2013. It is their experience and passion for the material that ultimately makes this book so valuable. I hope you enjoy reading it as much as I have.

Chris Beckett
SharePoint Solutions Specialist, Learning Consultant, Author, and Trainer
New Step Learning
Twitter: @sharepointbits
Web site: blog.sharepointbits.com
Email: chris@sharepointbits.com
Seattle, Washington
May 2013

Introduction

Microsoft SharePoint has come a long way since its original roots as a document management system in 2001. With the release of SharePoint 2007, Microsoft merged in the capabilities of the Microsoft Content Management Server 2002, and the potential to deploy SharePoint for web content management was born. Since that time, thousands of companies have built web sites using SharePoint 2007 and 2010.

With the release of SharePoint 2013, Microsoft has continued to evolve the web content management capabilities of SharePoint, making it one of the most mature, stable, scalable, and feature-rich platforms available for deploying and managing business web sites. One of the most exciting new capabilities is support for HTML5, opening up the potential to build cutting-edge web sites that provide the best user experience on the latest smart phones, tablets, and desktop browsers.

About This Book

This book aims to share with you how to leverage the power of two powerful technologies, HTML5 and SharePoint 2013, to build modern business web sites. Through the book we combine these technologies with a web design and development methodology referred to as "responsive web design" that allows a single web site to respond to differences in screen characteristics and browser capabilities.

The Need for Responsive Web Sites

The number of types of devices and browsers people are using to access the Internet just keeps growing. In addition to the rapid emergence of smart phones and tablets, web sites and applications are now being accessed from gaming consoles, televisions, ereaders, and more. You can even buy refrigerators today that can browse the web. These days, the browsers on these devices rival and sometimes even surpass the capabilities of desktop browsers; however it wasn't always this way.

The browsers embedded in the early generation mobile phones required simpler technologies. Wireless Application Protocol (WAP) was designed to allow mobile phones to access the Internet over high-latency, low-bandwidth mobile connections, and the browsers included in these devices were designed to display an alternative markup language called Wireless Markup Language (WML). Web sites rendered using WML used only basic text-based navigation and content. Organizations that wanted to support mobile devices were required to create an alternative web site using WML, and a precedent was born for the mobile-specific web site.

As mobile networks became faster and more reliable, and the browsers in the emerging generation of smart phones became closer in parity to desktop browsers, users abandoned the low-fidelity mobile web sites, and switched to viewing the full HTML versions of organization web sites. At the time, most business web sites were being designed to meet the lowest common denominator of desktops and network speeds. Typically, this was a fairly low-resolution monitor (often 800 × 600 pixels), and dial-up Internet connections or low-bandwidth broadband provided by early DSL and cable Internet providers. As broadband became more prevalent and desktop monitors increased in resolution, web sites evolved to the use of advanced plug-ins such as Flash for rich media, and the use of heavier graphics; mobile browsers again struggled to keep up.

The immense popularity of the Apple iPhone became the tipping point for many organizations in recognizing the need to provide a user experience tailored to the needs of mobile devices again. Some organizations started producing native applications to complement their web sites, and other organizations developed special versions of their web sites for specific smart phones (and later tablets like the iPad) by using a technique called "device detection" and redirecting users to web pages specifically designed for the devices' specific resolution and capabilities.

■ **Note** In 2013 the most common desktop resolution is 1024 × 768 pixels or higher, whereas the most popular mobile devices such as tablets have a resolution in excess of 2048 pixels across. Expect resolutions to only increase.

Today, however, increasingly we have a problem. Mobile devices are set to exceed the number of desktops accessing the Internet in 2013. As the variety of mobile devices that access the Internet increases, the ability to create a separate web site specific to each device becomes impossible. We need a better way! Responsive web design utilizes new capabilities of HTML5, notably improvements in CSS3 to create web sites that use fluid layouts to adapt to the capabilities of a specific browser or device. In a nutshell, a single web site can now provide a user experience tailored to the specific resolution and capabilities of their device without the need to produce specific page layouts for each device.

The Importance of HTML5

HTML5 is not a single technology or specification, but rather a loose marketing term for a broad collection of open (and not so "open") standards promoted and managed by a collection of standards bodies like the W3C and specific browser vendors. It encompasses changes to the next generation of HTML markup, enhancements to CSS, and new JavaScript APIs designed to enable a new generation of rich web sites and applications.

HTML5 is now widely supported by the world's leading technology vendors including Apple, Google, and Microsoft and the leading browsers including Firefox, Internet Explorer, Safari, Opera, and Chrome. Probably one of the most dramatic recent developments has been the wholehearted pivot by Microsoft to embrace the open standards of HTML5 for the next generation Internet Explorer 10, but to also place it front and center as the technology for developing the next generation of Windows 8 UI applications. Upon release IE 10 will be the most HTML5-compliant browser, and will no doubt continue to fuel competition across browser implementations. Although many of the HTML5 standards might not be finalized for many years, this kind of innovation and the industry investment being made is being driven by a number of important factors.

As an industry there is fervent recognition that web sites and applications need to work well, today and tomorrow, across the rapidly evolving capabilities of next-generation mobile devices and web-enabled consoles and appliances. Techniques such as the use of plug-ins like Adobe Flash and Microsoft Silverlight to support rich media and content presentation are not well supported on many of those devices. The refusal by Apple to support Adobe Flash, and the subsequent announcement by Adobe that they were abandoning a Flash Mobile runtime have clearly demonstrated the need for native browser capabilities to support enhanced capabilities that work, and perform well, across many platforms and computing architectures.

And no less important, organizations are looking to reduce the cost of developing and supporting web sites and applications. They are less supportive of vendor-specific tools and technologies, and the associated human resource costs of staffing the specialized skills required to leverage them. A significant advantage of HTML5 is the potential for ubiquitous access to sites and applications from anywhere, developing using standards-based technologies that are relatively simple and easy to learn. Increasingly, JavaScript will become the de facto programming language for developing the presentation layer of distributed applications. We are all JavaScript programmers now!

■ **Note** You can learn more about responsive web design, and details regarding how specific HTML5 capabilities support it by reading Chapter 2.

Why SharePoint 2013?

Microsoft SharePoint 2013 includes new features and capabilities to support many of the principles discussed in the last section, most important, better support for HTML5. It also includes significant enhancements to the Client Object Model, the programming API for accessing SharePoint from remote applications including in-browser with JavaScript and Ajax. This makes SharePoint a powerful platform for supporting rich and peformant web sites and applications without the need to program custom web services necessary to support client-side programming.

In addition to supporting the latest browser capabilities, business web sites also require a powerful server platform offering web content authoring and publishing, search, metadata, and rich media storage and streaming to satisfy business requirements. SharePoint 2013 includes significant improvements in capabilities that directly support the needs of leading-edge web sites including powerful improvements like continuous search crawling, improvements to the search keyword query language, metadata-driven site navigation, and more.

■ **Note**   You can learn about all the new improvements provided by SharePoint 2013 for web content management in Chapter 1.

Who Should Read This Book?

Over recent years, many traditional roles in information technology have become diffused by the "Do more with less" mantra being exercised today by organizations to remain competitive. Information technology professionals are frequently challenged with "stretch" assignments that challenge many of the traditional specializations such as project manager, designer, developer, and administrator.

- Are you a project manager responsible for managing the development of a business web site? This book will provide you with a step-by-step example of the typical activities and tasks involved in planning the development of a business web site with SharePoint 2013.

- Are you a web solution architect responsible for evaluating the ability of SharePoint 2013 to support the business requirements for a new business web site? This book will provide you with an overview of all the new changes in web content management in SharePoint 2013, and examples of how to use many of the most important new features.

- Are you a web designer responsible for designing a web site that will be deployed on SharePoint 2013? This book will show you how to import your web templates into SharePoint, how to take advantage of SharePoint metadata navigation, and how SharePoint can support responsive web designs using device detection.

- Are you a web developer who needs to add interactive elements to the web site that integrate with capabilities provided by SharePoint? This book provides examples of programming the SharePoint 2013 client object model providing a rich JavaScript API for accessing the advanced search, metadata, and other capabilities.

This book is primarily targeted for web designers and developers who are involved in building business web sites using SharePoint 2013 or SharePoint Online. However, for everyone, by choice or by circumstance, who is involved in the planning, architecture, design, development or deployment of a business web site using SharePoint 2013, this book is for you!

What You Need To Know

We have tried to make this book as relevant and useful to as wide an audience as possible. Through the book we provide step-by-step tutorials and samples of how to accomplish the tasks involved in building the web site that evolves through each chapter.

However, we cover some advanced topics in web design and development using leading-edge tools and technologies. To get the most of the topics covered, we recommend the following:

- An understanding of the basic technologies supporting the world wide web including HTTP and HTTPS, domain names and uniform resource locators (URLs), and the basics of how browsers interact with web servers over the Internet.

- Most important, successfully branding SharePoint requires good familiarity with HTML and CSS. It is also recommended that you have familiarity with programming in JavaScript as well as a working knowledge of jQuery. If you are looking to improve your general HTML and CSS skills we recommend any of the following resources:

  www.pluralsight.com
  www.lynda.com
  www.codecademy.com
  www.teamtreehouse.com

- An understanding of the features and capabilities of Microsoft SharePoint. Some hands-on experience using SharePoint sites, pages, lists, and libraries is also recommended.

Whatever your current level of experience, we are confident you will learn some valuable new skills and expertise by the time you are finished with this book.

How This Book Is Organized

The chapters in this book are divided into topics that can be read in any order, however, they have been ordered to follow a logical step-by-step process that incrementally builds an interactive and responsive website using SharePoint 2013.

Chapters 1 and 2 provide a brief introduction to the goals of the book, essential features of SharePoint 2013 for web content management, and a primer on HTML5 and responsive web design. Chapters 3 through 14 then demonstrate a typical web site development process while we incrementally build a sample web site.

Chapter 1: What's New in SharePoint 2013 Web Content Management

SharePoint 2013 introduces an exciting collection of new features and capabilities related to web content management. In this chapter we provide an overview of the new capabilities and how they improve on the web content management features carried forward from previous SharePoint releases. We also provide you a reference to how we use these features in subsequent chapters to build our example web site.

Chapter 2: Responsive Web Design and Development with HTML5

Responsive web design is a methodology, supported by new capabilities provided by HTML5 (primarily CSS3) that will enable the next generation of web sites to provide the best user experience across a wide variety of devices and browsers. In this chapter we introduce the reader to the fundamentals of HTML5, CSS3, and many of the new JavaScript APIs, and explain how these new features support designing and developing more responsive web sites.

Chapter 3: Designing a Responsive Web Site

Traditional web site analysis and design often followed a waterfall approach that focused on the design of static representations of web site pages. Responsive web design requires a new approach that recognizes that the traditional "pixel-perfect" web page has become much more difficult to achieve with the ever growing number of Internet-connected devices and their physical dimensions. Consider the different physical screen sizes and resolutions between smart phones, tablets, and different desktop monitor sizes. Tradition web page design might be replaced with a combination of multiple targeted web page dimensions and fluid layouts to match different device resolutions and orientations. In this chapter we demonstrate how to use wireframes and storyboards to demonstrate transitions between responsive layouts to communicate effectively with clients and web site stakeholders.

Chapter 4: Building a SharePoint HTML Master Page

SharePoint 2013 makes it easy for web designers without explicit knowledge of ASP.NET and SharePoint master pages to convert standard HTML web templates to SharePoint master pages using the new Design Manager. In this chapter, we demonstrate how to convert the HTML web site design template produced in Chapter 3 into a SharePoint-enabled master page using the new SharePoint 2013 Design Manager.

Chapter 5: Making Your Master Page Responsive

A "responsive" web design allows a single web site to dynamically present the best user experience for a variety of devices, browsers, screen resolutions, and orientations primarily using capabilities found in CSS3. This chapter demonstrates how to update an HTML master page that includes responsive web design principles by utilizing a responsive framework. We also see how we can further control our designs across different devices with CSS3 media queries as well as take a look at a new feature of SharePoint 2013, device channels.

Chapter 6: Building Site Structure and Navigation

Good navigation is one of the most important design elements of a web site contributing to a positive user experience. SharePoint 2013 has dramatically improved the ability to create dynamic navigation paths and site maps using the Managed Metadata Service. This new capability also provides improved human-friendly URLs that have long been the bane of SharePoint web sites. This chapter shows the reader how to design site structures and navigation with new features provided by SharePoint 2013 including Managed Metadata navigation. We also compare different types of navigation and multiple strategies when including them in a responsive site design.

Chapter 7: Building Page Layouts and Publishing Pages

Web pages created using the web content management publishing features of SharePoint are referred to as publishing pages, and they inherit layout and behavior from a page layout. Custom page layouts can be extended with custom content types to provide additional metadata as well as to provide a more consistent authoring experience. Most web sites will have a collection of page layouts for presenting different kinds of content such as a product catalog, or product details. Page layouts with custom content types are essential to allowing users to author content while controlling presentation. In this chapter we design and create a collection of page layouts required to support our example site along with a series of custom content types that are used throughout the example site.

Chapter 8: Publishing Cross-Site Content with Catalogs

To make it easier to share and publish content across multiple web sites, SharePoint 2013 introduces a new capability for cross-site publishing using catalogs. Catalogs are exposed through the search capabilities of SharePoint to allow content to be easily reused across multiple web sites such as your organization's extranet, intranet, and business web sites. In this chapter we demonstrate how to create a web site that exposes two catalogs, one of which integrates managed metadata navigation and the other which does not. These catalogs are used for content reusability, which can be surfaced through sites throughout a SharePoint farm.

Chapter 9: Integrating Search-Driven Content

One of the most powerful capabilities of SharePoint is "Search." The Search service in SharePoint is designed to scale to millions of content items and return search results with subsecond response times. One of the most common requirements for business web sites is to aggregate and display content such as news and events, recent updates, or popular content. In this chapter, we use the new Content Search web part to easily perform content aggregation and rollups for our example site, and show how to customize the presentation of the information.

Chapter 10: Building Rich Interactive Forms

Just about every web site occasionally needs to connect information from users including surveys, feedback, comments, or registration forms. HTML5 and jQuery provide the ability to provide rich interactive forms that support validation and error handling without requiring postbacks to the server. Although there are multiple methods to create forms in SharePoint 2013, in this chapter we implement a user event registration system using HTML5, jQuery, Bootstrap, and the new REST API.

Chapter 11: Uploading and Working with Files

Occasionally web sites need to provide users with the ability to upload files. Traditionally, HTTP and HTML have provided very limited support for accessing files on a client device. Uploading multiple files, particularly large files, typically required the use of a browser plug-in, Adobe Flash, or Microsoft Silverlight. In this chapter we show the reader how to combine the features of HTML5 and the SharePoint 2013 client object model to support advanced scenarios for working with files.

Chapter 12: Integrating Location-Based Features

One of the exciting features of the rapid adoption of advanced smart phones and tablet devices is the opportunity provided by GPS capabilities to support location-based features in your web sites or web applications. This chapter demonstrates how to utilize the new SharePoint Location metadata field and the HTML5 Geo-Location API to integrate maps and location-based features into the site.

Chapter 13: Integrating Feeds and Social Media

Many businesses are recognizing that the corporate web site needs to be an integrated component of their social marketing strategies, pushing and pulling information from the web site across social media channels like Facebook, LinkedIn, Twitter, and others. This chapter shows how to integrate remote feeds and social media features in your web site.

Chapter 14: Supporting Multilingual Web Sites

As more organizations pursue growth into an increasingly globalized marketplace for products and services, the need for web sites in multiple languages is growing. Potential customers appreciate organizations that make the effort to provide them information about products or services in their native language. An investment in a multilingual web site can produce measurable growth in company sales and customer satisfaction. This chapter shows you how to build multilingual sites using the Variations and Translation Services features in SharePoint 2013.

Appendix A: Configuring a Development Environment

To help you follow along with the step-by-step exercises in the book, this appendix helps you set up a development environment in case you do not already have access to one. We introduce both on-premise and cloud-based options that you can use for branding exercises as well as app development, as outlined in this book.

Tools You Will Need to Get Started

Through each of the chapters in this book we progressively build a working web site on SharePoint 2013. We encourage you to follow along with us through each chapter in your own environment. To support the design and development of web sites using SharePoint 2013 you will need the following tools and technologies:

- SharePoint 2013 Server. SharePoint 2013 comes in two editions: Foundation and Server. To access the web content management capabilities of SharePoint and follow along with the samples, you will need Site Collection Administrator access to a SharePoint 2013 Server web site. There are a variety of choices available to you including a web site on a preproduction server at your organization, a local installation of SharePoint 2013 (typically running as a virtual machine), a virtual server running in a hosted cloud environment like Amazon Web Services or Microsoft Windows Azure), or a trial or paid account on Microsoft Office 365.

- Web site editor. A web site editor will be required to manage and modify the branding elements of your SharePoint 2013 site collections. You are free to use your favorite web design editor, such as the popular Adobe Dreamweaver. The examples in the book use Adobe Dreamweaver and SharePoint Designer 2013, but you should be able to follow along with the tool of your choice.

- Adobe Dreamweaver. This web design tool by Adobe, currently in version CS6 as of this printing, is a powerful, general web design tool for building feature-rich web sites. With the addition of Design Manager in SharePoint 2013, Dreamweaver can now be used to modify most branding components of a SharePoint 2013 site.

- SharePoint Designer 2013. This free program is a Windows desktop application that you can download from Microsoft and is available in 32-bit and 64-bit versions. You should install whatever edition matches your operating system and office suite. Although not a full-fledged web site editor, SharePoint Designer 2013 provides access to branding files as well as additional access to SharePoint functionality such as file check out, check in, and publishing. SharePoint Design 2013 does not include a Design view or WYSIWYG editor, it only provides a Code view, providing the ability to edit your HTML, JavaScript, and style sheet code.

- NotePad++. This is another free program that is a simple yet powerful source code editing tool for many languages, including HTML, CSS, and JavaScript. This is a coder's tool, as there is no Design view, rather only a Code view.

- Any other web site editor tool including Notepad should work, although ideally you will want to use a tool that is HTML5 and CSS3 friendly.

- Microsoft Visual Studio 2012. This is Microsoft's premier development studio and comes in many editions including a free edition. To perform app development for SharePoint 2013, you will need Visual Studio 2012 Professional Edition or above. You can download a free trial of Visual Studio 2012 from Microsoft. Visual Studio is not required to build most of the web site described in this book, but it is required for app development as described in Chapter 12.

■ **Tip** To help you get started, we have provided step-by-step tutorials on setting up different types of development environments including cloud based environments such as those by Cloudshare and Microsoft Office 365. These are ideal for working through the book examples. For more information, see the Appendix.

Downloading the Source Code

The code for the examples shown in this book is available on the book's information page on the Apress web site (www.apress.com/9781430250289). The link can be located on the Source Code/Downloads tab underneath the Related Titles section of the page. You can also download the source code from this book's GitHub repository at http://sprwd.github.io/BookSourceCode/.

Demonstration Development Environment

As an added bonus, you can work through the examples in this book with a fully working demo virtual machine from Cloudshare, a cloud-based development environment provider. This allows you to get under the hood and see the material in this book in action, all set up and configured for you in a matter of minutes.

You can learn more about Cloudshare and the development environment that has been configured for this book in the Appendix. You can access the development environment now at http://sprwd.com/sprwd-cs-demo.

Social Community

We created a social community for you the readers and we the authors to come together, share stories and insights, ask questions and provide additional guidance and ideas as responsive design and SharePoint 2013 develop and mature. We decided to use the SharePoint Community SPYam at Yammer (https://www.yammer.com/spyam/). To access this community, join SPYam and then either search for the group "Pro SharePoint 2013 Branding and Responsive Web Development" or visit http://sprwd.com/spyam-sprwd.

What to know why we made the decisions we did? Ask us. Are you looking for supplemental material? Check out our group as we will provide additional examples, tips and tricks throughout the SharePoint 2013 life-cycle. This group will also be a central place to learn where we the authors will be speaking next so you can meet us in person. Join us on SPYam and keep the conversation and learning going.

Summary

Are you excited to get started? Whatever your background, we are sure this book will provide you with some new skills and experience to help you build better web sites with SharePoint 2013.

If you have been designing or building web sites using alternative content management platforms, this book will provide you with an excellent introduction to building sites with the web content management capabilities of Microsoft SharePoint. If you have been building fixed-width web sites with HTML 4.01 aimed at traditional desktop browsers, this book will introduce you to the exciting capabilities of HTML5, CSS3, and responsive web design and development. If you have been building static web sites, this book will provide an excellent primer to using JavaScript and some of the Web's most popular frameworks for building more performant and interactive web sites.

We really hope you enjoy this book and find it a valuable starting point on your journey toward building modern responsive web sites with SharePoint 2013.

■ ■ ■

CHAPTER 1

What's New in SharePoint 2013 Web Content Management

SharePoint 2013 introduces new and improved features for web content management that simplify how we design Internet sites and enhance the authoring and publishing processes for our organization. This chapter provides an overview of the new features for web content management in SharePoint 2013. We also look at how we will be using these new features in later chapters to build our example web site.

In this release of SharePoint, the product offers new content publishing features that enable us to reuse our content across many site collections. With deep integration between Search and Content Management, SharePoint now services dynamic web content across different site collections. We can create a piece of content once and then enable the content to be reused by other publishing sites. Instead of the traditional structured navigation, new in SharePoint 2013, the managed navigation feature allows us to use taxonomy to design site navigation based on business concepts without changing site structures. The new feature also allows us to create seach engine optimization (SEO)-friendly URLs derived from the managed navigation structure. To support multilingual content on a site, SharePoint 2013 now has an integrated translation service that lets content authors select content for human translation or machine translation.

Responsive web design is important in modern Internet sites. SharePoint 2013 has been rearchitected to provide better support for HTML5, CSS3, and JavaScript. With the rapid growth of mobile devices, we need to ensure our site can handle mobile browsers. For the first time, SharePoint provides the ability to target a different look and feel for different devices with the new device channel feature. There are times when we need to extend SharePoint to add rich interactive features to our site. SharePoint 2013 allows us to do that with significant enhancements and added features to the SharePoint Client Object Model. For content authors and designers, new features for publishing sites minimize the special SharePoint knowledge required to successfully design and brand a SharePoint site. Designers and developers now have the flexibility to use the tools and technologies with which they are familiar.

SharePoint 2013 offers new features in site design, authoring, presentation, content reuse, metadata-driven navigation, adaptive experiences, device channels, and client object model.

Search-Driven Publishing Model

A SharePoint site collection is a structure of sites that is made up of one top-level site and many sites below it. The sites in a site collection can share many features, resources, designs, and content to provide end users with a unified web site experience within the same site collection. Before SharePoint 2013, for the purpose of publishing, we often had to implement two site collections: one for authoring the content and one for production. We were restricted to service content from only a single site collection. We had to build custom solutions to get content across multiple site collections. Now with SharePoint 2013, we can create and publish content to be consumed in one or more publishing site collections.

SharePoint 2013 uses search to service dynamic web content on sites and to provide user-behavior-driven recommendations. We start by enabling a list or a library as a catalog. Then the content in the catalog gets crawled and added to the search index. The new Cross-site publishing feature uses search technology to retrieve content from the search index. Refer to the section "Cross-Site Publishing" later in this chapter for more information. The content can then be displayed in a target publishing site collection by using one or more Content Search web parts, which is also a new feature in SharePoint 2013. Refer to the section "Content Search Web Part" later in this chapter for more information.

The new content model for SharePoint 2013 sites is centered on two main components: search index and shared metadata. With the content stored in the search index, metadata stored in the Term Store database, and analytics stored in SharePoint database, all the published content can be serviced to users through query rules and a recommendation engine. See the sections "Analytics and Recommendations" and "Query Rules" later in this chapter for more information. When consuming published content, SharePoint can automatically generate rollup pages for different categories of the content, which can lead to the content's item detail pages, called Category pages. Refer to the section "Category Pages" later in this chapter for more information. Each of these pages is based on a template that can be customized by developers, known as a display template. See the section "Display Templates" later in this chapter for more information.

Cross-Site Publishing

New in SharePoint 2013, Cross-site publishing lets us store and maintain content in one or more authoring site collections, and the content can be displayed and serviced in different target site collections. When the content is changed in an authoring site collection, those changes are displayed on all site collections that are reusing this content as soon as the content has been recrawled.

■ **Tip** The Cross-site publishing feature is only available in the Enterprise edition of SharePoint 2013. This feature is not available on Office 365 as of now. For more up-to-date information on feature availability on SharePoint online and license requirements, refer to Microsoft TechNet at http://sprwd.com/dhmpvbk.

To enable a piece of content to be reused and shared, we need to activate the Cross-Site Collection Publishing feature on the authoring site collection containing the content. Similarly, to enable a target publishing site collection to consume published content, we also need to enable this feature on the target site collection. We can enable a site collection to use this feature on the site settings page by enabling the Cross-Site Collection Publishing site collection feature, as shown in Figure 1-1.

 Cross-Site Collection Publishing
Enables site collection to designate lists and document libraries as catalog sources for Cross-Site Collection Publishing.

Figure 1-1. *To use Cross-site publishing, enable the Cross-Site Collection Publishing feature*

■ **Note** You can learn more about Cross-site publishing in SharePoint 2013 in Chapter 8, when we demonstrate how to enable content in a list or library for reuse and how to consume the published content by a target site collection for our example site.

Content Catalog

SharePoint 2013 has added the ability to designate any library or list as a catalog. Once Cross-Site Collection Publishing is enabled on a site collection, we can enable any library or list as a catalog. We can use one or more catalog-enabled lists to store information or web content. Using Cross-site publishing allows this information to be displayed and reused in one or more publishing site collections.

A catalog is a helper feature that defines behaviors on the list or library to ensure the content is available as published catalogs via search. A catalog is registered within search for predefined queries. It tells search that the content is a catalog and is "published" across site collections. It also tells search not to remove the HTML markup in the index so that it can be used to serve as published pages directly from search results. This allows content authors to have a central content authoring site, working with products or articles in a list-like fashion, and rendering it in different ways to end users. Once a list or library has been enabled as a catalog, a result source is automatically created for the list or library. The result source for a list or library limits the search scope to the content within the library or list. This will become very useful, as we will see in later chapters, when we need to limit a query in the new Content Search web part, a feature that is a part of the search-driven publishing model in SharePoint 2013, to a particular list by using the list's result source.

■ **Note** To learn more about the Content Search web part, refer to Chapter 9.

Category Pages

When we need to display content in a catalog in the same manner, we can create a Category page. Category pages are page layouts that display structured content. As discussed previously, new in SharePoint 2013, the managed navigation feature enables us to design site navigation based on business concepts instead of static site structure. SharePoint uses a managed metadata service to define and manage terms and term sets that can now be used for site navigation. For more information on how to set up and use a managed metadata service in SharePoint 2013, refer to the Microsoft TechNet documentation at http://sprwd.com/meztskk.

■ **Note** To learn more about how to set up terms and term sets using the managed metadata service and how to create managed navigation using these terms, refer to Chapter 6, as we walk through the process of creating dynamic navigation for our example site.

We can associate a Category page with a specific navigation term in a term set that is used for managed navigation. When users click on a specific navigation term in the site navigation, they are routed to the corresponding Category page. The Category page has been configured with Content Search web parts. We can specify the query in the Content Search web part to use the current navigation term as part of the query. Then every time users browse to the Category page, the predefined query is automatically issued, and it returns and displays results from the search index.

Content Search Web Part

Previous versions of SharePoint used the Content Query web part (also known as CQWP) for content aggregation and rollup. The Content Query web part is still available in SharePoint 2013, but it can only aggregate data within a single site collection, it can only aggregate list information, and to change how results look, we had to customize the XSL of the web part. Similar to the function of the Content Query web part, SharePoint 2013 introduces the Content Search web part to allow developers and designers to pull content from many site collections. The new web part can return any content from the search index. Because the feature depends heavily on search functionality, it is important to note that the more often the search crawls, the more up-to-date the content is. In addition, SharePoint search only crawls major versions of content, not minor versions.

■ **Tip** The Content Search web part is ideal for aggregating content from many site collections, for major versioned content, and for frequently indexed content. If displaying instant content in a single site collection is a must, use the Content Query web part instead. If you want to display minor versions of the content in a single site collection, you need to use the Content Query web part instead. If you need to return results from a site that has been marked to not be indexed, you need to use the Content Query web part instead.

Each Content Search web part is associated with a search query and displays the results for that search query. The query can be designed to pull content based on values on the page or within the URL. The results are then exposed to the page in JSON format. We can then use display templates to change how search results appear on the page. Display templates are snippets of HTML and JavaScript that render the information returned by SharePoint.

■ **Tip** The Content Search web part feature is only available in the Enterprise edition of SharePoint 2013. It is also not available on Office 365 as of now. For more up-to-date information on feature availability on SharePoint online and license requirements, refer to Microsoft TechNet at `http://sprwd.com/dhmpvbk`.

To configure a Content Search Web Part, we have to first specify a query. This query is issued each time a user visits the page the web part is on. It is especially powerful when it is used in combination with managed navigation and Category pages, as we discussed earlier. We can restrict what results are returned from the web part by configuring the refiners and the query properties of the web part. We can restrict the results to content tagged with the current navigation term or content tagged with a static metadata term. The web part contains a query builder that helps us construct the query. The query builder also shows a real-time preview of the search result as we are configuring the web part. Figure 1-2 shows the query builder of the web part. The web part has restricted the results to return only items that have been tagged with the "Mobile" term. As shown in the search result preview, to the right of the query building, there are three results in the search index that have been tagged with the "Mobile" term.

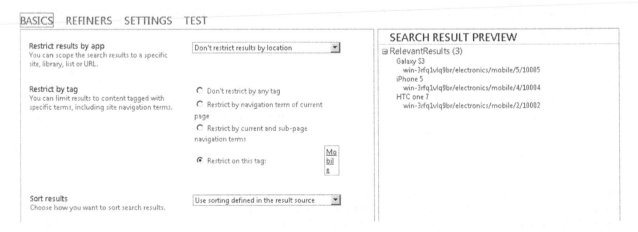

Figure 1-2. *Configure the Content Search web part to restrict results by using the current navigation term or static tag*

Once the query is defined, the web part also allows us to choose display templates to display the results. We can use the default out-of-the-box display templates offered by SharePoint. We can also create our own custom display templates by extending the basic display templates to customize the display of the results.

■ **Note** To learn more about how to configure the Content Search web part and how to create custom display templates, refer to Chapter 9.

Once we have configured all the properties for the web part, the web part will display a set of content that matches the query using the selected display template. Figure 1-3 shows an example of the displayed content.

Otay-Crossing

Otay was built with the traditional people in mind. People who opt for th…

Residential

Spruce Meadow

Spruce Meadow was built in 2001 right when the DotCom was at its peak…

Loft

Figure 1-3. *The Results web part will display a set of content from the Catalog using a defined display template*

■ **Note** You can learn more about the end-to-end process of search-driven publishing in SharePoint 2013 in Chapter 9, when we walk through how to publish content from an authoring site, how to consume the content from a target site, and how to customize the presentation of the aggregated content for our example site.

Product Catalog Site Collection Template

Before SharePoint 2013, when we needed to create sites that were heavy in web content, such as public-facing sites, blogs, or marketing sites, we created publishing site collections to leverage the SharePoint publishing features. Similar to publishing site collections, SharePoint 2013 offers a new publishing site collection template called Product Catalog. Content from Product Catalogs is not just pages and page layouts; it consists of published lists and libraries. The Product Catalog site collection has the Cross-Site Collection Publishing feature enabled by default, the Product content type created to be used for the content's content type, and the Product Hierarchy term set created for content tagging.

With a site collection that is created with the Product Catalog template, SharePoint guides us through all the steps necessary to set up a catalog of content. Following the guide, we need to first create site columns in the Product Catalog site for the properties of the publishing content so that the content can be searched by and filtered by these properties. For every set of content we plan to publish, we can combine similar properties to create corresponding site content types. The template already includes the default Product content type. Then for each type of content to publish, we can add site columns to the content's content type. To ensure all content is categorized in the product catalog, we can add terms to the Product Hierarchy term set for mapping. Populate content for all the lists and libraries that have been enabled as catalogs. Enable search to crawl the content. Finally in search, modify the managed properties settings so that users can query and refine search results based on the properties in the catalog.

■ **Note**   To learn more about the complete end-to-end process of cross-site collection publishing, refer to Chapter 8.

Refiners and Faceted Navigation

We just spent some time talking about aggregating content from various site collections. When a page has lots of results, to help users quickly browse to the specific content they are looking for, we can add refiners to the page. Refiners were introduced in SharePoint 2010. They are based on managed properties from the search index. To show refiners on results, we need to ensure the managed properties in the results have been enabled as refiners in search. In SharePoint 2013, with catalogs (published content), managed properties represent the properties of items in the catalog-enabled list or library. The old Refinement Panel web part can be used to help users narrow the content from different catalogs.

Faceted Navigation is a new feature in SharePoint 2013 that helps users browse for content more easily by filtering on refiners that are tied to terms in the navigation. We can configure different refiners for different terms in the navigation so that users can use different sets of properties to narrow content depending on the navigation term. With Faceted Navigation, users can find the relevant content for each category faster.

Earlier, we talked about creating a Category page for every category of the content. Each Category page is configured to show items in a category as represented by a term in the navigation. Using Faceted Navigation, we can configure different refiners for different terms (categories) in a term set without having to create additional pages by allowing different terms to share the same category page. For example, we have an Internet site for a restaurant. Our content is a catalog of dishes. A term set is used to categorize different types of dishes, such as appetizers and desserts. The same Category page is used for both terms. After we enable the managed properties of salad and ice cream as refiners, we then configure Faceted Navigation so that salad is shown as a refiner for appetizers and ice cream is shown as a refiner for desserts. The user will see friendly URLs for both appetizers and desserts—http://restaurantname/menu/appetizers and http://restaurantname/menu/desserts—but in fact, both of these URLs will route the user to the same category page with different refiners.

Analytics and Recommendations

In SharePoint 2013, there is a new Analytics Processing component that runs analytics jobs to analyze content in the search index and user actions that were performed on a site to identify items that users perceive as more relevant than others. The new functionality for displaying content recommendations based on usage patterns uses the information from the analytics. By including recommendations on a page, we can guide users to other content that might be relevant for them. For example, like Amazon, we can guide users to popular items in a category or inform them that users who viewed one item also viewed another specific item. User actions on the site are counted and analyzed. Analytics data can influence search relevance based on content usage. The data is deeply integrated with the search engine. Calculations are injected into the search index as sortable managed properties.

Developers can extend the analytics engine using custom events. We could change the weight of a specific event based on our own custom criteria. For example, when someone rates an item with a Like on Facebook, the recommendation weight is 5. When someone buys an item, the recommendation weight becomes 20.

We can guide users by adding recommendations to the search results page. We can show the user what other users who viewed this document also viewed by configuring the Recommended Items web part to display recommendations for the item the user is viewing. We can also show the user the most popular items in this category by configuring the Popular Items web part to display the most popular items that satisfy the query.

Query Rules

In SharePoint 2010, to improve relevance on specific queries, we could promote results to the top of the page by creating Search Keywords and Best Bets. Now in SharePoint 2013, both Search Keywords and Best Bets are replaced by Query Rules. With Query Rules, instead of matching specific queries, it infers what the user wants. For example, when a user searches for "holiday pictures," the Query Rules interprets it to show the user relevant image results with the word "holiday." When a user searches for "expense sheet," Query Rules promotes Excel spreadsheets that contain the word "expense." Instead of promoting specific results, it promotes blocks of results relevant to the user's query.

■ **Tip**   During an upgrade from SharePoint 2010 to SharePoint 2013, all existing Search Keywords will be automatically transformed into Query Rules. To create a Query Rule that acts like a Search Keywords feature, use the Query Matches Keyword Exactly condition when creating the Query Rule.

Each Query Rule has its own context, which refers to the set of content (Result source) to which the Query Rule applies. For example, we can create a Query Rule for all the local SharePoint sites or we can create one that only applies to all pages libraries. For the latter, when search is conducted against all pages libraries, the Query Rule created for that context will be applied.

Query Rules can be very powerful using all the different out-of-the-box conditions, and in addition, we can even create advanced conditions using regular expressions. For example, one of the out-of-the-box conditions for a Query Rule is Query Matches Dictionary Exactly, which means the Query Rule is applied when the query matches one of the terms in a term set. This can be very useful when we want to return results for searches against a category of products or a business unit. Another powerful condition that can guide users is Result type commonly clicked. With this condition, the Query Rule looks at the user's query. If people who executed the same query in the past found a particular result type (file type) useful, then the Query Rule applies. With this type of Query Rule, we can execute another query to return results of that result type (for instance, for a particular file type).

■ **Note**   To learn more about how to create your own Query Rules, refer to Chapter 9.

Metadata and Navigation

With the new Managed Navigation feature, we can now define the structure of our site by tagging the content with business terms, which ensures the navigation on the site is aligned with the content.

■ **Tip**   Managed Navigation is only available in the Standard and Enterprise editions of SharePoint 2013. It is also available on Office 365. For more up-to-date information on feature availability on SharePoint online and license requirements, refer to Microsoft TechNet at `http://sprwd.com/dhmpvbk`.

Taxonomies

Taxonomies and the Managed Metadata Service were introduced in SharePoint 2010. SharePoint uses the Managed Metadata Service to define and manage terms and term sets based on business logic, which can now be used for site navigation. For more information on how to set up and use the Managed Metadata Service in SharePoint 2013, refer to the Microsoft TechNet documentation at `http://sprwd.com/meztskk`.

SharePoint 2013 builds many new features on top of what SharePoint 2010 introduced. The most important change in managed metadata is the ability to create managed navigation using a term set. Anyone who has worked with managed metadata in SharePoint 2010 can recall only a restricted few users could have write permission to term sets. SharePoint 2013 enabled read and write permissions to groups of users. Term sets now have an "intended use" property to indicate if the term set should be used for tagging, search, navigation, and so on. In the past, term sets and terms were only accessible programmatically via server-side code. Now developers can work with term sets off the server by using client-side object model interfaces. New taxonomy management pages were added to reduce the number of people and instances needed to access the Term Store Manager Administration tool. SharePoint 2010 enabled administrators to copy and reuse terms. SharePoint 2013 introduces pinning, much like reuse, which blocks any changes where it is being reused. A term set or a set of terms can be pinned. Now all these features are available to us at the site collection level, not limited to just the central administration level.

Managed Navigation

In SharePoint 2013, the Managed Navigation feature enables us to create navigation based on taxonomy. We can drive our site navigation and URLs based on Term Store hierarchies derived from business concepts instead of site structures.

We can use the Taxonomy infrastructure to generate URLs and paths to content by using tagging and set the terms as navigation terms. Navigation Term sets are special term sets with the property of isNav. Navigation Term sets and Tagging Term sets can share the same terms. We can have a site collection level term set that can be shared outside of the site collection. We can combine portions of different term sets from different site collections to form the navigation of the whole site. When deciding on navigation, we can have a traditional structured navigation or we can use Managed Navigation.

We can have clean URLs and multilingual URLs for end users. We can copy the Navigation Term set and translate it into the same languages that are used for variations labels. In addition, Managed Navigation allows us to easily reorganize the content by modifying the term set instead of restructuring the actual content. With Managed Navigation, we can minimize the amount of physical pages for our site by using dynamic pages that are shared by multiple navigation terms. A single dynamic page can render different content for multiple navigation terms. Refer to the earlier section "Refiners and Faceted Navigation" for more information.

■ **Note**   You can learn more about Managed Navigation in SharePoint 2013 in Chapter 6 when we demonstrate how to design site structures and navigation with Managed Navigation.

Friendly URLs

It is important to ensure all web addresses for a modern web site are friendly URLs. Friendly URLs are easy to read and describe the content of the web page, which helps users remember the web address and helps describe the page to search engines.

Together with Managed Navigation and Category pages, we now have friendly URLs for our site. Another new Web Content Management capability in SharePoint 2013 is the native support for SEO. SharePoint 2013 allows content authors to provide SEO properties and metadata within the publishing pages.

We can use terms in a Navigation Term set to create friendly URLs. The URLs of category pages can be built from the terms of Navigation Term sets. Each friendly URL is relative to the root site URL. For example, we have a public site URL, http://spectorgroup.com. We can create a new term called Marketing within a term set called Departments. We want to navigate to the marketing Category page by using the friendly URL, http://spectorgroup.com/departments/marketing. We can use Managed Navigation to set the friendly URL of the Marketing term as http://spectorgroup.com /departments/marketing, and the actual marketing page can be anywhere in the site. When users click Marketing in the navigation, they only see a friendly URL, http://spectorgroup.com/departments/marketing, not the actual location of the marketing page.

Content Authoring, Design, and Branding Improvements

Responsive web design has been adopted widely to create web sites that can now provide a user experience tailored to the specific resolution and capabilities of their device without the need to produce specific page layouts for each device. Designers and developers can use the technologies and tools they already know and love for site design and branding.

Content Authoring

Before SharePoint 2013, there were very limited features that helped with content authoring. Any time users wanted to create rich interactive content, they either had to know how to write HTML code or had to create the content in the SharePoint designer. Neither option was ideal for corporate business users.

SharePoint 2013 includes many improvements that can enable an end user to create rich interactive content right within SharePoint. Content authors can now create content that has pictures, videos, rich formatting, Excel tables, and more in Microsoft Word, then copy the content from Word and paste it directly into a Rich Text Editor web part, Content Editor web part, or an HTML field control while SharePoint automatically semantically corrects HTML markup display in the styles defined by the site designer. For content authors who need to work with videos, SharePoint 2013 has new video content type and an improved video upload process. When the user uploads a video to an asset library, thumbnail preview images are automatically created. We can also choose a frame from the video to use as the thumbnail preview image.

■ **Note**   For automatic creation of thumbnail images, make sure to install the Desktop Experience feature on the SharePoint web front-end servers.

When users need to embed dynamic content from other sites, they can insert an iframe element into an HTML field on the page. Note that to allow end users to insert iframes on any page, site collection administrators need to customize the field security settings (HTML Field Security) on the site settings page by adding the referenced external domains in the list of default trusted external domains. If users need to display different-sized versions of an image on different pages, they can use the new Image Renditions feature, described next.

Image Renditions

Often, the same image needs to be used across a site in standard formats. We might need to ensure all the images are consistent in size. Content authors might need to crop target areas of pictures. In SharePoint 2013, we can generate different renditions of the same image from the same source file. Site owners can specify the height and width for all images and create multiple renditions of an image. When content owners want to use an image on a page, they can select the image and the rendition they want to add. When first requested, SharePoint generates the image according to the rendition and saves the images to the SharePoint web front-end server's disk for future requests.

■ **Note**   To use Image Renditions, we must enable the BLOB cache feature. For more information on how to configure BLOB cache, refer to `http://sprwd.com/46zufa6`.

Image previews for an image rendition are by default generated from the center of the image. We can adjust the image preview for an image by selecting and resizing the portion of the image we want to use. Image Rendition can improve site performance by using smaller versions of images, which will reduce the size of the file download required by the client. To use Image Rendition, click Image Renditions on the site settings page. Create a new image rendition by specifying a name and the width and height in pixels for the rendition. To use the rendition, add an image to a page, then click Edit Image Properties to select the image rendition to apply from a list of renditions. Another way to use an image rendition is to specify a value in the `RenditionID` property for an image field control. We can also use an image rendition by pointing the image URL to a URL that has the `RenditionID` parameter.

Branding

Branding in SharePoint has always been a huge undertaking. New features for publishing sites in SharePoint 2013 minimize the special knowledge required to successfully design and brand a SharePoint site. To brand a SharePoint site, designers can create a site design as they typically would by implementing HTML, Cascading Style Sheets (CSS), and JavaScript. Designers can create these design files using the design tool with which they are familiar, whether that is Adobe Dreamweaver, Microsoft Expression Web, or another HTML editor. Unlike before, you do not have to use SharePoint Designer or Visual Studio 2013 to brand a SharePoint site. Designers now have the flexibility to use the tools of their choice.

The process for web design in SharePoint 2013 is to start with tools like Dreamweaver. SharePoint 2013 allows developers and designers to copy non-SharePoint-specific design assets and upload them to SharePoint. Then, SharePoint infrastructure takes the HTML and CSS files uploaded and automatically converts them to SharePoint specific assets (*.master and *.aspx).

Figure 1-4 is a process flow diagram of design and branding in SharePoint 2013.

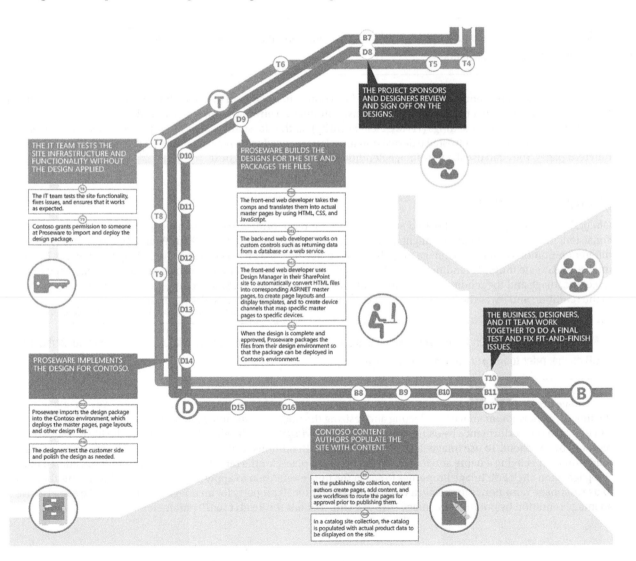

Figure 1-4. *A process flow diagram of design and branding in SharePoint 2013*

1. We start with the customer's project sponsors and the design agency review and sign off on the designs.

2. Then the design agency takes the comps and translates them into design files for the site using Dreamweaver or another HTML editor.

3. The designer then uses Design Manager in their SharePoint site to automatically convert HTML files into corresponding ASP.NET master pages, to create page layouts and display templates, and to create device channels that map specific master pages to specific devices. Design Manager, Display Templates, and Device Channels are dicussed in more detail later in this chapter.

4. Once the design is completed and approved, the design agency packages the files from the design environment into a design package so that the design can be deployed in the customer's environment.

5. The design package is deployed into the customer's environment, which deploys the master page, page layouts, and other design files.

6. Finally, we need to test and polish the design in the new environment as needed.

■ **Note**   To learn more about branding and how to convert a standard HTML web template into a SharePoint master page using new features in SharePoint 2013, refer to Chapter 4.

Device Channels

For the first time, SharePoint provides the ability to target a different look and feel for different devices with the new device channel feature. SharePoint 2013 allows us to design sites for multiple screens and browsers—desktop, tablet, mobile, and so on—all served from the same URLs to optimize search engine ranking. A new feature called device channels can help us map devices and browsers to the appropriate master pages, templates, layouts, or panels. For each device channel, we can define devices that are applicable to by adding device inclusion rules with user agent substrings (see Figure 1-5). Device channels are especially useful when we need to define a rendering that is optimal for a specific device.

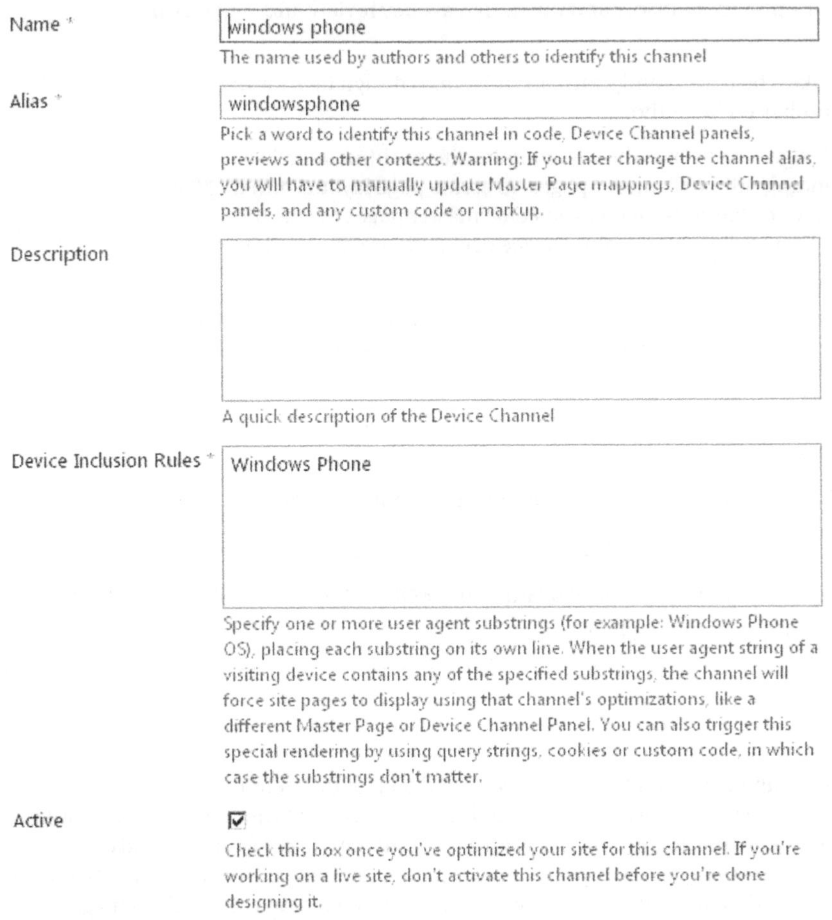

Name *

windows phone

The name used by authors and others to identify this channel

Alias *

windowsphone

Pick a word to identify this channel in code, Device Channel panels, previews and other contexts. Warning: If you later change the channel alias, you will have to manually update Master Page mappings, Device Channel panels, and any custom code or markup.

Description

A quick description of the Device Channel

Device Inclusion Rules *

Windows Phone

Specify one or more user agent substrings (for example: Windows Phone OS), placing each substring on its own line. When the user agent string of a visiting device contains any of the specified substrings, the channel will force site pages to display using that channel's optimizations, like a different Master Page or Device Channel Panel. You can also trigger this special rendering by using query strings, cookies or custom code, in which case the substrings don't matter.

Active

☑

Check this box once you've optimized your site for this channel. If you're working on a live site, don't activate this channel before you're done designing it.

Figure 1-5. *For each device channel, define devices that are applicable to by adding device inclusion rules with user agent substrings*

A channel can be associated with a master page, allowing for specific branding implementations for specific devices. If we need to create a separate look for the channel, we can customize an existing master page, then publish it before using it as a master page. Once we have the master page we want, we can set the master page for the site and then the master page we want to use for the specific channel.

We can selectively include or exclude portions of page layout for each channel. In the case where a device belongs to multiple channels, we can rank the channels so that devices with a higher ranking get the channel specifically for them first. All page layouts work with all the channels defined. To set the page layout designs apart between channels, we can use the Device Channel Panel control. The Device Channel Panel can be added to a page layout to control what content is rendered in which channel.

■ **Note** You can learn more about device detection in SharePoint 2013 in Chapter 5 when we show how to build a responsive web design to target specific devices.

Design Manager

One of the key features that will help us with branding in SharePoint 2013 is the new Design Manager feature. Design Manager provides one single place to upload design files, edit master pages, edit display templates to customize the display of search results, edit page layouts, publish and apply design, manage device channels for rendering of the site on mobile browsers, and export design packages. To launch Design Manager, shown in Figure 1-6, click Site Settings and then click Design Manager.

Electronics ▾   Home   ✎ EDIT LINKS

Design Manager: Welcome

1. Welcome
2. Manage Device Channels
3. Upload Design Files
4. Edit Master Pages
5. Edit Display Templates
6. Edit Page Layouts
7. Publish and Apply Design
8. Create Design Package

The Design Manager helps you create your own site design in SharePoint. Learn how SharePoint sites work

If you aren't creating your own design, you may instead want to choose from one of the following options:

- Import a complete design package
- Pick a pre-installed look

Otherwise, go ahead to the next step of the Design Manager. Get an overview

Figure 1-6. Use Design Manager to manage device channels, upload design files, edit master pages, edit display templates, edit page layouts, publish and apply design, and export design packages

Design Manager makes it easy to implement custom branded sites. First, designers can upload design assets (HTML, CSS, images, etc.) to Design Manager in a development environment. We can map the site collection as a network drive to upload the HTML version of the master page, upload CSS and JavaScript files, and access design files for editing. We can also edit SharePoint design files in Dreamweaver by opening the file from the mapped drive.

In SharePoint, designers can customize the master pages and page layouts with real-time preview of all the design components. When customizing the master page and page layouts, Design Manager provides a snippet gallery to make it easier for designers to add SharePoint components to the page. Design Manager generates HTML snippets of the controls so that they can be used in any web design tools. This ensures designers can use any web design tools because SharePoint and ASP.NET markups will be ignored in web design tools. Finally, when everything is completed, designers can export a design package as a *.wsp file to implement the custom branding in a production environment.

A design package contains all the content we have added or changed in the master page gallery, style library, theme library, device channels list, and page content types. Note that a design package does not include pages, navigation settings, or Term Store. In the new SharePoint environment, importing the design package will cause all the design assets in the design package to overwrite any existing files on the site, and the imported design will be applied as the current site design. The site's default and system master page, theme, and alternate CSS will all be set to the files in the design package.

Design Manager is available at the top-level site of a site collection. It is a feature that is part of the Publishing Portal site template. With Design Manager, we can add custom SharePoint components and ribbon elements. We can use several out-of-the-box SharePoint master pages and page layouts as our starting point to customize our own.

■ **Note**   You can learn more about how to convert a standard HTML web template into SharePoint master pages using the new Design Manager in SharePoint 2013 in Chapter 4.

Snippet Gallery

Designers can now configure SharePoint controls without knowing too much about SharePoint using the Snippet Gallery. We can quickly and easily add more functionalities to our site by adding many out-of-the-box SharePoint components to our pages. The Snippet Gallery is a page that shows us all the SharePoint components we need for the page we are designing. First we select a SharePoint component to add to the page, and then configure its properties, edit the generated HTML, and add CSS to brand the component. Then we can copy the resulting HTML snippet into our design files.

Display Templates

Before SharePoint 2013, to customize the display of search results, we had to write custom XSL to change the look and feel. It was also very limited in how much we could enhance. In SharePoint 2013, built on top of the Core Results web part, display templates can be used to design the presentation of search results. Use provided templates or create custom display templates to define the look and the overall structure of search results, to customize the look of groups of results, and to change how each result item is presented.

■ **Note** To learn more about how to create custom display templates, refer to Chapter 9.

Web Content Management Client Side Object Model

Because Web Content Management sites are based on SharePoint sites, lists, and libraries, developers can interact with the content by using standard SharePoint application programming interfaces (APIs). Before SharePoint 2013, to leverage Publishing namespaces, we had to leverage the server-side API. SharePoint 2013 exposes standard APIs to enable client-side and remote development opportunities. Developers can now interact with the content by using the Publishing and Taxonomy namespace in the client-side object model. Most of the server-side APIs are now available in corresponding client-side object model, Silverlight, and JavaScript assemblies. Some SharePoint APIs are even available in Windows Phone framework. To learn more about server-side API reference, client-side API reference, and JavaScript API reference in SharePoint 2013, refer to the Microsoft MSDN documentation at `http://sprwd.com/uqaibqq`.

■ **Note** You can learn more about the SharePoint 2013 client-side object model in Chapter 10 when we show how to build rich interactive forms and in Chapter 12 when we demonstrate how to use the JavaScript client object model to interact with SharePoint lists in a SharePoint App.

Support for Multilingual Sites

Although SharePoint 2010 supported building multilingual web sites using Variations, content translation required a fair amount of manual work. To export content for translation, we have to mark the column containing the content in the site as translatable. Export content for translation then exports all the content in the site to be translated, instead of providing a granular set of content to translate. After we choose Export Variation, all the content, variation information, and translatable field information will be exported into a content migration package. Identifying the content and the relevant fields to be translated is not straightforward. We have to first identify which field to translate by cross-referencing field IDs and then identifying which actual content should be translated.

In SharePoint 2013, the Variations feature continues to make content available to specific audiences on different sites based on the language settings of their web browser. Exporting and importing content for translation is much easier with the new translation package. Each translation package contains one file with source and target language information and the content to be translated. SharePoint 2013 now has an integrated translation service that lets content authors select content for human translation or specify content for machine translation (using the integrated Bing translator). These capabilities not only provide support for multilingual sites, but also ensure that content is created once and reused. After the content is first translated using Variations, the content in different languages is crawled. The result can be rendered in different languages for different audiences on different devices.

■ **Note**   The Machine Translation Service feature is available in all editions of SharePoint 2013. It is also available on Office 365. For more up-to-date information on feature availability on SharePoint online and license requirements, refer to Microsoft TechNet at `http://sprwd.com/dhmpvbk`.

Variations for Multilingual Sites

In SharePoint 2010, we could use Variations to make content available to users based on languages, devices, or branding needs. In SharePoint 2013, variation is used exclusively for multilingual sites. The Variations feature copies the content from a source variation site to one or more target variation sites to make the content available to different users across different sites. Users are redirected to the appropriate variable site based on the language setting in their browser. Content authors now have the ability to replicate an entire list or multiple labels on source variation sites to be propagated to target sites. It's important to note that list items such as documents, images, or announcements propagate independently from pages. The content author only needs to republish the content that was modified. SharePoint 2013 improves performance for variation by enabling bulk export of pages. It creates smaller export packages of content to allow for easy start and stop of the replication of content.

Integrated Translation Service

In SharePoint 2013, content can be automatically translated using the Bing translation service or by exporting the content in industry-standard XLIFF file format for third-party translation. After the content is translated, it can be imported back into SharePoint. We can export content for translation at a granular level, instead of at the site level. Each translation package contains one file with source and target language information as well as the content to be translated. In addition, the navigation taxonomy can be exported for external translation, which enables the site to have multilingual friendly URLs.

■ **Note**   You can learn more about support for multilingual web sites in SharePoint 2013 in Chapter 14 when we demonstrate how to build multilingual sites using the Variations, Machine Translation Service, and exporting content for third-party translation.

Summary

With the rapid growth of devices and browsers people use today to access the Internet, there is an immense need to build web sites that use responsive design to adapt to the capabilities of a specific browser or device. SharePoint 2013 has been rearchitected to provide better support for HTML5, CSS3, and JavaScript. For the first time, SharePoint provides the ability to target different devices. Also new to SharePoint, designers and developers have the flexibility to use the tools and technologies with which they are familiar. With significant enhancements to the client object model, SharePoint 2013 allows you to build rich interactive web sites. For the first time in SharePoint, you no longer need to develop custom solutions to service content across site collections. SharePoint 2013 introduces a cross-site publishing feature that works together with search to bring content together across site collections. For the first time in SharePoint, managed metadata is integrated with content publishing to allow you to drive your site navigation and to build friendly URLs based on Term Store hierarchies derived from business concepts instead of site structures.

■ ■ ■

CHAPTER 2

Responsive Web Design and Development with HTML5

Empty your mind, be formless. Shapeless, like water. If you put water into a cup, it becomes the cup. You put water into a bottle and it becomes the bottle. You put it in a teapot it becomes the teapot. Now, water can flow or it can crash. Be water my friend.

—Bruce Lee

This chapter is focused on providing you an overview of how responsive web design came into existence, starting with a trip down memory lane and then an idea of where we are going. The remainder of the chapter then focuses on the three core ingredients that make up any responsive web design, including a ramp-up on the latest HTML5, CSS3, and jQuery features. We then end the chapter with some key strategies in your solutions whether you are developing for SharePoint or not.

Our Scenario

In Chapter 3 we introduce the web design process and how it will apply to a scenario we build throughout this book. For now, let's look at an example of responsive web design in action based on the site this book uses to demonstrate branding and responsive web development on the SharePoint 2013 platform. In Figure 2-1 we can see the Specter Group site that we will be building for three primary groups of screen resolutions: desktop, tablet, and mobile. All three views leverage the same custom components but the visualization of the content changes based on the screen resolution.

Figure 2-1. *Specter Group web site in desktop, tablet, and mobile views*

As you can see based on the screen resolution of the browser and device, the same content will be displayed but visualized differently.

Through the rest of this chapter, we seek to help you understand, and teach the tools required to implement responsive web design and continue improving your skills.

Above the Fold

Remember when we first started building web sites, in the late 1990s, one of the first things that we'd do is browse the web to see if any sites would inspire us. For those web sites that awed us, we'd not only appreciate how beautiful the design was, but we'd also look at the source code to view how the designers leveraged HTML and CSS. At that time, HTML was still in its infancy, and the browser wars between Internet Explorer and Netscape Navigator were in full swing. Browser vendors were actually providing browser-specific HTML and CSS tags that swayed web designers to build sites that worked better in a specific browser versus another.

Web designers would proudly display a banner in the footer such as the once popular banner shown in Figure 2-2. This was a way to tell their visitors what browser would provide them the optimal experience.

Figure 2-2. *Typical banner you would see when viewing a site*

Targeting web sites for a specific browser worked well for web designers, as they did not have to build and test for multiple browsers. But how did visitors feel when they visited a site with a banner? The banner was a constant reminder that their browser was not properly equipped. Typically, they would get a gentle reminder to upgrade their browser; worse, the site would refuse to load. Seeing such a banner on a web site could make users cringe. Why? Designers were defining what browsers we could use to browse their sites, and in a sense, the Internet as a whole. This went against everything the web was envisioned for: a universally accessible resource. Aren't we glad that Tim Berners-Lee, inventor of the World Wide Web and director of the W3C, felt the same way?

> *Anyone who slaps a "this page is best viewed with Browser X" label on a Web page appears to be yearning for the bad old days, before the Web, when you had very little chance of reading a document written on another computer, another word processor, or another network.*

> —Tim Berners-Lee, *Technology Review* (July 1996)

The single most important optimization that you can do for any web site is to optimize what content they see above the fold. Figure 2-3 shows how little of the Specter Group site you would be viewing if it weren't for the recent advances made on viewports.

Figure 2-3. *Without the viewport defined, the left image is the limited section of the site (right image) you would be viewing*

Visually, the first viewable portion of any device's browser is called the viewport. As web developers, you have the ability to define the viewport. In the past, you had to design specifically for above the fold. Apple recognized this early on and provided a metatag named Viewport as part of their release of the iPhone. With the viewport not set, it was always a problem for web sites. You missed so much of the site that usually with previous smart phones, we had to squint, zoom, and pan web sites and try to click on links for sites that were not optimized. Smart phones have come of age but web sites are still lagging.

There's nothing wrong with optimizing for the common browsers that your visitors are using. However, for users who are still viewing your site on older browsers or mobile browsers, do the right thing and give them an alternative. It might not look as polished or as sophisticated, but as long as the site is functional, you've done your visitors a service. If you want to continue building a site that targets specific browsers, you are practicing browser-centric design, a slippery slope to follow.

In this chapter we investigate the general concepts of a current technique used to build both modern and stylish sites that are backward-compatible with older browsers, referred to as responsive web design. We review the origins of responsive web design and how it evolved. We'll also have a quick look at some of the new features of HTML5, CSS3, and jQuery that make responsive web design more practical. We continue by diving into the basics of what makes a site a candidate for responsive web design and finish with a look at some of the best practices of implementing responsive web design.

Change Is the Only Constant

Over the past decade, the popularity of mobile devices has made it far more important for web designers to keep mobile devices in mind when designing web sites. Mobile users are expected to outpace desktop users by the time you are reading this book. Whether it is mice and keyboards, phone keyboards, game consoles, or touch interfaces, users expect that when they interact with a web site it caters to their method of input. As the web grows to multiple device form factors, visitors want a unique experience regardless of the unique combination of form factor, input mechanism, browser, and screen resolution they are using. Web designers are continuing to evolve their design methodologies, so it is important to see where we came from, before we know where we are now and where we are going.

Graceful Degradation

When web development started gaining popularity, web designers leveraged the functionalities the latest web technologies had to offer and showcased them in modern browsers. This was great for those visitors who had modern browsers, but visitors with older browsers were unfortunately left behind. When browsers encountered tags that they didn't recognize or couldn't display, the browsers would not crash. Instead the markup was ignored and the browser would do its best to display the remaining web site markup.

The concept of graceful degradation was introduced as best practice for providing the best experience to users with the latest modern browsers. For those who didn't have a modern browser, web designers would not provide equivalents. Visitors with the latest modern browsers felt like first-class citizens and interacted with the site as web designers intended. Those without the latest web browsers were at least given a web site that degraded gracefully to a lower level of functionality.

One simple example of graceful degradation is the "alt" attribute for images. When the alt attribute is used properly, it displays a text alternative that conveys the same information as the image. Visitors who can't view the image or have browsers that can't display images get to see the alternate texts. Given that an image is worth a thousand words, it's still fair to say that the text equivalent is not aesthetically pleasing, which slightly degrades the user experience.

Although in theory graceful degradation seemed to make sense, what happened in practice was that web designers built sites for those with the most modern browsers. Visitors with older browsers were left with limited or reduced functionality as the web designers did not design or code sites that would in fact degrade gracefully. In essence, graceful degradation worked as a basic measure, but in practice it did not help.

Progressive Enhancement

Progressive enhancement, on the other hand, begins with the basic version of the site to ensure that it works on all browsers. Web designers can then add enhancements specifically for modern browsers. Progressive enhancement focuses on content first rather than functionality, which is important, as content is truly the only reason any one of us browse or build web sites in the first place. As a comparison, graceful degradation prioritized presentation and functionality before content and progressive enhancement prioritized content to the top of the web designer's priority list.

■ **Note** Aaron Gustafson wrote a great article, "A List Apart," detailing the differences between graceful degradation and progressive enhancement. For the use of Peanut M&M's as an analogy alone, it's well worth the read at http://sprwd.com/5rzfdkd.

Another factor that helped push progressive enhancement as a favorable approach over graceful degradation was how quickly older browsers were not supported by web designers. More often than not, web designers were asked to support older browsers. As we know, older browser versions and browser vendors render HTML and CSS tags differently. This is a battle web designers find it hard to win, as they are always trying to achieve pixel-perfect solutions. The argument went that it didn't make sense to be putting in twice the effort for a smaller subset of visitors who were still using older browsers. Focusing on content and ensuring that all visitors are able to view content in all browsers was a reasonable goal and any advanced functionality web designers wanted to make available could be tailored to the browsers that supported them.

The simplest example of progressive enhancement is the use of the external CSS style sheet. Modern browsers apply the external CSS style sheet to the site, whereas non-CSS browsers simply ignore it. For non-CSS browsers this means that only the content loads up and the browsers present it using built-in styles.

Progressive enhancement builds a rich experience on top of an accessible core without compromising that core. It improves on graceful degradation by prioritizing content over presentation. This is a great step forward and is still the basis of modern web design, but then mobile devices came along.

Separate Mobile Site

By the time progressive enhancement had become popular, the mobile phone revolution was gaining speed. Web designers were being sanctioned to build sites tailored for mobile devices, primarily by building separate mobile sites. They were even going so far as having separate mobile domains to tailor to mobile visitors. But it wasn't until the iPhone was introduced in 2007 that mobile usage really started gaining speed. Mobile sites all of sudden not only became mainstream, but web designers were starting to create feature-rich separate mobile sites tailored to the iPhone. In a matter of just a few years, web designers were now being asked to ensure that their sites were viewable and functional on multiple devices.

Creating separate mobile sites and ensuring that they worked on a multitude of devices was popular for a while. However, as the sheer number of smart devices grew, this approach simply became uneconomical. Web designers now had to consider the user experience for each variation of mobile device, browser, operating system, and display resolution, and how to best take advantage of each combination. Further complicating matters, web design had to be completely reimagined for the keyboard and touch interface.

The same code base typically wasn't used for both sites (larger and smaller devices) and because of that, development costs were higher. Web designers learned very quickly and this time around, they knew there had to be a better way. The problems faced in developing separate mobile sites ended up being the same problems web designers faced when developing sites for larger devices (i.e., different browsers on desktops).

■ **Note** There are benefits to creating mobile-specific sites. Read Nielsen Norman Group's recommendations, which are outlined in Mobile Site vs. Full Site at `http://sprwd.com/7ecobq`. What approach will you take for your project?

Responsive Web Design

Progressive enhancement, graceful degradation, and separate mobile sites all have their place in a web designer's toolbox. However, having web designers create specialized web sites for specific devices was not a favorable approach. Necessity is the mother of innovation, and web design needed a savior: Let us introduce responsive web design. Responsive web design is about developing a site from the beginning for all screen resolutions, browsers, and devices.

Responsive web design is all about building a web site that is resolution and device independent. It is an evolution of web design, rather than a revolution. Why? Primarily because the foundation of responsive web design stems from two existing web design approaches: graceful degradation and progressive enhancement. The term responsive web design was coined by Ethan Marcotte in the popular article at A List Apart, "Responsive Web Design" (`http://sprwd.com/3u6qod`), as an approach that popularized the use of flexible grid layouts, flexible images, and media queries into one unified methodology.

■ **Tip** Interested in diving straight into how responsive web design works in SharePoint 2013? Skip over to Chapter 5 to learn how to convert your fixed-width designs to be responsive.

If we are to truly have a responsive methodology to web design, we should design for the smallest viewport first and then progressively enhance the design and content for larger viewports. We can create one web site that adapts based on the features available on that device as well as screen size.

■ **Note** Learn more about the specifics of responsive web design in the section, "Responsive Web Design: The Core Ingredients" later in this chapter.

Adaptive Design

Does it stop at responsive web design? Not at all. Responsive web design is just the latest design principle in ever evolving web design methodologies. Keep in mind that responsive web design is not a silver bullet and has limitations as it is based around the fluid grid. What if we still want to build tailored or semi-tailored experiences for different viewports all in one site? Web designers started looking at the principles of responsive web design and including the principle of feature detection in progressive enhancement. This has evolved into a general methodology, adaptive web design.

As a web designer, wouldn't you want to keep an eye on your visitors and what device they are using to experience your site and how? Now that the site has been built from the ground up to leverage responsive web design based on device capabilities, browser capabilities, and browser resolution, what happens next?

Analytics and usage patterns are really the driving factor behind adaptive design. Don't we want to know what devices, browsers, and resolutions are most popular? Which ones are the least popular? Is there a segment of the site's visitors that have not been looked after? If so, is there a good enough reason for this? All these questions and more are important. After the site launch, there are quite a few opportunities you can take advantage of to adapt your current design; here are a few:

- *Feature detection.* Why not detect and apply only those features that the device and browser can handle? This is similar to progressive enhancement, but might differ because this does not only include improving the site based on available features, but possibly modifying the layout or content of the site based on the device.

- *Device APIs.* Take advantage of functionality device manufacturers provide via APIs to leverage device accelerometers and even functionality like near field communication (NFC) as part of the user experience that's provided to enhance the site visitors' experience.

- *Performance.* Having taken advantage of responsive web design, is there a large audience of members that need a targeted web design because of their low bandwidth? Why not consider a solution to address this for your users? This could be as simple as removing the use of images for navigation and instead using text and CSS.

- *Touch optimization.* Have you considered leveraging gestures to browse and interact with your web site? As more devices provide touch-focused user interface, why not have your web site take advantage of this?

- *Platform optimization.* One of the things you'll quickly learn is that you can start looking at analytics to view which device and operating system combination is most popular for visitors browsing your site. Why not provide them tips to have your web site be pinned on their mobile home page? If part of the site's marketing strategy is to provide a mobile application, why not suggest that to the visitors on their first visit.

Adaptive design and responsive web design are both paradigm shifts for many web designers to start building a single web site that tailors to different devices, browsers, and resolutions. It provides web designers the opportunity to focus on content first and then layer on functionality.

A web designer's design process never stops. It consistently continues to improve and the expectation is that it'll help us to keep improving our processes. As students of web design, let's ensure that we all take an oath to keep evolving, improving, responding, and adapting our designs and in turn, enriching the experience of those visitors who use our sites.

Responsive Web Design: The Core Ingredients

The three fundamental ingredients that make the responsive web design recipe are:

- *Fluid grid*. This is about building your designs on a grid so that it can adjust to different environments.

- *Flexible media (i.e., images)*. They can adapt to grow or shrink to fit with a flexible grid column, yet take it a step further and don't display (or even load) a higher resolution image, meant for the desktop, on a screen that is as small as a smart phone.

- *Media queries*. Driven by CSS, allow the web designers to apply different CSS style rules based on characteristics (most commonly the screen width).

Let's take a closer look into these three pillars of responsive web design.

Fluid Grid

As part of the creative design process, designers use a grid system to align and organize elements in a visually pleasing way on a particular page layout. The grid system uses a combination of margins, rows, and columns. The driving force behind leveraging a grid system in your designs is alignment. The alignment helps visitors recognize patterns and these patterns simplify designs to make them easily recognizable.

Building a grid system, in theory, is fairly easy. For instance, you start your design with a 1,000-pixel-wide container and you want to split it up into three (equally sized) columns. Each column would be one third the size of the container, or 333 1/3 pixel per column. That doesn't exactly add up, so we add 10-pixel margins on each side of every column. This means we also must subtract the 20 pixels from the width of each column. Adding the three columns, roughly 313 pixels wide for each column, 10 pixel margins on each side and we still end up with a container 999 pixels wide, not 1,000 pixels wide. You might continue this process to splitting your design to enforce structure using grids. Figure 2-4 shows how a sample of a site page might look with grids defining where the content can be placed.

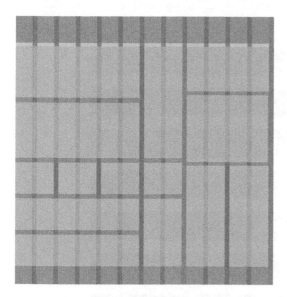

Figure 2-4. *Web page divided in a grid-based approach*

Taking a step back and looking at this image allows you to appreciate some of the beauty that can be achieved using a grid system.

You could continue the process of creating this pixel-perfect grid using HTML and CSS, but why go through all that trouble when someone else already has?

■ **Note**   The CSS visual model is all lines and boxes, which lends itself to the grid system. The advantage of CSS allows us to take a box—any box—and do with it what we want, independent of its surrounding boxes. Read more about the CSS basic box model from `http://sprwd.com/43caf3`.

Nathan Smith created the 960 Grid System as a simple way to lay out web sites using a grid that is 960 pixels wide. Using this system, the 960-pixel-width container can now be split into 12- or 16-column grids. In the 12-column version, shown in Figure 2-5, the narrowest column is 60 pixels wide. Each column after that increases by 80 pixels. Ten-pixel margins surround the container and a 10-pixel gutter is also included to separate the columns. Overall, this grid system was one of the most popular and helped pave the way for many different iterations.

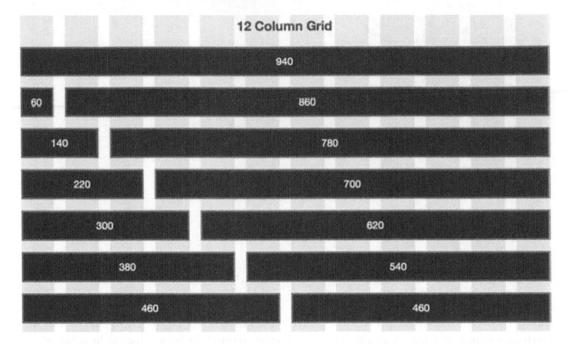

Figure 2-5. *12-column variation of the 960 Grid System*

The 960 Grid System helped many designers build their designs using the appropriate CSS classes. The CSS classes they used determined the width and surrounding margins for that column(s). With responsive web design, we are building for mobile first and adding features as the resolution increases. Fluid grids expanded on this concept with the grid system(s) in place, to allow for grid column widths to adapt dependent on the device viewport. If the viewport was 768 pixels or 1,200 pixels, the main container and its encompassing columns would adjust accordingly.

■ **Tip**   To learn more about CSS frameworks and the chosen framework in this book, refer to Chapter 5.

Media Queries

Media queries, an aspect of CSS, are not new. CSS2 have supported media-dependent styles but they were limited to basic media differentiations such as for screen or for print. As an example, in Listing 2-1 and Listing 2-2 we see two different methods using CSS2 standards to link to different style sheets based on the media or styles that reference media.

Listing 2-1. HTML <link> Tag Utilizing Value CSS2 Media Queries

```
<link rel="stylesheet" type="text/css" media="screen" href="styles-screent.css">
<link rel="stylesheet" type="text/css" media="print" href="styles-print.css">
```

Listing 2-2. HTML Styles Utilizing Value CSS2 Media Queries

```
<style type="text/css">
   @media screen {
      body {font-family: sans-serif; }
   }
```

```
@media print {
    body {font-family: serif; }
}
</style>
```

CSS3 builds on media queries previously available by allowing us to filter by more viewport values. Of most importance to responsive web design are viewport width filters. You don't necessarily have to have multiple style sheets to accommodate all the different screen sizes and browsers that your visitors might use. However, if you do prefer a different style for each design, you can use the code in Listing 2-3, for example, to do so.

Listing 2-3. In-Line Media Query

```
<link rel="stylesheet" media="screen and (max-device-width: 480px)" href="480px.css" />
<link rel="stylesheet" media="screen and (min-width: 600px)" href="large.css" />
```

For CSS3-capable browsers, the styles found in `small.css` will only be used if the maximum device width of the device is 480px. Two important notes are in order here. First, different browsers will handle a media query in a `<link>` tag differently. As an example, even though Firefox 9.0 and older versions support media queries, the `min-width` media query is not recognized but the rules inside the style sheets are still parsed and applied.

■ **Note** For information on which browsers support media queries, review `http://sprwd.com/puxa8x`.

Second, older browsers such as Internet Explorer 8.0, which do not support media queries, will ignore the media value and thus download and parse all linked to styles. This could be a problem, so for now, we will want to always include `@media` blocks in our style sheets as shown in Listing 2-4.

Listing 2-4. @media CSS3 Tag

```
@media screen and (max-width: 600px) {
    .sixhundredmaxwidth {
        clear: both;
        font-size: 1.3em;
    }
}
```

Going back to Listing 2-3, the `large.css` will only be loaded if the minimum width of the browser is 600px. There are those who prefer, for the sake of efficiency, to have a single CSS file that contains all the styles for different browsers and sizes. This eliminates the need for multiple requests for several different sheets. You can achieve media queries with each individual CSS declaration by using a `@media` CSS block as seen in Listing 2-4.

In this example we are specifying that the `sixhundremaxwidth` CSS class should only load when the maximum browser width is 600px. In Listing 2-5, we leverage the mobile handheld's ability to handle orientation for containers or sections labeled landscape.

Listing 2-5. Seek Orietation Feature for Intranet

```
@media screen and (orientation: landscape) {
    .landscape {
        width: 30%;
        float: right;
    }
}
```

27

There are many benefits to leveraging media queries in your web sites. Keep these basic techniques in mind as future chapters build on what we've just seen.

Flexible Media

Traditionally, any content (text, images, or video) on the web was designed to be suitable for a fixed-width experience. Now that you are building for a responsive web site, you need to start considering how media is going to be viewed on different viewports.

When designing for a responsive web site, say that your <h1> tag is styled with a font size of 26 pixels for the desktop view. What would the font size be for the tablet view or mobile view? You will need to account for font type that is proportionate to the sizes of the view. Similarly, the same thought process can be applied images, video, and other media.

In terms of text, it's a little bit easier to tame how content is viewed on different viewports. Everyone has his or her own approach, but one of the widely accepted best practices is to start with a base font size from which all other font sizes are proportioned.

■ **Note**   If you would like to dive deeper into text sizing, make sure you read the A List Apart article, "How to Size Text in CSS," at http://sprwd.com/99qqfnn.

Resizing a font is one thing, but trying to resize images and other forms of media introduces other problems. The first problem that you typically face is that if you have a fluid grid layout, media (e.g., images) are typically added using a fixed width. When you resize the image container, the image width does not change and therefore won't resize to fit within a fluid layout. There is a relatively easy fix to this problem that prevents images from exceeding the width of their containers, shown in Listing 2-6.

Listing 2-6. Flexible Image CSS Property

```
img {
    max-width: 100%;
}
```

A few years ago, defining the maximum width to 100 percent introduced issues with height and width aspect ratio. However, current browsers will resize images proportionally so that the image's aspect ratio remains intact. What's great about this simple approach is that we can actually apply this magic rule (max-width) to other media-ready elements (see Listing 2-7).

Listing 2-7. General Flexible Media Including Older Browser Support

```
img, embed, object, video {
    max-width: 100%;
    // support for IE5.5, IE6, IE7
    width: expression(this.width > 400 ? 400 : true);
}
```

This only works if your targeted browsers support the max-width property. Therefore, Listing 2-7 also includes code to support browsers, such as Internet Explorer 5.5, Internet Explorer 6.0, and Internet Explorer 7.0. However, we now run into our second problem. Even if you resize media on your site to dynamically fit within its container, you are still loading the same file for different devices.

■ **Tip** Although setting the video width to 100 percent is a good first step, you might want to go a step beyond and have height calculated based on the width. Read the article "Creating Intrinsic Ratios for Video" from A List Apart at `http://sprwd.com/2nbt2z`.

As a quick example of this download issue, say we have a large, high-resolution image we place on a particular page and say this image has a file size of 80k because it should display on a 960-pixel-wide design. If we intend to use this same image for a mobile device that has a 320-pixel-wide viewport, the mobile browser will still download the entire 80k image and resize it to fit the viewport. That is a large file to download considering how small it could be if instead we could have provided a smaller image. Furthermore, we might not have even wanted to display the large image at all on a smaller viewport. We'd try to hide the media using display: none. Despite the right intentions, a mobile browser might still download the image before it was hidden.

The second problem can be addressed by leveraging media queries. This means that you can have multiple images with different sizes for each device and browser combination. This obviously poses a different problem, as it can be burdensome to create so many variations of images. Proper planning would be required.

■ **Note** Loading device optimized media works when the browser supports it, but what happens when the visitor is using an older browser? SharePoint 2013 includes a new feature called Image Renditions. Learn more at `http://sprwd.com/46xffr`.

This was just a brief introduction to the three key elements of what makes responsive web design: fluid grids, flexible images, and media queries. The key to remember when designing your site is that responsive web design is not perfect. In the next section, we review a few of the gotchas and best practices when making responsive design part of your web development workflow.

Using the Right Tools

Responsive web design is a paradigm shift in designing web sites primarily because it gained momentum when the development languages matured and the web design community evolved. Responsive web design leverages a blend of different features from HTML5, CSS3, jQuery, and other web technologies that allow web sites to adapt to the device's environment.

You've had the opportunity to read how responsive web design evolved, and you've also had an opportunity to view screenshots of a sample site we build throughout this book that uses responsive design principles. Now, let's take the opportunity to go under the hood and learn how responsive web design is developed. Once you've become accustomed to the core functionality, we'll share some advice on how to continue adapting. Without these basic skills and an understanding of the underlying technologies, you will likely find it difficult to not only brand your SharePoint 2013 sites, but more important, brand them using responsive design principles.

HTML5

HTML5 is the latest markup standard that aims to improve how content is structured and presented. One of the biggest aims is to improve the markup language with support for the latest media. This section covers the new HTML5 features, and we look specifically at how the DOCTYPE has evolved and one of the biggest changes to come HTML5, semantic elements.

What's New in HTML5?

HTML5 offers many new features that have become popular or defined by the web design community. Here is a list of the key notable features:

- *Better browsers.* Browser vendors are encouraged more than ever to support web standards and even extend the functionalities of HTML5. This competition is and will continue to greatly benefit users.

- *Accessibility improvements.* ARIA attributes are included in the HTML5 standard to ensure that visitors have access to the same information regardless of how they browse the web.

- *Geolocation.* With the approval of the user, you can use his or her geographical position to help visitors plot their position on a map, such as finding the nearest coffee shop relative to a visitor's current location.

- *No third party API needed.* In the HTML5 world, when it is complete, plug-ins and third-party APIs will be second class. Your web browser will be the first-class citizen and most probably the only software you need to browse the web.

- *Video tag.* The popularity of YouTube, Netflix, and Hulu have driven built-in support for video streaming. More and more people want browsers to be able to stream video content as quickly and smoothly as possible. The HTML5 video tag provides a seamless video experience across all devices. Unfortunately like the third-party API feature, the video tag is still not widely supported in the same manner across different browsers and thus is not ready for prime time.

- *Awesome mobile support.* HTML5 on mobile devices supports advanced functionality similar to desktops, such as Offline Web Storage, GeoLocation API, Canvas Drawing, and CSS3 to name a few. HTML5 applications, like Windows Modern apps, can even run on mobile devices without a browser.

- *Immersive experiences.* HTML5 gives web designers much more control over the browser and allows them to develop games and applications that were once not possible in the browser. An example is `http://www.soul-reaper.com`, an HTML5 scroll book that uses the new `Canvas` tag, a part of HTML5.

- *Smart new canvas feature.* Taking advantage of what Apple started, the canvas element is a rectangle in your page where you can use JavaScript to draw almost anything (2D shapes, bitmap images, etc.) you want.

- *Form fields and validation.* There's no need to leverage existing JavaScript plug-ins to do form validation anymore. Validating form fields can now be handled with only HTML5. You'll also see a host of new form fields, everything from e-mail and telephone to autofocus.

- *Semantic tags.* Originally a hot topic of HTML5 allowing us to create any tag name we want such as `<header>`, `<footer>`, `<nav>`, `<section>`, and `<article>`, semantic tags, although nice for the web developer, have been declining in use on HTML5 sites as they are not well defined. For accessible sites we are often better off using ARIA attributes such as role rather than semantic tags such as `<nav>` or `<article>`.

It's worth noting that although HTML5 makes good on the promise of moving the web forward, the standard is still in the works. HTML5 is not one big feature but a collection of features. Many of the features (tags) just listed are supported by modern browsers but do not have widespread adoption.

Out of the many tags that are not ready for prime time, as previously mentioned, the HTML5 Video tag is not gaining support from major video-producing web sites because there is no standard video format. Users are not able to display full-screen video, and content protection issues exist. Feature support with other browsers is starting to pick up with browser vendors but there are some concerns from many inside and outside the industry.

With HTML5 you can accomplish a site's functionality natively without the need for plug-ins. Although we cannot detect for full HTML5 support, as support for HTML5 features increases, we can use tools to detect for "feature" support, meaning we can detect if say, geolocation, is available. Based on whether it is or is not, you can present the visitor different experiences with the site. In terms of HTML5 JavaScript API support, if your browser does not support it as of yet, your browser will still act as if these features are not present and simply run the JavaScript as before.

The full specification of HTML5 has not been confirmed, and likely will not be until 2020 or beyond, yet many of the major browsers have already started supporting HTML5 features. In the past, you needed multiple plug-ins to achieve many of the features visitors have learned to expect from web sites. Leveraging multiple custom plug-ins can be both a positive and a negative. The great thing to remember is HTML5 builds on the most successful format ever, HTML4.

What's a DOCTYPE?

At the top of every page, as per HTML standards, a DOCTYPE (short for document type declaration) defines for the browser which version of HTML you are using. All major browsers use DOCTYPEs to properly render web pages. The syntax in Listing 2-8 tells browsers whether CSS is stored externally and Listing 2-9 shows whether deprecated tags are used as well as external CSS.

Listing 2-8. HTML 4.01 Strict Syntax Tells the Browser That Presentational Markup Will Be Exclusively Stored in CSS Files

```
<!DOCTYPE HTML PUBLIC "-//W3C//DTD HTML 4.01//EN" "http://www.w3.org/TR/html4/strict.dtd">
<html>
    ...
</html>
```

Listing 2-9. XHTML 4.01 Transitional Syntax Adheres to the Strict Syntax But Deprecated Tags Are Allowed

```
<?xml version="1.0" encoding="UTF-8"?>
<!DOCTYPE html PUBLIC "-//W3C//DTD XHTML 1.0 Transitional//EN"
    "http://www.w3.org/TR/xhtml1/DTD/xhtml1-transitional.dtd">
<html xmlns="http://www.w3.org/1999/xhtml" xml:lang="en" lang="en">
    ...
</html>
```

If you are using an incomplete or outdated DOCTYPE, or no DOCTYPE at all, then most browsers switch to Quirks like mode, where the browser assumes you've written invalid markup and code.

■ **Note**   Document Type Definitions (DTDs) define the document structure with a list of legal elements and attributes. DOCTYPEs have always included reference DTDs as part of their definition. Two such examples of DTD are Strict and Transitional.

HTML5 still uses a DOCTYPE declaration but does not reference any DTD. There's no need to specify whether the doctype declaration is strict, transitional, frameset, or XHTML 1.1. This approach is so much better than what we had previously. All the DOCTYPE contains is the tag name of the root element of the document, HTML, as shown in Listing 2-10.

Listing 2-10. HTML5 Doctype Includes Only the Tag Name of the Toot Element of the Document

```
<!doctype html>
<html>
   ...
</html>
```

This is very simple doctype that will cause even browsers that don't support HTML5 to enter into standards mode. Standards mode means that popular HTML tags will still be supported, however, and if the browser does not support the new features of HTLM5 then the browser will ignore them.

SharePoint 2013 enforces XHTML compliance to ensure that an HTML document follows W3C best practices. Listing 2-11 shows how the HTML5 DOCTYPE should look in your HTML files, in particular HMTL files used by SharePoint 2013.

Listing 2-11. HTML5 Doctype to Make it SharePoint Compliant

```
<!DOCTYPE html>
<html>
   ...
</html>
```

■ **Tip** For your HTML document to be compliant with SharePoint 2013, the DOCTYPE tag must be in all caps.

Listing 2-12 shows a simple HTML5 document with minimum number of tags required.

Listing 2-12. Simple HTML5 Example

```
<!DOCTYPE html>
<html>
   <head>
      <title>Page Title</title>
   </head>
   <body>
      Content goes here....
   </body>
 </html>
```

As you'll notice the DOCTYPE declaration is clean and generally HTML5 has not changed what we've already learned.

The Semantic Web

HTML and browsers both have always been fairly forgiving when structure was not followed. Previously, in HTML4, we used <div> or <span> tags to signify different sections of the HTML page and we used other elements such as <h1>, <h2>, <h3>, <h4>, <h5>, or <h6> to provide heading titles as a quick example. If used well, div tags generally worked well to not only form a document structure, but also to style content within a particular <div> block. As you know, leveraging CSS between different div tags is easy as we just specify descriptive ID (unique per page) or CLASS values. We are all familiar with this knowledge, so to start, Listing 2-13 shows a sample HTML5-compliant document with HTML4 tags.

Listing 2-13. Sample HTML5 Document That Uses Only HTML4 Tags

```html
<!DOCTYPE html>
<html>
<head>
   <title>HTML5 compliant with HTML4 markup</title>
</head>
<body>
   <div id="header">logo</div >
   <div id="nav">item 1, item 2, item 3</div>
   <div class="article">
      <div class="section"></div>
   </div>
   <div id="sidebar">related links</div>
   <div id="footer">copyright</div>
</body>
</html>
```

The problem with HTML4 markup is that the `<div>` tag gets used for more than just defining a section. Anyone viewing the markup, let alone a browser rendering the page, might find it difficult to answer the question, "Is that `<div>` block a part of the outline of the page, defining a section or a subsection, and so on, or is it primarily used for presentational purposes such as for styling?" DIV elements gained quite a bit of popularity and it seems that the W3C was looking to supplement how `<div>` tags were be used and decided to include dozens of new tags, that is, these semantic tags.

The general mindset was that the use of `<div>` tags in HTML4 lacked the necessary semantics for describing the different sections. This "improper" use of `<div>` tags has a direct impact on accessibility and assistive technology but also sectioning (which is driven by the document outlining algorithm).

Over the course of the past decade, developers and designers have always developed sites to fit their needs. As the popularity of search engines has grown, their ability to understand unstructured HTML has improved as well. Search engines, like Google, were interested in knowing how sites were structured so that they could deliver better search results. Google embarked on this initiative to find out and interestingly enough, despite millions of sites being developed differently, Google found that majority of them follow a similar structure: header, navigation, body content, footer, and so on. The result of this research has been very helpful to support the vision of the "semantic web" of Tim Berners-Lee. He originally expressed his vision of the semantic web as follows:

> *I have a dream for the Web ... [in which computers] become capable of analyzing all the data on the Web—the content, links, and transactions between people and computers. A "Semantic Web," which should make this possible, ... the day-to-day mechanisms of trade, bureaucracy and our daily lives will be handled by machines talking to machines.*

> —Tim Berners-Lee, *Weaving the Web* (1999)

The vision of Berners-Lee, the interest in search engines that better understand content and return search results, and the need of the web designer community has driven the surge of microformats. With the general progression of the web, HTML5 now allows new semantic elements. The HTML5 specifications outline both textual and structural "semantic" elements, everything from the `<header>`, `<footer>`, `<nav>`, `<section>`, `<aside>`, and `<article>` to the `<meter>` and `<progress>` elements.

■ **Tip** Want to read more about the truth about structuring HTML5 and semantic tags? Check out *The Truth About HTML5* by Luke Stevens. An enlightening excerpt of this book is available at `http://sprwd.com/5pohtwg`.

We intend to use the semantic tags HTML5 provides throughout this book so let's discuss common ways in which new, popular HTML5 semantic tags are utilized. Besides the `<section>` element, there are many other commonly used tags that we have already mentioned but now define in greater detail.

- **section.** A section element defines a portion of your page that should create a new section of the outline of the page. Examples of sections would be chapters, the various tabbed pages in a tabbed dialog box, or the numbered sections of a thesis. A web site's home page could be split into sections for an introduction, news items, and contact information.

- **header.** A header element is intended to contain a site's top header bar, or a section's heading (an h1–h6 element or an hgroup element), but this is not required. The header element can also be used to wrap a section's table of contents, a search form, or any relevant logos.

- **nav.** The nav element represents a section of a page that links to other pages or to parts within the page.

- **article.** An article element represents a self-contained composition in a document, page, application, or site that is, in principle, independently distributable or reusable, for example, in syndication. This could be a forum post, a magazine or newspaper article, a blog entry, a user-submitted comment, an interactive widget or gadget, or any other independent item of content.

- **footer.** The footer element represents a footer for its nearest ancestor sectioning content or sectioning root element. A footer typically contains information about its section such as who wrote it, links to related documents, copyright data, and the like.

■ **Note**   Although new semantic tags are only available in HTML5, older browsers such as Internet Explorer 8 will render the content within a new HTML5 block. The catch is that the older browsers will not apply any styling to tags, or content within tags, it does not recognize. Fortunately for us, a quick, easy-to-deploy JavaScript fix named html5shiv was developed. Learn more at http://sprwd.com/3bttbp. Html5shiv provides us a backstop, thus giving us little reason not to use HTML5 tags if we want to.

Now that you've been acquainted with the new sectioning elements introduced by HTML5, where does that leave the `<div>` element? It is still recommended for backward compatibility if we do not wish to require html5shiv to allow HTML5 tags in older browsers. When an element is being used simply for styling purposes or as a convenience for scripting, a `<div>` element could still be used.

Taking our HTML4 example document from Listing 2-13, we can replace the div elements with the new elements: header, nav, section, article, aside, and footer (see Listing 2-14).

Listing 2-14. HTML4 Example Updated Using HTML5 Semantic Tags

```
<!DOCTYPE html>
<html>
<head>
    <title>HTML5 document</title>
</head>
<body>
    <header>...</header>
    <nav>...</nav>
```

```
<article>
    <section>
        ...
    </section>
</article>
<aside>...</aside>
<footer>...</footer>
</body>
</html>
```

This does not stop you from continuing to use `<div>` tags in your HTML5 markup; however, there are benefits to using the HTML5 semantic elements. First, you are providing structure to your web content. Another benefit is that with this structure in place, you can shift your focus to accessibility. You can add accessibility information to HTML elements using the Accessible Rich Internet Applications specification [WAI-ARIA]. This specification can be implemented in conjunction with HTML5 and will further promote accessibility features in your web sites. When considering leveraging WAI-ARIA attributes within your web sites, you'll have to consider when and when not to use similar HTML5 elements.

■ **Note**   To learn more about HTML and ARIA, please visit `http://sprwd.com/7jux6r`.

Your experience with HTML development provides you a solid foundation to leverage HTML5 features in your existing solutions; just make sure you use the HTML5 DOCTYPE.

In theory, the HTML5 specification makes sense, but in the real world it seems things were taken to an extreme when introducing new tags. The web design community doesn't see a value in these additional semantic tags because the core problem that existed with `<div>` tags will still exist. The core problem is the lack of education on how HTML documents should be structured. Introducing new elements is a good first step, but education on how to effectively leverage these new semantic elements should not be left to the web design community; rather, it should be driven by the W3C to ensure that everyone is on the same page. The W3C has tried to introduce a more semantic web with HTML5 and they might not have fixed the issue, but it appears as though it's an issue they want to tackle.

CSS3

We know that CSS stands for Cascading Style Sheets and that it's a markup language that alters, and gives style, to a web site. CSS gives us the ability to separate presentation from HTML markup and further allows us to reuse the styles defined in the CSS for all pages in your web site.

CSS Basics

Although we are assuming you are already familiar with basic CSS, we review a very simple example to make sure we are on the same "page" so to speak. The CSS provided in Listing 2-15 declares that all text within the paragraph `<p>` tag, wherever it is in your document, should be colored red.

Listing 2-15. Change Paragraph Text Color to Red

```
p { color: red; }
```

If you have multiple paragraphs of text that are inside <p> tags throughout your HTML page, they will all be colored red. Sometimes you want a bit more control. CSS gives us the ability to control which elements we style and which ones we don't. We can describe elements using IDs and classes. Both classes and IDs are ways of further clarifying which elements we're planning to alter. In Listing 2-16 we see HTML markup for two paragraphs defined by an ID attribute and a CLASS attribute and in Listing 2-17 we see how we can style the different paragraph blocks.

Listing 2-16. Paragraph Tag With ID Attribute and CLASS Attribute

```
<p id="intro">Introducing our latest solution. </p>
<p class="aside">Check out what else we have to offer</p>
```

Listing 2-17. CSS to Style IDs and CLASS Attributes

```
p#intro { font-size: 125%; }
p.aside { font-style: italic; }
```

What's the difference between classes and IDs? IDs are unique identifiers that should only show up once on the HTML page, whereas classes are not unique and can be used multiple times in a given page, such as the example in Listing 2-18.

Listing 2-18. CSS With Multiple CLASS Attributes and a Single Style ID

```
<p id="intro">Introducing our latest solution. </p>
<p class="aside">Check out what else we have to offer</p>
<p class="aside">Make sure you connect with our partners</p>
```

We obviously know that CSS is much more complex than this. If you'd like to learn more, there are hundreds of books dedicated to CSS and all its features.

■ **Note**   New to CSS? We recommend learning from veteran web developer and trainer Jeffrey Way, who has created a free video-based course, 30 Days to Learn HTML & CSS (see http://sprwd.com/8h3avv).

Let's go ahead and move on to some of the new CSS3 features.

New CSS3 Features

CSS3 offers a huge variety of new ways to impact your designs, which before required a combination of CSS and JavaScript. Like HTML5, the CSS3 specification is not yet complete and is instead being completed in modules. A few of the modules have been completed and are part of the specification, others are being finalized, and some are being depreciated. We'd like to bring your attention to a few features that are becoming a part of the CSS3 specification due to their popularity as well as their importance with responsive web design, which we use throughout the rest of this book.

Media Queries

We already reviewed media queries earlier in this chapter, but let us review them again because of their importance in responsive web design. Listing 2-19 shows how you can leverage media queries to apply a color background for a specific resolution.

Listing 2-19. Apply a Color Background if the Viewing Area Is Smaller Than 800px

```
@media screen and (max-width: 800px) {
   .class {
      background: #ccc;
   }
}
```

Media queries become even more powerful as you can combine conditions. You can add multiple conditions and even load your style sheets based on these conditions. Listing 2-20 provides an example of how you can load a specific style sheet based on the media type and device width.

Listing 2-20. Load a Different Style Sheet Based on Media Type and Maximum Device Width

```
<link rel="stylesheet" type="text/css" media="only screen and (max-device-width: 480px)"
   href="small-device.css" />
```

The conditions are not just limited to `width` or `max-device-width`; there's also `height`, `orientation`, and `resolution` to name just a few.

■ **Note**   Want to learn more about media queries and all for their different options? Read the W3C's recommendation on Media Queries at `http://sprwd.com/6zpojss`.

Keep in mind that using media queries for mobile devices does not mean you have a mobile optimized site. To be truly mobile optimized, your markup and media need to be refactored for mobile devices. That means media queries are great when you are designing the presentation for different media types, but it does not mean you are optimizing for them.

■ **Tip**   The Specter Group site presents content and navigation differently based on the viewport, but more can be done to optimize media. To learn more about this, make sure you read Chapter 6.

Browser-Specific Prefixes

Vendors who build browsers are free to implement extensions to the CSS specifications that are specific to their browsers. There are various reasons to support this flexibility, from adding new features to providing early access for CSS properties that have not been finalized by the W3C.

As an example, a common problem that web designers faced was how to have opacity implemented the same in all browsers (see Listing 2-21). Opacity is currently a part of the CSS3 specification, but few browsers actually supported it a few years back.

Listing 2-21. How to Achieve Opacity Across Major Browsers Using Vendor-Specific CSS

```
.opacity-test{
   background: red;
   filter: progid:DXImageTransform.Microsoft.Alpha(opacity=60);    /* IE filter extension */
   width:100%;              /* Required for IE filter */
   -webkit-opacity: 0.6;    /* Webkit extension */
   -moz-opacity: 0.6;       /* Mozilla extension */
   opacity: 0.6;            /* the correct CSS3 syntax */
}
```

The code in Listing 2-21 shows how to implement opacity in multiple browsers. Each browser will read this CSS differently. For example, Internet Explorer will use the `filter` property and ignore the other `opacity` declarations because it does not recognize them. Older Gecko browsers that don't understand the CSS3 opacity property will respect the `–moz-opacity` property. Safari will respect the `-webkit-opacity` property. Finally the CSS3 `opacity` property will be respected by modern browsers. Of course, a browser that doesn't support element opacity will ignore the entire CSS block, which we as web designers might have to consider as well.

There are many other examples of browser-specific CSS extensions that are now part of the CSS3 specifications. Another great example is Resizing (see Listing 2-22). Resizing gives the user control to resize a specific container's vertices: Horizontal, vertical, or both vertices are supported.

Listing 2-22. Resize CSS3 Property

```
.resizable {
        padding: 10px;
        border: 1px solid;
        resize: both;
        overflow: auto;
}
```

If you applied this CSS class to a container (e.g., a textarea), the visitor will have the ability to resize the container from the bottom right, as shown in Figure 2-6.

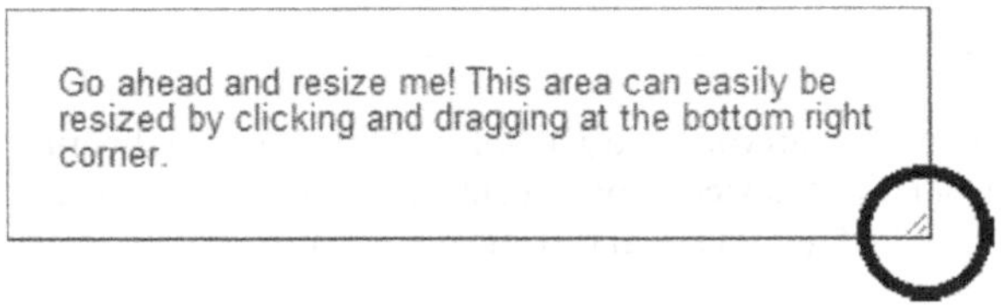

Figure 2-6. *Resizable text box that allows users to change their height and/or width*

There are many more features that have been added to the CSS3 specification that have removed the need for JavaScript, jQuery, and even effects that were only possible using images. JavaScript has been vastly popular for a number of reasons, including its ability to animate elements. CSS3 includes support for transitions and transforms. This functionality is gaining popularity as performance on mobile browsers is far better than using jQuery functions such as "animate." This is the benefit for a lot of the new CSS3 features and this goes beyond transition and transform. Other notable new CSS3 features are the following:

- border-radius gives you the ability to control the roundness of borders around containers.

- box-shadow allows you to add shadows to any container.

- text-shadow lets you add shadows to text elements.

We hope these features have intrigued you enough to learn more about CSS3 and what the specifications have to offer.

■ **Note**   Want to learn more about CSS3? Visit `http://sprwd.com/qoyqnpw`.

---

jQuery and Responsive Web Design

Now that you have a basic knowledge of HTML and CSS, we would like to bring your attention to one of the most popular JavaScript libraries, jQuery. If you are not already familiar with jQuery, it is a lightweight, very well supported JavaScript library that lives by the motto, "Write less, do more." From day one, the purpose of jQuery has been to make it easier to use JavaScript on your web site. jQuery takes a lot of common tasks that require multiple lines of JavaScript code to accomplish and wraps it into methods that you can call with a single line of code. The ease of use, popularity, and vast feature set of jQuery has meant that it's the best tested cross-browser library. There's a lot of good to be said about jQuery because much of its functionality has been included in HTML5 specifications.

jQuery Basics

Although other JavaScript libraries exist, jQuery is by far the most popular and has been wildly adopted as a part of many web sites. It has become so popular that many of the big companies use it, including Google, Microsoft, IBM, and Netflix. If you are new to this side of the world, let's take the opportunity to go through a few basic jQuery scripts.

■ **Note** Although the demo site we build throughout this book uses jQuery extensively and includes many additional jQuery plug-ins, jQuery itself is not required for many responsive sites. That being said, we highly recommend you become comfortable with jQuery, as it is not too difficult to use, and many responsive techniques such as responsive navigation will rely on jQuery (see Chapter 6).

Including the jQuery Library

jQuery is provided as a single JavaScript file from `<jquery.org>`, although you can use a minified or developer version of the JavaScript file. We recommend the minified version for performance issues. Because this is just a JavaScript file, we can load it via a `<script>` tag in our HTML `<head>` section. A growing trend has been to add this and other JavaScript files just before the ending `</body>` tag to help increase page load time. For SharePoint we suggest adding your jQuery library reference to your `<head>` section, as we might want to include additional jQuery plug-ins to specific page layouts, and it is much easier to add these to the `<head>` section as well.

■ **Note** Learn how to link to the jQuery library using SharePoint 2013's new HTML master pages found in Design Manager, discussed in Chapter 4.

Another popular technique to link to a jQuery library is to use a Content Delivery Network (CDN) such as Google or Microsoft's ASP.NET code CDN. Listing 2-23 shows how to link to a CDN to load the jQuery library and also provide an additional method to load a local copy of the jQuery Library.

Listing 2-23. A Method to Load the jQuery First by CDN Using a Local Copy as a Backup

```
<html>
<head>
    <title>...</title>
    <script src="//ajax.aspnetcdn.com/ajax/jQuery/jquery-1.9.1.min.js"></script>
    <script>window.jQuery || document.write('<script src="/js/jquery-1.9.1.min.js"><\/script>')</script>
</head>
```

```
<body>
...
</body>
</html>
```

■ **Tip**   Using a CDN for libraries can provide high performance and high availability for common objects across sites such as the jQuery library. However, always provide a link to a local cached version as a fallback.

Changing Styles

Now that we have linked to jQuery, our site can begin including jQuery code. As a starting point, let's take a look at how selectors work with jQuery. Imagine your HTML5 markup's body tag includes a <div> tag with CLASS attribute's value set to boxes. There's content inside the <div> container and you'd like change the font color. Yes, you could do this with CSS as well, but for the sake of simplicity, let's assume we want to use jQuery instead (see Listing 2-24).

Listing 2-24. Change Font Color With jQuery

```
...
<body>
<div class="boxes">
    <!—some content-->
</div>
<script>
    $(".boxes").css("font-color", "red");
</script>
</body>
...
```

jQuery allows for the use of chaining functions as well as calling functions within functions. For our next example, let's take the same <div> in Listing 2-24, but using the jQuery hover function, we change the background color over the <div> to green whenever a site visitor hovers over the <div> and switch it back to transparent on hover-out (see Listing 2-25).

Listing 2-25. jQuery Hover Example

```
<script>
    $('.boxes').hover(function() {
      $(this).css('background-color','green');
    }, function() {
      $(this).css('background-color','transparent');
    });
</script>
```

Changing the DOM

jQuery's power doesn't stop at just modifying CSS styles on the fly but also the document object as we saw in Listing 2-25. Listing 2-26 is another quick example that toggles content visibility.

Listing 2-26. Toggle Displaying Content

```
...
<body>
<h1>Showing and Hiding</h1>
<p>With jQuery, it's easy to show and hide elements dynamically.</p>
<h2>Item One</h2>
<p>Lorem ipsum dolor sit amet, consectetur adipiscing elit.</p>
<h2>Item Two</h2>
<p>Lorem ipsum dolor sit amet, consectetur adipiscing elit.</p>
<h2>Item Three</h2>
<p>Lorem ipsum dolor sit amet, consectetur adipiscing elit.</p>
<script>
    $(function() {
        $('h2').next('p').hide();
        $('h2').click(function(e) {
           $(this).next('p').toggle();
        });
    });
</script>
```

When you click one of the headings, it pops open, moving the remaining content down the page. Clicking the same heading hides the paragraph again. Each heading and its related paragraph work independently of the others, all thanks to just a few lines of jQuery (see Figure 2-7).

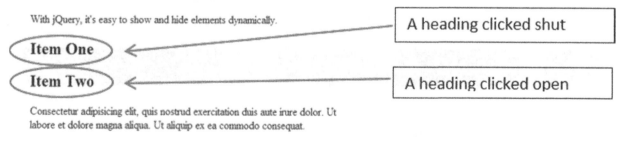

Figure 2-7. *Leverage jQuery to toggle content visibility*

This is not a book on jQuery, but hopefully if you are not already familiar with jQuery this extremely brief introduction gives you an idea of the power and ease. jQuery is useful in building feature-rich responsive sites on SharePoint. Learn more about jQuery at jquery.org. Although there are hundreds of additional online and print-based resources, we recommend *Pro jQuery* by Adam Freeman (Apress, 2012) and *Pro SharePoint with jQuery* by Phill Duffy (Apress, 2012). Even though *Pro SharePoint with jQuery* is geared toward SharePoint 2010, we think you might find it useful with SharePoint 2013 as well.

Responsive and jQuery

Why jQuery? CSS3 media queries do a decent job of resizing the overall layout, but CSS won't help when we need to resize and optimize all of those individual elements and features. This includes navigation controls, forms, images, sliders, and carousels that all need to be optimized. We quickly look at two uses for jQuery in helping with responsive web design although there are almost countless other examples.

Feature Detection

Resizing containers to fit within a screen resolution is relatively straightforward with CSS3 and media queries. The difficult part comes when the screen resolution isn't the only thing you'd like to be inquiring about. Mobile devices have introduced functionality that includes items like rotation, device width, and even device orientation, which media queries are not currently able to handle. With that being said, the industry standard is feature detection.

JavaScript frameworks like Modernizr, jQuery, and jQuery Mobile can directly test browser support for HTML and CSS features. These frameworks, if given access, can also identify the device or browser user agent to properly alter the design to fit your needs.

■ **Note**   We will use Modernizr in the demo solution we build throughout this book to provide feature detection for features such as mobile navigation.

Menu to a Drop-Down for Small Screens

We mentioned previously that navigation is a notorious struggling point for responsive web design and SharePoint does not make it any easier. In Chapter 6 we review navigation in detail, and we see how we can leverage jQuery, including additional jQuery plug-ins to help make a top navigation bar respond to different screen resolutions (see Figure 2-8).

Figure 2-8. *Using jQuery to manage responsive navigation. The top image shows the desktop view and the bottom image shows the mobile view*

Keep Adapting Responsibly

We might wish that all web browsers provided the same functionality, but we learned a long time ago this is not the case. Initially bandwidth was an issue, but when modems gave way to DSL, Cable, T1, fiber, and other dedicated Internet connections, bandwidth became less of a concern to many web developers for desktop users. To add to our complexities in delivering a good experience to our web site visitors, we must once again consider precious bandwidth for our less connected mobile friends. Just because we can do something with HTML5, CSS3, and jQuery does not necessarily mean we should. Take advantage of technology appropriately based on necessity, not based on considering older browsers, slower hardware, and limited bandwidth.

The approach of detecting browser and device width via media queries is not perfect and relying on jQuery is hazardous if the client browser does not have JavaScript enabled. Once you start coding a web site design, you will run into a common dilemma: Should you use multiple CSS files or have one CSS file with media queries within it? What do we do with no support for CSS3 and JavaScript disabled? We should practice responsible HTML, CSS, and JavaScript coding principles now if never before. The best solution is to code responsibly and make use of CSS fallbacks that allow the browser to ignore CSS properties that it doesn't recognize, nor a design that requires JavaScript.

CSS Style Sheet or Style Sheets?

If we have multiple CSS style sheets, we can use <link> tag-based media queries to help filter what style sheets should load on a particular client device, but as we mentioned different browsers treat <link> tag-based style sheets differently. Further, more files to download increases the number of HTTP requests that the client makes on every page load. Each page request has overhead, not only in CPU cycles but also additional packet overhead.

On the other hand, having one style sheet that utilizes media queries to handle all devices is not advantageous, as it forces low bandwidth or mobile devices to download and process the complete CSS style sheet, much of which it won't need.

A robust solution centers on a "mobile first" strategy. In this strategy, we build toward mobile devices first; thus we start by building for mobile users and limited display devices and add on functionality as devices allow. (Sounds like progressive enhancement, doesn't it? Are you starting to see how many methodologies are related?) In this case our first style sheet would be a basic or base style sheet that requires no media devices and at most helps style our fluid grid site so that it can scale in a basic manner on any device without the need for CSS3 or JavaScript.

Our next series of style sheets would be linked to using <link> tags with included media queries. We could include style sheets for mobile, tablet, and desktop enhancements. Why include a mobile style sheet? We might want to include additional CSS3 tagging, transactions, and so on, that could require JavaScript-based feature detection, or we simply want to increase the mobile browsing experience with additional enhancements if allowed. We must remember that our additional style sheets should also include media queries in case a browser decides to, or is unable to, filter by the <link>-based media query. Refer to Listing 2-27 for an example of linking to multiple style sheets and Listing 2-28 for an excerpt of the style sheets themselves.

Listing 2-27. Linking to Multiple Style Sheets

```
<!DOCTYPE html>
<html>
<head>
    <title></title>
    <link rel="stylesheet" type="text/css" href="basic.css" />
    <link rel="stylesheet" type="text/css" media="all and (max-width: 767px)" href="mobile.css" />
    <link rel="stylesheet" type="text/css" media="all and (min-width: 768px) and (max-width: 959px)"
        href="tablet.css" />
    <link rel="stylesheet" type="text/css" media="all and (min-width: 960px)" href="desktop.css" />
</head>
...
</html>
```

Listing 2-28. basic.css, mobile.css, tablel.css, and desktop.css Style Sheets

```
basic.css
body {
    font-family: sans-serif;
    color: #222;
    font-size: .6em;
}

mobile.css
/*any screen smaller than most tablets*/
@media all and (max-width: 767px) {
    body {
        color: #444; /*change the font color*/
        font-size: .8em;
    }
}

tablet.css
/*any screen between most tablets and a minimal desktop experience based on a 960px grid*/
@media all and (min-width: 768px) and (max-width: 959px) {
    body {
        color: #666; /*change the font color*/
        font-size: .95em;
    }
}

desktop.css
/*any screen based on a general desktop experience with a max width of 1200px*/
@media all and (min-width: 960px) {
    body {
        color: #888; /*change the font color*/
        font-size: 1.1em;
    }
}
```

The simplicity of this approach provides us the ability to limit the bytes downloaded, yet at the same time provides a reasonable experience on most any device. This is easy in theory but difficult in practice as sites grow in complexity, which changes the way most web developers have been building web sites; that is, focusing on the desktop experience.

■ **Note**   Throughout this book, each chapter builds on the last. For this reason our case study relies on one primary style sheet that uses media queries. This one style sheet allows us to easily highlight what additional CSS styles were required at each step of our design process. Ideally we would utilize the process just described, but in practice, for teaching purposes, this adds an extra level of unnecessary complexity.

My Site Requires JavaScript

Don't forget that a site should at least load and be functional without requiring JavaScript. This might mean our CSS, by default, should hide some aspects of our site, such as rotating banners based on our minimal site requirements. If you "require" JavaScript you are doing some of your potential visitors a disservice. If you are running a public-facing site on SharePoint, you can limit the damage inflicted when a visitor accesses your site yet doesn't allow JavaScript. There's an advantage to limiting your reliance on JavaScript, as it provides improvements for search engine optimization as well as accessibility. For your site administrators, you will have to require JavaScript, as much of SharePoint's administrative functionality is driven off of the Office Suite bar and the ribbon.

Once you have finished the primary build of your site, you might find it advantageous to minimize and combine your JavaScript and jQuery plug-ins into one large `.js` file. Even if all plug-ins and scripts are not required on every page, once the script has been downloaded, most browsers will cache this file. Further, keep in mind that the fewer files our page downloads, the fewer HTTP requests your site visitors make. This is beneficial, as it will help improve performance and page load time.

There's Always a Better Approach

Responsive web design as a methodology is still improving and is often supplemented with additional design theories that we have already reviewed including adaptive web design, mobile first, and in SharePoint 2013, supplemented with separate mobile, like features found in device channels. It is important to remember that there is no silver bullet approach; rather, each project is unique and might use a combination of approaches to achieve the desired outcome. Here's what you can do to tailor user experiences to your visitors:

1. Review your traffic logs and determine what mobile devices are accessing your site today.

2. Test your site on those devices and determine where the experience breaks down.

3. Develop an action plan to address the issues that you face. Focus on the critical path and test.

Once you've addressed this, pat yourself and your team on the back and when you're ready, go back go to Step 1 and start again, as the landscape will likely have changed and you do not want to be left behind.

Summary

In this chapter we provided an overview of web design methodologies and their evolution. The web design community has come along from graceful degradation and progressive enhancement to where we are now, responsive web design. Responsive web design is a different approach to building web sites and it's important for designers to understand the pros and cons before they start diving into the specifics.

What's truly amazing is that there are only three core ingredients for responsive web design: fluid grid, media queries, and flexible media. Starting with building a design based on a grid so that your designs have structure. Making that grid fluid helps when you start taking advantage of media queries to present content for different viewports. Once both of these elements are in place, you can then start looking at making your media content flexible for each viewport. These three elements are simple in principle, but implemented together and effectively they can drastically improve the user experience for your visitors.

We wanted to continue empowering you and further expand your knowledge by introducing you to leveraging HTML5, CSS3, and jQuery features. For any professional web designer, these three web technologies are at the core of the toolbox. You'll find leveraging these three standards will ensure your web site takes advantage of specifications that aim to greatly improve the web. In turn, you'll be building toward a semantic (structured) web that will help all of your visitors including those who need assistive technologies to view the web.

Responsive web design is a fairly young web technology and in an agile fashion, it'll continually evolve to become better. This chapter ends with guidance and best practices to consider. The list is not exclusive, and it will continually be updated. We encourage you to do the same; that is, keep adapting responsively.

Now that we have this knowledge, we can continue on to Chapter 3, where we guide you through the process of capturing requirements for a web site that uses responsive web design and how this fits into your design workflow. We use this plan along with our understanding of the underlying technology throughout the rest of this book, learning how we can combine responsive web design and SharePoint 2013 into one cohesive unit.

CHAPTER 3

■ ■ ■

Designing a Responsive Web Site

Any seasoned web professional knows that planning prior to implementation is key to the success of any project. Planning a web site project is a critical task and possibly the most important. It helps us gain focus and clarity by defining objectives for the project, and forces us to solidify the overall goals for what the stakeholder hopes to achieve, considering the end user experience. Planning a SharePoint web site project also requires considering the implementation of the various SharePoint-specific features.

To successfully build a web site, we start with information gathering. This requires learning about and understanding the goals of our users, and the tasks they need to carry out to ensure we fulfill their needs. This might seem simple, but often it is challenging to understand how a user will respond, or what specific experience he or she might have. Further, this might require us to challenge our assumptions about our users.

This chapter aims to walk you through the process of designing a SharePoint 2013 public web site for a fictitious company we will call Specter Group, a construction and architecture firm. Although this process isn't SharePoint-specific, it is certainly great to follow when building public-facing web sites as well as organizational intranets and extranets on SharePoint 2013 as the chosen Web Content Management (WCM) platform, and we highly recommend you do this to increase the probability of success of your project. We approach this process applying a user-centered design method, providing you with examples of the exercises that are typical along the way, including responsive design wireframing for tablet and mobile devices.

Our Scenario

Specter Group has requested that we build them a new public-facing Internet site built on the SharePoint 2013 platform. They have ideas of what their web site's aims are, but they are not detailed. In this scenario we walk through the site design and planning process, a general process for any web site including intranets, extranets, and public-facing sites. Using user-centered design, we review user analysis, task analysis, information architecture, and finally wireframing, site design and site mockups. By the end of this process we expect to have enough guidance and site design materials so that we can hand off the web site build-out process to the web development team.

The SharePoint Web Site Design Approach

There have been many techniques developed throughout the years to help design any sort of product, many of which have also been adapted for designing web sites. One such technique, activity-centered design, focuses on the activities of the user while using given software. A second method, contextual design, is taught as a medium to teach user-centered design; its core principle is to understand a user's intent, drives, and desires within the context of using the software or product in question. The other fairly common approach is task analysis, which is based on the concept that no matter what, users will always be executing tasks on the web site, and it helps to thoroughly understand the steps in the execution of these tasks, sometimes in person, as the user is actually using the web site.

Our preferred method is the user-centered design (UCD) methodology, which focuses on catering to the users rather than forcing the users to change how they do things using the product (or at times causing users to experience frustration). This is a great approach to follow when building a web site. But what exactly is UCD? Microsoft provides a great explanation:

> *This philosophy, called user-centered design, incorporates user concerns and advocacy from the beginning of the design process and dictates that the needs of the user should be foremost in any design decisions.*

> —Microsoft Corporation
> (http://sprwd.com/26h2wop)

It is this philosophy or methodology that we use throughout this chapter to discover who our web site audience is. Knowing that, we can determine web site features that ultimately cater to their needs and make the web site both relevant and valuable to them. We focus on key activities (see the section "Key User-Centered Design Activities We Use" later in this chapter) that help determine our web site structure and navigation all the way to a point where we have wireframes and full-fidelity mockups at the end of this chapter.

The Return on Investment of Usability

Given the extensive time dedicated to usability, some might wonder if it is really worth investing a considerable amount of time in figuring out the best user experience (UX) possible, and if a healthy return on investment (ROI) exists. In other words, can a project stakeholder justify spending such time in conducting usability testing and design?

For e-commerce sites, it is typical to get a sense of ROI by analyzing the number of transactions, visitors, and abandoned shopping carts on the web site. Regardless of whether your web site is an e-commerce site or an informational site, there is most likely a way to measure its success. For example, to measure the ROI for a corporate intranet that has a technical support ticketing feature, you can compare how many ticket submissions versus phone calls happen within a certain time frame. Another metric would be tracking the speed with which support tickets are resolved or closed.

In the case of our web site project, we know Specter's first goal is to showcase properties available to prospects, so tracking how many people actually purchased (the conversion rate) would be a one of the metrics to have in determining the ROI.

Key User-Centered Design Activities We Use

For our web site project, we'd like to walk you through the UCD process in the context of planning a SharePoint 2013 public-facing web site, using only select activities from the process as outlined in the following list. These activities are the bare minimum in our mind and certainly can be augmented to fit your particular web site project. We start by formulating the vision, goals, and objectives that will help drive the rest of the activities.

1. *Vision, goals, and objectives*: To create a user-centric web site, we must first clearly define the organization's vision, goals, and objectives. To do this, we might find that an organization can answer key questions, such as these: Who are the users of our web site? What are their goals or tasks when visiting our web site?

2. *User analysis*: In this activity we focus on learning who our web site users are, their characteristics, interests, and maybe even their experience level. This information is then used to develop user-specific *personas* that we use to inform our UCD.

3. *Task analysis*: Once we've defined our audience or identified our users, we must understand the tasks they will carry out when visiting our web site. This activity focuses on determining some of the key *user tasks* based on the type of user. In other words, we identify what our users are trying to achieve when visiting our web site.

4. *Information architecture and interaction design*: This activity focuses on ensuring our users can find what they need in the most efficient manner. The *structure, navigation,* and *taxonomy* used for the site all play a key role in ensuring we allow users to find what they need quickly. The web site goals help us determine the information architecture, as we know the user's goals and have gone through task analysis activities as well.

5. *Wireframing and design*: This activity focuses on a simple representation of our information architecture and interaction design. It illustrates key features, content, and typically navigation. It also visually calls out page features with brief explanations of the page elements. *Wireframes* help all project members, including developers and project managers, understand what the product will look like; however, this is not meant to dictate how the web site ultimately will look. *Design comps*, or mockups of how the site will look, add detail and provide a sense of what the look and feel of the site will be.

■ **Note** This chapter outlines a simple, agile, and yet effective UCD process you can use when planning your web site. You can go through as much iteration as needed to achieve the desired outcome. For an extensive list of UCD activities and additional guidance, visit `www.usability.gov`.

Vision, Goals, and Objectives

One problem often encountered within a project is unclear objectives and goals. Many times, there are multiple people working on a web site project, each of whom has a different idea of the overall objectives and goals. Having a clear understanding about the user needs and business goals is necessary prior to developing any mockup or snippet of code if we are to expect a successful outcome.

Our first task is to write a statement to describe Specter Group's business goals, although typically the project sponsor or project managers on the business side will have articulated this for us. Specter Group created the following statement for their web site business goals.

BUSINESS GOALS

The purpose of the new Specter Group web site is to showcase the various construction projects to prospective buyers of properties currently being built with the purpose of enticing them and ultimately converting them to actual buyers. Our secondary goal is to build a community comprised of property owners, and connect them with their respective neighbors to promote more interaction and bring each community closer. We envision our community members staying up-to-date with their community while on the go, and for that matter, we would like to ensure the new Specter web site allows for a seamless user experience on mobile devices.

The business goals statement does not cover the intended purpose for the intended user audience; it also does not provide details on what end users can expect to get out of the web site. Therefore we then need to articulate end users' expectations and needs. The user needs statement can be written by stakeholders or in other cases project managers who have a clear understanding of the vision of the web site. Specter Group created the following user needs statement.

USER NEEDS

Specter web site members will need the ability to communicate with their neighbors in a casual and effective way via blog posts, announcements, or discussion boards. In addition, members will need the ability to share pictures with their community as desired. Users who are not members will need to be able to view property information, blog posts, and news that Specter Group publishes on the Specter public web site.

User Analysis and Persona Development

The user analysis activity within the UCD process is considered one of the core activities, as it is the means to get to know our audience, and how they will use the web site. To do that, we start creating personas. A persona is a fictional characterization of a web site user. The use of personas first surfaced in 1998 in the book titled *The Inmates Are Running the Asylum* by Alan Cooper, and shortly thereafter was widely adopted in various software projects due to its effectiveness. As time went by, further proof surfaced of the benefits of using personas.

Developing sample personas will help our design process in keeping a very realistic perspective of our users and what they can accomplish on the SharePoint web site, be it an intranet, extranet, or public-facing web site such as the Specter site. For example, in our analysis, if we were to ask ourselves, "Is Oliver, a community member, able to participate on a discussion on a community he does not belong to?" we can immediately start thinking about the need to plan permissions and roles for each community within SharePoint. Asking that kind of question and other relevant questions when doing analysis can help develop the web site features in alignment with the user's expectations as you can imagine.

■ **Note**   We cover specific use tasks or scenarios later in this chapter to help you understand what each persona can potentially do while visiting the Specter public web site, but first we will craft our personas to gain insight on our web site audience.

How does one create a persona? Personas can be as simple as a paragraph or a full-blown profile that can include demographics such as age, gender, income, name, technical experience level, a picture, and other characteristics. For the Specter web site, we realized there are at least three personas: a public web site user, a community member, and the web site administrator. Let's start by describing what the public web site user's characteristics look like.

Public Web Site User

We know that Specter's web site is public; however, one of the goals is to reach out to those people who have purchased a property and encourage them to join the online community created for their neighborhood. This persona is crafted in a way to reflect that type of person, as shown in Table 3-1.

Table 3-1. *Public Web Site Persona*

Full Name	Dylan Roberts
Job Title	Marketing Director
Income	$150,000/year
Description	Dylan is a 37-year-old husband and father of 2 girls. He lives in the suburbs of New Jersey. He majored in liberal arts, yet his career is in the marketing field. Dylan and his wife are looking for a house as their family is growing and they've outgrown a two-bedroom condominium they currently live in. He has many concerns, and some include the ability to find a place where he can feel connected with his community or neighbors and a safe place to live.
	He is most likely heard saying things like "Where can I view the floor plans and details for this property I'm seriously considering purchasing?"
	As a marketing director, he is well versed on how to use the web and various tools to get things done, including the task of looking for a potential new home.

Community Member

A member of the Specter web site needs to efficiently communicate with his or her community. We accomplish this by allowing the member to post news, add new discussion topics, and add new blog posts. Table 3-2 shows the community member persona.

Table 3-2. *The Community Member Persona*

Full Name	Oliver Sparks
Job Title	Entrepreneur, Owner of Sparks Management Consulting, Inc.
Income	$1,000,000/year
Description	Oliver is a 30-year-old professional. He holds a PhD in robotics, and is very comfortable using multiple platforms and software programs (even X Terminal in Linux). He has a dedicated T1 line to his home office, as he runs his business from home. Oliver currently owns one of the most prestigious properties in a community built by Specter Group, Spruce Meadows, which is located along the Southern California Pacific Coast, in the city of Malibu.
	Likely you will hear him say things like "How can I ask other members what security measures they've taken?"
	One of his concerns is security within the property he owns, as his company contracts with government entities and works with many proprietary software programs internally developed that are of a sensitive nature.

Specter Web Site Administrator

The web site administrator shown in Table 3-3 has the capability to add, edit, and delete various types of content including blog posts, news, and new community web sites. Having content structured correctly in addition to an intuitive authoring site is paramount for this role to be successful.

Table 3-3. Specter Web Site Administrator Persona

Full Name	Rebecca Le-Smith	
Job Title	Sr. Administrative Assistant, Specter Group	
Income	$100,000/year	
Description	Rebecca is a 26-year-old, well-educated employee at Specter Group.	
	She currently manages content on the existing Specter public web site and is involved in the redesign project.	
	Her concerns are ease of use and ensuring it is not a daunting task to manage the new web site content. She also cares a lot about reusing content and artifacts within the web site, such as news images, and other generic content to reduce duplication of things, hence saving her valuable time while authoring content.	
	You most likely will hear her say things like, "I am working on authoring the content for our upcoming property's floor plan and basic information on the site and publishing it soon."	

Task Analysis and Persona Task Definitions

The next activity within our process is to identify the common tasks for our users. We've created our personas, so we can now use them in the context of the user tasks.

User tasks help us understand the potential interaction between a user and the system, in our case the Specter Group web site and related community sites. Depending on the complexity and needs of a project, task analysis can range from "casual" to what is known as "fully dressed." We want to keep things relatively simple and therefore have decided to document things using the casual approach, which has minimal information, yet is invaluable in our design process.

User Tasks

We start by asking ourselves relevant questions that can help determine what the common user tasks are for a given persona. For example, what are the users trying to accomplish on the web site?

If we were to come up with at least one task per persona for the Specter web site, this is what each task might look like.

PUBLIC WEB SITE USER

Dylan would like to get familiar with the upcoming properties Specter Group is showcasing on the web site. He browses to the Communities home page, and views properties by type. He then is able to preview all properties of that type and see a primary picture, description, and year built. Dylan then proceeds to fill out the contact form on the Specter web site to inquire on a property.

COMMUNITY MEMBER

Oliver recently experienced a theft and wants to post an alert to his community members about this incident. He browses his community web site and posts a new discussion board topic and later receives responses from his neighbors. Oliver obtains helpful tips, and awards a badge to his neighbor Sally after she provided him with a helpful tip.

WEB SITE ADMINISTRATOR

Rebecca wants to showcase an upcoming property on which Specter Group is finalizing construction. She logs into the web site, and she then creates a new community web site. She proceeds to add a primary picture, a description, year built, and location for use on a map. She then publishes the home page and all artifacts.

These tasks are simple, yet effective in providing insight as to the expectations of each user on the web site. Typically one can develop one to five tasks per persona if the system is simple, and 15 or more per persona for complex systems.

Information Architecture and Interaction Design

Now that we have gone through the process of creating personas and user tasks, we can start looking at how our users will find information on our web site. When we think of web application development we should be thinking of two main principles: interaction design and information architecture. Interaction design (IxD) is used to describe possible user behavior and defining how the web site will accommodate and respond to that behavior. Information architecture, as we've seen earlier, is focused on the categorization of information and determining how to present the information to our users.

The practice of information architecture is mostly used to create organizational and navigational systems (in our case the web site) that allow users to move through the web site content efficiently and intuitively.

Because the practice of information architecture calls for creating categorization schemes, we've created ours and mapped them directly to the end users' needs. The basic information structure unit is a called a *node* and this node can be a group of information or an actual piece of information. For example, on the Specter web site, this can be a blog that holds all posts or it can be a blog post.

For the communities' information architecture we used a top-down approach and started with the broadest category or node called "Communities" (global navigation menu item), which in our case is a group of information. The second-level node is the actual community and the most granular piece of information we deal with at this level is items such as a blog post or news article.

Site Structure

The wireframing or skeleton of the site can define the placement of many user interface elements, but the structure defines how users arrive to a page and where they will end up when they have completed their tasks (see the section "Wireframing and Design" later in this chapter).

The site structure we have come up with is shown in Figure 3-1. The information is presented in a way that directly reflects the web site objectives as previously discussed (see the section "Vision, Goals, and Objectives" earlier in this chapter).

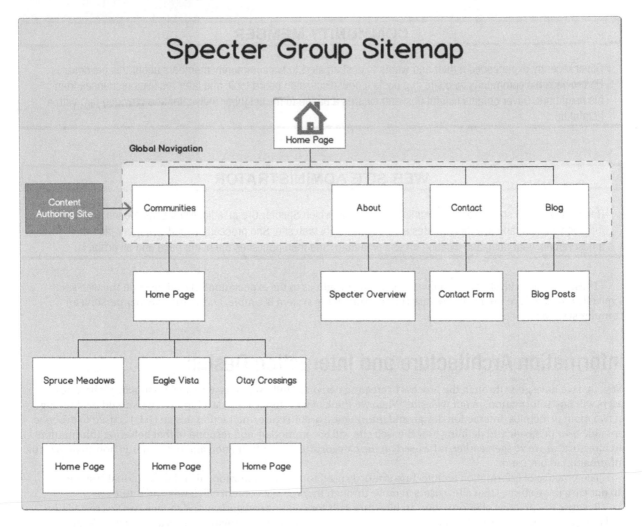

Figure 3-1. *Specter Group site map structure*

After learning about the Specter Group needs and the intended audience, as well as the overall site objectives, we started exploring how to present the main pieces of information via the global navigation. The global navigation is highlighted using a dotted section on Figure 3-1. The global navigation options are very few, and this is intentional as we feel the user has clear options to select from to immediately go to the main content areas regardless of whether the user is public or a registered member.

■ **Tip** One key element of building a proper site navigation and structure is to label artifacts appropriately. This plays an important role in ensuring users do not get lost on the web site and can efficiently find information with minimal effort.

Because we are building a SharePoint web site, we must plan and think of SharePoint-specific features to implement; one of them is the authoring of content. Therefore on our site map we've depicted where the content is authored and published. This authoring web site is where content such as floor plans, blog posts, and news items is authored and then published to the Specter Group public web site. This directly affects how we can make use of the new Cross-Site Collection Publishing feature and how we choose to configure it.

This stage of the design process is also a great time to start planning the SharePoint logical design, which includes among other things, site collections, sites, and content databases to ensure proper capacity and permissions planning. Any design team on a SharePoint implementation should be at least thinking of the SharePoint-specific planning involved to ensure the highest rate of success on any given implementation.

■ **Note**   Given the site map structure, you will notice there is an authoring site. This maps to the new SharePoint 2013 Cross-Site Collection Publishing feature, which you can learn more about in Chapter 8.

Global Navigation

Providing our users with the ability to navigate to areas that matter the most to them is essential, and the navigation element is the vehicle to achieve this. You can think of the navigation as the mechanism to the information architecture and structure we previously designed. There are common challenges in designing the proper or optimal navigation to any web site, and SharePoint web sites certainly are no exception. In fact, if you've played with SharePoint enough, you'd agree; it has a plethora of menu options and links on any given page that can easily confuse a user.

You can see from our example, shown in Figure 3-2, that we've designed the navigation on our site based on three basic principles:

1.   We must allow users to get from one web page to another intuitively.

2.   We should make it easy for users to sense how menu items are related to each other.

3.   We should ensure the navigation element helps users understand what the relationship is between the menu item they clicked on, and the page they actually landed on; it should be obvious.

Figure 3-2. *Specter web site global navigation*

In our experience, most sites provide more than one navigation element, each one with a different purpose. Some of those could be social navigation bars or a site map and breadcrumbs as shown in Figure 3-2.

Planning web site navigation based on the principles we've already outlined is key. SharePoint navigation planning also requires special attention; this stage in the design process allows us to think of what type of navigation we might opt to use and why. Questions that we must inevitably ask ourselves are the following:

•   Do we use static term-driven navigation or a hierarchy-based navigation?

•   Do we use metadata navigation for some of the global navigation nodes?

If the client needs an ecommerce site, it might make sense to leverage the new metadata navigation to provide the list of products and product details. Imagine then using the new display templates customized to add a "Purchase" button, for example. The possibilities are endless. Understanding the many new navigation options in SharePoint 2013 at the design stage will certainly yield greater success and a product that is intuitive to use from an end user's perspective.

■ **Tip** Refer to Chapter 6 for an in-depth, step-by-step exercise on how to build web site navigation on SharePoint 2013 and Chapter 9 to learn more about display templates and how to create them.

Taxonomy

Even if the structure of the web site is perfectly represented, web site users must still understand the vocabulary; that is, labels, terminology, or descriptions to help them find the information they are looking for within our site structure. Our intention should be to use the same language with which our users are familiar.

The Specter web site project certainly is a candidate for this metadata or common vocabulary. A great example of using this metadata within the Specter web site project is creating the definition of what a community is; in other words, we need to provide information about the information, which is exactly what the term *metadata* means. Table 3-4 shows us the metadata that describes a Specter Community.

Table 3-4. The Specter Community Metadata

Label	Type
Community Name	Text
About	Multiline text
Year built	Number
Location	Geolocation
Property Type	Options:
	• Commercial
	• Residential
	• Beachfront
	• Loft

■ **Tip** See Chapter 7 for a step-by-step exercise on implementing the metadata, term sets, and page layouts for the Specter Group web site on SharePoint 2013.

There are more benefits to having metadata created. What are some of those? Once the metadata is in place, the web site search engine can use it to refine searches, and different types of content can be connected or rolled up, filtered, and presented in a single page. On the site map listing, each community makes use of the metadata listed in Table 3-4 and this allows for construction of the navigation and other elements of the site.

As we go through planning our taxonomy, we must start thinking of some of the benefits and reasons why we need to carefully plan this as it relates to the SharePoint side of things. Some of those are the following:

- The ability to tag content that can be rolled up via search WebParts to leverage the new search-driven content features.

- The ability to customize the search user experience including the advanced search page, results page, and adding refiners to drill down on content results.

- Using terms, for example, allows for quick changes across the web site(s), sometimes to directly address compliance.

- Consistent use of corporate terminology.

Some of the specific SharePoint components we might start planning at this stage include the managed metadata service application, terms and term sets, content types, enterprise keywords, and the metadata hub, as a central location from where all managed metadata is syndicated across all web applications.

Planning these SharePoint components within the site structure and taxonomy planning stage can easily allow for the project team to draft configuration design documents specific to SharePoint as well.

Wireframing and Design

The structure is in place, and now it needs refinement. We now start identifying the elements of the interface, elements such as pages and the components within them. This activity is referred to as interface design and it will help make our web site structure more concrete as we are putting a visual representation to the conceptual structure previously developed. This includes refining the appropriate navigation spaces and the content areas within the pages. We start by creating wireframes, or a representation of a site void of imagery, typography, and normally of actual content. Wireframes allow us to see where elements on a given web page will go without having to worry about what the final site will actually look like. We complete what the final site will look like during the design phase after wireframes have been created and approved.

■ **Tip** For wireframing, we've used the popular Balsamiq Mockups software available for PC and Mac at http://balsamiq.com. There are also many free add-on controls (including the Bootstrap Grid System) and you can purchase the desktop version or use their web-based version.

Site Template (Skeleton)

The surface of a web site, or the end result, typically the imagery, buttons, photographs, and other elements, is what is on top of the skeleton or wireframe of a site. The skeleton or wireframe defines and optimizes the arrangement of these elements for maximum impact or to reach the intended effect.

Wireframing is the first step in solidifying what the user interface will look like. Having navigation in place, we now need to come up with conceptual wireframes of what the pages a user arrives at will look like.

One of the greatest challenges in designing interfaces is ensuring we show the most important information to the users as they navigate the interface. Good interface design practices ensure that the most relevant information is presented to the user so that he or she does not have to struggle to find it, but instead finds it readily available. This can be done by making some of the most important or relevant elements on the page larger or more prominent, such as news article titles or a login button.

The General Site Elements

We believe the most direct method of explaining wireframe is by example. Using the information we have gathered thus far for the Specter Group web site, we now proceed by creating wireframes. Our first wireframe is the overall site template that will be used for the base of our SharePoint 2013 HTML Master Page, and it covers general site elements such as the header, main content area, and footer. These components are annotated as shown in Figure 3-3.

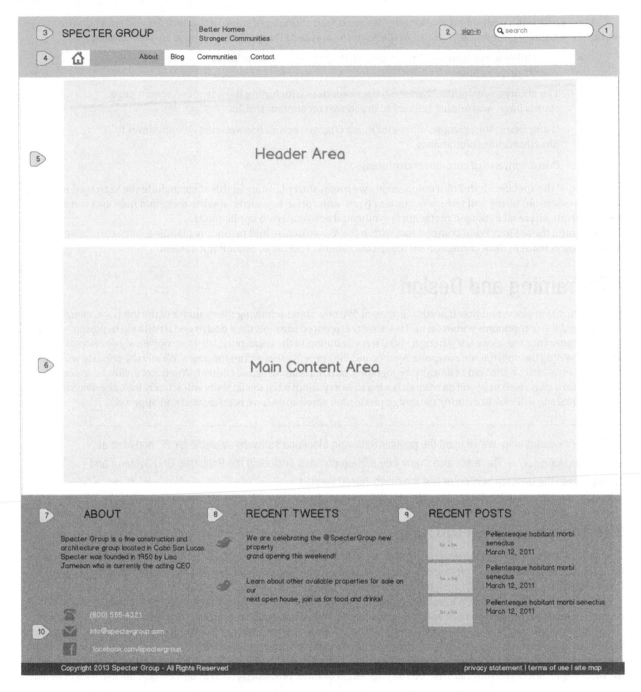

Figure 3-3. The Specter Group web site template shows each component and how it will appear

---

■ **Tip** See Chapter 4 for a walkthrough on creating an HTML Master Page in SharePoint 2013 and Chapter 5 for a step-by-step guide on incorporating responsive design with SharePoint 2013 Master Pages.

The following list provides more detail on the required capabilities for each component as per the Specter Group web site design requirements:

1. Search Box: Allows for searching across the entire Specter web site.

2. Login: This button appears when the user is not logged in. When the user is in fact logged in, the standard user actions SharePoint menu is shown.

3. Specter Logo Image

4. Top Navigation: This top displays the first-level pages of the Specter web site. The Communities menu displays existing Communities via a fly-out menu.

5. Header Area: This area can be used to add widgets.

6. Main Content Area: This is the standard main content area.

7. About: This is static text.

8. Recent Tweets: This widget shows the most recent tweets from Specter's Twitter handle.

9. Recent Posts: The most recent blog posts published by Specter that are tagged "Public" will be shown here.

10. Contact Information

The Responsive Wireframing Approach

Specter Group is interested in catering to the audience that heavily uses their mobile devices to browse for properties for sale as an example. They are also interested in making sure community members can access the web site on the go and post news, share pictures, or add discussion topics via their mobile devices. To satisfy this requirement, we have also worked on an approach to visualize how the web site will look on the various supported widths of mobile devices which include tablets, desktops, laptops, and smart phones, as shown in Figure 3-4.

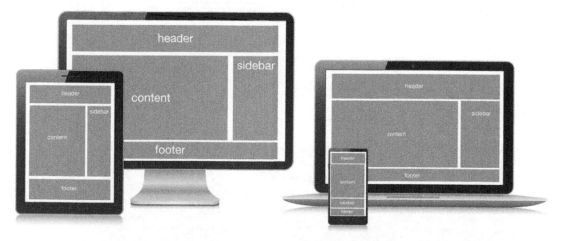

Figure 3-4. Responsive design wireframing caters to various screen sizes and adjusts content elements accordingly

■ **Tip** For an introduction to responsive web design, take a look at Chapter 2. Refer to Chapter 5 for a step-by-step guide on making an HTML master page responsive.

Supported Mobile Views

The full desktop experience is shown in Figure 3-5, supporting up to 1200×800 resolution. When viewing the Specter web site (see Figure 3-6) on tablets such as an iPad, several components adjust in size, including the logo. A smart phone view, such as for an iPhone (see Figure 3-7) is where we see a dramatic change in the user interface; all sections are adjusted to the mobile device width, including the logo. The top navigation now uses a drop-down list, and the footer content is rearranged appropriately and increases the overall height of our view. The user must scroll down to continue viewing the content.

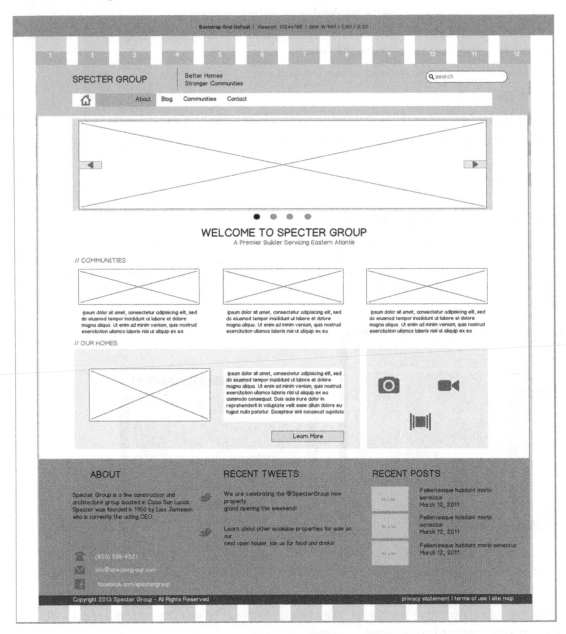

Figure 3-5. *Full desktop wireframe of Specter Group home page*

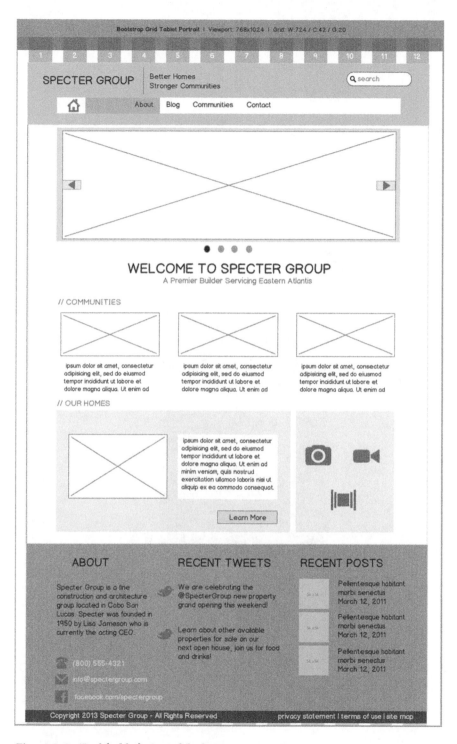

Figure 3-6. *iPad (tablet) view of the home page*

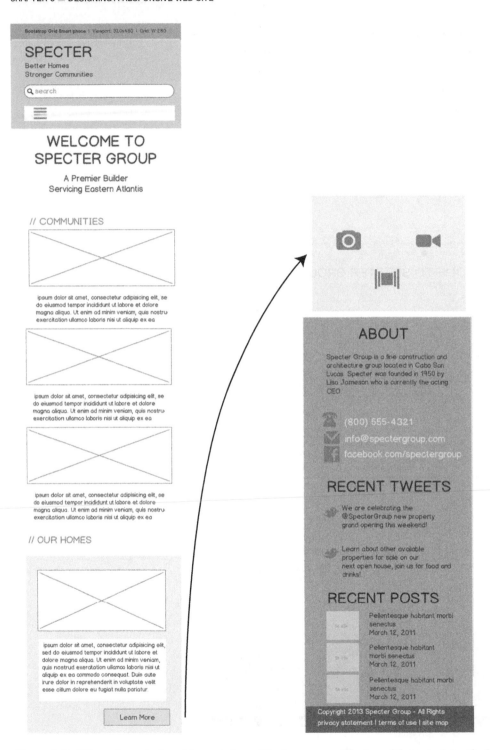

Figure 3-7. *iPhone (smart phone) layout view of the home page. The top of the page is on the left and the bottom is on the right*

You will notice how we include a grid system as part of our responsive design wireframing; this is a great way to visualize how the various elements on a page adjust as the screen dimensions change.

Wireframing Top-Level Pages

Building on the general wireframe created in Figure 3-4, expanded on to show the home page in Figure 3-5, and finally optimized for mobile devices in Figure 3-6 and Figure 3-7, we now look at other wireframe layouts for additional subpages. This section describes the top-level page layouts for the Specter Group web site. These layouts map to the SharePoint 2013 publishing page layouts and therefore serve as our blueprint for building publishing page layouts for the Specter web site.

What Is a SharePoint Publishing Page Layout?

What is a SharePoint page layout and how does it relate to the site template, otherwise known as the HTML master page within SharePoint 2013? We can think of the HTML master page as the site template, from which all site pages are derived. The page layout is actually just handling the content, whereas the HTML master page or site template handles the overall header, footer, and other common page elements. The master page and page layout are merged at runtime to render our page as shown in Figure 3-8.

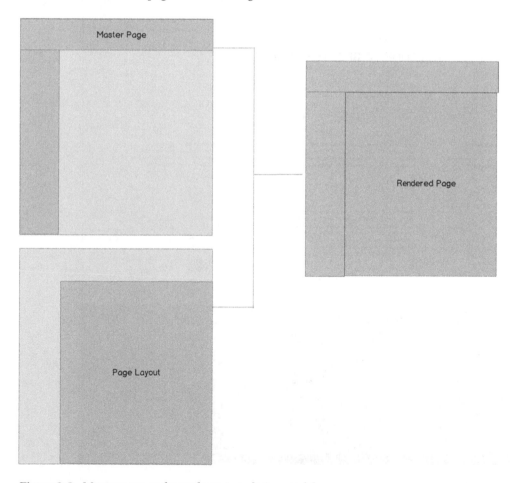

Figure 3-8. Master page and page layout rendering model

■ **Tip** For a detailed walkthrough on creating the custom publishing page layouts, see Chapter 7.

Home Page

This is the landing page to which first time visitors and newly registered members are taken. It is also the default page a member is redirected to when signing in. The home page has two main sections, a header area and a main content area (see Figure 3-9).

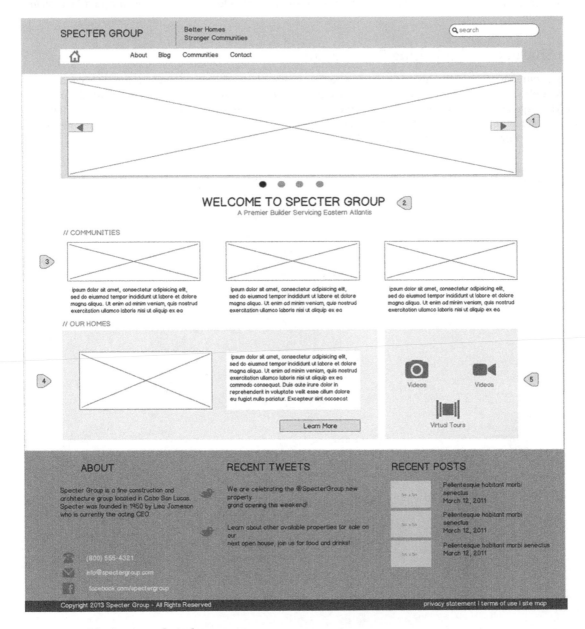

Figure 3-9. The Specter web site home page

1. News gallery: The news gallery displays Specter Group news articles that are public and are viewable by nonregistered users. Each news item has a picture and short blurb. The news gallery is displayed as a slider.

2. Page title: This component can be edited when the page is in edit mode.

3. Communities: This area displays the latest communities with basic descriptions.

4. Our Homes: This area features a residential home with a description and a button to obtain more details.

5. Media: This section has links to photos, videos, and virtual tours for various properties.

Blog Page

The Blog page displays recent blog posts published by Specter Group and is rendered as shown in Figure 3-10. The blog categories are also retrieved and displayed on the right side.

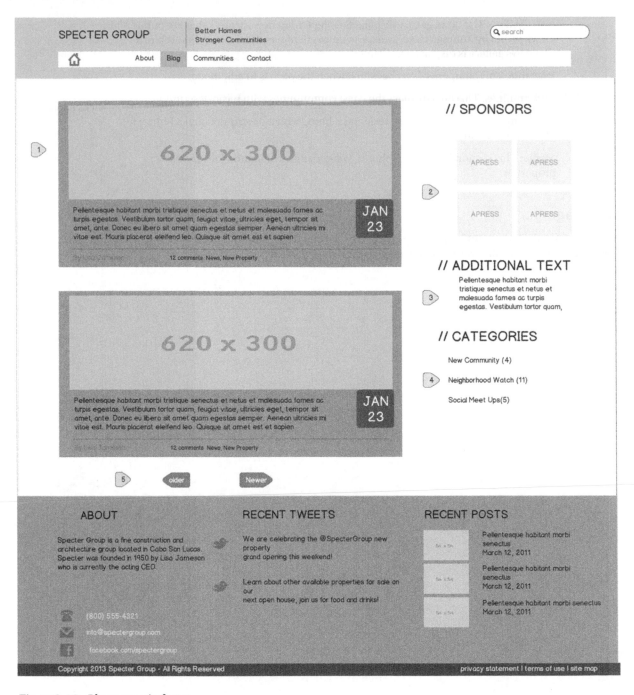

Figure 3-10. *Blog page wireframe*

General Site Page

This layout is used to create additional site pages; it uses the Specter custom branding background within the content area as shown in Figure 3-11.

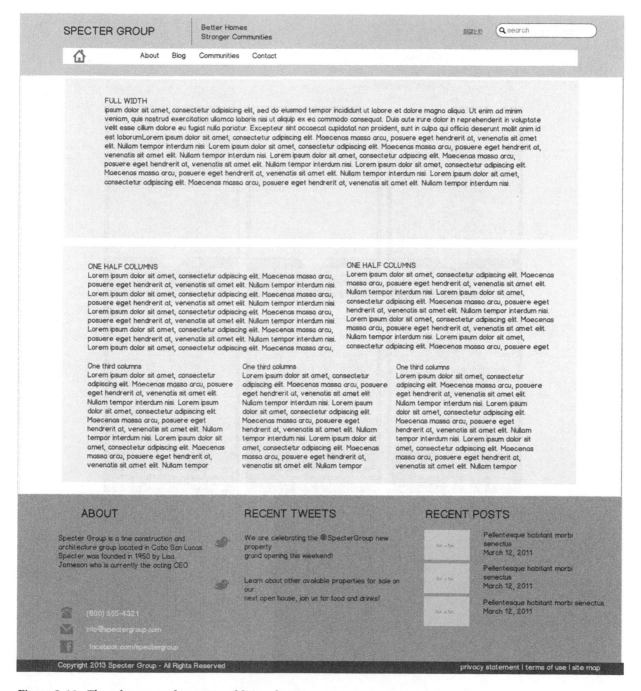

Figure 3-11. *The subpage used to create additional pages*

Communities Page

The Communities page showcases the Specter properties using an elegant filtering (see Figure 3-12) mechanism that allows a user to view properties by type such as Loft, Residential, Beachfront, and Commercial.

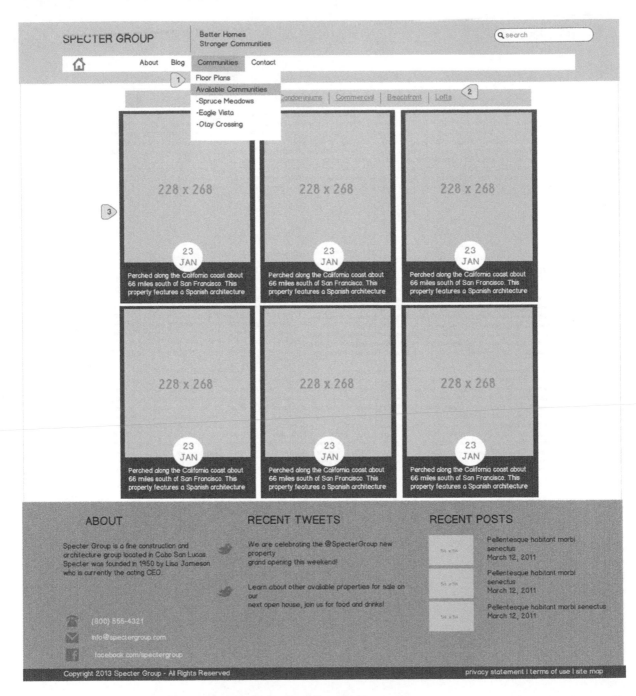

Figure 3-12. *Communities home page on the Specter public web site*

■ **Tip** You will learn how to filter and roll up the content we've been planning for using SharePoint 2013 new Cross-Site Publishing features and search-driven WebParts in Chapters 8 and 9.

1. The top navigation Communities label takes the user to this view. When a user hovers over the menu, however, a fly-out menu displays all community web sites, and clicking on any of those will take the user to the home page of said community.

2. Each property is rendered with a main picture, year built, and a brief overview.

Community Site Home Page

Each community will have the same capabilities and features as described on the home page section. The community home page wireframe is shown in Figure 3-13. The home page allows a community member access to all features available, such as creating a news article, creating a blog post, or adding a new discussion topic. A member also has the ability to share pictures or videos that are viewable via the media slider in the top section of the home page.

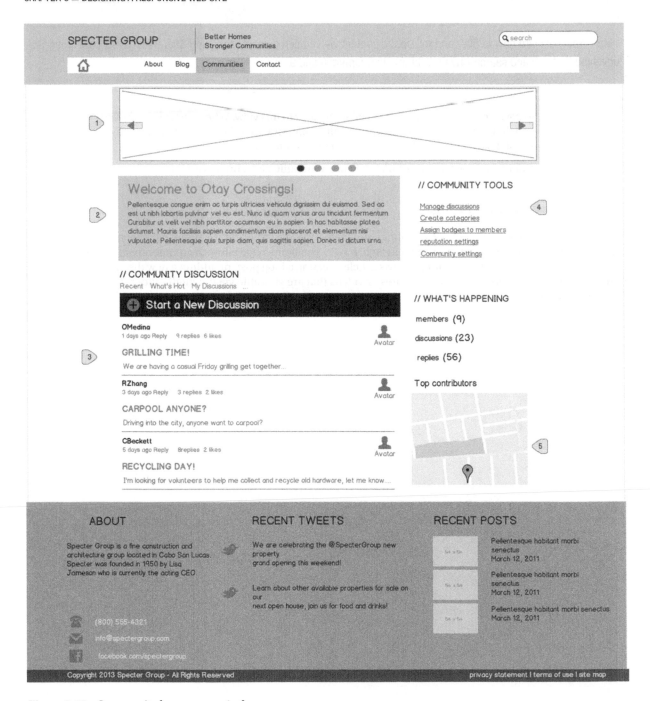

Figure 3-13. *Community home page wireframe*

1. Community media slider: This component shows pictures and videos shared by community members.

2. Community welcome and overview: This area allows for display of an overview about the community.

3. Discussion board: This area displays the latest discussions and allows users to easily create new ones.

4. Community Tools: This section allows for setting preferences and changing overall settings for a community.

5. Map: This map displays the actual location of the community with a pin. When a user clicks on the pin, a bubble displays the community address details.

■ **Tip** For a step-by-step walkthrough on implementing geolocation (Item 5 in the preceding list), see Chapter 12 on how to integrate the new Geolocation field and HTML5 geolocation features in SharePoint 2013.

Design Comps

Once the wireframes have been created and approved, it is time to create the mockup or high-fidelity composition (comps) of how the web site will appear. This, of course, is an important step as we need the project sponsor buy-in. Full-fidelity compositions are typically implemented using tools of the trade such as Adobe Photoshop or Adobe Fireworks. Creating design comps is often the first truly "fun" phase of a web site design project (if you are the web designer) as you and the stakeholders finally get to see what the final web site will look like. This can be an exciting process with many opinions.

Unfortunately design comps are often the first phase for many projects (see the Tip that follows). By following the UCD process, however, including IA and wireframing, you should have such a good idea of how the web site will look by the time you get to design comps. This allows you to focus on design, imagery, typography, and polish, impressing everyone with a web site design that is not only highly functional and meets the goals of the business, but also looks outstanding.

■ **Tip** Design comps are often the first aspect of a project you or the project sponsor might want completed, but skipping the previously outlined steps including user analysis, task analysis, information architecture, and in-depth wireframing will provide a shaky foundation that no amount of "pretty paint" in a design comp can fix. One other thing to consider is that comps take more time to create and therefore iterations are lengthier, as opposed to wireframes. You have been warned!

The intent of producing design comps is to show all the pieces working together, and at this point we can see a one-to-one correlation between the components on the wireframe and the design comp. This is also where the stakeholder has a first look at the overall new design. We can see the new styles, typography, and global elements as well as the brand or identity applied, as seen in Figure 3-14.

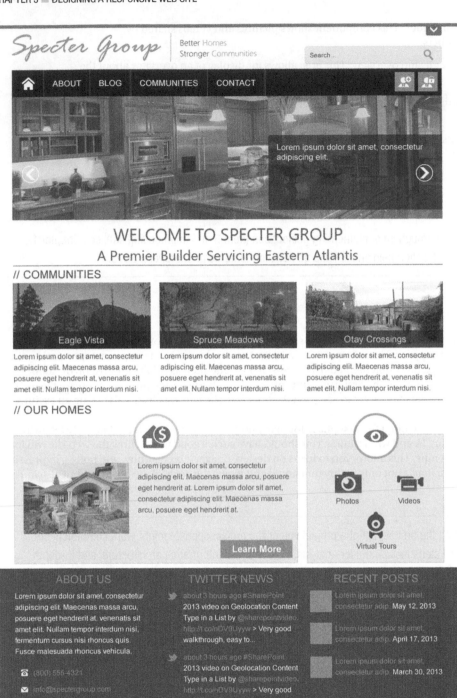

Figure 3-14. *Full-fidelity mockup of the site template*

The following comp showcases the new look of the Specter web site that follows the wireframe concepts and translates them into a full-fidelity comp.

■ **Note** You will notice we are not providing comps for all top-level pages, nor are we delving into how to generate CSS and HTML from the PSD or even creating Photoshop files, as this is outside the scope of this book. You can download and review all PSD comps including the full HTML version of the entire site for our book resource site at `https://github.com/SPRWD`.

Summary

In this chapter we have walked through the general process of planning a web site, practical for public-facing web sites, intranets, and extranets. As a demonstration, we used this process to provide the web site planning of the fictitious Specter Group public-facing web site using elements of the UCD approach. We walked through crafting examples of the business objectives and pivoted on those to further build the user analysis to understand our audience. We reviewed the importance of information architecture and site structure and the use of wireframes to bring a visual representation of that architecture, and finally to produce full-fidelity design comps.

In Chapter 4 we walk through the process for creating a SharePoint HTML master page based on the HTML handed off by the design team, which includes artifacts such as CSS and images. Chapter 5 then walks you through step-by-step instructions on how you can integrate the Twitter Bootstrap Responsive Grid System that comes with the framework on the custom HTML master page we create.

CHAPTER 4

■ ■ ■

Building a SharePoint HTML Master Page

If you have worked with past versions of SharePoint you will know firsthand that SharePoint has improved both dramatically and also gradually over the years. If you worked with Microsoft SharePoint 2003, you might recall that you had to use Microsoft FrontPage 2003 to brand a site. Although the tool was made for the task, it lacked ease of use and it was still difficult to brand multiple sites. With the release of WSS 3.0 and Microsoft Office SharePoint Server 2007, SharePoint was completely revamped on top of the .NET 2.0 framework, thus allowing SharePoint to make use of .NET 2.0 features such as master pages and page layouts. We were also given a new SharePoint site development and branding tool, SharePoint Designer 2007, a tool more integrated with SharePoint.

SharePoint 2010 brought more improvements in terms of branding capabilities. Web designers could now push the envelope and not only make SharePoint take on a corporate brand, but also include cutting-edge web site design trends by incorporating AJAX and other frameworks. SharePoint 2010 included the customization tool SharePoint Designer 2010, with additional capabilities to customize sites including the ability to aggregate various data sources to create custom views using XSLT and XML. Unfortunately it was still the only tool that could be used to customize SharePoint and it was not a tool that would always fit into the design process that many designers were accustomed to. For example, when a web designer wanted to take a Photoshop mockup and slice it into an HTML web page, he or she needed a prototype built first in a web design tool such as Adobe Dreamweaver. The process of combining a prototype and SharePoint still required yet another tool, SharePoint Designer.

Enter SharePoint 2013. The product has been enriched with new technologies including client-side APIs using standards such as REST and JSON, JavaScript, CSS, and HTML5. The branding capabilities and the process to brand a web site have also changed. SharePoint 2013 includes the new Designer Manager, a powerful new web-based designer tool available in SharePoint 2013 sites that have the Publishing feature by default. SharePoint 2013 introduces the new concept of HTML master pages and HTML page layouts. This is quite different from the previous master pages one could build on SharePoint 2010, which were built with the underlying .NET 2.0 master pages framework.

■ **Note** Although we walk you through the process of creating an HTML master page, you can still build traditional master pages without the need to create an HTML master page by simply using an out-of-the-box master page as a starting point.

In this chapter we dive into the Design Manager and see how we can take advantage of HTML master pages to make it easier to brand SharePoint. With this new model of generating master pages, SharePoint generates new, special markup when it converts an HTML design into an HTML master page, and we review this markup in detail. If you have customized SharePoint 2010 master pages, you are likely aware of content placeholders and how we had to manage them. In this chapter we also learn how with HTML master pages, SharePoint internally tracks all content placeholders for us. We review many tricks that will help you work with HTML master pages and finish with an overview of how Design Manager will also help us package our custom branding for easy redeployment to other site collections, such as moving our branding from a development environment to a production environment. Clearly, Microsoft realized that aligning SharePoint to the process designers are used to would provide value and increase overall adoption.

Our Scenario

In Chapter 3 we walked through the planning and design process recommended for any web site project. Using the fictitious Specter Group as a case study, we produced wireframes and design comps for the Specter Group web site. We ended with an HTML web site prototype based on the Specter Group requirements.

■ **Note**   You will notice that Chapter 3 did not cover the design activity of creating the CSS and HTML files from our PSD or Adobe Photoshop design file, as it is outside the scope of this book and in fact, part of a greater design process. Check out a great visual representation of this process at `http://sprwd.com/73hvkga`, and specifically Step D9. Download the entire Specter Group HTML prototype at `https://github.com/SPRWD`.

In this chapter we walk through the process of transforming an HTML prototype (i.e., HTML, CSS, Images, and JavaScript) to a SharePoint 2013 HTML master page in a new SharePoint 2013 site with Publishing enabled. We will continue using our Specter Group case study as our working example. We introduce the new Snippet Gallery that we will use to add code snippets to further enhance an HTML master page with SharePoint-specific controls such as the login control, our standard SharePoint logo control, and a SharePoint search box. The outcome will be the following:

- A deployed master page with supporting artifacts that we will then use in Chapter 5 to convert our design to leverage responsive design features.

- In Chapter 6 we will learn how to include the horizontal and vertical navigation snippet to provide navigation in our HTML master page.

- The Specter Group also requires that a branding solution be easily transferred from a development environment to a production environment so we will introduce Design Manager's Design Package, a new browser-based tool that provides us the ability to quickly package and deploy custom branding.

In our example, we have gone through the process of "cutting up" (which this book does not cover as it is outside the scope of the book) the design using Photoshop and Dreamweaver. We now have the HTML, JavaScript, CSS, and images files often returned to us from our design department all contained in a folder. See the Tip below for information on how to download this example package. In our scenario our web design team came back with an HTML5-ready, jQuery-enhanced site with all of the bells and whistles. They used standard grid-based coding techniques that have been common for the last few years, of course without responsive design in mind, as that is too foreign for them. No worries, we have you covered.

■ **Tip**   See Chapter 5 for insight on the standard grid coding techniques and making the Specter HTML master page responsive. Also be sure to download the web site HTML prototype and other source code at `https://github.com/SPRWD/BookSourceCode` as we will be using this throughout the book.

Why Do We Need an HTML Master Page Anyway?

Being involved on SharePoint projects for many years now, we have certainly noticed the one aspect of the project that always ends up being a top priority for project sponsors is the branding of an intranet, public web site, or extranet built on top of SharePoint. It turns out that most companies do not want to have the out-of-the-box look and feel; they want to have the opportunity to personalize and brand their web site initiatives.

SharePoint allows for companies to brand their SharePoint web sites by building custom master pages or a template that handles the look and feel, header, and footer, thereby completely changing how the SharePoint web site looks.

■ **Note**   We do not cover themes or composed looks as part of our step-by-step guide in this book, primarily because this book focuses on building public-facing and more complex intranet and extranet solutions with SharePoint 2013. Themes and composed looks are the preferred branding tool for collaboration sites such as team sites, but do not provide the customization tools often needed for more sophisticated SharePoint 2013 sites.

Getting Started

Before you are ready to convert a general HTML page design to an HTML master page, you will want to have your pure HTML web site prototype ready, which includes the sample pages, CSS, JavaScript, images, and other artifacts that the design uses.

■ **Tip**   One way to know your HTML site prototype is ready is to test it by opening up the index.html page on your browser. You should be able to browse the sample pages, scripts should be working, and CSS should be applied accordingly.

In Figure 4-1 you can see the folder structure of our HTML site prototype; it contains all of the site HTML sample pages, CSS, JavaScript, and images. We are now ready to convert our first HTML page to a SharePoint 2013 HTML master page.

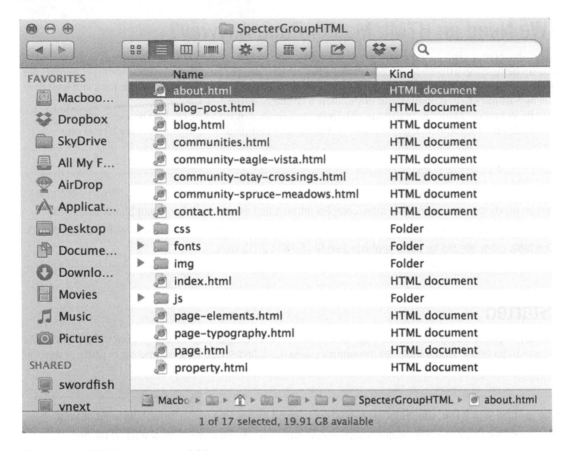

Figure 4-1. HTML protoype site folder structure

About Our Design Environment

Because we no longer are required to use SharePoint Designer to work with branding artifacts, we want to walk you through the branding experience using a common tool, and we chose Adobe Dreamweaver (CS6 in fact), as this tool is popular with web developers and designers. We are also executing our branding exercise on a MacBook Pro, as we know many designers use this platform in conjunction with the Adobe Creative Suite, and to demonstrate how the activity of branding SharePoint 2013 is no longer dependent on Microsoft tools. You might be wondering if Dreamweaver is officially supported by SharePoint 2013. We are happy to let you know that it is fully supported on both Mac and PC. With SharePoint 2013, the Web Distributed Authoring and Versioning (WebDAV) protocol now makes it possible to use tools such as Microsoft Expression Web, Adobe Dreamweaver, and Microsoft Visual Studio, in addition to SharePoint Designer 2013, to connect to and manipulate site files. Although WebDAV has been used since SharePoint 2001, it was used mostly to issue search queries, officially at least. With SharePoint 2013, Microsoft opened it up to allow other tools to communicate via this protocol with SharePoint and actually modify files for the purposes of branding.

■ **Note** In December 2012, Microsoft announced that Expression Studio would no longer be a stand-alone product. Expression Blend would be wrapped into Visual Studio and Expression Web would no longer be upgraded; therefore we believe web designers will more likely be inclined to use Dreamweaver. If you run into a slow performance issue when using Dreamweaver, be sure to take a look at a potential resolution to this at `http://sprwd.com/vvft7mi`.

To get started, we give you an overview of the new Design Manager, which is the web-based tool we use throughout this exercise.

Introducing Design Manager

With the new process for branding SharePoint 2013 comes a new set of features that help execute this activity. Design Manager is one of those new features and is part of the improved Publishing feature available on publishing sites by default and on other sites such as team sites by activating the Publishing feature via Site Settings.

■ **Note** Publishing is only available in SharePoint Server 2013 and above; that is, not in SharePoint Foundation 2013. Also, using Design Manager on nonpublishing sites (even after activating the Publishing feature) is not officially supported.

Design Manager is one of the most exciting new features as it relates to the branding aspect of SharePoint. Design Manager is accessible directly from the new Settings menu (similar to the old Site Actions menu) as well as from the Site Settings page. When you navigate to the Design Manager page, you will notice there are several tasks, although in our opinion you do not have to perform them in that order, and you generally won't. See Figure 4-2 for a view of the Design Manager's left menu, specifically option 3, Upload Design Files. Designers can leverage this tool throughout the design cycle to carry out various tasks, such as creating and editing HTML master pages and deploying the supporting artifacts. In addition, the Design Manager interface allows you to manage device channels, edit display templates, edit page layouts, and create a design package.

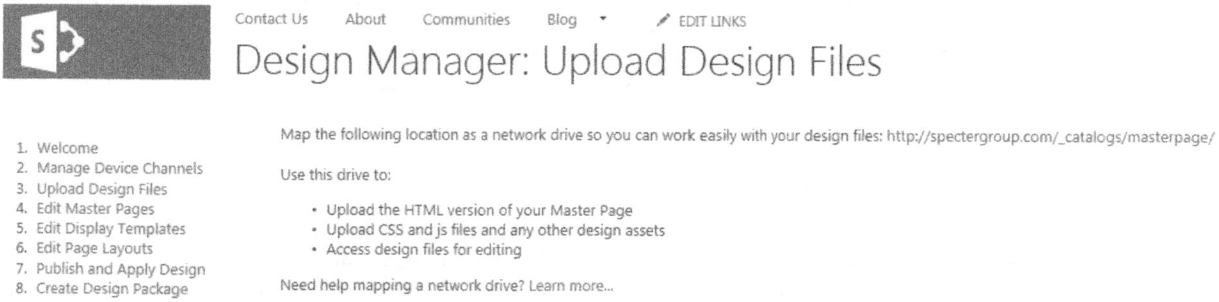

Contact Us   About   Communities   Blog ▾   ✎ EDIT LINKS

Design Manager: Upload Design Files

1. Welcome
2. Manage Device Channels
3. Upload Design Files
4. Edit Master Pages
5. Edit Display Templates
6. Edit Page Layouts
7. Publish and Apply Design
8. Create Design Package

Map the following location as a network drive so you can work easily with your design files: http://spectergroup.com/_catalogs/masterpage/

Use this drive to:

- Upload the HTML version of your Master Page
- Upload CSS and js files and any other design assets
- Access design files for editing

Need help mapping a network drive? Learn more...

Figure 4-2. *Design Manager tasks and guidance*

■ **Tip** To learn how to create display templates, see Chapter 9. See Chapter 7 to learn how to create page layouts.

Because we review the many options available to us in Design Manager throughout this book, we jump right in here and start working on our master page. Don't worry, we return to Design Manager many times and will learn all of the different tools available. To begin working with our master page, we will work through the first few steps, although the order of executing these steps does not necessarily reflect the numbered order shown in Figure 4-2. Our order reflects our experience of what is appropriate for most scenarios including ours and it is as follows:

1. Prepare the HTML file for conversion to an HTML master page.

2. Map the Master Page Gallery to a local drive and upload the Design folder that contains all of the site HTML, CSS, JavaScript, and Images.

3. Create an HTML master page from an HTML prototype.

4. Modify the HTML master page: Fix common warnings, clean up newly created HTML master page files, and make common CSS adjustments.

5. HTML master page SharePoint-generated markup: Review the markup.

6. Add snippets from the Snippet Gallery.

7. Publish and assign the newly created HTML master page as the site master page.

8. Create design package (optional) for reusability on other site collections.

Preparing an HTML File for Conversion to an HTML Master Page

The first step in building an HTML master page is to ensure that your HTML file meets all the following conditions:

- The HTML file must be XML-compliant, which unfortunately is not the same as HTML5 compliant. There are many simple XML validation tools available that can assist you, such as `http://validator.w3.org/`. As an example, HTML5 allows a doctype of `<!doctype html>` whereas to be XML-complaint for Design Manager, the doctype must be in all capital letters, such as `<!DOCTYPE html>`.

- Your `<html>` tag must be a simple `<html>` tag; you cannot use the popular IE conditional opening solution such as:

```
<!--[if lt IE 7]> <html class="no-js lt-ie7" lang="en"> <![endif]-->
<!--[if IE 7]>    <html class="no-js lt-ie8" lang="en"> <![endif]-->
<!--[if IE 8]>    <html class="no-js lt-ie9" lang="en"> <![endif]-->
<!--[if gt IE 8]><!--> <html class="no-js" lang="en"> <!--<![endif]-->
```

This should be just

```
<html class="no-js" lang="en">
```

- Be careful what styles you apply to the `<html>` and `<body>` tags, as all elements of a SharePoint page, including the ribbon, reside within the `<body>` block. You might want to consider applying your "global" styles to a main wrapper, or wait until after the conversion and apply your styles to the ID, `s4-workspace` or `s4-bodyContainer`, both added and used by SharePoint.

- The `<head>` code block should not contain any `<style>` tags. All styles should be placed in external style sheets, linked to by a `<link>` tag. All `<style>` tags in the `<head>` will be removed during conversion.

- A reference to a jQuery library should be place in the `<head>` section before the `</head>` tag. For SharePoint, one reason this is recommended is in case you need to dynamically load additional jQuery plug-ins within page layouts.

- If you intend to include a web font, in your HTML file, add `ms-design-css-conversion="no"` to your `<link>` tag:

```
<link rel='stylesheet' href='http://fonts.googleapis.com/css?family=Sintony'
                ms-design-css-conversion="no" />
```

- Remove all `<form>` tags, as SharePoint allows only one `<form>` tag that it will handle for us.

- Review your HTML and place comments around blocks of HTML that will be replaced with snippets (more on snippets later in this chapter) such as where you will replace HTML from the HTML file with SharePoint components such as navigation, a search box, and the main content area. We use tags such as `<!--search snippet-->` and `<!--end search snippet-->` around an HTML block in our HTML file that we intend to replace with a Search Box snippet.

- Finally consider the file name of the HTML file you intend to use as your master page. Although `index.html` and `default.html` are both valid, they will create master pages named `index.master` and `default.master`. We are going to rename our sample HTML file we will convert later in this chapter to `SpecterGroup.html`.

Map the Master Page Gallery to a Local Drive and Upload Design Files

Before we convert our master page, we want to upload all other branding assets such as style sheets, images and JavaScript files. Uploading the files to our SharePoint site can be done in multiple ways. One option is to upload the entire folder and contents via a web browser, although this is only helpful when you are uploading multiple files using Internet Explorer due to the fact the ActiveX control to upload multiple files only exists on IE. A second option is using the steps we outline next that correspond to Step 3 in Design Manager, which involves mapping a local drive to the Master Page Gallery. A third option is to use SharePoint Designer 2013, which is similar to how we would have uploaded files with SharePoint Designer 2010.

An important consideration is the new recommendation that all branding assets now be added to the Master Page Gallery. This is very different than how we used to use the Style Library document library for storing branding assets such as style sheets and images.

■ **Tip** To maintain organization of our branding files in the Master Page Gallery, we can create a subfolder in the Master Page Gallery for each branding initiate such as `/_catalogs/masterpage/spectergroup`. This is the approach we've chosen.

Map the Master Page Gallery to a Local Drive

To map the Master Page Gallery to a local drive on our MacBook Pro, we follow these steps. If you are on a PC, follow the traditional network drive mapping steps.

1. Navigate to Design Manager in a browser and click on Step 3, Upload Design Files. On the Upload Design Files page shown in Figure 4-2, obtain the location of your Master Page Gallery. Although Figure 4-2 provides a location of `http://www.spectergroup.com/_catalogs/masterpage`, for this exercise, we are using the following URL: `http://192.168.3.105:4500/_catalogs/masterpage`. You will, of course, be provided your own local SharePoint location by Design Manager.

2. We need to map this URL to a local drive, on the Mac, using the Finder, select Go ➤ Connect to Server or (Command + K).

3. In the Server Address text field, paste the URL from Step 1 and press + to add it to the Favorite Servers list as shown in Figure 4-3.

Figure 4-3. *Mapping Master Page Gallery as a local drive dialog box on the Mac where Adobe Dreamweaver is installed*

4. Click Connect. A successful connection will open up the entire masterpage folder. You might get a credential box (see Figure 4-4); if so, simply provide your domain account and password.

Figure 4-4. *Credential box seen while mapping shared drive on a Mac*

To authenticate with SharePoint, you must enter your domain credentials. For example, in the credentials box shown in Figure 4-4, one can type the username in the format of Contoso\James.Hall and the corresponding password. Be sure to select the Registered User option.

■ **Tip**   To map the Master Page Gallery to a network drive on a Windows platform, see `http://sprwd.com/ywwpzx`.

Upload Design Files to the Master Page Gallery

Using the connection we created in the previous section, we may now upload our Design files to the Master Page Gallery.

Drag and drop your local folder with all branding artifacts; in our case this is a folder we named `SpecterGroup` which contains CSS, Images, and JavaScript files to the newly mapped drive. You do not want to copy over all of your HTML files yet, only the primary HTML page, the one we wish to use as our basis for our HTML master page.

■ **Note**   You might notice all Design files including the style sheets, images, and JavaScript files are being placed in the Master Page Gallery. This is different than in SharePoint 2010, where we would use the Style Library. Best practices with SharePoint 2013 are to now use the Master Page Gallery to store all branding assets including style sheets, images, and JavaScript files.

At this point, the `Specter` folder and all of its content is uploaded to the Master Page Gallery as shown in Figure 4-5.

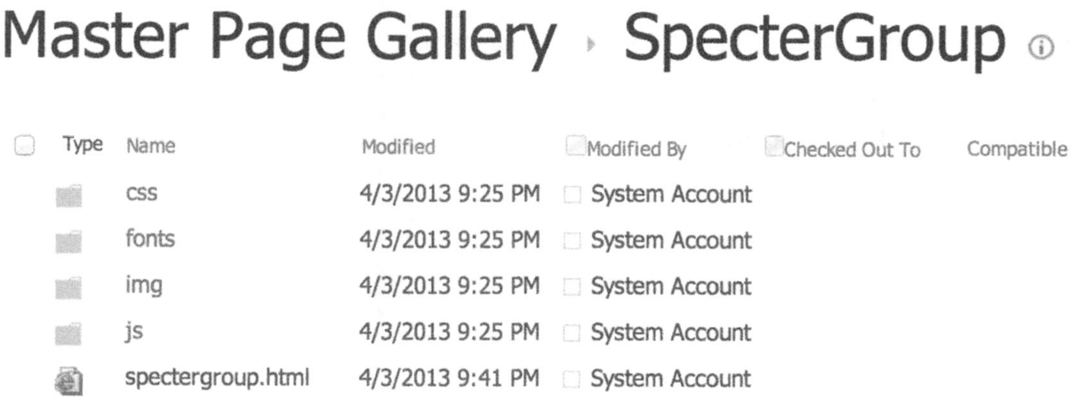

Master Page Gallery › SpecterGroup ⓘ

	Type	Name	Modified	Modified By	Checked Out To	Compatible
☐		css	4/3/2013 9:25 PM	☐ System Account		
		fonts	4/3/2013 9:25 PM	☐ System Account		
		img	4/3/2013 9:25 PM	☐ System Account		
		js	4/3/2013 9:25 PM	☐ System Account		
		spectergroup.html	4/3/2013 9:41 PM	☐ System Account		

Figure 4-5.   *The Specter Group Design folder uploaded to the Master Page Gallery*

■ **Tip**   We still must publish a major version of all branding assets before they are available to all users. We suggest publishing all the files in bulk via the Content and Structure Tool found in the Site Settings. You will need to go into each subfolder, as sadly SharePoint does not publish items recursively. You can also use the browser or SharePoint Design to publish files as well. A huge bonus is that we do not have to always check out, check in, and then publish any longer; we can skip ahead and just publish a major version.

Create a Dreamweaver Site

Design Manager does not cover this step; however now that we've mapped the SharePoint Master Page Gallery location to a local drive, we are able to create a Dreamweaver site and set the Local Site Root folder to the folder we previously uploaded.

Follow these steps:

1. Launch Dreamweaver, and select Site ➤ Manage Sites. The New Site dialog box opens.

2. On the bottom right of the dialog box, select New Site.

3. Type the site name (something descriptive helps).

4. Browse to the local mapped folder (the folder from our previous exercise) and select that as the Local Site Folder.

5. In the Files pane, you should see all of your files. You are now ready to edit your files as shown in Figure 4-6.

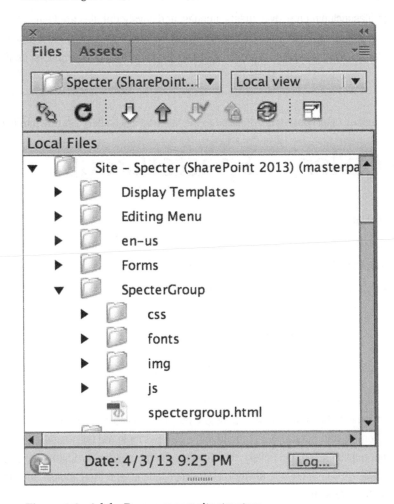

Figure 4-6. *Adobe Dreamweaver site structure*

At this point we have connected to the Master Page Gallery by mapping a local drive, which uses WebDAV in the background. We then used this mapped folder to upload our entire design folder. We created a site in Dreamweaver and mapped its root to the Master Page Gallery local drive that contains our Specter Group Design folder. So now we are able to quickly make edits to the HTML files and other artifacts directly in the Master Page Gallery. Our next task is to actually convert our HTML file into an HTML master page.

■ **Tip**　We uploaded only one .html file, `spectergroup.html`. We took `index.html` provided by the design team and renamed it `spectergroup.html` so that when the HTML master page is generated, it is named appropriately; that is, not `index.html` and `index.master`, respectively.

Create an HTML Master Page from an HTML Prototype

We can now convert our HTML prototype to a SharePoint-friendly HTML master page. Navigate once again to Design Manager in a browser and select Step 4, Edit Master Pages. This page provides a list of currently available HTML master pages and presents us with two additional options as shown in Figure 4-7. You might also notice that Design Manager provides us two HTML master pages out of the box, oslo and seattle. We ignore these here, although they might come in handy if we want to see a working example of an HTML master page.

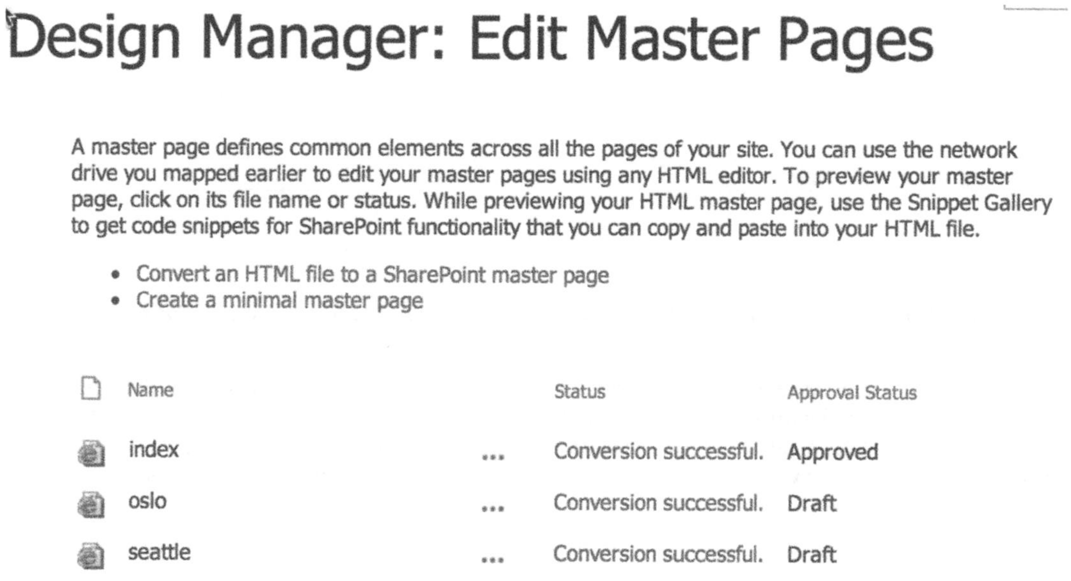

Design Manager: Edit Master Pages

A master page defines common elements across all the pages of your site. You can use the network drive you mapped earlier to edit your master pages using any HTML editor. To preview your master page, click on its file name or status. While previewing your HTML master page, use the Snippet Gallery to get code snippets for SharePoint functionality that you can copy and paste into your HTML file.

- Convert an HTML file to a SharePoint master page
- Create a minimal master page

☐	Name		Status	Approval Status
▣	index	...	Conversion successful.	Approved
▣	oslo	...	Conversion successful.	Draft
▣	seattle	...	Conversion successful.	Draft

Figure 4-7. Design Manager's Edit Master Pages page

The first option is to convert an HTML file into a master page, which is what we will be doing throughout this guide. The second option allows us to start with the minimal master page, which allows for a designer to start from the bare minimum and progressively build the master page by incorporating the design.

Convert an HTML Prototype to an HTML Master Page

Proceed with the conversion: On the Edit Master Pages page (see Figure 4-7) click Convert an HTML file to a SharePoint master page. An Asset Picker modal dialog box appears. Browse to the folder where your HTML file is located (i.e., /_catalogs/masterpage/SpecterGroup), select the HTML file you wish to convert to an HTML master page, and click Insert. In our case we've selected the file called SpecterGroup.html within our folder, as shown in Figure 4-8.

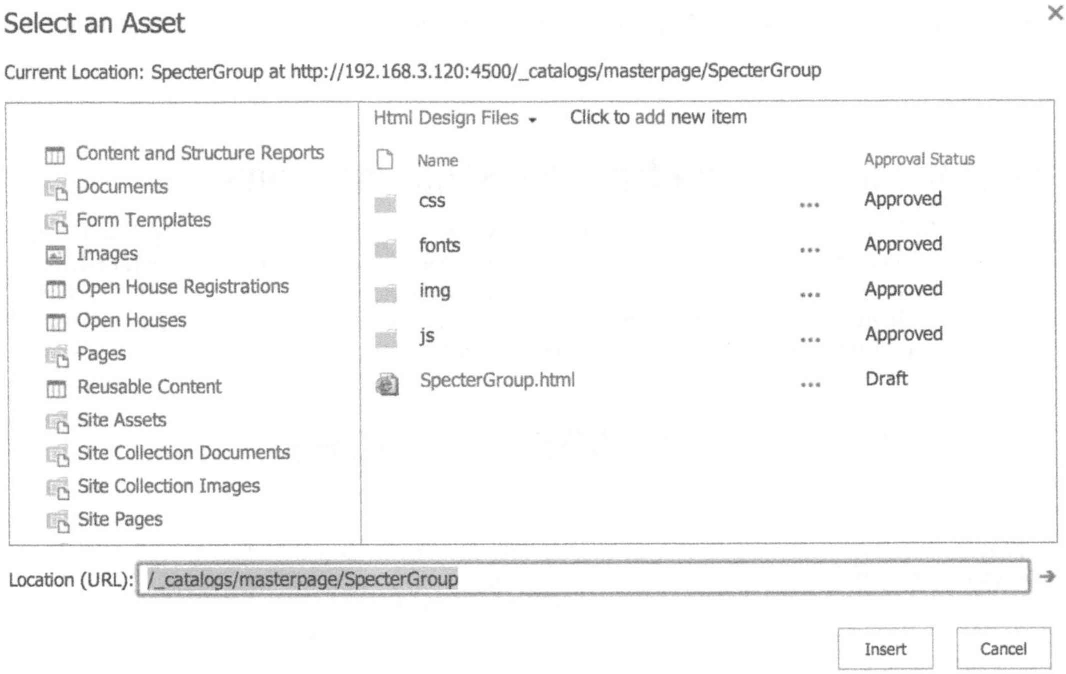

Select an Asset   ×

Current Location: SpecterGroup at http://192.168.3.120:4500/_catalogs/masterpage/SpecterGroup

Html Design Files ▾	Click to add new item		
Name			Approval Status
css		...	Approved
fonts		...	Approved
img		...	Approved
js		...	Approved
SpecterGroup.html		...	Draft

- ▥ Content and Structure Reports
- ▧ Documents
- ▧ Form Templates
- ▣ Images
- ▥ Open House Registrations
- ▥ Open Houses
- ▧ Pages
- ▥ Reusable Content
- ▧ Site Assets
- ▧ Site Collection Documents
- ▧ Site Collection Images
- ▧ Site Pages

Location (URL): /_catalogs/masterpage/SpecterGroup → →

[Insert] [Cancel]

Figure 4-8. *Selecting an HTML file to convert to an HTML master page via the Asset Picker modal dialog box*

Once we select the HTML file, SharePoint then generates a .master file that it associates with the HTML file. The HTML file itself is now associated with a content type called HTML Master Page (new to SharePoint 2013). This content type has a column named Associated File that is used to flag the association, as shown in Figure 4-9. When you make changes to the .html file, for example, in Dreamweaver, the changes are automatically reflected in the linked .master file due to this new association.

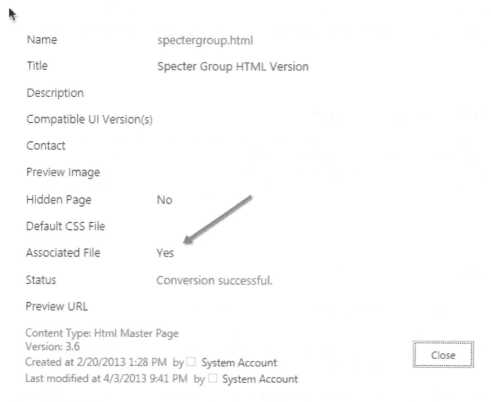

Figure 4-9. *HTML master page properties: This HTML master page is associated with a corresponding .master file*

Under the hood, during this initial conversion, SharePoint modifies the HTML file and adds various snippets and comments (more on this later), which, once saved, are converted to ASP.NET code in the .master file. The Design Manager (and Adobe Dreamweaver) effectively ignores any ASP.NET code in the HTML file.

■ **Caution**   Once an HTML file is associated with a .master file, you should never edit the .master file directly; SharePoint handles this file for us. If you ever wish to disassociate the HTML file from the .master file so that moving forward you only update the .master, simply change the value of the Associated File column and set it to NO in the page properties for the HTML master page. Doing so means that changes made to the HTML master page will not be reflected in the .master file.

Work Directly with the .master Master Page

Once we have converted our HTML to an HTML master page, and the corresponding .master file has been created for us, there is no reason why we can't work directly with the .master file. This, of course, means we have to disassociate the HTML file from the .master file, at which point only the .master file is the one to edit and update. In this case we would treat the .master just as we did with previous versions of SharePoint, as the .master is an ASP.NET master page, allowing us to add .NET components, and so on. Just be aware that we would also need to concern ourselves with required content placeholders as well as other SharePoint requirements. For this reason we stick with the HTML master page for the remainder of this book.

■ **Caution**   If you decide to reassociate the HTML master page file with the .master after it has been edited, all of your changes to the .master file will be overwritten.

Modifying an HTML Master Page

Once Design Manager completes the process of converting a general HTML page to an HTML master page, we will be returned to the Edit Master Pages page. This page shows a list of HTML master pages including the one we just converted. If all goes well, we will see a message next to our new HTML master page that reads Conversion Successful. If there was a problem converting an HTML page to an HTML master page, we will see a Warnings and Errors message, similar to Figure 4-10. To view details on these warnings and errors, click the link.

SpecterGroup ✳   •••   Warnings and Errors.   Draft

Figure 4-10. *HTML master page listing with conversion issues*

Fixing Common HTML Master Page Warnings and Errors

Fixing warnings and errors might be difficult or it might be easy. You might have to rewrite your original HTML file. If it was coded correctly, you will just need to massage it into place with SharePoint. You can make changes directly to your HTML master page in your web editor and as you save changes, refresh the Preview page in your browser to see if that helped fix your issues.

Click on the Name or Status of our new HTML master page to view any warnings and errors as well as preview the rendered HTML master page right from Design Manager. This is helpful to detect any problems that need to be fixed. Should your master page have any errors or warnings, these will also display in this area just below the black Ribbon for a particular HTML master page you preview. See Figure 4-11 for a sample error message.

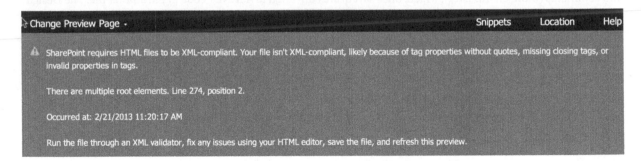

Figure 4-11. *Sample errors and warnings message after an HTML master page conversion*

Our web design team provided us an HTML file that was not quite in the format SharePoint 2013 requires, so our conversion had errors. You can see the exact message we get when clicking on the HTML master page in Figure 4-11.

■ **Note**   Our example master page was specially crafted to highlight common conversion errors even though the HTML file was created using standard, common HTML practices. We want to highlight the most common warnings and errors you might encounter. We did not follow our own advice previously in this chapter in the section "Preparing an HTML File for Conversion to an HTML Master Page".

Let's quickly investigate this error message as although it is cryptic, it does supply some valuable information. First, the message tells us that the HTML file must be XML-compliant. Even though we intend to use HTML5, Design Manager requires that HTML master pages be XML-compliant so that it can properly parse each file. Our first step might be to run our original HTML file through an XML validator. If we do this, we will find that our sample HTML file is in fact XML-compliant.

Let's move on down the line and see that there are multiple root elements on line 274. Open the converted HTML master page, in our case SpecterGroup.html in Dreamweaver and look around line 274 for a problem. Review Listing 4-1 for a compact view of the converted HTML. Line 274 is at the bottom. The problem we immediately encountered is that SharePoint added a second <head> block to the end of the file. This was added because we did not define a proper <html> element after our DOCTYPE. SharePoint is quite strict and currently will not accept the popular technique of using IE <!--if--> comments to provide additional class elements for IE 8 and earlier.

■ **Tip**   Always make sure that you have a valid <head> opening tag, as Design Manager converts this to a special Head control in the associated .master file.

Listing 4-1. The HTML Source for the Newly Converted HTML Master Page (Some Code Has Been Removed for Simplicity)

```
<!DOCTYPE html>
<!-- paulirish.com/2008/conditional-stylesheets-vs-css-hacks-answer-neither/ -->
<!--[if lt IE 7]> <html class="no-js lt-ie9 lt-ie8 lt-ie7" lang="en"
      xmlns:mso="urn:schemas-microsoft-com:office:office"
      xmlns:msdt="uuid:C2F41010-65B3-11d1-A29F-00AA00C14882"> <![endif]-->
<!--[if IE 7]><html class="no-js lt-ie9 lt-ie8" lang="en"> <![endif]-->
<!--[if IE 8]><html class="no-js lt-ie9" lang="en"> <![endif]-->
<!--[if gt IE 8]><!--><html class="no-js" lang="en"><!--<![endif]-->
<head>
      <meta charset="utf-8" />
      <title>Specter Group HTML Version</title>
      <meta name="description" content="" />
      <!-- Rest of head section removed-->
</head>
<body>
      <!-- HEADER -->
      <header>
            <!--header removed-->
      </header>
      <!-- ENDS HEADER -->
```

```
        <!-- nav -->
        <nav id="topnav">
                <!--top nav removed-->
        </nav>
        <!-- ends nav -->

        <!-- MAIN -->
        <div role="main" id="main">
                <!--main content area removed-->
        </div>
        <!-- ENDS MAIN -->

        <footer>
                <!--footer removed-->
        </footer>
</body>
</html>
<head>
<!--[if gte mso 9]><xml>
<mso:CustomDocumentProperties>
<!--properties removed-->
</mso:CustomDocumentProperties>
</xml><!--[endif]-->
</head><!--[if gt IE 8]>
```

In our example, the first error we need to fix has to do with the duplicate <head> tag SharePoint added at the time of the conversion. The next thing we need to do is replace the top <head> section attempting to target IE versions with a standard <head> tag. So we will remove the additional <head> block added after the closing </html> tag and replace the first few lines of the HTML Master Page as seen in Listing 4-2.

Listing 4-2. Valid DOCTYPE, <html>, and <head> Tags for an HTML Master Page

```
<!DOCTYPE html>
<html class="no-js" lang="en">
<head>
```

After we save our HTML master page in our web editor and refresh the Preview page we get a successful conversion with no warnings or errors as shown in Figure 4-12.

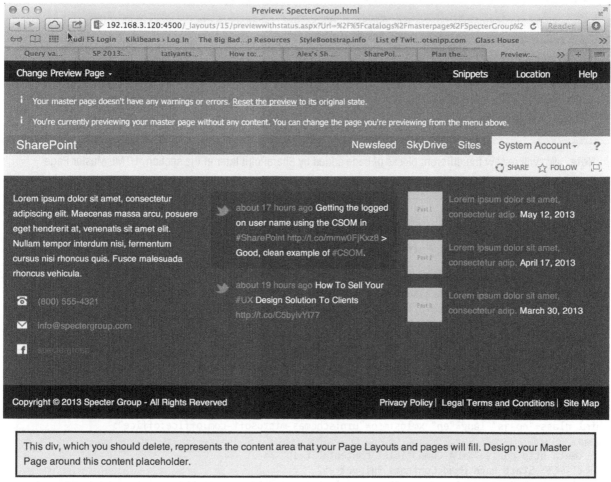

Figure 4-12. *Successful HTML Master Page conversion: Note the yellow box at the bottom*

You might encounter additional errors and warnings depending on how XML-compliant and valid your original HTML file is. You will need to work through each error message displayed until Design Manager reports no more errors with your HTML master page. As soon as the conversion is successful, Design Manager will completely rewrite your original HTML file, adding in a whole series of new tags, comments, and content blocks.

Clean Up a Newly Converted HTML Master Page

Once you have successfully converted an HTML file to an HTML master page, there are a few clean-up issues that you will want to handle before you get into adding additional SharePoint functionality such as snippets. First we look at the primary ContentPlaceHolder and second we look at common styling techniques.

■ **Note**   Learn about snippets later in this chapter, in the section "Snippets and the Snippet Gallery."

Let's look at our newly converted HTML master page, which you can see in Listing 4-3. Note that we have removed blocks of code that in general are required but decrease readability at this time. Pay special attention to a new <div> with a data-name of ContentPlaceHolderMain added at the bottom of Listing 4-3. This <div> created the yellow box shown at the bottom of Figure 4-12.

■ **Note**   We will review the different blocks of code added by SharePoint later in the section "HTML Master Page SharePoint-Generated Markup," including how to parse what each block is adding.

Listing 4-3. Our Sample Converted HTML Master Page

```
<?xml version="1.0" encoding="utf-8"?>
<!--SPG:
This HTML file has been associated with a SharePoint Master Page (.master file) carrying the same
name. While the files remain associated, you will not be allowed to edit the .master file, and any
rename, move, or deletion operations will be reciprocated.

To build the master page directly from this HTML file, simply edit the page as you normally would.
Use the Snippet Generator at http://192.168.3.120:4500/_layouts/15/ComponentHome.aspx?... to create
and customize useful SharePoint entities, then copy and paste them as HTML snippets into your HTML
code.  All updates to this file will automatically sync to the associated Master Page.
-->
<!DOCTYPE html[]>
<html class="no-js" lang="en" xmlns:mso="urn:schemas-microsoft-com:office:office">
<head>
    <meta http-equiv="X-UA-Compatible" content="IE=10" />
    <!--CS: Start Page Head Contents Snippet-->
    <!--SPM:<%@Register Tagprefix="SharePoint" Namespace="Microsoft.SharePoint.WebControls" -->
    <!--SPM:<%@Register Tagprefix="WebPartPages"
        Namespace="Microsoft.SharePoint.WebPartPages" -->
    <!--SID:00 -->
    <meta name="GENERATOR" content="Microsoft SharePoint" />
    <meta http-equiv="Content-type" content="text/html; charset=utf-8" />
    <meta http-equiv="Expires" content="0" />
    <!--MS:<SharePoint:RobotsMetaTag runat="server">-->
    <!--ME:</SharePoint:RobotsMetaTag>-->
    <!--Remainder of head removed for brevity-->
</head>
<body>
    <!--CS: Start Ribbon Snippet-->
    <!--SPM:<%@Register Tagprefix="SharePoint"
        Namespace="Microsoft.SharePoint.WebControls" -->
    <!--SPM:<%@Register Tagprefix="wssucw" TagName="Welcome" -->
    <!--MS:<SharePoint:SPSecurityTrimmedControl runat="server"
            HideFromSearchCrawler="true">-->
        <!--Removed for brevity-->
```

```
    <!--ME:</SharePoint:SPSecurityTrimmedControl>-->
    <div id="ms-designer-ribbon">
        <!--Removed for brevity-->
    </div>
    <!--CE: End Ribbon Snippet-->
    <div id="s4-workspace">
        <div id="s4-bodyContainer">
            <!-- HEADER -->
            <header>
                <!--Removed for brevity-->
            </header>
            <!-- ENDS HEADER -->
            <!-- nav -->
            <nav id="topnav">
                <!--Removed for brevity-->
            </nav>
            <!-- ends nav -->
            <!-- MAIN -->
            <div role="main" id="main">
                <div class="wrapper">
                    <!--main content placerholder, use the following
                    html as sample content for content placeholder-->
                    <!--Removed for brevity-->
                    <!--end content placeholder-->
                </div>
            </div>
            <!-- ENDS MAIN -->
            <footer>
                <!--Removed for brevity-->
            </footer>
            <div data-name="ContentPlaceHolderMain">
                <!--CS: Start PlaceHolderMain Snippet-->
                <!--SPM:<%@Register Tagprefix="SharePoint"
                    Namespace="Microsoft.SharePoint.WebControls" -->
                <!--MS:<SharePoint:AjaxDelta ID="DeltaPlaceHolderMain"
                        IsMainContent="true" runat="server">-->
                    <!--MS:<asp:ContentPlaceHolder ID="PlaceHolderMain" runat="server">-->
                        <div class="DefaultContentBlock" style="border:medium black solid; background:yellow;
                                color:black;>
                            This div, which you should delete, represents the content area that your Page Layouts
                                and pages will fill. Design your Master Page around this content placeholder.
                        </div>
                    <!--ME:</asp:ContentPlaceHolder>-->
                <!--ME:</SharePoint:AjaxDelta>-->
                <!--CE: End PlaceHolderMain Snippet-->
            </div>
        </div>
    </div>
</body>
</html>
```

We first want to handle the yellow box added to the bottom of our HTML master page. Figure 4-13 shows the entire code for the `ContentPlaceHolderMain` `<div>` element, which essentially wraps the entire ASP.NET `PlaceHolderMain` element on our HTML master page.

Figure 4-13. *ContentPlaceHolder DIV element that corresponds to the .NET control ContentPlaceHolder*

The block within `<div data-name="ContentPlaceHolderMain">` is a `ContentPlaceHolder` snippet. We learn more about snippets later in this chapter. For now, this snippet maps directly to a `ContentPlaceHolder` .NET control that we are used to from SharePoint 2010.

A `ContentPlaceHolder` in a master page is essentially a .NET control that may be overwritten by a page layout. Most elements in a master page are fixed for all pages that utilize the master page but content placeholders provide a mechanism we can use to provide specific areas of a master page that a page layout can customize. Content placeholders may also contain default "content," including additional .NET controls that a particular page will display by default but that a page layout might override.

■ **Note**   Learn how to customize the content in content placeholders in page layouts in Chapter 7.

In our case, the `ContentPlaceHolder` with an ID of `PlaceHolderMain` is the primary `ContentPlaceHolder` used throughout SharePoint as the placeholder where all "Main" content will go.

Cut the entire `<div>` block highlighted in Figure 4-13 to your clipboard so that you can move it to its proper place in the HTML master page. In our case, we want this block contained within the `<div class="wrapper">` block found within `<div id="main">`. Refer to Listing 4-3.

Within `<div class="wrapper">` you will see two important comments,

```
<!--main content placerholder, use the following html as sample content for content placeholder-->
```

and

```
<!--end content placerholder-->
```

These comments were added by the web design team and help us know where SharePoint components should go. We will see how they are useful to figure out where other snippets may go such as the logo snippet, the navigation snippet, and the search box snippet. These types of comments are also helpful within page layout code blocks as well, as there are also many snippets available to page layouts.

After we paste the `<div>` in our clipboard within the preceding comments we should see code similar to Listing 4-4.

Listing 4-4. ContentPlaceHolder PlaceHolderMain Moved to Within Our "Main" Div

```
<!-- MAIN -->
<div role="main" id="main">
    <div class="wrapper">
        <!--main content placerholder, use the following html as sample content for content placeholder-->
        <div data-name="ContentPlaceHolderMain">
            <!--CS: Start PlaceHolderMain Snippet-->
            <!--SPM:<%@Register Tagprefix="SharePoint" Namespace="Microsoft.SharePoint.WebControls" -->
            <!--MS:<SharePoint:AjaxDelta ID="DeltaPlaceHolderMain" IsMainContent="true" runat="server">-->
                <!--MS:<asp:ContentPlaceHolder ID="PlaceHolderMain" runat="server">-->
                    <div class="DefaultContentBlock" style="border:medium black solid; background:yellow;
                            color:black;>
                        This div, which you should delete, represents the content area that your page layouts'
                        and pages will fill. Design your master page around this content placeholder.
                    </div>
                <!--ME:</asp:ContentPlaceHolder>-->
            <!--ME:</SharePoint:AjaxDelta>-->
            <!--CE: End PlaceHolderMain Snippet-->
        </div>
        <!--end content placerholder-->
    </div>
</div>
<!-- ENDS MAIN -->
```

■ **Note**   You can replace the entire `<div>` block with the class `"DefaultContentBlock"` with preview content, possibly from your original HTML file. This "preview" content will only be displayed while previewing an HTML master page, as although it is the default content for `PlaceHolderMain`, this `ContentPlaceHolder` content will always be replaced by a SharePoint Page.

After moving the `<div>` that represents the main `PlaceHolderMain` to the appropriate location within your HTML master page, your preview of your HTML master page will look similar to Figure 4-14.

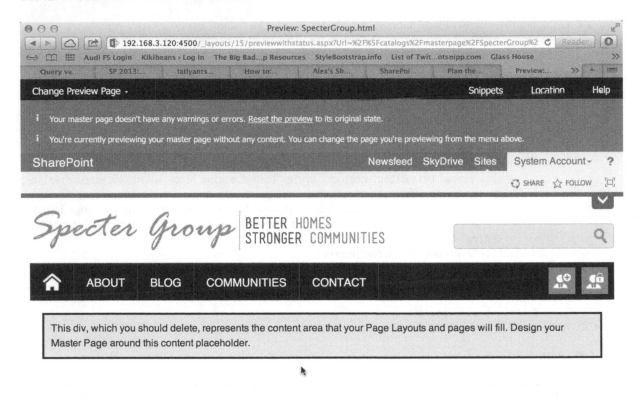

Figure 4-14. *The PlaceHolderMain DIV within the correct location on our HTML master page*

Common Style Sheet Adjustments for HTML Master Pages

When SharePoint converts your HTML master page, it adds a bunch of controls and other markup. These include the ribbon and the s4-workspace and s4-bodyContainer divs you might recognize from SharePoint 2010 days. These new components are contained within divs and as such have additional styling applied to them by SharePoint. As this styling might not work for us, we will review a few common aspects of an HTML master page you might wish to customize.

We will use Firebug in Firefox to help track down the styles we wish to change and provide any updated styles in our custom style sheet, that is, /~catalogs/masterpage/SpecterGroup/css/styles.css. Using the techniques we review in the next two subsections, you should be able to track down any HTML element or style you wish to update on your custom HTML master page.

General Page Padding

Often you might want a footer that reaches all of the way down to the bottom of the browser window. One of the changes that SharePoint makes to our HTML master pages appears to add additional padding to the bottom of our footer. Refer to Figure 4-15, where we can see this additional padding and notice how we use Firebug to find where this padding is coming from.

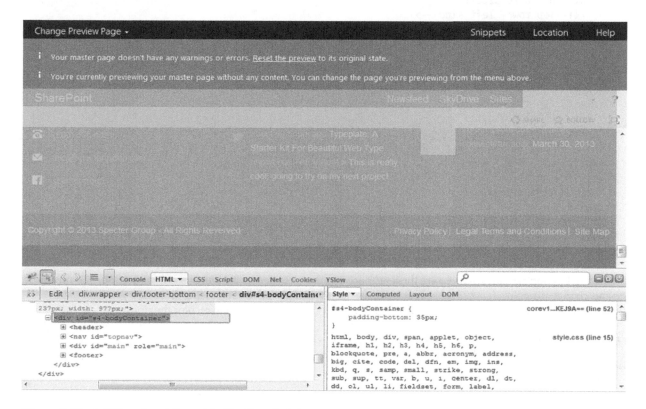

Figure 4-15. *Additional padding added by SharePoint*

We can see that the `core15.css` style sheet provided by SharePoint 2013 adds a bottom padding of 35px to the s4-bodyContainer div. Listing 4-5 shows the style we add to our custom style sheet to remove this bottom padding.

Listing 4-5. Remove the Bottom Padding from the s4-bodyContainer

```
#s4-bodyContainer {
        padding-bottom: 0px;
}
```

Recolor the Suite Bar

Changing the color of the Suite Bar to match your branding is another easy task using a browser developer tool such as Firebug and a few custom styles. Listing 4-6 shows the HTML generated by SharePoint for the Suite Bar, and using Firebug we can select these different elements until we find which elements define specific aspects of the ribbon.

Listing 4-6. Main HTML Generated by SharePoint to Generate the Ribbon and Inner Components That Include the Suite Bar

```
<div id="ms-designer-ribbon">
  <div>
    <div id="suiteBar" class="ms-dialogHidden noindex">
      <div id="suiteBarLeft">
        <!--Top row - left side -->
      <div id="suiteBarRight">
        <!--Top row - right side -->

      <div>
    </div>
    <div id="s4-ribbonrow" style="height: 35px;">
      <div id="globalNavBox">
        <!--second row-->
      </div>
    </div>
    <div id="notificationArea" class="ms-notif-box">
      <!--Notification box-->
    </div>
    <div id="DeltaPageStatusBar"></div>
  </div>
</div>
```

Using Firebug, we can see there are three primary divs that provide the building blocks for the Suite Bar on which we can change the color: IDs suiteBarleft, suiteBarRight, and globalNavBox. Using these IDs, you can create custom styles similar to Listing 4-7 that you can add to your custom style sheet to recolor the ribbon.

Listing 4-7. Custom Styles to Restyle the Suite Bar

```
#suiteBarLeft {
    background-color: #993300;
}
#suiteBarRight {
    background-color: #e5e5e5;
}
.ms-core-suiteLink-a:hover {
    background-color: #009899;
}
#globalNavBox, .ms-clientcontrol-chromeheader {
    background-color: #e5e5e5;
}
```

The styles in Listing 4-7 change the top left Suite Bar(#suiteBarLeft) from blue to our branding color of burgundy, the top right ribbon (#suiteBarRight) and the second bar of the ribbon (#globalNavBox, .ms-clientcontrol-chromeheader) to a darker gray, and then finally we change the color of the hover color for links in ribbon to a different dark gray. These results are shown in Figure 4-16.

Figure 4-16. *Suite Bar styles, second row highlighted by Element Selector in Firebug*

Changing Suite Bar Text

We suspect one common need will be to change the ribbon's text that appears on the top left (see Figure 4-16), which says SharePoint. In our case, we wanted to change it to read Specter Group. Our approach is to ask our PowerShell Guru to make a change via the SharePoint 2013 PowerShell command line.

The PowerShell command to execute is:

1.   Go to Start ➤ SharePoint 2013 Management Shell.

2.   On the command line, type the following:

```
$specterWebApp = Get-SPWebApplication "http://spectergroup.com"
$specterWebApp.SuiteBarBrandingElementHtml = "Specter Group"
$specterWebApp.Update()
```

After we execute this command and browse the web site we see the change as shown in Figure 4-17.

Figure 4-17. *The new tagline or label now says Specter Group instead of SharePoint*

HTML Master Page SharePoint-Generated Markup

Now we have converted an HTML file to an HTML master page and not only fixed a few common issues, but also saw how to use browser tools to help us customize additional SharePoint elements. Let's take a closer look at what SharePoint did to our HTML master page. When we convert a plain HTML file into an HTML master page, there is a considerable amount of markup added to our file. This all is related to the new way of generating SharePoint .master master pages and keeping both the HTML master page and its associated .master file in sync.

Also all content added by SharePoint to a successfully converted HTML master page is contained within the standard HTML comment blocks, <!-- and -->. These comments are very important and how they start tells us a lot about for what SharePoint intends to use that particular comment. Let's look at the special markup descriptions first, then review what is added to the <head> and <body> blocks.

Markup Descriptions

The following list outlines the various types of markup with a brief explanation of what they are. We cover more detail on where exactly these appear within the HTML master page file shortly.

- <!--SPM:...-->: SharePoint Markup. This allows for registering the server-side controls that have the SharePoint namespace.

- <!--CS:...--> and <!--CE:...-->: Comment Start and Comment End. This is used throughout the code that SharePoint outputs so that it is easy to identify where each major component starts and ends such as the Head, Ribbon, and Main Content. Comments can be safely removed if you do not want them.

- <!--MS:...--> and <!--ME:...-->: Markup Start and Markup End. Markup Start allows you to start any valid HTML or .NET control tag that you want sent directly to the .master file without Design Manager touching it. Most often you will see this used to start and end a particular .NET control such as a ContentPlaceHolder or other SharePoint control, but it could also be used for HTML tags as well, such as <!--MS:<script type="text/javascript">--> and <!--ME:</script>-->. You will always need a Markup End command somewhere after a Markup Start command.

- <!--PS:...--> and <!--PE:...-->: Preview Start and Preview End. HTML tags within a Preview block are only used while previewing an HTML master page in the Preview view or within a web design tool such as Dreamweaver. Preview blocks are not required but might help while building an HTML master page as they provide what a particular snippet "could" look like.

- There are also two reserved ID tags, <!--SID:00 --> and <!--SID:02 -->. These are reserved snippets that make our HTML master page more readable.

Markup Added to the <head> Tag

The <head> tag includes various added markup blocks. The first block we'd like to point out is the Document Properties or <mso> tags, added just before the </head> tag. The Document Properties keep track of metadata including the file association and the conversion status. The Design Manager also uses these properties to determine and set those values once there are no errors on our page. Listing 4-8 shows this specific markup for our conversion.

■ **Note**   For the most part, we don't need to edit the markup that is generated by SharePoint; our intention is to provide you with information about what this is. We do add snippets, however, and those use this markup.

Listing 4-8. Sample <mso> Metadata Block Found in an HTML Master Page, Simplified

```
<!--[if gte mso 9]><xml>
<mso:CustomDocumentProperties>
    <mso:HtmlDesignFromMaster msdt:dt="string"></mso:HtmlDesignFromMaster>
    <mso:HtmlDesignStatusAndPreview msdt:dt="string">
        http://192.168.3.120:4500/_catalogs/masterpage/SpecterGroup/SpecterGroup.html, Conversion
        successful.</mso:HtmlDesignStatusAndPreview>
    <mso:ContentTypeId msdt:dt="string">
        0x0101000F1C8B9E0EB4BE489F09807B...</mso:ContentTypeId>
    <mso:HtmlDesignAssociated msdt:dt="string">1</mso:HtmlDesignAssociated>
    <mso:HtmlDesignConversionSucceeded msdt:dt="string">True</mso:HtmlDesignConversionSucceeded>
    <mso:HtmlDesignPreviewUrl msdt:dt="string">
        http://192.168.3.120:4500/pages/default.aspx, /pages/default.aspx</mso:HtmlDesignPreviewUrl>
</mso:CustomDocumentProperties>
</xml><![endif]-->
```

The other markup that is added to the <head> tag is a combination of comments and snippets that include the out-of-the-box SharePoint JavaScript and CSS as well as the registration of the required assemblies as shown in Listing 4-9. Again we have simplified some of the tags for readability. If you worked with SharePoint 2010 master pages you will likely recognize many of tags within the <!--MS--> blocks, and if you were to open the associated .master file, you will see how all of the Markup Start tags related one-to-one with .NET controls.

Listing 4-9. The Core <head> Content Markup Added by SharePoint

```
<!--CS: Start Page Head Contents Snippet-->
<!--SPM:<%@Register Tagprefix="SharePoint" Namespace="Microsoft.SharePoint.WebControls" %>-->
<!--SPM:<%@Register Tagprefix="WebPartPages" Namespace="Microsoft.SharePoint.WebPartPages" %>-->

<!--SID:00 -->
<meta name="GENERATOR" content="Microsoft SharePoint" />
<meta http-equiv="Content-type" content="text/html; charset=utf-8" />
<meta http-equiv="Expires" content="0" />
<!--MS:<SharePoint:RobotsMetaTag runat="server">-->
<!--ME:</SharePoint:RobotsMetaTag>-->
<!--MS:<SharePoint:PageTitle runat="server">-->
  <!--MS:<asp:ContentPlaceHolder id="PlaceHolderPageTitle" runat="server">-->
    <!--MS:<SharePoint:ProjectProperty Property="Title" runat="server">-->
    <!--ME:</SharePoint:ProjectProperty>-->
  <!--ME:</asp:ContentPlaceHolder>-->
```

```
<!--ME:</SharePoint:PageTitle>-->
<!--MS:<SharePoint:StartScript runat="server">-->
<!--ME:</SharePoint:StartScript>-->
<!--MS:<SharePoint:CssLink runat="server" Version="15">-->
<!--ME:</SharePoint:CssLink>-->
<!--MS:<SharePoint:CacheManifestLink runat="server">-->
<!--ME:</SharePoint:CacheManifestLink>-->
<!--MS:<SharePoint:PageRenderMode runat="server" RenderModeType="Standard">-->
<!--ME:</SharePoint:PageRenderMode>-->
<!--MS:<SharePoint:ScriptLink language="javascript" name="core.js" OnDemand="true"
runat="server">-->
<!--ME:</SharePoint:ScriptLink>-->
<!--additional references to OOTB JavaScript files-->
<!--MS:<SharePoint:CustomJSUrl runat="server">-->
<!--ME:</SharePoint:CustomJSUrl>-->
<!--MS:<SharePoint:SoapDiscoveryLink runat="server">-->
<!--ME:</SharePoint:SoapDiscoveryLink>-->
<!--MS:<SharePoint:AjaxDelta id="DeltaPlaceHolderAdditionalPageHead" Container="false"
runat="server">-->
  <!--MS:<asp:ContentPlaceHolder id="PlaceHolderAdditionalPageHead" runat="server">-->
  <!--ME:</asp:ContentPlaceHolder>-->
  <!--MS:<SharePoint:DelegateControl runat="server" ControlId="AdditionalPageHead">-->
  <!--ME:</SharePoint:DelegateControl>-->
  <!--MS:<asp:ContentPlaceHolder id="PlaceHolderBodyAreaClass" runat="server">-->
  <!--ME:</asp:ContentPlaceHolder>-->
<!--ME:</SharePoint:AjaxDelta>-->
<!--MS:<SharePoint:CssRegistration Name="Themable/corev15.css" runat="server">-->
<!--ME:</SharePoint:CssRegistration>-->
<!--MS:<SharePoint:AjaxDelta id="DeltaSPWebPartManager" runat="server">-->
  <!--MS:<WebPartPages:SPWebPartManager runat="server">-->
  <!--ME:</WebPartPages:SPWebPartManager>-->
<!--ME:</SharePoint:AjaxDelta>-->
<!--CE: End Page Head Contents Snippet-->
```

Markup Added to the <body> Tag

Within the <body> block, the major additions are found just after the opening <body> tag and one final block added to the bottom, which we reviewed earlier. In Listing 4-10 you can see the first block added to the <body> tag. Take special note of <!--SID:02 {Ribbon}-->, which we learned is a reserved, compressed snippet to ease readability, and the <!--MS:<SharePoint:SPSecurityTrimmedControl>--> tag, which we revisit later in the section "Sign In Snippet".

Listing 4-10. Markup Added to <body> Tag, Simplified

```
<!--CS: Start Ribbon Snippet-->
<!--SPM:<%@Register Tagprefix="SharePoint" Namespace="Microsoft.SharePoint.WebControls" %>-->
<!--SPM:<%@Register Tagprefix="wssucw" TagName="Welcome" %>-->
<!--MS:<SharePoint:SPSecurityTrimmedControl runat="server" HideFromSearchCrawler="true"
    EmitDiv="true">-->
  <div id="TurnOnAccessibility" style="display:none" class="s4-notdlg noindex">
    <a id="linkTurnOnAcc" href="#" class="ms-accessible ms-acc-button" onclick="...">
      <!--MS:<SharePoint:EncodedLiteral runat="server" text="&lt;%$Resources:wss, &&gt;" >-->
```

```
      <!--ME:</SharePoint:EncodedLiteral>-->
    </a>
  </div>
  <div id="TurnOffAccessibility" style="display:none" class="s4-notdlg noindex">
    <a id="linkTurnOffAcc" href="#" class="ms-accessible ms-acc-button" onclick="...">
      <!--MS:<SharePoint:EncodedLiteral runat="server" text="&lt;%$Resources:wss%&gt;">-->
      <!--ME:</SharePoint:EncodedLiteral>-->
    </a>
  </div>
<!--ME:</SharePoint:SPSecurityTrimmedControl>-->
<div id="ms-designer-ribbon">
  <!--SID:02 {Ribbon}-->
  <!--PS: Start of READ-ONLY PREVIEW (do not modify) -->
    <div class="DefaultContentBlock" style="background:rgb(0, 114, 198); color:white;
overflow:hidden;">
      The SharePoint ribbon will be here when your file is either previewed on or applied to your
site.
    </div>
  <!--PE: End of READ-ONLY PREVIEW -->
</div>
<!--MS:<SharePoint:SPSecurityTrimmedControl runat="server" AuthenticationRestrictions="...">-->
  <!--MS:<wssucw:Welcome runat="server" EnableViewState="false">-->
  <!--ME:</wssucw:Welcome>-->
<!--ME:</SharePoint:SPSecurityTrimmedControl>-->
<!--CE: End Ribbon Snippet-->
```

Right after the closing ribbon snippet comments, two <div> tags are added as well, as shown on Listing 4-11. All content is wrapped around these divs and again to those with experience with SharePoint 2010, these will look very familiar. The s4-workspace div is primarily used by SharePoint to control the scrolling space beneath the ribbon and is also used to replace the browser <body> scrollbars. SharePoint will handle the width and height of s4-workspace so we would recommend that most styling you might apply to the <body> tag be applied to s4-bodyContainer instead.

Listing 4-11. The Two Primary container <div>s Added to the <body> Tag

```
<div id="s4-workspace">
     <div id="s4-bodyContainer">
```

Previewing With a New or Existing Page

Notice the black ribbon at the top of the preview page. The Change Preview Page drop-down menu is on the left end and contains two options, Select Existing and Create New. The first option allows you to quickly select from an existing content page to preview your newly created HTML master page. The second option allows you to create a new page to preview your HTML master page.

When we select the first option, we are presented with a dialog box, shown in Figure 4-18, that allows us to either type a URL or use a Generic Preview, which omits some of the content placeholders. In our case, we chose to preview within an existing page so we can provide the full URL of http://192.168.3.105:4500/Pages/Default.aspx. This would populate our Preview with whatever content had been entered at our default.aspx page. Figure 4-19 shows the outcome.

Select Existing Page for Previewing   ✕

⦿ URL: | http://192.168.3.120:4500/pages/default.as ✕ |

If you know what page you want to use for previewing, type the URL here. You can choose any kind of page: a search-driven page or a static page.

◯ Generic Preview

The generic preview will show you some of the SharePoint placeholders but not any page content.

| OK | | Cancel |

Figure 4-18. *Select Preview Page modal dialog box*

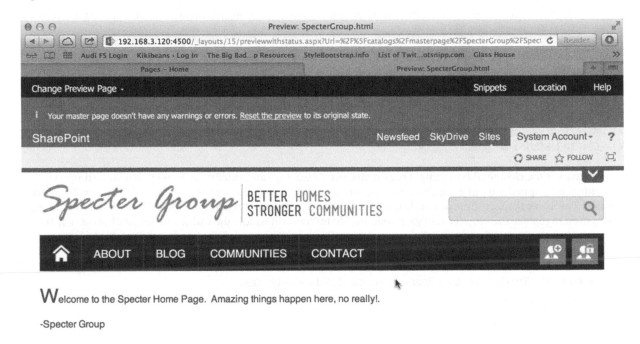

Figure 4-19. *Prevewing the HTML master page by providing the URL of the Default.aspx page*

Selecting the Create New option allows us to create a new page, select a page layout, and then preview our new master page.

■ **Note**   We learn all about page layouts in Chapter 7.

Snippets and the Snippet Gallery

HTML master pages only allow standard HTML; they do not allow for .NET or SharePoint controls. We have already been referring to them, but the Design Manager solves this issue by providing snippets, which allow us to customize our HTML master pages with SharePoint and .NET controls and components. Snippets allow us to insert various SharePoint ASP.NET controls wrapped within the snippet markup and configure them via the Design Manager web-based tool without the need to edit the master page (.master) directly as we were accustomed to with SharePoint 2010.

We can access the Snippet Gallery by clicking Snippets, found at the top right of the HTML master page Preview page. There are various components available to us, as shown in Figure 4-20. The components available to us are grouped into the categories of Navigation, Administration, Containers, WebParts, and Custom ASP.NET Markup.

Figure 4-20. *Snippet Gallery snippets available to HTML master pages*

■ **Note**   The Snippet Gallery was not designed to be an end-all, be-all for all .NET and SharePoint controls that can or should be added to a master page. These are intended to be the most widely used ones. Using the Custom ASP.NET Markup snippet allows us to convert any .NET or SharePoint control to a snippet for insertion into our HTML master page.

■ **Note**   Refer to Chapter 7 for an in-depth review of page layout snippets and the Snippet Gallery.

Now that we have successfully created our HTML master page, we want to start adding in SharePoint components such as the Site Logo, Sign In and Search Box snippets.

■ **Tip**   We will leave a very important snippet, the Top Navigation snippet, until Chapter 6, where we will look into navigation in general and see how to fully utilize the Top Navigation snippet.

Site Logo Snippet

We start with a very simple snippet, the Site Logo snippet. Referring to Figure 4-20, we see that the Site Logo snippet is found in the Administration group.

1. Go to Design Manager and select Edit Master Pages.

2. Click your HTML master page. In our case SpecterGroup.html, which at this point should be in Draft state. Clicking takes you to the Preview Page.

3. Click on the Snippets Ribbon option on the top right.

4. On the Design Ribbon, under Administration, click Site Logo.

5. There are many settings that we can configure, and common ones include the following. Be sure to click Update after changing settings to update the HTML snippet.

    a. Under Customization - Site Logo (SPSimpleSiteLink), make the following changes:

       Appearance ➤ CssClass: Remove any classes, as we will provide our own styling to the logo link.

       Navigation ➤ NavigateURL = ~sitecollection (Valid values for NavigateURL include ~site and ~sitecollection).

    b. Under Customization - Site Logo (SiteLogoImage), make the following changes:

       Appearance ➤ CssClass: Remove any classes, as we will provide our own styling to the logo image.

       Misc ➤ LogoImageURL = /_catalogs/masterpage/spectergroup/img/logo.gif (You can change this URL to your own default logo location).

6. Copy the HTML snippet from the text box on the left and paste it into your HTML master page. Because this is the logo, we want to replace the logo block from our HTML prototype. Refer to Listing 4-12 for an example of the Site Logo HTML snippet added to our HTML master page.

■ **Note** The container <div>, <div data-name="SiteLogo">, and the Comment Start Markup, <!--CS: Start Site Logo Snippet-->, are not required and can be removed. <!--PS:--> tags can be removed as well, but might affect Preview.

Listing 4-12. Site Logo Snippet Within HTML of HTML Master Page

```
<div id="logo">
  <!--logo snippet-->
  <div data-name="SiteLogo">
    <!--CS: Start Site Logo Snippet-->
    <!--SPM:<%@Register Tagprefix="SharePoint" Namespace="Microsoft.SharePoint.WebControls" %>-->
```

```
<!--MS:<SharePoint:AjaxDelta runat="server" BlockElement="True">-->
  <!--PS: Start of READ-ONLY PREVIEW (do not modify)--><!--PE: End of READ-ONLY PREVIEW-->
  <!--MS:<SharePoint:SPSimpleSiteLink runat="server" CssClass="" ID="x531"
      NavigateUrl="~sitecollection">-->
    <!--PS: Start of READ-ONLY PREVIEW (do not modify)--><!--PE: End of READ-ONLY PREVIEW-->
    <!--MS:<SharePoint:SiteLogoImage runat="server" CssClass=""
        ID="x1daed9c2757141c2a871aeda8b6384df"
        LogoImageUrl="/_catalogs/masterpage/spectergroup/img/logo.gif">-->
      <!--PS: Start of READ-ONLY PREVIEW (do not modify)-->
      <img id="ctl00_x1daed9c2757141c2a871aeda8b6384df" name="onetidHeadbnnr0"
          Src="/_catalogs/masterpage/spectergroup/img/logo.gif" alt="Specter Group" />
      <!--PE: End of READ-ONLY PREVIEW-->
    <!--ME:</SharePoint:SiteLogoImage>-->
    <!--PS: Start of READ-ONLY PREVIEW (do not modify)-->
    <!--PE: End of READ-ONLY PREVIEW-->
  <!--ME:</SharePoint:SPSimpleSiteLink>-->
  <!--PS: Start of READ-ONLY PREVIEW (do not modify)-->
  <!--PE: End of READ-ONLY PREVIEW-->
<!--ME:</SharePoint:AjaxDelta>-->
<!--CE: End Site Logo Snippet-->
</div>
<!--end logo snippet-->
</div>
```

7. Save the HTML master page and preview in Design Manager. The default Site Logo control now replaces the static link to our logo image, as shown in Figure 4-21.

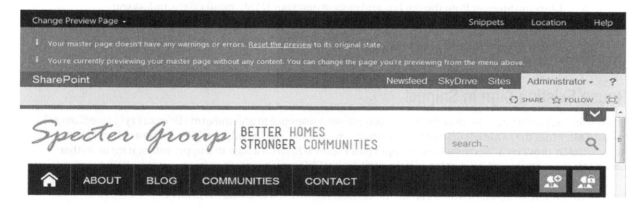

Figure 4-21. *Site Logo snippet added to HTML master page*

Sign In Snippet

As you recall from Chapter 3, we are building a publishing public web site for Specter Group. Therefore, we need to allow users to log in. To do this, we can use the Sign In snippet, which is found in the Administration category on the Design Manager Ribbon, as shown in Figure 4-22. This is a security trimmed control and essentially the same as the previous SharePoint 2010 control, which was available via SharePoint Designer 2010.

Figure 4-22. *Sign In snippet available in the Administration group*

Follow these steps to add the Sign In snippet to your master page:

1. Go to Design Manager and select Edit Master Pages.

2. Click your HTML master page, in our case the SpecterGroup.html, which at this point should be in Draft state. Clicking takes you to the Preview page.

3. Click the Snippets Ribbon option on the top right.

4. On the Design Ribbon, under Administration, click Sign In.

5. Copy the Snippet from the text box and paste it into your HTML master page, unless you need to provide any changes to the configuration first.

6. Save the HTML master page and preview it in Design Manager.

Reuse Existing Sign In Snippet

If you refer back to Listing 4-10, near the bottom you will see a reference to a SharePoint:SPSecurityTrimmedControl tag and after that the same wssucw:Welcome we just saw with the Sign In snippet. This is true as SharePoint automatically provides a "Security Trim" snippet (see Figure 4-20) with a Sign In snippet within it for us so that an HTML master page will have a sign in link out of the box. We can reuse this.

In Figure 4-20, we can see two icons at the right of the top navigation bar, one for a Register button and another for a Login button. In Listing 4-13 we can see the original HTML used to create these links.

Listing 4-13. HTML from HTML Prototype for Registration and Login Buttons

```
<div class="site-access cf">
  <ul>
    <!--anonymous only snippet-->
    <li>
      <a href="#"><img src="img/icon-register.png" alt="Register" /></a>
    </li>
    <!--anonymous only snippet-->
    <li>
```

```
      <!--welcome / login snippet-->
      <a href="#"><img src="img/icon-login.png" alt="Login" /></a>
      <!--end login snippet-->
    </li>
  </ul>
</div>
```

■ **Tip**   Notice the `<!--anonymous only snippet-->` and `<!--welcome / login snippet-->` comments in Listing 4-13. Refer to the earlier section, "Preparing an HTML File for Conversion to an HTML Master Page" for an explanation of why we add these kinds of comments in HTML prototypes.

Let's now move (not copy) the SharePoint:SPSecurityTrimmedControl snippet and its wssucw:Welcome snippet from Listing 4-10 into the HTML from Listing 4-13. The results can be seen in Listing 4-14 and Figure 4-23. You will notice in Figure 4-23 that the Registration button disappeared, which makes sense as the Security Trim snippet will hide the link for nonanonymous users, which we as designers are most definitely not. Therefore, we only see the Welcome control with the standard drop-down menu.

Listing 4-14. HTML Master Page With Snippets from Listing 4-10

```
<div class="site-access cf">
  <ul>
    <!--MS:<SharePoint:SPSecurityTrimmedControl runat="server"
        AuthenticationRestrictions="AnonymousUsersOnly">-->
      <li>
        <a href="#"><img src="img/icon-register.png" alt="Register" /></a>
      </li>
    <!--ME:</SharePoint:SPSecurityTrimmedControl>-->
      <li>
        <!--MS:<wssucw:Welcome runat="server" EnableViewState="false">--><!--ME:</wssucw:Welcome>-->
      </li>
  </ul>
</div>
```

Figure 4-23. *The Registration link and Sign In snippet*

Style the Sign In Snippet

You can style the Sign In link or button a few different ways. One way is to provide a CssClass to the Sign In snippet before you add it and then provide that special class and its styles to your style sheet. Another method is to simply use the CssClass that the Welcome control will add for a Sign In link, .ms-signInLink.

In Listing 4-15 you can see how we reference the Sign In link only within our navigation bar. We provide a fixed width and height, forcing the element to display as a block. We then move the text outside of this block to hide the text and provide a background image. The result is the same as seen in Figure 4-23, but now the Sign In link actually directs a visitor to the site Sign In process.

Listing 4-15. Custom Style for Anonymous Sign In Link or Button

```
nav .site-access .ms-signInLink {
    width: 43px;
    height: 43px;
    display: block;
    text-indent: -1000px;
    overflow: hidden;
    background: transparent url('../img/icon-login.png') no-repeat 0 0;
    line-height: 1em;
    padding: 0px;
}
```

Search Box Snippet

We end our foray into master page snippets for now with a look at the Search Box snippet. The Search Box snippet provides us access to SharePoint's search box control so that we can provide a search box on our sites. In our HTML prototype, we provided a static search box that we can see in Listing 4-16. In Figure 4-21, you can view what this search box looks like.

Listing 4-16. Static Search Box from HTML Prototype

```
<div class="searchbox">
  <!--search snippet-->
    <div id="searchInputBox">
      <input id="header-search" name="header-search" type="text" autofocus="autofocus"
          placeholder="search..." accessKey="S" value="" />
      <a title="Search" href="javascript: {}"><img src="img/icon-search.png" alt="Search" /></a>
    </div>
  <!--end search snippet-->
</div>
```

Follow these steps to add the Search Box snippet to your master page:

1. Go to Design Manager and select Edit Master Pages.

2. Click your HTML Master Page, in our case the SpecterGroup.html, which at this point should be in Draft state. Clicking takes you to the Preview page.

3. Click the Snippets Ribbon option on the top right.

4. On the Design Ribbon, under Navigation, click Search Box.

5. Copy the snippet from the text box and paste it into your HTML master page unless you need to provide any changes to the configuration first. We are going to provide styling to the Search Box based on existing classes and HTML. Refer to Listing 4-17 to view how this snippet appears in our HTML master page. Note that we removed the containing `<div data-name="SearchBox">` and `<!--PS:-->` tags for simplicity.

Listing 4-17. Search Snippet in HTML Master Page

```
<div class="searchbox">
  <!--search box snippet-->
  <!--CS: Start Search Box Snippet-->
  <!--SPM:<%@Register Tagprefix="SearchWC" Namespace="Microsoft.Office.Server.Search.WebControls"
      Assembly="Microsoft.Office.Server.Search, Version=15.0.0.0, Culture=neutral,
      PublicKeyToken=71e9bce111e9429c"%>-->
    <!--MS:<SearchWC:SearchBoxScriptWebPart UseSiteCollectionSettings="true"
        EmitStyleReference="false" ShowQuerySuggestions="false" ChromeType="None"
        UseSharedSettings="true" TryInplaceQuery="false" ServerInitialRender="true" runat="server">-->
      <!--PS: Start of READ-ONLY PREVIEW (do not modify)-->
        <!--removed-->
      <!--PE: End of READ-ONLY PREVIEW-->
    <!--ME:</SearchWC:SearchBoxScriptWebPart>-->
  <!--CE: End Search Box Snippet-->
  <!--end search box snippet-->
</div>
```

6. Save the HTML master page and preview it in Design Manager. Refer to Figure 4-24.

Figure 4-24. *Search Box snippet added to HTML master page*

We can see in Figure 4-24 that the styling from our HTML prototype search box did not transfer over to our Search Box snippet. This is not uncommon, as snippets often will code their contents using different HTML and class structure than a design team might expect. Styling the search box takes a little more work than styling a sign in button, as we need to override styling for the search container, the input box, and the search button. Using Firebug we can quickly drill into the HTML tags and find the styles that we need to override. Refer to Listing 4-18 for our overriding styles and Figure 4-25 for the end result.

Listing 4-18. Custom Styles to Style the Search Box Snippet

```css
header #SearchBox .ms-srch-sb-border, header #SearchBox .ms-srch-sb-borderFocused {
    background: #e5e5e5 none;
    border: 1px #c2c2c2 solid;
    border-radius: 5px;
    -moz-border-radius: 5px;
    -webkit-border-radius:5px;
    height: 38px;
    display: block;
}
header #SearchBox .ms-srch-sb-borderFocused {
    border-color: #009899;
}
header #SearchBox .ms-srch-sb input[type=text]{
    border: 0px;
    width: 170px;
    height: 28px;
    padding: 5px 10px;
    font-size: 16px;
    line-height: 1em;
    color: #333;
    background: transparent none;
    display: inline-block;
    vertical-align: top;
}
.ms-srch-sb > .ms-srch-sb-searchLink {
    height: 24px;
    width: 22px;
    display: inline-block;
    margin: 0px;
    padding: 7px 0px 5px;
    vertical-align: top;
    -webkit-transition: all 0s ease;
    -moz-transition: all 0s ease;
    -o-transition: all 0s ease;
    transition: all 0s ease;
    background: transparent url('../img/icon-search.png') no-repeat 0px 6px;
}
.ms-srch-sb > .ms-srch-sb-navLink  {
    background: transparent none;
    padding: 0px;
    margin:  7px 10px 5px 0;
}
.ms-srch-sb > .ms-srch-sb-navLink img {
    display: block;
}
.ms-srch-sb > .ms-srch-sb-searchLink:hover {
    background: transparent url('../img/icon-search.png') no-repeat 0px -70px;
}
.ms-srch-sb > .ms-srch-sb-searchLink img {
    display: none;
}
```

Figure 4-25. *HTML master page with search styling from Listing 4-18 applied*

In Listing 4-18, we include six primary overrides. The first CSS block overrides the styling for the search area container by providing a new background color, rounded border, and border color. The second block provides a new border color to the search box on hover. The third block provides styling to the actual input box itself, and the final three blocks modify how the search "go" link or search button display.

Publishing and Assigning a Site Master Page

Once you have reached a point in the design cycle where the HTML master page meets the design standards and requirements, you will need to publish a major version of your HTML master page (as well as all other branding assets). To publish your newly created master page and related artifacts, you can use SharePoint Designer or a browser. If you choose to use a browser, you can use the Content and Structure Tool located at /_layouts/15/sitemanager.aspx in your environment or found on the Site Settings page (Site Administration ➤ Content and structure). This allows for bulk publishing files instead of doing it one file a time. Once all files have been checked in and published you are ready to set your master page as the default.

You only need to check in the HTML master page (i.e., SpecterGroup.html) and not the .master file (i.e., SpecterGroup.master). SharePoint will handle the publishing of the .master file for you if you check in and publish your HTML master page.

■ **Caution** If for some reason you are not able to view certain images, or scripts are not working on your master page, ensure you have published a "major version" of all files. The Content and Structure Tool does not publish items recursively; therefore, you must publish files under each subfolder.

After all assets including the HTML master page have been published, you now need to tell SharePoint to use it. To do this, simply go to the Site Settings ➤ Master Page under Look and Feel. You only change the Site master page for now as this is the same as the Custom master page that publishing pages use. The System master page is the master page used by system pages such as the Site Settings pages. We leave this as the default master page for now.

The drop-down menu next to the Site master page should show your published master pages. If your custom master page(s) are not listed, go back and make sure you published a major version. See Figure 4-26 for our list of master pages. Select the SpecterGroup/SpecterGroup master page and save our settings. Our site should now be using the Specter Group master page on standard publishing pages found in the "pages" library.

Site Master Page Settings ⓘ

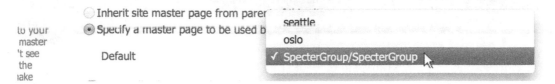

Figure 4-26. Published master page shown on the available drop-down menu

---

■ **Caution**   Although our custom master page resides in a folder we named SpecterGroup, it should still show up on the available ones via the drop-down list as shown in Figure 4-26. If you do not see your master page, please ensure you have published a major version.

Creating a Design Package

More often than not, there is a need to share design artifacts across SharePoint instances, such as when moving a branding solution from a development farm to a production farm. When you need to, simply create a Design Package (Step 8 of Design Manager as shown in Figure 4-27). SharePoint creates a WSP or Solution file that contains all of your artifacts, such as images, JavaScript, CSS, and the master page. Once you save this file, it is available on the Solution Gallery of the Site Collection you are working on. In addition, you are given a link to download this Design Package right from the Design Manager.

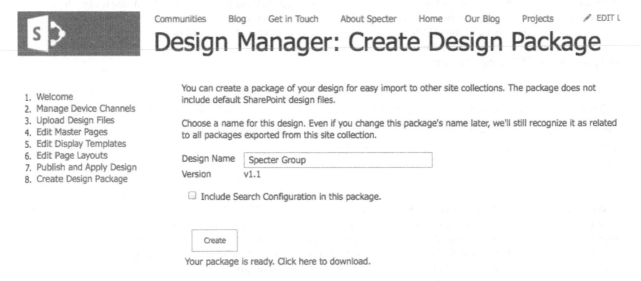

Figure 4-27. Create a Design Package via Design Manager

> ■ **Note**   A Design Package is supposed to contain only modifications (unghosted) assets and files in your SharePoint site including modifications to the Master Page Gallery (master pages, page layouts, images, CSS, and JavaScript files) as well as custom lists, libraries and even content types and content columns. We learn about page layouts and content types in Chapter 7.

Are you curious to know exactly what is included in the Design Package file? If so download the WSP file to your workstation and rename it with a .cab extension for Windows or .zip for a Mac. Open it using the appropriate application (we used Zipeg on the Mac). As shown in Figure 4-28, the contents of the solution include a feature that deploys all the actual files assigning them the Design File content type as expected.

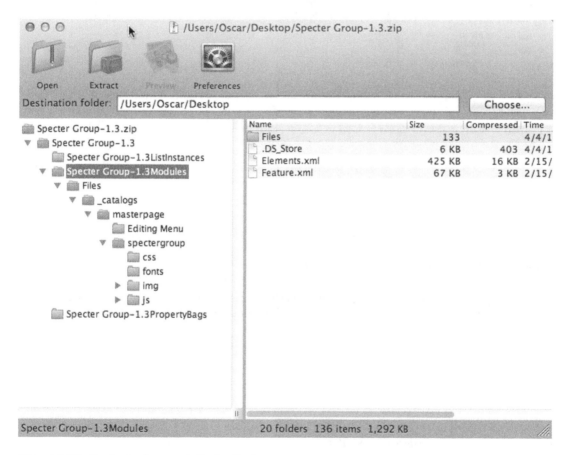

Figure 4-28.   *Contents of a sample Design Package*

The Specter Group artifacts are within the original folder we uploaded, shown in Figure 4-29, which includes the HTML master page and the .master file as well as the JavaScript, CSS, and images.

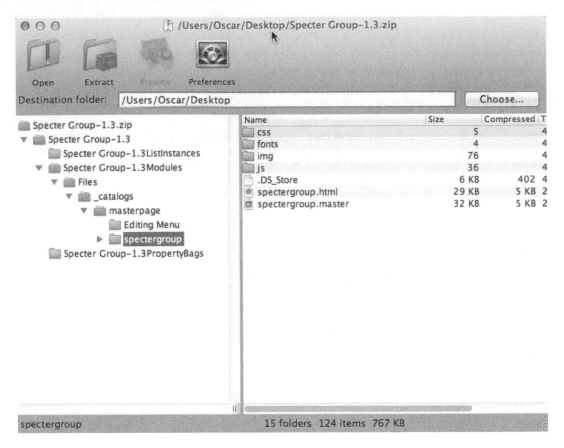

Figure 4-29. *Design Package Master Page Gallery module contents*

Each artifact is deployed with the corresponding content type; in the case of a CSS file it is deployed as a Design File, as shown on Figure 4-30, which was found in the elements.xml file for the Specter Group module.

```
<File Url="style.css" Type="GhostableInLibrary" Level="Draft" Path="style.css" ReplaceContent="true">
  <Property Name="ContentTypeId" Value="0x010100C5033D6CFB8447359FB795C8A73A2B1900CE5834B5E7B6064DA85F508A4BBEA8C7" />
  <Property Name="FileLeafRef" Value="style.css" />
  <Property Name="ContentType" Value="Design File" />
  <Property Name="_ModerationStatus" Value="3" />
  <Property Name="FileDirRef" Value="_catalogs/masterpage/VintageSpecter/css" />
  <Property Name="FSObjType" Value="0" />
</File>
```

Figure 4-30. *Design File content type assigned to CSS files*

Because a WSP file is just a .cab, we could also use a .cab builder to repackage the Design Package in case we want to make any additional changes. As an example, there might be a few branding assets included in the Design Package that you do not want to deploy to your production environment. You can unpackage the Design Package to your workstation, modify the module's elements.xml file to remove the files you do not wish to deploy, and then finally repackage the cab using a .cab builder, renaming the final package with a .wsp extension. Please note that this is an advanced process that is not well supported. The recommended path to create a custom Design Package would be to use Visual Studio and create a feature.

Summary

In this chapter we walked through the steps necessary to create a SharePoint 2013 HTML master page from an HTML prototype. We showed you how to connect a development and design tool other than SharePoint Designer to a SharePoint site using WebDAV. Using this connection and the new Design Manager tool provided in SharePoint 2013, we uploaded our branding assets including our HTML prototype to our SharePoint site. Once the assets were uploaded we converted our HTML prototype to an HTML master page.

After running into and solving common conversion errors, we looked at the converted HTML master page to investigate what SharePoint had to do to associate our HTML master page with a .master master page. We continued on by leveraging the new Snippet Gallery to add snippets to our HTML master page and then concluded by publishing our master page and finally creating a Design Package to ease redeployment of our branding initiative.

In our next chapters we walk through the process of making an HTML master page responsive, followed by a look into navigation, page layouts, and content types.

■ ■ ■

CHAPTER 5

Making Your Master Page Responsive

The previous chapter walked us through importing an HTML prototype and its related branding assets into SharePoint 2013 using Design Manager. Now, what would you end up with? A newly branded site on one of the most powerful WCM platforms available on the market. It is a fairly impressive feat for a process that used to take expert SharePoint designers weeks or more to complete with previous versions of SharePoint.

Now that we've converted our design files using the SharePoint 2013 Design Manager, this chapter is going to take a standard master page and apply the core responsive web design principles that were discussed in Chapter 2. Before we dive into the actual work, we'll share the benefits of creating your own CSS framework versus one that's already been created. We then break down the process of adapting your master page to be responsive by splitting the work into major sections. Last but not least, we close this chapter by sharing solutions to some of the common issues when dealing with older browsers, SharePoint 2013 and responsive design principles.

Our Scenario

As stated in Chapter 3, Specter Group wishes to have a new public-facing web site built on the SharePoint 2013 platform that site visitors may access from any device, from desktops to smart phones. The decision was made to capitalize on responsive web design principles that would utilize only one branding effort, yet at the same time adapt to any viewport. A site design was created based on traditional web design practices and converted to a SharePoint 2013 HTML master page (Chapter 4). Specter Group further required that this be a responsive site, so we must convert the HTML master page's HTML and CSS to use responsive design properties such as the fluid grid and flexible media.

The Promise of a One Web

One of the biggest challenges (perhaps even the biggest challenge) in responsive design is how a web site's mobile layout can achieve content parity. Content parity is part of the W3C's "One Web" philosophy, also known as thematic consistency of resource identified by a URI:

> *Whereby content should be accessible on a range of devices irrespective of differences in presentation capabilities and access mechanism.*

—Mobile Web Best Practices 1.0
(http://sprwd.com/45dij34)

This quote says that it is alright to optimize the presentation of content as long as the content remains accessible in some way, shape, or form.

Rome wasn't built in a day, and neither are web sites. You understand that. Over the years, we've all gone through the painstaking process of building web sites from scratch; learning about the different CSS and JavaScript classes, controls, and constructs. Try out hacks and invent some of our own. We've even learned to love some of the plug-ins and frameworks delivered by others. This process has helped us understand how to build better web sites. Looking at what others use to build their own sites has also taught us how to include tricks into our own personal framework.

We wanted to write a book that would give everyone, beginners as well as experienced designers, an opportunity to build a responsive web site together, no matter where you were in your career or your project. Our hope is to educate you on the process that we felt would give you a breadth of experience as well as share some of the lessons learned.

In this chapter, we are going to continue our journey by converting a fixed-width design that treats nondesktop users as second-class citizens to one that treats every browser regardless of device as a first-class citizen. Here's to the web, where we all stand up and demand equality regardless of our choice in device, operating system, resolution, or browser: One web!

Responsive Design in Principle

Responsive web design was inspired by Nicholas Negroponte's concept of responsive architecture, in which the structure changes its shape, form, color, or character responsibly based on environmental conditions. Responsive web design is a "write once, run everywhere" style of building web sites. How you start to build it is just as important as what you end up with. As they say, before you know where you're going, you have to know where you came from.

We start with a look at different approaches to building a responsive site. In particular, there are two approaches you can take to converting your design to become responsive: starting from scratch, or using an existing framework.

Building a Responsive Site from Scratch

You could take the approach of going through the tedious task of creating your own responsive framework. Taking this approach gives you greater flexibility to change it easily whenever design preferences or requirements change. The most important value that comes out of building your own CSS framework is that instead of spending time learning someone else's framework, you focus on learning something more valuable: CSS specifications. Your own design and thus code would be optimized for your specific solution, but every time you want to add another feature, you would have to build it from scratch.

If this is your first foray into designing a responsive site, particularly one built on SharePoint 2013, we highly recommend you hold off on building your own responsive framework from scratch, primarily because of the effort involved. There's no point in building a perfectly optimized solution that is three months too late. There are many benefits to building your own, but this book isn't focused on helping you build your own framework. The goal for this book is about providing value and to get you up to speed quickly on building a responsive web site in SharePoint 2013. In the next section, "Leverage a Responsive Framework," we have a look at our second option, which builds on leveraging a preexisting framework.

If you are set on creating your own responsive framework, or simply do not want to use any framework and just code a fluid grid that contains your content, we would like to give you a few recommendations. As a starting point we'd recommend dividing your style sheets into multiple files. This way you can build your style sheets one step at a time. Here's a sample of how you could break down the style sheets:

- `reset.css`: Includes CSS to reset all padding, margins, and border values as each browser treats the box model differently.

- `base.css`: Includes the core styles that will be used throughout the site.

- `typography.css`: All styles that are related to text styles, header tags, and so on.

- `layout.css`: All styles related to the structure of the page.

- `form.css`: All styles related to forms.

- `table.css`: All styles related to tables.

- `browser.css`: You can actually create a separate CSS file for each browser.

- `print.css`: Styles used when the visitor wants to print the page.

One of the things that we truly enjoyed when we first started designing web sites was building the underlying framework from scratch. In the long run, the process would take us longer but it helped us to understand the plumbing of how things fit together. We also didn't inherit bugs or flaws that were created by someone else. On the flip side, though, we might miss bugs and flaws in our design or implementation that might have been handled or solved in an existing framework.

This again is advice for those of you who are adventurous and learning. Here are a few tips to consider before moving your style sheets into production:

- Combine them into one style sheet. This will improve performance, as the browser only has to download one file.

- Test on browsers. If your project does not allow you to do usability testing, at least test your solution in the most popular browsers that you expect will be used on your web site.

- Follow specifications. The general approach is to first follow the CSS specifications and then look at best practices that make sense for your site.

- Clean code. Ensure that your code is clean, well structured, and properly documented. It'll go a long way toward troubleshooting any errors.

- Validate your code. W3C provides a validation service, `http://validator.w3.org`, to ensure the technical quality of web pages. It's a first step to check your site for well-formed markup, which helps with browser compatibility and site usability.

Leverage a Responsive Framework

We want to focus on showcasing the capabilities of responsive design, leveraging a preexisting framework that would get us started quickly. There are quite a few prebuilt and well-supported responsive frameworks and most any of them could be converted to work with SharePoint 2013. The following sections list some of the more popular CSS frameworks that have helped us rapidly develop web sites in the past. These frameworks have been helpful because they eliminate our need to re-create a feature-rich structure for every web site project, and to top it off, responsive layouts are a part of each framework.

Zurb Foundation

Zurb Foundation (`http://foundation.zurb.com/`) is a 12-column, future-friendly responsive grid framework that includes dozens of styles and elements to help you quickly put together clickable prototypes. Foundation lets you quickly put together page layouts for mobile devices and the desktop. The grid is built to create a rock-solid experience on all kinds of devices with the exact same markup. Foundation has a simpler, less bloated feel to it, compared to the other frameworks, which we really appreciate. It really is amazingly easy to download it and start turning out web pages in no time.

Foundation includes a download customization tool that we can use to customize the foundation framework to only include features that we want. This allowing us to have an even leaner framework geared around our specific needs. There are example demos as well as extensive online documentation and a good size user-base.

Skeleton

Skeleton (http://www.getskeleton.com/) is a small collection of CSS and JavaScript files that has built its foundation on a 960-pixel-wide grid. It seamlessly scales down to downsized browser windows, tablets, and mobile phones (in both landscape and portrait). Skeleton is fairly lightweight and is primarily used for building responsive web sites. Its focus is to provide a responsive framework that is mobile-friendly. The boilerplate template is appealing if your web site is light on features or you want a bare-bones framework you can build on.

Skeleton is so lean to begin with that there are no automated framework customization tools and the online documentation is not a full as Zurb Foundation. There is a sizable user base, but a smaller one than for Foundation at the time of this publication.

Twitter Bootstrap

Bootstrap from Twitter (http://twitter.github.com/bootstrap/) is a front-end CSS toolkit for rapidly developing web applications. It is a collection of CSS and HTML conventions.

This framework is a Swiss Army knife for developers, as it contains dozens of tools and utilities. Depending on your individual project, some you'll find very useful and others you'll never touch. Bootstrap is specifically built to be used for quickly building sites as well as giving you the opportunity to make it your own. Bootstrap provides a breadth of features that makes it easy for any novice to leverage its features and build a site fairly quickly.

A full download of the Bootstrap framework is quite large and most likely will include tools, plug-ins, and other components you will never use. There is a very powerful online customization tool that gives you options galore, allowing you to strip down Bootstrap to just the essentials. The Bootstrap site contains ample documentation and the user base is by far the most widespread of the different frameworks. There are quite a few additional plug-ins and add-ons that have been created by the Bootstrap community, most of which can easily be ported to Bootstrap.

It is for these reasons that we selected the Bootstrap framework as the recommended framework for this book. This does not mean that the other frameworks won't work for your project, nor does it mean that you cannot follow along with the web design process we continue throughout this book. Almost all popular frameworks contain a grid with columns, so you will be primarily replacing Bootstrap markup with your framework markup as you work through our examples.

Additional Important Frameworks

Besides taking advantage of CSS frameworks, you also want to take advantage of JavaScript frameworks. They can dramatically improve your development time, as many of the problems we will face have been faced by others and they have provided solutions.

jQuery

jQuery has become a major tool for any web development nowadays. It's the most popular JavaScript library not just because it contains functionality to navigate the DOM, create animations, and handle events, but it also allows you to create custom plug-ins on top of jQuery. We use jQuery extensively throughout our responsive development process. You can download the latest jQuery library at (jquery.org) .

Modernizr

Modernizr is a favorite JavaScript framework and one that is widely used by the development community. Modernizr is a powerful JavaScript library that provides web designers a quick and lightweight library to detect features available in browsers, such as CSS3 and HTML5 features. As an example, we can use Modernizr to detect if a browser allows for the CSS3 "transition" style. If "transition" is available, using additional CSS alone, we can provide additional CSS markup that will only be implemented by those browsers that support the style.

Keep Learning

Once you start looking at existing frameworks you will start seeing the value of leveraging the expertise of experienced designers and developers in your projects. Typically, hundreds if not thousands of developers and designers have spent time testing the frameworks, reporting bugs, and providing fixes. Frameworks are a product of the community's efforts and you'd be hard pressed not to consider this an option.

Bootstrap was selected as the primary CSS framework for our demonstrations as it provided more features, documentation, and community support than the other frameworks. The framework encompasses quite a few features, and it does provide the ability to download only what you need for your project.

These frameworks are here to help ease the learning curve, so why not use them? After all, you might learn a thing or two about the way these frameworks leverage CSS and JavaScript. We recommend that you add these to your arsenal of development tools. By leveraging numerous frameworks and features, you will be able to convert and build a responsive site relatively quickly.

Now that we've looked at the two different development strategies, let's dive into the process of converting a fixed-width HTML master page to a fully responsive HTML master page.

Be Like Water

Adapting a general web site to be responsive can be a fairly easy task if your original HTML prototype already leveraged Bootstrap. This would not be unusual because of the popularity of Bootstrap, but we must assume our design team didn't know any better and gave us an HTML prototype built on no framework. Therefore, if our HTML prototype did not leverage Twitter Bootstrap, and thus our HTML master page did not either, we might need to rewrite some of the HTML markup to take advantage of the framework.

We've distilled the process into three primary steps to integrate a framework and make your existing fixed-width designs responsive:

1. Prepare your design. Download the framework's files and add them to your solution.

2. Leverage the grid system. Adapt your design to follow the grid system, one container at a time.

3. Make it responsive. Take advantage of the framework to ensure that it's responsive.

Follow along as we take the steps to device freedom.

Prepare Your Design for a Framework

To prepare your design, you need to download your framework files, in this case the Bootstrap files, and add them to your solution.

Download the Framework

Launch your browser and open http://twitter.github.com/bootstrap/. To download the entire Bootstrap framework, click the large Download button in the middle of the home page, or our recommendation, click Customize in the top navigation menu so that you can build your own download package. On the Customize and Download page, click Toggle All found just to the right of "1. Choose components." This will deselect all the components that are a part of Bootstrap so that we can add back in only those that we want. For the bare minimum, we suggest the following components, as seen in Figure 5-1.

Figure 5-1. *Selected minimal Twitter Bootstrap CSS framework components*

- Scaffolding
    - Grid system
    - Layouts
- Responsive
    - Visible/hidden classes
    - Narrow tablets and below (<767px)
    - Tablets to desktops (767-979px)
    - Large desktops (>1200px)
    - Responsive navbar

You might want to also include the following additional components.

- Scaffolding
    - Normalize and reset
    - Body type and links
- Components
    - Button groups and dropdowns
    - Navs, tabs and pills
    - Navbar

- Breadcrumbs
- Pagination
- JS components (all of them)

Next, scroll down to the jQuery plug-ins, and click Toggle all. We are not planning on using any of the Bootstrap jQuery plug-ins in this book, but you might want to include some of them so that you can use them throughout your web site build out.

■ **Note**　Before you add a component or jQuery plug-in, do yourself a favor and research that particular component or plug-in first and try to determine if you are actually going to use it or not. If you do not think you are going to use it, don't include it.

Now go ahead to the bottom of the page and click Customize and Download. If you did not customize the Twitter Bootstrap download as documented earlier, you'd be adding a lot of unnecessary files and page weight to your project. We can get a minimal very feature-rich custom `bootstrap.min.css` down to 22 kb (370 kb smaller than the full download).

■ **Note**　By clicking the big button that says Download Bootstrap, you add a total of 392 KB to your branding solution, based on Twitter Bootstrap version 2.3.0. Later in this chapter, we review how you can take a look at performance.

Add a Framework to Your HTML Master Page

Adding your framework assets, most likely consisting of at least a CSS style sheet or two, possibly some images, and a JavaScript file or two, should follow the same process we used in Chapter 4.

■ **Note**　Refer to Chapter 4 if you wish to review how to connect to your SharePoint site using WebDAV. For the following walkthrough, the master page and associated files are stored in the Master Page Gallery SpecterGroup directory (i.e. `/_catalogs/masterpage/SpecterGroup/`).

With Bootstrap, once you extract the framework package that you downloaded in the previous section to your workstation, open your SharePoint Master Page Gallery in your preferred method, be it Dreamweaver, SharePoint Designer, Windows Explorer, or something else. We recommend adding your framework assets to the same location as your custom HTML master page, in our case `/_catalogs/masterpage/SpecterGroup`. For our example of Bootstrap, Bootstrap files should be fairly easy to move into our branding solution folder structure, as our solution from Chapter 4 has a similar directory naming convention to how Bootstrap is structured (the `css` folder contains style sheets, the `js` folder contains JavaScript files, and the `img` folder contains images). You might find it easier to match your branding solution to a framework's directory structure rather than the other way around.

■ **Tip**　Once you have uploaded your framework assets to your SharePoint Master Page Gallery, do not forget to publish a major version of all new files.

Alternative Design File Deployment Locations

Although best practices include deploying all design files to the Master Page Gallery, there are other locations that you still might consider for your particular solution. We are only talking about your design files, such as your style sheets, images, and JavaScript files, though, as your master pages and page layouts (Chapter 7) should always be placed in your Master Page Gallery.

As mentioned in Chapter 4, you could also use your site collection's Style Library to house design files, although that is not recommended because the Style Library is geared for only your root web in your site collection, whereas each site and subsite could have its own Master Page Gallery. If you intend to have only one master page for an entire site collection, the Style Library might be a good location for your design files.

You may also deploy design files directly to the SharePoint server file system; that is, the SharePoint hive. Your SharePoint hive, often referred to as the 15 hive for SharePoint 2013, is a folder structure found on each SharePoint server in your farm, normally located in `C:\Program Files\Common Files\Microsoft Shared\Web Server Extensions\15`. Access to this folder normally requires server Administrator privileges as well as access to the server console itself. Deploying design files to the proper Layouts folder, `C:\Program Files\Common Files\Microsoft Shared\Web Server Extensions\15\TEMPLATE\LAYOUTS`, might require custom code. This option affects the entire server and all web applications that are hosted on that server. Any SharePoint site can use any design file that is deployed to the Layouts directory. The advantage of the Layouts directory is that the information is stored in the file system and not in a particular web applications database. The obvious downside is that it might be difficult to customize files stored in the Layouts folder as well as much more difficult to package and redeploy your branding solution.

■ **Tip**   Refer to Chapter 4 for a review of design packages, a new feature of SharePoint 2013 that allows you to easily create and deploy branding solutions.

Link an HTML Master Page to a Framework

At this point we have added our framework files (i.e., the Bootstrap framework), into SharePoint, so now let's update our solution to reference our framework. With your web editor of choice, such as Dreamweaver, open your HTML (i.e., `/_catalogs/masterpage/spectergroup/SpecterGroup.html`) for editing. You must add a `<link>` to your framework style sheet, `bootstrap.min.css`, which we placed in the `/_catalogs/masterpage/spectergroup/css` folder, somewhere in the `<head>` section of your HTML master page. We recommend adding the link to your framework before any other style sheets you might have already included, allowing you to override the framework if you need to instead of having the framework override your custom styles.

In Chapter 4 we assumed the HTML prototype properly links to a style sheet using the common `<link>` tag, but with SharePoint there are actually three ways in which SharePoint designers can add references to style sheets.

Use the SharePoint:CssRegistration Control

The `SharePoint:CssRegistration` server control generates a `<link>` element into the resulting HTML page that applies the specified style sheet. This has benefits over the HTML markup, as it gives you control over the order in which a CSS style sheet is applied (before or after other CSS files). This is the same way we could link to a style sheet with SharePoint 2010 sites, although with HTML master pages we must use the Design Manager Markup. Listing 5-1 shows valid methods in which to use a `SharePoint:CssRegistration` control in a HTML master page (or HTML page layout, refer to Chapter 7). Invalid or non-recommended ways to use a `SharePoint:CssRegistration` control are shown in Listing 5-2.

Listing 5-1. Vaild Snippet Markup for SharePoint:CssRegistration Control

```
<!--MS:<SharePoint:CssRegistration Name="/_catalogs/masterpage/spectergroup/css/bootstrap.css"
  runat="server">-->
<!--ME:</SharePoint:CssRegistration>-->

<!--MS:<SharePoint:CssRegistration Name="/_catalogs/masterpage/spectergroup/css/bootstrap.css"
  After="Themable/corev15.css" runat="server">-->
<!--ME:</SharePoint:CssRegistration>-->

<!--SPM:<SharePoint:CssRegistration Name="/_catalogs/masterpage/spectergroup/css/bootstrap.css"
  runat="server" />-->

<!--MS:<SharePoint:CssRegistration
  Name="&lt;% $SPUrl:~sitecollection/_catalogs/masterpage/spectergroup/css/bootstrap.css %&gt;"
  After="Themable/corev15.css" runat="server">-->
<!--ME:</SharePoint:CssRegistration>-->
```

Listing 5-2. Invalid Snippet Markup for SharePoint:CssRegistration Control

```
<!--MS:<SharePoint:CssRegistration
  Name="<% $SPUrl:~sitecollection/_catalogs/masterpage/spectergroup/css/bootstrap.css %>"
  After="Themable/corev15.css" runat="server">-->
<!--ME:</SharePoint:CssRegistration>-->

<!--MS:<SharePoint:CssRegistration Name="css/bootstrap.css" runat="server">-->
<!--ME:</SharePoint:CssRegistration>-->

<!--SPM:<SharePoint:CssRegistration
  Name="<% $SPUrl:~/_catalogs/masterpage/spectergroup/css/bootstrap.css%>" runat="server" />-->

<!--SPM:<SharePoint:CssRegistration Name="/_catalogs/masterpage/spectergroup/css/bootstrap.css%>"
  runat="server"></SharePoint:CssRegistration>-->
```

■ **Tip**   Refer to Chapter 4 for a review of Design Manager Markup (i.e., snippets).

In Listing 5-1 we see how we can use `<!--MS:-->``<!--ME:-->` blocks as well as the `<!--SPM:-->` block. We can also see how we can use the `CssRegistration` control `After` property to specify a style sheet after which this style sheet should always load. Also note, though, that we always have to provide a full path to the style sheet.

In Listing 5-2 we see that we should not provide a relative URL to the style sheet, nor can we use `<% SPURL:~sitecollection/ ...%>` to provide a variable path based on the site collection location. Further, when we use the `<!--SPM:-->` block, the closing tag must be included in the opening tag. If you intend to create redeployable design packages, you will find it best to use the `SharePoint:CssRegistration` control with `&lt;% SPURL:~sitecollection/ ...%&gt;` as this will allow a CSS style sheet to be accessible no matter the location of the site collection.

Use an Alternative CSS URL

We still have the ability to set one Alternate CSS style sheet via Site Settings (Site Settings ➤ Look and Feel ➤ Master Page). This approach allows site administrators to lock down one specific style sheet, but only one style sheet. This is not practical when the customizations to the design are not just style based, typically covered by a CSS file, versus structural changes, which is where master pages and page layouts come into play.

Use the HTML <link> Tag

The HTML <link> tag is generally the easiest way to link to a style sheet with HTML master pages. It does not take advantage of any benefits that SharePoint's server tags provide such as caching, control over cascading, or access to dynamic CSS file paths. On the plus side, SharePoint will handle the directory path for us assuming that the style sheets are in a subdirectory of the HTML master page. Refer to Listing 5-3 for an example.

Listing 5-3. Standard <link> Tag

```
<link rel="stylesheet" href="css/bootstrap.min.css" />
```

The Alternative CSS URL provides a less than ideal method to link to a framework style sheet, although the SharePoint:CssRegistration control would be okay if we used a name with a value of <% SPURL:~sitecollection/ ...%>. Because the SPURL name is less clear than a <link> tag, and SharePoint will handle the full href path to our style sheet in HTML master pages with a <link> tag, the <link> tag is our preferred method to move forward. In our HTML master page we will find our other links to style sheets and add our new link just before them. In Listing 5-4 we can see a portion of our new <head> section with a link to our framework added, which is no different than adding a general style sheet reference in a generic HTML file.

■ **Note** Depending on how you downloaded your framework, you might have a framework style sheet and another style sheet to provide responsive functionality. In Listing 5-3 we link to one custom Bootstrap style sheet that contains the primary framework as well as responsive overrides. In Listing 5-4 you can see how we instead link to the entire Bootstrap framework as well as Bootstrap's second "responsive" style sheet. We recommend a custom Bootstrap framework as linked to in Listing 5-3, but linking to the original, full Bootstrap might be helpful during development.

Listing 5-4. HTML to Reference Framework Style Sheet in <head>

```
<head>
  <!--beginning removed for simplicity-->
  <!--DC:Specter Group Bootstrap Version-->
  <meta name="description" content="" />

  <!--Our framework stylesheet-->
  <link rel="stylesheet" href="css/bootstrap.css" />
  <link rel="stylesheet" href="css/bootstrap-responsive.css" />

  <!--originally included stylesheets-->
  <link rel="stylesheet" href="css/superfish.css" />
  <link rel="stylesheet" href="css/nivo-slider.css" />
  <link rel="stylesheet" href="css/isotope.css" />
  <link rel="stylesheet" href="css/elements.css" />
  <link rel="stylesheet" href="css/style.css" />
  <!-- Modernizr enables HTML5 elements &#38; feature detects for optimal performance.
    Include html5shiv 3.6. Our version is a custom build.
    Create your own custom Modernizr build: www.modernizr.com/download/ -->
  <script src="js/modernizr-2.6.2.custom.js">//<![CDATA[//]]>
  </script>
  <!--remaining head bloc removed for simplicity-->
</head>
```

By including these references, we are giving our site the opportunity to take advantage of all the hard work that's been put into Bootstrap. What impact does this have now though? With the current addition of your framework style sheet, there will likely be little visual change. However, as you start browsing the site, you'll notice some issues here and there. A common issue with many frameworks including Bootstrap and in particular Bootstrap's Responsive add-on is that many SharePoint images and icons might break. The ribbon might start breaking (see Figure 5-2) and many fonts, content, and form elements could look incorrect. Every framework is different and its element resets might cause different issues. We view common SharePoint/Bootstrap conflicts in the section "Fix Common Responsive Issues with SharePoint" later in this chapter.

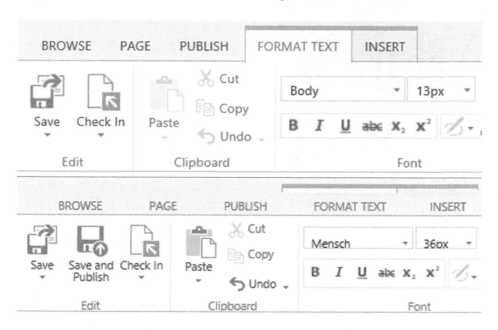

Figure 5-2. *The top image shows how the ribbon styling looks without any custom styles and the bottom image shows how the ribbon looks after custom styling is applied*

We've included the reference to our framework but we haven't changed our design files to take advantage of it fully. Let's do this next.

Leveraging the Grid System

Bootstrap, like many other CSS frameworks, takes advantage of grids, which allow you to stack content elements on top of one another as well as next to each other. This grid system provides web designers with a structured approach to design. Previously, web site developers used HTML tables to design web sites. In today's design world, tables for layout are considered obsolete. There were rendering issues across different browses, they provided too much baked-in "style" with the HTML itself, which is a big no-no, and finally they do not scale well for mobile devices. It made sense for the web development community to look for something to replace them.

Grid-Based Design

The way any grid system works is that containers are stacked horizontally. Each single container contains one or more rows and each row contains one or more columns. What really gives the grid-based design flexibility is that you can include a container inside a column. Most grid frameworks include this functionality so now a column can have its own set of rows and columns. Refer to Figure 5-3 for an example of containers that contain rows and columns.

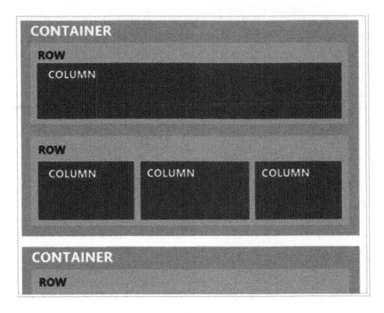

Figure 5-3. Sample grid with containers, rows, and columns

With Bootstrap's fixed-width grid system, each row container allows up to 12 columns with a total width of 940 pixels. Each column's width is 60 pixels and there's 10 pixels of padding on either side of each column, thus 20 pixels of padding between any two columns. Figure 5-4 shows how this works.

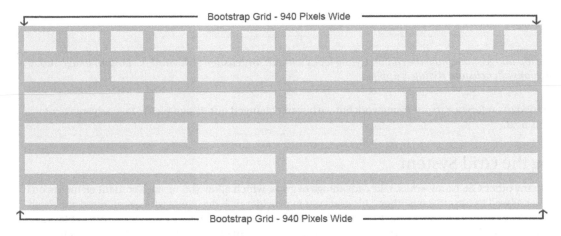

Figure 5-4. Bootstrap's grid system based on 60-pixel-wide columns

---

■ **Note** Although the fixed container is 940 pixels wide, with the Bootstrap responsive features included the grid will adapt between 724 and 1,170 pixels wide. For viewports less than 767 pixels wide, the columns instead stack vertically and become fluid to fill up the entire width of the viewport.

Basic Bootstrap Grid

Keep in mind that a CSS grid is essentially built on the row and span (column) methodology. To implement a grid using CSS, the steps are as follows.

1. Create a div container that will hold all your markup inside of it. This typically is in the form of a primary div such as `<div class="container">...</div>`.

2. Inside the div container, start creating your markup using a series of row containers.

3. Within each row, create one or more span (column) div containers as well as nested rows to break a column into even more rows and columns.

Given that Bootstrap uses a 12-column grid, make sure that each row you create, including nested rows with columns, has a total of 12 spans (columns).

In Listing 5-5 we create a simple Bootstrap-driven grid that has two rows. The first row will have one column that spans the length of 12 column units. The second row will have two columns, the first column spans the length of 3 column units and the second column spans the length of 9 column units.

Listing 5-5. Sample Bootstrap Grid with Two Rows

```
<div class="container">
  <div class="row">
    <div class="span12">
      Row 1 - column 1
    </div>
  </div>
  <div class="row">
    <div class="span3">
      Row 2 - column 1
    </div>
    <div class="span9">
      Row 2 - column 2
    </div>
  </div>
</div>
```

As long as you ensure each row's set of column(s) spans a total of 12 column units, you're in good shape. The key is to realize that you can build simple and quite complex layouts using this grid system that combines multiple containers, multiple rows, and multiple spans.

■ **Tip** To learn more about the Bootstrap scaffolding, visit the Bootstrap documentation at `http://sprwd.com/d73xauy` for more examples, as well as a deeper look at the underlying HTML.

Add Bootstrap to an HTML Master Page

Updating an HTML master page to fully utilize a grid-based framework can be difficult without a well-laid plan. The best way to describe the process is for us to go through our sample Specter Group solution. Remember that most popular grid frameworks use similar tagging so the methodology would be similar. We go through our HTML master page we created in Chapter 4 and recently updated in the earlier section, "Prepare Your Design for a Framework," and now transform the HTML to leverage the Bootstrap framework, section by section.

Follow along and you can apply the same principles to convert your designs to use any framework.

■ **Tip** You can download the finished source code for this conversion as well as all source code created in this book at `http://sprwd.github.io/BookSourceCode/`. Or check out a working demo of the converted HTML master page in a Cloudshare virtual machine at `http://sprwd.com/sprwd-cs-demo`.

Divide an HTML Master Page into Rows and Columns

Our approach to converting our markup over to Bootstrap, or any framework for that matter, will be to divide and conquer. We'll start with the containers and then we'll split the design into rows. Once we've addressed that, we'll split each row into columns.

The first step is to divide the design visually into major components. Previewing our master page from Chapter 4, we can see the following major components:

- Header: Contains the Specter Group logo, tagline, search, and the social media drop-down list.

- Top Navigation: Contains the home button, navigation items, registration, and login icons.

- Main Content: This will vary based on the page layout that we are on.

- Footer: Contains the About Us, Twitter News, Recent Posts, Copyright, and Legal related links.

By starting here, we can convert this design over to Bootstrap fairly quickly and have a working prototype.

What we'd want to do is go through each major component's div container and add `<div class="container">...</div>` around the content. Once you've done that, you'll want to look at each container and split that into rows and columns. Because we are dealing with only the master page at this time, each container (Header, Top Navigation, Main Content, and Footer) will map over well to individual rows. See Figure 5-5.

Figure 5-5. *Specter Group home page split into major components*

For each row, you'll want to split it into columns, as long as the number of columns totals 12 for each row. In Figure 5-6 you can see visually that each row of columns is split to provide a sum total of 12. If our HTML markup follows a grid-based design, the conversion over to Bootstrap should work fairly painlessly.

Figure 5-6. *Specter Group home page split into rows and columns*

■ **Note**   Notice in Figure 5-6 the main content area is one column with a span of 12. We look at page layouts in more detail in Chapter 7.

In Listing 5-6 we can see the original HTML structure from our HTML master page in Chapter 4, although much of the "content" has been removed for the sake of simplicity.

Listing 5-6. Type HTML Structure without a Grid Framework

```
<body>
    <div id="s4-workspace">
      <div id="s4-bodyContainer">

          <!-- HEADER -->
          <header>
             <!-- header wrapper -->
             <div class="wrapper cf">...</div>
             <!-- ENDS header wrapper -->
          </header>
          <!-- ENDS HEADER -->

          <!-- nav -->
          <nav id="topnav">
             <!--navigation wrapper-->
             <div class="wrapper cf">...</div>
             <!--end navigation wrapper-->
          </nav>
          <!-- ends nav -->

          <!-- MAIN -->
          <div role="main" id="main">
             <!--Main content wrapper-->
             <div class="wrapper cf">...</div>
             <!--end Main content wrapper-->
          </div>
          <!-- ENDS MAIN -->

          <footer>
             <!-- wrapper -->
             <div class="wrapper cf"></div>
             <!--end wrapper-->
             <!-- bottom footer-->
             <div class="footer-bottom">
                <div class="wrapper cf"></div>
             </div>
             <!--end bottom footer-->
          </footer>
       </div>
    </div>
</body>
```

Now that we have seen visually how we want to divide our page and understand the process of taking any design and converting it to a grid-based framework, we can move into the details part of this chapter. We walk through breaking up each primary section in Listing 5-6 one section at a time. A few quick notes are in order, though. We will not touch the SharePoint provided s4-workspace or s4-body-Container divs, as all SharePoint pages will need those. Second, we leave the HTML5 tags, <header>, <nav>, and <footer> as larger wrappers. This will not cause a problem with our grid as long as we leave the width set to "auto," which is the default, for these three tags.

Bootstrap and the Header

Referring to Listing 5-6, we can find the <header> block near the top of the document. We can see it has one primary wrapper div. Let's look at more of the <header> HTML in Listing 5-7.

Listing 5-7. Header Code After Design Manager Conversion

```
<header>
   <!-- header wrapper -->
   <div class="wrapper cf">
      <div id="logo">
         <!--logo snippet-->
      </div>
      <div class="tagline">
         <!--h2 tag lines-->
      </div>
      <div class="searchbox">
         <!--search box snippet-->
      </div>
      <div class="social cf">
         <!--social icons-->
      </div>
   </div>
   <!-- ENDS header wrapper -->
</header>
```

What we need to do is change the class attribute value of the first div container, from wrapper cf to container to provide for our fixed container. For each container, we must have a row container, so we will add a new div, <div class"row"> right after the <div class="container">. We'll want to close the row container by adding a </div> before the end of the container div.

Now that we've wrapped the logo, tagline, searchbox, and social containers in Bootstrap's container and row components, it's time to wrap each of the smaller components into columns. The logo and tagline will be wrapped around by <div class="span8"> container and the searchbox will be wrapped around by <div class="span4">.

What about the div, social? We are throwing a curve ball here. You can add containers into a row if you want that will not be a span, but only if that div has a position of absolute or fixed, because we need to take the additional div outside of the flow of a row's columns. In our case, <div class="social cf"></div> has an absolute position and thus will not ruin the flow of the columns.

Refer to Listing 5-8 for the updated <header>.

Listing 5-8. Header Tag Converted to Leverage Bootstrap Framework

```
<header>
    <div class="container ">
        <div class="row ">
            <div class="span8">
                <div id="logo">
                    <!--logo snippet-->
                </div>
                <div class="tagline">
                    <!--h2 tag lines-->
                </div>
            </div>
            <div class="span4">
                <div class="searchbox">
                    <!--search box snippet-->
                </div>
            </div>
            <div class="social cf">
                <!--social icons-->
            </div>
        </div> <!--end row-->
    </div> <!--end container-->
</header>
```

Bootstrap and Navigation

Although we dive much deeper into navigation in Chapter 6, let's see how to prepare the main navigation container to be Bootstrap friendly. Before we make changes to our Top Navigation, let's have a quick look at the code in Listing 5-9.

Listing 5-9. Top Navigation Code after Design Manager Conversion

```
<nav id="topnav">
    <div class="wrapper cf">
        <!--nav snippet-->
        <div class="nav">
            <!--Navigation List-->
        </div>
        <!--end nav snippet-->
        <!--MS:<SharePoint:SPSecurityTrimmedControl runat="server"
            AuthenticationRestrictions="AnonymousUsersOnly">-->
            <div class="site-access cf">
                <!--Site access links-->
            </div>
        <!--ME:</SharePoint:SPSecurityTrimmedControl>-->
    </div>
</nav>
```

As we saw from Figure 5-6, the top navigation should be wrapped around in a single container, with a single row and span (12 column units wide), as shown in Listing 5-10.

Listing 5-10. Nav Tag Converted to Leverage Bootstrap Framework

```
<nav id="topnav">
   <div class="container ">
      <div class="row ">
         <div class="span12">
            <div class="navbar navbar-inverse">
               <div class="navbar-inner">
                  <div class="container">
                     <a class="btn btn-navbar" data-toggle="collapse" data-target=".nav-
                        collapse">
                        <span class="icon-bar"></span>
                        <span class="icon-bar"></span>
                        <span class="icon-bar"></span>
                     </a>
                     <div class="nav nav-collapse collapse">
                        <!--nav snippet-->
                     </div>
                     <!--end class nav-->
                  </div>
                  <!--end container-->
               </div>
               <!--MS:<SharePoint:SPSecurityTrimmedControl runat="server"
                     AuthenticationRestrictions="AnonymousUsersOnly">-->
               <div class="site-access cf">
                  <!--site access links-->
               </div>
               <!--ME:</SharePoint:SPSecurityTrimmedControl>-->
            </div>
         </div><!--end span 12-->
      </div> <!--end row-->
   </div> <!--end container-->
</nav>
```

> ■ **Note** Listing 5-10 provides further framework code to utilize Bootstrap Navbar components. Refer to Chapter 6, or you can learn more about Bootstrap Navbars at `http://sprwd.com/zdpdxn`.

Bootstrap and Main Content

The Main Content of a particular page will be defined by page layouts (Chapter 7) or system pages that SharePoint provides for us. This being the case, our HTML master page only needs to provide us one primary container, row, and column. Refer to Listing 5-11 for the original HTML that utilized a wrapper and Listing 5-12 now using the Bootstrap framework.

Listing 5-11. Main Content Code after Design Manager Conversion

```
<div role="main" id="main">
   <div class="wrapper cf">
      <!--main content placerholder-->
   </div>
</div>
```

Listing 5-12. Main Content Converted to Leverage Bootstrap Framework

```
<div role="main" id="main">
   <div class="container ">
      <div class="row ">
         <div class="span12">
            <!--main content placerholder-->
         </div>
      </div>
   </div>
</div>
```

There are a few trade-offs that we are making in Listing 5-12. In particular, we are assuming that there will not be a Quick Launch (Vertical Navigation) in the HTML master page. This can be problem for an HTML master page that you intend to use as a System (Default) master page as well as a Site (Custom) master page. System pages often require the Quick Launch for additional navigation and simply removing it from the master page might cause those system pages to no longer function correctly.

One solution would be to divide the "main" row into two columns, the left for the Quick Launch and the right for the main content placeholder. Refer to Listing 5-13 for the HTML, and refer to Chapter 6 to learn how to add additional snippets such as the Vertical Navigation (Quick Launch) snippet. The catch with this layout is, if we want to have a page layout that does not include the Quick Launch, how can we remove this only for specific page layouts? We review this in Chapter 7, but you need to know now that you need to prepare your master page first depending on your requirements.

Listing 5-13. Main Content with an Additional Column for the Quick Launch

```
<div role="main" id="main">
   <div class="container ">
      <div class="row ">
         <div class="span3">
            <!–Vertical Navigation Snippet-->
         </div>
         <div class="span9">
            <!--main content placerholder-->
         </div>
      </div>
   </div>
</div>
```

Bootstrap and a Footer

Now that we've gone through the process of using the Bootstrap-specific CSS classes, the last major container is the Footer. Again referring to Figure 5-6, we see that the Footer is actually broken into two rows, the top row having three columns and the second row having two columns.

Let's split up the Footer into smaller chunks so that we can work through this easily. To start with, we'll want to make sure that all content inside the Footer is wrapped inside a container. Our converted design already has two places where there exists a div container with two class attributes wrapper and cf. Replace both of these with a CSS class container to take advantage of Bootstrap's grid system.

Now that we have our container defined around our two pieces of content, we can break up the rest of the footer design into two rows and columns. We'll do that for each row of content and further define column spans (where applicable).

It is not uncommon to have used unordered lists (`<ul><li>` blocks) for columns in a design without a framework, which is what we see in our footer's first primary row that has three columns. We remove this list-based approach yet keep the tags for the content, and added spans; that is, `<div="span4">`. Our second Footer was much easier, as it only had two columns, so we can add `<div class="span6">` around each container. Listing 5-14 shows you the code for the footer after the conversion and Listing 5-15 shows you how the code looks after integrating it with Bootstrap.

Listing 5-14. Footer Code after Design Manager Conversion

```
<footer>
    <!-- wrapper -->
    <div class="wrapper cf">
        <ul class="cols cf">
            <li class="col">
                <div class="col-block">
                    <!--left column-->
                </div>
            </li>
            <li class="col">
                <div class="col-block">
                    <!--middle column-->
                </div>
            </li>
            <li class="col">
                <div class="col-block">
                    <!--right column-->
                </div>
            </li>
        </ul>
        <!-- ENDS columns -->
    </div>
    <!--end wrapper-->
    <!-- bottom footer-->
    <div class="footer-bottom">
        <div class="wrapper cf">
            <div class="copyright">
                <!--copyright-->
            </div>
            <div class="sitemap">
                <!--sitemap list-->
            </div>
        </div>
    </div>
    <!--end bottom footer-->
</footer>
```

Listing 5-15. Footer Converted to Leverage Bootstrap Framework

```
<footer>
    <div class="container ">
        <div class="row ">
            <!--columns-->
            <div class="span4">
                <!--left column-->
            </div>
            <div class="span4">
                <!--middle column-->
            </div>
            <div class="span4">
                <!--right column-->
            </div>
            <!-- ENDS columns -->
        </div>
        <!--end row-->
    </div>
    <!--end container-->

    <!-- bottom footer-->
    <div class="footer-bottom">
        <div class="container ">
            <div class="row ">
                <div class="span6 copyright">
                    <!--copyright-->
                </div>
                <div class="span6 sitemap">
                    <!--sitemap list-->
                </div>
            </div>
        </div>
    </div>
    <!--end bottom footer-->
</footer>
```

Make It Responsive

Now that we have referenced Twitter Bootstrap files in our new design and converted each of the major containers to leverage Bootstrap, it is finally time to start making the site responsive. By leveraging a framework like Bootstrap, the general process is extremely quick and easy, although SharePoint will add a few more curve balls our way that we will need to handle.

First we need to make sure that our framework is set for responsive design. In Listings 5-3 and 5-4 we provided two different methods to link to the Bootstrap framework to provide responsive functionality but your framework might already have it included, or you might need to link to yet another style sheet. Refer to the section "Add a Framework to Your HTML Master Page" earlier in this chapter for further guidance.

The Viewport Meta Tag

Before we turn on the responsive grid, we need to set up the viewport properly. We already know that the viewport is the screen or monitor on which we are viewing a site. For desktop browsers, your viewport is your browser window; with mobile devices, your viewport is normally the full width of the given screen.

When the iPhone was developed, Apple knew that many sites would not be mobile friendly for a while so there had to be a way to view a non mobile friendly site on a small screen. They came up with panning and zooming, thus allowing you to pan around a given page and then zoom in and zoom out as necessary. But at what zoom level or pixel width should the page first load?

Traditionally on mobile devices, a mobile device will assume that a given page is not mobile ready and thus should be rendered as if on a desktop. This likely would be in the 960-pixel-wide range, but zoomed out so that the user can see the entire site, even if it is extremely small. The user can then zoom in on a particular part of the page and pan as necessary.

But what about those of us who have considered mobile devices and do not want a mobile device to try to figure anything out? A new meta tag has been provided that most mobile devices recognize that gives us the ability to tell a device to set the site width to the viewport's native width, and start the zoom at 100% (see Listing 5-16).

Listing 5-16. Viewport Meta Tag

```
<meta name="viewport" content="width=device-width, initial-scale=1.0" />
```

The meta tag in Listing 5-16 tells the browser to adjust the viewport (the visible part of the browser where your web site loads) to be the same width as the device when the user loads your page in the device's browser. Then, with the initial-scale option, it tells the browser to proportionally zoom the page to best display the web site for that device screen size. In Listing 5-17 we see how we add this to our HTML master page <head> section.

Listing 5-17. Viewport Meta Tag in HTML Master Page <head>

```
<!DOCTYPE html[]>
<html class="no-js" lang="en">
    <head>
        <meta http-equiv="X-UA-Compatible" content="IE=10" />
        <meta name="description" content="" />

        <meta name="viewport" content="width=device-width, initial-scale=1.0" />

        <!--CS: Head Contents Snippet-->

        <!--Our stylesheets-->
        <link rel="stylesheet" href="css/bootstrap.css" />-->

        <!-- Our scripts-->
        <script src="js/modernizr-2.6.2.custom.js">//<![CDATA[//]]>
        </script>

        <!--[if gte mso 9]>
        <xml>
            <mso:CustomDocumentProperties>
                <!--Document properties-->
            </mso:CustomDocumentProperties>
        </xml>
        <![endif]-->
    </head>
    <!--rest of HTML MasterPage-->
```

Media Queries

Bootstrap, by default, includes targeted media queries starting with smaller smart phones and working its way up to a large display, viewports that are 1,200 pixels across and wider. Basically, each media query changes the size of the columns to reflow the layout to something more appropriate for the viewport. Table 5-1 lists the viewport sizes that Bootstrap supports natively.

***Table 5-1.** Viewports Bootstrap Responsively Supports Out of the Box*

Label	Layout Width	Column Width	Gutter Width
Phones	480px and below	Fluid columns, no fixed width	
Phones to tablets	767px and below	Fluid columns, no fixed width	
Portrait tablets	768px and above	42px	20px
Default	980px and up	60px	20px
Large Display	1,200px and up	70px	30px

■ **Note** Review media queries in detail in Chapter 2.

The first media query (480 pixels and below) targets smart phones and pretty much breaks everything down to a single, 100 percent width column. This might be a bit oversimplified for your tastes, but the beauty of frameworks like this is that they're only suggestions; you're encouraged to customize to your heart's content.

The next media query targets portrait tablets with a range of 480 to 767 pixels, then up to 980 pixels for portrait tablets and on up to standard desktops and large displays. For the static grid, individual columns start at 70 pixels wide, then jump down to 60 pixels and finally down to 42 pixels before going 100 percent width for mobile (see Figure 5-7).

***Figure 5-7.** Column widths based on viewport and media query*

Because Bootstrap has media queries built in, your project might have a need to develop custom media queries. Listing 5-18 shows an example of media queries that target specific viewports.

***Listing 5-18.** Base Sample Media Queries*

```
/** Large Desktop */
@media (min-width: 1200px) { ... }

/** Portrait tablet to landscape and desktop */
@media (min-width: 768px) and (max-width: 979px) { ... }
```

```
/** Landscape phone to portrait tablet */
@media (max-width: 767px) { ... }

/** Landscape phone and lower */
@media (max-width: 480px) { ... }
```

At this point we have added the Bootstrap framework including adding the responsive components. We then included the viewport meta tag. Figure 5-8 shows what our Specter Group site looks like now at different resolutions. Many of the changes that you are seeing are due to developers specifying how the different elements interact.

Figure 5-8. *Specter Group site at 960 pixels, 768 pixels, and 320 pixels wide*

Continually testing a responsive site design in multiple devices can be very time consuming. Fortunately there are a few different tools available to us. No matter what, if you need to make sure your site responds correctly on a given device you will need to test it on that device.

First, you can always resize your browser window on your development workstation with any modern browser including Internet Explorer 9 and above. If you did everything right, your site should shrink with your browser window.

A second method, and our preferred method because it integrates with Firebug really well, is the Responsive Design View (Ctrl+Shift+M) available in current versions of Firefox. To find this, load your page in Firefox and go to Tools ➤ Web Developer ➤ Responsive Design View or press Ctrl+Shift+M. Your page will now load in a window within your browser window. At the top left you can get the exact dimensions of a viewport on which you would like to preview your site. Plus you have the ability to use Firebug to figure out how styles are being applied to every element on your page.

From Fixed to Fluid

We hope by now you are starting to see the power of a framework to provide the base frame on which we can build a responsive site. We were able to quickly convert our fixed-width site to a responsive site by adding Bootstrap, then after breaking up our site design into rows and columns and providing a viewport meta tag, we had a responsive site.

Bootstrap still has more to offer. At the highest level, Bootstrap provides two types of containers:

1. A container CSS class that has a fixed width based on a default of 940 pixels, or modified based on media queries.

2. An alternative container-fluid CSS class has a fluid width that is based on percentages.

We used container for all of our main component areas but what if we fluid containers, rows, and columns? All we need to do now is go back through our HTML master page and append -fluid after each container and row value. Let's take an example from one of the sections we just completed, the Footer. Refer to Listing 5-19 for the Footer now with fluid containers.

Listing 5-19. Footer Converted from Responsive Fixed Widths to Fluid

```
<footer>
    <div class="container-fluid">
        <div class="row-fluid ">
            <!--columns-->
            <div class="span4">
                <!--left column-->
            </div>
            <div class="span4">
                <!--middle column-->
            </div>
            <div class="span4">
                <!--right column-->
            </div>
            <!-- ENDS columns -->
        </div>
        <!--end row-->
    </div>
    <!--end container-->

    <!-- bottom footer-->
    <div class="footer-bottom">
        <div class="container-fluid ">
            <div class="row-fluid ">
                <div class="span6 copyright">
                    <!--copyright-->
                </div>
                <div class="span6 sitemap">
                    <!--sitemap list-->
                </div>
            </div>
        </div>
    </div>
    <!--end bottom footer-->
</footer>
```

As you can see in Listing 5-16, we simply changed the class attribute value for the container wrapper from `container` to `container-fluid` and also changed the class attribute values for each from `row` to `row-fluid`. The site design will now flow to always fill up the entire viewport.

Fix Common Responsive Issues with SharePoint

At this point we should have a fully fluid, responsive HTML master page. We have provided no additional custom styles besides the Bootstrap framework based on the HTML prototype provided to us. If we now preview the HTML master page with just Bootstrap included and the basic grid applied, we will see quite a few layout issues arise. Most of these layout issues are common across many frameworks and you would likely run into some of these with your own custom responsive grids as well.

We now review common issues with responsive design and SharePoint. Each issue starts with a screenshot or "problem" followed by an explanation as to what is happening and, most important, the CSS necessary to fix the problem. Most of the CSS we provide will work to fix the general issue described, although some of our solutions have styles specific to Bootstrap and our sample design. It is our aim that the explanation of the cause of each problem along with our fix will enable you to provide the specific styling necessary for your particular problems.

Images and Icons

The first problem that will likely jump out at you with a responsive framework is that the ribbon appears completely broken, as shown in Figure 5-9. Because like a majority of public-facing sites, 95+ percent of your users are visitors, it's fine if you disable many SharePoint features (like the ribbon) for the front end of a public-facing SharePoint site. For your content editors and administrators, who rely heavily on the ribbon, though, this is completely unacceptable, so it needs to be fixed.

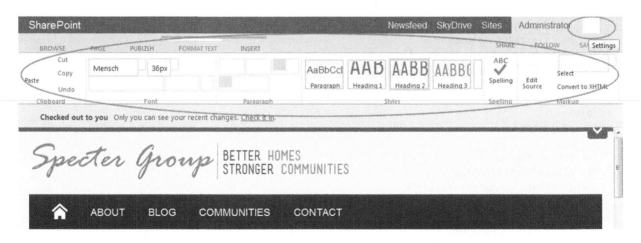

Figure 5-9. Disappearing images from the ribbon and elsewhere throughout the web site

The Explanation

Probably the most common and frustrating problem with responsive frameworks and SharePoint is the frameworks need to do two things. First, most responsive frameworks reset the box-sizing style to "border-box" instead of "content-box".

■ **Tip**   To learn more about box-sizing, refer to `http://sprwd.com/gamhnty`.

In a nutshell, box-sizing allows us to specify how we want the browser to calculate the CSS box model. In particular, should the "width" of a box or container include padding and the border, or is the width just what is inside of the padding? Content-box means that the specified width and height do not include margins, borders, or padding. Border-box, on the other hand is similar to how Internet Explorer determines width and height when a document is rendered in Quirks mode, meaning the width and height include the border and padding, but not the margin.

Why does all of this matter? Well, for most responsive frameworks to work, we want to provide a specific width, possibly a fluid width, of a container, but still provide a fixed padding. With a content-box this is not possible, as the ratio of the width to the padding is an unknown variable.

The second issue causing the ribbon grief is that frameworks will reset all images to max-width 100 percent and width to auto. This ensures that an image will never fall outside of a given container (row and column), at the same time allowing the image to scale to a container. With the ribbon, that just wreaks havoc.

The Fix

The general fix is quite easy, although there are some special cases to consider. First, we need to reset our box-sizing to content-box for all elements because that is what SharePoint expects. Now that breaks the grid, so we can turn the box-sizing back to border-box for any row or container that begins with the phase "span," such as span1, span4, span12, and so on.

Second, reset the images as well to no max-width but use a similar trick as for the box-sizing by allowing images within our framework columns to reset to use responsive properties.

Finally there are special cases where SharePoint uses its own containers that begin with "span," thus we need to provide additional overrides for the site actions as well as a few list pages. Listing 5-20 shows the code for repairing the images in the ribbon.

Listing 5-20. Custom Styles Fixing Responsive Images in Ribbon

```
*, *:before, *:after {
    -webkit-box-sizing: content-box; /*border-box causes many issues with SP*/
    -moz-box-sizing: content-box; /*border-box causes many issues with SP*/
    box-sizing: content-box; /*border-box causes many issues with SP*/
}
* [class^="span"], * [class^="span"]:before, , * [class^="span"]:after {
    -webkit-box-sizing: border-box; /*re-enable border-box for framework spans*/
    -moz-box-sizing: border-box; /*re-enable border-box for framework spans*/
    box-sizing: border-box; /*re-enable border-box for framework spans*/
}
img {
    max-width: none;
    width: auto;
}
* [class^="span"] img {
    max-width: 100%; /*for images inside span grid*/
}
#scriptWPQ2 img, img.ms-webpart-menuArrowImg, #applist img {
    /*within a span may still need to have width of image not 100% for SP2013 OOTB features/imges*/
    width: auto;
    max-width: none;
}
```

```
.ms-siteactions-imgspan {
    float: none;
    margin: 0px;
}
```

Figure 5-10 shows what the ribbon looks like after this code has been applied.

***Figure 5-10.** Ribbon icons and other SharePoint images fixed*

Ribbon Spans and Ribbon Drop-Down Menus

Now that the ribbon image issues have been solved, look at Figure 5-10 again. Notice anything wrong with the tabs in the upper left? How about the font drop-downs?

The Explanation

It so happens that the tabs are inside of containers that start with the phrase "span" again. Because Bootstrap reset spans to float left, this will cause problems with our tabs. Other frameworks might not have this issue, but you might find your framework breaks other SharePoint elements for similar reasons.

The drop-downs are causing issues because Bootstrap resets the styling of many form elements. Using Firebug we can quickly find out what styles need updating.

The Fix

Because we know that any span in the ribbon, such as the div with an ID of s4-ribbonrow, should not use our framework, we only need to override any container that starts with the keyword "span" to not float. We also reset the margin and line height to fit what SharePoint would prefer.

As for the input field, because ribbon input elements contain the same class, we can narrow down a style to just inputs within the ribbon and override their padding and height to again what SharePoint prefers. Listing 5-21 shows these changes.

Listing 5-21. Custom Styles to Fix Ribbon Layout Issues

```
#s4-ribbonrow [class*="span"] {
    float: none;
    margin-left: 0px;
    line-height: 1.2em;
}
input.ms-cui-cb-input {
    height: 14px;
    padding: 3px 7px 2px;
}
```

Figure 5-11 shows the ribbon with the fixes applied.

Figure 5-11. *Ribbon tabs and drop-down menus fixed*

Stop Fluid Behavior for Extra Large Viewports

In a previous section of this chapter, "From Fixed to Fluid," we reset our containers and rows so that they would be fluid. In general this is very much what responsive is all about. But how is your site going to look on very wide viewports, say viewports 1,600 pixels wide or larger? Do you really want your images to scale to that large? How about if we limit our site to grow to no more than 1,200 pixels wide for now?

The Explanation

The containers themselves are set to grow indefinitely so we are going to have to override this. We are going to have to be careful, though, because we cannot provide a blanket reset to all `container-fluid` tags to provide a fixed max width because what if we have containers within containers?

The Fix

The fix is easy: All we need to do is provide a max width to `container-fluid` elements that are directly after our own main containers such as `header` and `nav` and `footer`, as shown in Listing 5-22. We can use the same max-width in our `#main` container as well. We are placing this in a media query because we ideally want the left and right margin set to auto only when we are setting the max-width style.

Listing 5-22. Set a Maximum Width of a Fluid Web Site

```
@media (min-width: 1200px) {
   header > .container-fluid, nav#topnav > .container-fluid, footer > .container-fluid,
   .footer-bottom > .container-fluid {
      max-width: 1160px;
      margin-left: auto;
      margin-right: auto;
   }
   #main {
      max-width: 1200px;
      margin-left: auto;
      margin-right: auto;
   }
}
```

Rotating Images

jQuery-based rotating banners and images are very popular and there are many that are now responsive friendly. Even so, there might be an issue with how images transition from one to the other. In Figure 5-12 we can see that as the second image is sliding in both the height and width are scaling, when ideally there should be no scaling at all.

Figure 5-12. *Rotating images improperly transitioning*

The Explanation

Yet again the framework's reset of all image properties is getting in our way. We will use a similar trick as when we fixed the ribbon icons here as well.

The Fix

All we need to do is tell the images within the slider that their height should be fixed to the container height, as shown in Listing 5-23. Using the containing class of our slider, we specify a height for only images within our sliders.

Listing 5-23. Force a Set Height for Rotating Images

```
.theme-nivo-specter .nivoSlider img {
    height: 100% !important;
}
```

In Figure 5-13 we can see how our incoming image is not scaling its height any longer.

Figure 5-13. *Rotating image with a fixed height*

Misplaced Elements

When developing an HTML prototype, it might be very common to create our own wrappers and containers that have grid-like behaviors. We might then have a need for absolute positioned elements within a particular wrapper, which is, of course, not a problem assuming that our wrapper has a "position" of relative or absolute. But what happens when you replace your wrappers within a framework container, row, or column? Normally these containers do not have a position of relative associated with them, so if you need to position a child element within a grid container, row, or column, you will have to do some additional work.

There are quite a few of these issues in our demo design because of how the HTML prototype was built to reflect the design requirements for Specter Group. We will look at one particular issue, the Search box. If you refer to Figure 5-11, look in the header toward the right and you will notice that the Search box is missing. Let's see what we can do to fix that.

The Explanation

If you don't set a particular container, row, or column to have a CSS position of absolute or relative, a child container with an absolute position will be positioned based on the first element in its ancestry with a relative position. This could produce an unexpected result, which is exactly what is happening with our Search box.

The Fix

All we need to do is make sure that the container (container, row, or column) of an absolute positioned element is set to relative and the child element should appear where we want it. You can see in Listing 5-24 that we set the `container-fluid` that appears right after `<header>` to be relative, so any element in its lineage would be positioned based on that `container-fluid`.

Listing 5-24. Fix Absolutely Positioned divs in a Grid Framework

```
header > .container-fluid {
    position: relative;
}
header .searchbox {
    bottom: auto;
    right: auto;
    position: relative;
    float: right;
    margin-top: 60px;
    text-align: left;
    width: 260px;
}
header #searchInputBox input[type=text]{
    box-shadow: none;
    transition: none;
    -moz-transition: none;
    -webkit-transition: none;
}
```

What we decided to do, though, was to have the Search box not be absolutely positioned, but rather float to the right and use padding to get into the right space. We made this decision because we wanted it to always flow within the fluid container. We also provided a few additional styles to remove some of the styling SharePoint provides to search boxes.

Take a look at Figure 5-14. The Search box is now in the correct place, but we see that the Social bar tab just above and to the right of the Search box does not have the correct padding to the right. This element is positioned absolutely to the `container-fluid` but remember that Bootstrap uses 20-pixel padding, so we will simply move the tab over a full 20 pixels to match, as shown in Listing 5-25.

Figure 5-14. Rotating image with a fixed height

Listing 5-25. Account to Framework Padding

```
header .social {
    right: 20px;
}
```

Not Enough Padding or Spacing Between Rows and Columns

What if you want more padding or spacing between rows and columns? We can see in Figure 5-15 that our footer does not have the spacing we are looking for, nor are the Heading elements centered.

Figure 5-15. *Improper spacing between rows and columns*

The Explanation

This is another common problem when transitioning from our own HTML coding to a framework. If you recall from the earlier section in this chapter, "Bootstrap and a Footer," we moved our footer columns from an unordered list to Bootstrap span columns. The styling applied to the unordered list must be moved over to the footer spans now.

The Fix

All we really need to do is take the styling that we had applied to the footer unordered list and replace many of the ul and li elements with span4 as we are using a three-column layout, as shown in Listing 5-26. As for the footer-bottom block, we simply need to specify additional padding to the Bootstrap container we added.

Listing 5-26. Provide Additional Padding and Margins for Grid Elements

```
footer {
    padding-top: 10px;
}
footer .span4 h1, footer .span4 h2, footer .span4 h3, footer .span4 h4,
      footer .span4 h5,  footer .span4 h6 {
    font-weight: normal;
    margin-bottom: 20px;
    padding-bottom: 0;
    padding-top: 0;
    text-align: center;
}
footer .footer-bottom  .container-fluid {
    padding: 15px 20px;
}
```

```
footer .footer-bottom p, footer .footer-bottom li {
    font-size: 13px;
}
footer .footer-bottom .copyright, footer .footer-bottom .sitemap {
    min-height: 0px;
}
footer .footer-bottom  .sitcmap {
    text-align: right;
}
```

Figure 5-16 shows the fixed footer.

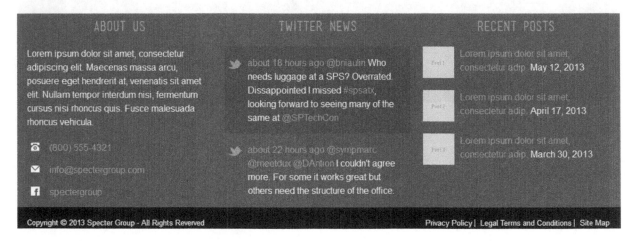

Figure 5-16. *Grid spacing reset for specific elements*

Smaller Viewport Layouts Break

A responsive framework provides most of the tools we need to make the grid itself responsive, but that does not mean all of the elements of our web site will scale the way we want them to. Custom media queries come to the rescue.

Our design requires a few different fixes for multiple viewports, so we look at the header for an example. In particular we look at the logo, tagline, and Search box and see how these elements react at different viewport widths. In Figure 5-17, note how the header looks in 768-pixel- and 320-pixel-wide viewports in comparison with the header in Figure 5-14.

Figure 5-17. *Broken layouts on 768- and 320-pixel-wide viewports*

The Explanation

Just because we use rows and columns does not mean our elements within these rows and columns will scale in a graceful manner. We will need to provide our own styles within media queries to help fix our layout based on different viewport widths.

■ **Note** Ideally all elements will be within their own rows and columns and would scale automatically, but in practice that is often not the case.

The Fix

Using breakpoints of viewports under 979 pixels (tablets), under 767 pixels (small tablets), and under 479 pixels (smart phones), we will scale particular elements and change their positioning. In Listing 5-27, look at how we scale the logo. First we tell the logo container to always only take up only 50 percent of the width of the column, yet the image inside should always fill up the entire #logo container. For small tablets, provide additional margin at the top and left of the logo so that it does not butt up right next to the viewport frame.

Listing 5-27. Media Query Enclosed Styles Providing Layout Fixes for the Header

```
@media (max-width: 979px) {
   header #logo {
      width: 50%;
   }
   header #logo img {
      display: block;
      width: 100%;
      max-width: 100%;
      height: auto;
   }
}
```

```css
    header .tagline h2 {
        font-size: 20px;
    }
    header .searchbox {
        margin-top: 50px;
    }
}
@media (max-width: 767px) {
    header #logo img {
        margin: 10px 0px 0px 5px;
    }
    header .tagline h2 {
        font-size: 16px;
    }
    header .searchbox {
        margin: 10px 1% 10px;
        float: left;
        width: 98%;
    }
    header #searchInputBox input[type="text"] {
        width: 80%;
    }
    header .searchbox a {
        float: right;
        margin-right: 2%;
    }
    header .social {
        right: 1%;
    }
}
@media (max-width: 479px) {
    header .tagline {
        background: transparent none;
        display: block;
        margin: 5px 10px;
        min-height: 0px;
        padding: 0px;
        vertical-align: top;
    }
    header .tagline h2 {
        font-size: 16px;
    }
}
```

Also check out the search box. Once we hit the smaller tablet viewports we no longer float the block right, but rather float it left. Further we tell the element to fill up 98 percent of the width of the column, thus making the search scale to the entire column now.

Figure 5-18 shows these fixes.

Figure 5-18. *Fixed layouts on 768- and 320-pixel-wide viewports*

Using the preceding techniques we can provide additional styles to our different media queries to fix other layout issues that we encounter with different viewports. This includes issues elsewhere on our HTML master page, such as the footer and particular content blocks. You might even decide to hide elements at particular viewports by simply setting an element's display property to "none." See Listing 5-28, where we hide the tagline for smart phones and how that would look in Figure 5-19.

Listing 5-28. Hide the Tagline for Viewport Less Than 479 Pixels Wide

```
@media (max-width: 479px) {
    header .tagline {
        display: none;
    }
}
```

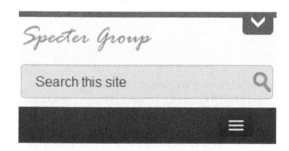

Figure 5-19. *The tagline has been hidden for small viewports*

Other Hints and Suggestions

You will certainly find that moving to a responsive grid will cause new problems that you must work through one by one. If your original HTML prototype was created well, then moving over styles that reference your specific grid containers, rows, and columns should not be too difficult with the help of a developer tool such as Firebug. Don't forget about the Responsive Design View in Firefox as well (Tools ➤ Web Developer ➤ Responsive Design View or Ctrl+Shift+M).

You might also have noticed that in many of our fixes, we used our HTML5 elements to help narrow our styles to specific containers or rows. Using our own specific wrapper elements or even adding additional IDs or classes to grid elements will help you target styles to specific elements without accidently breaking other aspects of your web site.

■ **Tip** Refer to this book's Github repository at `https://github.com/SPRWD` to see the entire updated style sheet in the Chapter 5 folder.

Dealing with Older Browsers

Let's share some of the challenges that you'll face when dealing with older browsers and the options available to handle each challenge.

Here is a tip to keep in mind: You can either have a design that tries to accomplish all functionality in older browsers, or you can create individual master pages targeted for specific browsers. You don't have to deliver a pixel-perfect version of your site for all browsers. As long as the core functionality is accessible, that's a great starting point. Instead, you can start with design iterations that might look the same but will most probably have limited functionality. As long as your visitors can view the same content and have the navigation controls to navigate the site, you are a step ahead.

Be Progressive Across All Browsers

A common concern among developers is ensuring that their sites render the same across all browsers, including older ones such as Internet Explorer 8 and older. That might not always be necessary, as a better route is to consider progressively enhancing your site by offering a solid working baseline experience to users with legacy browsers while providing a richer interface to those users with modern browsers. It's an uphill battle to have your site look pixel perfect in all browsers and it is a battle you aren't going to win. If you know you have to target a particular older browser in your organization such as Internet Explorer 7, then there might be a need to invest the time to verify your site works on that browser at the level you require. Otherwise, look to develop for IE 8+ and you will hit more than 98 percent of your site's visitors.

HTML5Shiv

One popular workaround to allow HTML5 semantic tags in legacy browsers is to use JavaScript. A JavaScript workaround was discovered by Sjoerd Visscher and it enabled styling for HTML5 elements by non-HTML5 browsers such as IE 8 and older. Why is this a problem for HTML5 elements? Browsers typically won't apply styling to elements that they don't recognize.

To use this script, simply download html5shiv from `http://sprwd.com/33hgajz` and add a link to the JavaScript library in your code (ideally minified). Refer to Listing 5-24. The caveat here is that you must include the link to html5shiv before the `<body>` element (i.e., in the `<head>`).

Another common linking method is to use a Content Delivery Network (CDN) such as `http://html5shiv.googlecode.com/svn/trunk/html5.js`. Many JavaScript libraries such as Modernizr (`http://modernizr.com/`) already include html5shiv, so you might notice that we do not have to link directly to html5shiv in our examples because we are relying on Modernizr.

■ **Tip** Modernizr is a JavaScript library that provides HTML5 and CSS3 feature detection.

Because we only use html5shiv for IE 8 and older, there is a special tag we can provide that tells particular versions of IE that they should process the following HTML, whereas other browsers will ignore it. We also use this conditional HTML coding in Listing 5-29.

Listing 5-29. Conditional Reference to html5shiv

```
<head>
...
<!--[if lt IE 9]>
   <script type="text/javscript"
       src="http://html5shiv.googlecode.com/svn/trunk/html5.js"></script>
<![endif]-->
...
</head>
```

■ **Tip** Including JavaScript files after style sheets helps with performance as it tells the browser that it should load style sheets before JavaScript files. Many even recommend placing JavaScript files just before the closing `</body>` tag because of performance, but with SharePoint and especially jQuery libraries and plug-ins, it is recommended that you add script links to the `<head>`.

Browser Upgrade Notification

Another option, although we agree it does not quite strike an accord with the One Web philosophy, is to detect what browser your visitors are using and prompt them to upgrade their browser, as shown in Figure 5-20. As you might expect, there's JavaScript already available that does this work for you.

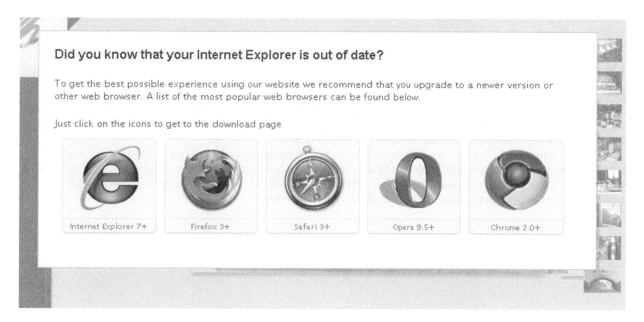

Figure 5-20. *Did you know that your browser is out of date?*

This is an interesting option because you are supporting the stance that users should upgrade to newer browsers. This is a bold, yet possible stance to take when it's a public-facing site and your list of supported browsers has to constantly grow. At some point you might have to let older browsers go, although hopefully using a progressively enhanced site, your site will still function on older browsers. For an intranet this might be harder to enforce, as there could be other reasons why you must support older browsers.

To enable this browser upgrade notification, download the solution zip file that contains the JavaScript as well as a few images from http://sprwd.com/g7qpixw and save them to your project solution library. In your master page, right after the <body> element, add the code shown in Listing 5-30.

Listing 5-30. Adding the Browser Upgrade Notification Script

```
<body>
    ...
    <!--[if lte IE 6]>
        <script src="js/ie6/warning.js"></script> <script>window.onload=function()
{e("js/ie6/")}</script>
    <![endif]-->
    ...
</body>
```

■ **Tip** Keep in mind that after you add any new solution, jQuery code, or CSS that you should test SharePoint functionality. This is even more true when you start mixing different versions of the same framework, like jQuery. SharePoint 2013 leverages jQuery 1.7 and your custom jQuery solutions might leverage the latest jQuery version. Test and test again.

Device Channels

Device channels are a new feature added to SharePoint 2013, originally designed as an updated approach to developing mobile-friendly sites. Previous versions of SharePoint included a Mobile View. This was very limiting and only designed for collaboration sites, not publishing sites. We briefly introduced device channels in Chapter 1, but let's investigate them a little further and see how they can help us.

Device channels allow us to map devices and browsers to appropriate master pages. For each device channel, we can define devices that are applicable to it by adding device inclusion rules with user agent substrings, and then we associate a master page with each device channel (see Figure 5-21). Device channels are especially useful when we need to define a web site rendering that is optimal for a specific device.

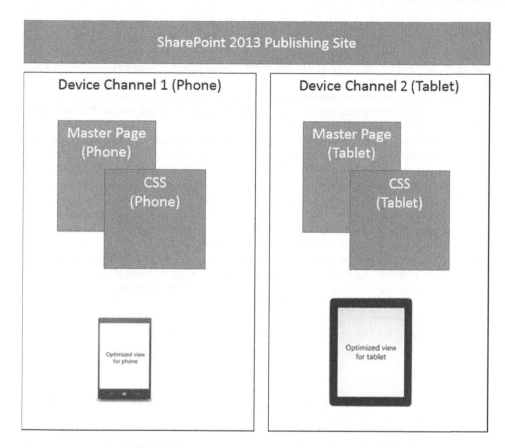

Figure 5-21. *Device channels may be mapped to devices, each with its own master page, CSS, and so on*

All of this means we can create a custom master page for a series of one or more devices and tailor that particular master page specifically for those devices. All of our master pages, for all of our device channels, would still reside on one site, and would use the same content, content pages, and page layouts. Device channels allow you to customize page layouts by the use of device channel panels.

Device channels provide us a hybrid approach of a separate mobile site without the need for actually creating a separate site for each tailored interface, just a tailored master page and possibly customized page layouts.

Device Channels and Responsive Web Design

If device channels are designed to provide mobile views, you might ask yourself why we are bothering with responsive web design.

The first answer to that question is that because a device channel is mapped to devices (i.e., user agents), then what do we do with the ever increasing number of devices? Do you want to try to manage that list? We sure do not.

Second, there are no standards for viewport widths, so we might have to create a device channel for so many different viewport widths it could quickly become unmanageable.

Third, you have to maintain each master page for each device channel. One branding effort can be difficult enough to build, test, debug, and maintain; adding channels means multiplying that effort.

Responsive web design is not perfect by any means, and device channels do provide the advantage of tailored designs for specific browsers or devices. It is our opinion that the positives of an adaptive site design regardless of the browser and viewport is generally preferable to a rigid design that must be manually adapted and mapped to specific devices.

When We Might Use Device Channels

Device channels definitely can have their place in the web designer's process. The opportunity is great to leverage the functionality of device channels provided by SharePoint 2013 and build a master page or master pages tailored to specific browsers or devices.

We propose two possible sound reasons why device channels might come in handy. Remember that device channels are mapped to the user agent and not an actual device. This means we can map to not just an iPhone, but to a specific browser version such as IE 7 or IE 8 regardless of the device.

Let us say that before you begin developing your web site you analyze existing web traffic logs and find that a very large percentage of your users are accessing your web site using a specific device, say a Surface Pro. You could create a solution that includes two device channels, one for most visitors and a second specifically for Surface Pro users. This second device channel might not need to be responsive, nor would you have to provide much client-side feature detection because you know what features are and are not available. A device channel just for this specific device might open the doors to a truly unique experience for specific visitors. If you are building an intranet or extranet, you might know that your web site users will only be using either a specific desktop browser or a specific smart phone to access your web site. If that is the case, then device channels might once again make sense.

Device channels could also be leveraged to provide a lighter or less feature-rich version of a site design that works well in, say, Internet Explorer 8 or older. This way you could create a device channel mapped to an HTML5 master page for most visitors with modern browsers that is responsive and a second device channel just for older versions of IE that does not use HTML5, CSS3, and maybe even limits JavaScript as well.

There are likely many more good reasons why device channels might make sense for your organization and we expect some interesting insights into special cases for device channels over the next few years.

Create a Device Channel

We now walk through how to create a device channel in SharePoint 2013. You'll first want to browse to the Design Manager in a browser by clicking the Settings icon and then selecting Design Manager.

From the left navigation menu, select the menu item 2. Device Channels, as shown in Figure 5-22. The Manage Device Channels page will load. Click Create a Channel, found just under the main page title, to create a new device channel.

Figure 5-22. Manage Device Channels page

The New Device Channel dialog box will appear, as shown in Figure 5-23. You will need to enter information related to your custom device channel:

1. In the Name text box, enter a name for the device channel.

2. In the Alias text box, enter an alias for the device channel.

■ **Note** The alias must be alphanumeric characters and cannot contain spaces. You will use the alias to refer to the device channel in code and in other contexts.

---

3. In the Description text box, enter a brief description of the devices or browsers that the channel will capture.

4. In the Device Inclusion Rules text box, enter the user agent substrings for the channel. A request for a web page will use this channel if any of the strings that you provide match any part of the user agent string of the requesting agent.

    As an example, Windows Phones have user agent strings that contain the substring "Windows Phone". If you wanted a device channel for all Windows Phones, a Device Inclusion Rule need only contain the rule, "Windows Phone" and not the entire long user agent, Mozilla/5.0 (compatible; MSIE 9.0; Windows Phone OS 7.5; Trident/5.0; IEMobile/9.0).

5. If you are ready to make the channel available to render pages, select the Active check box.

6. Once you have entered in all of the required information, click Save to save your new device channel.

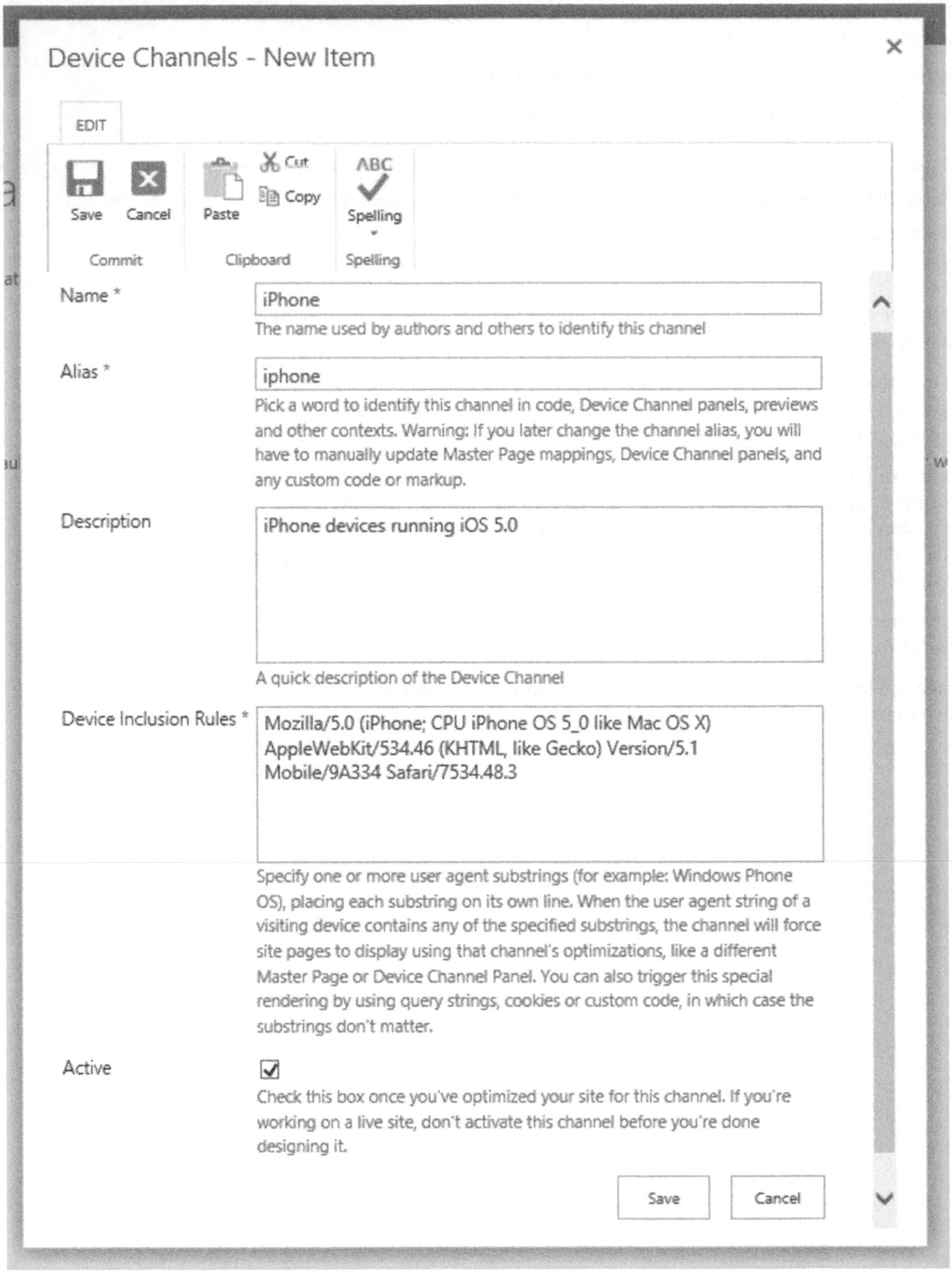

Device Channels - New Item   ✕

EDIT

💾	✕	📋	✂ Cut	ABC
Save	Cancel	Paste	📋 Copy	✓ Spelling ▾
Commit		Clipboard		Spelling

Name *
iPhone

The name used by authors and others to identify this channel

Alias *
iphone

Pick a word to identify this channel in code, Device Channel panels, previews and other contexts. Warning: If you later change the channel alias, you will have to manually update Master Page mappings, Device Channel panels, and any custom code or markup.

Description
iPhone devices running iOS 5.0

A quick description of the Device Channel

Device Inclusion Rules *
Mozilla/5.0 (iPhone; CPU iPhone OS 5_0 like Mac OS X) AppleWebKit/534.46 (KHTML, like Gecko) Version/5.1 Mobile/9A334 Safari/7534.48.3

Specify one or more user agent substrings (for example: Windows Phone OS), placing each substring on its own line. When the user agent string of a visiting device contains any of the specified substrings, the channel will force site pages to display using that channel's optimizations, like a different Master Page or Device Channel Panel. You can also trigger this special rendering by using query strings, cookies or custom code, in which case the substrings don't matter.

Active
☑
Check this box once you've optimized your site for this channel. If you're working on a live site, don't activate this channel before you're done designing it.

Save   Cancel

Figure 5-23. Sample device channel created for iPhones

■ **Note** If you'd like to see an exhaustive list of user agent strings, go to `http://sprwd.com/narb3md`. To view the user agent string for your browser and device combination, browse to their home page at `http://sprwd.com/aaxtzbp`.

Assign a Master Page to a Device Channel

Once a device channel has been configured and a master page has been created that a particular device channel should use, it is time to assign the master page to the device channel. In Chapter 4, we showed you how to assign a master page as a Site (custom) master page. Once you have more than one device channel, that master page settings page will allow you to assign a master page per device channel.

Open your Site Settings page in a browser and under Look and Feel click Master Page.

On your Site Master Page Settings page, next to Site Master Page, you should see each device channel you created, as shown in Figure 5-24. You can now set any valid, published master page to each device channel. Notice that you can only set a specific site master page to each device channel, and your system master page will be the same for all devices. This means that all system pages and other pages that use the system master page will always use the same master page.

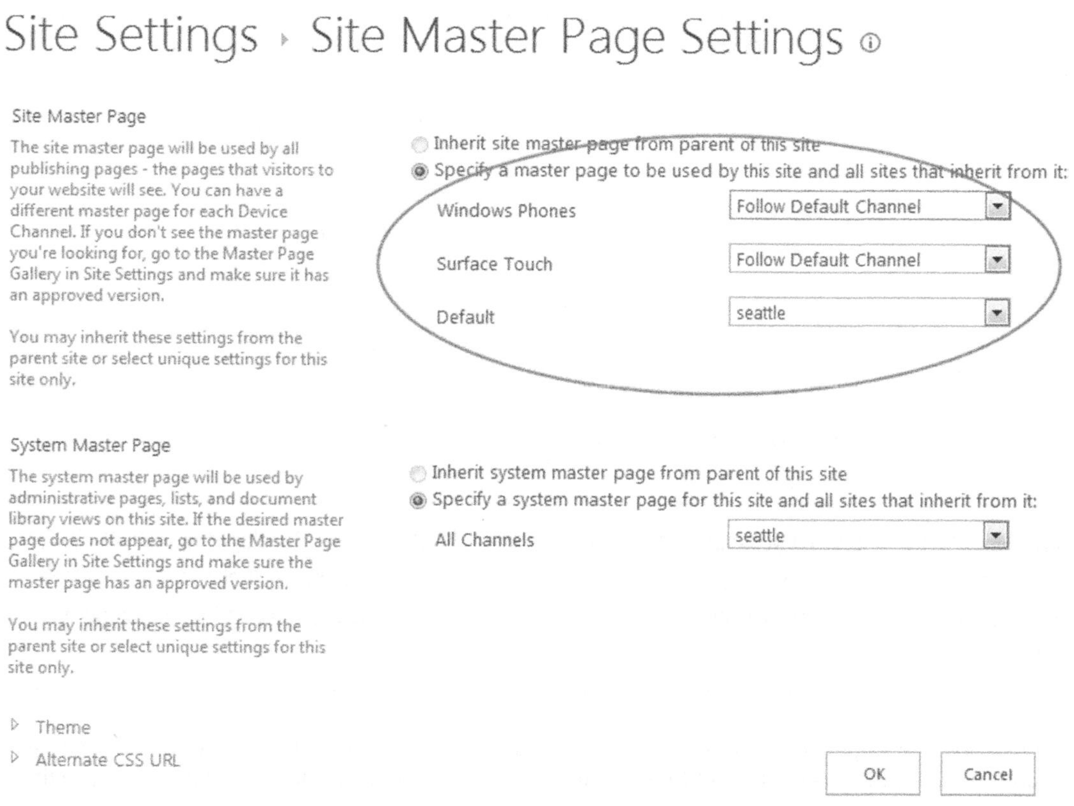

Site Settings ▸ Site Master Page Settings ⓘ

Site Master Page

The site master page will be used by all publishing pages - the pages that visitors to your website will see. You can have a different master page for each Device Channel. If you don't see the master page you're looking for, go to the Master Page Gallery in Site Settings and make sure it has an approved version.

You may inherit these settings from the parent site or select unique settings for this site only.

○ Inherit site master page from parent of this site
◉ Specify a master page to be used by this site and all sites that inherit from it:

Windows Phones	Follow Default Channel ▾
Surface Touch	Follow Default Channel ▾
Default	seattle ▾

System Master Page

The system master page will be used by administrative pages, lists, and document library views on this site. If the desired master page does not appear, go to the Master Page Gallery in Site Settings and make sure the master page has an approved version.

You may inherit these settings from the parent site or select unique settings for this site only.

○ Inherit system master page from parent of this site
◉ Specify a system master page for this site and all sites that inherit from it:

All Channels	seattle ▾

▷ Theme
▷ Alternate CSS URL

[OK] [Cancel]

Figure 5-24. Set master pages for specific device channels

Changing Your User-Agent String

When a browser requests a web page from a web server, a browser will send along a user-agent (UA) string that identifies the browser type and version to the web server. The chosen UA string will be sent across the network as a header in every request. Many web sites change their appearance based on user strings, which, as we have mentioned, is also how device channels work.

For development and testing purposes, changing your user-agent string could be very beneficial and there are a variety of browser-specific tools you can use to accomplish this. As an example, in Internet Explorer 10, we can change the user-agent string by enabling the Developer Toolbar by pressing F12 and then selecting a different browser mode from Tools ➤ Change user agent string, as shown in Figure 5-25.

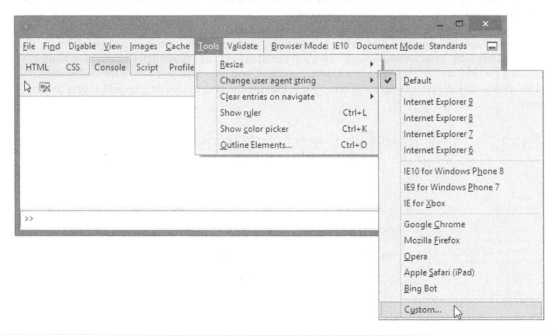

Figure 5-25. *Change the user agent in Internet Explorer using the IE Developer Toolbar*

■ **Note**   In Internet Explorer 8, 9, and 10, you can press F12 to open the Internet Explorer Developer Toolbar. It's fairly similar in functionality to Firebug for Firefox and other browser-specific web developer toolbars. It allows you to select nodes within the DOM, view and edit properties, and so on, which comes in very handy when trying to understand how HTML markup helps build sites.

The Internet Explorer Developer Toolbar is a powerful tool similar to Firebox for Firebug. If you would like to see how your site is rendered in a previous version of Internet Explorer, you can change the Browser Mode setting on the IE Toolbar.

Summary

In this chapter we looked at different options to use to integrate responsive design theories with our SharePoint 2013 HTML master pages. We looked at creating a responsive infrastructure from scratch but quickly realized leveraging an existing responsive framework such as Twitter Bootstrap would alleviate much of the hassle of creating the initial responsive skeleton or grid. We reviewed how we can go about merging an existing HTML master page with a framework and then looked at common problems or concerns that might arise when moving to responsive design. We finished with a look at how to handle older browsers, including a look at device channels and how they might be useful.

In the next two chapters we continue the process of building the basic framework of our responsive site by first looking at navigation and then continuing on to page layouts.

Summary

CHAPTER 6

∎ ∎ ∎

Building Site Structure and Navigation

In this chapter we review common types of navigation a site might incorporate, including horizontal navigation, vertical navigation, footer-based navigation, and social media icon bars. We investigate different options available to us in SharePoint 2013 that can assist us with integrating and managing these different navigation components. With the addition of managed metadata-driven navigation in SharePoint 2013, we can build even more custom, complete navigation structures, still managed by SharePoint, than we could with SharePoint 2010. By the end of the chapter we will have learned how to configure a SharePoint 2013 web site to allow for managed metadata-driven navigation as well as how to modify an HTML master page and other branding elements to include responsive-friendly navigation elements.

We start this chapter with a review of site structure planning and navigation methods available in SharePoint 2013. We continue with a deep dive into term stores and managed metadata. If you are already familiar with managed metadata and term stores, you can skip ahead to the rest of this chapter, specifically the sections "How SharePoint 2013 Builds the Navigation Bar" and "Style and Make the Navigation Bar Responsive."

∎ **Note**   This chapter focuses on managed metadata-based navigation. To learn how to configure navigation for cross-site publishing, please refer to Chapter 8.

Our Scenario

The public Specter Group web site requires multiple forms of navigation including a primary top horizontal navigation bar as well as footer-based navigation. Specter Group wants to leverage the latest tools in SharePoint 2013 to help manage their navigation structure throughout their web site solution. Finally, any navigation component added to the web site must fit within the responsive framework chosen for this project. Navigation must be visible as well as fully functional across multiple devices with different limitations of available features.

Determine Site Structure

A prerequisite to successful site navigation that enables your site visitors to find content relevant to their needs begins with a site map. Your site map is a list of site web pages, sites, and other documents that will be contained in your site. Normally a site map is represented as a hierarchical tree, providing a tree of logically connected branches and nodes, displaying how pages are connected. Once you have an understanding of what pages will exist within a site, you can begin to build a strategy to provide navigation within your site.

∎ **Note**   To review information architecture and a sample site map, refer to Chapter 3.

Primary Navigation Methods in SharePoint 2013

Before we dive into methods of branding our site navigation, we must begin by investigating available navigation management methods. SharePoint 2013 provides two primary tools that we can use to help manage our site navigation: structured navigation and managed navigation. We can also create custom, possibly nonmanaged navigation methods that include panels, bars, and tool panes we code directly into master pages and page layouts as well as our own .NET navigation providers.

Managed Navigation

SharePoint 2013 introduces a new method of managing our navigation. We can now use managed metadata and the Managed Metadata Service to build taxonomies or terms and term sets to build our navigation structure.

■ **Note**   Learn how to use the Term Store for managed navigation later in the chapter in the section "Using the Term Store for Navigation."

Pros

1. Based around your taxonomy. You can build your navigation based around your own organization's language and terms.

2. Complex navigation structures. Your term set and list of terms can be as simple or complex as your business requirements.

3. Friendly URLs. Managed navigation allows you to use specific friendly URLs such as /a-new-article instead of /post.aspx?ID=12.

4. Separation of site structure and navigation structure. Your site navigation need not be tied to your site structure. This allows you to create navigation around business concepts without having to rearrange your site.

5. Customize with a browser or with code. You can manage your navigation term store via the browser although because managed navigation leverages the Managed Metadata Service, a comprehensive API exists that you can use to manage terms and term sets.

6. Term set management can be delegated to specific users based on sets or subsets of terms.

Cons

1. One term set per site. You can link a site to only one term set, so if you want to have your global navigation and current navigation both use managed navigation, they must use the same term set. You can specify if you want a particular term displayed in the global navigation, current navigation, or both.

2. No audience targeting. Unlike with structured navigation (covered in the next section) where you can target navigation items to specific users and groups, managed navigation does not currently provide the same functionality. All valid navigation nodes will be displayed to all site visitors.

3. Link to a page. Term-driven pages with a friendly URL must link to a page; they may not link to general libraries such as a document library.

4. Unique term sets. A term set can be linked to only one site. If you want to reuse a term set you must first create a second term set and then pin terms from one term set to another. Learn how to share term sets across sites in the section "Share Managed Navigation Across Site Collections" later in this chapter.

5. Term Store Management browser compatibility. At the time of publication of this book, you should only manage your term store with Internet Explorer 8 or newer.

Structured Navigation

Structured navigation was the primary navigation management method available in SharePoint 2010 and is still available in SharePoint 2013. Structured navigation depends on the site structure or site map of your site. We are allowed to specify if we want to include subsites, site pages, or sibling sites and if we want to simply inherit the structured settings from a particular site's parent site. We can also insert custom headings, links and, sublinks within our site structure navigation.

Pros

1. Automatically based on site structure. Structured navigation uses the structure or site map of your site. Once you configure your site to use structured navigation, depending on your settings, as sites and pages are added to your site collection, your navigation bars will automatically reflect your changes.

2. Audience targeting. You can specify a specific audience or group of users that should be shown a particular navigation node. This allows you to easily create different site navigation dependent upon who visits a given page.

3. Browser-based management. You manage your structured navigation in a browser.

4. Custom links. Although the primary navigation is based on your site structure, you can also add additional links, headings, and links within headings.

5. Similar rendered HTML. SharePoint 2013 uses a similar HTML structure for structured navigation as for managed navigation.

Cons

1. Based on site structure. Yes, this is a con as well as a pro, depending on your site requirements. If you want to rearrange your navigation, you will have to rearrange your site structure. This can often be difficult with more complex site navigation requirements. Additionally, business requirements may dictate your navigation structure be different than your site structure.

2. All sites, subsites, and pages are included. With structured navigation, if you select to include pages, all pages (or published pages in publishing sites) are included. Note that you can hide subsites from being included.

3. Custom link hierarchy. You can only have up to two levels of custom links. You can create custom headings where headings can be either text or links. Headings can have child links but headings cannot have child headings. This means you can only have two levels of custom links.

4. No structure sharing. Structured navigation may not be shared across site collections, nor may be it used by other sites, only inherited by direct descendent child sites.

Custom Navigation

You will find no requirement that you must use SharePoint to manage your site navigation. You can always create your own navigation bars (i.e., top navigation or current navigation) using HTML or HTML5 that you include directly in your master pages and page layouts. You could also create your own site map provider, your own .NET controls, or even a new SharePoint 2013 App. Although navigation not managed by SharePoint is beyond the scope of this book, we continue our review of the pros and cons of custom navigation.

Pros

1. Complete control. You can decide exactly how you want your navigation to appear, including your own HTML rendering as well as navigation data sources.

2. Overcome SharePoint navigation obstacles. Custom site map providers can help overcome issues of managed or structured navigation. Custom web parts, controls, or SharePoint 2013 Apps can provide missing functionality.

Cons

1. New pages or sites might require assistance. If you hard-code your navigation into your master page, say using an unordered list of navigation items, new pages, new sites, or modifications to your site structure might require modifications to your master page.

2. Custom code required. Building your own site map providers or navigation apps will most likely require Visual Studio 2012 and custom coding.

3. Future compatibility. Custom navigation solutions are less likely to be compatible with future versions of SharePoint. You might need to rebuild your custom navigation solutions if you upgrade your site to a new version of SharePoint.

■ **Note** The custom code component of custom navigation will cause most SharePoint deployments to decide to use structured navigation or the new managed navigation provided in SharePoint 2013. Because structured navigation was originally introduced in SharePoint 2010, we focus our attention on managed navigation through the remainder of this book. Branding structured navigation and managed navigation is the same, as both methods render the same HTML markup we see later in this chapter in the section, "How SharePoint 2013 Builds the Navigation Bar."

Using the Term Store for Navigation

SharePoint 2010 provided tools to help manage navigation, both global navigation (i.e., the top, horizontal navigation bar) and the current navigation (i.e., the left, vertical navigation bar). We were limited to either having SharePoint manage navigation for us based on the site structure, using structured navigation, or we had to use static navigation based on a list of links, groups, and sublinks. Structured navigation allowed SharePoint to manage navigation based on our site structure but was limiting because it strictly followed how we created the hierarchy of our sites, subsites, and pages. A problem could arise when we needed to create site hierarchies for governance reasons that did not directly relate to how we want navigation structured. If we instead went with static navigation based on a list of links, groups, and sublinks, we had to manually manage our navigation menus and we were limited to only one level of dynamic navigation. Finally, with either method, we were unable to create search engine friendly URLs, such as http://www.spectergroup.com/about instead of http://www.spectergroup.com/pages/aboutus.aspx.

SharePoint 2013 provides a new tool for navigation management that helps solve some of these issues, along with providing us the added functionality of linking to catalogs and catalog categories, by allowing us to use managed metadata and a term store to store and manage our navigation. Additional improvements include the ability to provide SEO-friendly URLs to their actual sites such as our previous example, http://www.spectergroup.com/about.

What Is Metadata-Driven Navigation?

The quick and dirty definition of metadata as used by SharePoint boils down to data about data. SharePoint 2010 introduced the Managed Metadata Service, which allowed us to store term sets (words) as well as provide central location to store content types (Chapter 7). Term sets allowed us to create a hierarchy of terms for our sites, site collections, and web applications that were unique to our business needs. SharePoint 2013 looks to leverage the Managed Metadata Service and in particular term sets to drive our navigation. Our site navigation can link to a particular term set in a Managed Metadata Service, and then each term in the term set corresponds to a particular node in the navigation structure. Further, each node can have a set of properties that define how it will be displayed and utilized.

Before we get to how to link a site to a term set, we must first look at term stores and the Managed Metadata Service. Because multiple site collections, across web applications even, can share the same navigation term set, configuration and storage of term sets must occur at a central location, i.e. the farm. In particular, term sets are managed by the Managed Metadata Service, which we configure in Central Admin.

A default installation of SharePoint 2013 includes the creation of a standard Managed Metadata Service Application. Your SharePoint administrator might have also already configured this for you, but if not, you will need to create and configure a Managed Metadata Service Application to utilize the SharePoint 2013 metadata-driven navigation.

■ **Note**   The Managed Metadata Service provides valuable tools to help manage and maintain your site taxonomy. We review how to use managed metadata for navigation, a small but important use of the Managed Metadata Service. To learn about managed metadata, term store management, taxonomy, and how to make a general plan for your site, visit http://sprwd.com/zujbab.

Configure the Metadata Hub

Before you can use metadata-driven navigation you need to make sure that your site can access the Managed Metadata Service and that the Application Pool and Managed Metadata Web Service have been started in your SharePoint farm. Often this will be handled by an organization's SharePoint farm administrator, but when the designers are also the farm administrators, we will quickly review the process to enable managed metadata.

To quickly check to see if your farm has been configured for managed metadata, log in to the root of your project site collection as a site collection administrator and navigate to your site collection's Site Settings page (Settings ➤ Site Settings on the ribbon). On the Site Settings page, in the Site Administration section, click Term store management.

If the Term Store Management Tool page displays an error, "The Managed Metadata Service or Connection is currently not available. The Application Pool or Managed Metadata Web Service may not have been started. Please Contact your Administrator," as shown in Figure 6-1, you or your SharePoint farm administrator will either need to set up and configure the Managed Metadata Service, or there is an issue with how the Managed Metadata Service was configured. Fixing a broken Managed Metadata Service is beyond the scope of this book, but we can easily create a new Managed Metadata Service instance.

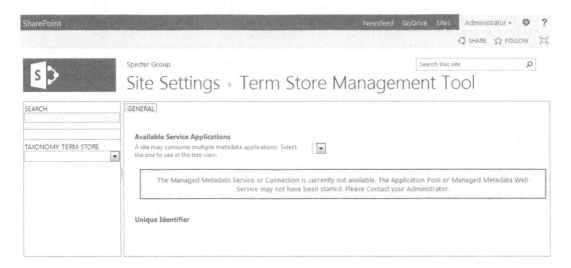

Figure 6-1. *Site Collection Term Store Management Tool error, with no Managed Metadata Service available*

Configure the Managed Metadata Service

Configuring the Managed Metadata Service for your farm requires access to Central Administration as well as access to a database that will store metadata. Otherwise the process is simple and straightforward.

1. Log in to SharePoint 2013 Central Administration with a user account that has farm administrator permissions.

2. You need to make sure that the Managed Metadata Web Service has been started first. Click Application Management on the left menu, then under the Service Applications section, click Manage services on server.

3. On the Services on Server page, make sure that Managed Metadata Web Service has a status of Started. If its status is Stopped, click Start to start the Managed Metadata Web Service.

4. Click Application Management on the left menu, then under Service Applications, click Manage service applications.

5. On the Service Applications page, on the ribbon within the Create section, click New, then in the New drop-down list, click Managed Metadata Service. A Create New Managed Metadata Service dialog box, shown in Figure 6-2, opens.

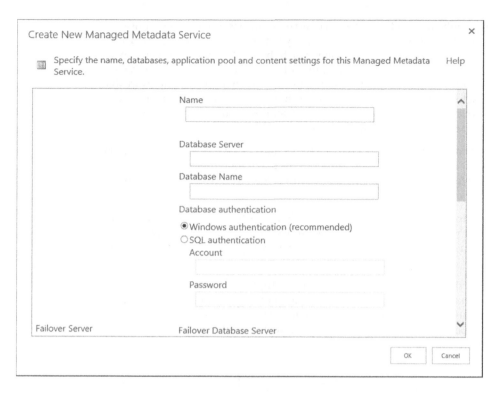

Figure 6-2. *Create New Managed Metadata Service dialog box*

6.   Provide values as requested by the dialog box:

   a.   Name: The name of this unique Managed Metadata Service in your farm. You might have multiple metadata service applications running in your farm and your site can use multiple metadata service applications as well. For our case, we name this new instance Specter Managed Metadata.

   b.   Database Server: This is the name of the database server you wish to have store your Managed Metadata Application for this instance. This does not have to be the same database server as the one hosting your SharePoint 2013 sites.

   c.   Database Name: This is the name of the database you would like created on your database server. This must be a unique database name for each metadata service application. In our case we want this new instance to create a new database named Specter Managed Metadata DB.

   d.   Database authentication: You must provide an account that has access to your database server to create the new database and have access to the database itself.

   e.   Failover Database Server: This is the location of your failover database server if you have one. This is not required and for our installation we leave this blank.

   f.   Application Pool: Either select an existing application pool that you would like this metadata service application to use, or create a new one. If you create a new one you also need to provide the authentication credentials for this new pool to use. In our case we are going to create a new application pool named SharePoint - Specter Managed Metadata.

g. Content type hub: Managed metadata also serves as the backbone for enterprise content types. This facility in SharePoint allows you to manage content types in a single site collection, known as the content type hub, which may then be consumed by other site collections. You may provide the URL of the site collection you wish to associate as the Content Type Hub for this Managed Metadata Service. Be aware that additional setup is required in the content type hub site collection and changing a hub is not trivial. In our case we leave this blank for now, although in Chapter 7 we review how to configure a content type hub.

h. Report syndication import errors from Site Collections using this service application: Select this check box if you wish web applications that import the content types from the content type hub associated with this service to log errors that might occur on import or export of content types.

i. Add this service application to the farm's default list: Select this check box if you wish to add this service application to the Default proxy group of your farm. New web applications automatically create connections to service applications in the Default proxy group.

7. Click OK to create the new Managed Metadata Service Application. It might take a few minutes for SharePoint to create your new service, but once the process has been completed, you should see your new service listed in the Service Application List (see Figure 6-3). A common error might include incorrect or invalid credentials for your database or application pool.

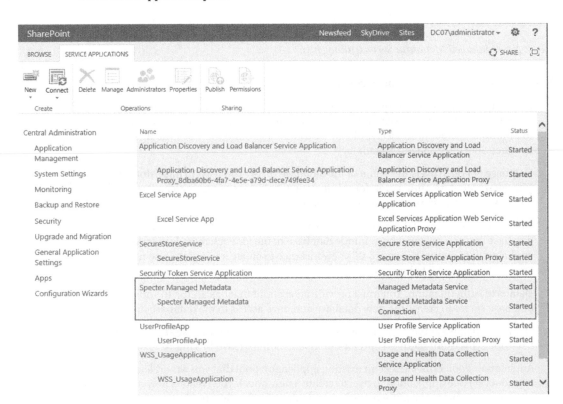

Figure 6-3. *After the new Managed Metadata Service Application has been created*

8. By default, a new Managed Metadata Service will be available to all web applications. You can configure a web application's Service Applications to not link to your new Managed Metadata Service if you need to. Navigate to Application Management ➤ Manage web applications ➤ Select your web application ➤ Service Connections (on the ribbon).

■ **Note** It might take a few minutes before you can use the Managed Metadata Service in your site collection.

At this point your site collection will have access to your new Metadata Service Application. Return to the root of your site collection, and navigate to the Term Store Management Tool (Site Settings ➤ Site Administration ➤ Term Store Management). You should now see your new metadata service application (see Figure 6-4).

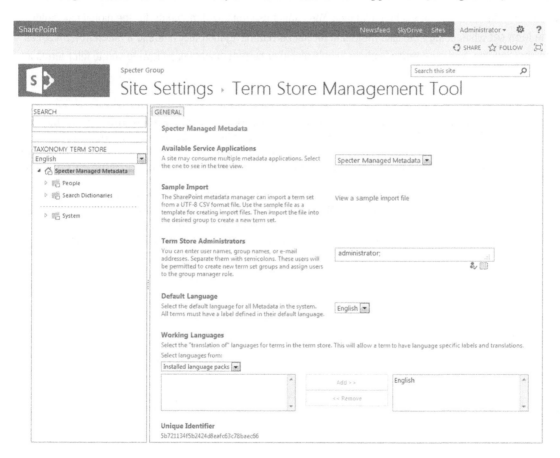

Figure 6-4. *Term Store Management Tool with available Metadata Service Application*

■ **Tip** PowerShell fans can configure a metadata service application using PowerShell. Learn more about how to use PowerShell cmdlets for metadata management from `http://sprwd.com/3fqk8uf`.

Create a Term Set

Once you have your Managed Metadata Service application configured on your farm and you have linked your web application to at least one metadata service application, you are ready to create a term set for your site navigation. In this walkthrough, we are going to create a term set that we intend to use for our top, global navigation bar.

■ **Tip** A site can only link to one term set for navigation. You cannot use managed metadata for the global navigation that binds to one term set while using managed metadata for the current navigation that binds to a different term set all within the same site. You can configure terms to show in only global or current navigation, allowing you to filter terms in one term set.

Within a particular site, there are multiple ways to load your site's Term Store Management Tool. One is the general method we have already used in the previous section: Use your Site Settings page, and within the Site Administration section, click Term store management. You may also access the Term Store Management Tool directly from the Navigation Settings page. A link to the Navigation Settings page is also found on the Site Settings page within the Look and Feel section under Navigation.

On the Navigation Settings page, if either the Global Navigation or Current Navigation has been selected to use Managed Navigation, a new section appears, Managed Navigation: Term Set. This section allows you to select the term set you wish this site to use for managed navigation. Beneath the term set selection box you will find a Term Store Management Tool link, shown in Figure 6-5, that also takes you directly to the Term Store Management Tool page.

Figure 6-5. *Term Store Management Tool access via Navigation Settings*

■ **Note** As of the printing of this book, Internet Explorer 9+ should be used to utilize the Term Store Management Tool, as many settings appear not to save correctly in other browsers.

Once you load the Term Set Management Tool, you should see a page similar to what we saw in Figure 6-4. You are now ready to add your Term Set. For this walkthrough, we will add a Term Set to the metadata service application, "Specter Managed Metadata" created in the previous section.

1. In the Term Store Management Tool, in the navigation pane found to the left, hover over and right-click your metadata service application, in our example, Specter Managed Metadata. In the drop-down menu that appears, click New Group to create a new group to hold our navigation term set. You can skip this step if you already have a group in which you wish to place your term set.

   If a drop-down menu does not appear when you click your metadata service application, you most likely do not have permissions to administer your application. Your account must be included in the Term Store Administrators list, seen in Figure 6-4.

2. For your new group, provide a group name. In our example we create a group named Navigation that will hold our navigation term set for our site and any other site or site collection that might require its own term set for navigation.

3. Once your new group has been created, the group's General tab will appear to the right. You can customize the group name, provide a description for this group, and manage group managers and contributors. This allows you to provide management rights to those users or user groups that need management access to this metadata group.

4. To create a new term set under your new group, right-click your new group and select New Term Set in the group drop-down menu.

5. A new term set appears under your Group. Provide your term set with a name, in our example Specter Global Navigation.

6. Once the term set has been created, its properties will appear to the right. The different properties found within each tab are explained in detail, but the two important properties we are most concerned with are found on the Intended Use and Custom Sort tabs.

   a. Click the Intended Use tab and select the Use this Term Set for Site Navigation check box. This allows this term set to be made available on our site's navigation settings page. This setting also provides additional properties for our terms within the term set that are unique to navigation. Click Save to update the term set.

   b. Click the Custom Sort tab and select Use custom sort order. This setting allows you to sort your terms manually so that they are listed in your navigation bar in the order you intend, not alphabetically by default. Once you add terms you can either return to this tab to modify the sort order of your terms or reorder your navigation terms directly in the navigation bar.

■ **Note**   We review managing navigation terms in the navigation bar later in this chapter in the section "Managing Navigation Quick Edit Mode."

---

7. You are now ready to add terms to your term set. Right-click your term set and on the term set drop-down list, click Add Term to add a new term. Once the term has been created, provide it a name and press Enter. You can now add another term, or right-click the term to create a child term. You can add as many terms, child terms, grandchild terms, and so on, as needed. Figure 6-6 shows our example term set with a series of terms that will be used by the Specter Group for its global navigation.

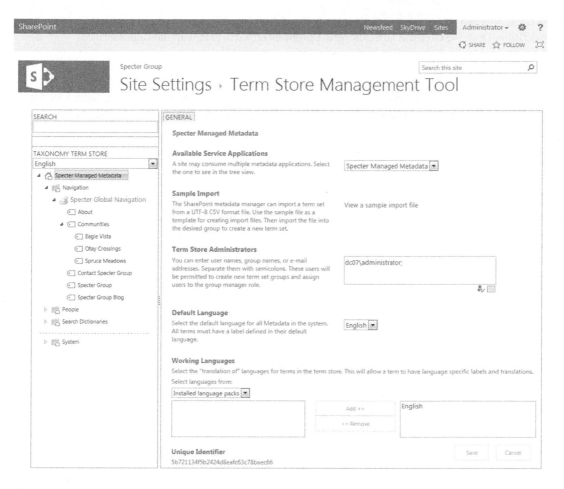

Figure 6-6. *Specter Global Navigation Term Set with related terms corresponding to the site map*

■ **Note**   For every term created, it would be best to have already created a new page that the term will reference, although this is not required. To learn how to create content pages from OOTB and custom page layouts, refer to Chapter 7.

Managing Terms

In the previous section we created a term set in our metadata service application. We then created terms and child terms that matched our site map as described in Chapter 3. You might notice that the term names we provided are not necessarily what we want displayed in our navigation bar. Further, the order of navigation terms is not correct. Once your terms have been created, you can manage term properties as well as the order of terms via the Term Store Management Tool.

By default, when you provide a term its name, your navigation bar will display the term name. To configure a particular term's properties, click a particular term in the left navigation pane of the Term Store Management Tool to load that term's property list. In this example we click the Specter Group term found under the Specter Global

Navigation term set we created in the previous section. This term is supposed to represent the Home link we require in our global navigation. Once we click this term, the term's property tabs will load with the General tab preselected.

■ **Note** The Navigation and Term-Driven Pages tabs are only available in term sets that have been configured for the Intended Use of Use this Term Set for Site Navigation. Review the earlier section "Create a Term Set" to see how to set this term set property.

Term Properties General Tab

The General tab shown in Figure 6-7 contains general properties for each term. For the purposes of general navigation, you will likely not need to modify any general properties. Note that the Default label contains the title that will appear in the term list for this term while also serving as the default value displayed in a navigation bar. This can be overwritten in the Navigation tab.

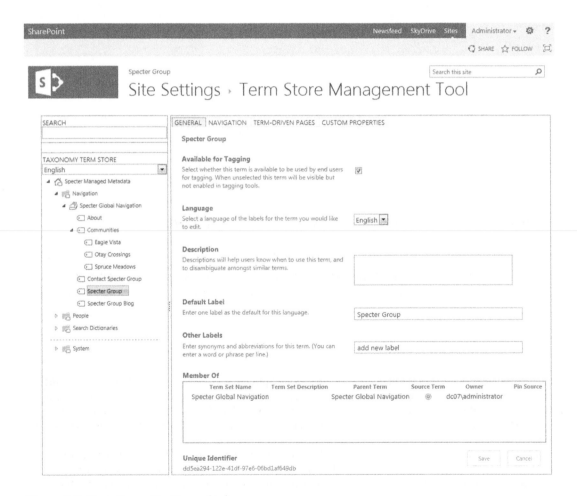

Figure 6-7. *Term Properties General tab*

Term Properties Navigation Tab

The Navigation tab shown in Figure 6-8 contains the core properties for configuring how a term will act within a navigation bar.

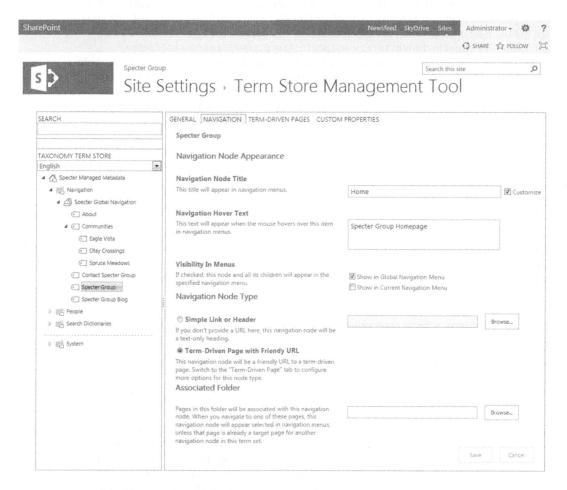

Figure 6-8. *Term Properties Navigation tab*

- Navigation Node Title: This title is what will appear in navigation menus. To customize this title you will need to select the Customize check box next to the title and then modify the title. Because we do not want to display Specter Group for a link back to our home page, we customize this title to Home.

- Navigation Hover Text: The text, if any, that should appear when the mouse hovers over this term in the navigation menu. This is optional but we set this to Specter Group Homepage.

- Visibility in Menus: These two options allow us to solve a potential issue with managed metadata-driven navigation for global and current navigation. Remember that a particular site can only link to one term set for navigation. If you want to use managed navigation for both global and current navigation, but you require different menu items in each navigation menu, you can use the Visibility in Menus options to select where this particular term should be displayed.

As an example, when you would like this term to only display in the global navigation, clear Show in Current Navigation Menu. In our case we want the home link to only show in the global menu so we clear Show in Current Navigation Menu.

- Navigation Node Type: Here we can set how we want this navigation node to link to its URL or page. If you want to link to a relative or absolute URL like we did in SharePoint 2010, or if you want to link to an outside URL, select Simple Link or Header and then provide a URL to the right. Examples might include `http://www.spectergroup.com/pages/contact.aspx`, `/pages/contact.aspx`, or even just `contact.aspx`. Because the navigation menu could appear on any page level of your site, it is recommended to always provide an absolute URL, though, never a relative URL. Note that there are cases when relative paths might be beneficial, including when you wish to develop your site in one location yet deploy it to a production environment.

■ **Tip** If this particular node needs to be a header and not a clickable link to another page, select Simple Link or Header and leave the address box to the right empty.

- If, on the other hand, you would like to create a friendly URL for this term, for example, instead of linking to `http://www.spectergroup.com/pages/about.aspx` to link to the About page you would like a friendly URL of `http://www.spectergroup.com/about`, select Term-Driven Page with Friendly URL. You can configure this friendly URL on the Term-Driven Page tab.

■ **Note** A friendly URL must have a target page within the current site collection. If you want to link a term to another site collection, even within the same web application, you will need to configure this term to use Simple Link or Header. You may not use a friendly URL to link to the other site collection's pages. However, a single content page can have multiple friendly URLs.

- Associated Folder: Often when browsing through a site, it is helpful for visitors to know what section of the site they are in. One common method is to highlight the node in the navigation bar that relates to the section they are currently viewing. As an example, say a visitor is on the Spruce Meadows page in the community area. It might be helpful to highlight the Community tab in the navigation menu. Because friendly URLs are no longer directly associated with site structure, the Associated Folder allows you to set a folder that contains pages that should highlight this navigation node when a site visitor navigates to one of the folder's pages.

- The folder in question does not have to exist in your site structure; rather the folder may exist in your site structure (i.e., /pages) or only in friendly URLs. As an example, refer to the two pages in Table 6-1 along with Figure 6-8 for a visual example.

Table 6-1. Example Friendly URLs With Their Associated Target Pages

Term	Friendly URL	Target Page
Communities	/communities	/pages/communities.aspx
Spruce Meadows	/communities/spruce-meadows	/pages/spruce-meadows.aspx

If the Associated Folder for the term Communities is set to /communities, then whenever a visitor navigates to /communities/spruce-meadows, the term Communities in the navigation bar is highlighted as SharePoint adds the class "selected" to the Communities list item in the rendered HTML.

■ **Tip** Before switching to a different Term Property tab, be sure to click Save at the bottom of the existing tab to save any changes you made.

Term Properties Term-Driven Pages Tab

The Term-Driven Pages tab shown in Figure 6-9 contains properties that allow us to configure what the friendly URL looks like and what page should actually be loaded when a visitor navigates to this friendly URL.

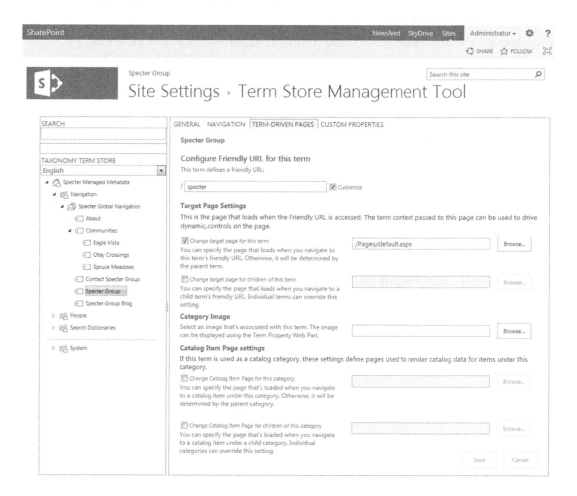

Figure 6-9. *Term Properties Term-Driven Pages tab*

- Configure Friendly URL for this term: By default, the friendly URL will be the term name with spaces replaced by - and other special characters removed. If you would like to customize the friendly URL, select the Customized check box and provide the new friendly URL. In our case we change specter-group to just home. This gives us an absolute URL of `http://www.spectergroup.com/home`, although we only need to provide "home" in the friendly URL text box.

- Target Page Settings: You can override an existing default target for this term that might have been set by its parent by providing a target page for this term, say `/pages/default.aspx` for our home page. Remember that the target page must be local to the current site collection. You may also provide a default target for all child terms of this particular term. Child terms can always override this default target on their own Term-Driven Pages tab.

- Category Image: If you would like to associate an image with this term, you can set the location of that image. By default this image will not be displayed in a navigation menu, nor would it be displayed on a particular page associated with this term, but you can reference and display this image using the Term Property Web Part.

- Catalog Item Page settings: The last two settings on this tab provide the targets for pages that are loaded when this term is used as a catalog category. In the case of our global navigation, this is not needed and thus is ignored.

Customize Term Order

When you first create a term set, then add terms to the term set, terms will be automatically sorted alphabetically. This is also true of child terms added to parent terms. Normally the terms will need to be sorted manually and fortunately this is an easy task. To provide a custom order for a set of terms, click the parent term set or term depending on which level you wish to order. In our example, we click the Specter Global Navigation term set to order its child terms. Note that ordering the child terms under the Communities term can be handled the same way. Once the term set (or term) properties loads, click the Custom Sort tab to load the properties page, which allows us to customize the sort order.

■ **Note**   Only terms with child terms will display the Custom Sort tab.

To provide your own custom sort order, select Use custom sort order. As soon as you do, the child terms will appear below the sort options, allowing us to set the order in which we want the terms displayed. The lower the number, the sooner on the list it will appear. Click Save to save your term order. In Figure 6-10, notice the old sort order highlighted on the left and the new sort order we wish highlighted to the right. In Figure 6-11 you can see the new sort order of the terms, highlighted on the left.

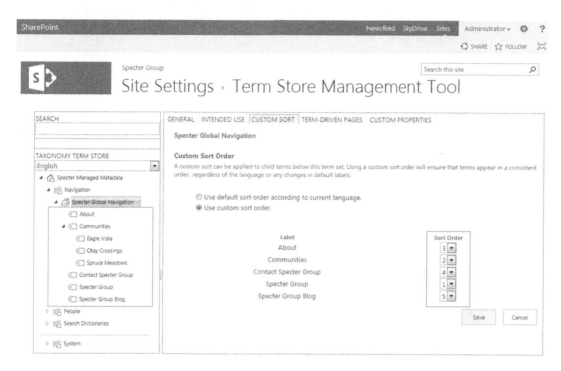

Figure 6-10. *Custom Sort tab*

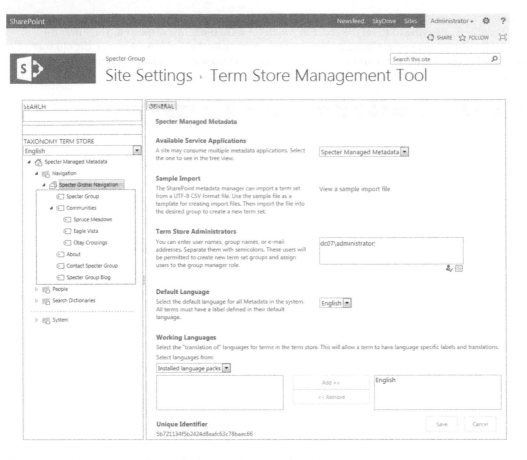

Figure 6-11. *Custom sorted terms in Specter Group navigation term set*

Set a Term Set for Navigation

At this point we have created and configured a metadata service application in our SharePoint 2013 farm to store our term sets. We then created a term set using the Term Store Management Tool within our working site collection. We finally created, configured, and ordered our set of terms that represents the site map we created in Chapter 3. It is now time to modify our site's navigation properties to use our term set.

1. From your root site in your site collection, navigation to your Site Settings page.

2. In your root site's Site Settings page, in the Look and Feel section, click Navigation to load your site's Navigation Settings page.

3. Configure Global Navigation to use Managed Navigation: The navigation items will be represented using a Managed Metadata term set.

4. Once you select the Managed Navigation option, a new section appears lower down on the Navigation Settings page entitled Managed Navigation: Term Set (see Figure 6-12). You should already see your Managed Metadata Service, in our case Specter Managed Metadata. Drill down the settings tree until you see your navigation term set, in our case Specter Global Navigation, found in the Navigation group.

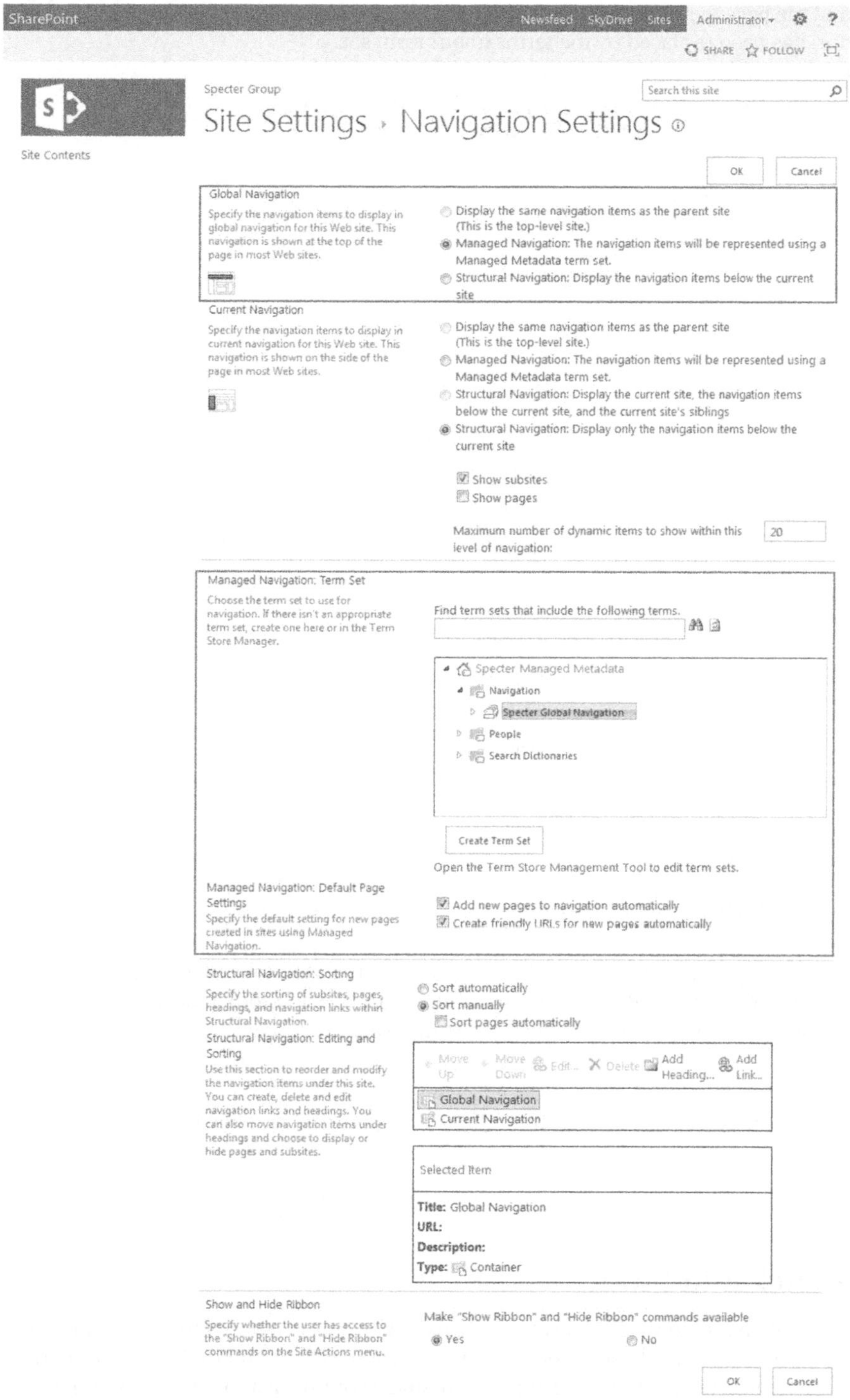

Figure 6-12. Navigation Settings configured to use managed navigation for global navigation

5.   Click OK at the bottom of the page to save your settings. Referring to Figure 6-13, notice that the global navigation has been replaced by the terms in our term set.

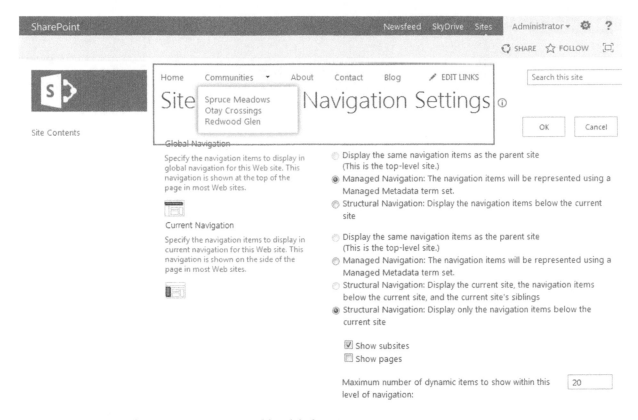

Figure 6-13. Managed navigation term set used for global navigation

By default, new pages you add to your site after you have configured your site to use managed navigation will automatically be added to your term set and friendly URLs will also be generated. You can modify these settings by clearing the check boxes within the Managed Navigation: Default Page Settings section.

■ **Note**   You can also create a new term set as well as open the Term Store Management Tool directly from the Navigation Settings page.

Managing Navigation Quick Edit Mode

An excellent addition to managed navigation includes the ability to managed a navigation bar directly inline, meaning that if you are logged into your site with an account with sufficient permissions, you will see an Edit Links button to the right of (or below) your navigation menu. This gives you the ability to manage your navigation menus without having to return directly to the Term Store Management Tool. Using the inline Edit Links feature, you can show and hide links, rename a link's display title, reorder links by dragging and dropping them in place, manage submenu links, and even add new links.

■ **Note**   Once a link has been created you can only edit the target URL using the Term Store Management Tool.

If you wish to create a new link with a friendly URL you need to use the Term Store Management Tool. Quick Edit mode does not give you all of the tools associated with the Term Store Management Tool, but it does provide access to many features you might require when quickly updating the navigation. We review the available Quick Edit Mode actions next. Review Figure 6-14 for a visual example.

Figure 6-14. *Managed navigation Quick Edit mode key elements and actions*

Show or Hide a Link

A visible link will include an open eye icon as marked by Visible Link in Figure 6-14. When you click this icon, the link is hidden in the standard navigation menu and the icon is replaced with a closed eye icon, as marked by Invisible Link in Figure 6-14. Clicking this closed eye icon causes a link to again be displayed.

Edit a Link Title

Click a link title to enter an edit mode to rename the link as well as to review the link's target URL or friendly URL.

Reorder Links

If you click a link title, you can drag the link anywhere else in the navigation menu, including moving the link to a submenu, by hovering over the submenu's parent link. This causes the submenu to appear so that you can drop the link into the submenu.

Managed Submenu Links

A down arrow will appear to the right of a link that has a submenu. If you click that arrow, the submenu appears and you can manage submenu links in the same manner as you manage top-level links. If a submenu link has an arrow pointing to the right then this sublink has its own submenu. Click the right arrow to make its submenu appear.

Add New Links

There are two ways to add new links via Quick Edit mode. The first is to drag and drop a link into the menu where the text Drag and drop link here is displayed. The second way is to click (+) link found at the right of the Quick Edit menu. When you click (+) link, an Add a link dialog box appears, allowing you to provide the display text as well as the target URL. If you wish to link to a friendly URL that does not yet have a term associated with it, you will need to create the link via the Term Store Management Tool.

Share Managed Navigation Across Site Collections

A limitation to managed navigation is that a term set can only be used by one site, unless subsites are configured to use the parent site's navigation. Primarily this will cause a problem when two or more site collections are supposed to have the same navigation menu. When you attempt to configure a site to use a term set for managed navigation already used by a different site, the error shown in Figure 6-15 will appear.

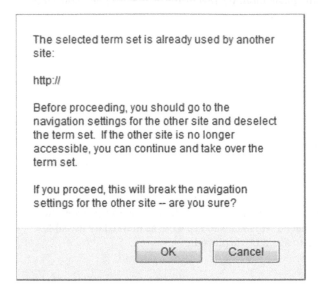

The selected term set is already used by another site:

http://

Before proceeding, you should go to the navigation settings for the other site and deselect the term set. If the other site is no longer accessible, you can continue and take over the term set.

If you proceed, this will break the navigation settings for the other site -- are you sure?

OK   Cancel

Figure 6-15. *Warning when attempting to use a term set for a second site*

If you click OK, the first site that was using this term set for managed navigation will no longer display the navigation menu for which the term set was being used.

Fortunately term sets offer a solution. When term sets were first introduced in SharePoint 2010, an option to reuse a term was available. Reusing a term would create a linked term within two term sets. An administrator could then modify a reused term in any term set and all replicated terms would be updated. SharePoint 2013 provides for reusing terms, but it also provides a new option, pinning a term. When you pin a term from one term set to another, the pinned term, in the destination term set, is created as read only. Changes to properties are only allowed at the source term. When used for a term in a term set that is intended for navigation, this holds true, although properties in the Navigation and Term-Driven tabs can be updated in each term and changes are not replicated.

■ **Note**   To learn how to reuse a term set in cross site publishing, please refer to Chapter 8.

Reuse Terms with Pinning

Creating a term set for each site collection in an overall web site strategy using pinning is simple to set up, although a few pitfalls exist. First, you have to create and manage a term set per site collection. You will only have to pin first-tier terms to the destination term set, as child terms will automatically be replicated. Second, if you intend to use friendly URLs, the friendly URL will always include the path to each site collection, which would mean you will have multiple apparent paths to a particular page, even if only one target page exists.

As an example of this concern, consider our About Us page with a physical location of www.spectergroup.com/pages/aboutus.aspx. We can create a term, About Specter, with a friendly URL of "about," which translates to www.spectergroup.com/about and a target URL of /pages/aboutus.aspx. Remember that the target page for a friendly URL has to be a relative path; it cannot be an absolute URL.

If we create a second term set for our Communities subsite collection, and then pin the About Specter term to the second term set, all properties stay the same. When you navigate to the Communities site collection and click About in the navigation menu, you will notice that you are directed to the address www.spectergroup.com/sites/community/about, not www.spectergroup.com/about. Both friendly URLs have the same target (i.e., www.spectergroup.com/pages/aboutus.aspx) but different visible URLs. This is normally not an issue for site visitors but is worth considering.

Follow these steps to create a term set with pinned terms from a source term set.

1. In the Term Store Management Tool, right-click the Navigation group we created in the previous section and click New Term Set. Provide a new name and press Enter.

2. Configure this term set just as we did in the earlier section, "Create a Term Set."

3. Right-click the new term set and click Pin Term with Children. A dialog box will appear that displays your Taxonomy Term Store. Click the Navigation term group and notice that term sets are listed, except the term set to which you are attempting to pin a term. This is expected, as you cannot pin a term within the same term set. Expand the terms in the source term set, in our case Specter Global Navigation, and select a parent term to pin. Click OK.

4. The term from the source term set is now pinned in your destination term set. Notice the icon next to the pinned term in both the source and destination term sets. The source term displays an icon that tells you this term is being reused. The destination term displays an icon showing that it is a pinned term. Refer to Figure 6-16 for an example of pinned terms. If you click either the source or destination term, on its General tab, at the bottom, you also can see membership information, including how the term is shared and pinned.

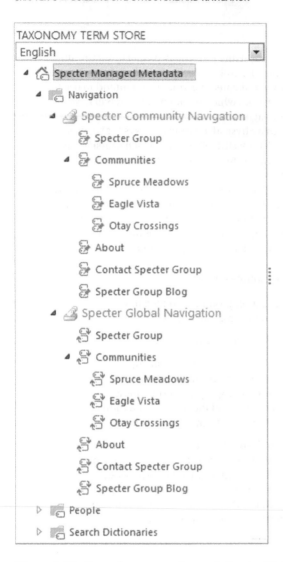

Figure 6-16. Terms from source term set, Specter Global Navigation, pinned to the destination term set, Specter Community Navigation

5. Repeat step 3 for each top-level term in your source term set to replicate your term set structure.

6. You can now configure your other site collection to use this new term set for its managed navigation by following the steps previously outlined in the earlier section "Set a Term Set for Navigation."

How SharePoint 2013 Builds the Navigation Bar

Before we can begin successfully styling SharePoint's global navigation as well as its current navigation, it is important to know how SharePoint renders the navigation in HTML. First, both the global navigation menu and the current navigation menu use very similar HTML. The primary difference between the two being a class that SharePoint adds to the containing div just before the menu's root unordered list, either `ms-core-listMenu-horizontalBox` for the global navigation in horizontal display mode or `ms-core-listMenu-verticalBox` for the current navigation in vertical display mode. If you have branded navigation menus in SharePoint 2010 in the past, then the HTML and associated CSS in SharePoint 2013 will look similar.

Add the Top Navigation Snippet to a Master Page

Before we can look at the HTML SharePoint generates, we must first add the Top Navigation snippet to our HTML master page. Load Design Manager in a browser, navigate to 4. Edit Master Pages, and click the master page to which you wish to add the Top Navigation snippet. Once the Master Page Preview page loads, click Snippets in the upper right corner.

■ **Note**   For an in-depth review of the Snippet Gallery available for master pages in Design Manager, refer to Chapter 4.

In the Snippet Gallery, click the Top Navigation icon found in the Navigation section of the ribbon to load the Top Navigation component. As we saw in Chapter 4, we can customize the snippet in the right pane. The HTML we need to add to our master page is located at the bottom left under HTML Snippet. Before we copy the HTML snippet to the clipboard, we need to make a few changes. Refer to Figure 6-17 for an overview of the Top Navigation snippet in the Snippet Gallery and Table 6-2 for explanations of the properties.

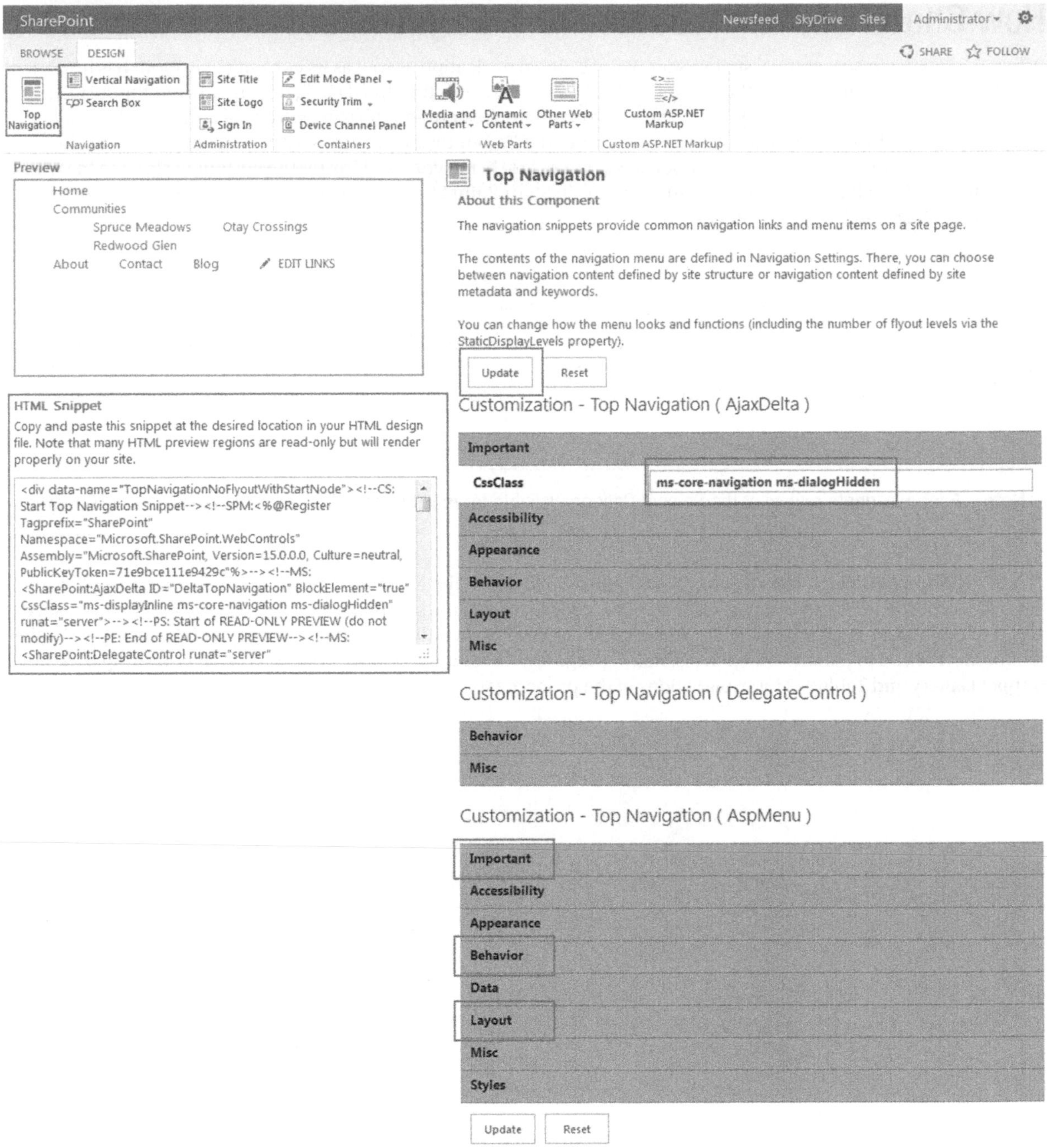

Figure 6-17. *In Design Manager's HTML master page Snippet Manager, configure the Top Navigation snippet*

Table 6-2. *Explanations of the Top Navigation Properties*

Property	Explanation
CssClass (Top Navigation (AjaxDelta))	We remove ms-displayinline as that class will cause the navigation items to include display: inline-block, which we do not require based on how our navigation was prototyped.
AdjustForShowStartingNode	By setting this to true, the number of static display levels is corrected when you have only one static level of navigation based on managed navigation, but two levels for structured navigation.
StaticDisplayLevels	We normally would show two levels of navigation at all times with structured navigation, whereas with managed navigation we actually only want to show one. By setting this property to 2 and AdjustForShowStartingNode to true, this Top Navigation snippet works for both structured and managed navigation. In general the StaticDisplayLevels property sets how many levels of your navigation structure to show as static links.
CssClass (Top Navigation (AspMenu))	If we want to add a class to the direct parent of our navigation unordered list, we can set the CssClass for the AspMenu.
MaximumDynamicDisplayLevels	We are requesting that up to two additional levels of navigation are displayed in dynamic menus. In general the MaximumDynamicDisplayLevels property sets how many levels, after the static levels are displayed, to then show as dynamic menus.
RenderingMode	There are two rendering modes, List and Table. Table is the SharePoint 2007 rendering mode that generates a table for the navigation bar. We prefer the navigation bar be rendered as an unordered list.

1. Under Customization - Top Navigation (AjaxDelta), select Important and set CssClass to ms-core-navigation ms-dialogHidden.

2. Under Customization - Top Navigation (AspMenu), make the following changes:

    a. Important ➤ AdjustForShowStartingNode = True

    b. Important ➤ StaticDisplayLevels = 2

    c. Appearance ➤ CssClass = nav-container

    d. Behavior ➤ MaximumDynamicDisplayLevels = 2

    e. Layout ➤ RenderingMode = List

3. Click Update to update the HTML Snippet window. We can now copy and paste the HTML snippet to our master page.

■ **Note**   We investigate static and dynamic levels of navigation in greater detail in the section "Static Levels and Dynamic Levels" later in this chapter.

To add the Top Navigation snippet to our master page, we open our custom master page we added and updated in Chapters 4 and 5 in our web site editor tool. We need to find the location where the Top Navigation snippet should go, so we look for the HTML comment <!--nav snippet-->, and its corresponding end tag, <!--end nav snippet--> (see Listing 6-1).

Listing 6-1. Original Static Navigation From Master Page

```
...
<!--nav snippet-->
<ul class="root">
  <li class="current-menu-item"><a href="index.html">HOME</a></li>
  <li><a href="about.html">ABOUT</a></li>
  ...
</ul>
<!--end nav snippet-->
...
```

■ **Note** During the HTML prototype phase of your project, it is best to include HTML comments that will help you find components that should be replaced by snippets similar to `<!--nav snippet-->`.

We are now ready to replace the HTML in Listing 6-1 with the Top Navigation snippet we just created, which should look like Listing 6-2.

Listing 6-2. Top Navigation HTML Snippet Added to Our Custom Master Page (Preview HTML and Some Properties Removed for Readiblity)

```
...
<div class="nav nav-collapse collapse">
  <!--nav snippet-->
  <!--CS: Start Top Navigation Snippet-->
  <!--SPM:<%@Register Tagprefix="SharePoint" Namespace="Microsoft.SharePoint.WebControls" %>-->
  <!--MS:<SharePoint:AjaxDelta ID="DeltaTopNavigation"
        CssClass="ms-core-navigation ms-dialogHidden">-->
    <!--PS: Start of READ-ONLY PREVIEW (do not modify)--><!--PE: End of READ-ONLY PREVIEW-->
    <!--MS:<SharePoint:DelegateControl runat="server" ControlId="TopNavigationDataSource">-->
      <!--PS: Start of READ-ONLY PREVIEW (do not modify)-->...<!--PE: End of READ-ONLY PREVIEW-->
      <!--MS:<Template_Controls>-->
        <!--MS:<asp:SiteMapDataSource SiteMapProvider="SPNavigationProvider" ID="topSiteMap">-->
        <!--ME:</asp:SiteMapDataSource>-->
      <!--ME:</Template_Controls>-->
    <!--ME:</SharePoint:DelegateControl>-->
    <a name="startNavigation"></a>
    <!--MS:<asp:ContentPlaceHolder ID="PlaceHolderTopNavBar" runat="server">-->
      <!--MS: <SharePoint:AspMenu ID="TopNavigationMenu" runat="server" DataSourceID="topSiteMap"
          UseSimpleRendering="true" Orientation="Horizontal" StaticDisplayLevels="2"
          AdjustForShowStartingNode="true" MaximumDynamicDisplayLevels="2"
          CssClass=" nav-container"> -->
        <!--PS: Start of READ-ONLY PREVIEW (do not modify)-->...
        <!--PE: End of READ-ONLY PREVIEW-->
      <!--ME:</SharePoint:AspMenu>-->
    <!--ME:</asp:ContentPlaceHolder>-->
    <!--PS: Start of READ-ONLY PREVIEW (do not modify)--><!--PE: End of READ-ONLY PREVIEW-->
  <!--ME:</SharePoint:AjaxDelta>-->
  <!--CE: End Top Navigation Snippet-->
  <!--end nav snippet-->
  <!--used if we want to have a select dropdown for nav on mobile-->
```

```
  <div id="nav-select-holder">
  </div>
</div>
...
```

Save the master page and load your home page in a browser. We are assuming that the custom master page has been set as your site's Custom Master Page. The top navigation will probably not look correct. We learn how to style our top navigation in the section "Style and Make the Navigation Bar Responsive" later in this chapter. If we open the source view of our home page in the browser and look for the comment `<!--nav snippet-->` again, we see that the Top Navigation snippet produced the HTML code in Listing 6-3. We have removed IDs as well as other HTML properties or tags that are not important for our understanding of the HTML and each tag's associated classes or styling.

Listing 6-3. HTML Produced by SharePoint When Rendering the Top Navigation Snippet

```
<div class="nav nav-collapse collapse">
  <!--nav snippet-->
  <div id="DeltaTopNavigation" class="ms-core-navigation ms-dialogHidden">
    <a name="startNavigation"></a>
    <div id="" class="nav-container noindex ms-core-listMenu-horizontalBox">
      <ul class="root static">
        <li class="static"><a class="static" href="/home"><span>
            <span class="menu-item-text">Home</span></span></a></li>
        <li class="static">...<!--Additional top level links-->...</li>
        <li class="static"><a class="static" href="/communities"><span>
            <span class="menu-item-text">Communities</span></span></a>
            <ul class="static">
              <li class="dynamic"><a class="dynamic" href="/communities/spruce-meadows"><span>
                  <span class="menu-item-text">Spruce Meadows</span></span></a></li>
              <li class="dynamic">...<!--Additional community links-->...</li>
            </ul>
        </li>
        <li class="static"><a class="static" href="/contact"><span>
            <span class="menu-item-text">Contact</span></span></a></li>
      </ul>
    </div>
  </div>
  <!--end nav snippet-->
</div>
```

There are a few aspects of this HTML that we want to pay attention to. First, notice how all of our top-level links (Home, Communities, About, etc.) are all within the same `<ul>` tag. This is a benefit of managed navigation because with structured navigation this is not the case. With structured navigation, Home is the only top-level list item; the other top-level links are actually in a sublist. This can cause branding difficulties that managed navigation helps avert. Refer to Listing 6-4 to see a standard structured navigation menu rendered by SharePoint in the next section.

■ **Note**   To learn more about the difference between structured navigation HTML and how static and dynamic levels play a different role in HTML, review the next section, "Static Levels and Dynamic Levels."

Also in Listing 6-3, look in the first `div` with the ID of `DeltaTopNavigation`. Notice the class value, `"ms-core-navigation ms-dialogHidden"` is the same that we set in Customization - Top Navigation (AjaxDelta) ➤ Important ➤ CssClass. Look down to the next `div`, the `div` with the ID of `""` (i.e. it has no ID). Notice how this class value contains "nav-container", which we set in Customization - Top Navigation (AspMenu) ➤ Appearance ➤ CssClass. Many snippets might have different properties that can affect specific elements of itself both before and after final rendering to the client browser.

The rendered HTML in Listing 6-3 is much more responsive friendly. Next, notice the containing div has an ID of DeltaTopNavigation. We can use this ID to help style the navigation elements for only this top navigation menu if we do not want to style all unordered lists with a class of ms-core-listMenu-horizontalBox the same. The remaining HTML appears just as it did in SharePoint 2010. Static list items will always have a class static applied to them and list items with dynamic children will also contain the class dynamic-children. A dynamic unordered list will contain the class dynamic as will its child list items and child anchor tags. Using a combination of these classes we can quickly brand the navigation menu as well as make it responsive which we cover in the section "Style and Make the Navigation Bar Responsive" later in this chapter.

Static Levels and Dynamic Levels

Two important settings for how navigation will function include the number of static and dynamic levels you wish to display in a navigation menu. When you create a navigation snippet, either top or vertical, within the Customization - Top Navigation (AspMenu) section, under Important you can set the number of StaticDisplayLevels. Under Behavior you can set the number of MaximumDynamicDisplayLevels. If you consider the hierarchy of links in your navigation structure, you can consider the level of a given link as the distance it is from the top-most level, which starts at 1. In our term set, Home, About, Blog, Community, and Contact are all at level 1 and the three links under Community are at level 2. Our StaticDisplayLevels setting dictates how many static levels to show on the navigation menu, meaning navigation items to always show. The MaximumDynamicDisplayLevels setting thus controls how many levels should be displayed in dynamic menus under our static items.

With managed navigation, this creates a beneficial outcome that we can use to our advantage. In particular in SharePoint 2010 and SharePoint 2013 structured navigation, the home page was always considered the first static level and all of our other top-level links were the second static level of navigation. The catch is that the second static level is an unordered list of list items, but was included in the first level's first list item. This rendered the HTML in Listing 6-4.

Listing 6-4. Sample HTML Rendering of Structured Navigation (Certain Tags and Tag Properties Removed for Simplicity)

```
<div class="nav nav-collapse collapse">
    <!--nav snippet-->
    <div id="DeltaTopNavigation" class="ms-core-navigation ms-dialogHidden">
        <a name="startNavigation"></a>
        <div id="" class="nav-container ms-core-listMenu-horizontalBox">
            <ul class="root static">
                <li class="static"><a class="static">Home</a>
                    <ul class="static">
                        <li class="static">...<!--Additional top level links-->...</li>
                        <li class="static"><a class="static">Communities</a>
                            <ul class="static">
                                <li class="dynamic"><a class="dynamic">Spruce Meadows</a></li>
                                <li class="dynamic">...<!--Additional community links-->...</li>
                            </ul>
                        </li>
                        <li class="static"><a class="static">Contact</span></span></a></li>
                    </ul>
                </li>
            </ul>
        </div>
    </div>
</div>
```

```
    <!--end nav snippet-->
    <!--used if we want to have a select dropdown for nav on mobile-->
    <div id="nav-select-holder"></div>
</div>
```

Having a list and a sublist of items that should all be displayed at the same level can cause a headache in responsive design. We might want to collapse the navigation for smaller devices based on a particular node's navigation level. We have to somehow handle the fact that the first two levels count as the first level and all additional levels of navigation are displayed one level at a time.

With managed navigation, we can have all static links on one level, thus alleviating many of our initial headaches. The rendered HTML in Listing 6-3 is much easier to style, as all top-level links are in our root unordered list. This also allows us to leverage the Bootstrap framework to make the navigation bar responsive.

Style and Make the Navigation Bar Responsive

In the preceding section, we added the Top Navigation snippet to our master page in Design Manager. We then looked at the HTML SharePoint generates when it renders the Top Navigation snippet. We must now view the top navigation in the browser, fix any style issues that arise when using SharePoint for our navigation instead of static navigation, and finally look at how to make our navigation responsive.

Style the Navigation Bar

We saw in Listing 6-3 how SharePoint 2013 renders navigation in HTML. Let us now look at how this looks in a browser and fix any styles that SharePoint might have tweaked (see Figure 6-18).

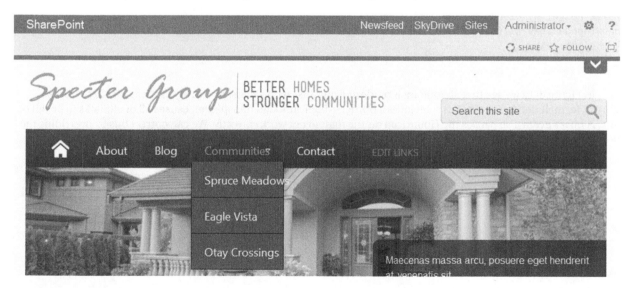

Figure 6-18. *Top Navigation as displayed in a browser after snippet insertion*

■ **Tip**   Although our examples that follow might be specific to our demo design, the theory and practice we use to solve these problems will help you solve specific problems you run into when converting your navigation to managed navigation with SharePoint.

Here are the known issues: The navigation menu has been dropped down by one pixel. The drop-down arrow rendered by SharePoint for Communities should be hidden or moved to the right. The drop-down menu does not appear correct. The Edit Links font color is incorrect and there are spacing issues in Quick Edit mode. We review each problem and how to fix it. The replacement CSS is provided in Listing 6-5.

Listing 6-5. CSS Updated to Fix Layout of Top Navigation Snippet Rendered HTML

```
/*top nav*/
/*center menu*/
nav#topnav .ms-core-listMenu-horizontalBox {
   display: block;
}
/*hide or provide padding for downdown arrow*/
nav#topnav .ms-core-listMenu-horizontalBox .dynamic-children.additional-background {
   padding-right: 20px;
   /*background: transparent none;*/ /*unhide to hide the down arrow*/
}
/*remove border from menu items*/
nav#topnav .ms-core-listMenu-horizontalBox li.static > .ms-core-listMenu-item {
   border: none;
}
/*correct location of dropdown menu*/
nav#topnav .nav ul.root > li ul {
   border: none;
   top: 54px !important;
}
/*fix height of dropdown menu list items*/
nav#topnav .nav ul.root > li ul li a {
   height: 25px;
}
```

In Figure 6-19 we see that SharePoint is rendering our links with a class, ms-core-listMenu-horizontalBox. This style, included in corev15.css, includes a border, which although transparent, causes all of our links to be out of line. A hover event also causes the Home icon on the right to not work correctly. We can correct this by overriding the border style to "border: none;".

Figure 6-19. *Additional border on items*

Figure 6-20 shows that SharePoint adds a span with class `dynamic-children` for list items with dynamic menus. Normally this would have right padding to provide space for the arrow, but our styles are overriding this, as we removed the padding and margin for all children of unordered lists within nav#topnav `.nav`. We can either add space for the down arrow or hide the down arrow. In our walkthrough, we will add the right padding back in by providing a more targeted style, nav `.navbar` `.nav` `.dynamic-children.additional-background`.

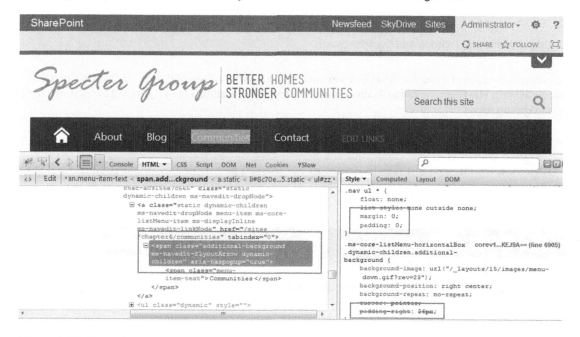

Figure 6-20. *Drop-down arrow span*

Figure 6-21 shows us two problems that must be addressed: The drop-down menu placement is incorrect and the drop-down menu itself is not the correct size. As we see highlighted in Figure 6-21, SharePoint provides drop-down functionality that is overriding our menu placement as well as drop-down menu width. We can solve this by overriding nav#topnav .nav ul.root > li > ul as well as children of dynamic menus with nav#topnav .nav ul.root ul.dynamic ul.dynamic.

Figure 6-21. *Drop-down menu location and border*

Using the same technique of using our developer toolbar, we can find the causes of the Edit Links and Quick Edit mode style issues as well. The CSS required to fix these issues is provided in Listing 6-6. In Figure 6-22 we can see the corrected top navigation menu.

Figure 6-22. *Top navigation in inline Edit mode with updated CSS*

Listing 6-6. CSS Updated to Fix Layout of Top Navigation While in Inline Edit Mode

```
/*edit links font*/
nav#topnav .nav .ms-metadata {
    font-size: inherit;
    font: inherit;
    color: #fff;
}
/*images within nav should not use respponsive properties*/
nav#topnav .nav img {max-width: none;}
nav#topnav .nav .ms-navedit-hidespan {display: block;}
/*force the edit node text icon into a box*/
nav#topnav .nav a.ms-navedit-hidelink {
    padding: 21px 0px 0px !important;
    margin: 0px !important;
    display: block !important;
    overflow: hidden !important;
    height: 17px !important;
}
/*remove border added to node table*/
nav#topnav .nav .ms-core-listMenuEdit, nav#topnav .nav .ms-core-listMenuEdit:hover {
    border: none;
}
/*edit node text padding*/
nav#topnav .nav .ms-navedit-hiddenAppendArea {
    padding: 20px 10px 10px;
    color: #F3E4C8;
}
/*edit link node text on dynamic menus requires background*/
nav#topnav .nav .dynamic .ms-navedit-deletelinkCell {
    background: #333333 none;
}
/*add a link should float left*/
nav#topnav .nav .ms-navedit-addNewLink {
    display: inline-block !important;
}
/*bump save and cancel buttons down*/
nav#topnav .nav .ms-navedit-editButton {
    margin-top: 20px;
}
nav#topnav .nav .ms-core-listMenu-horizontalBox span.ms-list-addnew-imgSpan16 {
    vertical-align: middle;
    margin-right: 5px;
}
/*reset the first node to not show a home icon, rather text*/
nav#topnav .nav ul.root > li.ms-navedit-dropNode:first-child {
    height: auto;
    padding: 0px;
}
nav#topnav .nav ul.root > li.ms-navedit-dropNode:first-child a {
    background: transparent none;
    height: auto;
```

```
  overflow: visible;
  padding: 21px 20px;
  text-indent: 0;
  white-space: nowrap;
  width: auto;
}
/*end quick edit mode*/
```

Make the Navigation Bar Responsive

The general problem we are attempting to solve when making a navigation menu responsive is how our navigation menu will work on mobile devices or devices that have a smaller viewport. Further, how can we display a complex navigation structure that works well for desktop users as well as mobile users? To compound our problems, we must also consider what functionality is available on any given client, most pertinent to navigation, the hover or mouse-over event. Many tablets and other mobile devices do not include the ability to react to a hover action so our navigation must take this into account. By default, the top navigation bar SharePoint generates for us depends on a hover event for a drop- down menu to appear and we must handle this first. After we see how we can trap the hover/mouse-over event, we will cover three methods of making a navigation bar responsive with their pros and cons: floating navigation, drop-down navigation, and collapsing navigation.

Hover and Mouse-Over Navigation and SharePoint

Multi-tiered navigation menus often provide access to submenus via a hover or mouse-over event. If you have worked with the SharePoint 2010 top navigation menu, this will be familiar to you, as this was how SharePoint 2010 provided access to submenus. In the previous section we mentioned that the HTML produced by SharePoint when rendering the navigation control is the same for SharePoint 2010 and SharePoint 2013. This would lead us to conclude that access to submenus would be the same as well, and we would be correct.

As we have already mentioned, we cannot depend on a client device, such as a smart phone or tablet, having a hover or mouse-over event. More generally, not all of your site visitors will have a mouse any longer. We need a way to supplement SharePoint's top navigation menu to provide a way to click an icon to open a submenu. If we want to use the Top Navigation snippet we will have to add JavaScript code to provide this functionality.

In Listing 6-7 through Listing 6-9, we will once again leverage jQuery to supplement SharePoint's OOTB navigation. We will grab an instance of the top navigation menu, then looping through each menu item, check to see if any child menu items are available. If so, we modify the parent item to provide a click event as well as the hover event to cause a menu to appear or disappear.

In Listing 6-7, we trigger our `BindTopNav` function after our document is ready by using the alias safe `jQuery(document).read(function($) {});` function. In `BindTopNav` we remove the `s4-tn` class as SharePoint 2013 adds styles that we do not want to have to worry about. We then grab a reference to our navigation unordered list, `#topnav ul.root`. Using this reference, we loop through every anchor tag (link) that includes the class `dynamic-children` that SharePoint adds to any menu item with a submenu.

For each such anchor found, we bind a new jQuery hover event to the anchor's parent `li` element, and then bind a jQuery click event to not only the anchor but also anchor's child span as well. We need to use a little math to determine where the user clicked (or touched), be it the anchor text or the down arrow. In Listing 6-8 and Listing 6-9 we introduce our custom `HoverTopNav` function as well as our custom `DropTopNav` function.

Listing 6-7. jQuery to Override the SharePoint OOTB Top Menu Hover Drop-Down

```
jQuery(document).ready(function($) {
   BindTopNav($);
});
function BindTopNav($) {
   /*grab top nav SP generated list*/
   var u = $('#topnav ul.root');
   if (u.length > 0) {
      /*loop through every nav item that has dynamic children*/
      u.find('a.dynamic-children').each(function() {
         /*get current link parent li and first child span*/
         var l = $(this).parent('li');
         var s = $(this).children('span').eq(0);
         /*override parent li hover event to show dropdown*/
         l.hover(
            function () {HoverTopNav($, $(this),'');},
            function () {HoverTopNav($, $(this),'o');}
         );
         /*trap link click*/
         $(this).bind('click',function(e) {
            /*do math to determine if click was the link text, or the dropdown arrow*/
            var w = $(this).outerWidth(true);
            var s = $(this).children('span').eq(0);
            var rs = parseInt($(this).css("padding-right")) + parseInt($(this).css("margin-right"))
+
                  parseInt(s.css("padding-right")) + parseInt(s.css("margin-right"));
            var x = e.pageX - $(this).offset().left;
            if (x > (w-rs))
               DropTopNav($, $(this));
            else
               return true;
            return false;
         });
         /*need to trap link span too for some browsers*/
         s.bind('click',function(e) {
            /*do similar math to determine if click was link text or arrow*/
            var w = $(this).outerWidth(true);
            var rs = parseInt($(this).css("padding-right")) + parseInt($(this).css("margin-right"));
            var x = e.pageX - $(this).offset().left;
            if (x > (w-rs))
               DropTopNav($, $(this).parent('a').eq(0));
            else
               window.location.href = $(this).parent('a').eq(0).attr('href');
            return false;
         });
      });
   }
}
```

Now that we have bound our new hover and click events to our navigation bar, we need to tell the client browser what to do on a hover or click event. In Listing 6-8 we call the DropTopNav function unless the mobile navigation button, .navbar .btn-navbar-close, is displayed. If this button is displayed then we are showing our mobile navigation, meaning that we do not want any hover events for our navigation menu.

Listing 6-8. jQuery HoverTopNav Function

```
/*triggered when a nav link is hovered*/
function HoverTopNav($, l, a) {
    if (l.length > 0) {
        var m = $('.navbar .btn-navbar-close');
        if (m.length > 0) {
            /*only down dropdown on hover if not mobile nav view*/
            if (m.css('display') != 'inline-block')
                DropTopNav($, l.children('a.dynamic-children').eq(0), a);
        }
    }
}
```

In Listing 6-9 we see the function, DropTopNav introduced in Listing 6-8. DropTopNav takes the link that was clicked and either hides or shows the link's submenu by switching the submenu's "display" style to either "none" or "block". The function also adds a class selected to the link that was clicked if the submenu is displayed in case we wish to provide additional styling to the link.

Listing 6-9. jQuery DropTopNav Function Drops or Hides a Dynamic Menu

```
/*triggered when a nav link is clicked*/
function DropTopNav($, l, a) {
    if (l.length > 0) {
        var u = l.siblings('ul').eq(0);
        if (u.length > 0) {
            /*if the sub menu is hidden, then show or vice-versa*/
            if (l.hasClass('selected') || (a=='o')) {
                u.css('display','none');
                l.removeClass('selected');
                u.find('ul.dynamic').css('display','none');
                u.find('a.dynamic-children').removeClass('selected');
            }
            else {
                u.css('display','block');
                l.addClass('selected');
            }
        }
    }
}
```

Floating Navigation

Floating navigation provides an easy, almost do-nothing approach to responsive navigation. The navigation menu items float within their container so with larger viewport widths, say widths over 768 pixels, this normally means a standard navigation menu. On a tablet or mobile device, the navigation menu items might not appear on one line, so we allow additional elements to float to the next line as seen in Figure 6-23. Using media queries, we can also create an additional breakpoint (i.e., 480 pixels) so that with smaller viewports display each menu item on its own line.

Figure 6-23. *Mobile view with floating navigation*

The pros of floating navigation include simplistic and straightforward navigation for the end user as well as the benefit of not requiring the use of JavaScript or jQuery.

Unfortunately, floating navigation does not work well if you intend to have drop-down submenus, as you can see in Figure 6-23. Drop-down menus would require secondary-level navigation. Further, the navigation might take up valuable real estate at the top of a site on a mobile device.

Implementing Floating Navigation

Floating navigation assumes a few basic tenets, that being that the menu items are floating and that the container holding the menu items will grow as menu items require additional lines. In Listing 6-10 we introduce the straightforward HTML code adding floating navigation in our sample master page.

Listing 6-10. Top Navigation HTML for Floating Navigation for All Views (Top Navigation Snippet Has Been Removed But Would Be Same as in Listing 6-2)

```
<div class="nav">
  <!--nav snippet-->
  <!--CS: Start Top Navigation Snippet-->
  ...
  <!--CE: End Top Navigation Snippet-->
  <!--end nav snippet-->
</div>
```

If we compare Listing 6-10 with Listing 6-2, we see that we removed nav-collapse and collapse from the first div class, as we do not need Bootstrap collapsing navigation. Our navigation items already float left within their container, so all that remains for us is simple styles to remove additional borders so that hanging borders do not appear on smaller viewports. The styles are provided in Listing 6-11.

Listing 6-11. Floating Navigation for All Viewports

```
/*floating navigation*/
/*top level nav container show no long float and should have grow in height as needed*/
nav#topnav {
    height: auto;
}
/*require that each menu item display inline*/
nav#topnav .nav ul.root > li {
    display: inline-block;
    border: none;
}
/*remove any border so we do not have hanging borders*/
nav#topnav .nav ul.root > li a {
    border: none;
}
/*end floating navigation*/
```

We do not need to use media queries, as we will have our top navigation float for all viewports. If you intend to have a different type of navigation bar for large and small viewports, you might need to use media queries if you only require mobile top navigation to float. Besides setting the primary nav container (nav#topnav) height to grow as menu items float to a second or more lines, we also force list items to display as an inline block. Finally we set a menu item padding to take less space than in a desktop view, while still providing a mobile-friendly button to click.

Drop-Down Navigation

Drop-down selection list navigation afforded an early approach to handle issues encountered with floating navigation in mobile and tablet views, implemented as a <select> list in HTML as seen in Figure 6-24.

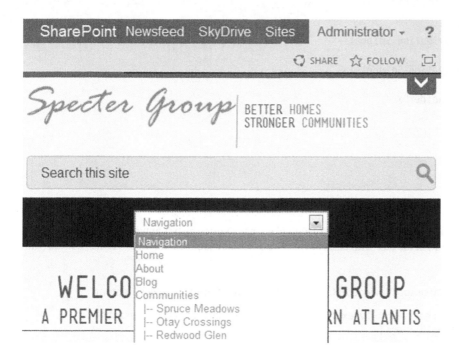

Figure 6-24. *Drop-down navigation in mobile view*

There are two leading ways of implementing drop-down navigation for mobile devices, one being to create a second navigation structure in the master page, then containing both navigation bars in a separate div. Using media queries, we could code which menu should be shown at what viewport width. This is not a recommended approach, as we have to create the second navigation menu, which is not only difficult with SharePoint, but also requires a visitor to download two versions of your navigation menu.

A second approach uses JavaScript to build the mobile drop-down navigation menu based on the primary navigation menu at the client side. A drawback to this approach includes the requirement of JavaScript or jQuery, but is far easier to maintain in the long run.

Implementing Drop-Down Navigation

Drop-down navigation for narrow viewports requires that we first add a container or tag where we will insert our <select> menu (see Listing 6-12). We then use a JavaScript function (see Listing 6-13) to parse our top navigation menu, create a new select HTML element, update the select tag to include navigation nodes from our primary navigation menu, and finally add the select menu to our page. Our last step includes updating our style sheet to provide the client properties as to when each menu should be displayed or hidden, as well as to provide general styling to the two menus (see Listing 6-14).

Listing 6-12. Top Navigation HTML for Drop-Down Navigation in Mobile Views (Top Navigation Snippet Has Been Removed But Would Be Same as in Listing 6-2)

```
<nav id="topnav">
  <div class="navbar">
    <div class="navbar-inner">
      <div class="container">
        <div class="nav nav-select">
```

```
        <!--nav snippet-->
        <!--CS: Start Top Navigation Snippet-->
        ...
        <!--CE: End Top Navigation Snippet-->
        <!--end nav snippet-->
        <div id="nav-select-holder">
        </div>

      </div>
    </div>
  </div>
</div>
</nav>
```

Notice how we added a new class, nav-select to the div with class, nav. Notice also that we added a new div with ID nav-select-holder at the end of the div with class nav-select. Our nav-select-holder div will contain our select element.

Listing 6-13. jQuery/JavaScript to Parse Top Navigation List Menu, Create and Populate Select Element

```
// Responsive Combo Navi - Alternative, only execute if select element container exists
if ($("#nav-select-holder").length > 0) {
  // Create the drop-down base
  $("<select id='comboNav' />").appendTo("#nav-select-holder");
  // Create default option "Navigation"
  $("<option />", {
     "selected": "selected",
     "value"   : "",
     "text"    : "Navigation"
  }).appendTo("#nav-select-holder select");

  // Populate drop-down with menu items
  $("#topnav .nav li a.menu-item").each(function() {
     var el = $(this);
     var lev = el.parents('ul').length;

     $("<option />", {
        "value"   : el.attr("href"),
        "text"    :  (lev < 2) ? el.text(): '|-- ' + el.text(),
        "style"   : 'padding-left: ' + ((lev-1) * 10) + 'px'
     }).appendTo("#nav-select-holder select");
  });
  $("#comboNav").change(function() {
     location = this.options[this.selectedIndex].value;
  });
}
```

> ■ **Note** Listing 6-13 required jQuery and must be called during the page load event, such as within a jQuery(document).ready(function($) { }); block.

Listing 6-14. *CSS With Media Query for Smaller Viewports for Drop-Down Navigation*

```
/*topnav mobile drop-down fixes */
/*hide the select menu for default viewports*/
nav#topnav #nav-select-holder {
    display: none;
}
/*use Media Query to apply additional styling for smaller viewports*/
@media (max-width: 979px) {
    /*force the height of the main nav bar*/
    nav#topnav .navbar-inverse .navbar-inner {
        height: 59px;
    }
    /*hide the normal navigation bar*/
    nav#topnav .nav-select ul.root {
        display: none;
    }
    /*display the select navigation container*/
    nav#topnav .nav-select #nav-select-holder  {
        display: block;
        text-align: center;
        padding-top: 10px;
    }
    nav#topnav .nav-select #nav-select-holder  select {
        margin: 5px 0px;
    }
}
/*end topnav mobile drop-down fixes */
```

Using the media query, @media (max-width: 979px), our CSS code will only fire on viewports with widths less than 980px (standard tablets). We hide the standard, default navigation menu and show our drop-down navigation and finally provide additional spacing around our select element to provide for a cleaner look.

Collapsing Navigation

Collapsing navigation strives to solve many of the issues of a multileveled navigation structure and hover limitations while still providing a navigation menu that fits a site's branding without having to resort to a Select menu that might look out of place. The theory of collapsing navigation states that when a viewport width hits a certain pixel threshold, the navigation menu should collapse into a single line with a menu icon that will provide a one-click action to cause the navigation menu to expand. Submenus are hidden as well, but a submenu icon could appear next to its parent menu item, allowing a site visitor the ability to drill down the navigation tree. Based on our Specter Group site, let's look at collapsing navigation in practice in a mobile view in Figure 6-25.

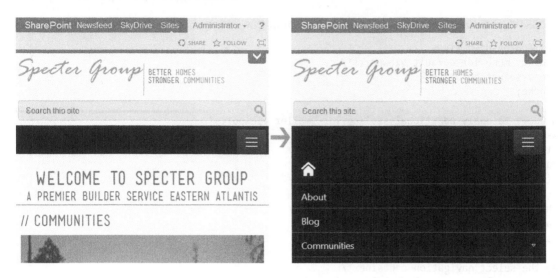

Figure 6-25. *Collapsing navigation (hidden and displayed) in mobile view*

Collapsing navigation can often be difficult to implement, as it requires a similar setup as drop-down navigation but must also include additional functionality to allow for the expansion of submenus. Fortunately the Bootstrap framework contains built-in functionality to provide collapsing navigation once we configure the navigation snippet properly and provide a few extra fixes.

Implementing Collapsing Navigation

Collapsing navigation in Bootstrap does not require additional code on our part assuming proper HTML is added to our master page to provide for the first-level navigation expansion icon. We review the HTML for Bootstrap collapsing navigation (see Listing 6-15) as well as additional CSS required to style the collapsing menu (see Listing 6-16).

Listing 6-15. Top Navigation HTML for Bootstrap-Based Collapsing Navigation in Mobile Views (Top Navigation Snippet Has Been Removed But Would Be Same as in Listing 6-2)

```
<nav id="topnav">
    <div class="container-fluid">
        <div class="row-fluid">
            <div class="span12">
                <div class="navbar navbar-inverse">
                    <div class="navbar-inner">
                        <div class="container">
                            <a class="btn btn-navbar" data-toggle="collapse" data-target=".nav-
                                collapse">
                                <span class="icon-bar"></span>
                                <span class="icon-bar"></span>
                                <span class="icon-bar"></span>
                            </a>
                            <div class="nav nav-collapse collapse">
                                <!--nav snippet-->
                                <!--CS: Start Top Navigation Snippet-->
                                ...
```

```
                                <!--CE: End Top Navigation Snippet-->
                                <!--end nav snippet-->
                        </div>
                    </div>
                </div>
            </div>
        </div>
    </div>
</nav>
```

There are two blocks of code we must examine closely. The first is an anchor tag that we add just before our div with class nav. This anchor tag provides us a button we can use to show or hide the collapsing navigation. It includes three icon bars that has become a standard "menu" icon. The second modification is the addition of two classes to our nav div, which now includes the nav-collapse and collapse classes that are provided in the Bootstrap CSS.

Listing 6-16. CSS With Media Query for Smaller Viewports for Bootstrap-Based Collapsing Navigation

```css
@media (max-width: 979px) {
    /*allow the top nav container to grow as menu grows*/
    nav#topnav {
        height: auto;
    }
    nav#topnav .navbar-inverse .navbar-inner {
        border: none;
        height: auto;
    }
    nav#topnav .navbar .nav {
        float: none;
        margin: 0px;
    }
    /*remove the right border, add a top border, and have each nav item display one per line*/
    nav#topnav .nav ul.root > li {
        border-right: none;
        border-top: 1px solid #2F2F2F;
        display: block;
        float: none;
        height: auto;
        background: #000 none;
    }
    nav#topnav .nav ul.root > li:first-child, nav#topnav .nav ul.root > li a {
        padding: 15px 20px;
        border-top: none;
    }
    /*for links with dynamic children, provide remove from drop-down arrow*/
    nav .navbar .nav .dynamic-children.additional-background {
        padding-right: 10% !important;
        width: 90%;
        display: block;
        background-image: url('/_layouts/15/images/menu-down.gif');
    }
```

```
/*turn off any hover event*/
nav#topnav .nav  ul.root > li:hover > ul, nav#topnav .nav  ul.root ul > li:hover > ul {
    display: none;
}
/*do not allow inline editing of links while in mobile view*/
.ms-core-listMenu-horizontalBox > .ms-core-listMenu-root > .ms-listMenu-editLink {
    display: none !important;
}
/*set dynamic menus to not float*/
nav#topnav .nav ul.root ul.dynamic, nav#topnav .nav ul.root ul.dynamic ul.dynamic {
    float: none !important;
    left: auto !important;
    top: auto !important;
    position: relative !important;
}
nav#topnav .nav ul.root > li ul li a {
    padding: 15px 20px;
    border-top: none;
}
}
```

Using the media query, @media (max-width: 979px), our CSS code will only fire on viewports with widths less than 980px (standard tablets). We hide the standard, default navigation menu and display the collapse menu icon. Bootstrap handled the menu icon so that when clicked, a navigation menu appears. The remaining CSS styles provided reformat the menu items to appear one per line with a divider between each line.

Other Mobile-Friendly Navigation Methods

There are quite a few other techniques to provide navigation functionality on nondesktop devices besides the three we reviewed. Some of these include off-canvas navigation and Hide 'n Cry (attributed to Brad Frost; see bradfrostweb.com).

Off-Canvas Navigation

With off-canvas navigation, the navigation menu is hidden off canvas, or outside of the viewport of the client device. When a menu icon is clicked, the navigation will slide in to the viewport screen, often "pushing" the content of the site out of the way. This is a popular menu system seen in many mobile apps. Off-canvas navigation provides a modern approach to mobile-first web site design that also allows for complex navigation structures as the navigation menu can be provided in its own window.

In Figure 6-26 we see to the left our normal collapsing navigation similar to Figure 6-25. To the right we see what happens when a user clicks the menu icon. The entire site shifts to the left (or it could be to the right) and the menu appears from "off canvas."

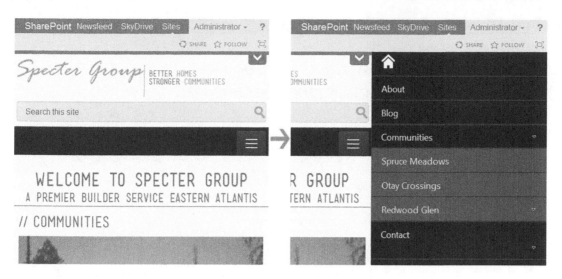

Figure 6-26. *Off-canvas navigation*

Hide'n Cry

Hide 'n Cry is the name of a method attributed to Brad Frost (bradfrostweb.com). The theory behind this method is that we simply hide the navigation for mobile viewers because we want to limit what they can do with the site. This does not appear to be a valid solution for most web sites, but might be feasible for certain sites. A slight corollary is to create a greatly reduced navigation menu for mobile visitors. This provides some navigation to mobile users but goes against the general theory of responsive web design, which holds that content available to a desktop user ideally is available to mobile users as well.

Other Forms of Navigation

There are additional common forms of navigation that you are probably familiar with that are also natively available in SharePoint 2013, or are easy to add. Let's review a few of these.

Current Navigation

Current navigation in SharePoint 2013 is what we used to call Quick Launch navigation in SharePoint 2010. Current navigation is often a vertical bar or column navigation menu, normally placed on the left or right side of a web page. Current navigation used to be very common on all pages of a web site, including the home page, but current trends are to not include a vertical navigation bar on the home page.

In SharePoint 2013, current navigation can be configured in a similar manner as global navigation by browsing to the Navigation Settings page, found in the Look and Feel section of your Site Settings page. You can configure current navigation to inherit current navigation settings from its parent, managed navigation, and two types of structured navigation (refer to Figure 6-27).

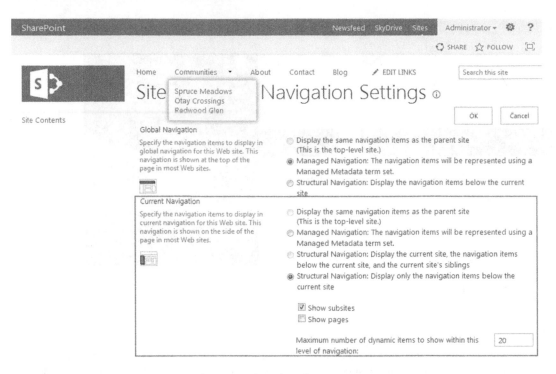

Figure 6-27. *Current navigation configuration found on the Navigation Settings page*

Remember that a site can only link to one term set for managed navigation, meaning that if you intend to have both global and current navigation use managed navigation, you will need to create your terms in your term set carefully and correctly configure your term properties.

■ **Note**   To learn how to configure managed navigation, review the section "Using the Term Store for Navigation" earlier in this chapter.

As with the Top Navigation snippet, you can find the Vertical Navigation snippet in the master page Snippet Gallery (see Figure 6-28).

Figure 6-28. *Vertical Navigation snippet in the master page Snippet Gallery*

As with the Top Navigation snippet, quite a few properties are available for customizing the Vertical Navigation snippet, although the important properties include CssClass, as well as the static and dynamic levels properties. These properties provide similar functionality to the Top Navigation snippet. Once you have configured your snippet, you are ready to copy and paste the generated snippet code to either your master page or your page layouts, even if you wish to only have vertical navigation on specific pages.

Normally the current navigation snippet is added to the master page so that it can be shared across all pages in your site. For collaboration sites this is desirable, but for publishing sites, we might only want vertical navigation on particular page layouts. If you include the vertical navigation in the master page, then your custom page layouts that should not include the vertical navigation will have to hide it somehow. The common method is to use an inline style, but in a responsive framework, this can cause undesirable flickering as well as problems with grid columns. We address how to implement hiding a vertical navigation menu in a page layout in Chapter 7.

Another interesting aspect of the current navigation is the added ability in SharePoint 2013 for Focus on Content. In Figure 6-29 notice the new icon highlighted on the right. If you click this icon on a page using an OOTB master page, the current navigation should be hidden and your content area fills up the remaining space. Click the icon again and your current navigation should reappear. This "magic" is performed by SharePoint with the simple addition of the class ms-fullscreenmode added to the main <body> tag. You can utilize this OOTB ribbon function and the class added for you to hide and display your custom current navigation as well as other aspects of your site design.

Figure 6-29. *Focus on Content button in ribbon*

■ **Note**   To learn how to add the current navigation to a page layout as well as hide the current navigation in a page layout if the current navigation menu is included in the master page, refer to Chapter 7.

Breadcrumb Navigation

Breadcrumb navigation has been with us for a long time and its inclusion in web sites comes and goes with the trends. Breadcrumbs provide the ability to assist visitors with where they currently are on the site, and in particular how they got there. Breadcrumbs provide a quick representation of where the current page exists in the site structure of the site and where each parent node of the current page is displayed along with a link. See Figure 6-30 for an example of breadcrumb navigation.

Figure 6-30. *Breadcrumb navigation*

The obvious place to go looking for the breadcrumb snippet is the Snippet Gallery, but you will find there is not a breadcrumb snippet readily available. You need to create your own snippet from custom ASP.NET markup. This is an advanced topic that requires some understanding of ASP.NET controls.

To help you get started, you can use code and controls SharePoint provides out of the box. In particular code blocks are already provided in OOTB master pages such as `seattle.master` found in the `/~catalogs/masterpage` library. If you open `seattle.master` and look for the breadcrumb ASP.NET markup, you will find the ASP.NET code shown in Listing 6-17.

Listing 6-17. ASP.NET Code From seattle.master That Generates Breadcrumbs

```
<SharePoint:AjaxDelta id="DeltaPlaceHolderPageTitleInTitleArea" runat="server">
    <asp:ContentPlaceHolder id="PlaceHolderPageTitleInTitleArea" runat="server">
        <SharePoint:SPTitleBreadcrumb
            runat="server"
            RenderCurrentNodeAsLink="true"
            SiteMapProvider="SPContentMapProvider"
            CentralAdminSiteMapProvider="SPXmlAdminContentMapProvider">
            <PATHSEPARATORTEMPLATE>
                <SharePoint:ClusteredDirectionalSeparatorArrow runat="server" />
            </PATHSEPARATORTEMPLATE>
        </SharePoint:SPTitleBreadcrumb>
    </asp:ContentPlaceHolder>
</SharePoint:AjaxDelta>
```

It would be nice if you could copy and paste this directly to our HTML master page, but you cannot because HTML master pages might not include ASP.NET controls. You must first convert this to a snippet.

1. Open the Snippet Gallery for your master page.

2. Click the Custom ASP.NET Markup icon in the ribbon.

3. This will load the Create Snippets From Custom ASP.NET Markup. Paste the ASP.NET code from Listing 6-17 in the text box at the lower right of the page. Click Update to update the HTML Snippet.

4. The HTML Snippet will update with the HTML-friendly code in Listing 6-18. You can now copy and paste this to your HTML master page.

5. You can use these steps to quickly generate a snippet based on any ASP.NET markup.

Listing 6-18. HTML Snippet Generated by the Snippet Gallery for a Breadcrumb

```
<!--CS: Start Create Snippets From Custom ASP.NET Markup Snippet-->
<!--SPM:<SharePoint:AjaxDelta id="DeltaPlaceHolderPageTitleInTitleArea" runat="server">-->
<!--SPM:  <asp:ContentPlaceHolder id="PlaceHolderPageTitleInTitleArea" runat="server">-->
<!--SPM:     <SharePoint:SPTitleBreadcrumb runat="server" RenderCurrentNodeAsLink="true"
       SiteMapProvider="SPContentMapProvider"
       CentralAdminSiteMapProvider="SPXmlAdminContentMapProvider">-->
<!--SPM:        <PATHSEPARATORTEMPLATE>-->
<!--SPM:           <SharePoint:ClusteredDirectionalSeparatorArrow runat="server" />-->
<!--SPM:        </PATHSEPARATORTEMPLATE>-->
<!--SPM:     </SharePoint:SPTitleBreadcrumb>-->
<!--SPM:  </asp:ContentPlaceHolder>-->
<!--SPM:</SharePoint:AjaxDelta>-->
<!--CE: End Create Snippets From Custom ASP.NET Markup Snippet-->
```

If you add the HTML Snippet in Listing 6-18 to your custom master page, load a page in the browser, and view the source HTML, you will find a breadcrumb similar to Listing 6-19 or Listing 6-20. Notice that the separator image and spans are different between the two listings, as you have to provide special styling for each type of breadcrumb even though they both come from the same SPTitleBreadcrumb control. In particular in Listing 6-19, all breadcrumb nodes are contained within their own span, whereas in Listing 6-20 only the separator image is contained within its own span.

Listing 6-19. Rendered Breadcrumb Navigation: Type One With Some Properties Removed for Feadability

```
<span id="DeltaPlaceHolderPageTitleInTitleArea">
   <span>
      <a href="#"><img alt="Skip Navigation Links" /></a>
      <span>
         <a href="/_catalogs/masterpage/Forms/AllItems.aspx">Master Page Gallery</a>
      </span>
      <span>
         <img src="/_layouts/15/images/spcommon.png?rev=23">
      </span>
      <span>
         <a href="/_catalogs/masterpage/Forms/AllItems.aspx">Specter Group</a>
      </span>
      <a id="ctl00_PlaceHolderPageTitleInTitleArea_ctl00_SkipLink"></a>
   </span>
</span>
```

The HTML provided in Listing 6-20 will be most commonly found in Site Settings pages, whereas the HTML provided in Listing 6-19 will be common throughout content pages, lists, and libraries.

Listing 6-20. Rendered Breadcrumb Navigation: Type 2 With Some Properties Removed for Readability

```
<span id="DeltaPlaceHolderPageTitleInTitleArea">
   <a href="settings.aspx">Site Settings</a>
   <span>
      <span>
         <img src="/_layouts/15/images/spcommon.png?rev=23">
      </span>
   </span>
   Site Master Page Settings
</span>
```

To add a breadcrumb to the example master page we have been using throughout this chapter to produce the results in Figure 6-30, we must add Listing 6-17 to the master page as well as provide additional styling.

In Listing 6-21, we add the snippet from Listing 6-18 to our master page above our header's search box.

Listing 6-21. Add Breadcrumb Snippet to Master Page

```
<header>
    <!--header container, row, logo, etc. removed-->
    <div class="span4">
        <div class="sp-breadcrumb">
            <!--CS: Start Create Snippets From Custom ASP.NET Markup Snippet-->
            <!--Snippet from Listing 6-18-->
            <!--CE: End Create Snippets From Custom ASP.NET Markup Snippet-->
        </div>
        <div class="searchbox">
            <!--search box snippet-->
            <!--end search box snippet-->
        </div>
    </div>
    <!--end header container removed-->
</header>
```

SharePoint provides OOTB styling for breadcrumbs but we want to ensure that the breadcrumb matches our branding. Listing 6-22 provides additional styles for the breadcrumb navigation. The styles help position the breadcrumb above the search box, modify the text and link colors to match our branding, and finally provide media queries to reshape the breadcrumb depending on the viewport.

Listing 6-22. Styles for Breadcrumb Navigation

```
/*target the right span in the header. Allows us to position breadcrumb*/
header .span4 {
    position: relative;
}
/*position the breadcrumb in the header*/
.sp-breadcrumb {
    display: block;
    position: absolute;
    right: 0px;
    top: 30px;
    color: #444;
    white-space: nowrap;
}
/*fix bootstrap image resize issue for seperator image*/
.sp-breadcrumb img {
    max-width: none;
    width: auto;
}
/*change links and text to match branding*/
.sp-breadcrumb a {
    color: #009899;
}
```

```
@media (max-width: 979px) {
   /*for tablets, descrease font size and move up with search box*/
   .sp-breadcrumb {
      font-size: 14px;
      top: 24px;
   }
}
@media (max-width: 767px) {
   /*for smaller devices, drop breadcrumb to its own line*/
   .sp-breadcrumb {
      position: relative;
      right: auto;
      top: auto;
      padding: 0px 10px;
   }
}
```

At this point your breadcrumb should look similar to Figure 6-30, although the separator image will be different. We now provide CSS to make two additional changes. The first modification we will make includes changing the separator image. The second change we will make is we want to hide the navigation for tablet and mobile views based on the Bootstrap model.

Change the Separator Image

To change the image that separates the breadcrumb hierarchical items, we can provide our own PathSeparatorTemplate to the SPTitleBreadcrumb control in Listing 6-18. Unfortunately this will not always work, as SharePoint renders the breadcrumb in different ways depending on the page, as we saw in Listing 6-19 and Listing 6-20. We fix this by providing a PathSeparatorTemplate as well as a separator class to the SPTitleBreadcrumb control as seen in Listing 6-23.

Listing 6-23. Breadcrumb Snippet With Separator Class and New Separator Template

```
<!--CS: Start Create Snippets From Custom ASP.NET Markup Snippet-->
<!--SPM:<SharePoint:AjaxDelta id="DeltaPlaceHolderPageTitleInTitleArea" runat="server">-->
<!--SPM:  <asp:ContentPlaceHolder id="PlaceHolderPageTitleInTitleArea" runat="server">-->
<!--SPM:     <SharePoint:SPTitleBreadcrumb runat="server" RenderCurrentNodeAsLink="true"
        SiteMapProvider="SPContentMapProvider"
        class="breadcrumb-separator"
        CentralAdminSiteMapProvider="SPXmlAdminContentMapProvider">-->
<!--SPM:        <PATHSEPARATORTEMPLATE>-->
<!--SPM:          <asp:Image id="BCSeperator" runat="server" GenerateEmptyAlternateText="true"
                        ImageUrl="/_catalogs/masterpage/img/breadcrumb-separator.png" />-->
<!--SPM:        </PATHSEPARATORTEMPLATE>-->
<!--SPM:     </SharePoint:SPTitleBreadcrumb>-->
<!--SPM:  </asp:ContentPlaceHolder>-->
<!--SPM:</SharePoint:AjaxDelta>-->
<!--CE: End Create Snippets From Custom ASP.NET Markup Snippet-->
```

To provide our own separator image for all breadcrumbs, we can use the styles provided in Listing 6-24. We can add additional styling that acts differently if the breadcrumb includes a wrapper span with a class of sp-breadcrumb-separator.

Listing 6-24. CSS to Change the Breadcrumb Separator Image

```
/*separator image*/
/*hide the OOTB separator image*/
#DeltaPlaceHolderPageTitleInTitleArea > span > span img{
   display: none;
}
/*a second-level span should only contain the separator, so provide our image*/
#DeltaPlaceHolderPageTitleInTitleArea > span > span {
   background: transparent url('../img/breadcrumb-separator.png') no-repeat 0 6px;
   margin: 0px 0px 0px 5px;
   width: 8px;
   height: 17px;
   display: inline-block;
}

/*if breadcrumb-separator container exists, we have to provide different styles*/
/*display, move image out of the way and provide a new background that uses our separator image*/
#DeltaPlaceHolderPageTitleInTitleArea > span.breadcrumb-separator > span img{
   text-indent: -9999px;
   overflow: hidden;
   background: transparent url('../img/breadcrumb-separator.png')
      no-repeat 0 6px;
   margin: 0px 5px;
   width: 8px !important;
   height: 17px !important;
   display: inline-block !important;
}
/*second-level span may include text or separator, so we need to reset its styles*/
#DeltaPlaceHolderPageTitleInTitleArea > span:first-child > span,
#DeltaPlaceHolderPageTitleInTitleArea > span.breadcrumb-separator > span {
   background: transparent none;
   margin: 0px;
   width: auto;
   height: auto;
   display: inline;
}
```

The first two styles provide an alternate separator image for pages that render the breadcrumb in HTML similar to Listing 6-20. The first style hides any img found within a span that is a direct descendant of DeltaPlaceHolderPageTitleInTitleArea. The second style allows for a direct descendant span of DeltaPlaceHolderPageTitleInTitleArea to be an inline block with a fixed width and height that has a background image set by the background property.

The next two styles provide overrides for those cases where the breadcrumb has spans surrounding each of the breadcrumb nodes as shown in Listing 6-18. The first of these two styles uses the separator image that SharePoint provided, but moves the images out of the way and provides a new background. The second style resets the breadcrumb spans to flow inline without set dimensions. Your breadcrumb should now look exactly like Figure 6-30.

Hide Breadcrumb Navigation for Tablet and Mobile Views

Although the breadcrumb navigation rendered by SharePoint is responsive friendly, as it will float and stack elements as the viewport width shrinks, what if we wanted to simply hide the breadcrumb navigation on mobile devices? You could use the style shown in Listing 6-25.

Listing 6-25. CSS to Hide the Breadcrumb Navigation in Tablet and Mobile Views

```
<style>
@media (max-width:979px) {
   #DeltaPlaceHolderPageTitleInTitleArea {
      display: none;
   }
}
</style>
```

Using media queries, you can create a media query that states that if the viewport in question is less than 980 pixels wide then apply the following styles, the styles in question being to hide the div container holding our breadcrumb navigation.

Footer Navigation

The footer navigation bar is normally not a particular snippet that you add to a master page, but rather a section in and of itself where you might place active as well as static links, content, contact information, a map, and so on. As an example, the Specter Group required a footer navigation bar that included common links, contact information, and a live Twitter feed, as highlighted in Figure 6-31.

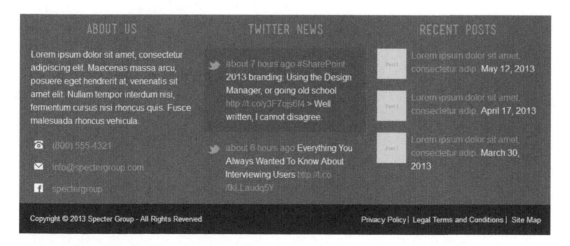

Figure 6-31. *Specter Group primary footer*

■ **Note**   Refer to Chapter 5 for an in-depth look at the footer and how to make it responsive.

We can see that much of the footer is actually used for social functions, which we cover in greater detail in Chapter 13, including how to include a Twitter feed. What we see in the rightmost column though is an extension of a navigation menu bar. Although these navigation items are static links not handled by SharePoint, we can use this type of space for important links that we want to provide on every page throughout our site, but are not important enough to take up valuable resources at the top of each web page.

Other common uses of footer bars and footer navigation include providing a space for an aggregated link farm for outside sites or space for disclaimers and use policies. You could even manage your footer navigation using managed metadata by using jQuery to parse navigation links from your primary or current navigation and including them in your footer navigation. You could also forego your top navigation or current navigation and use the Top Navigation or Horizontal Navigation snippets in your footer instead.

Summary

In this chapter we reviewed the new navigation structure provided in SharePoint 2013, that being metadata-driven navigation. This huge improvement over previous versions of SharePoint provides outstanding ability to modify and maintain a site's navigation as well as share a navigation structure across multiple site collections. Once the managed metadata store is configured in the farm, a term set can be quickly created, utilized, and even customized in line with browser-based tools.

We then looked at the top navigation snippet, added this to a HTML master page and saw common methods of styling a SharePoint navigation menu. We reviewed how to make a horizontal navigation bar responsive as well as considered caveats for different methods. We finished with a look at additional forms of web site navigation, including vertical navigation, a breadcrumb, footer navigation, and a social toolbar.

■ ■ ■

CHAPTER 7

Building Page Layouts and Publishing Pages

In this chapter we investigate how to add content pages to our site and how content pages link to page layouts whether they be out-of-the-box (OOTB) or custom page layouts. We begin with a look at content types, both OOTB and custom, that we will leverage when creating custom page layouts. We review the value and properties of content types and why we create our own custom content types, as well as where they are stored in SharePoint 2013. We review OOTB page layouts as well as create custom HTML page layouts using Design Manager. We also learn how to link page layouts to both OOTB and custom content types. We continue with a look at the properties of a page layout that allow it to be responsive, and conclude by learning how to utilize a page layout in a new content page.

■ **Note** Learn how to use custom content types with Cross-Site Collection Publishing in Chapter 8.

Our Scenario

Public-facing web sites normally intend to provide information to visitors, and the public Specter Group web site is no different. Specter Group requires different types of web pages based on the type of information a particular page should contain. Specter Group also wants to not only make a web page easy to edit by an author, but also control what kind of content may be placed on a particular page type. By using content types and page layouts, we will build a custom content type stored in the Managed Metadata Hub we created in Chapter 6 that our custom page layouts will use to provide a diverse set of page layouts authors can use when creating content pages. Of course, all custom page layouts must flow within our responsive framework as well.

An Introduction to Layouts and Content Types

Page layouts provide web developers the ability to control how content will be displayed on a particular content page. Recall that master pages control the outside shell of a site, such as the header, footer, general background, and navigation. Page layouts provide the layout or flow for the given "content" on a particular page. Page layouts are stored by SharePoint in the Master Page Gallery and are only available when the site collection-based Publishing Infrastructure feature and site-based Publishing feature are enabled. Sites without Publishing enabled, such as collaboration sites, use the "text layout" or "wiki layout." The "text layout" limits our ability to provide reusable, custom layouts and are thus normally not acceptable for public-facing sites or larger Intranets and Extranets.

> ■ **Note** Learn how to create a responsive master page in Chapter 5 and responsive navigation in Chapter 6.

There are at least fifteen OOTB page layouts provided in SharePoint 2013. If you worked with the SharePoint 2010 publishing infrastructure, the SharePoint 2013 OOTB page layouts will look similar. You can view a list of available OOTB page layouts multiple ways, including the following: (1) via the Master Page Gallery in a browser, (2) by connecting to your site using WebDav and using a web editor such as Dreamweaver to view the ~sitecollection/_catalogs/masterpage directory, or (3) by loading your site in SharePoint Designer 2013 and viewing the Page Layouts Site Object (seen in Figure 7-1).

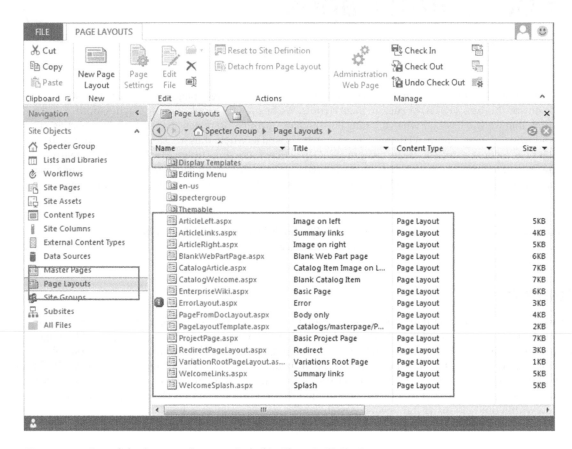

Figure 7-1. *Out-of-the-box page layouts viewed in SharePoint Designer 2013*

> ■ **Note** Two OOTB page layouts are hidden by default, PageLayoutTemplate.aspx and VariationRootPageLayout.aspx.

All page layouts must be linked to a content type. A valid page layout content type should have as its parent content type the "Page" content type or another content type that inherits from the "Page" content type, such as the "Article Page" content type. We must understand content types before we can truly understand how page layouts work. Specifically we must know what content types are, how they are built and stored, and how they are utilized by page layouts.

> ■ **Note** If you are familiar with content types, content type hubs, and the Managed Metadata Service, skip ahead to the page layout sections later in this chapter including "Out-of-the-Box Page Layouts," "Custom Page Layouts," and "Making a Page Layout Responsive."

Content Types

Content types were first introduced in WSS 3.0/SharePoint Server 2007/MOSS and have become the cornerstone of all content in SharePoint 2013. Effectively all content in one way or another is associated with a content type. A content type defines the attributes or metadata that an object in SharePoint may contain or store. All lists and libraries are associated with a content type, thus any item that is created for a list or library will have the ability to store and utilize content associated with each attribute within the associated content type.

We can visualize content types by comparing an individual content type to a simple spreadsheet, in particular the first header row of a spreadsheet. We refer to each attribute of a content type as either a Content Type Column or Content Type Field, which we can think of as a column header in a spreadsheet. A column or field can be configured to store many types of data including text, numbers, dates or time, choices, HTML, images, GPS location, managed metadata, and more. Refer to Figure 7-2 for a full list of OOTB column types. You can even create your own column types to store your own types of data. To further our analogy of content types and spreadsheets, an actual spreadsheet would equate to the list where the list data is stored in cells within the spreadsheet, but our column headers (e.g., content type) specify the columns' names and types of data each column may store.

Site Columns ▸ Create Column ⓘ

Name and Type

Type a name for this column, and select the type of information you want to store in the column.

Column name:

The type of information in this column is:

- ⦿ Single line of text
- ○ Multiple lines of text
- ○ Choice (menu to choose from)
- ○ Number (1, 1.0, 100)
- ○ Currency ($, ¥, €)
- ○ Date and Time
- ○ Lookup (information already on this site)
- ○ Yes/No (check box)
- ○ Person or Group
- ○ Hyperlink or Picture
- ○ Calculated (calculation based on other columns)
- ○ Task Outcome
- ○ Full HTML content with formatting and constraints for publishing
- ○ Image with formatting and constraints for publishing
- ○ Hyperlink with formatting and constraints for publishing
- ○ Summary Links data
- ○ Rich media data for publishing
- ○ Managed Metadata

Figure 7-2. *OOTB column types as provided by ~ sitecollection/_layouts/15/fldnew.aspx*

■ **Note**   We present content types only in regard to basic Web Content Management. For a deeper look at content types and Enterprise Content Management with SharePoint, consider *Practical SharePoint 2010 Information Architecture* by Ruven Gotz (Apress, 2012; `www.apress.com/9781430241768`). Although written for SharePoint 2010, the information is still useful for SharePoint 2013.

Content types also provide the ability to inherit from existing content types, which in turn can inherit from other content types. Just as in programming inheritance, inheritance in SharePoint's content types allows content types to reuse its parent content type columns without having to readd them themselves. In fact all content types but one will inherit from a previously defined content type. The one root content type in SharePoint is the System content type that has an ID of 0x, and then only one content type exists that inherits from the System content type, the Item content type with an ID of 0x01. In general, all other content types including custom content types will inherit from either the Item content type or from one of its many descendants.

■ **Tip**   Learn more about Base content type hierarchy at `http://sprwd.com/86zebtp`.

Content types are a very powerful tool, used for much more than just WCM, and an in-depth review is beyond of the scope of this book. Moving forward we consider content types only in their basic form and in regard to how they can be used in a WCM system.

■ **Tip**   Learn how to plan content types at `http://sprwd.com/a3cfg6x`.

Content pages stored within our SharePoint 2013 Publishing sites are stored within a Pages library. The Pages library, as with all lists and libraries in SharePoint 2013, inherits a primary content type, in this case the Document content type. The Pages library has been configured to allow multiple content types and by default the Page content type. A particular list item, or content page stored within the Pages library, can also be associated with any additional content type allowed by the Pages library.

■ **Note**   The Page content type has the following content type inheritance. System ➤ Item ➤ Document ➤ System Page ➤ Page (self).

We can create our own custom page content types that we can then include in our Pages library and then have our custom page layouts inherit from those custom page content types.

Where to Store Custom Content Types

All content types must be stored within SharePoint. Although content types are a site-level feature, multiple storage locations exist for storing content types. OOTB content types are stored within the SharePoint farm itself. If we want to create custom content types, we have an option as to where to create them, depending on where we would like them to be accessible. We may store content types in a site, a site collection or in a content type hub. A site may inherit content types from its parent site, thus where we store a content type will dictate where a given content type may be used.

Custom Content Types Stored in a Site

At the most shallow level, a custom content type can be created and stored in a given site. Once the content type has been created in a site, it would then be available for use in that site and any descendent site as well. If we want to create a custom content type that its parent sites will not see or be allowed to use, then a custom content type stored within a site might be a good solution. If, on the other hand, all sites within a site collection should use and share a given custom content type, storing a custom content type within a subsite will fail.

Custom Content Types Stored in a Site Collection

Moving one level deeper, a custom content type may be created and stored in the root site of a site collection. Essentially this is the same as storing a content type in a site as previously discussed, just note that storing a content type in a site collection's root site makes that content type available throughout the entire site collection. If we want to share a custom content type across site collections, for example in Cross-Site Collection Publishing, we will need a deeper way to store our custom content types.

___

■ **Note**   We review Cross-Site Collection Publishing in detail in Chapter 8.

___

Custom Content Types Stored in a Content Type Hub

SharePoint 2013 provides a mechanism for us to create content types that can be shared across site collections or even web applications, via a content type hub. A content type hub is a site collection, with its set of OOTB and custom content types, linked to a particular Managed Metadata Service Application. We can then associate other web applications with a Managed Metadata Service Application to inherit the content type from the content type hub.

___

■ **Note**   You can learn more about the Managed Metadata Service in Chapter 6.

___

The value of a content type hub includes the ability to create a custom content type once that can then be used across multiple site collections. We will find this invaluable when configuring and utilizing Cross-Site Collection Publishing.

Configuring a Content Type Hub

As we just saw, a content type hub is a site collection that is referenced by a Managed Metadata Service Application. In Chapter 6 we reviewed how to create and manage a Managed Metadata Service Application that we then linked our web application to. We will now carry this process one step further and link our Managed Metadata Service Application to a site collection that will store custom content types that may be utilized across multiple web applications and site collections. The content type hub site collection could be any site collection in your SharePoint farm including your Central Admin site collection, and you can create as many content type hubs as you need, although you will need to create a new Metadata Service Application for each content type hub you require. In the case of Specter Group requirements, we want to be able to modify our custom content types without having to log into the Central Admin site collection, so we are going to have our authoring site collection (`authoring.spectergroup.com`) be our content type hub for our entire Specter Group site architecture.

Prerequisite

A content type hub is associated with a Managed Metadata Service Application. To learn how to create a Managed Metadata Service Application, refer to Chapter 6. The site collection that will store the content types that you wish to be in your content type hub must already have been created. This site collection does not yet need to have your custom content types at this point. Because by default a Managed Metadata Service Application is made available to all web applications, we will assume this is still the case. Second, the site collection that will be the content type hub must also have the site collection feature Content Type Syndication Hub already enabled.

■ **Note**   Each content type hub included in your SharePoint farm will require its own Managed Metadata Service Application.

A site collection may be configured as a content type hub for a particular Managed Metadata Service in Central Admin:

1. Verify the site collection feature Content Type Syndication Hub has been enabled for the site collection that will become a content type hub.

   a. Navigate to the Site Collection Features page found on the Site Settings page of the site collection that will become the content type hub.

   b. Activate the feature Content Type Syndication Hub if it is not yet active (see Figure 7-3).

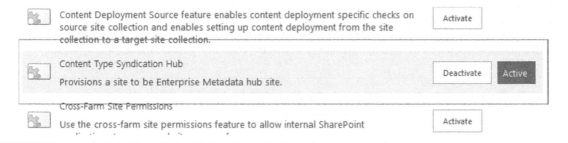

Figure 7-3. *Verify the Content Type Syndication Hub feature is active*

2. Open Central Admin and click Application Management in the left menu.

3. Found in the Service Applications group, click Manage service applications.

4. Scroll down the list of applications and find the Managed Metadata Service your web application(s) are configured to use for their managed metadata, in our case, Managed Metadata Service. Now click Properties in the ribbon, found in the Operations group.

5. In the Service's Properties dialog box, scroll to the bottom and provide the full URL of the site collection that will be your content type hub (see Figure 7-4).

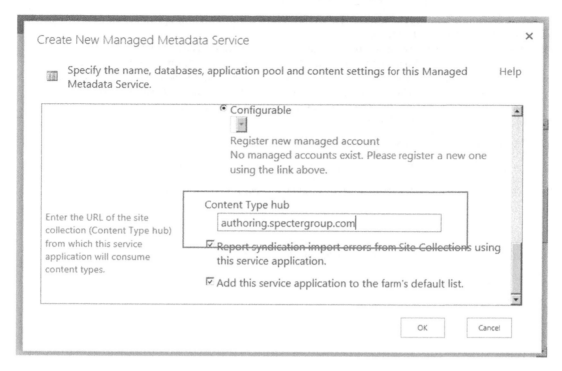

Figure 7-4. *Providing a content type hub site collection*

6. Click OK to save your changes.

All web applications that have a service connection to this Managed Metadata Service are now using this site collection's list of content types as a content type hub. We are now ready to create custom content types that we want shared across site collections and even web applications.

Creating a Custom Content Type

As we have mentioned, custom content types are associated with a site, a site collection, or a content type hub. The process of creating a custom content type will always be the same no matter where we store the content type because a content type hub is just a site collection. When we add custom content types to a site collection, we are simply creating our custom content types in the root site of a site collection.

■ **Note**   We review adding a custom content type via a browser. You can also deploy content types via features developed in Visual Studio as well as create content types with PowerShell, but these topics are beyond the scope of this book.

Creating a Custom Content Type Column

Before we create a custom content type, let us review the structure of content types. Again consider a content type as a spreadsheet of data. In this spreadsheet the columns represent the different types of information we can store and the row represents a particular item or document associated with this content type. A given column must be associated with a field, and that field dictates the type of content that column may store. SharePoint provides an extensive list of content type columns, which we saw in Figure 7-2.

Although there is a large list of site columns already available, there are reasons why you might want to create your own custom site columns for your custom content types. You might want site columns named a particular way or maybe you want to set the default value to your own calculated value. A common reason for a custom column is to provide a custom list of choices or to link a column to managed metadata. In the next example, we will create a custom site column. We want our custom site columns to be available in our content type hub; therefore, we will create the custom site column in our authoring.spectergroup.com root site.

1. Open the site in which you want to add a custom site column.

2. Click the Settings icon and then Site settings in the Settings drop-down list.

3. On the Site Settings page, under Web Designer Galleries, click Site columns, as shown in Figure 7-5.

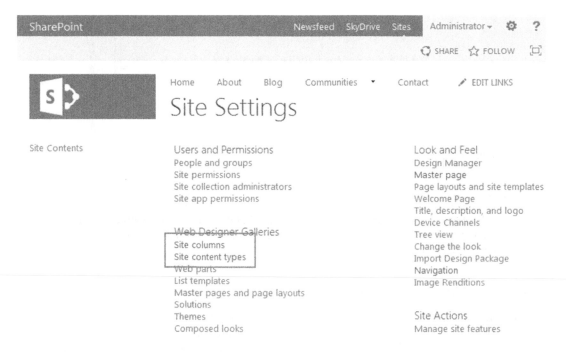

Figure 7-5. *Site Settings ➤ Site columns and Site content types location*

4. You will see a list of all site columns currently available to this site. Click Create at the top of the Site Columns page shown in Figure 7-6.

Figure 7-6. *Site Settings ➤ Site Columns ➤ Create button*

5. The Create Column page will appear, allowing you to configure your custom site column. A full explanation of every possible site column setting is beyond the scope of this book. In our example, we wish to create a custom site column to store the property type of a particular property. Refer to Figure 7-7 for our custom column property values.

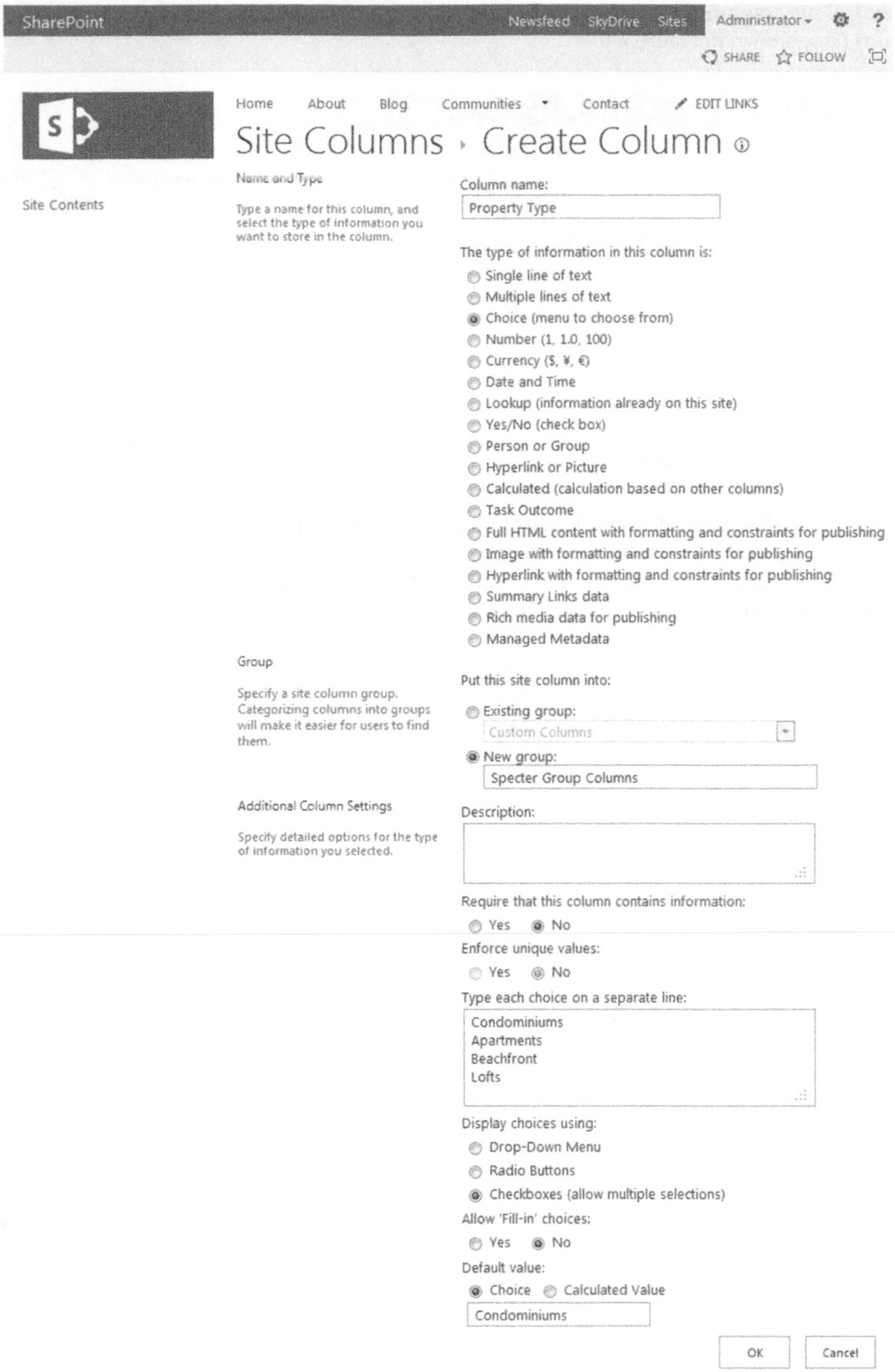

SharePoint   Newsfeed   SkyDrive   Sites   Administrator ▾   ⚙   ?

◯ SHARE   ☆ FOLLOW   ⌐

Home   About   Blog   Communities   ▾   Contact   ✎ EDIT LINKS

Site Columns › Create Column ⓘ

Name and Type

Type a name for this column, and select the type of information you want to store in the column.

Site Contents

Column name:

Property Type

The type of information in this column is:

- ◯ Single line of text
- ◯ Multiple lines of text
- ◉ Choice (menu to choose from)
- ◯ Number (1, 1.0, 100)
- ◯ Currency ($, ¥, €)
- ◯ Date and Time
- ◯ Lookup (information already on this site)
- ◯ Yes/No (check box)
- ◯ Person or Group
- ◯ Hyperlink or Picture
- ◯ Calculated (calculation based on other columns)
- ◯ Task Outcome
- ◯ Full HTML content with formatting and constraints for publishing
- ◯ Image with formatting and constraints for publishing
- ◯ Hyperlink with formatting and constraints for publishing
- ◯ Summary Links data
- ◯ Rich media data for publishing
- ◯ Managed Metadata

Group

Specify a site column group. Categorizing columns into groups will make it easier for users to find them.

Put this site column into:

- ◯ Existing group:

  Custom Columns   ▾

- ◉ New group:

  Specter Group Columns

Additional Column Settings

Specify detailed options for the type of information you selected.

Description:

Require that this column contains information:

◯ Yes   ◉ No

Enforce unique values:

◯ Yes   ◉ No

Type each choice on a separate line:

```
Condominiums
Apartments
Beachfront
Lofts
```

Display choices using:

- ◯ Drop-Down Menu
- ◯ Radio Buttons
- ◉ Checkboxes (allow multiple selections)

Allow 'Fill-in' choices:

◯ Yes   ◉ No

Default value:

◉ Choice   ◯ Calculated Value

Condominiums

[OK]   [Cancel]

Figure 7-7. Sample custom column properties

■ **Note**   A column name must be unique within the site in which you are creating the custom column, including any inherited column names.

6.   Click OK to create your new column.

Creating a Custom Content Type

Creating a custom content type is not much more difficult than creating a custom column. Custom content types may be created via the browser, by a custom feature included in an app developed in Visual Studio or with PowerShell. In our case we use a browser to provide a visual, direct example.

■ **Note**   Because redeploying a content type created in the browser is difficult, content types that need to be shared should be placed in your content type hub.

1.   Open the site in which you want to add a custom content type and navigate to the Site Settings page.

2.   On the Site Settings page, under Web Designer Galleries, click Site content types.

3.   You will see a list of all content types currently available to this site. Click Create at the top of the Site Content Types page (see Figure 7-8).

Figure 7-8. *Site Settings ➤ Site Content Types ➤ Create button*

4.   The New Site Content Type page will appear. Here you can provide the necessary properties to create your custom content type. Refer to Figure 7-9 for our sample custom content type property values.

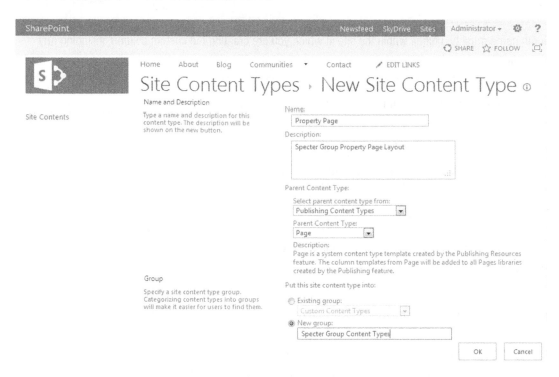

Figure 7-9. *Custom content type properties*

■ **Note**   All custom content types must inherit from an existing content type. In our example we wish to create a new content type that inherits from the Page content type, as we will be using this content type for custom page layouts. Therefore we select a parent content type group of Publishing Content Types with a parent content type of Page.

---

5.   Click OK to create your new content type.

Once a content type has been created, you can return to the Site Contents Type page (`~site/_layouts/15/mngctype.aspx`) and view your custom content type within the content type group you selected or provided. Remember, all subsites of the site you create a content type in can reference the custom content type. Further, if this content type was created at the root site of a site collection configured as a content type hub, all web applications connected to the Managed Metadata Service Application using this site collection will also have access to this content type once replication has completed.

■ **Tip**   SharePoint will generate a content type ID for a custom content type. A content type ID provides information regarding its inheritance. To learn more about custom IDs, please refer to `http://sprwd.com/7d79dsn`.

Out-of-the-Box Page Layouts

As we have already stated, there are fifteen page layouts provided by SharePoint 2013 for sites with the Publishing feature enabled, although two of these page layouts are hidden by default. We find that for custom public-facing sites as well as many intranets and extranets, custom page layouts are required, especially when creating responsive sites.

Ideally we will attempt to utilize OOTB assets provided by SharePoint 2013. In particular, we have seen how OOTB content types can serve as a basis for our custom content types. The same is true for OOTB page layouts. Having examples of how page layouts employ content types to expose metadata can help provide a starting place for our own custom page layouts.

■ **Note**   OOTB page layouts are page layouts, not HTML page layouts. SharePoint 2013 does not provide any OOTB HTML page layouts, although we can easily create one. We review HTML page layouts later in this chapter in the section "Custom Page Layouts with Design Manager."

For a list of the seven OOTB page content types used by OOTB page layouts, refer to Figure 7-10. In Figure 7-11 we can see the thirteen visible OOTB page layouts.

Page Layout Content Types

Article Page	Page	Specter Group
Catalog-Item Reuse	Page	Specter Group
Enterprise Wiki Page	Page	Specter Group
Error Page	Page	Specter Group
Project Page	Enterprise Wiki Page	Specter Group
Redirect Page	Page	Specter Group
Welcome Page	Page	Specter Group

Figure 7-10. *The seven OOTB content types used by the thirteen OOTB page layouts*

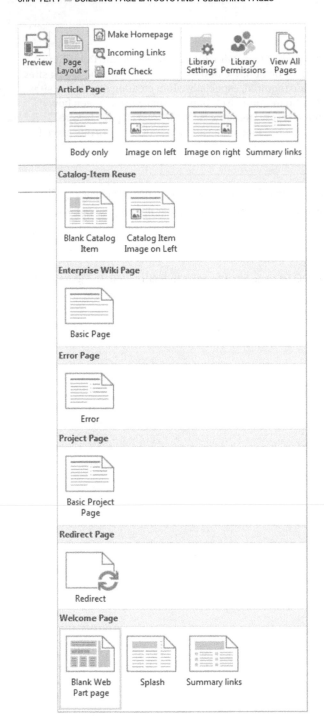

Figure 7-11. *The thirteen visible OOTB SharePoint 2013 page layouts*

All page layouts, including the two hidden ones, can be viewed in a site collection's Master Page Gallery as well, as seen in Figure 7-12. Note that page layouts all end with the extension .aspx.

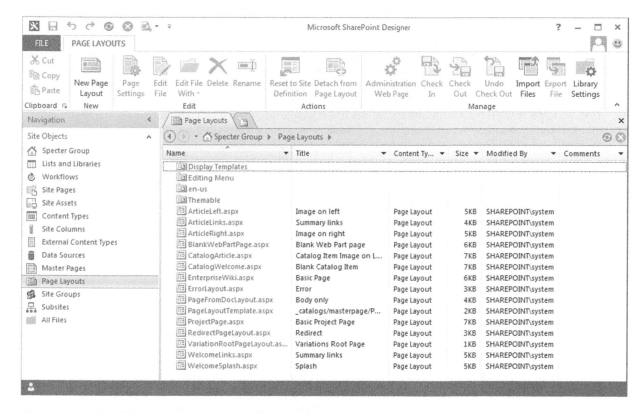

Figure 7-12. All OOTB page layouts as seen in the Master Page Gallery

Custom Page Layouts

OOTB page layouts might provide the layouts and metadata we need for sites built with SharePoint, but more often than not, we require customized page layouts that can store and display custom content and metadata. Custom page layouts tied together with existing or custom content types can satisfy these goals while still leveraging the power of SharePoint and its publishing infrastructure. This is not to say that OOTB page layouts do not provide a great resource, as you might find an OOTB page layout that is close to what you need. All that a page layout might need are a few minor modifications. No problem: You can create a content type that inherits from the Page content type, or even from the page content type that you want to customize, create a copy of the page layout you wish to customize, associate it with your custom content type, and finally customize your new page layout.

■ **Tip** You should never edit an OOTB file provided by SharePoint, including the OOTB master pages, page layouts, or content types. Always create your own copy of the original and create a new content type that inherits from an existing content type. If a patch or service pack for SharePoint is applied, OOTB files and assets might be overwritten, and thus you might lose your modifications.

Previous versions of SharePoint provided the ability to create and utilize custom page layouts. With the addition of Design Manager, managing page layouts has become easier and thus makes them more useful. In the world of responsive design, custom page layouts become a necessity, as we need to control our responsive grid. Although OOTB page layouts in SharePoint 2013 use a div-based structure, we would prefer to leverage a framework's structure. Custom page layouts also provide us the chance to tap into the power of custom content types that allow our page layouts to store metadata for a given layout.

There are two preferred methods to create and manage a page layout. First we can work directly with a .NET .aspx page layout in the Master Page Gallery. Better yet, we can take advantage of Design Manager and work with HTML page layouts. We examine both techniques and at the same time see how we can use both an OOTB page layout content type as well as the custom content type we created earlier in this chapter.

After we learn how to create page layouts, we will link our page layouts to their content types. Using SharePoint Designer and Design Manager we will reference and surface our content type field values for editing, displaying, or both. Finally we will expand our example site by creating new pages for Specter Group that use our custom page layout linked to our custom content type. Both scenarios build on the master page and navigation we already built in Chapter 5 and Chapter 6.

■ **Note**   To review how to add a content type, refer to the section "Content Types" earlier in this chapter.

Custom Page Layouts Without Design Manager

Custom page layouts were available to us in SharePoint 2010 and we can work with custom page layouts in SharePoint 2013 in a similar fashion. Page layouts are stored in the Master Page Gallery. When we connect to a site collection using a web editor tool such as SharePoint Designer, we can not only see all of our page layouts, but easily create and manage custom page layouts. When we create our own custom page layouts, we do not always have to create a custom content type for that page layout. In fact it is often best to utilize an existing content type if it has the columns our page layout requires and if it's being used in a similar manner as other page layouts that are associated with the content type.

Therefore in our first example of creating a custom page layout, we create a custom page layout for the Specter Group About page. The page requirements include one left-aligned image, a container to hold text along with the page title, and finally two web part zones beneath the content box. Because the requirements for this page only require a page image as well as one large rich text editor, we use the existing Article Page content type. We will start by looking at the HTML only version of this page provided by our design team at the end of Chapter 3 as seen in Figure 7-13.

// ABOUT SPECTER GROUP

Lorem ipsum dolor sit amet, consectetur adipiscing elit. Maecenas massa arcu, posuere eget hendrerit at, venenatis sit amet elit. Nullam tempor interdum nisi. Lorem ipsum dolor sit amet, consectetur adipiscing elit. Maecenas massa arcu, posuere eget hendrerit at, venenatis sit amet elit. Lorem ipsum dolor sit amet, consectetur adipiscing elit. Maecenas massa arcu, posuere eget hendrerit at, venenatis sit amet elit. Nullam tempor interdum nisi. Lorem ipsum dolor sit amet, consectetur adipiscing elit. Maecenas massa arcu, posuere eget hendrerit at, venenatis sit amet elit. Lorem ipsum dolor sit amet, consectetur adipiscing elit. Maecenas massa arcu, posuere eget hendrerit at, venenatis sit amet elit. Nullam tempor interdum nisi. Lorem ipsum dolor sit amet, consectetur adipiscing elit. Maecenas massa arcu, posuere eget hendrerit at, venenatis sit amet elit.

// LEFT COLUMN

Lorem ipsum dolor sit amet, consectetur adipiscing elit. Maecenas massa arcu, posuere eget hendrerit at, venenatis sit amet elit. Nullam tempor interdum nisi. Lorem ipsum dolor sit amet, consectetur adipiscing elit. Maecenas massa arcu, posuere eget hendrerit at, venenatis sit amet elit. Lorem ipsum dolor sit amet, consectetur adipiscing elit. Maecenas massa arcu, posuere eget hendrerit at, venenatis sit amet elit. Nullam tempor interdum nisi. Lorem ipsum dolor sit amet, consectetur adipiscing elit. Maecenas massa arcu, posuere eget hendrerit at, venenatis sit amet elit. Lorem ipsum dolor sit amet, consectetur adipiscing elit. Maecenas massa arcu, posuere eget hendrerit at, venenatis sit amet elit. Nullam tempor interdum nisi. Lorem ipsum dolor sit amet, consectetur adipiscing elit. Maecenas massa arcu, posuere eget hendrerit at, venenatis sit amet elit.

// RIGHT COLUMN

Lorem ipsum dolor sit amet, consectetur adipiscing elit. Maecenas massa arcu, posuere eget hendrerit at, venenatis sit amet elit. Nullam tempor interdum nisi. Lorem ipsum dolor sit amet, consectetur adipiscing elit. Maecenas massa arcu, posuere eget hendrerit at, venenatis sit amet elit. Lorem ipsum dolor sit amet, consectetur adipiscing elit. Maecenas massa arcu, posuere eget hendrerit at, venenatis sit amet elit. Nullam tempor interdum nisi. Lorem ipsum dolor sit amet, consectetur adipiscing elit. Maecenas massa arcu, posuere eget hendrerit at, venenatis sit amet elit. Lorem ipsum dolor sit amet, consectetur adipiscing elit. Maecenas massa arcu, posuere eget hendrerit at, venenatis sit amet elit. Nullam tempor interdum nisi. Lorem ipsum dolor sit amet, consectetur adipiscing elit. Maecenas massa arcu, posuere eget hendrerit at, venenatis sit amet elit.

Figure 7-13. *About Us page mockup*

In Listing 7-1 we can see the HTML that provides the structure and content for the About Us page seen in Figure 7-13.

Listing 7-1. HTML Mockup of About Us Content Area

```
<!-- page-content -->
<div class="page-content">
   <!-- entry-content -->
   <div class="section noborder cf">

      <h2 class="heading">About Specter Group</h2>

      <div class="floatleft">
         <img src=http://placehold.it/300x200&text=About+Specter+Group+Image
            alt="" />
```

```
      </div>
      <p>Lorem ipsum dolor sit amet, consectetu...<!--additional content--></p>

      <!-- 2 cols -->
      <div class="one-half">
          <h4 class="heading">Left column</h4>
          <p>Lorem ipsum dolor sit amet, consecte...<!--additional content--></p>
      </div>
      <div class="one-half last">
          <h4 class="heading">Right column</h4>
          <p>Lorem ipsum dolor sit amet, consect...<!--additional content--></p>
      </div>

      <div class="clearfix"></div>

      <!-- ENDS 2 cols -->
   </div>
   <!-- ENDS section -->
</div>
<!-- ENDS page-content -->
```

To create a new .NET .aspx page layout, follow these steps.

1. Open the root site of your site collection in SharePoint Designer 2013.

2. In the Site Objects left pane, click All Files. Navigate to _catalogs and then to its subfolder, masterpage.

3. We can create a new page layout from scratch, or by copying an existing page layout. An obvious choice should be to copy from the PageLayoutTemplate.aspx page layout. This OOTB page layout was designed as a starting place for custom page layouts. In our case, it would be advantageous for us to use one of the preexisting article page layouts, as our page layout requires a similar layout as the ArticleLeft.aspx page layout.

4. Right-click ArticleLeft.aspx and select Copy.

5. We recommend keeping branding assets organized by branding effort. For this example, paste the page layout copy in the spectergroup folder we created in Chapter 4, i.e. ~sitecollection/_catalogs/masterpage/spectergroup.

6. A new copy of ArticleLeft.aspx is now in your spectergroup folder. To rename this file, right-click ArticleLeft.aspx and select Rename. Rename this file about-pagelayout.aspx.

7. Right-click about-pagelayout.aspx and select Edit in Advanced Mode so that you can edit the page layout.

Review the code in Listing 7-2 for the updated about-pagelayout.aspx contents. Note that we only updated the PlaceHolderMain ContentPlaceHolder, so only that aspect of the code is provided in Listing 7-2. Further, you will notice no snippets like we saw in previous chapters, as we are not using the Design Manager at this point. All of the code for .aspx page layout is HTML and ASP.NET markup. We replaced title and content blocks with a combination of SharePoint controls such as EditModePanel, TextField, FieldValue, RichImageField, and WebPartZone to provide a page layout that can house content, images, and additional web parts as required by page authors.

Listing 7-2. PlaceHolderMain of about-pagelayout.aspx

```
<asp:Content ContentPlaceholderID="PlaceHolderMain" runat="server">
    <!-- page-content -->
    <div class="page-content">
        <!-- entry-content -->
        <div class="section noborder cf">

            <PublishingWebControls:EditModePanel runat="server"
              PageDisplayMode="Edit" CssClass="edit-mode-panel">
              <SharePointWebControls:TextField runat="server" FieldName="Title"/>
            </PublishingWebControls:EditModePanel>
            <PublishingWebControls:EditModePanel runat="server"
              PageDisplayMode="Display">
              <h2 class="heading">
                  <SharePointWebControls:FieldValue id="PageTitle"
                      FieldName="Title" runat="server"/>
              </h2>
            </PublishingWebControls:EditModePanel>

            <PublishingWebControls:EditModePanel runat="server"
              CssClass="edit-mode-panel">
              <SharePointWebControls:TextField runat="server"
                  FieldName="SeoMetaDescription"/>
            </PublishingWebControls:EditModePanel>

            <div class="floatleft">
              <PublishingWebControls:RichImageField
                  FieldName="PublishingPageImage" runat="server"/>
            </div>

            <PublishingWebControls:RichHtmlField FieldName="PublishingPageContent"
                runat="server"/>

            <!-- 2 cols -->
            <div class="one-half">
              <WebPartPages:WebPartZone runat="server" Title="LeftZone"
                  ID="LeftColumn">
                <ZoneTemplate></ZoneTemplate>
              </WebPartPages:WebPartZone>
            </div>
            <div class="one-half last">
              <WebPartPages:WebPartZone runat="server" Title="RightZone"
                  ID="RightColumn">
                <ZoneTemplate></ZoneTemplate>
              </WebPartPages:WebPartZone>
            </div>

            <div class="clearfix"></div>
            <!-- ENDS 2 cols -->
        </div>
```

```
        <!-- ENDS section -->
    </div>
    <!-- ENDS page-content -->
</asp:Content>
```

If you compare the HTML prototype layout in Listing 7-1 with the page layout in Listing 7-2, you will notice that the basic HTML structure of the two blocks of code is essentially the same. They both use the same div structure. The difference is that the "content" from Listing 7-1, such as the heading `<h2 class="heading">About Specter Group</h2>`, has been replaced by SharePoint controls. We will break down the changes that we had to make to produce Listing 7-2.

■ **Note**   We discuss creating content pages and linking them to our custom page layouts later in this chapter, in the section "Creating and Publishing New Pages Based on Custom Page Layouts."

- The main heading of the page, `<h2 class="heading">About Specter Group</h2>`, gets replaced with three different types of SharePoint controls. The first control, EditModePanel, found in the `Microsoft.SharePoint.Publishing.WebControls` namespace, provides a panel that appears only while in edit mode or display mode. By default the EditModePanel will only display in edit mode unless the PageDisplayMode property is set to "Display". These panels are used to allow an author to edit the page heading while in edit mode, yet display the heading in an `<h2>` tag while in display mode.

- The next controls used are the FieldValue and TextField controls, both found in the `Microsoft.SharePoint.WebControls` namespace. These controls will either display the value of a metadata field (FieldValue) or provide a text box (TextField) to edit the metadata field while in edit mode.

- The main page layout image from Listing 7-1 gets replaced by another control, RichImageField, also found in the `Microsoft.SharePoint.Publishing.WebControls` namespace. This control will display an image while in display mode. While in edit mode an author has the ability to replace the image, all within the browser. This image control can be seen in Figure 7-14, where the text "Click here to insert a picture from SharePoint." is displayed.

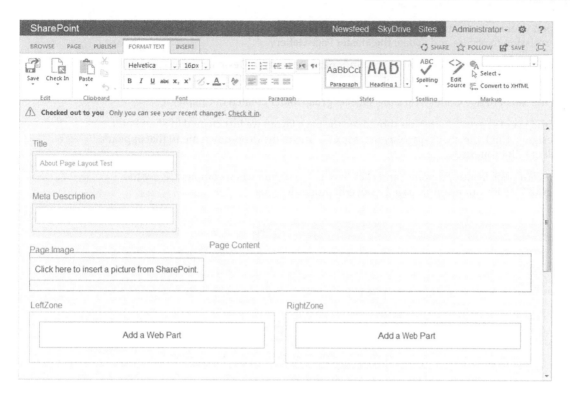

Figure 7-14. *Sample page layout, about-pagelayout.aspx, applied to an empty content page while in edit mode*

- The third interesting block in Listing 7-2 is the `RichHtmlField` control. As you might be able to notice, this too is in the `Microsoft.SharePoint.Publishing.WebControls` namespace. Just like the `RichImageField`, the `RichHtmlField` will display the contents of the field it is tied to. In our case this is the `PublishingPageContent` field in our pages associated content type. While in edit mode though, an author is provided a rich text editor. In Figure 7-14, the Page Content control has been highlighted. Notice how the ribbon includes text formatting tools.

- The final block of code in Listing 7-2 of interest replaces the two columns of text below the image. To provide for more flexibility, Listing 7-2 uses two `WebPartZone` controls found in the `Microsoft.SharePoint.WebPartPages` namespace. Web part zones allow for a large number of web parts within each zone, including the Content Editor Web Part, Content Search Web Parts, and much more. We could have created custom fields in a custom content type and displayed the field values instead. `WebPartZone` controls provide more flexibility to page authors, but possibly too much control. If a content block in a page layout will only contain text, you will lean toward custom fields, whereas if a content block requires a large number of web parts, a `WebPartZone` would be more appropriate.

Editing Page Layout Properties

Before we can use a page layout for a particular content page, we must first set its properties. We can accomplish this via the browser.

■ **Note** At a minimum, be sure to review and set the content type for a new page layout.

1. Open your site collection in a browser. You must log in with an account that has permission to access and update the Master Page Gallery.

2. Navigate to your site collection Site Settings page. In the Web Designer Galleries section, click Master pages and page layouts.

3. In the Master Page Gallery, click the spectergroup folder created in Chapter 4.

4. In the spectergroup folder you should see the page layout we just created in SharePoint Designer. Click the about-pagelayout.aspx file and in the drop-down menu that appears, select Edit Properties.

5. Set your page layout properties and click Save in the ribbon when complete. Refer to Figure 7-15 for our example page layout edit properties page.

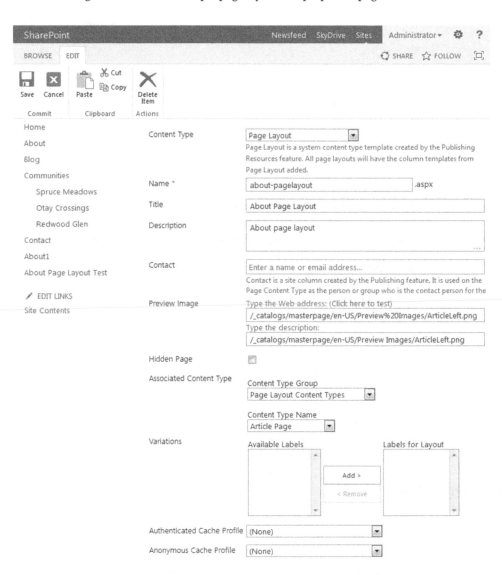

Figure 7-15. *Edit the page layout properties*

a. Content Type: We can set the primary content type for this file. In our case this must be Page Layout, although when working with Design Manager we will see how we can use a different content type.

b. Name: This is the file name. We will leave this the same, but if you wish to rename the file, you can change the Name property.

c. Title: The title of this page layout as displayed throughout the site. Because we copied this page layout from the `ArticleLeft.aspx` OOTB page layout, the Title will have been preset. We want to change this to a title that is more meaningful. Our title will be About.

d. Description: The optional description of the page layout.

e. Contact: Provide the name or e-mail address of the primary contact for this page layout.

f. Preview Image: You can provide a preview image and description for this page layout. Learn how in the section "Creating a Page Layout Preview Icon" later in this chapter.

g. Hidden Page: If this check box is left cleared, this page layout will be hidden. We will leave this cleared.

h. Associated Content Type: Here is where we actually specify what content type we wish to link this page layout to. In this case we want this page layout associated with the Article Page content type found in the Page Layout Content Types group.

i. Variations: If we have variations of our site, we can set labels here. We review multilingual sites and variations in Chapter 14.

j. Cache Profiles: You can set cache profiles to increase page load performance. We will leave both fields set to (None).

Publishing a Page Layout

Before a page layout can be available for use by a content page, the page layout must be checked in and published. In the days of SharePoint 2010, out of the box there was a strict check-in, publish, and approval workflow. In SharePoint 2013 this has been simplified to a single step. You might start to notice that you do not have to check out a file to begin editing it either. SharePoint 2013 still allows us to check out and check in files, but this is no longer a requirement.

1. In your browser, navigate to the `spectergroup` folder in the Master Page Gallery.

2. Click the `about-pagelayout.aspx` file (see Figure 7-16).

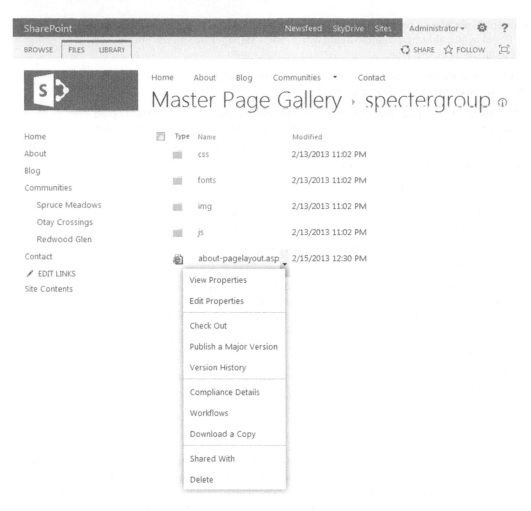

Figure 7-16. *Publishing a page layout in the Master Page Gallery*

- If you did not check out this file before editing its properties, click Publish a Major Version to publish a major version of this page layout.

- If you did check out this file before editing its properties, click Check In.

  a. In the Check in dialog box, select the Major version (publish) option, decide if you wish to keep the file checked out, and add any comments.

  b. When you are ready, click OK to check in and publish a major version.

Your page layout is now ready for use by content pages. We review how to utilize a page layout in a content page in the later section, "Creating and Publishing New Pages Based on Custom Page Layouts."

■ **Note**   If you make a change to a page layout, you must publish a major version before other users, including anonymous users, observe your modifications including changes to code or properties.

Creating a Page Layout Preview Icon

In the earlier section "Editing Page Layout Properties," we discussed one of the properties, the Preview Image property. Every page layout can be associated with a preview or thumbnail image that is useful when distinguishing one layout from the next in the page layout preview pane. We will see how quickly we can create a page preview icon, which will improve the authoring experience and provide a better branded site.

To get started, we should first see what preview icons SharePoint 2013 provides us. Your preview icons can be stored almost anywhere in your site collection, although you will find SharePoint's default preview icons in your Master Page Gallery. For U.S. English installations, you will find preview icons in ~sitecollection/_catalogs/ masterpage/en-us/PreviewImages. For other language packages you will need to replace en-us with your standard language code.

Complete the following steps to create a page preview icon:

1. Using WebDAV, or SharePoint Designer if you wish, open your site collection and navigate to ~sitecollection/_catalogs/masterpage/en-us/PreviewImages. We recommend opening the PreviewImages folder in Windows Explorer using WebDAV because you can more easily manipulate files using external tools.

2. There exist approximately eleven preview icons used by OOTB master pages and page layouts. Create a copy of a preview image (WelcomeTOC.png in this case) to provide a template image to work with. Select WelcomeTOC.png, copy it to the clipboard, and then paste the file back into the same directory. Select the newly created file and rename it SpecterAbout.png.

3. Open your preview icon in your favorite image editor (we use Photoshop for this walkthrough). You will notice that a page layout icon image has a resolution of 72 px by 54 px at ~96 dpi. The icon itself is smaller, leaving a padding around all sides. Using Photoshop we can make this icon appear however we like, although ideally we want it to resemble the page layout it will represent. For the About page we created the icon in Figure 7-17 and placed in the PreviewImages folder.

Figure 7-17. *Custom About page layout preview icon*

4. We can now edit the properties of our page layout to link to our new preview icon. Refer to the earlier section, "Editing Page Layout Properties," to learn how to update page layout properties.

Creating a custom preview icon for a custom page layout or even a custom master page is not necessary, but authors and administrators appreciate the consistent user interface, which we know always helps drive user adoption through an improved user experience.

Custom Page Layouts With Design Manager

As we saw with mpster Pages, the Design Manager opens up a new technique in which we can create, modify, and manage page layouts. No longer are we stuck with the .NET .aspx page and SharePoint Designer. Now we can take an HTML-only page created during the mockup phase (i.e., created by our design department, or even created by an outside agency) and quickly integrate this into SharePoint.

■ **Note**   Remember that Design Manager allows us to quickly create a design package as well to quickly package and redeploy a branding initiative to another site collection, say, when moving from a development site to a production site.

When we converted our HTML page to a master page in Chapter 4, we uploaded the HTML file to the Master Page Gallery. SharePoint then converted this HTML file to an HTML master page for us with its corresponding .master file. With page layouts we have to follow a slightly different technique because a page layout in Design Manager must be first associated with a master page.

In this walkthrough we are going to expand on our Specter Group site by converting a Specter Property page prototype to a page layout in Design Manager. We will link this page layout to the custom content type we created earlier in this chapter. We will review the original HTML file to find what part of the source will be a part of our page layout. We will then create a new page layout in Design Manager and move this to our spectergroup folder in the Master Page Gallery. After the page layout file has been created, we will modify the page layout to include the property layout by using snippets to access additional SharePoint content. Finally we will link the page layout to our custom content type and make our page layout available for use by a content page.

Preparing an HTML Prototype for Page Layout Conversion

Remember how when we created a master page in Design Manager in Chapter 4, we had to separate the aspects of a page between that which is a part of the master page and that which is a part of the page content? We had to move a ContentPlaceHolder markup tag added by Design Manager from the bottom of the converted master page to its proper location, and then move what would become the sample content into this ContentPlaceHolder preview section. When you create a new page layout, you will be transferring the content aspect of a given HTML prototype into a page layout. This is why it is a best practice to include SharePoint component placement comments in the original HTML prototype to make this transfer easier with less confusion.

■ **Note**   To review how to convert an HTML page into a master page in Design Manager, refer to Chapter 4.

For the scenario just outlined, we start by looking at the HTML-only version of this page provided by our design team at the end of Chapter 3, as seen in Figure 7-18. We limit our look at just what is a part of the page layout and not what would be a part of the master page.

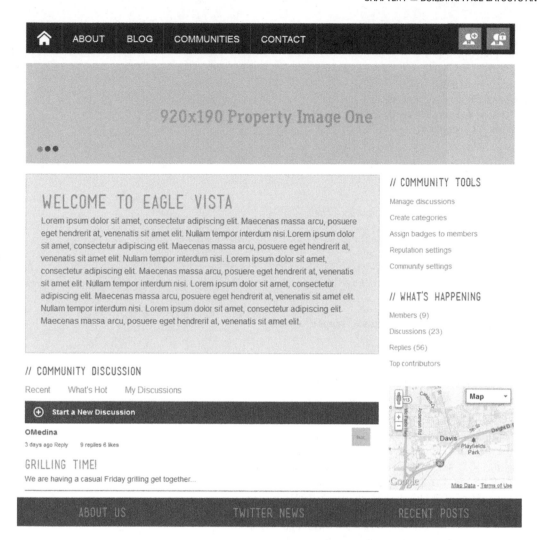

Figure 7-18. *Sample property page layout without full header and footer*

In Listing 7-3 we can see the HTML required for just the page layout portion of Figure 7-18.

Listing 7-3. HTML Mockup, General Property Page (Some HTML Has Been Removed for Brevity)

```
<!--Page content-->
<!-- SLIDER -->
<div class="slider-wrapper theme-nivo-specter theme-default slider-community">
   <div class="ribbon"></div>
   <div id="slider-property" class="nivoSlider">
      <img src=http://placehold.it/920x190&text=920x190+Property+Image+One
        alt="" />
      <!--more images - removed for brevity-->
   </div>
</div>
<!-- ENDS SLIDER -->
```

```html
<div id="posts-list" class="community-listing cf">
   <!--community listing-->
   <div class="page-content cf">
      <article>
         <!-- property content -->
         <h2>Welcome to Eagle Vista</h2>
         <p>Lorem ipsum dolor sit amet, consectetur adipiscing elit...</p>
         <!-- end property content -->
      </article>
   </div>
   <!-- end community list -->

   <div id="comments-wrap">
      <h4 class="heading">Community Discussion</h4>

      <ul class="comments-links-horizontal">
         <li><a href="#">Recent</a></li>
         <li><a href="#">What's Hot</a></li>
         <li><a href="#">My Discussions</a></li>
      </ul>

      <div class="toggle-trigger"><i class="simple"></i>
         Start a New Discussion
      </div>
      <div class="toggle-container form">
         <!--new discussion form - removed for brevity-->
      </div>

      <ol class="commentlist">
         <li class="comment even thread-even depth-1" id="li-comment-1">
            <div id="comment-1" class="comment-body cf">
               <img alt='' src='http://placehold.it/560x300&text=Avatar'
                  class='avatar avatar-35 photo' />
               <div class="comment-author vcard">OMedina</div>
               <div class="comment-meta commentmetadata">
                  <span class="comment-date">3 days ago  </span>
                  <span class="comment-reply-link-wrap">
                     <a class='comment-reply-link' href='#'>Reply</a>
                  </span>
                  <span class="comment-replies">9 replies</span>
                  <span class="comment-likes">6 likes  </span>
               </div>
               <div class="comment-inner">
                  <h4><a href="#">Grilling Time!</a></h4>
                  <p>We are having a casual Friday grilling get together...</p>
               </div>
            </div>
         </li>
         <!--Additional comments - removed for brevity -->
      </ol>
   </div>
</div>
<!--end post listing-->
```

```html
<!-- sidebar -->
<aside id="sidebar" class="community-listing">
    <ul>
        <li class="block">
            <h4 class="heading">Community Tools</h4>
            <ul>
                <li class="page-item"><a href="#">Manage discussions</a></li>
                <!--additional tools-->
            </ul>
        </li>
        <li class="block">
            <h4 class="heading">What's Happening</h4>
            <ul>
                <li class="cat-item"><a href="#" title="title">
                    Members<span class="post-counter">(9)</span></a>
                </li>
                <!--additional links - removed for brevity -->
            </ul>
        </li>
        <li class="block">
            <div id="map_canvas"></div>
            <!-- GOOGLE MAPS Script - removed for brevity-->
        </li>
    </ul>
</aside>
<!-- ENDS sidebar -->
<!--end page content-->
```

Creating a New Page Layout in Design Manager

HTML mockup pages cannot be converted directly to page layouts as we did with master pages because a page layout only contains content, markup, and other HTML for content placeholders in the master page. We saw this same structure in page layouts not managed by Design Manager in the earlier section, "Custom Page Layouts Without Design Manager." In Design Manager, we manage an HTML-only file associated with the HTML Page Layout content type. This HTML file is in turn associated with the actual .aspx page layout that we do not manage, nor can we edit.

■ **Note**   We only manage the HTML page layout; we do not, nor should not, manage or edit the associated .aspx page layout ourselves.

The HTML page layout that we manage is built from a master page we select when we create the HTML page layout. This allows the HTML page layout to contain all of the HTML necessary to manage the layout using any HTML editor such as Dreamweaver, at the same time having additional code necessary to allow Design Manager to know how to create the associated .aspx page layout. Because SharePoint would have difficulty knowing where the content within an HTML mockup resides, we cannot convert an HTML mockup in Design Manager. We must create a new page layout and then add our content and layout to this new page layout to meet our needs. Once we create an HTML page layout, we can create a copy of just this HTML page layout and Design Manager will automatically associate it with its own .aspx page layout.

To create a new page layout using Design Manage, follow these steps:

1. Open Design Manager in a browser. In the left menu in Design Manager click Edit Page Layouts.

2. On the Edit Page Layouts page, click Create a page layout found in the middle of page.

3. A Create a Page Layout dialog box opens. You need to provide a name, the master page on which this page layout should be based, and finally the content type this page layout should use. For our example, we use the following settings.

    a. Name: Community Property.

    b. Master Page: spectergroup/spectergroup (notice how Design Manager includes the folder that Master Page is found in as well).

    c. Content Type: Property Page (Your page layouts may be associated with whichever content type you require, assuming that the content type is based on the Page content type, or based on another content type that has the Page content type in its lineage.)

4. Click OK to create the new page layout.

Once the page layout has been created you should see a page similar to Figure 7-19. The page layout was added to your Master Page Gallery so you can use your web editor (SharePoint Designer, Dreamweaver, etc.) to access the .html file.

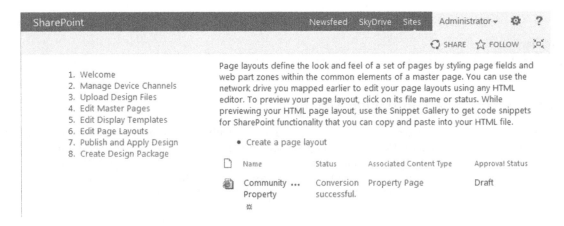

Figure 7-19. *A new page layout in Design Manager*

SharePoint will automatically set the file name of your new page layout to be the same as the name you provided when creating the page layout. Spaces will be replaced with the underscore (_) character. For our example, SharePoint creates a page layout with a file name of Community_Property.html.

In the next few subsections we review how to move the page layout to our branding folder as well as how to modify the page layout and use page layout snippets.

Moving a Page Layout to Another Location in Design Manager

As we just noticed when creating a page layout in Design Manager, the page layout was added to the root of the Master Page Gallery. Often you will want to move your page layouts to a specific branding directory, in our demo the `spectergroup` subfolder in the Master Page Gallery. Moving a page layout is not difficult, but there is a correct way to do it.

1. The key to moving a page layout in Design Manager is to note that you only need to move the .html file; Design Manager will handle the .aspx file for you. Open the Master Page Gallery in SharePoint Designer, or even quicker, map your Master Page Gallery as a drive in Windows Explorer.

2. Find the page layout you wish to move, in our case `Community-Property.html`, cut (Ctrl-c) the file, and move it to your clipboard. Notice how the space in our page layout title Community Property was replaced with a hyphen for our page layout file name.

3. Navigate to the subdirectory to which you wish to move the page layout, in our example, `spectergroup`, and paste (Ctrl-v) the `Community-Property.html` file.

4. After the transfer has been completed, refresh the folder and you will see that not only did your .html file get transferred, but the .aspx file was moved as well.

Just to be clear, we only need to move the .html page layout and not the .aspx file. Design Manager handles the .aspx file for us. Once we move the .html page layout, Design Manager automatically removes the original .aspx file and creates a new .aspx for us in our subdirectory.

Customizing a Page Layout

Now that we have our blank page layout in the correct folder, it is time to customize it. Let's start by reviewing the page layout created for us by Design Manager. Open the Master Page Gallery in your web editor or Windows Explorer. We want to open the .html file we just created. In our case we need to drill down to the `spectergroup` folder and open the `Community_Property.html` page layout. Have we said this enough? Do not touch the .aspx file.

Look at the HTML code of the page layout, and you will see much of the HTML from the master page. Beware that just because this looks like a fully valid HTML file, it is not. Just like with standard .aspx page layouts, in HTML page layouts, you can only edit content within content placeholders. Content placeholders are easy to find.

Start by reviewing the `<head>` section. Right away you will notice comment tags that start with `<!--MS:<asp:ContentPlaceHolder...>` similar to the one shown in Listing 7-4.

Listing 7-4. Sample ContentPlacerHolder Comment Code in HTML Page Layout Managed by Design Manager

```
<!--MS:<asp:ContentPlaceHolder id="PlaceHolderPageTitle" runat="server">-->
  <!--MS:<SharePoint:ProjectProperty Property="Title" runat="server">-->
  <!--ME:</SharePoint:ProjectProperty>-->
  <!--CS: Start Page Field: Title Snippet-->
  <!--SPM:<%@Register Tagprefix="PageFieldFieldValue"
      Namespace="Microsoft.SharePoint.WebControls"
      Assembly="Microsoft.SharePoint, Version=15.0.0.0, Culture=neutral,
      PublicKeyToken=71e9bce111e9429c"%>-->
    <!--MS:<PageFieldFieldValue:FieldValue
        FieldName="fa564e0f-0c70-4ab9-b863-0177e6ddd247" runat="server">-->
    <!--ME:</PageFieldFieldValue:FieldValue>-->
  <!--CE: End Page Field: Title Snippet-->
<!--ME:</asp:ContentPlaceHolder>-->
```

■ **Important**   When editing an HTML page layout, you can only change content found within the tags:

```
<!--MS:<asp:ContentPlaceHolder id="PlaceHolderID" runat="server">-->
```

```
<!--ME:</asp:ContentPlaceHolder>-->
```

Do not edit or modify any HTML or code outside of a `ContentPlaceHolder` block as it will be ignored.

Page layouts will contain many `ContentPlaceHolder` tags that correspond to the content placeholders found in the Master Page. In fact if there is a content placeholder in the master page that was not included automatically when the page layout was created, you can add the following block to your page layout; just replace `"PlaceHolderID"` with the actual "ID" from the master page for the correct `ContentPlaceHolder` you wish to add:

```
<!--MS:<asp:ContentPlaceHolder id="PlaceHolderID" runat="server">-->
<!--ME:</asp:ContentPlaceHolder>-->
```

Let's look at how Design Manager processes the code block in Listing 7-4 in the page layout's .aspx file. Open the corresponding .aspx file, in our example `Community_Property.aspx`, in your editor. It is fine to open an .html page layout's corresponding .aspx file, we will just not edit the .aspx file. Look for the ID `PlaceHolderPageTitle`. You will find this ID is now in an `<asp:Content>` tag as shown in Listing 7-5.

Listing 7-5. Content Block, PlaceHolderPageTitle Found in .aspx Page Layout

```
<asp:Content runat="server" ContentPlaceHolderID="PlaceHolderPageTitle">
    <SharePoint:ProjectProperty Property="Title"
        runat="server">
    </SharePoint:ProjectProperty>
    <PageFieldFieldValue:FieldValue
        FieldName="fa564e0f-0c70-4ab9-b863-0177e6ddd247"
        runat="server">
    </PageFieldFieldValue:FieldValue>
</asp:Content>
```

If you worked with page layouts in SharePoint 2010 this will look very familiar to you. Design Manager took the tag

```
<!--MS:<asp:ContentPlaceHolder id="PlaceHolderPageTitle" runat="server">-->
```

and converted this to the correct ASP.NET markup:

```
<asp:Content runat="server" ContentPlaceHolderID="PlaceHolderPageTitle">.
```

Design Manager then took the Markup Start (MS) tags and created their corresponding ASP.NET markup, in our case the `Sharepoint:ProjectProperty` and `PageFieldFieldValue:FindValue` tags.

You should notice one other interesting comment tag in Listing 7-4, `<!--SPM:` (SharePoint Markup). This tag allows us to register assemblies, such as SharePoint assemblies or even our own custom assemblies, that our markup requires. In the preceding example, we are registering the namespace `Microsoft.SharePoint.WebControls` found in `Microsoft.SharePoint` assembly because we want to use the `FieldValue` control. To access controls found within a namespace, a tag prefix must be provided. In this example a tax prefix of `PageFieldFieldValue` was provided. This means we can now use the `FieldValue` control with the tag `< PageFieldFieldValue:FieldValue />`.

The `<!--SPM:` comment allows us to register different namespaces and tag prefixes throughout our page layout. In fact it is a best practice to always register all tag prefixes needed within a given content placeholder. Design Manager will handle any case in which you register the same tag prefix in the same namespace in one page layout for you.

Further down our example HTML page layout you will find the `<body>` tag. Here exist a few more `<!--MS:<asp:ContentPlaceHolder>-->` comment tags. In our example we see the code shown in Listing 7-6.

Listing 7-6. Body Tag in HTML Page Layout (Certain Tags Have Had Some Properties Removed for Brevity)

```
<body>
    <!--MS:<asp:ContentPlaceHolder ID="PlaceHolderTopNavBar" runat="server">-->
        <!--MS:<SharePoint:AspMenu ID="TopNavigationMenu" runat="server">-->
            <!--PS: Start of READ-ONLY PREVIEW (do not modify)-->
            <!--PE: End of READ-ONLY PREVIEW-->
        <!--ME:</SharePoint:AspMenu>-->
    <!--ME:</asp:ContentPlaceHolder>-->
    <!--MS:<asp:ContentPlaceHolder ID="PlaceHolderPageTitleInTitleArea"
        runat="server">-->
        <!--CS: Start Page Field: Title Snippet-->
        <!--SPM:<%@Register Tagprefix="PageFieldFieldValue"%>-->
        <!--MS:<PageFieldFieldValue:FieldValue
            FieldName="fa564e0f-0c70-4ab9-b863-0177e6ddd247" runat="server">-->
        <!--ME:</PageFieldFieldValue:FieldValue>-->
        <!--CE: End Page Field: Title Snippet-->
    <!--ME:</asp:ContentPlaceHolder>-->
    <!--MS:<asp:ContentPlaceHolder ID="PlaceHolderMain" runat="server">-->
        <div>
            <!--CS: Start Page Field: Title Snippet-->
            <!--SPM:<%@Register Tagprefix="PageFieldTextField"%>-->
            <!--SPM:<%@Register Tagprefix="Publishing" %>-->
            <!--MS:<Publishing:EditModePanel runat="server"
                CssClass="edit-mode-panel">-->
                <!--MS:<PageFieldTextField:TextField
                    FieldName="fa564e0f-0c70-4ab9-b863-0177e6ddd247"
                    runat="server">-->
                <!--ME:</PageFieldTextField:TextField>-->
            <!--ME:</Publishing:EditModePanel>-->
            <!--CE: End Page Field: Title Snippet-->
        </div>
    <!--ME:</asp:ContentPlaceHolder>-->
</body>
```

■ **Note** If you select an OOTB content type when creating an HTML page layout, the `PlaceHolderMain` `ContentPlaceHolder` will contain snippets to some content type columns. These snippet blocks are not included when creating a HTML page layout associated with a custom content type but can be quickly added with snippets. Learn more about snippets later in this chapter in the section "Page Layout Snippets."

By now the HTML in Listing 7-6 should look familiar. There are three ContentPlaceHolder blocks within the <body> tag, the first two replacing our top navigation bar, PlaceHolderTopNavBar, and the second replacing the Title in the header, PlaceHolderPageTitleInTitleArea. These two might be of interest to us, but if you look in our HTML master page this page layout uses, you will find that these content placeholders are not referenced. That is strange, isn't it?

If you open the associated .master file for our master page, though, you will find these two content placeholders at the bottom of the .master file, but with their visibility property set to false, thus hiding the content placeholder. If you worked with master pages in SharePoint 2010, you might remember that you can never remove a content placeholder from a master page just because you are not going to use it. Rather you had to hide it somehow because the content placeholder may still be referenced and is thus needed. Design Manager handles content placeholders we do not intend to use so we do not have to concern ourselves with unused content placeholders with Design Manager. Another plus!

Because we are not using PlaceHolderTopNavBar and PlaceHolderPageTitleInTitleArea, we can remove them from our <body> section. We now need to add our actual layout to the final Content Placeholder, PlaceHolderMain. If we review the PlaceHolderMain ContentPlaceHolder, we will see there is already a snippet, or snippets, provided. In Listing 7-6 a snippet is included to display the page title. We are going to replace this for now with the content layout from our mockup HTML provided in Listing 7-3. When this is complete, the <body> section will look similar to Listing 7-7. If everything goes correctly, this HTML page layout should look the same as Figure 7-18 when viewed in Design Manager's Page Layout Preview. Refer to Figure 7-20 for the beginning of such a view.

Listing 7-7. New Body Section (Many Tags Have Had Properties Temoved for Brevity)

```
<body>
    <!--MS:<asp:ContentPlaceHolder ID="PlaceHolderMain" runat="server">-->
        <!--Page content-->
        <!-- SLIDER -->
        ...
        <!-- ENDS SLIDER -->

        <div id="posts-list" class="community-listing cf">
            <!--community listing-->
            ...
            <!-- end community list -->

            <div id="comments-wrap">
            ...
            </div>
        </div>
        <!--end post listing-->

        <!-- sidebar -->
        <aside id="sidebar" class="community-listing">
        ...
        </aside>
        <!-- ENDS sidebar -->
        <!--end page content-->
    <!--ME:</asp:ContentPlaceHolder>-->
</body>
```

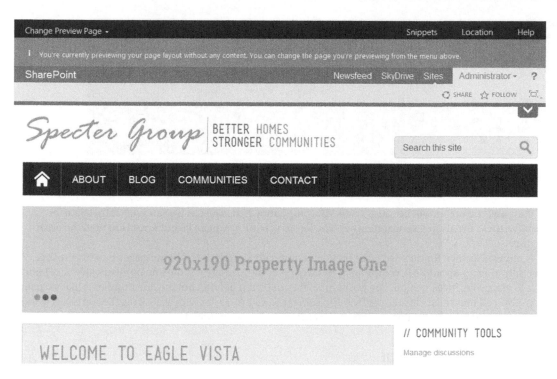

Figure 7-20. *Community property page layout with static page content, viewed in Design Manager's Page Layout Preview*

A few notes are in order. First, we did remove the Title snippet. We cover snippets in the next section. The content placeholder now has only static content; there is no way to use this page layout for a content page and have that content page have its own content. This, too, will be solved with page layout snippets. Third, you do not need to copy and paste HTML from a mockup HTML file. You could skip the prototype stage and create your page layout directly in the HTML page layout file. Finally later in this chapter we show how to copy an HTML page layout to speed up the process of creating a new page layout in the section, "Copying an HTML Page Layout From an Existing Page Layout."

HTML Page Layout Errors and Warnings

Just as we saw when converting an HTML mockup to an HTML master page in Chapter 4, our HTML page layouts can also contain errors that SharePoint will reject. SharePoint will throw errors and warnings on the Edit Page Layouts page in Design Manager. Detailed error messages are available on a Page Layout Preview page. See Figure 7-21 for a common page layout error.

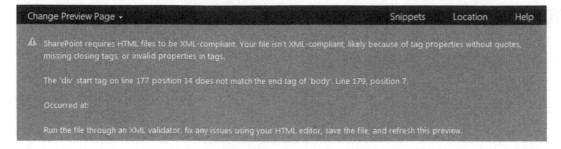

Figure 7-21. Sample HTML Page Layout Preview Error Message

More often than not, the errors will be caused by XML compliancy issues just as we saw with HTML master pages. We find and fix these errors in a similar manner. The key to solving any page layout error is to read the error message thoroughly.

SharePoint is not well known for detailed error messages, but with SharePoint 2013 messages have improved. In Figure 7-21, we see an error about XML compliancy, but what is of more interest is the line numbers given, 177 and 179. That is where to start your investigation. The position might not be too helpful, but the line number is likely close. Remember that in XML, all tags must close either by self-closing (i.e., <link />) or with a close tag (i.e., <div></div>).

For more information on fixing common errors and warnings, refer to Chapter 4.

Publishing an HTML Page Layout

Before an HTML page layout can be used by a content page, a major version of the HTML page layout must be checked in and published. This can be accomplished in a similar manner as for page layouts not managed by Design Manager. The Design Manager can also be used to publish a page layout.

To check in and publish a major version of a HTML page layout, follow these steps.

1. Open Design Manager in a browser and click Edit Page Layouts in the left menu.

2. On the Edit Page Layouts page, next to the page layout you wish to publish, you will see an ellipsis (…). This symbol is used by SharePoint 2013 to reference a menu for a particular item. Click … next to the page layout you wish to publish and a page layout property dialog box opens. In this dialog box, click … found in the lower left.

3. In the drop-down that appears, click Publish a Major Version to publish this page layout, thus making it available for content pages.

■ **Note** If you customize a page layout after it has been published, you must publish a major version again before all users will see your modifications.

Page Layout Snippets

Page layout snippets provide access to SharePoint and .NET controls in HTML page layouts. These snippets are exactly like the HTML master page snippets covered in Chapter 4, and in fact we have already seen page layout snippets in the previous section.

We continue our example by expanding on the HTML page layout code block we created in Listing 7-7. We can use snippets to allow our content pages that use our page layout to have dynamic content.

First we review the different snippets available to us and then we create a few snippets and add them to our page layout.

Available Page Layout Snippet Overview

We need to load the Snippet Manager for the page layout we wish to update.

1. Open Design Manager in a browser and in the left menu click Edit Page Layouts.

2. On the Edit Page Layouts page, click Conversion Successful next to the page layout you wish to update. If you don't see Conversion Successful, refer to the earlier section, "HTML Page Layout Errors and Warnings."

3. The Preview Page Layout will load, providing a preview of the page layout. In the Preview ribbon, shown in Figure 7-22, click Snippets, which will load the Snippet Gallery in a new tab.

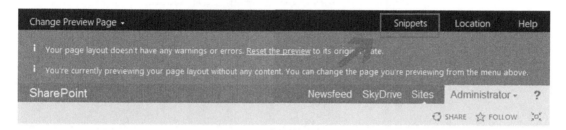

Figure 7-22. *Page Layout Preview Page, Snippet Gallery location*

The Snippet Gallery provides us access to a very large set of snippets that we can heavily customize, copy, and paste into our HTML page layout. The snippets are broken into four main sections: Page Fields, Containers, Web Parts, and Custom ASP.NET Markup, as shown in Figure 7-23.

Figure 7-23. *Snippet Gallery snippet categories*

■ **Note**   Once you customize a snippet's attributes, be sure to click Update at the bottom of the customization page before copying the HTML snippet code to the clipboard.

Page Fields

The Page Fields section contains one snippet type, that being page fields. Page fields provide us access to all fields within the content type and its lineage that this page layout is associated with. The list of page fields will change depending on which content type a page layout is associated with. Clicking on the Page Fields icon causes a list of fields to appear. You may select a particular field you wish to make available on a page layout. Once you load a page field, there are quite a few attributes you can customize in the Behavior and Misc menus found to the right. Refer to Figure 7-24 for a list of page fields for the Article Page content type along with the page field properties.

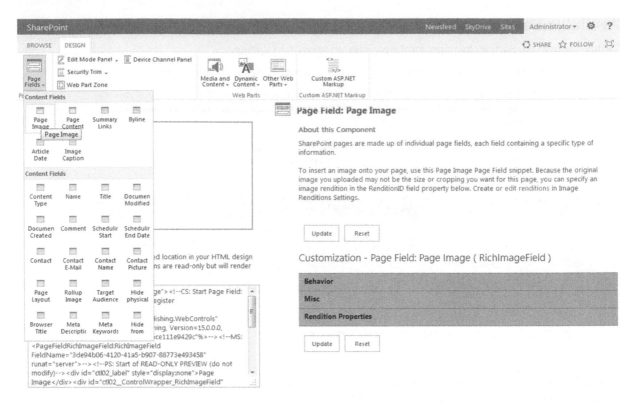

Figure 7-24. *Snippet Manager: List of page fields for Article Page content type*

Containers

You will find four snippet types within the Containers section, these being snippets that are designed as containers that might hold other snippets, web parts, content, markup, and so on. Therefore once you add one of these container snippets to your page layout, you can further customize them by adding additional markup and other snippets, within its code block.

- Edit Mode Panel: The Edit Mode Panel provides the ability to control if a particular block of code will be displayed only in edit mode, or in display (regular) mode. This is often used to allow access to edit metadata such as the page title, meta description, keywords, and other such page fields that would not be displayed on the content page, but should be editable without having to load the content page's properties.

- Security Trim: The Security Trim container allows us to control if a particular block of code will be displayed based on the permission level of the current user. We can create blocks that will show or hide a block of code to all users, only anonymous users, or only authenticated users. Once we select the Authentication Restriction, we can then provide a further level of permission requirements based on whether a particular user has permissions to perform a specific action. This is another powerful container if we want to provide additional information or controls for, say, authors only.

- Web Part Zone: This is self-explanatory. The Web Part Zone snippet allows us to create a web part zone for our page layout that authors can use to add web parts as needed via the browser, unique to each content page.

- Device Channel Panel: Device channels are new to SharePoint 2013 and allow us to create a particular channel that is associated with a device, say an iPad, Surface tablet, Windows Phone, and so on. Device channel panels allow us to create a particular panel in a page layout that can be associated with a particular device channel. The content, HTML code and snippets added to a particular device channel panel would only be displayed for that device channel.

■ **Note**   To learn more about device channels and device channel panels please refer to `http://sprwd.com/yysdg3` or Chapter 5.

Web Parts

The Web Parts container provides us access to many web parts available in SharePoint. Each web part snippet can be heavily customized as with other snippets.

- Media and Content: Web parts that provide quick access to media such as the Image Viewer Web Part and content such as the ever popular and seemingly boundless Content Editor Web Part.

- Dynamic Content: Web parts that provide access to dynamic content based on your SharePoint site's existing content or structure. Examples include the Content Query Web Part we used in previous versions of SharePoint as well as the new, extremely powerful Content Search Web Part. We review the Content Search Web Part in more detail in Chapter 9 in conjunction with search-driven content.

- Other Web Parts: A very long set of other common Web Parts that we might need, including the HTML Form Web Part, Social Collaboration Web Parts, and additional Search Web Parts.

Custom ASP.NET Markup

The final section of snippets, the Custom ASP.NET Markup section, provides access to one snippet. The Custom ASP. NET Markup provides us the ability to have the Snippet Manager convert any ASP.NET markup we might have and need in our page layout in a snippet-friendly format. This could be very useful if you are moving over ASP.NET markup from your existing SharePoint 2010 page layouts. Although you could create the proper snippet code yourself using the `<!--MS-->` comment code, the Custom ASP.NET Markup generator will make this process much easier and take care of the details for you. This tool is the final catch-all that will allow us to create a snippet based on existing ASP. NET markup or from a custom Web Part.

Customizing a Page Layout with Snippets

Now that we have seen all of the available snippets available for page layouts, we look at how we select a particular snippet, customize its properties, and finally add a snippet to a page layout. For this demonstration we take the page layout we created in Listing 7-7 and replace the static content with the proper snippets.

In each section, we review which snippet we choose, the page layout HTML code block it replaces, as well as any attributes we customized. At the end we look at the final page layout `<body>` tag.

Editing Title and Meta Description

We would like to edit the page title and meta description inline, but this should only be visible while in edit mode. We therefore generate an Edit Mode Panel and then add two page fields. The snippets are found in the Snippet ribbon (see Figure 7-24). Also note that we are looking to create the same controls we described previously in "Custom Page Layouts Without Design Manager," just using Design Manager's snippet syntax.

1. We need to add an Edit Mode Panel snippet. This snippet will eventually contain our page field snippets. In the ribbon's Containers section, click the down arrow next to Edit Mode Panel. In the drop-down list, select Show only in Edit Mode to generate an Edit Mode Panel that will only display while in edit mode.

2. For page fields, look in the Page Fields section and click the Page Fields icon. This will cause a drop-down to appear (see Figure 7-24). Under Content Fields, select Title. Once you generate this snippet and copy the HTML snippet to your HTML page layout, return to the Content Fields section and create a Meta Description Page Field snippet as well.

■ **Note**   When you create page field snippets, SharePoint will link to your page field by its Content Type ID, such as fa564e0f-0c70-4ab9-b863-0177e6ddd247 for Title. You can replace this ID with the text-based FieldName. You can also remove duplicate ‹!--SPM: tags if they register the same namespaces.

Refer to Listing 7-8 to see how the page field snippets we generated earlier can be included within a Edit Mode Panel snippet.

Listing 7-8. Snippet Code for Page Title and Meta Description in Edit Mode Panel

```
<!--SPM:<%@Register Tagprefix="Publishing"
    Namespace="Microsoft.SharePoint.Publishing.WebControls"
    Assembly="Microsoft.SharePoint.Publishing, Version=15.0.0.0,
    Culture=neutral, PublicKeyToken=71e9bce111e9429c"%>-->
<!--MS:<Publishing:EditModePanel runat="server" CssClass="edit-mode-panel">-->
    <!--SPM:<%@Register Tagprefix="PageFieldTextField"
        Namespace="Microsoft.SharePoint.WebControls"
        Assembly="Microsoft.SharePoint, Version=15.0.0.0, Culture=neutral,
        PublicKeyToken=71e9bce111e9429c"%>-->
    <!--MS:<PageFieldTextField:TextField FieldName="Title" runat="server">-->
    <!--ME:</PageFieldTextField:TextField>-->

    <!--MS:<PageFieldTextField:TextField FieldName="SeoMetaDescription"
        runat="server">-->
    <!--ME:</PageFieldTextField:TextField>-->
<!--ME:</Publishing:EditModePanel>-->
```

Rotating Images

There are quite a few methods we could utilize to display a jQuery-based rotating banner in a page layout. The SharePoint 2013 way would be to use the Content Search Web Part and a custom list to store rotating images. We could create a custom list based on a custom content type to store images. A Content Search Web Part could then be generated to query a filtered list of images and using display templates we could have SharePoint format the proper JavaScript and jQuery code necessary for the rotating banner to work. We review this type of process in Chapter 9 on search-driven content.

For now, we generate and include a simple Web Part Zone that an author could use to add a Content Editor Web Part, a Content Search Web Part, and so on, to provide the actual rotating banner in a content page.

In the Snippet ribbon, within the Containers section, click Web Part Zone, and keep the default properties. Listing 7-9 shows the snippet for a general Web Part Zone.

Listing 7-9. Snippet Code for Web Part Zone

```
<!--SPM:<%@Register Tagprefix="WebPartPages"
    Namespace="Microsoft.SharePoint.WebPartPages"
    Assembly="Microsoft.SharePoint, Version=15.0.0.0, Culture=neutral,
    PublicKeyToken=71e9bce111e9429c"%>-->
<!--MS:<WebPartPages:WebPartZone runat="server" AllowPersonalization="false"
    ID="x5bb499f3b1df4f469fd12354190fd2a1" FrameType="TitleBarOnly"
    Orientation="Vertical">-->
    <!--MS:<ZoneTemplate>--><!--ME:</ZoneTemplate>-->
<!--ME:</WebPartPages:WebPartZone>-->
```

Editing and Displaying Field Columns

To display a content type column in both edit and display modes, we can use the same Page Fields snippet we saw before. Note that based on the column type, Design Manager might render a slightly different snippet for us. Let's look at the Page Content column and add that to our page layout.

In the Snippet ribbon, in the Page Fields group, click the Page Fields icon. Under Content Fields, select Page Content. Keep the default properties for the snippet. In Listing 7-10 we can see the snippet code generated for our Page Content field.

Listing 7-10. Snippet Code for Page Field With a RichHTMLField Control

```
<!--SPM:<%@Register Tagprefix="PageFieldRichHtmlField"
    Namespace="Microsoft.SharePoint.Publishing.WebControls"
    Assembly="Microsoft.SharePoint.Publishing, Version=15.0.0.0,
    Culture=neutral, PublicKeyToken=71e9bce111e9429c"%>-->
<!--MS:<PageFieldRichHtmlField:RichHtmlField
    FieldName="PublishingPageContent" runat="server">-->
<!--ME:</PageFieldRichHtmlField:RichHtmlField>-->
```

Notice how although we used the same Page Field snippet for the Title and Page Content column, Design Manager knew to create the correct control for the Page Content field. The proper control for the Title field is a TextField control, whereas for the Page Content field, we must use the RichHtmlField control. Design Manager is able to use the field's content type to generate the correct control.

Sample Page Layout With Snippets

The remaining snippets in our sample page layout are a combination of what we have seen along with Content Search Web Parts for the discussion and What's Happening, which we discuss in greater detail in Chapter 9. A Summary Links Web Part or the Summary Links column could be used for Community Tools. Review Listing 7-11 for a complete overview of the sample page layout; for readability, we refer to previous listings so as not to repeat ourselves. We have also removed some additional properties of the snippets, so be sure to re-create your own snippets from the Snippet Manager.

Listing 7-11. Final Page Layout Body Tag With Some Tag Properties Removed for Brevity

```
<body>
    <!--MS:<asp:ContentPlaceHolder ID="PlaceHolderMain" runat="server">-->
    <!--Page content-->
    <!--Listing 7.8 goes here-->

    <!-- SLIDER -->
    <!--Listing 7.9 goes here-->
    <!-- ENDS SLIDER -->

    <div id="posts-list" class="community-listing cf">
        <!--community listing-->
        <div class="page-content cf">
            <article>
                <!-- property content -->
                <!--Listing 7.10 goes here-->
                <!-- end property content -->
            </article>
        </div>
        <!-- end community list -->

        <div id="comments-wrap">
            <h4 class="heading">Community Discussion</h4>

            <ul class="comments-links-horizontal">
                <li><a href="#">Recent</a></li>
                ...
            </ul>

            <div class="toggle-trigger"><i class="simple"></i>Start a New
                Discussion</div>
            <div class="toggle-container form">
                <!-- CSOM or Form Web Part snippet-->
            </div>

            <!--NOTE: Content Search Snippet coding shorted for brevity-->
            <!--CS: Start Content Search Snippet-->
            <!--SPM:<%@Register Tagprefix="spsswc"
                Namespace="Microsoft.Office.Server.Search.WebControls"%>-->
            <!--SPM:<%@Register Tagprefix="a2e"
                Namespace="Microsoft.Office.Server.Search.WebControls"%>-->
            <!--MS:<spsswc:ContentBySearchWebPart runat="server" ...>-->
            <!--ME:</spsswc:ContentBySearchWebPart>-->
            <!--CE: End Content Search Snippet-->
        </div>
    </div>
    <!--end post listing-->

    <!-- sidebar -->
    <aside id="sidebar" class="community-listing">
        <ul>
```

```
      <li class="block">
       <h4 class="heading">Community Tools</h4>

       <!--NOTE: Summary Links Snippet coding shorted for brevity-->
       <!--CS: Start Page Field: Summary Links Snippet-->
       <!--SPM:<%@Register
            Tagprefix="PageFieldSummaryLinkFieldControl"%>-->
       <!--MS:<PageFieldSummaryLinkFieldControl:SummaryLinkFieldControl
            FieldName="SummaryLinks">-->
       <!--ME:</PageFieldSummaryLinkFieldControl:SummaryLinkFieldControl>-->
       <!--CE: End Page Field: Summary Links Snippet-->

      </li>
      <li class="block">
         <h4 class="heading">What's Happening</h4>

         <!--Use Content Search Web Part and Display Templates-->
         <!--NOTE: Content Search Snippet coding shorted for brevity-->
         <!--CS: Start Content Search Snippet-->
         <!--SPM:<%@Register Tagprefix="spsswc"
              Namespace="Microsoft.Office.Server.Search.WebControls"%>-->
         <!--MS:<spsswc:ContentBySearchWebPart runat="server"
              AlwaysRenderOnServer="False" ...>-->
         <!--ME:</spsswc:ContentBySearchWebPart>-->
         <!--CE: End Content Search Snippet-->

      </li>
    </ul>
  </aside>

  <!-- ENDS sidebar -->
  <!--end page content-->
  <!--ME:</asp:ContentPlaceHolder>-->
</body>
```

In Figure 7-25 we can see how a content page that utilizes this page layout would appear while in edit mode.

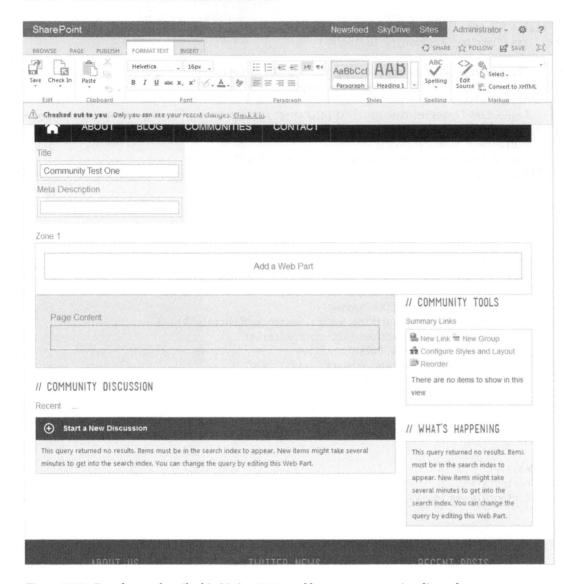

Figure 7-25. *Page layout described in Listing 7-11, used by a content page in edit mode*

HTML Page Layout Limitations and Considerations

There are a few known HTML page layout limitations that could preclude their extended use in certain branding deployments.

Inline Scripts and Styles

Inline scripts and inline styles within a ContentPlaceHolder block, such as in Listing 7-12, can cause results you might not expect.

Listing 7-12. Inline < script > and < style > Blocks in HTML Page Layout

```
<!--MS:<asp:ContentPlaceHolder ID="PlaceHolderMain" runat="server">-->
   <style type="text/css">
      #sideNavBox {
         display: none;
      }
   </style>
   <script>
      jQuery.ready(function($) {
         $('#sideNavBox').css('display','none');
      });
   </script>
<!--ME:</asp:ContentPlaceHolder>-->
```

In Listing 7-13 we see how the <style> and <script> blocks from Listing 7-12 are parsed and interpreted by Design Manager when it generates the .aspx page layout.

Listing 7-13. Converted < script > and < style > Blocks in .aspx Page Layout

```
<asp:ContentPlaceHolder ID="PlaceHolderMain" runat="server">
   <style type="text/css">
      //<![CDATA[
      #sideNavBox {
         display: none;
      }
      //]]>
   </style>
   <script>
      //<![CDATA[
      jQuery.ready(function($) {
         $('#sideNavBox').css('display','none');
      });
      //]]>
   </script>
<!--ME:</asp:ContentPlaceHolder>-->
```

Unfortunately for us, what the //<![CDATA[//]]> block does is turn the inline style as well as the JavaScript into comments in most browsers. This obviously won't work if we want to include inline styles or scripts in HTML page layouts.

Fortunately we can use snippet markup to get around this limitation, as seen in Listing 7-14.

Listing 7-14. Inline < script > and < style > Blocks in HTML Page Layout Using SharePoint Markup

```
<!--MS:<asp:ContentPlaceHolder ID="PlaceHolderMain" runat="server">-->
   <!--MS:<style type="text/css">-->
      #sideNavBox {
         display: none;
      }
   <!--ME:</style>-->
```

```
<!--MS:<script>-->
    jQuery.ready(function($) {
        $('#sideNavBox').css('display','none');
    });
<!--ME:</script>-->
<!--ME:</asp:ContentPlaceHolder>-->
```

Disassociating an HTML Page Layout

We have seen that HTML page layouts are useful for managing our site page layouts. We have also seen that HTML page layouts have limitations. You might also find additional frustrations with your particular branding requirements around XML validation or long inline scripts or styles. You might decide to package your branding in your own custom feature instead of a design package. To make this deployment more direct you might want to include only the .aspx page layout in your feature. None of these concerns should mean that HTML page layouts should be ignored.

SharePoint allows us to disassociate an HTML page layout with its corresponding .aspx file. Once the HTML page layout is disassociated, we may edit the .aspx page layout directly. Disassociation also means that edits to the HTML page layout will not be realized by your sites. Be aware that any modifications you make to the .aspx file would be overwritten if you ever wish to reassociate the .html and .aspx files again.

To disassociate a HTML page layout follow these steps.

1. Open the Master Page Gallery in a browser (Settings ➤ Site Settings ➤ Web Designer Galleries ➤ Master pages and page layouts).

2. In the Master Page Gallery, find the HTML page layout file you wish to disassociate with the .aspx file. In our example, we drill down to the spectergroup subfolder and find the CommunityProperty.html file.

3. Hover over the HTML page layout and click the down arrow to open the file's menu.

4. On the drop-down menu that appears, select Edit Properties to load the HTML page layout's properties page.

5. Scroll down near the bottom of the properties page and find the Associated File check box (see Figure 7-26). If you clear this check box and save the settings then your HTML page layout and its corresponding .aspx file are not long associated.

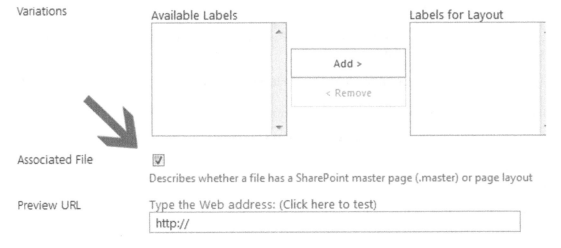

Figure 7-26. *HTML page layout edit properties, Associated File property*

You can now edit the .aspx page layout directly and any changes made to the .html HTML page layout will not be reflected by the .aspx page. As already mentioned, if you edit the HTML page layout's properties again to reestablish the Associated File status, any changes you made to the .aspx page layout will be overwritten.

Even if you plan to not use HTML page layouts as your long-term method to manage page layouts, HTML page layouts might still be useful when converting your prototype to page layouts. HTML page layouts allow you to treat your page layout as a functioning web page instead of just content placeholders during development. Further, initially adding SharePoint and .NET controls with snippets is often easier then looking up a valid control elsewhere. Utilize Design Manager and HTML page layouts to get started and then disassociate a layout if you need more control.

Copying an HTML Page Layout From an Existing Page Layout

We previously stated that you cannot convert a mockup HTML file to an HTML page layout in Design Manager. Instead we showed how to create an HTML page layout, move it to a subfolder, and finally modify the HTML page layout in a web editor using snippets and custom code. Let's say that you have a page layout already built in Design Manager but wish to create a similar new page layout. You can create a new page layout based on a copy of an existing page layout.

1. Open the Master Page Gallery in SharePoint Designer or even in Windows Explorer using WebDAV.

2. Find the HTML page layout you wish to copy. For our example we create a copy of CommunityProperty.html in the spectergroup subfolder.

3. Copy the .html file (i.e., CommunityProperty.html) to the clipboard, then paste this back into the same folder. This will create a new file, CommunityProperty - Copy.html. Refresh the folder to see this new file.

■ **Note**   As with moving HTML page layouts, we only want to select and copy the .html file; we let Design Manager handle the .aspx for us.

---

4. Right-click the CommunityProperty - Copy.html file to rename it, say to CommunityPropertyRental.html. Notice that Design Manager will also rename the .aspx file for us as well.

5. Return to Design Manager in a browser and navigate to the Edit Page Layouts page. You will see your new page layout listed. If you edit its properties you will see that it will have the same properties as the page you copied this from including its associated content type. You can now edit the new HTML page layout, just do not forget to publish a major version when you are done.

Making a Page Layout Responsive

In Chapter 5 we reviewed how to convert a standard site into a responsive site utilizing a framework, in our case the Twitter Bootstrap framework. As we saw in Chapter 5, a framework is not necessary in responsive design, but can definitely help the process of creating a responsive site by prebuilding a grid that provides responsive features.

Because the master page provides the basic responsive features of a general site, including the general wrapper, header, footer, and primary navigation, let us now consider what we need to do within a page layout to further the responsive aspects of a given content page.

A Responsive Page Layout

A page layouts primary function is to replace the `PlaceHolderMain` `ContentPlaceHolder` snippet. The other content placeholders available within a page layout are important and may provide us ample opportunity to customize a particular page, but most content and layout will be placed in the `PlaceHolderMain` `ContentPlaceHolder`. There are two different methods of coding a master page to work with page layouts to allow it to be responsive; we can provide a wrapper container in the master page that itself has responsive styling, or we can force the page layouts to provide their own responsive nature.

We next consider an example. In the Bootstrap framework we provide a container div, and within this container we can have rows and within each row a mix of twelve columns. Bootstrap, as with most frameworks, provides this sort of row and column grid structure. Now let's say that we only provide the container in the master page and we force the page layouts to provide the rows and the span columns. Not a problem; this should work just fine. As we have learned, the row-fluid within Listing 7-16 would get placed inside of the `PlaceHolderMain` seen in Listing 7-15.

Listing 7-15. HTML Master Page With Only a Container Around PlaceHolderMain

```
<div class="container-fluid">
   <!--MS:<SharePoint:AjaxDelta ID="DeltaPlaceHolderMain" IsMainContent="true" runat="server">-->
      <!--MS:<asp:ContentPlaceHolder ID="PlaceHolderMain" runat="server">-->
      <!--ME:</asp:ContentPlaceHolder>-->
   <!--ME:</SharePoint:AjaxDelta>-->
</div>
```

Listing 7-16. HTML Page Layout With Primary Row in PlaceHolderMain ContentPlaceHolder

```
<!--MS:<asp:ContentPlaceHolder ID="PlaceHolderMain" runat="server">-->
   <div class="row-fluid">
      <div class="span3">
         <!--left column in page layout-->
      </div>
      <div class="span9">
         <!--right column in page layout-->
      </div>
   </div>
<!--ME:</asp:ContentPlaceHolder>-->
```

The potential issue for this approach is twofold. First, OOTB page layouts might not work correctly within the framework because they will not have any framework-based rows and spans to provide for a responsive site. Second, non-page-layout-based pages such as any site settings or list pages will also not have responsive properties built in, again, directly within the framework. It is possible to provide additional CSS to account for these deficiencies, but it is not ideal.

Now, let us consider if we provide both the container, a primary row, and even initial spans within the master page itself and let page layouts provide subrows and subspans. This is an interesting approach that offers a new technique. Here any non-page-layout-based page will be forced to have all of its content bound within a responsive framework-based span, while page layouts could then have subrows and subspans to provide additional rows and columns.

In Listing 7-17 we have an HTML master page that provides a framework-based, responsive, full-width column. This one column contains the content placeholder, `PlaceHolderMain`. The partial HTML page layout provided in Listing 7-18 then provides a subrow and subcolumns that will replace the HTML master page's `PlaceHolderMain`.

Listing 7-17. HTML Master Page With Only a Container Around PlaceHolderMain

```
<div class="container-fluid">
   <div class="row-fluid">
      <div class="span12">
         <!--MS:<SharePoint:AjaxDelta ID="DeltaPlaceHolderMain"
               IsMainContent="true" runat="server">-->
            <!--MS:<asp:ContentPlaceHolder ID="PlaceHolderMain"
               runat="server">-->
            <!--ME:</asp:ContentPlaceHolder>-->
         <!--ME:</SharePoint:AjaxDelta>-->
      </div>
   </div>
</div>
```

Listing 7-18. HTML Page Layout With Primary Row in PlaceHolderMain ContentPlaceHolder

```
<!--MS:<asp:ContentPlaceHolder ID="PlaceHolderMain" runat="server">-->
   <!--some content, additional snippets, etc could replace this comment-->
   <div class="row-fluid">
      <!--Then another row could be added to provide additional columns-->
      <div class="span3">
         <!--left column in page layout-->
      </div>
      <div class="span9">
         <!--right column in page layout-->
      </div>
   </div>
<!--ME:</asp:ContentPlaceHolder>-->
```

Why would we do this? An easy example is if site requirements included the need for left navigation based on SharePoint's built in quick launch or vertical navigation that is included in the v4 master as well as SharePoint 2013 Seattle and Oslo master pages. If we wanted to build one master page for both our custom and default master pages, then we would need to include the left, vertical navigation bar for site setting and site pages, while building a mechanism for custom page layouts to hide the left navigation. This is what we see in OOTB page layouts such as Welcome page layouts that provide an inline style in an `<asp:Content>` tag to hide the left navigation bar while making the main content div full width.

In general there are a few key points to keep in mind while making the content areas in a page layout responsive. First, review Chapter 5. Adding a framework such as Bootstrap to an HTML mockup is basically the same with a master page as it is for a page layout. In particular you will separate the components of your page layout into your grid.

As an example we will take the HTML we added to our HTML page layout in Listing 7-2 and integrate Bootstrap's rows and columns grid. Based on the HTML master page in Listing 7-14, the new HTML page layout is found in Listing 7-19.

Listing 7-19. PlaceHolderMain of About-pagelayout.aspx With Bootstrap

```
<!--MS:<asp:ContentPlaceHolder ID="PlaceHolderMain" runat="server">-->
   <!-- page-content -->
   <div class="row-fluid">
      <div class="span12 page-content">
         <!--title and meta description in edit mode-->
         <!--Listing 7.8 goes here-->
```

```
<!-- entry-content -->
<div class="row-fluid section noborder">
   <div class="span12">

      <!--Main image, floating to the left-->
      <div class="floatleft">
        <!--SPM:<%@Register Tagprefix="PageFieldRichImageField"
             Namespace="Microsoft.SharePoint.Publishing.WebControls"
             Assembly="Microsoft.SharePoint.Publishing,
             Version=15.0.0.0, Culture=neutral,
             PublicKeyToken=71e9bce111e9429c"%>-->
        <!--MS:<PublishingWebControls:RichImageField
             FieldName="PublishingPageImage" runat="server">-->
        <!--ME:</PublishingWebControls:RichImageField>-->
      </div>

      <!--Content from page layout Content Type Meta Data-->
      <!--SPM:<%@Register Tagprefix="PageFieldRichHtmlField"
           Namespace="Microsoft.SharePoint.Publishing.WebControls"
           Assembly="Microsoft.SharePoint.Publishing, Version=15.0.0.0,
           Culture=neutral, PublicKeyToken=71e9bce111e9429c"%>-->
      <PublishingWebControls:RichHtmlField
           FieldName="PublishingPageContent" runat="server"/>

      <!-- 2 cols -->
      <div class="row-fluid section noborder">
         <div class="span6">
            <!--Web Part Zone with ID: LeftZone-->

            <!--SPM:<%@Register Tagprefix="WebPartPages"
                 Namespace="Microsoft.SharePoint.WebPartPages"
                 Assembly="Microsoft.SharePoint, Version=15.0.0.0,
                 Culture=neutral, PublicKeyToken=71e9bce111e9429c"%>-->
            <!--MS:<WebPartPages:WebPartZone runat="server"
                 AllowPersonalization="false" ID="LeftZone"
                 FrameType="TitleBarOnly" Orientation="Vertical">-->
               <!--MS:<ZoneTemplate>--><!--ME:</ZoneTemplate>-->
            <!--ME:</WebPartPages:WebPartZone>-->
         </div>
         <div class="span6">
            <!--Web Part Zone with ID: RightZone-->

            <!--SPM:<%@Register Tagprefix="WebPartPages"
                 Namespace="Microsoft.SharePoint.WebPartPages"
                 Assembly="Microsoft.SharePoint, Version=15.0.0.0,
                 Culture=neutral, PublicKeyToken=71e9bce111e9429c"%>-->
            <!--MS:<WebPartPages:WebPartZone runat="server"
                 AllowPersonalization="false" ID="RightZone"
                 FrameType="TitleBarOnly" Orientation="Vertical">-->
               <!--MS:<ZoneTemplate>--><!--ME:</ZoneTemplate>-->
```

```
        <!--ME:</WebPartPages:WebPartZone>-->
      </div>
    </div>
    <!-- ENDS 2 cols -->
  </div><!--end span12-->
  </div><!--end sub row-->
  </div><!-- ENDS page-content -->
  </div><!-- ENDS fluid-row-->
<!--ME:</asp:ContentPlaceHolder>-->
```

When we compare Listing 7-2 with Listing 7-19, we replaced all SharePoint controls with snippets. We also added a primary row and within this row a primary column that is twelve columns wide. We had to move the Title to above the "section" because we wanted to create another row to hold just the float left image and the text to its right.

For our `<!-- 2 cols -->` we add a subrow split into two equal width columns, again totaling twelve columns wide. Leveraging the framework for our grid relieves us yet again of the nitty-gritty of the responsive nature our of site design.

Consider How a Page Layout Will Respond

Creating a simple page layout with responsive design properties in mind is fairly straightforward, as we just saw in Listing 7-19. The primary goal is to break up the content area of your prototype into rows and columns. More complex page layouts might require more considerations.

Flow of Content on the Page and in the HTML

The horizontal and vertical flow of content and content containers may differ between viewports. As an example, take the current navigation, often placed on the left side of a web site when seen on a standard desktop monitor. Now consider where you might want that left navigation to appear on a mobile device. If this left navigation is added to the first Bootstrap span within a row, then by default this navigation menu would appear above other content on a mobile device.

Because the left navigation might not be as important as the content on a mobile device, or imagine a left navigation with many menu items, we might want to have this left navigation move below the main content. With Bootstrap this is not easy OOTB because the framework does not provide us the toolset to move elements in this manner.

One option might be to leave the left navigation above the main content. Then using a media query, collapse the left navigation in a mobile view similar to what we saw in Chapter 6 with collapsing navigation. Another option might be to utilize a media query once again and take the left navigation out of the flow of content by setting the position of the left navigation to "absolute," also providing positioning styles such as "bottom" and "left," to move the navigation to the bottom of the content box.

The best option is to consider the flow of content during your wireframing, mockup, and prototyping stages so that when it is time to add your framework to your prototype, you have already made the difficult decisions.

Viewport Utilization

Ideally page layouts will utilize a particular viewport to its fullest. There are seemingly a countless number of viewport resolutions, from the smaller smart phones to very wide monitors with well over 2,000 pixels across. Designers should strive to utilize as much of the vertical viewport space as possible and attempt to limit the vertical scrolling. With page layouts that might have a large amount of content in any given content page, this might be difficult to achieve, but it should be your goal.

As prices for larger monitors continue to fall and older desktops are replaced, we can assume that a larger portion of our site visitors will have viewports in excess of 1,200 pixels across. Be sure to consider how your site will work and function with these larger viewports, as leaving large gutters of unused space to the left and right of your main content could be a waste. Further it might distract from the look of your site. In Figure 7-27, notice the extra wide white space on either side of the site content on a wide monitor. This extra space can be distracting but could also be used to pull more content above the fold.

Figure 7-27. *Sample site as viewed on a extra wide monitor*

■ **Note**   Need help knowing what resolutions to target? Besides searching your own web site logs, `w3schools.com` maintains a summary of their visitors' resolutions over the years at `http://sprwd.com/42kklqh`. You might also want to try `StatCounter.com`, which maintains browser and resolution statistics compiled every month at `http://sprwd.com/d2z6vcv`.

Content Container Vertical Dimensions

Continuing the thread of using a viewport to its fullest, you might also want to consider the vertical utilization of your page layouts. As an example, consider a landing page page layout. Landing pages might often contain many blocks of teaser content that is not intended to tell the whole story. Rather, these tease blocks are intended to help site visitors find the content they are looking for.

On larger viewports these blocks of teaser content might take up one-third to one-half the vertical space of a page on a desktop monitor. On a smart phone, this could cause excessive vertical scrolling. If your design allows, you could add maximum heights to some content containers and hide the overflow using a media query targeted toward smaller resolution viewports.

In Listing 7-20 we see a specific row within a HTML page layout. This may go within the `PlaceholderMain` `ContentPlaceHolder` and there could be additional rows before and after.

Listing 7-20. HTML Page Layout Excerpt With Three Columns

```
<!--additional rows before this row-->
<!-- Row with three Bootstrap fluid columns -->
<div class="row-fluid mobile-contain-height">
   <!--SPM:<%@Register Tagprefix="WebPartPages"
        Namespace="Microsoft.SharePoint.WebPartPages"
        Assembly="Microsoft.SharePoint, Version=15.0.0.0, Culture=neutral,
        PublicKeyToken=71e9bce111e9429c"%>-->
```

```
<div class="span4">
   <!--Web Part Zone with ID: ColumnOne-->
   <!--MS:<WebPartPages:WebPartZone runat="server"
        AllowPersonalization="false" ID=" ColumnOne"
        FrameType="TitleBarOnly" Orientation="Vertical">-->
      <!--MS:<ZoneTemplate>--><!--ME:</ZoneTemplate>-->
   <!--ME:</WebPartPages:WebPartZone>-->
</div>
<div class="span4">
   <!--Web Part Zone with ID: ColumnTwo-->
   <!--MS:<WebPartPages:WebPartZone runat="server"
        AllowPersonalization="false" ID=" ColumnTwo "
        FrameType="TitleBarOnly" Orientation="Vertical">-->
      <!--MS:<ZoneTemplate>--><!--ME:</ZoneTemplate>-->
   <!--ME:</WebPartPages:WebPartZone>-->
</div>
<div class="span4">
   <!--Web Part Zone with ID: ColumnThree-->
   <!--MS:<WebPartPages:WebPartZone runat="server"
        AllowPersonalization="false" ID=" ColumnThree "
        FrameType="TitleBarOnly" Orientation="Vertical">-->
      <!--MS:<ZoneTemplate>--><!--ME:</ZoneTemplate>-->
   <!--ME:</WebPartPages:WebPartZone>-->
</div>
</div><!--end row-->
<!--additional rows, etc-->
```

With Bootstrap, the three columns provided in the divs with the class "span4" in Listing 7-20 will not float next to each other in mobile viewports. On tablets the vertical scrolling might be minimal depending on the web parts that are added to the web part zones. But let's say we want to limit the maximum height of a span4 div in Listing 7-20 for viewports under 600 pixels wide. With the help of the additional class we added at the top, mobile-contain-height and a media query, this is simple. The media query and styles are provided in Listing 7-21.

Listing 7-21. Media Query and Styles for Maximum Height Containers in Mobile Views

```
/*style only for viewports under 600 pixels wide*/
@media (max-width: 599px) {
   /*target just span4 containers within .mobile-contain-height*/
   .mobile-contain-height .span4 {
      max-height: 200px; /*set a maximum height*/
      overflow-y: hidden; /*hide any additional overflow*/
   }
}
```

Hiding the Current Navigation in a Page Layout

A new feature added to the SharePoint 2013 ribbon is the Focus on Content icon found in the ribbon and highlighted in Figure 7-28. In the OOTB master pages, when this icon is clicked, the left navigation bar is hidden and the main content fills in the space. This is accomplished with some very simple JavaScript provided by SharePoint along with the addition of one class to the main <body> tag. This one class added when Focus on Content is selected is ms-fullscreenmode.

Figure 7-28. *The new Focus on Content feature in SharePoint 2013*

Using this additional class, we can provide a simple style to hide the horizontal navigation. When working with a grid, though, we must also consider how to tell our main content column or columns to fill in the additional space.

Listing 7-22 shows the HTML for the PlaceHolderMain ContentPlaceHolder. This HTML page layout includes the Vertical Navigation snippet rather than the snippet being included in the master page. The general principle will work for either location of the snippet but is dependent on how the grid is applied to the master page and page layouts. Listing 7-22 assumes the PlaceHolderMain ContentPlaceHolder from Listing 7-14.

Listing 7-22. HTML Page Layout With Vertical Navigation

```
<div class="row-fluid">
    <div class="span3" id="sideNavBox">
        <!--CS: Start Vertical Navigation Snippet-->
        <!--For simplicity we removed the default vertical navigation snippet-->
        <!--CE: End Vertical Navigation Snippet-->
    </div>
    <div class="span9" id="mainbody">
        <!--replace with additional page layout content areas and column-->
    </div>
</div>
```

In Listing 7-22 the Quick Launch in the form of the default Vertical Navigation snippet is bound to the first three columns. We supply the left three column container with the ID sideNavBox. This ID is the new OOTB ID for the left navigation in SharePoint 2013. We include a second container that spans nine columns, which we also provided a new ID of mainbody.

When the Focus on Content icon is clicked, the left navigation will automatically hide because we provided the ID of sideNavBox. What we would like to add is a style that will tell our mainbody div to not span nine columns, but rather to span twelve columns. It would be difficult to replace the class span9 with span12, so instead we can simply add span12 properties to the ID mainbody when the <body> tag includes ms-fullscreenmode. See Listing 7-23 for this style.

Listing 7-23. Style to Increase Width of Content for Focus on Content

```
/*override #mainbody from a span9 to the properties of a span12
.ms-fullscreenmode #mainbody {
    width: 100%;
}
```

Creating and Publishing New Pages Based on Custom Page Layouts

At this point we have reviewed content types and how we can use them in conjunction with page layouts. We investigated how we can manage our page layouts using Design Manager as well as what special considerations are needed to make page layouts responsive within our master pages. We are now ready to use our custom page layouts in a content page.

Creating a New Content Page

Start by loading the default page of the site you wish to add a content page. In this example we are going to add the About page to our root web.

1. Click the settings icon in the ribbon and click Add a page.

2. In the Add a page dialog box, you must give your new page a name. This will be translated to the file name of the page; the title of the page can be changed at a later time. The name for our example will be About.

After the new content page has been created, it will be associated with your default page layout. We will learn how to manage visible and default page layouts in the section "Verifying and Controlling a Page Layout's Availability" later in this chapter.

3. To change the page layout for the page we just created, while in edit mode, in the ribbon, click the Page tab. When the Page ribbon appears, in the fourth section entitled Page Actions, click Page Layout.

4. A drop-down list will appear displaying all valid page layouts. Select the page layout you wish this page to use.

■ **Note** If your custom page layout does not appear in the Page Layout drop-down list, ensure that you published a major version of the custom page layout. If you have and the page layout still does not appear, refer to the section "Verifying and Controlling a Valid Page Layout's Availability" later in this chapter.

---

5. Click Save on the ribbon to save the page.

You can also add a new content page directly in the Pages document library.

1. Load the default page of the site to which you wish to add a new content page.

2. Click the Settings icon on the ribbon and click Site contents.

3. Your Site Contents page will load. Under Lists, Libraries, and other Apps, click the Pages Library.

4. To add a new page, on the ribbon, click Files.

5. On the Files ribbon, click New Document, and then click Page.

6. The Create Page page will load. You can now provide the Title and Description as well as the page's file name. Finally you set the page layout you wish this new content page to utilize. When you have entered the required information, click Create to create the page.

7. The Pages library will appear once the page has been created. You can click on the new page's title to load the content page so that you can begin editing the page's content.

■ **Tip** You can have your custom content types appear in the New Document drop-down list by customizing the Pages document library list of allowed content types.

Checking in and Publishing a Content Page

After you create a new content page, it will not be available to all users until you publish the page. There are two primary methods to check in and publish a content page, although this process might vary depending on any workflows that might have been created. We review two OOTB methods of publishing content pages.

Note that OOTB, the Publishing workflow in SharePoint 2013 has been simplified. You might not need to check in, publish, and approve a content page as you did OOTB with SharePoint 2010. This could be changed by your site administrator based on your organization's requirements. We review the OOTB simplified workflow.

Publish a Page via a Content Page Ribbon

A content page can be checked in and published directly from the ribbon on the content page you wish to publish. In fact in SharePoint 2013 you can skip checking in a content page and publish in one step. Refer to Figure 7-29 for a content page ribbon.

Figure 7-29. *Content page Publish tab and Publish icon*

1.   Load the content page you wish to publish.

2.   If there is a version of the page to publish, the content page will be checked out, or checked in without having been published. Either way, the ribbon will load with the page. The last tab should be Publish. Click Publish to load the Publish ribbon.

3.   On the Publish ribbon, click the Publish icon.

4.   The content page has been published and should be available to visitors.

Publish a Page via the Pages Library

Alternatively, a content page can be checked in and published directly in the Pages document library.

1.   Load the Pages library as we did when creating a new content page.

2.   Next to the content page you wish to publish, click the ellipsis (...) to load the content page properties popup. On the properties popup, click the ellipses (...) found in the bottom bar.

3. On the Page menu, click Check In.

4. In the Check In dialog box, select Major version (publish). If you would like to keep the file checked out even after publishing it, select Yes under Retain your check out after checking in. Finally provide comments if you wish before clicking OK to check in and publish a major version.

Verifying and Controlling a Valid Page Layout's Availability

Often you will find a need to control which page layouts should be available within a given site, on a site-by-site basis. We have seen how we can hide a page layout by editing a given page layout's properties, but that will hide the page layout for the entire site collection. What if you wish to hide a page layout within a particular site? What if you wish to hide OOTB page layouts quickly without having to edit each page layout's property, or remove the actual page layout from the site collection? There is a mechanism available to us to control which page layouts are available in a given site as well as control which page layout is the default page layout for new content pages.

■ **Tip**   If a page layout is not available when selecting the page layout for a content page, and yet the page layout has a published major version, the page layout might have been hidden using the following process.

---

1. Navigate to your site's Site Settings page (Settings ➤ Site Settings on the ribbon).

2. On the Site Settings page, under Look and Feel, click Page layouts and site templates.

3. On the Page Layout and Site Template Settings page, you can set which site templates this site and all subsites (if you wish) can use.

4. You can also set which Page Layouts are available; that is, all page layouts, inherit allowed page layouts from this site's parent, or only specific page layouts. If you select Pages in this site can only use the following layouts:, you can select and Add the specific page layouts you wish to make available to this site. If you also select Reset all subsites to inherit these preferred page layout settings, all subsites will be updated with this site's preferred page layout settings.

5. You can also set the default page layout for new content pages.

6. Click OK to save your Page Layout settings.

Summary

In this chapter we started with an overview of content types and how they relate to page layouts. We reviewed where content types are stored and how we can leverage a Content Type Hub to centrally store our custom content types across sites, site collections, and web applications. We continued by reviewing OOTB page layouts, how to create custom page layouts, and how to bind a custom page layout to a custom content type. Leveraging the power of responsive design, we utilized OOTB page layouts as well as modified custom page layout with snippets that produce content type field data that looks good and provide an optimized version based on device viewport.

■ ■ ■

CHAPTER 8

Publish Cross-Site Content with Catalogs

The core of any Web Content Management (WCM) solution ultimately is content. We find that having the ability to effectively manage and reuse your web site's content is paramount. We can expect to have a large amount of content over time and this will eventually (and inevitably) affect the web site back end in terms of capacity and performance if not planned accordingly. Therefore, planning for reusable content can pay off in the long term. SharePoint 2010 had a built-in feature that allowed content owners to reuse content; one could save snippets of text such as copyright and footer content. When creating or editing pages, the Ribbon provided access to this reusable content, which could then be inserted into the publishing page. This capability still exists in SharePoint 2013; however, this is quite limited and not enough, as it does not cover other content type such as media and images that are prime candidates for reusability.

In addition, SharePoint 2010 had the Content Deployment feature, which allowed the controlled publishing of content from one site collection to another or from Farm A to Farm B. Content deployment could be as granular as a page, for example. Content deployment could also be scheduled. We believe SharePoint 2013 Cross-Site Collection Publishing effectively replaces the Content Deployment feature.

In Chapter 1 we introduced you to cross-site publishing; this chapter aims at further acquainting you with the feature by providing you with additional insight. The second portion of this chapter walks you through a step-by-step exercise in implementing cross-site publishing in the context of the Specter Group Cross-Site Publishing scenario as cross-site collection publishing is best explained with a concrete example. Using the theories, concepts, and examples provided, you should be able to adapt the examples to your specific projects.

Our Scenario

Up to this point, the solution we have been building throughout this book has all of the major branding applied, but only has basic content pages within the http://spectergroup.com site itself. Recall in Chapter 3 that we discussed how content would be authored in one site collection, yet consumed by the public site, found in a separate site collection. It is now time to build the authoring and content presentation solution using cross-site collection publishing, Content Search web parts, and display templates.

About Cross-Site Publishing

Cross-Site Collection Publishing is a new SharePoint 2013 feature that allows for authoring content in one or more site collections, and then surfacing or displaying the content to one or more other site collections. Cross-Site Collection Publishing essentially replaces the need for content deployment introduced in previous versions of SharePoint. In particular, in SharePoint 2010, content created in one site collection could not be easily surfaced in another site collection without third-party tools or content deployment. With Cross-Site Collection Publishing in SharePoint 2013, this limitation no longer exists. Content in one site collection can be quickly surfaced in another site collection.

The new content model for SharePoint 2013 sites is centered on two main components: search index and shared metadata. With the content stored in the search index, metadata stored in the Term Store database, and analytics stored in the SharePoint database, all the published content can be surfaced to users through query rules and the recommendation engine after the content is crawled and added to the search index that catalog result sources leverage. The cross-site publishing feature uses search technology to retrieve content from the search index as the content gets crawled and added to the search index. The content can then be displayed in another site collection by using web parts, in particular the new Content Search web part or the Search Results web part.

Catalogs themselves can be Pages Libraries as well as selected lists in which cataloging is enabled and configured. Figure 8-1 shows the diagram of how cross-site publishing works.

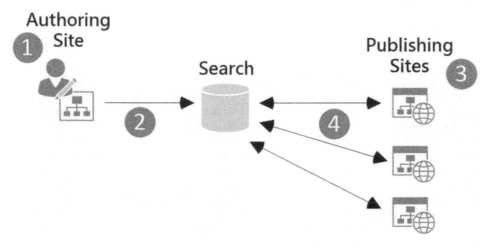

Figure 8-1. *How cross-site publishing works*

1. Content is authored (publishing pages, lists, asset libraries).

2. SharePoint 2013 Search crawls the content and builds the index.

3. The publishing site pages are viewed, and search queries previously configured on Content Search web parts and Search Results web parts are triggered.

4. Results are returned and viewed on publishing page, which contains the Content Search and Search Results web parts. Items are displayed via display templates.

Why Use Cross-Site Publishing?

One of the key benefits of using Cross-Site Collection Publishing is the ability to reuse different types of content across sites. There are many other benefits of using this feature, which include the separation in how content is authored and how or where the content is actually presented. There are also no boundaries for sharing content across various SharePoint object levels (i.e., site collections and web applications). Authored content can be publishing pages that themselves contain embedded media such as pictures and other metadata dictated by the page layout as well as content found in lists and libraries.

Cross-Site Publishing Possible Scenarios

Although different situations all have specific needs, the scenarios identified and described in Table 8-1 will satisfy many publishing needs. Of course, at times, using cross-site publishing will not make sense at all; for example, when simplicity and authoring content in place is sufficient and there is no need to reuse content. Again, however, these scenarios are frequently useful. In this chapter, we implement the Internet Site scenario.

Table 8-1. *Cross-Site Publishing Scenarios*

Scenario	Details
Internet Site	Cross-site publishing can be used to create an e-commerce web site that contains typical products and details. The navigation of the entire product catalog can be driven by metadata and can be filtered or refined. All content is developed within an internal authoring site and shared with anonymous users outside of the firewall as is typical of any public web site.
Intranet Site	Cross-site publishing can be used to author all of an intranet's content within an authoring site collection. It can then be published to a separate site collection where all employees have access to consume said content and have read-only permissions.
Extranet Site	Imagine deploying a Partner Extranet, content is authored internally by a small group of authors. Content is then published to the Partner Extranet web site, which can have very different permissions, say based on the Partner type.
Multilingual Site	Imagine the ability to author your public web site in multiple languages such as Spanish, Italian, and English. You can do exactly that by using cross-site publishing together with the variations and translation features to create multiple sites that show translated content for said languages or locales and still reuse or share other content applicable to all web sites. Each web site can then have its own appropriate URL; for example, the Spanish web site can be www.spectergroup.mx or the Italian version could be www.spectergroup.it.

■ **Tip**   Sometimes, depending on the cross-site collection publishing scenario, you might wish to share the same branding on both the authoring and the consumer sites. To do this, you could opt to create a design package and deploy this across the consuming sites. See Chapter 4 on how to create a design package.

Cross-Site Publishing Limitations

There are some limitations, gotchas, and constraints when using cross-site publishing that you should be aware of before jumping in head first (see Table 8-2). Knowing these limitations up front can save you time on future projects that you might think are good candidates for cross-site publishing.

Table 8-2. *Cross-Site Publishing Limitations*

Limitation	Comment
Content Indexing	Cross-site publishing is dependent on content indexing; therefore it is not shown until the content is crawled. SharePoint 2013 does have continuous crawling capabilities which can be configured to crawl in short intervals. There is also full and incremental crawl.
	Note: You must run a full crawl prior to creating any result sources and when the catalog definition is changed.
Term Set Version Control	Making changes to terms is affected immediately, therefore there might be a scenario where content is not authored yet, but the terms have been added.
No Approval	Lists do not have approval workflow, therefore the use of versioning is highly recommended so that the index only picks up the items that have major versions approved. Alternatively, simply do not add items to lists if you are not ready to publish.

Catalogs and Cross-Site Collection Publishing

A core component of Cross-Site Collection Publishing is catalogs. What exactly do we mean by catalogs? Catalogs, as used by Cross-Site Collection Publishing, can be any SharePoint list or library that will be shared across site collections. A list or library is configured as a catalog by being set as a shared catalog via a particular list's List settings. Pages libraries, lists, and asset libraries must be configured as catalogs to be able to reuse content across site collections.

Once a catalog has been shared, a consuming site can connect to it by using the Catalog Connections setting found under Site ➤ Site Administration ➤ Manage Catalog Connections. Then by using search-driven web parts and specific queries to retrieve items from a given catalog result source, the consuming web site can display content as needed. This content can also be rendered via special pages that are automatically created by SharePoint called category and category item pages. The category page displays the catalog items when a user clicks on an item; it is displayed using the category item page. SharePoint also creates a category page layout and category item layout automatically at the time of connecting to a shared catalog.

Introduction to the Content Search Web Part

As we mentioned, the catalog contents are consumed via the new Content Search web part, which are placed on any given page within a publishing site. The Content Search web part is extremely powerful and contains a configuration panel to highly customize the queries as shown in Figure 8-2; one can test queries instantaneously to ensure results are returned and can easily configure refiners, sorting, and other query settings.

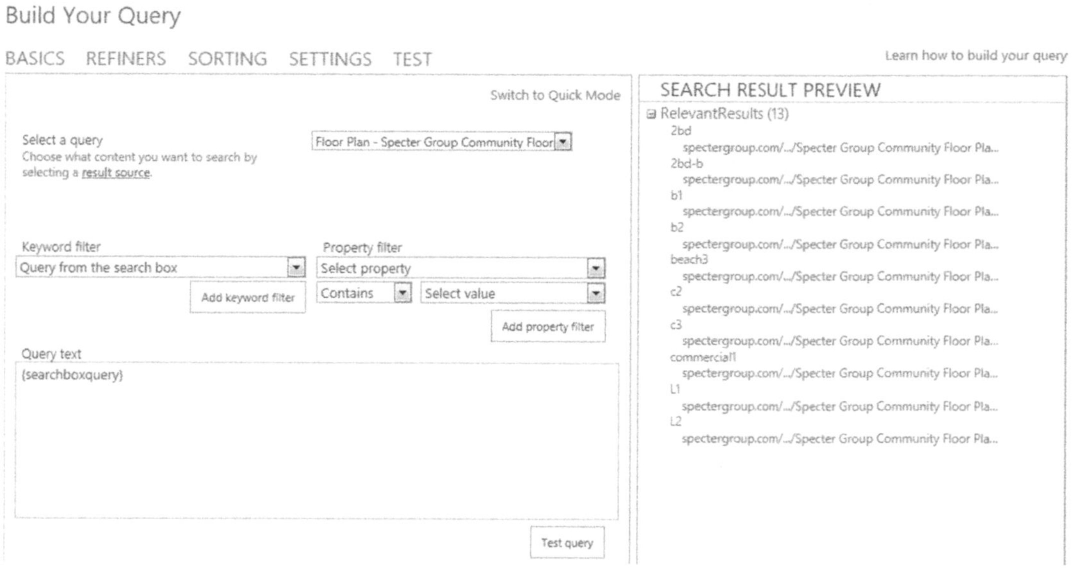

Build Your Query

BASICS   REFINERS   SORTING   SETTINGS   TEST   Learn how to build your query

Figure 8-2. *Content Search web part query configuration panel*

■ **Tip**   Get an in-depth overview of the Content Search web part, display templates, and query rules in Chapter 9.

Overview of Display Templates

Because Cross-Site Collection Publishing depends on search and search results, a method is needed to control how search results get displayed on a given page. Display templates allow for custom rendering of search-driven content that resides in the result source created automatically by SharePoint when connecting to a shared catalog. SharePoint comes with several display templates that generally meet our needs. However, when branding a SharePoint site, there is a high likelihood a custom one will need to be created to display items branded appropriately. See the section "Applying Branding to Search Results with Display Templates" later in this chapter to learn how to create and brand your own display templates.

Another way to look at display templates is in the context of how we used to surface indexed data in SharePoint 2010, that being the Content Query web part. If you have used the Content Query web part in SharePoint 2010 (it is still available in SharePoint 2013), then you might have worked with the XSLT style sheets that the Content Query web part relied on to display query results. Display templates in Design Manager seek to replace XSLT, which few developers ever learned, with more standard HTML. We get into the specifics of creating display templates later in this chapter as well as in Chapter 9, as Cross-Site Collection Publishing and display templates are at the heart of the new WCM paradigm in SharePoint 2013.

There are two kinds of components that help render catalog contents via the Content Search web part. There is a Control display template, which handles the rendering of the entire filtered result, and an Item display template, which renders each individual item. These two templates are set in the web part tool pane as shown in Figure 8-3.

Figure 8-3. *The Content Search web part configuration tool pane shows the two kinds of display templates*

You can find the out-of-the-box display templates in the Master Page Gallery in a folder called Display Template. You also can browse to ~sitecollection/_layouts/15/DesignDisplayTemplates.aspx, i.e. http://spectergroup.com/_layouts/15/DesignDisplayTemplates.aspx, in a browser for a list of all display templates. In addition to selecting the display templates, the Content Search web part allows you to specify the metadata or managed properties you would like to display. In this chapter's walkthrough you will learn how to surface your own metadata and display it using your own look and feel.

■ **Tip**   To learn more about creating display templates, see Chapter 9.

Tagging Terms and Metadata

Items in a catalog must be tagged with metadata or terms. Once crawled, the search index adds this metadata, which can then be used in the consuming site collection via the Content Search web part configuration pane. In addition, a term set field can be used for managed navigation in the consuming site.

It is worth nothing that SharePoint 2013 automatically creates managed properties for site columns that are part of the metadata contained within a catalog. Also all managed properties that are automatically created are of type Text. There is a specific format SharePoint uses when it automatically creates managed properties. Table 8-3 shows the naming conventions.

Table 8-3. *Partial List of Managed Properties Automatically Created for Site Columns*

Site Column Type	Crawled Property	Managed Property	Returned Format
Single line of text	ows_q_TEXT_SiteColumnName	SiteColumnNameOWSTEXT	Exact value
Date and Time	ows_q_DATE_SiteColumnName	SiteColumnNameOWSDATE	Sample format: YYYY-MM-DDTHH:MM:SSZ

Publishing Image	ows_q_IMGE_SiteColumnName	SiteColumnNameOWSIMGE	Returns an HTML image tag, for example:
			`<img alt=""`
			`src="http://spectergroup.com/`
			`PublishingImages/logo.jpg" />`

■ **Tip** Automatic creation of managed properties is not supported for site columns of type Lookup, Calculated, Summary Links data, and Rich media data for publishing. For a full list of managed properties automatically created for site columns visit `http://sprwd.com/22hg4qu`.

Cross-Site Publishing Use: Case Example

We will further show how Cross-Site Collection Publishing can be used by extending our example site. The Specter Group authoring site will be located at `http://authoring.specter.com`; this is where all content is authored. The public web site located at `http://spectergroup.com` has to consume the content from the authoring site. The pages and blog lists required to store content are stored in the authoring site and these lists are configured as catalogs so that they can be indexed properly by the search index. In our scenario, we will fully leverage the Publishing features and hence will use publishing page layouts and content pages.

Our solution will also include a globally accessible assets repository, otherwise we might run into a problem of broken image links between the authoring and public sites. Therefore, we have created a separate web application with a single site collection and anonymous access enabled. This assets site can contain all media assets, which will allow for authors to pick and choose media to include in content and the source URL used within the Content Search web part will not appear broken. The authoring site collection is configured to use the Suggested Browser Locations to point to the global assets site collection located at `http://assets.spectergroup.com`. Figure 8-4 shows the different web applications used in the solution.

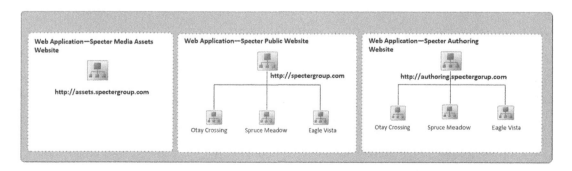

Figure 8-4. *The web applications we are using include Assets, Public Website, and Authoring Site*

Now that we've given you a more complete overview of the sample Specter Group Cross-Site Collection Publishing solution, we walk you through the steps to implement Cross-Site Collection Publishing and related steps for our specific scenario. The following list gives the overall process in order. We then break down each step throughout the remainder of this chapter.

1. Configuring the authoring site collection.

    a. Configure the pages library as a shared catalog.

    b. Configure the blog list as a shared catalog.

2. Configuring the consuming site collection.

    a. Connect to the blog catalog, integrating navigation.

    b. Change the metadata displayed on the blog category page.

    c. Connect to the communities catalog without integrating navigation.

    d. Create landing pages for the communities catalog.

    e. Create the community detail page.

    f. Set the community detail URL.

    g. Configure catalog navigation for communities.

    h. Apply the Specter Group branding via display templates.

        i. Create the List control.

        ii. Create the Item display template.

■ **Note** Please ensure you have the required metadata, as we mentioned earlier, prior to catalog content being available for a consuming site. Content must be tagged with the appropriate metadata. Chapter 6 walked through the process of creating the community content type as well as term sets.

Both the Specter Group content type and the ability to leverage catalogs with managed navigation require us to have a global term set. Depending on your term set configuration, you can share terms on the site navigation. Figure 8-5 shows the structure we have come up with for the Communities term set. The Specter Group community content type contains metadata columns that map to nodes such as Property Type, which are used to fill in metadata when creating new property pages and other artifacts such as images to allow tagging them with the appropriate community.

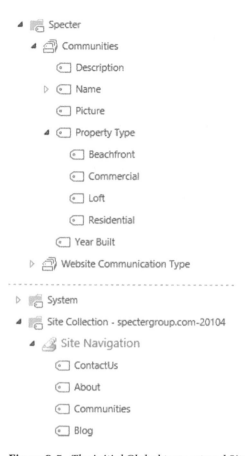

Figure 8-5. *The initial Global term set and Site Collection term set*

The term set nodes under the Site Collection ➤ Site Navigation group includes the term "Blog". We use this term later in this chapter to leverage the metadata navigation for the blog catalog when we configure the catalog connection on the Specter Group public web site (the consuming site). This will allow us to browse all blogs and blog entry details with dynamically built category pages, which we also discuss in more detail in the following section.

Configuring Cross-Site Publishing for Specific Content an Authoring Site Collection

In Chapter 3 we came up with the design comps that showed various dynamic content, such as for communities and blog posts. This section walks you through the process of enabling and configuring cross-site publishing for each of these items, in addition to ensuring these are displayed as per the branding requirements. There are two catalogs we configure on our authoring site collection: Specter Community and Specter Blog Post.

1. New Community information (Pages Library): This is the standard publishing pages library, which makes use of page fields and layouts and our Specter Group community content type.

2. Specter Blog Posts (Posts List): This is the standard posts list that resides within the blog subsite on the authoring site collection.

■ **Note** Refer to Chapter 9 for detailed instructions on configuring search for cross-site publishing.

Add a Suggested Browser Location

As stated earlier, while authoring content, users need the ability to pick media assets. We can leverage suggested browser locations on the Authoring Site so that content authors are able to easily pick media assets via the SharePoint Asset Picker modal window.

To add a suggested location, navigate to the Site Settings page on the main site of the authoring site collection and follow these steps:

1. Under Site Collection Administration, click Suggested Browser Locations to load the Suggested Content Browser Locations page.

2. Click New item to open the new form page.

3. Provide a display name, URL, and optional description of the suggested browser location, as shown in Figure 8-6.

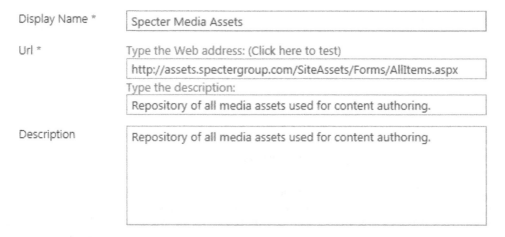

Figure 8-6. The configured suggested browser location on the authoring site

4. Click Save to save the suggestion location.

Configuring Catalog Sharing

We first configure the Community catalog. This catalog enables sharing of actual publishing pages as a catalog. The pages library uses the custom content type Specter Community. The publishing page also contains image field controls that will enable authoring of new community pages with text and embedded images.

Configure the Pages Library to Use the Community Content Type

To start, we add the community content type to the pages library and then create a new publishing page. We follow these steps for adding the content type:

1. Go to Site Settings ➤ Site Content, then select the Pages Library Settings as shown in Figure 8-7.

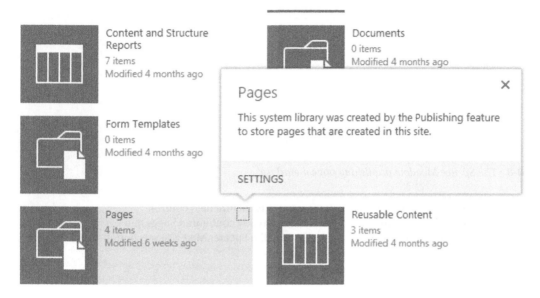

Figure 8-7. *Under Site Content, single-click Pages Library, then click the Settings link on the modal dialog box*

2. Click Add from existing site content types to add the Specter Community content type.

Now that we have the Specter Community content type added to the pages library, we create a new publishing page to create the Spruce Meadow Community or property.

■ **Tip**   See Chapter 7 to learn how to create page layouts and content types, and how to enable them on your site.

---

1. Go to Site Settings ➤ Add Page, and provide a page name in the modal dialog box. Then in page edit mode, fill in the appropriate metadata as shown in Figure 8-8.

Figure 8-8. *The Spruce Meadow publishing page metadata*

2. To select a picture for this community, click the Community Picture field control.
    The Asset Picker dialog box will appear, but because we already configured Suggested
    Browser Locations, at the top left of the dialog box we see the Specter Media Assets option
    as shown in Figure 8-9.

Select an Asset

Current Location: Images at http://authoring.spectergroup.com/PublishingImages

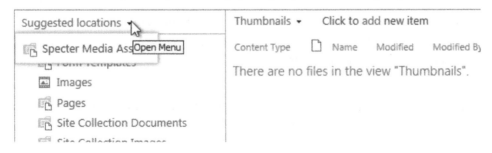

Figure 8-9. *The Specter Media Assets location available via the Asset Picker dialog box*

3. When you click the Specter Media Assets location, you are able to browse to the Assets Library where all media is stored (see Figure 8-10) and directly select a picture for the Spruce Meadow Community. You will notice that the location URL is `http://assets.spectergroup.com/SiteAssets,` which is the central repository previously configured and available to all web sites. See the section "Cross-Site Publishing Use: Case Example" earlier in this chapter for details. Select the image you wish to associate with this page and then click Insert.

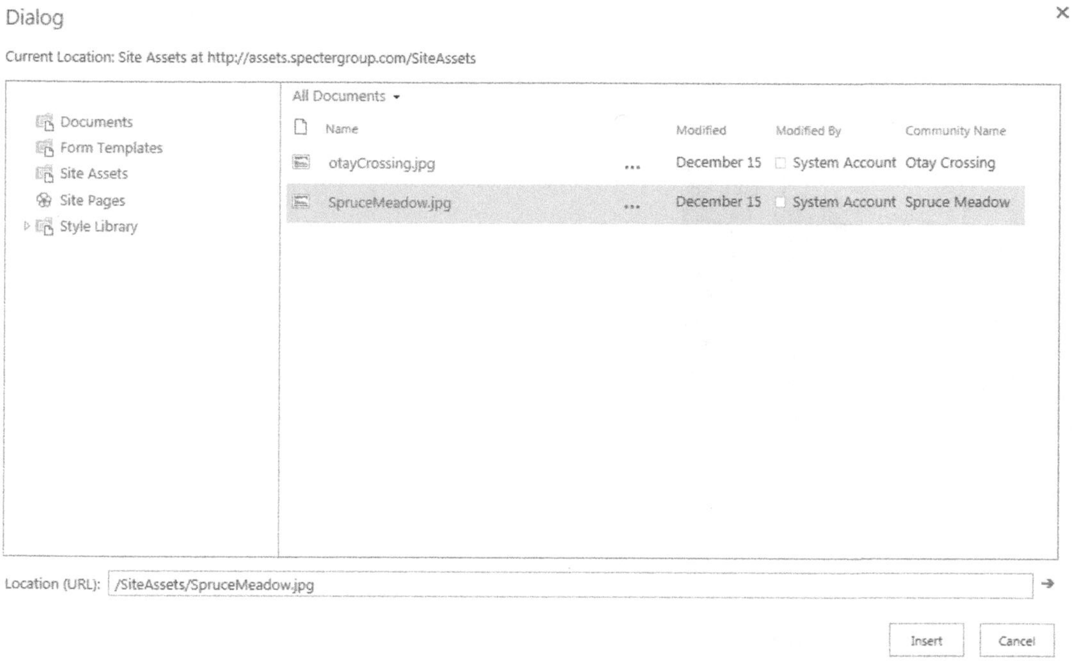

Figure 8-10. *The Specter Media Assets location*

At this point the Specter Group community page for Spruce Meadow has all metadata filled in, including a picture, and it is ready to be saved and published. The page in edit mode is shown in Figure 8-11. We've created pages for other properties and have tagged and published them to ensure they are aggregated on the next search crawl.

Figure 8-11. *The newly created Spruce Meadow Community page*

Configuring the Catalog on the Pages Library

The next step is to configure the pages library and enable it for catalogs. We are using this library to author and publish new Specter Group communities. To do this, follow these steps:

1.   On the authoring site, go to Site Settings ➤ Site Content. When the Site Content loads, hover over the right side of the pages library (see Figure 8-12) and click the ellipsis. Then click Settings.

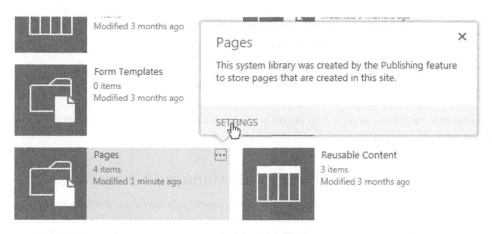

Figure 8-12. *Use the ellipsis shortcut to get to the Pages Library Settings*

2. Under General Settings, click Catalog Settings to open the screen shown in Figure 8-13.

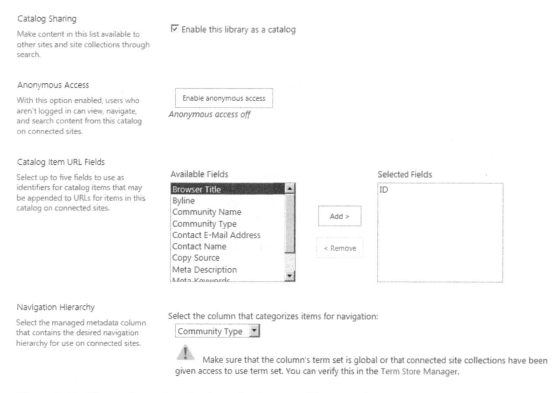

Figure 8-13. *The catalog settings for the authoring pages library used to create new Specter communities*

3. For Catalog Sharing, select the Enable this library as a catalog check box.

4. In the Catalog Item URL Fields section, select the ID field.

5. In the Navigation Hierarchy section, select the column Community Type metadata column, as this categorizes our communities accordingly and will help drive navigation on the public web site.

At this point the settings for this catalog are as shown on Figure 8-13 and this library is ready to be crawled. We configure the Blog Catalog next.

Configuring Catalog Sharing for Integration with Managed Navigation

The blog posts are authored on a subsite within the authoring site collection. This is also the Cross-Site Collection Publishing example we use to integrate with managed navigation. One of the key requirements from Specter Group was to have an image for each blog post. We simply add the existing site column Page Image, which is also used on publishing pages, but most certainly can be used on our blog post. Our first step is to configure the catalog. To accomplish this, follow these steps while on the authoring blog subsite.

1. On the authoring site, go to Site Settings ➤ Site Content. When the Site Content loads, hover over the right side of the blog library and click the ellipsis. Then click Settings.

2. Under General Settings, click Catalog Settings.

3. Select the Enable this library as catalog check box.

4. Under Anonymous Access, enable anonymous access.

5. Under Catalog Item URL Fields, select the ID field (this is the best option as it is unique).

When to Enable Catalog Anonymous Access

In what scenario would it make sense to enable anonymous access for a catalog? This can be helpful when we are sharing catalogs with a public web site so anonymous users would be able to see the catalog content once it is indexed. However, if we enabled anonymous access but wish to change individual item permissions within our catalog, the search system will respect said permissions. Therefore the search system will not show these items to anonymous users, yet will still make them available to the specific users and groups as specified by the specific item permissions. This is helpful to know when planning catalogs.

The catalog configuration is now completed, and it should look like the one shown in Figure 8-14.

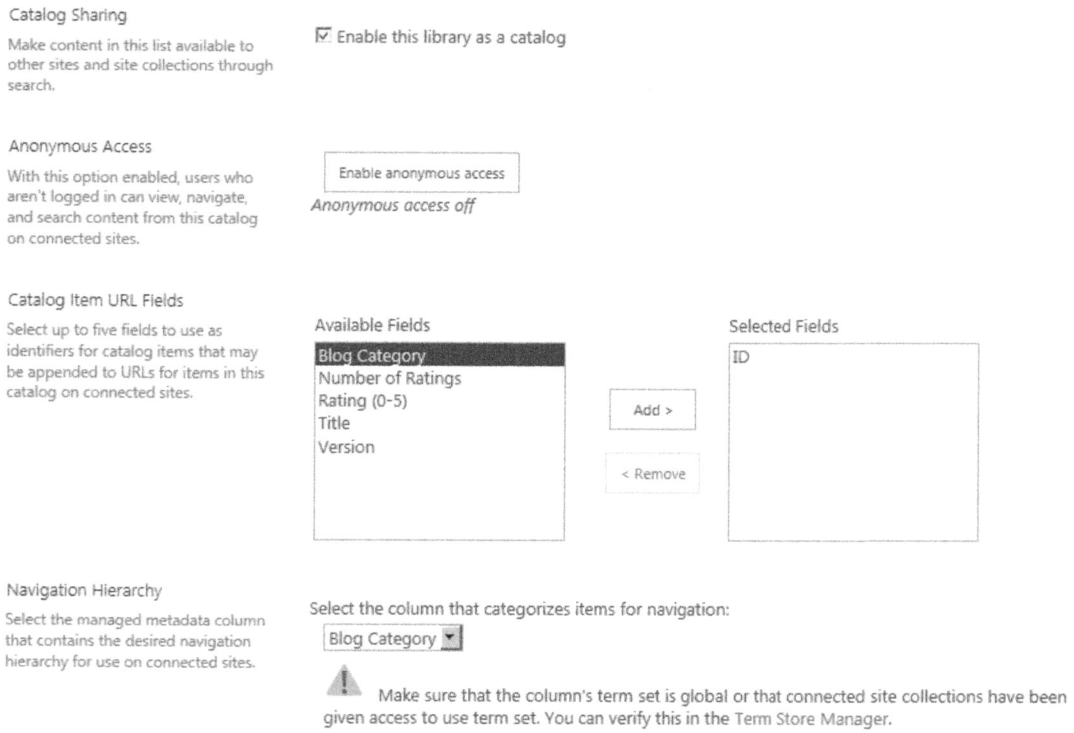

Catalog Sharing

Make content in this list available to other sites and site collections through search.

☑ Enable this library as a catalog

Anonymous Access

With this option enabled, users who aren't logged in can view, navigate, and search content from this catalog on connected sites.

Enable anonymous access

Anonymous access off

Catalog Item URL Fields

Select up to five fields to use as identifiers for catalog items that may be appended to URLs for items in this catalog on connected sites.

Available Fields

Blog Category
Number of Ratings
Rating (0-5)
Title
Version

Add >

< Remove

Selected Fields

ID

Navigation Hierarchy

Select the managed metadata column that contains the desired navigation hierarchy for use on connected sites.

Select the column that categorizes items for navigation:

Blog Category ▾

⚠ Make sure that the column's term set is global or that connected site collections have been given access to use term set. You can verify this in the Term Store Manager.

Figure 8-14. *Posts SharePoint list catalog configuration*

Augmenting the Out-of-the-Box Posts List

Out of the box, the SharcPoint posts list does not provide a blog post image; therefore we can add the Site Column, Page Image. Also, to be able to browse posts by a given category on the Specter Group public web site, we can create a global term set (see Figure 8-15) that outlines these categories and adds it as a metadata column to the posts list. This in turn allows us to specify the metadata column as the one used to categorize blog posts.

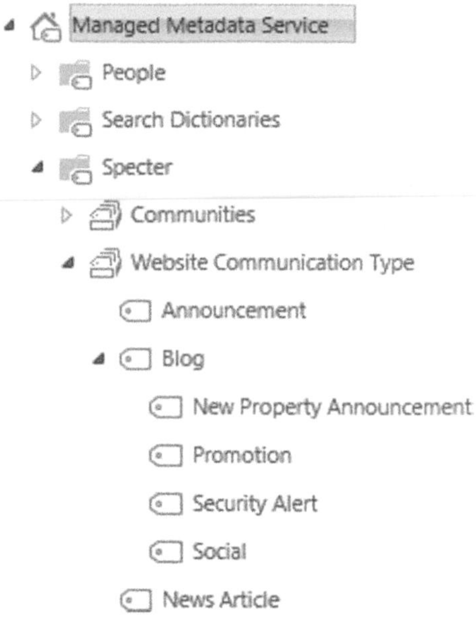

Figure 8-15. *The Specter Global Group, which contains the Website Communication Type term set, which contains the Blog term and child blog category terms*

In addition, due to an issue with post HTML content not being escaped when shown on the catalog consuming site, we add the publishing page content column as well.

With this configuration in place, blog posts are now able to be tagged, published, and shared as a catalog, provided we run a full crawl on our search crawler. Once the search crawler runs, this catalog is available and can be consumed by the Specter Group public web site.

■ **Tip**   Learn how to configure a search in Chapter 9.

Configuring a Web Site for Catalog Consumption

The second part of configuring Cross-Site Collection Publishing is on the consuming web site. In our case this is the Specter Group public web site. Each of the catalogs we created on the authoring site in the previous section is now available to connect to, assuming the search crawler has run. Remember that the two catalogs we configured are slightly different, as the communities catalog does not use managed metadata navigation, whereas the blog catalog does. We walk through connecting to the blog catalog (with managed metadata navigation) first, followed by the community catalog.

Connecting to the Catalog with Managed Metadata Navigation

Now that we've configured our shared catalogs within our authoring portal, we next configure the connection to these catalogs for use by the Specter Group public web site.

Catalog connections are managed at the site collection level. On the content consuming site (i.e., the public site), follow these steps.

1. Go to Site Settings and under Site Administration, click Manage Catalog Connections.

2. Click Connect to Catalog. Refer to Figure 8-16, which shows the available catalogs. Notice the Blog - Posts and Specter Authoring Portal - Pages catalogs.

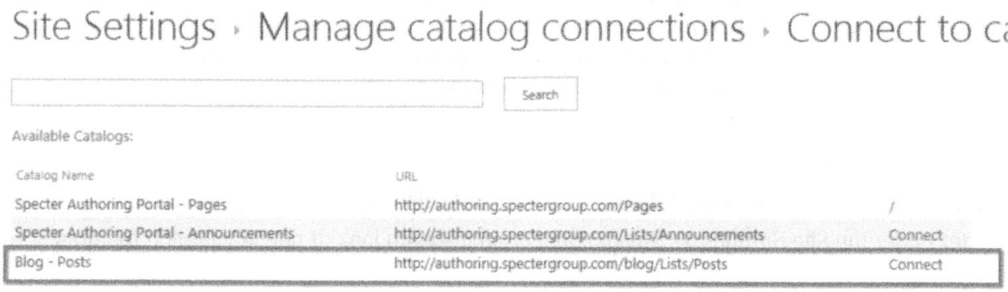

Site Settings ⟩ Manage catalog connections ⟩ Connect to catalog

	Search

Available Catalogs:

Catalog Name	URL	
Specter Authoring Portal - Pages	http://authoring.spectergroup.com/Pages	/
Specter Authoring Portal - Announcements	http://authoring.spectergroup.com/Lists/Announcements	Connect
Blog - Posts	http://authoring.spectergroup.com/blog/Lists/Posts	Connect

Figure 8-16. *The available Blog - Posts catalog previously set up on the authoring portal is shown on the Specter public web site*

3. To the right of the catalog to which you wish to connect, in this case, Blog - Posts, click Connect.

4. You can now configure the connection. Refer to Figure 8-17, which shows the first two options, in particular how to integrate the connection and how the navigation hierarchy should be configured.

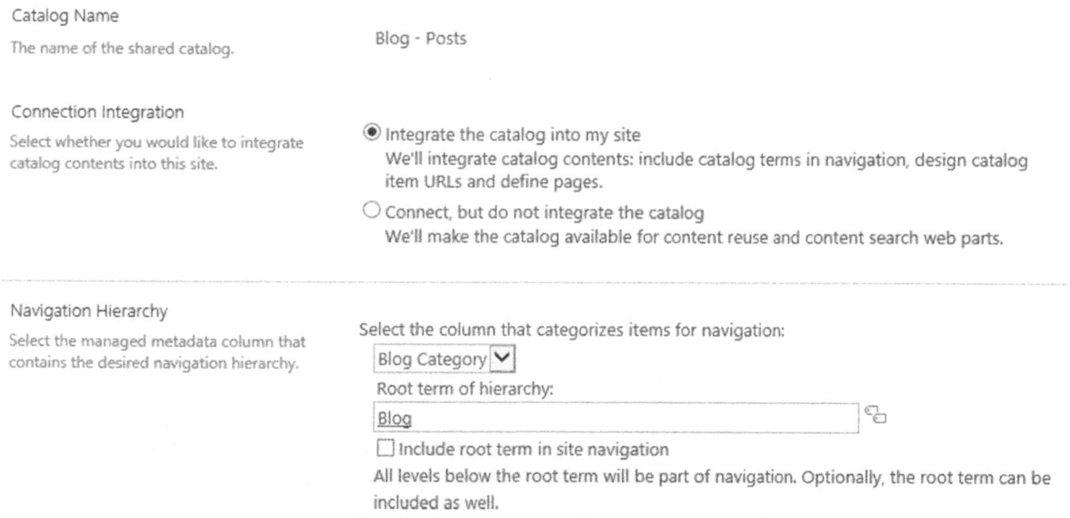

Catalog Name

The name of the shared catalog.   Blog - Posts

Connection Integration

Select whether you would like to integrate   ◉ Integrate the catalog into my site
catalog contents into this site.   We'll integrate catalog contents: include catalog terms in navigation, design catalog
                                                            item URLs and define pages.

                                                        ○ Connect, but do not integrate the catalog
                                                            We'll make the catalog available for content reuse and content search web parts.

Navigation Hierarchy

Select the managed metadata column that   Select the column that categorizes items for navigation:
contains the desired navigation hierarchy.   Blog Category ▾

                                                        Root term of hierarchy:

                                                        Blog

                                                        ☐ Include root term in site navigation
                                                        All levels below the root term will be part of navigation. Optionally, the root term can be
                                                        included as well.

Figure 8-17. *Blog catalog connection configuration shows the first two options: connection integration and navigation hierarchy*

5. Under Connection Integration, select the Integrate the catalog into my site option because we are looking to be able to navigate blog posts driven by the categories. When this option is selected, there are many options that can be configured and we walk through those in the next steps.

6. Under Navigation Hierarchy, ensure the metadata column Blog Category is selected in the drop-down list. The root term of the hierarchy is automatically selected for you. It is the one previously configured on the global term set. You do not want to include this root term on the site navigation if you already have a local term on your site navigation. In our case, in Chapter 6 we added the term "blog" to the navigation menu, so we would leave the Include root term in site navigation check box unchecked.

■ **Tip**   If you choose to include the root navigation node, SharePoint automatically creates the site navigation. You can then change the order under the Site Settings ➤ Navigation. For an in-depth look at new navigation features, see Chapter 6.

Once this configuration option is in place, the terms from the global term set labeled "Blog" will be shared with the local site navigation node labeled "Blog" and will appear with a pin icon in the Term Store Management Tool, as shown in Figure 8-18.

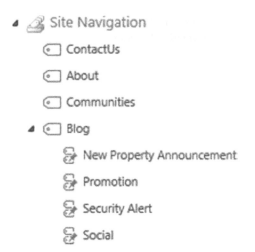

Figure 8-18. Blog Post category terms pinned to the Site Navigation Blog term set

The next configuration is Navigation Position. This option is extremely useful in our case, as the Specter Group public web site already contains a managed navigation node named Blog.

7. Our objective is to drop the blog categories under this node and allow for browsing the posts by category. Therefore, select the Select an alternate location in site navigation option as shown in Figure 8-19, and browse or type the name of the node you wish to drop the categories under. The intellisense should pick up the site navigation Blog node so you can select it.

Navigation Position

Choose where this catalog is integrated into site navigation.

○ Add to navigation root
The catalog's navigation will begin at the root level of the site

◉ Select an alternate location in site navigation
Position the catalog below the root of site navigation.

| b |

Suggestions
Blog [Site Navigation]

Navigation Pinning

For site navigation to reflect changes to the original term set, pin the category terms. Only the owner of the original term set will be able to add, remove, or move around category terms.

Figure 8-19. Navigation position allows flexibility in integrating the Catalog Navigation and positioning it exactly where we need to, in our case the Blog existing global navigation node

The next important aspect of configuring the catalog connection is the Catalog Item URL Behavior and Catalog Item URL Format shown in Figure 8-20. Both are equally important.

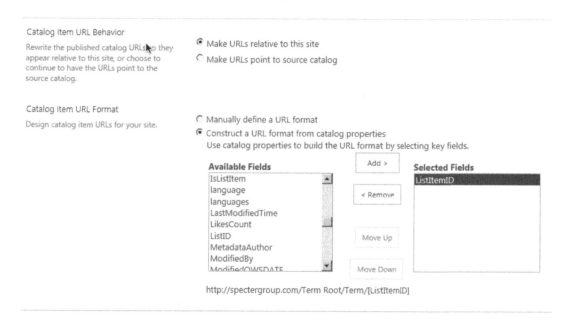

Catalog Item URL Behavior

Rewrite the published catalog URLs so they appear relative to this site, or choose to continue to have the URLs point to the source catalog.

◉ Make URLs relative to this site
○ Make URLs point to source catalog

Catalog Item URL Format

Design catalog item URLs for your site.

○ Manually define a URL format
◉ Construct a URL format from catalog properties
Use catalog properties to build the URL format by selecting key fields.

Available Fields
IsListItem
language
languages
LastModifiedTime
LikesCount
ListID
MetadataAuthor
ModifiedBy
ModifiedOWSDATE

Add >
< Remove
Move Up
Move Down

Selected Fields
ListItemID

http://spectergroup.com/Term Root/Term/[ListItemID]

Figure 8-20. The Blog Catalog URL behavior and format configuration settings

8. Because we do not want users to browse to the authoring portal when clicking on a blog post, proceed to configure the Catalog Item URL Behavior and select the Make URLs relative to this site option.

9. For Catalog Item URL Format, select the second option to construct the URL based on the catalog properties and select the ListItemID field. This field is the unique identifier for a particular blog post. You will notice the URL preview underneath, which tells us how our navigation will look based on the original terms selected. In our case, this is the public site base URL followed by the Blog term root followed by the selected Category followed by the ID of the blog post.

Now that we have connected to our blog catalog, we see the dynamic navigation under the global site navigation with each blog category underneath the original blog node as the label (shown in Figure 8-21). You will also notice how SharePoint automatically builds a breadcrumb based on the selected blog category.

Figure 8-21. *The new blog catalog managed navigation and the blog post displayed below it*

Using the Category and Category-Item Pages

When we create a connection to any catalog, SharePoint has the capability to create two key pages that are used to browse the catalog. These two pages are the category page and the category-item page. In addition to these two pages, two corresponding page layouts are provisioned and the category and category-item pages are created based on these layouts. In the example from the previous section, with our blog catalog, SharePoint automatically created page layouts named `Category-Blog.aspx` and `CatalogItem-Blog.aspx` as shown in Figure 8-22 at the time when we connected to the catalog.

Figure 8-22. *Auto-provisioned HTML page layouts for the blog catalog connection*

We have the ability to customize these pages at various levels. We can customize the page layout or we can choose to only modify the page for a specific category. In Figure 8-23 you can see the modal dialog box that is displayed when a new category page is created.

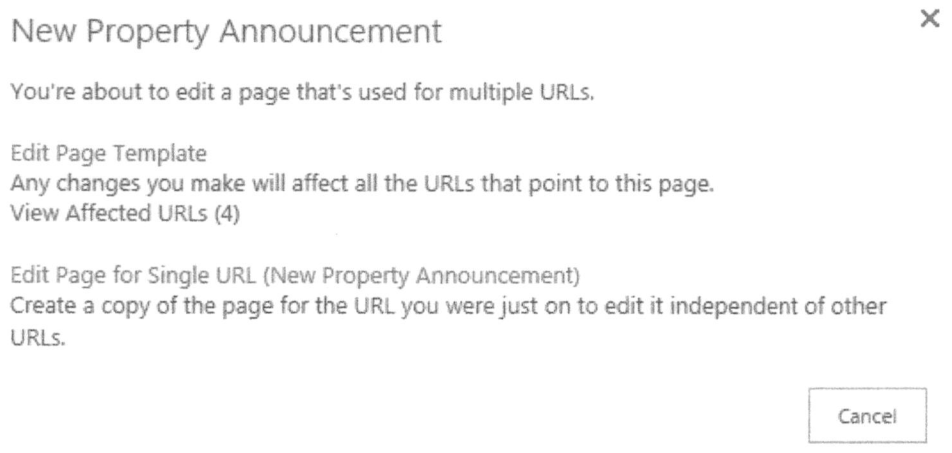

New Property Announcement ✕

You're about to edit a page that's used for multiple URLs.

Edit Page Template
Any changes you make will affect all the URLs that point to this page.
View Affected URLs (4)

Edit Page for Single URL (New Property Announcement)
Create a copy of the page for the URL you were just on to edit it independent of other
URLs.

Cancel

Figure 8-23. When editing the Category page, SharePoint displays available editing options

---

■ **Tip** Whenever we disconnect from a catalog, there is some manual cleanup work that must be completed.
This includes deleting the category and category-item pages that reside within the pages library. Further, you must
remove the two corresponding page layouts that were automatically created and are found in the Master Page Gallery.
Finally, you must manually delete the terms previously shared under a navigation node if the catalog included managed
metadata similar to our example blog list. Removing all of these artifacts will allow you to connect to the catalog again
without potential problems if you need to re-create the connection.

Changing Metadata Displayed on a Category Page

By default, a category page might not display all of the metadata your scenario requires. In our scenario, the blog
metadata displayed by default on the catalog consuming page is not enough. The category page only displays the
image and title (see Figure 8-21). How about if you would like to display additional metadata such as the following:

- Title
- Body text
- Picture
- Published date
- Published by
- Comment count

To change what metadata is displayed you can edit the category page template or page layout via the web browser.
Browse to a blog post category and place the page in editing mode. A dialog box very similar to Figure 8-24 will appear.
Click Edit Page Template so that all related categories reflect your change. Once in edit mode, determine what metadata
you can display by using the diagnostic view available in the configuration pane of the SharePoint content search web
part. Yes, the content search web part is actually used within the category page to display the catalog content. This allows
you to map columns and view the detailed information on the output as shown in Figure 8-24.

Figure 8-24. The category page contains the Content Search web part, which can be further configured, including displaying additional metadata by mapping custom columns that are part of our custom content type

■ **Tip** The SharePoint user interface calls a category page layout a template, which can be confusing given the fact that template is used to refer to other capabilities or features. To be clear, it is a page layout and we are in fact editing the page layout when we opt to edit the category page template.

■ **Caution** You will notice that the blog body content HTML is not escaped when using the multiple line of text column, which is used by default on the posts list.

To ensure the blog post body HTML is escaped, we have decided to add the publishing page content column to the posts list and use that to enter the content of a post. This in return outputs the HTML correctly when displaying posts via the Content Search web part using Cross-Site Collection Publishing.

Connecting to a Catalog without Integrating Navigation

Now that we have seen how to connect to a catalog with managed metadata navigation, we want to look at how connecting to a catalog without integrated navigation might be different. In our example, the Specter Group communities catalog does not leverage the catalog navigation. We connect to the communities catalog, and then we show the properties and required metadata styled as per the Specter branding in combination with using the Content Search web part and a custom display template.

■ **Note** Because the communities catalog does not integrate with navigation, we manually create the pages to view communities including the community detail page.

To get started, first connect to the communities catalog you previously shared on the authoring site by following these steps:

1. On the consuming site, go to Site Settings. Under Site Administration, click Manage Catalog Connections.

2. Click Connect to a Catalog. If the communities catalog was configured properly and crawled by the search indexer, it will appear as shown in Figure 8-25.

Available Catalogs:

Catalog Name	URL	
Specter Authoring Portal - Pages	http://authoring.spectergroup.com/Pages	Connect

Figure 8-25. *The communities catalog available on the Specter public web site*

3. Click Connect and then under Connection Integration, select the Connect, but do not integrate the catalog option, as shown in Figure 8-26. Using this configuration you are able to use the specific Content Reuse web parts available in the Snippet Gallery.

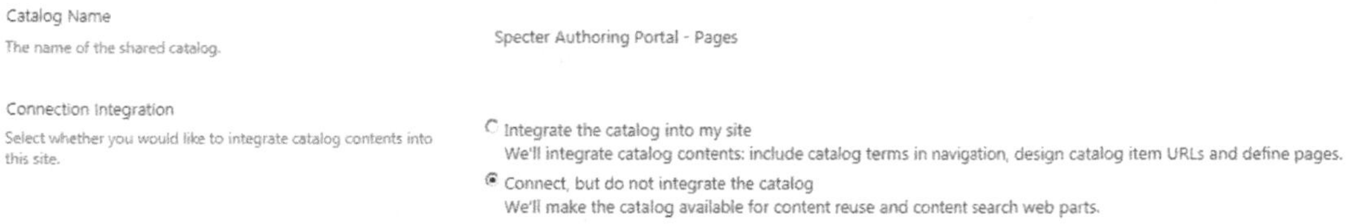

Catalog Name
The name of the shared catalog.   Specter Authoring Portal - Pages

Connection Integration
Select whether you would like to integrate catalog contents into   ○ Integrate the catalog into my site
this site.   We'll integrate catalog contents: include catalog terms in navigation, design catalog item URLs and define pages.
                                                                     ● Connect, but do not integrate the catalog
                                                                         We'll make the catalog available for content reuse and content search web parts.

Figure 8-26. *Communities catalog integration options*

4. All other options are unavailable at this point, so click OK to complete the connection.

■ **Note** Because we did not integrate the communities with the Specter Group web site (including catalog item navigation), there will be problems if we simply insert a Content Search web part onto a page. The page will display the catalog contents, but if you hover over any item, you will notice the URL to the item was only partially generated. This is because we must further configure the catalog.

---

5. Go back to the catalog settings on the consuming site and set the Catalog Item URL Behavior to Make URLs relative to this site as shown in Figure 8-27.

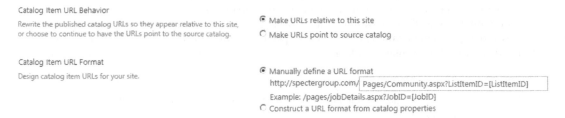

Figure 8-27. Community catalog URL behavior and format configuration

6. Under the Catalog Item URL Format, select the Manually define a URL format option and set the text box value also shown in Figure 8-27. Notice the custom page `Community.aspx`, as you will need to create that as well. (See the next section, "Creating Landing Pages for a Catalog.")

One can think of category pages as the ones responsible for displaying the list of data items, and the category-item page as the item detail page. This is very much like the typical ASP.NET data-driven web application pattern. In fact, we can also use the QueryString to pass the item ID to the details page, again much like traditional data-driven web applications.

Creating Landing Pages for a Catalog

As we saw earlier, SharePoint creates catalog landing pages only when we do in fact integrate with navigation at the time of connecting to a catalog. Because we did not integrate navigation for our communities catalog, we must manually build the appropriate pages where users can see all communities and the community detail page. In the following sections we see how we can create a catalog landing page and a catalog details page and define a catalog detail URL.

Creating a Category Landing Page

Our first step is to create the page that a user will go to when browsing friendly URLs for a catalog, in our case the communities catalog.

■ **Note** These are in fact the equivalent of the category pages previously discussed, except we are creating them manually.

We create a page where we will display all of the communities via the search-driven web part. We call this page Communities and add it to the global navigation on our site.

1. Go to Settings ➤ Add Page on the top right. When the Add Page modal dialog box appears, type the name Communities.

2. Select the appropriate page layout you wish to use. Review Chapter 7 if you want to create a new page layout.

3. Once the page has been created, edit the page and insert a Content Search web part found under the content rollup category in the Web Part Gallery as shown in Figure 8-28.

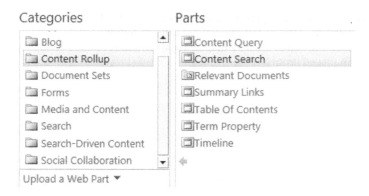

Figure 8-28. *The Content Search web part is used to display communities from the catalog*

■ **Note**   We use the Content Search web part as it contains richer capabilities to query result sources, some of them being the catalogs we've enabled and that are automatically created by SharePoint. You might consider using the Recently Changed Items web part under the "Search-Driven Category," but it does not contain the result sources when building a query.

Our next step is to configure the Content Search web part to display the communities catalog content. To do this, edit the newly added web part settings.

1. In the Configuration pane, under Search Criteria, click Change Query. A Change modal dialog box will appear.

2. Under Basics, select the Result Source named Specter Authoring Portal - Pages Results, which is the result source automatically created when you connected to this catalog. Once you select this result source, the catalog content is retrieved, as shown in Figure 8-29. In our example, we immediately see two communities in the Search Result Preview pane as these two communities were previously added.

Build Your Query

BASICS   REFINERS   SETTINGS   TEST

Learn how to build

Switch to Advanced Mode

SEARCH RESULT PREVIEW

⊟ RelevantResults (2)

Otay-Crossing
spectergroup.com/Pages/Community.aspx?ListItemID=5

Spruce Meadow
spectergroup.com/Pages/Community.aspx?ListItemID=4

Select a query
Choose what content you want to search by
selecting a result source.

Specter Authoring Portal - Pages Results (Site ▾)
Blog - Posts Results (Site Collection)
Documents (System)
Items matching a content type (System)
Items matching a tag (System)
Items related to current user (System)
Items with same keyword as this item (System)
Local Video Results (System)
Pages (System)
Pictures (System)
Popular (System)
Recently changed items (System)
Recommended Items (System)
Specter Authoring Portal - Pages Results (Site Collection)
Wiki (System)

Restrict by tag
You can limit results to content tagged with
specific terms, including site navigation terms.

Add additional filters
Using syntax as if you were creating your own
query, add additional filters and search terms
here.

Figure 8-29. *Selecting the communities catalog and previewing results*

3. The catalog contents are displayed using the standard display template, which is specified in the web part tool pane. You can now configure additional metadata to display by editing the Content Search web part settings as shown in Figure 8-30. To display the community picture, you can include the appropriate managed property.

⊟ Display Templates   Help

Control

| List with Paging | ▾ |

Item

| Picture on left, 3 lines on right | ▾ |

☑ Don't show anything when there are no results.

⊟ Property Mappings

☑ Change the mapping of managed properties for the fields in the Item Display Template.

Picture URL

| CommunityPictureOWSIMGE | ▾ |

Link URL

| Path | ▾ |

Line 1

| Title | ▾ |

Line 2

| AboutOWSMTXT | ▾ |

Line 3

| owstaxIdCommunityx0020Type | ▾ |

Figure 8-30. *Search web part metadata configuration for communities catalog*

At this point we can see the communities including the picture and some of the metadata, as shown in Figure 8-31.

Otay-Crossing

Otay was built with the traditional people in mind. People who opt for th...

Residential

Spruce Meadow

Spruce Meadow was built in 2001 right when the DotCom was at its peak...

Loft

Figure 8-31. *Content Search web part configured to retrieve Specter Group communities catalog results using an out-of-the-box display template*

Creating a Category-Item Page

When a user clicks on a given category for a category landing page, a category detail page for that specific category should load. For us, when visitors land on the community landing page created in the previous section and they click on a specific community, we want to be able to display further details. To do this, we first create a new publishing page and call it Community as shown on Figure 8-32.

Add a page

Give it a name

Community

Find it at http://spectergroup.com/community

Create   Cancel

Figure 8-32. *Creating the Community details page*

On this page we insert a Content Search web part as we did in the previous section; however, the web part configuration is a bit different. Our objective for this web part is to retrieve the value of the URL QueryString passed to the page so that we can display the specific community details. One of the new features of the Content Search web part allows us to do this by specifying the QueryString name as shown in Figure 8-33 in the web part's query builder. In addition, we ensure we select the appropriate results on the drop-down menu to only show items from the communities catalog.

Build Your Query

BASICS   REFINERS   SETTINGS   TEST   Learn how to build your query

Switch to Advanced Mode

SEARCH RESULT PREVIEW

⊟ RelevantResults (1)
    Otay-Crossing
        spectergroup.com/Pages/Community.aspx?ListItemID=5

Select a query
Choose what content you want to search by selecting a result source.

Specter Authoring Portal · Pages Results (Sit ▼

Restrict by tag
You can limit results to content tagged with specific terms, including site navigation terms.

◉ Don't restrict by any tag

○ Restrict by navigation term of current page

○ Restrict by current and child navigation terms

○ Restrict on this tag:

Add additional filters
Using syntax as if you were creating your own query, add additional filters and search terms here.

ListItemID={QueryString.ListItemID}

Figure 8-33. *Content Search web part configured to retrieve only one item as per the URL QueryString*

Once we have configured the Content Search web part and then click on a given community, the detail page displays additional information or metadata.

■ **Tip** To learn more about full text queries and available variables when working with the Content Search web part, refer to Chapter 9 or visit `http://sprwd.com/ffqhxnr`.

Defining a Category-Item Page URL

During our catalog configuration, we specified that the URL behavior was to make URLs relative to the current site. We can easily validate this configuration by hovering over any of the catalog items on the category landing page and verifying the catalog item URL. In our case, if we hover over the Spruce Meadow community, as shown in Figure 8-34, we see the browser status bar displays the URL to this item's detail page and passes the `ListItemID`, as previously configured.

Announcement

Promotion

Security Alert

Social

✎ EDIT LINKS

Site Contents

Spruce Meadow

Spruce Meadow was built

Loft

`http://spectergroup.com/Pages/Community.aspx?ListItemID=4`

Figure 8-34. *The community catalog item URL format and behavior as previously configured and pointing to the Community.aspx custom page*

Configuring Catalog Navigation for Catalogs without Integrated Navigation

Our last step is to configure the Specter Group web site term labeled "Communities" so that when a user clicks on it via the top navigation, the link goes to a page we specify that displays all of the communities. To do this, go to Site Settings, and click Term Store Managed. With the Term Store Management Tool, expand the site navigation term set, and then click on the term labeled Communities. On the navigation tab, select the Simple Link or Header option. To provide a link to the communities page, you can either browse the web site and pick the page, or simply type it in the textbox as shown in Figure 8-35. Click Save and your top navigation now includes a Community link that points to the communities page.

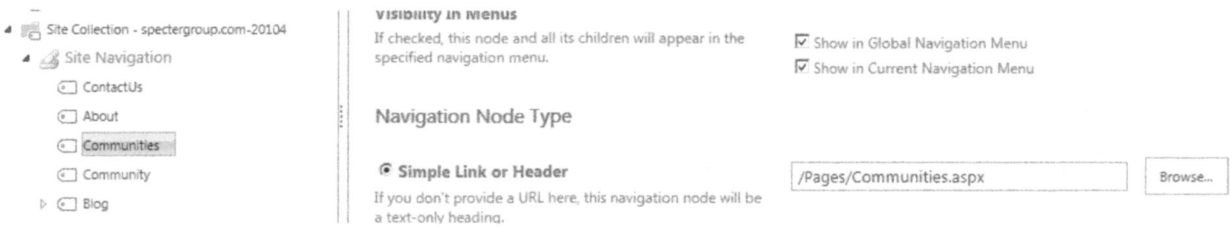

Figure 8-35. *Site navigation Communities node static page configuration*

Applying Branding to Search Result with Display Templates

Now that we have the communities catalog completely set up we are able to style it according to the previously created Specter Group design. To achieve this, we need to create two key components. The first is a list Control display template, and the second is an Item display template. Together these two display templates allow us to place and style Content Search web part results.

■ **Tip**　For in-depth coverage on how to create list Control and Item display templates, see Chapter 9.

Creating a Custom List Control Display Template

A list Control display template is used once per search results to wrap the collection of returned items. Each item in turn is displayed using an Item display template, once per item. Our objective is to use the appropriate HTML markup so that the entire collection of items is displayed as per the Specter Group design.

1. To create a new list control, it is best practice to start with an existing display template. You can make a copy of an existing Control display template by navigating to the Master Page Gallery ➤ Display Templates ➤ Content WebParts folder.

2. Make a copy of the Control_List.html file, and rename it Control_List_Specter.html. The full HTML source code for the out-of-the-box Control_List.html file is shown in Listing 8-1.

Listing 8-1. The Full HTML Source Code for the Out-of-the-Box Control_List.html File

```
<html xmlns:mso="urn:schemas-microsoft-com:office:office"
      xmlns:msdt="uuid:C2F41010-65B3-11d1-A29F-00AA00C14882">
<head>
<title>List</title>
<!--[if gte mso 9]><xml>
<mso:CustomDocumentProperties>
<mso:TemplateHidden msdt:dt="string">0</mso:TemplateHidden>
<mso:MasterPageDescription msdt:dt="string"><!--a description--></mso:MasterPageDescription>
<mso:ContentTypeId msdt:dt="string">0x010100203...</mso:ContentTypeId>
<mso:TargetControlType msdt:dt="string">;#Content Web Parts;#</mso:TargetControlType>
<mso:HtmlDesignAssociated msdt:dt="string">1</mso:HtmlDesignAssociated>
</mso:CustomDocumentProperties>
</xml><![endif]-->
</head>
<body>
```

```
<!--
Warning: Do not try to add HTML to this section.
Only the contents of the first <div>
inside the <body> tag will be used while executing
Display Template code. Any HTML that
you add to this section will NOT become part of your Display Template.
-->
<script>
    $includeLanguageScript(this.url,
        "~sitecollection/_catalogs/masterpage/Display Templates/Language Files/
        {Locale}/CustomStrings.js");
</script>
<!--
    Use the div below to author your Display Template.Here are some things to keep in mind:
    * Surround any JavaScript logic as shown below using a "pound underscore"
     (#_ ... _#) token inside a comment.
    * Use the values assigned to your variables using an "underscore pound equals"
     (_#= ... =#_) token.
-->

<div id="Control_List">
    <!--#_
    if (!$isNull(ctx.ClientControl) && !$isNull(ctx.ClientControl.shouldRenderControl) &&
            !ctx.ClientControl.shouldRenderControl()) {
        return "";
    }
    ctx.ListDataJSONGroupsKey = "ResultTables";
    var $noResults = Srch.ContentBySearch.
        getControlTemplateEncodedNoResultsMessage(ctx.ClientControl);
    var noResultsClassName = "ms-srch-result-noResults";
    var ListRenderRenderWrapper = function(itemRenderResult, inCtx, tpl) {
        var iStr = [];
        iStr.push('<li>');
        iStr.push(itemRenderResult);
        iStr.push('</li>');
        return iStr.join('');
    }
    ctx['ItemRenderWrapper'] = ListRenderRenderWrapper;
    _#-->
    <ul class="cbs-List">
        _#= ctx.RenderGroups(ctx) =#_
    </ul>
    <!--#_
    if (ctx.ClientControl.get_shouldShowNoResultMessage()) {
    _#-->
        <div class="_#= noResultsClassName =#_">_#= $noResults =#_</div>
    <!--#_
    }
    _#-->
</div>
</body>
</html>
```

■ **Note** SharePoint will automatically generate and sync the corresponding .js file, which has the same name.

Looking at the original entire HTML code in Listing 8-1, toward the bottom you will find the <UL> tag used to render the groups as shown in the following snippet. Our task is to change the class name and ID used to match our Specter Design. The out-of-the-box list control HTML code used to wrap items is shown in Listing 8-2.

Listing 8-2. Control Template HTML that Wraps and Calls the Item Templates

```
<ul class="cbs-List">
    _#= ctx.RenderGroups(ctx) =#_
</ul>
```

Our task is to change the class name and ID used to match our Specter Group design. The out-of-the-box list control HTML code used to wrap items is shown in Listing 8-2.

3. The Specter Group design uses the <UL> tag as well, but we must specify a different class name and we change the HTML to look like Listing 8-3.

Listing 8-3. The New Class Name Specified for the HTML Code That Wraps Items

```
<ul id="filter-container" class="feature cf">
    _#= ctx.RenderGroups(ctx) =#_
</ul>
```

4. One thing we would like to make sure is that when we are specifying this custom control via the Content Search web part tool pane, the appropriate name shows up in the drop-down list that allows for selecting the available list controls. To do this, we simply change the <Title> tag contents at the top of the Control_List_Specter.html file. In our case, we named it Specter Communities List and can be seen in Figure 8-36 as found in the Content Search web part tool pane.

Figure 8-36. *The new Specter list control available via the drop-down list in the Content Search web part tool pane*

5. At this point, we have finished creating our custom list Control display template so we are ready to save and publish it.

Creating a Custom Item Display Template

We just saw how to create a list Control display template that is used to wrap a list of items returned by a Content Search web part. Creating a custom Item display template that is used once per item returned is not any more difficult. Again, we start by creating a copy of an existing Item display template and then modify this custom template as required.

We start with making a copy of the Item_Large_Picture.html, which can also be found in the Master Page Gallery under the /Display Templates/Content WebParts folder. We make a copy of the existing Display Template and rename it Item_LargePicture.html. Most of the HTML markup provided in the Item display template will stay the same as it is used by SharePoint to configure the file. We only want to change the HTML markup right before the last closing </DIV> tag to render the item as shown in Listing 8-4.

Listing 8-4. The HTML Markup That Uses the Custom Specter Classes to Render the Item

```
<span class="_#= specterPropertyType =#_">
   <a href="_#= linkURL =#_" class="thumb" >_#= pictureMarkup =#_
   <div class="date"><div class="d">_#= date =#_</div>
       <div class="m">_#= month =#_</div></div>
   </a>
   <div class="caption">_#= specterPropertyType =#_</div>
</span>
```

Because our master page includes the appropriate style sheet (refer to Chapter 5 and Chapter 7), our Item display template renders a particular item as expected and is shown in Figure 8-37.

Figure 8-37. *Custom display template shows the Specter community item from the catalog*

■ **Tip**   For a more in-depth look at how display templates work, see Chapter 9.

Summary

In this chapter we walked you through a step-by-step exercise on configuring Cross-Site Collection Publishing from the Specter Group authoring site to the public web site. We designed our solution to include a globally available media assets repository that is accessible via the asset picker while authoring content. Our solution included the use of publishing pages that use a custom content type, which demonstrates how you can use Cross-Site Collection Publishing in a real-world project. We then walked you through configuring catalog connections on the Specter Group public web site for consumption for authored content. We demonstrated how to retrieve custom metadata using the Content Search web part and display it using the Specter Group branding with custom display templates. We finished with a look at how display templates are deployed and available via the settings panel of Content Search web parts.

■ ■ ■

CHAPTER 9

Integrating Search-Driven Content

In Chapter 1, we introduced new features in SharePoint 2013 that use the power of search to surface dynamic content across sites. SharePoint 2013 is the first release of SharePoint to fully integrate FAST search into the core product. In this chapter, we learn how to integrate dynamic content from other sites and present the content with the same user interface by utilizing new out-of-the-box search web parts as well as HTML, JavaScript, CSS, display templates, query rules, and result types. We first review how to get content from other sites by using the new SharePoint 2013 cross-site publishing feature. Then we create a content rollup solution by creating custom display templates for SharePoint's Content Search web part. Last, we look at how to fine-tune search queries and customize the display of results in search. We demonstrate how to use query rules and result types to improve the search experience.

Our Scenarios

For the public Specter Group site, we have two scenarios that use search-driven content.

In the first scenario, we want to show potential buyers a rollup of all the available Specter Group properties for sale from all the communities, such as floor plans, description, and property type. Because only builders and architects at Specter Group can author and manage floor plans, we want to have a dedicated and separate site just for floor plans (`www.spectergroup.com/sites/floorplan`). Meanwhile, we want to present all the floor plans to site visitors of `www.spectergroup.com` in a seamless manner. To accomplish this, we need to perform the following steps (for a process diagram of the scenario, refer to Figure 9-1):

1. We need to make the floor plan content in the authoring site available to search so that other sites can consume the content.

2. We need to ensure search is periodically indexing the authoring content to ensure the dynamic content is up to date.

3. From the public `spectergroup.com` site, we need to consume the floor plan content from search.

4. From the public `spectergroup.com` site, we need to customize the display of the rolled up content.

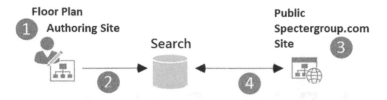

Figure 9-1. Content publishing process for Spectergroup.com floor plans

In this chapter, we focus on the design and the implementation of the solution for this scenario. First we demonstrate how to pull the floor plan content from the Floor plan site collection. Then, we will show how to customize the content search web part on the Floor Plans page to display search results with our own design using custom display templates.

In the second scenario, we want to customize the search experience when users search for "floor plans". We are going to create a query rule and a result type for floor plans, such that when users search for the keyword "floor plans", the following things happen:

- We will show a block of results that are all floor plans.

- We will promote a few beachfront properties to the top of the results if the current month is in the summer.

- We will render the block of results for floor plans with its own user interface to distinguish these results from all other results in the list.

In this chapter, we look at how to fine-tune search queries and customize the display of floor plan results in search. We demonstrate how to use query rules and result types to improve the search experience.

Publishing Content to Search

In Chapter 8, we used the Cross-Site Collection Publishing feature to allow http://spectergroup.com to consume publishing pages and page layouts from http://authoring.spectergroup.com. For more information on how to set up cross-site publishing, refer to Chapter 8. In this chapter, we look at how to use the Cross-Site Collection Publishing feature to consume content, such as documents. Then in the section "Custom Display Templates for Specter Design" later in this chapter, we demonstrate in detail how to customize the display of results by creating custom display templates.

■ **Note**   Learn how to configure and use Cross-Site Collection Publishing in Chapter 8.

Configuring Content for Search

Before we can consume the floor plan content, we need to make sure the content is available to SharePoint search. The floor plan content resides in a picture library called Specter Group Community Floor Plans in the http://spectergroup.com/sites/floorplan site collection. Table 9-1 shows the metadata that describes a floor plan document. For more information on Specter Group TermSets and the Managed Metadata feature, refer to Chapter 7.

Table 9-1. *Specter Group Community Floor Plan Metadata*

Label	Type
Community Name	Managed Metadata (mapped to Name terms in Communities TermSet): • Eagle Vista • Otay Crossing • Spruce Meadow
Property Type	Managed Metadata (mapped to Property Type terms in Communities TermSet): • Beachfront • Commercial • Residential • Loft
Title	Single line of text
Description	Multiline text
Last Modified	Date time
Picture	Image file

As shown in Table 9-1, all floor plan documents have a set of properties that describe each floor plan. Because we are working with search, we need to think about how to expose these properties to SharePoint search so that users can search against them and view these properties in the search results. To ensure these properties can be searched against and can be used as refiners and filters, we need to create Search Managed Properties for each floor plan property. To learn how to create managed properties, refer to the section "Creating Search Managed Properties for Content" later in this chapter, where we demonstrate how to create a search managed property, `SpecterPropertyType`, based on the Managed Metadata column property type. We later use the `SpecterPropertyType` managed property as a refiner and a filter in our solution.

As floor plan files are added to the library, users identify and tag metadata (such as Community Name and Property Type information) for each file (see Figure 9-2).

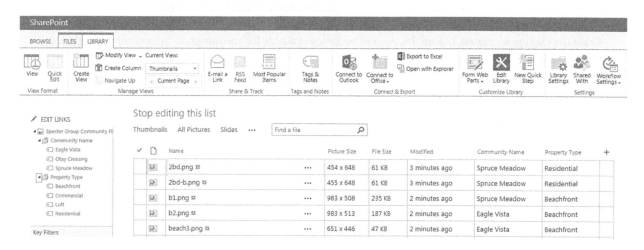

Figure 9-2. *To enhance search ability of content, tag content with metadata when authoring content*

Once the content is ready for publishing, we need to enable the content's library as a catalog. For the purpose of demonstration, please refer to Chapter 7 for detailed steps for configuring a catalog.

■ **Note**   Before we can enable a library as a catalog, we need to enable the Cross-Site Collection Publishing feature. For more information on how to get started with Cross-Site Collection Publishing and how to configure a library as a catalog, refer to Chapter 8.

After we configure the catalog, the Catalog Settings page should look like Figure 9-3, which shows the top section of the page.

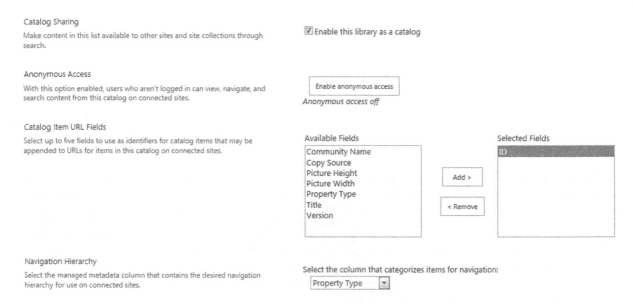

Figure 9-3. *Catalog Settings page for Specter Group Community Floor Plans document library*

Once the catalog is created, before this content becomes available for consumption from other site collections, we must perform a full or an incremental crawl on the content source.

1. From Central Administration, navigate to the SharePoint Search Service application.

2. Click the arrow next to the content source you want to crawl.

3. Select Start Full Crawl (see Figure 9-4).

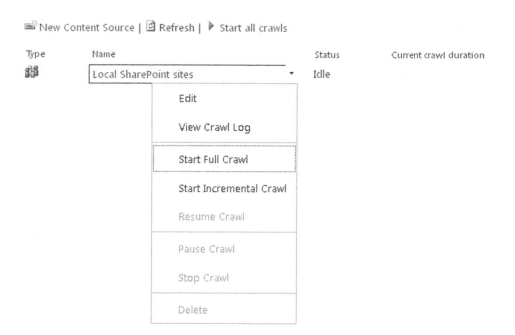

🖼 New Content Source | 🖺 Refresh | ▶ Start all crawls

Type	Name	Status	Current crawl duration
🏢	Local SharePoint sites ▾	Idle	

Edit

View Crawl Log

Start Full Crawl

Start Incremental Crawl

Resume Crawl

Pause Crawl

Stop Crawl

Delete

Figure 9-4. *Perform a full or an incremental crawl to get all new content and updates in search index*

To ensure the target site gets fresh and up-to-date content, we need to configure the Search Service application to make sure SharePoint search is continuously crawling content in the authoring site, as seen in Figure 9-5. For more information on how to configure and schedule full crawl, incremental crawl, and continuous crawl in SharePoint search through Central Administration, refer to http://sprwd.com/6uhfguy.

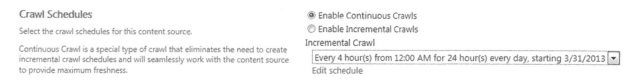

Crawl Schedules

Select the crawl schedules for this content source.

Continuous Crawl is a special type of crawl that eliminates the need to create incremental crawl schedules and will seamlessly work with the content source to provide maximum freshness.

◉ Enable Continuous Crawls
○ Enable Incremental Crawls

Incremental Crawl

Every 4 hour(s) from 12:00 AM for 24 hour(s) every day, starting 3/31/2013 ▾
Edit schedule

Figure 9-5. *From Central Administration, enable continuous crawls on the content source that contains this catalog to ensure freshness of the content*

■ **Tip**   Cross-site publishing is dependent on the search feature to index the content. New and updated content is only available for consumption after it has been crawled. In a production environment, we need to make sure SharePoint search is continuously crawling the authoring sites to get the latest content to appear in the consuming sites quicker. If the Search Service application gets corrupted or gets deleted for some reason, we need to configure the consuming site to reconnect to the catalog to reestablish connection with the content.

Creating Search Managed Properties for Content

Now that we have the content and the properties of the content available in the search index, we can create search managed properties for each property we want to use as refiners and filters.

1. Similar to SharePoint 2010, to get the content's properties, referred to as crawled properties, we need to perform a crawl of the content.

2. Once the crawled properties are available in search, we can create new managed properties that map to the corresponding crawled properties.

3. After we have created the new managed properties, we have to do another crawl on the content to get the property-value mapping established.

4. In the case where we want to perform a full crawl on just a library, the site collection administrator can go to the library settings and mark the library for a full crawl during the SharePoint farm's next scheduled crawl.

    a. On the Catalog Settings page, click the Advanced settings page link shown in Figure 9-6 to configure full reindexing of the content.

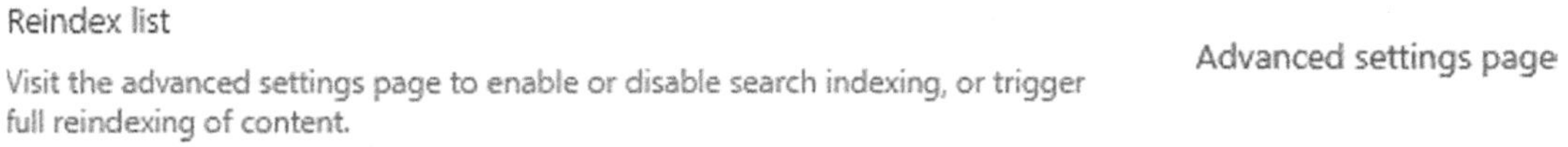

Reindex list

Visit the advanced settings page to enable or disable search indexing, or trigger full reindexing of content.

Advanced settings page

Figure 9-6. *Enable full indexing of content in the library*

    b. To trigger a full reindex of the content during the next schedule crawl, on the Advanced Settings page, click Reindex Document Library (see Figure 9-7).

Reindex Document Library

Click the Reindex Picture Library button to reindex all of the content in this document library during the next scheduled crawl.

Reindex Document Library

Figure 9-7. *Mark the library for a full crawl during the next scheduled crawl*

5. To create new search managed properties, navigate to Central Administration.

6. From Application Management ➤ Manage Service Applications, select the current Search Service application (see Figure 9-8).

Search Service Application	Search Service Application	Started
Search Service Application	Search Service Application Proxy	Started

Figure 9-8. *Navigate to SharePoint Central Administration's current Search Service application*

7. On the Search Administration page, click Search Schema under the Queries and Results group shown in Figure 9-9.

Queries and Results
Authoritative Pages
Result Sources
Query Rules
Query Client Types
Search Schema
Query Suggestions
Search Dictionaries
Search Result Removal

Figure 9-9. Click Search Schema to view Managed Properties page

8. Once the Managed Properties page is loaded, click New Managed Property below the filter (see Figure 9-10).

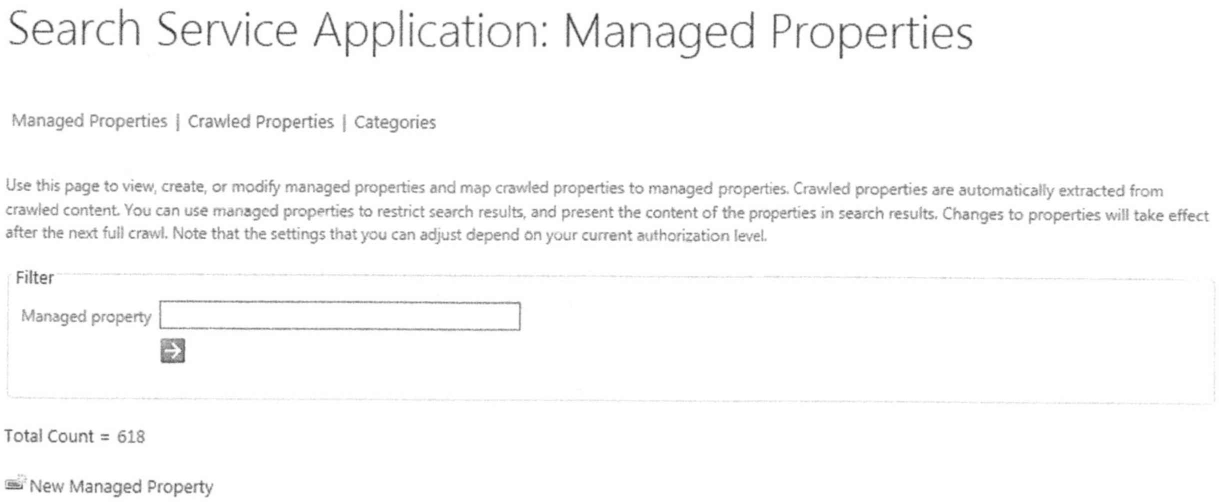

Search Service Application: Managed Properties

Managed Properties | Crawled Properties | Categories

Use this page to view, create, or modify managed properties and map crawled properties to managed properties. Crawled properties are automatically extracted from crawled content. You can use managed properties to restrict search results, and present the content of the properties in search results. Changes to properties will take effect after the next full crawl. Note that the settings that you can adjust depend on your current authorization level.

Filter

Managed property [   ]

Total Count = 618

New Managed Property

Figure 9-10. Create a new managed property from the Managed Properties page

9. Next, enter a name and select a data type (Text) for the new managed property, SpecterPropertyType (see Figure 9-11).

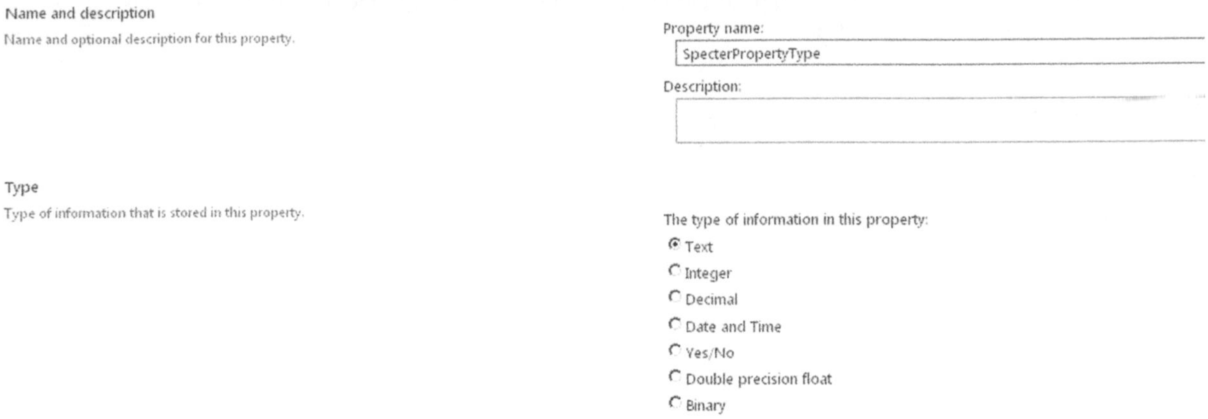

Name and description

Name and optional description for this property.

Property name:

SpecterPropertyType

Description:

Type

Type of information that is stored in this property.

The type of information in this property:

○ Text

○ Integer

○ Decimal

○ Date and Time

○ Yes/No

○ Double precision float

○ Binary

Figure 9-11. Create new managed property page

10. Next, we need to ensure the property is searchable by checking the Searchable check box, as shown in Figure 9-12. Now users can query against the content containing this property.

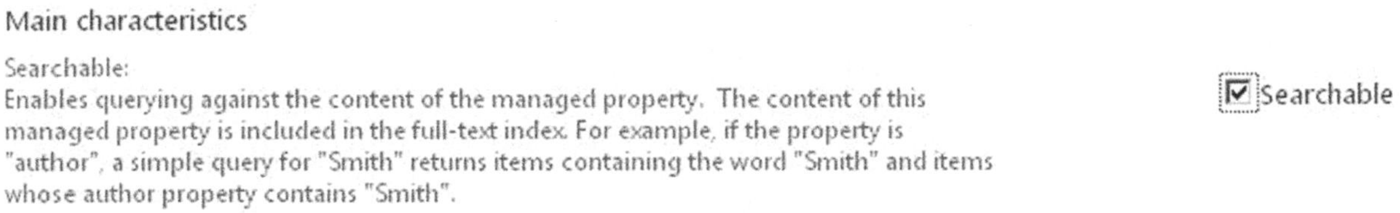

Main characteristics

Searchable:

Enables querying against the content of the managed property. The content of this managed property is included in the full-text index. For example, if the property is "author", a simple query for "Smith" returns items containing the word "Smith" and items whose author property contains "Smith".

☑ Searchable

Figure 9-12. Mark the new managed property as searchable

11. Then, we need to configure the property as Queryable to allow users to make queries specifically against the new managed property (see Figure 9-13).

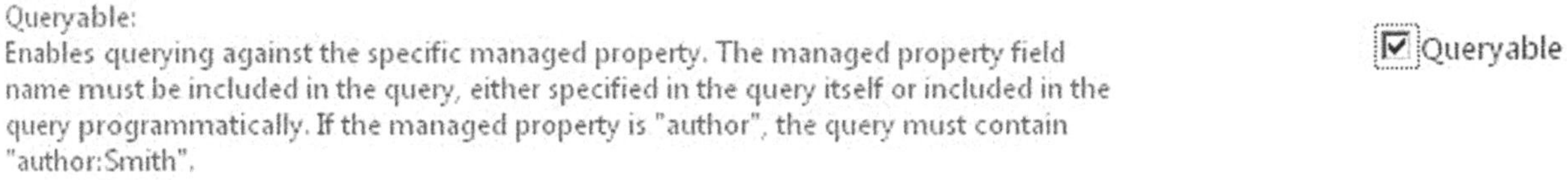

Queryable:

Enables querying against the specific managed property. The managed property field name must be included in the query, either specified in the query itself or included in the query programmatically. If the managed property is "author", the query must contain "author:Smith".

☑ Queryable

Figure 9-13. Mark the new managed property as queryable

12. Besides allowing users to query against the property, we also need to ensure the property can be retrieved as part of the search result if it contains relevant data that need to be displayed (see Figure 9-14).

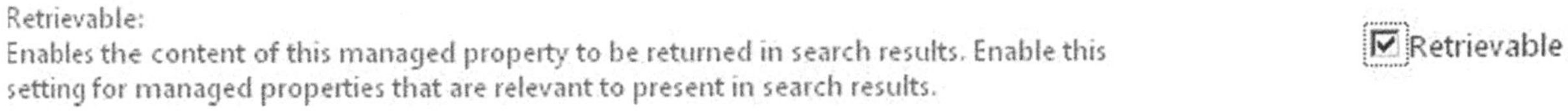

Retrievable:

Enables the content of this managed property to be returned in search results. Enable this setting for managed properties that are relevant to present in search results.

☑ Retrievable

Figure 9-14. Mark the new managed property as retrievable

13. In the case where the managed property is mapped to a column that allows multiple values, it's a good idea to select the Allow multiple values check box as shown in Figure 9-15, so that each tagged value will be stored as a separate key/value pair in the managed property.

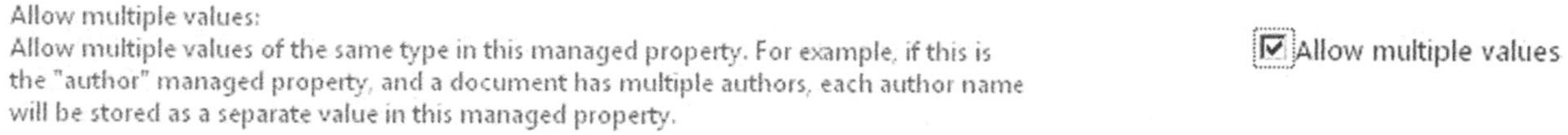

Allow multiple values:
Allow multiple values of the same type in this managed property. For example, if this is the "author" managed property, and a document has multiple authors, each author name will be stored as a separate value in this managed property.

☑ Allow multiple values

Figure 9-15. Mark the new managed property to allow multiple values to be mapped

14. If the managed property is going to be used as a refiner for users to refine search results, then we need to select Yes - active from the Refinable drop-down list seen in Figure 9-16.

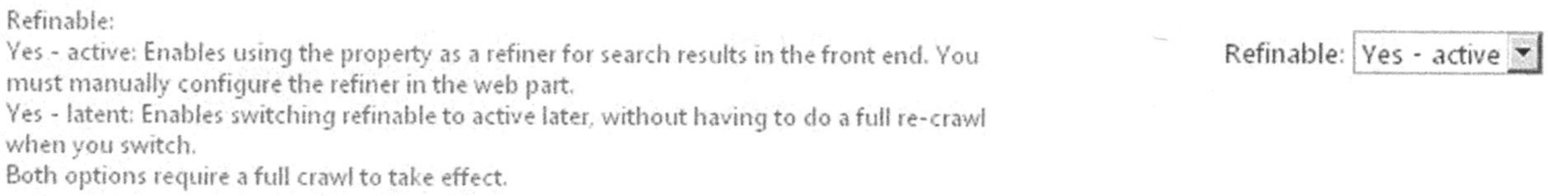

Refinable:
Yes - active: Enables using the property as a refiner for search results in the front end. You must manually configure the refiner in the web part.
Yes - latent: Enables switching refinable to active later, without having to do a full re-crawl when you switch.
Both options require a full crawl to take effect.

Refinable: Yes - active ▼

Figure 9-16. Mark the new managed property as refinable

15. Finally, we need to map the new managed property with a crawled property returned from the most recent full crawl of the search content. Under the Mappings to crawled properties section, click Add a Mapping to the right (see Figure 9-17).

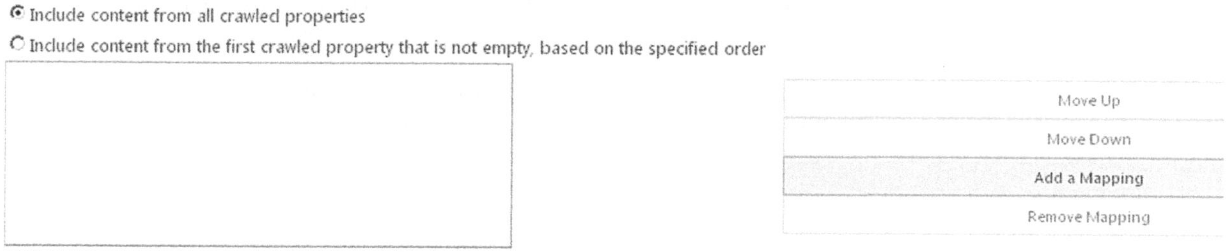

⊙ Include content from all crawled properties
○ Include content from the first crawled property that is not empty, based on the specified order

| Move Up |
| Move Down |
| Add a Mapping |
| Remove Mapping |

Figure 9-17. Map the new managed property with a crawled property

16. Once the Crawled property selection page is launched, enter a keyword of the crawled property (name of the column from the Floor plan library). Then click Find to get all the crawled properties containing the key word (see Figure 9-18). Note the crawled property name is the same as the SharePoint internal property name for the library column of Property Type.

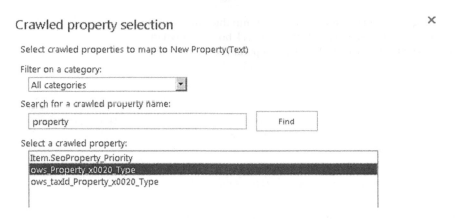

Figure 9-18. *Find the crawled property, then map to it*

17. Click OK to create the managed property. New in SharePoint 2013, we can quickly verify the creation of the new managed property by providing a keyword in the filter box on the Managed Properties page. Then the new managed property should be shown on the page as seen in Figure 9-19.

Property Name	Type	Multi	Query	Search	Retrieve	Refine	Sort	Mapped Crawled Properties
SpecterPropertyType	Text	Yes	Yes	Yes	Yes	Yes	No	ows_Property_x0020_Type

Figure 9-19. *Quickly find the new managed property and view its properties*

18. Once we are done creating all the new managed properties, we need to navigate to the Content Sources page from the Search administration to perform a full crawl.

    a. From Central Administration, navigate to the SharePoint Search Service Application.

    b. Click the arrow next to the content source you want to crawl.

    c. From the shortcut menu, click Start Full Crawl as shown in Figure 9-20 to ensure all new managed properties contain data so that we can query against them.

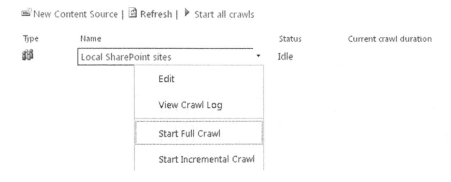

Figure 9-20. *Start a full crawl to get values for the new managed properties*

Getting Content from a Catalog

Now that we have the content as well as new managed properties in the search index, we need to make the content available for users to see in the Specter Group public-facing site. For our scenario, we need to enable the Specter Group public-facing site to connect to the Floor Plan catalog created in the previous section.

1. On the Specter Group public-facing site, click Site Settings.

2. Under Site Administration, click Manage catalog connections.

3. Click the Connect to a Catalog link on the page to view all the available published catalogs.

4. For our scenario, click the Connect link next to the Floor Plan - Specter Group Community Floor Plans catalog in Figure 9-21.

Floor Plan - Specter Group Community Floor Plans   http://spectergroup.com/sites/floorplan/Specter Group Community Floor Plans   Connect

Figure 9-21. *From the Specter Group public-facing site, connect to the published Floor plan catalog*

■ **Note** For more information on how to configure and connect to a catalog, refer to Chapter 8.

---

5. The catalog configuration process makes the content available in the Specter Group public-facing site. When connecting to a catalog, we have the option to integrate the catalog with the whole site by selecting Integrate the catalog into my site or we can select Connect, but do not integrate the catalog to allow less integration. Because we are exposing the Floor plan content specifically on one page, the Floor Plans page, we will not be integrating with the Specter Group public-facing site's navigation. Select the Connect, but do not integrate the catalog option shown in Figure 9-22.

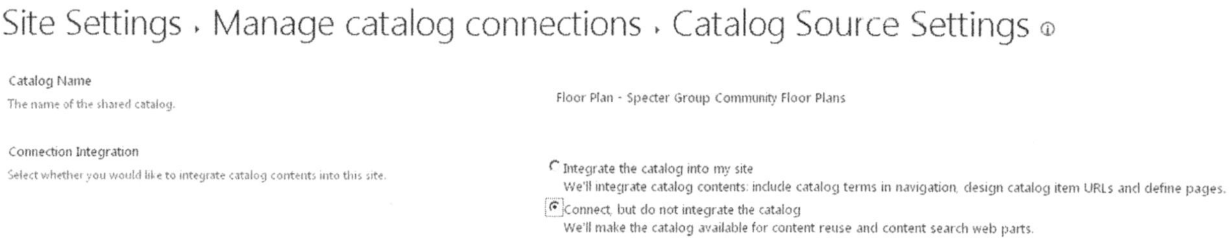

Site Settings › Manage catalog connections › Catalog Source Settings ⓘ

Catalog Name
The name of the shared catalog.

Floor Plan - Specter Group Community Floor Plans

Connection Integration
Select whether you would like to integrate catalog contents into this site.

○ Integrate the catalog into my site
We'll integrate catalog contents: include catalog terms in navigation, design catalog item URLs and define pages.

⦿ Connect, but do not integrate the catalog
We'll make the catalog available for content reuse and content search web parts.

Figure 9-22. *Connect to the catalog without integrating navigation*

6. Because we are presenting the search results to public users, they will not have access to the authoring site, `http://spectergroup.com/sites/floorplan` site collection. Under the Catalog Item URL Behavior section, ensure the Make URLs relative to this site option is selected as shown in Figure 9-23.

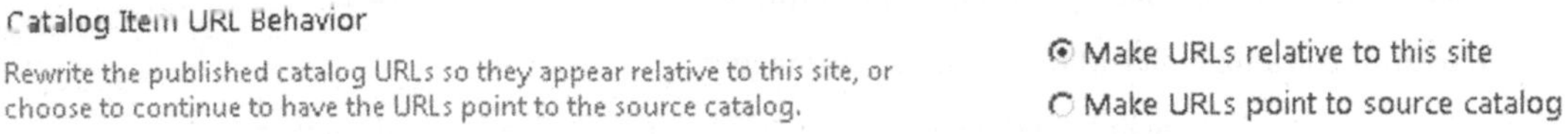

Catalog Item URL Behavior

Rewrite the published catalog URLs so they appear relative to this site, or choose to continue to have the URLs point to the source catalog.

⦿ Make URLs relative to this site

○ Make URLs point to source catalog

Figure 9-23. Make catalog item's URL relative to the Specter Group public-facing site

■ **Note**   For more information on how to create catalog item pages for a catalog, refer to Chapter 8.

Creating a Content Rollup Solution

In the following sections, we create a page for content rollup. We add a Content Search web part and configure it to get the right results by using the Query Builder.

Creating a Landing Page for Floor Plans

First, we need to create a landing page for our floor plans so that users can view all floor plans by navigating to the `http://spectergroup.com/communities/floor-plans` URL or by clicking Floor Plans on the Home Page menu flyout as shown in the wireframe in Chapter 3 and Figure 9-24.

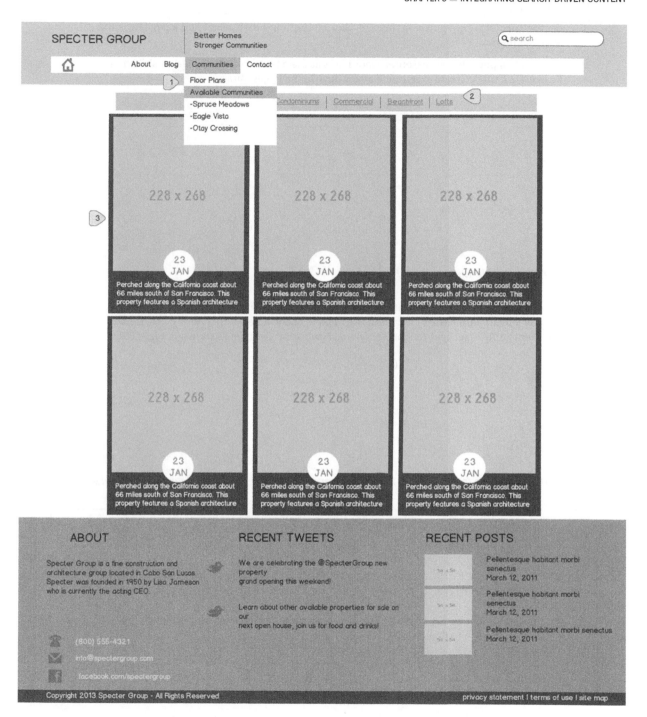

Figure 9-24. *Wireframe for Floor Plans landing page and menu flyout*

1. On the Specter Group public-facing site, click Site Settings, then select Add a page from the shortcut menu.

2. In the Add a page dialog box, enter Floor Plans as the name of the new page, as shown in Figure 9-25. Click Create to generate a new page in the Pages library.

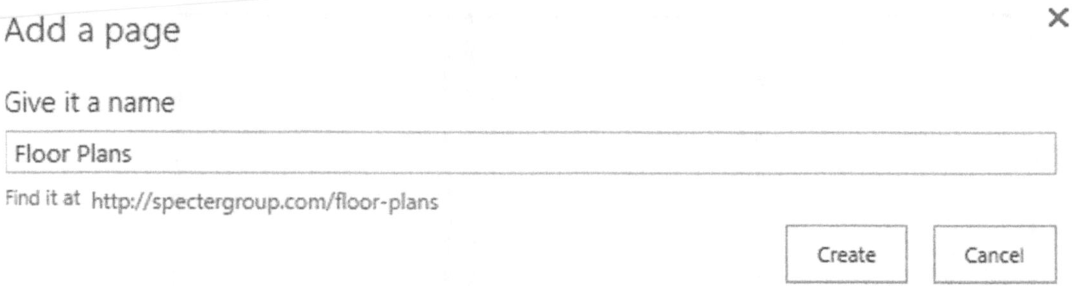

Add a page   ✕

Give it a name

> Floor Plans

Find it at http://spectergroup.com/floor-plans

                                   [Create]   [Cancel]

Figure 9-25. Create a new landing page for Floor Plans

3. For navigation, because we are using the Specter Global Navigation TermSet for the Specter Group public site's navigation, we need to create a new term, Floor Plans, under the Communities term in the Specter Global Navigation TermSet as shown in Figure 9-26.

▲ 🗗 Specter Global Navigation

      ⊙ About

▲ ⊙ Communities

      ⊙ Floor Plans

Figure 9-26. Add a new term for Floor Plans under the Communities term in the global navigation TermSet

---

■ **Note**   For more information on how to configure navigation using the Managed Navigation feature, refer to Chapter 6.

---

4. We need to configure the new page to use a friendly URL that maps to the new term in the site navigation. Navigate to the new page and click Edit Page in the upper right corner.

5. To configure the page's friendly URL, on the top ribbon, on the Page tab, click the Page URLs icon, as seen in Figure 9-27.

Figure 9-27. *Configure the page's friendly URL by clicking the Page URLs icon*

6. On the Page URLs page, add a friendly URL that is mapped to the Communities ➤ Floor Plans term in the navigation (see Figure 9-28).

Page URLs

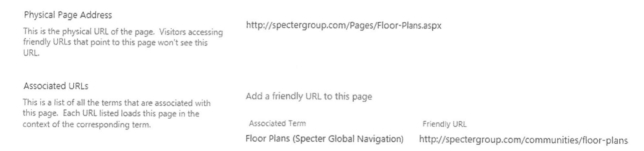

Physical Page Address

This is the physical URL of the page. Visitors accessing friendly URLs that point to this page won't see this URL.

http://spectergroup.com/Pages/Floor-Plans.aspx

Associated URLs

This is a list of all the terms that are associated with this page. Each URL listed loads this page in the context of the corresponding term.

Add a friendly URL to this page

Associated Term	Friendly URL
Floor Plans (Specter Global Navigation)	http://spectergroup.com/communities/floor-plans

Figure 9-28. *On the Page URLs page, add a friendly URL that maps to the Floor Plan term in the navigation TermSet*

Exposing Search Results Using Content Search Web Part

Now that we have the Floor Plan's landing page as well as its friendly URL configured, we need to add the Content Search web part to the page to display all the results from the Floor Plan catalog.

1. On the Floor Plans page, click the Settings icon at the top right corner of the page, then select Edit Page from the shortcut menu, as shown in Figure 9-29.

Figure 9-29. *To add a web part to a page, we must first edit the page*

2. Once the page is in the edit mode, click the inside of the Page Content area on the page.

3. On the ribbon at the top of the page, click the Insert tab, then select the Web Part icon to add a web part to the page.

4. Under Categories, select Content Rollup, then select Content Search web part, as shown in Figure 9-30. Click Add at the bottom right of the ribbon to add the web part to the page.

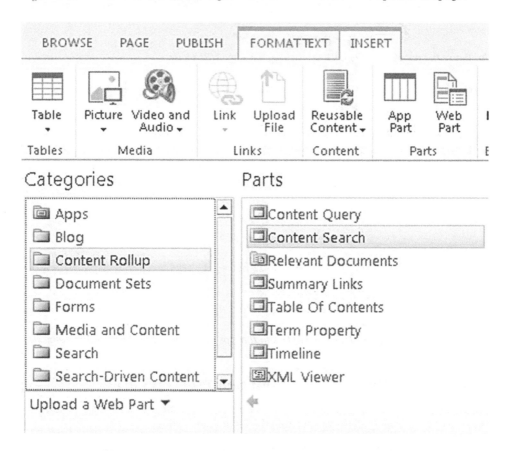

Figure 9-30. *Add a Content Search web part to the content rollup page*

5. Once the web part is on the page, at the top right corner of the web part, click the down arrow to the left of the check box. Then select Edit Web Part from the drop-down menu to configure the web part (see Figure 9-31).

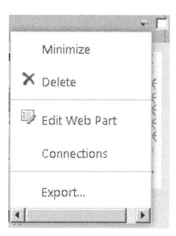

Figure 9-31. *To configure the web part, we must select Edit Web Part*

Now that we have the Content Search web part on the page, we next need to configure the web part.

Query Building

The Content Search web part allows you to restrict the results by limiting the query to a given set of content, whether it's content from the search index or content from the site collection. To get to the right content, we need to formulate the query just right and we need to ensure the query works under different dynamic conditions for different users.

1. The web part configuration panel shows up on the right side of the page.

2. Launch Query Builder to get the results you want. In the Properties section, click Change query to launch Query Builder to specify your query. You can also specify how many results to show in the web part (see Figure 9-32).

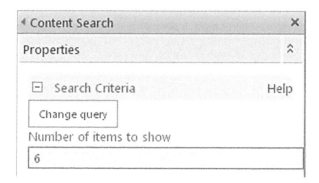

Figure 9-32. *Click Change query to launch Query Builder*

The full-screen Query Builder allows users to create and test queries without having to learn keyword query syntax. It shows a real-time preview of the search result on the right. It is also fully integrated with result sources and query rules. The web part allows dynamic values to be substituted at query time to enable query by dynamic values such as the current user's profile properties or the current web's properties.

3. On the Basics tab, click the drop-down control next to Select a query (see Figure 9-33). Note there are many options for contents to choose from. Most of the result sources are content stored in the current site collection; for instance, all documents using the Documents content type stored in the Specter Group public-facing site. If you do not see your result source in the list, click the result source link below Select a query.

BASICS	REFINERS	SORTING	SETTINGS	TEST

Switch to Quick Mode

Select a query
Choose what content you want to search by
selecting a result source.

Floor Plan - Specter Group Community Floor ▼

Figure 9-33. *In Query Builder, select a result source for its query*

a. To view all the available result sources in the site collection, under Select a query click the result source link or navigate to Site Settings, then click Result Sources.

b. By default, SharePoint sets Local SharePoint Results as the default result source. If you want to set a different result source as the default source for the site, on the Manage Result Sources page, click a result source, then select Set as Default from the drop-down menu shown in Figure 9-34.

Site Settings › Manage Result Sources

Use result sources to scope search results and federate queries to external sources, such as internet search engines. After defining a result source, configure search web parts and query rule actions to use it. Learn more about result sources.

Result Sources replace Search Scopes, which are now deprecated. You can still view your old scopes and use them in queries, but not edit them.

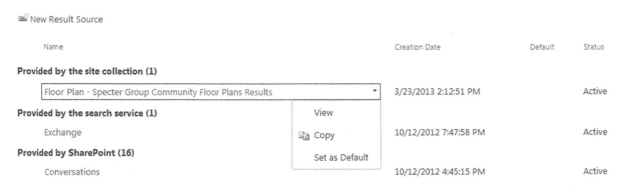

⊟ New Result Source

Name	Creation Date	Default	Status
Provided by the site collection (1)			
Floor Plan - Specter Group Community Floor Plans Results ▼	3/23/2013 2:12:51 PM		Active
Provided by the search service (1)	View		
Exchange	📋 Copy 10/12/2012 7:47:58 PM		Active
Provided by SharePoint (16)	Set as Default		
Conversations	10/12/2012 4:45:15 PM		Active

Figure 9-34. *Select a resource source as the default source for the site*

4. Back in Query Builder, we select the Floor Plan catalog we published in the previous section as our result source. Notice the search result preview pane to the right automatically displays all the relevant results from that result source, in this case, floor plans (see Figure 9-35).

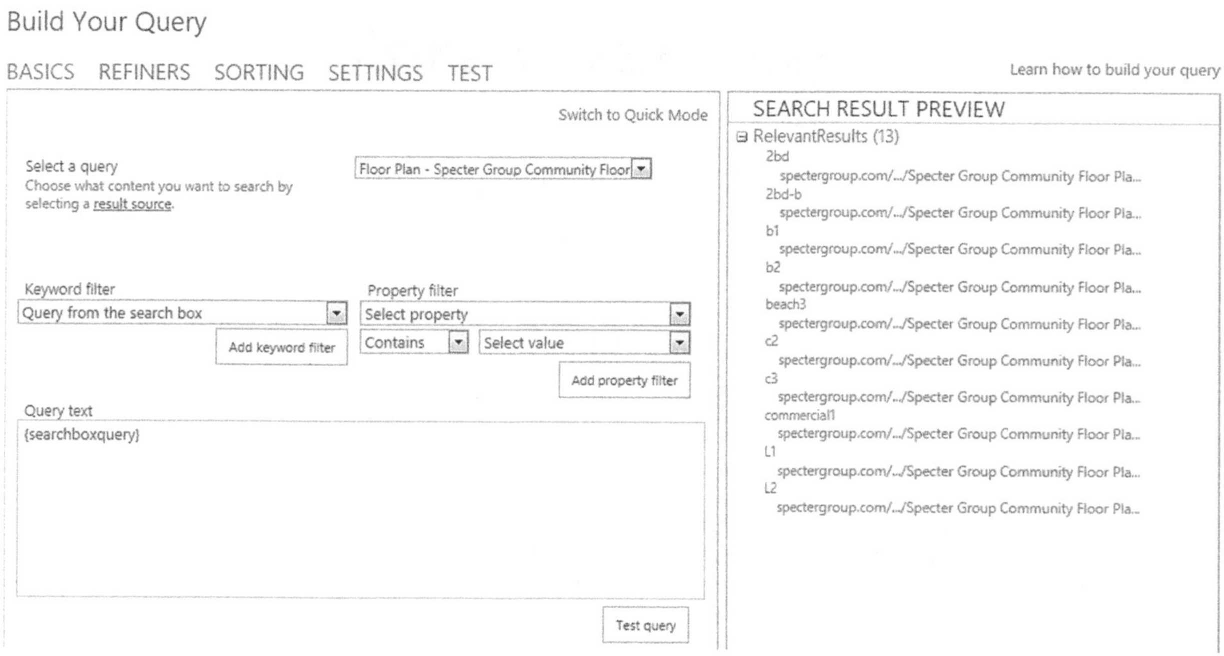

Build Your Query

BASICS   REFINERS   SORTING   SETTINGS   TEST   Learn how to build your query

Switch to Quick Mode

SEARCH RESULT PREVIEW

Select a query
Choose what content you want to search by
selecting a result source.

Floor Plan - Specter Group Community Floor ▾

⊟ RelevantResults (13)
    2bd
        spectergroup.com/.../Specter Group Community Floor Pla...
    2bd-b
        spectergroup.com/.../Specter Group Community Floor Pla...
    b1
        spectergroup.com/.../Specter Group Community Floor Pla...
    b2
        spectergroup.com/.../Specter Group Community Floor Pla...
    beach3
        spectergroup.com/.../Specter Group Community Floor Pla...
    c2
        spectergroup.com/.../Specter Group Community Floor Pla...
    c3
        spectergroup.com/.../Specter Group Community Floor Pla...
    commercial1
        spectergroup.com/.../Specter Group Community Floor Pla...
    L1
        spectergroup.com/.../Specter Group Community Floor Pla...
    L2
        spectergroup.com/.../Specter Group Community Floor Pla...

Keyword filter
Query from the search box ▾
Add keyword filter

Property filter
Select property ▾
Contains ▾   Select value ▾
Add property filter

Query text
{searchboxquery}

Test query

Figure 9-35. *In Query Builder, select a result source and specify terms to limit the query. The Search result preview automatically updates as the the query changes*

5. In Query Builder, we can also construct filters to trim down the results. For our scenario, we leave the filters blank, as we want to have all the results returned.

6. For the sort order of our results, we can pick from any of the options in the Sort results drop-down list. For example, for an e-commerce site we could select the ViewLifeTimeUniqueUsers option to get the most popular items. For our scenario, we select the Last Modified option to sort results in descending order to show the most recent properties at the top (see Figure 9-36).

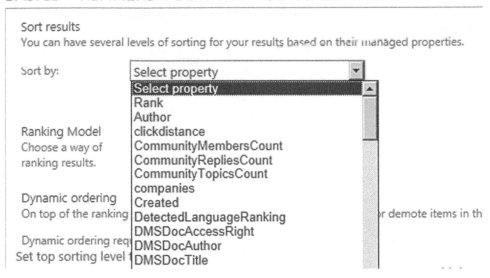

Figure 9-36. *Define sort order for results*

7. To add refiners, we can use our new managed properties to refine our search query. Click the Refiners tab. From the list of refiners, select the new managed property, SpecterPropertyType. Note in Figure 9-37 that all the values for the managed property are automatically populated in the list for you to choose from (e.g., Residential, Commercial, Loft, and Beachfront).

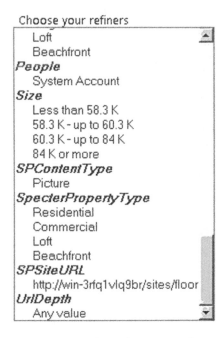

Figure 9-37. *Select refiners to use for your results*

8. From the list of refiners, select Residential under SpecterPropertyType to create a refiner. Click Apply. Note that the results shown in the search result preview on the right in Figure 9-38 are automatically updated with fewer results based on the new refiner. For our scenario, however, we leave the Refiners blank because we want to show all of the floor plans.

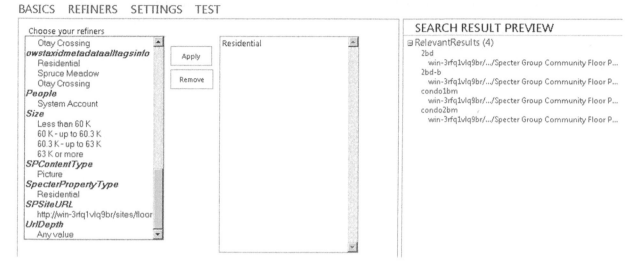

Figure 9-38. *Using managed properties as refiners will filter out search results*

9. At this point, looking at the results returned in the search result preview, we are pretty confident with the query we have built. Click the Test tab. There you can take a look at the query text the web part has constructed based on your preferences (see Figure 9-39).

Figure 9-39. *System-generated query based on configurations specified in Query Builder*

10. Click OK to apply your changes for the query. This closes the Query Builder and allows us to continue to configure the rest of the Content Search web part.

Introduction to Display Templates

SharePoint 2013 uses Display templates in search web parts to display search results. Each display template controls what managed properties to show and how to render them in the web part.

■ **Note**   Display templates are only available to Search web parts. For example, the Content Query web part cannot use display templates because it is not search-driven.

Display templates can be used to control the format and presentation of search results. We can also use display templates when we want to customize how content displays on our site. There are two major types of display templates: Control and Item (see Figure 9-40).

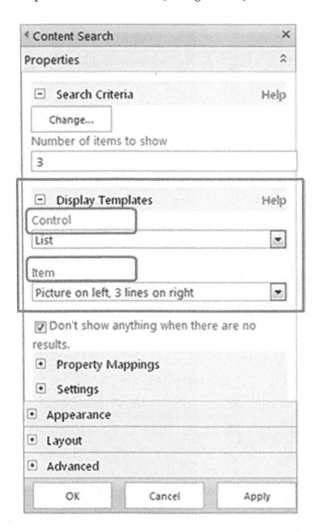

Figure 9-40.   *In the Content Search web part configuration tool pane, select a Control display template and an Item display template for the web part*

- A Control template is used to provide HTML to customize how the overall structure of search results is presented. This template defines the look and feel around the results, the layout of the results, paging options if any, the display of results count, a heading for the list if any, and even the display of when no results are found. For more information about how to create a custom Control display template, refer to the section "Creating a Custom Control Display Template" later in this chapter.

- Item templates provide HTML that determines how each result item is displayed. This template defines the look and feel of each item, the managed properties to display for each item, and the display of each managed property. It might be displaying text, images, or videos. Every item in the search result set is going to render the item display template once. So, the item display template creates its section of HTML as many times as the number of results. For more information about how to create a custom Item display template, refer to the section "Creating a Custom Item Display Template" later in this chapter.

Less common types of display templates include the Hover over template and the Filter template. Hover over templates are used to customize the look and feel of an item to show additional values when users hover over the result. For example, hover over templates for people results show additional user profile properties and hover over templates for document results show document previews. Filter templates are used when you want to show options for filtering the search results by configuring the refiners.

Out-of-the-Box Display Templates

SharePoint offers various out-of-the-box display templates to provide rendering of results.

1. Continue with the Content Search web part used in our scenario. Moving down the web part configuration panel, in the Display Templates section, for Control display template, choose the List Control display template from the list of out-of-the-box Control display templates shown in Figure 9-41. The List template shows all the results in a list.

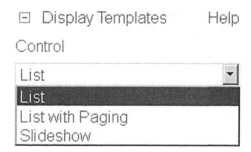

Figure 9-41. *From the list of out-of-the-box Control display templates, select the List Control display template to use for the rendering of the structure of the entire result set*

For out-of-the-box Control display templates, List with Paging is useful when dealing with a large result set that needs to be displayed across multiple pages. The Content Search web part has a limit of displaying 50 items per page. The Slideshow Control display template is useful when dealing with images in the result set, such that they can be displayed in a slideshow format.

2. For the Item display template section, choose the Large picture Item display template from the list of out-of-the-box Item display templates (see Figure 9-42).

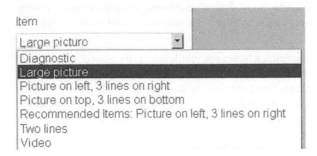

Figure 9-42. From the list of out-of-the-box Item display templates, select the Large picture Item display template to use for the rendering of a result item

The Large picture Item display template shows all the results in a single-column list with a thumbnail image as well as a hover-over effect.

Although for our scenario, we are using the Large picture display template, note there are other out-of-the-box Item display templates:

- Diagnostic is useful for debugging and troubleshooting our search-driven solution as it provides a diagnostic view of all the mapped managed properties and the values used in the web part.

- The Picture on left, 3 lines on right, Picture on top, 3 lines on bottom, and Recommended Items display templates are useful when dealing with images in the result set, such that the results can be displayed in a single-column list of thumbnail images and text.

- The Two lines display template is useful when dealing with documents or lists in the result set, such that they can be displayed in a single-column list of text and an image for the document type.

- The Video display template is useful when dealing with video files, such that they can be displayed in a horizontal layout with thumbnails of the files and the text below the image.

■ **Note**   For more information on all different types of out-of-the-box display templates, refer to http://sprwd.com/5nbp9ss.

---

3. Click Apply on the tool pane of the Content Search web part. Reload the page, which should then look similar to Figure 9-43.

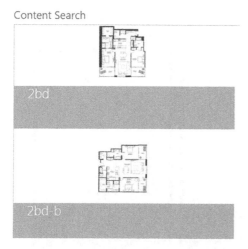

Figure 9-43. *Floor Plans page with out-of-the-box display templates*

Specter Design Components

We have configured the Content Search web part to get the right results from the Floor Plan catalog to appear on our Specter Group public-facing site and we have demonstrated the look and feel with out-of-the-box display templates. Let's enrich the end user experience. In SharePoint 2010, if you wanted to change the look and feel of a particular search result item, it required a lot of work to modify the XSLT of the Core Results Search web part. Now we have the ability to craft the perfect look in HTML, CSS, and JavaScript by creating custom display templates in SharePoint 2013.

Before we create custom display templates, let's review the design we would like to use for our floor plan page and the different components of the design. Figure 9-44 shows the design wireframe from Chapter 3 that we use to display the floor plans.

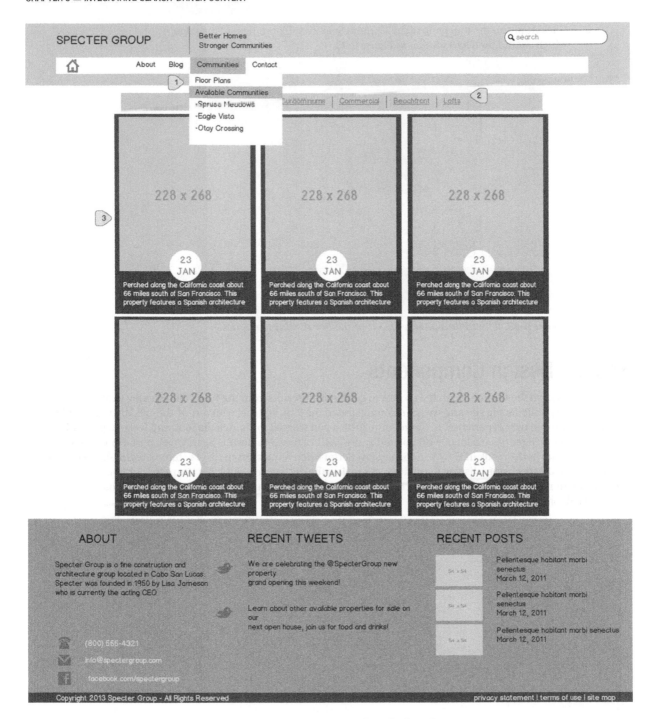

Figure 9-44. *Design wireframe for the floor plan landing page as described in Chapter 3*

This wireframe is the design we want to apply to the floor plans. The different components of the design are listed in Table 9-2. The list describes markup of all the components as well as how each component can be mapped into SharePoint.

Table 9-2. *Design Components and Mappings in SharePoint*

Component	Type	File	SharePoint Artifacts
Background for page	CSS	`style.css`	Custom Master Page: `/Spectergroup/Spectergroup.html`
Style for each search result item	CSS	`style.css`	CSS file in the Master Page Gallery: `/Spectergroup/css/style.css`
Style for the entire result set block	CSS	`Style.css`	CSS file in the Master Page Gallery: `/Spectergroup/css/style.css`
Structure for the entire block of results	HTML tag: `<ul>`	`Control_List_Specter`	Custom Control display template in the Master Page Gallery: `/Display Templates/Content Web Part/Control_List_Specter.html`
Content for each result item	HTML tag: `<li>`	`Item_LargePicture_Specter`	Custom Item display template in the Master Page Gallery: `/Display Templates/Content Web Part/Item_LargePicture_Specter.html`
Display properties for each result item	JavaScript	Inline JavaScript in `Item_LargePicture_Specter`	Custom Item display template in the Master Page Gallery: `/Display Templates/Content Web Part/Item_LargePicture_Specter.html`

Because we have covered how to create custom master pages in Chapters 4 and 5, we focus here on the rest of the components in the design.

Display templates are used to tell SharePoint what content we want to show and how we want the content to be rendered on the page dynamically. During runtime, SharePoint renders HTML tags and CSS class to render the search results based on the configurations in the display templates. Before we dive into creating custom display templates, we need to first understand how we are styling our results so that they look like the wireframe design. Display templates render results as an HTML list, made of a `<ul>` tag and many `<li>` tags for each result item. To style the result set and each item in the set, we need to add a CSS class to style them.

To reference the CSS used for each design component, use the numbered items in Figure 9-45 and reference the corresponding Listings as outlined here.

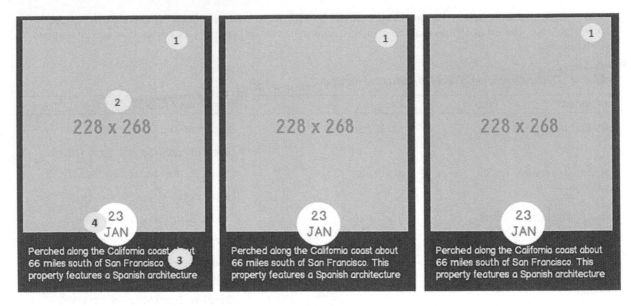

Figure 9-45. *CSS for each design component to style the result set*

1. Style to set the layout of the result set in a three-column table (Listings 9-1 and 9-2).

2. Style for the thumbnail image of the item (Listing 9-3).

3. Style for the caption of the item (Listing 9-4).

4. Style for the date of the item (Listing 9-5).

As we described in Table 9-2, we have style elements for the entire result set. To set the width of the entire result set and the layout of the results in a table layout, add the following CSS for the <ul> tag with the feature class.

Listing 9-1. CSS to Set the Width and Layout of the Entire Result Set

```
.feature {
        width: 940px;
        display:table;
}
```

Each item in the list has a CSS class to reference for its style. To set the background and width for each item and to set the layout of the results as inline-block so that results are rendered in a three-column table, add the following CSS for the <li> tags under the <ul> tag with the feature class.

Listing 9-2. CSS to Set the Background, Width, and Layout of Each Item in the Results List

```
.feature li {
        background: #333333 none;
        margin-bottom: 20px;
        margin-left: 13px;
        position: relative;
        width: 300px;
        display:inline-block;
}
```

To configure the display of the thumbnail of each item, we need to add the following CSS to `style.css`.

Listing 9-3. CSS to Set the Display of Thumbnail Images of Each Item

```
.feature li .thumb {
        display: block;
        position: relative;
        width: 280px;
        margin: 10px;
}
.feature li .thumb img {
        max-width: 100%;
}
```

To configure the style of the caption and padding for the caption under the thumbnail of each item, add the following CSS.

Listing 9-4. CSS to Set the Style of Caption for Each Item

```
.feature li .caption {
        padding: 20px 10px 20px 10px;
        text-align: center;
        color: #fff;
}
```

To configure the style of the background area for the date and month values for each item, add the following CSS. Note, border-radius creates the top semicircle.

Listing 9-5. CSS to Set the Style of the Date for Each Item

```
.feature li .thumb .date {
        background: none repeat scroll 0 0 #fff;
        display: block;
        position: absolute;
        left: 110px;
        bottom: -25px;
        width: 60px;
        height: 50px;
        float: left;
        padding-top: 10px;
        font-family: mensch;
        border-radius: 40px;
        -moz-border-radius: 40px;
        -webkit-border-radius:40px;
}
.feature li .thumb .date div {
        display: block;
        font-size: 20px;
        line-height: 20px;
        text-align: center;
}
```

Custom Display Templates for Specter Design

In the previous section, we walked through the steps of implementing our design with an HTML list of items. Now, let's see how we can integrate the design into SharePoint by creating custom display templates that can be used by the Content Search web part.

Display Template Basics

Before we dive into implementations of our own display templates, let's review the basics of working with display templates.

Display Template Hierarchy

As discussed earlier, SharePoint uses two basic types of display templates to render results. When the Control display template and the Item display template are combined, the HTML output generated looks like Figure 9-46.

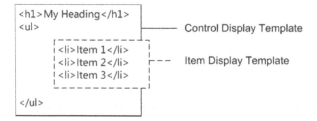

Figure 9-46. *HTML output after adding a Control display template and an Item display template*

To see what a Control display template generates during runtime, from your browser, inspect the entire result set on the page by clicking on the border of the result set. As you can see in Figure 9-47, the out-of-the-box Control_List Control display template (used in the previous section) renders a `<ul>` tag with the `cbs-List` class, which is included in the `Searchv15.css` file. This display template tells SharePoint the layout and structure of the results.

■ **Note**   The content inside of the `<ul>` tag is configured by the Item display template and the hover over content is configured by the Hover display template.

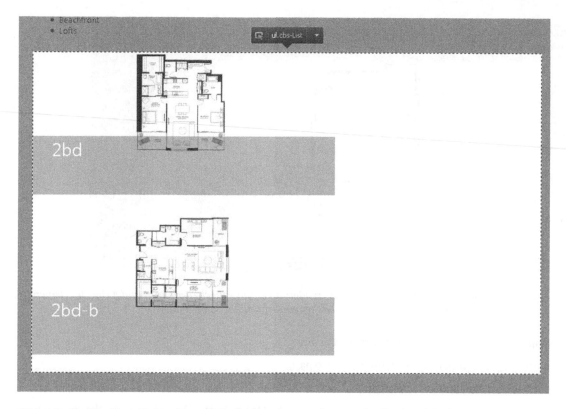

Figure 9-47. *The Control_List Control display template renders a <ul> element with the cbs-List class for the layout of the results on the page*

Similarly, to see what an Item display template generates during runtime, from your browser, inspect a result item on the page by clicking on the border of the item. As you can see in Figure 9-48, the out-of-the-box Item_LargePicture Item display template (used in the previous section) renders an empty <li> tag, and under the <li> tag, there is a <div> tag with the cbs-largePictureContainer class, which is included in the Searchv15.css file. This display template tells SharePoint what properties to display for the item and how to display it.

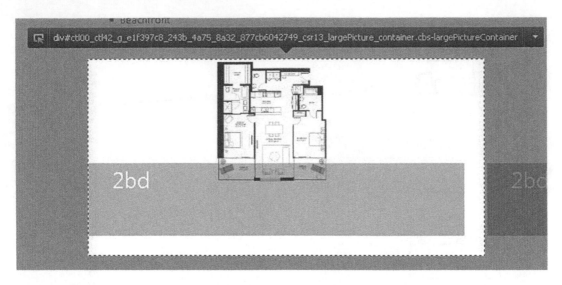

Figure 9-48. *The Item_LargePicture Item display template renders an empty <li> element, and under the <li> element, there is a <div> tag with the cbs-LargePictureContainer class for each result item on the page*

Display templates work in a hierarchy in the following order:

1. Control display template is called once per web part.

2. Item template is called once per item.

Each level in the hierarchy has an associated content type in the Master Page Gallery. To identify the content type for each display template file, use the appropriate prefix in the file name. For example, `Control_ListWithPaging.html` and `Control_ListWithPaging.js` are files associated with the List with Paging Control display template residing in the Master Page Gallery. To find all the files associated with an out-of-the-box display template, we can follow this file naming convention to find the associated files in the Master Page Gallery.

In Figure 9-49, there is a list of out-of-the box Control display templates in the Display Templates folder under the Master Page Gallery. Note that when configuring the Content Search web part, each option in the Control display template drop-down list maps to an HTML display template file in the Master Page Gallery. For example, from the editor pane of the Content Search web part, the List with Paging option refers to the `Control_ListWithPaging.html` and `Control_ListWithPaging.js` files and the Slideshow option refers to the `Control_Slideshow.html` and the `Control_Slideshow.js` files.

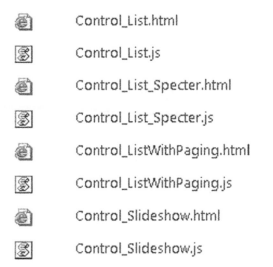

Control_List.html

Control_List.js

Control_List_Specter.html

Control_List_Specter.js

Control_ListWithPaging.html

Control_ListWithPaging.js

Control_Slideshow.html

Control_Slideshow.js

Figure 9-49. *Out-of-the-box Control display templates*

■ **Note**   All display templates consist of an HTML file and a SharePoint-generated JavaScript file. When creating or updating a display template, we should always modify the content in the HTML file, never the JavaScript file. Once the changes are made in the .html file, SharePoint compiles the changes into a .js file that has the same name as the .html file. SharePoint uses the new .js file to render the web part on the page. In the HTML file, we can add placeholders for where the managed properties and custom properties created in JavaScript should be displayed, and then SharePoint will emit the values during runtime.

Figure 9-50 shows a list of out-of-the-box Item display templates. Note that each one of these files maps to an option in the Item drop-down list below the Display Templates section in the configuration pane of the Content Search web part; for example, the Large picture option map to the Item_LargePicture.html and Item_LargePicture.js files and the Picture on left, 3 lines on right option map to the Item_Picture3Lines.html and Item_Picture3Lines.js files.

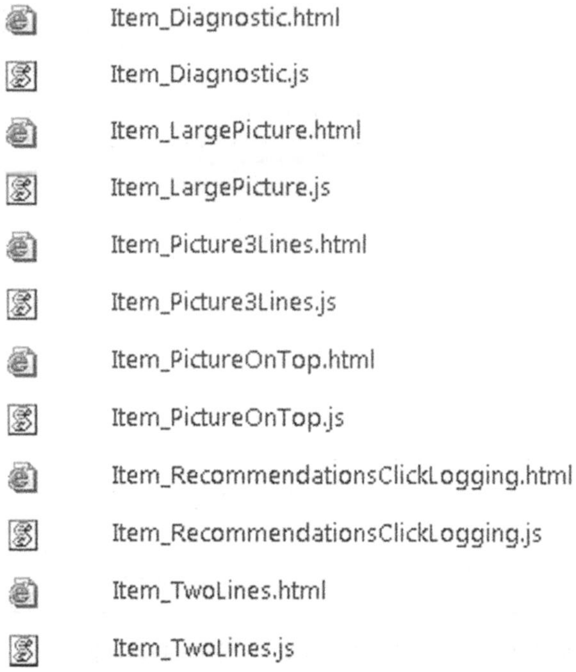

Item_Diagnostic.html

Item_Diagnostic.js

Item_LargePicture.html

Item_LargePicture.js

Item_Picture3Lines.html

Item_Picture3Lines.js

Item_PictureOnTop.html

Item_PictureOnTop.js

Item_RecommendationsClickLogging.html

Item_RecommendationsClickLogging.js

Item_TwoLines.html

Item_TwoLines.js

Figure 9-50. *Out-of-the-box Item display templates*

■ **Note**   For the purpose of this chapter, we are focusing on display templates for Content web parts. If you want to learn more about all the display templates and their HTML and JavaScript files, including display templates for Search and Refiners, refer to `http://sprwd.com/5nbp9ss`.

As a side note, when we configure to consume a catalog from a publishing site, if we choose to let the catalog integration process create category pages, then the default category page created by SharePoint contains a Content Search web part. The default Control display template for the Content Search web part on the default category page is List with Paging, which is mapped to the Control_ListWithPaging files in the Master Page Gallery. The default Item display template used by that Content Search web part is Picture on top, 3 lines on bottom, which is mapped to the Item_Picture3Lines files in the Master Page Gallery.

Creating a New Display Template

The recommended approach to create a custom display template is to create a new HTML file for a new display template that is based on an existing display template. We do not want to override any out-of-the-box display templates because we want to keep the out-of-the-box design intact in case we want to use it again or use it as a reference design.

There are four components to implement when creating a custom display template.

1.   We need to specify all the managed properties we want to retrieve at query time so that we can use these properties in our HTML.

2.   We can externalize and add all the JavaScript and CSS files we use in the display template.

3. For any inline JavaScript we use in the display template, we need to make sure they are below the first `<div>` tag in the display template.

4. Within the custom display template, we need to add HTML markups to render the results.

■ **Note** To create a new display template, always make the changes in the `.html` file; never make any changes directly in the `.js` file. For the conversion process to succeed, always make sure the `.html` file is XML compliant. For example, unclosed tags such as `<br>` instead of `<br/>` will make the HTML file XML noncomplaint.

For our custom display template, first we make a copy of an existing display template that has the same Content type and is similar to the look and feel we want to create. Based on our design as described in the section "Specter Design Components" earlier in this chapter, we need to customize how the entire search result set looks as well as the rendering of each individual search result. Therefore, we need to create a custom Control display template and a custom Item display template.

1. On the Specter Group public-facing site, click Site Settings.

2. Click the Master Pages and page layouts link.

3. Under the Master Page Gallery library, click the `Display Templates` folder. Then under the `Display Templates` folder, click the `Content Web Parts` folder. Within the `Content Web Parts` folder, you will see all the out-of-the-box display templates and their `.html` and `.js` files (refer to Figures 9-49 and 9-50).

   For our custom display template, we make our own `.html` file; the `.js` file is generated automatically when we upload the `.html` file.

4. Download a local copy of the `Control_List.html` file and a copy of the `Item_LargePicture.html` file.

5. Rename these local copies `Control_List_Specter.html` and `Item_LargePicture_Specter.html`, respectively.

6. Open the files in any HTML designer, Dreamweaver, SharePoint Designer, Visual Studio, or Notepad for editing.

■ **Note** We do not get the full WYSIWIG experience in our HTML editor as we do not get the style sheets and images used in the site.

Display Template Structure

Before we make any changes to our custom display templates, let's review the basic structure of a display template. Please follow along with this section by referencing the local copy of the custom display template file. There are four main sections of a display template:

1. Title section: At the top of the HTML file, the `<title>` tag is used to identify the display name of this display template as seen in search web parts. For an example, refer to Figure 9-51.

```
]<html xmlns:mso="urn:schemas-microsoft-com:office:office" xmlns:msdt="uuid:C2F41010-65B3-11d1-A29F-00AA00C14882">
]<head>
<title>List Specter</title>
```

Figure 9-51. An example of the Title section in display templates

2. Header section: Below the `<title>` tag, there is an `<xml>` tag with a group of elements in CustomDocumentProperties that can be modified in the display template to provide SharePoint information about this display template. For example, one of the most commonly referenced elements is the `ManagedPropertyMapping` element. It maps fields exposed by search result items to properties available for JavaScript. This property is used to provide SharePoint the list of managed properties it needs to reference in this display template (see Listing 9-6). The `ManagedPropertyMapping` element is only used in Item display templates.

Listing 9-6. An Example of the ManagedPropertyMapping Element in Display Templates

```
<mso:ManagedPropertyMapping msdt:dt="string">
        'LastModifiedTime':'LastModifiedTime',
        'Specter Property Type'{Specter Property Type}:'SpecterPropertyType',
        'Picture URL'{Picture URL}:'PublishingImage;PictureURL;PictureThumbnailURL',
        'Link URL'{Link URL}:'Path',
        'Line 1'{Line 1}:'Title',
        'Line 2'{Line 2}:'Description',
        'SecondaryFileExtension',
        'ContentTypeId'
</mso:ManagedPropertyMapping>
```

■ **Note** Not all elements are used in every display template. For a list of CustomDocumentProperties elements, refer to http://sprwd.com/79gd4jr. To learn more about the ManagedPropertyMapping element, refer to the section "Creating Search Managed Properties for Content."

---

3. Script section: Within the `<body>` tag, you will see a `<script>` tag, which is used to reference JavaScript and CSS files outside of the display template. To add a reference to outside JavaScript files that are part of the current site collection, we need to do the following:

   `$includeScript(this.url, "~sitecollection/_catalogs/masterpage/custom.js");`

To add a reference to an outside CSS file that is in a location relative to the current display template, we need to do the following:

`$includeCSS(this.url, "../../style.css");`

4. DIV section: Below the `<script>` tag, there is a `<div>` tag. This `<div>` tag is never rendered on the page. All the HTML or JavaScript code we want to render on the page must be included inside of this `<div>` tag.

■ **Note**   To learn more about how to add content to the DIV section, refer to Listing 9-11.

Basics of Working with JavaScript, HTML, and CSS

When creating custom display templates, we often need to work with JavaScript, HTML, and CSS to provide customizations. To see examples of how these are used, refer to the following two sections.

Inline JavaScript is very useful when we need to create variables to hold data and then output values in the HTML markup. When creating inline JavaScript in display templates, for it to execute, we need to add the JavaScript code after the first <div> tag in the template and it needs to be added between an opening and closing tag set. This is specific to display templates.

```
<!--#_ and _#-->
```

In HTML markup, to view the value of a managed property or a variable created from inline JavaScript, we need to enclose the code in an opening and closing tag set.

```
_#= somefield =#_
```

To access the current SharePoint context, use the ctx object. To access information of the current search result item, use the ctx.CurrentItem object. This object contains references to all of its managed properties. To get a managed property's value of a result item, use the following in the HTML section:

```
_#=ctx.CurrentItem.SpecterPropertyType=#_
```

To work with managed properties as local variables in JavaScript, we can reference the property as follows:

```
var myPropertyType = "This is for property type: " + ctx.CurrentItem. SpecterPropertyType + ".";
```

■ **Tip**   When creating the display template, it's much faster and easier to test the look and feel by keeping the style tags under the <style> tag in the <head> section of the display template. Once the design is completed, we can move the style tags to a separate CSS file, then reference the CSS file in the <script> tag.

Creating a Custom Control Display Template

For our scenario, let's see how we can integrate the design we have implemented in the section "Specter Design Components" earlier in this chapter with our custom display templates. Let's start with the Control display template.

1.   At the top of the Control_List_Specter.html file, change the value inside the <title> tag, which is the name displayed in the Display Template drop-down list when configuring the Content Search web part. We change it to List Specter as shown in Figure 9-52.

```
}<html xmlns:mso="urn:schemas-microsoft-com:office:office" xmlns:msdt="uuid:C2F41010-65B3-11d1-A29F-00AA00C14882">
}<head>
<title>List Specter</title>
```

Figure 9-52. Define a name for the custom Control display template

Recall from Chapter 4 that we created a custom style sheet, `style.css`, which contains custom styles for the site. The file was then added to the Specter Group public-facing site's Master Page Gallery and has been included in the master page so that it can be referenced throughout the site.

2. From Listing 9-1, we created CSS code blocks based on the Specter design components for displaying search results. To tell SharePoint to use those CSS styles, we need to add all the CSS code blocks created earlier to the `style.css` file.

3. Because the Floor Plan landing page is using the Specter Group master page, `style.css` has already been included. If you decide to create a separate CSS file that is not included in the master page, you would need to include the CSS file within the `<script>` section of the display template, as described in step 3 in the section "Display Template Structure" earlier in this chapter.

4. From the CSS code block in Listing 9-1, to ensure a list of items is displayed in a three-column table, we need to add the `feature` class to the list. To do this, we need to update the custom Control display template file, `Control_List_Specter.html`, to ensure the `<ul>` tag within the `<div>` tag in the display template is using the `feature` class, as shown in Listing 9-7.

Listing 9-7. Add the Feature Class to the <ul> Tag to Ensure Results Are Displayed in a Three-Column Table

```
<ul class="feature">
        _#=ctx.RenderGroups(ctx) =#_
</ul>
```

5. We will leave the rest of the display template as is. Calling the `ctx.RenderGroups(ctx)` function triggers the rendering of all the search results.

   At this point, we have made all the necessary changes for the custom Control display template, Control_List_Specter, to render results in a three-column table. For other scenarios, if you have a different look and feel for the search results block, you would need to add specific CSS and HTML markup in the custom Control display template HTML file.

6. From the custom Control display template file, save the `Control_List_Specter.html` file and upload it to the same location as the rest of the display templates.

7. After uploading the file, note the Content Type is automatically selected as Control Display Template as a result of the file naming convention (see Figure 9-53). Also note that the title is automatically generated with the same text as the one we have indicated in the `<title>` tag in the HTML file. Under Target Control Type, make sure the Content Search Web Parts check box is selected, as this display template is specifically created for the Content Search web part. Click Save.

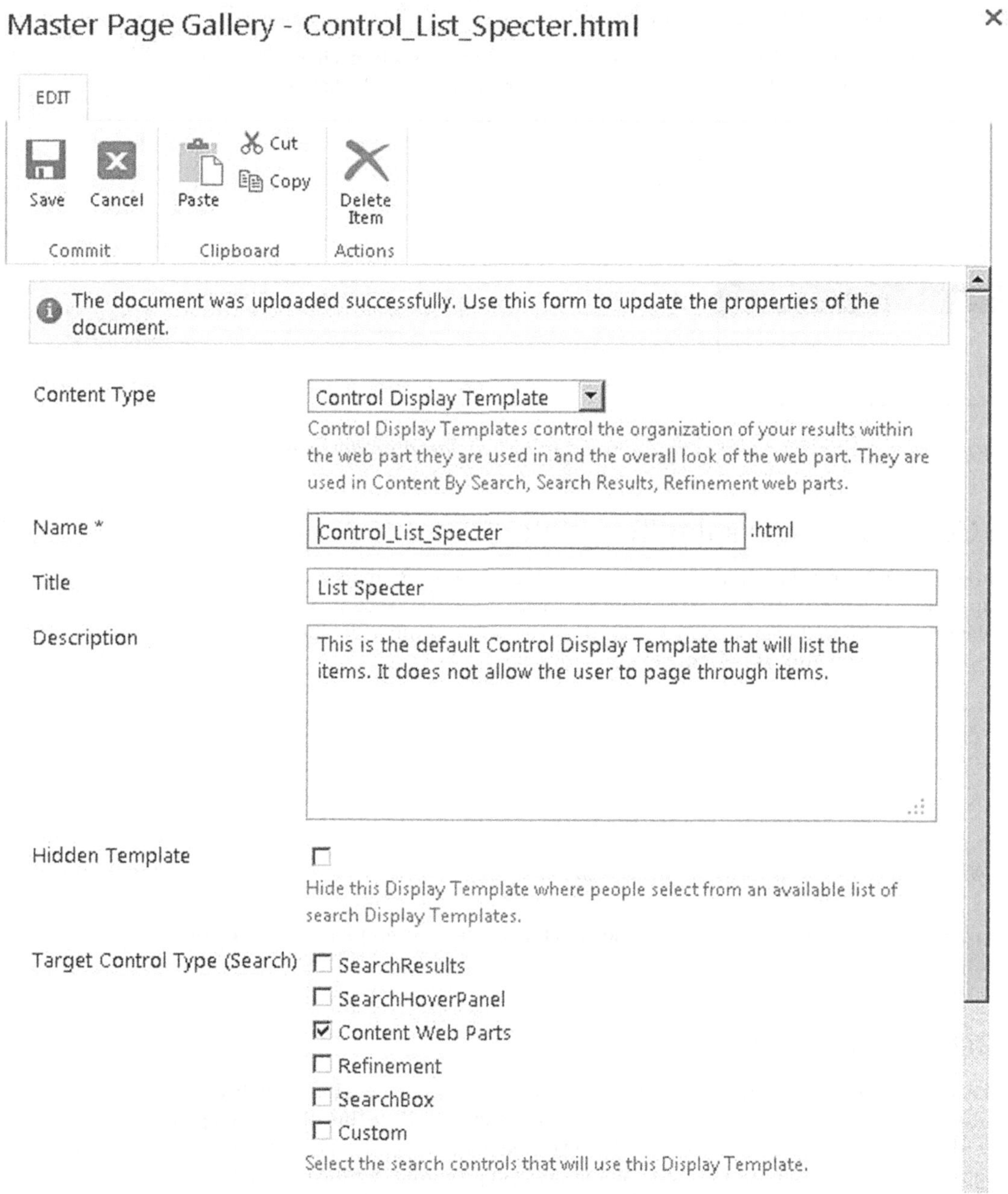

Master Page Gallery - Control_List_Specter.html ✕

EDIT

💾 Save	✕ Cancel	📋 Paste	✂ Cut 📋 Copy	✕ Delete Item
Commit		Clipboard		Actions

ⓘ The document was uploaded successfully. Use this form to update the properties of the document.

Content Type

| Control Display Template ▼ |

Control Display Templates control the organization of your results within the web part they are used in and the overall look of the web part. They are used in Content By Search, Search Results, Refinement web parts.

Name *

| Control_List_Specter | .html

Title

| List Specter |

Description

| This is the default Control Display Template that will list the items. It does not allow the user to page through items. |

Hidden Template

☐

Hide this Display Template where people select from an available list of search Display Templates.

Target Control Type (Search)
☐ SearchResults
☐ SearchHoverPanel
☑ Content Web Parts
☐ Refinement
☐ SearchBox
☐ Custom

Select the search controls that will use this Display Template.

Figure 9-53. *Properties to set when uploading a custom display template file to the Master Page Gallery*

As soon as the file is uploaded, a corresponding .js file is created next to the HTML file. Let's verify the Control_List_Specter display template was created correctly.

8. Navigate to the Floor Plan page and click Edit Page.

9. Edit the Content Search web part on the page.

10. In the web part tool panel on the right, in the Display template section, click the Control drop-down list. The new display template List Specter should be in the list as shown in Figure 9-54.

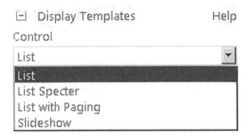

Figure 9-54. *New display template is added to the Control display template drop-down list in the web part*

Creating a Custom Item Display Template

Next, we customize the rendering of each search result by creating our own Item display template.

From the top of the `Item_LargePicture.html` page we created in a prior section, the value inside the `<title>` tag is the name displayed in the Item display template drop-down list when configuring the Content Search web part. We change it to Specter Large picture as in Figure 9-55.

```
Item_LargePicture_Specter.html*   ⊡ ✕
⊟ <html xmlns:mso="urn:schemas-microsoft-com:office:office" xmlns:msdt="uuid:C2F41010-65B3-11d1-A29F-00AA00C14882">
⊟ <head>
    <title>Specter Large picture</title>
```

Figure 9-55. *Define a name for the custom Item display template*

With the Item display template in place, next we need to tell the display template what to display for each item and how to display it.

Adding Search Managed Properties

Every Item display template contains information about the managed properties it needs to display. To update the managed properties referenced in the display template, we need to change the value of the ManagedProperty Mapping field, as shown in Listing 9-8. We need to add a tag called `mso:ManagedPropertyMapping` to include any out-of-the-box managed properties as well as any custom managed properties we have created in search (such as the one we created in the section "Creating Search Managed Properties for Content" earlier in this chapter). The ManagedPropertyMapping tag is a comma-separated list of managed property names and the properties in the UI to which they are mapped (see Listing 9-8). The UI properties can be mapped to multiple managed properties, other than the ones specified using the Property Mappings section of the Content Search web part tool pane.

For example, within the ManagedPropertyMapping tag, both `PictureURL` and `PictureThumbnailURL` are mapped to Image URL.

```
'Image URL': 'PictureURL;PictureThumbnailURL', 'Line 1':'Title', 'Line 1 Link':'Path',...
```

For our custom Item display template, we need to add two managed properties (see Listing 9-8).

Listing 9-8. Add Managed Properties to the Display Template and Map the Property to a Property in the UI

```
<mso:ManagedPropertyMapping msdt:dt="string">
        'LastModifiedTime':'LastModifiedTime',
        'Specter Property Type'{Specter Property Type}:'SpecterPropertyType',
        'Picture URL'{Picture URL}:'PublishingImage;PictureURL;PictureThumbnailURL',
        'Link URL'{Link URL}:'Path',
        'Line 1'{Line 1}:'Title',
        'Line 2'{Line 2}:'Description',
        'SecondaryFileExtension',
        'ContentTypeId'
</mso:ManagedPropertyMapping>>
```

1. Add the out-of-the-box managed property, LastModifiedTime, to show users the date the property was posted.

2. Add the custom managed property, SpecterPropertyType, to display the property type as a caption for each floor plan.

Adding Inline JavaScript

As mentioned earlier all the HTML and JavaScript code we want to render on the page must be included inside of the first <div> tag.

Continue with the Item_LargePicture.html page, below the first <div> tag, and add the inline JavaScript code in Listing 9-9 to get data for each item.

Listing 9-9. Inline JavaScript Added to the Custom Item Display Template to Get Data for Each Result Item

```
var encodedId = $htmlEncode(ctx.ClientControl.get_nextUniqueId() + "_largePicture_Specter_");
var linkURL = $getItemValue(ctx, "Link URL");
linkURL.overrideValueRenderer($urlHtmlEncode);
var line1 = $getItemValue(ctx, "Line 1");
var line2 = $getItemValue(ctx, "Line 2");
var pictureURL = $getItemValue(ctx, "Picture URL");
var pictureId = encodedId + "picture";
var pictureMarkup = Srch.ContentBySearch.getPictureMarkup(pictureURL, 468, 220,
                                ctx.CurrentItem, "cbs-largePictureImg", line1, pictureId);
var specterPropertyType = $getItemValue(ctx, "SpecterPropertyType");
var lastModifiedTime = $getItemValue(ctx, "LastModifiedTime");

var m_names = new Array("Jan", "Feb", "Mar",
    "Apr", "May", "Jun", "Jul", "Aug", "Sep",
    "Oct", "Nov", "Dec");

var d = new Date(lastModifiedTime);
var date = d.getDate();
var d_month = d.getMonth();
var month = m_names[d_month];
```

For the purpose of demonstration, let's break the inline JavaScript in our solution into three sections.

- Get properties for the current item:

  - Get the encoded client ID of the current result item

    ```
    var encodedId = $htmlEncode(ctx.ClientControl.get_nextUniqueId() + "_largePicture_Specter_");
    ```

  - Get the encoded URL of the detail page for the current item. linkURL is derived from the Link URL UI property, which is mapped to the Path managed property in our solution

    ```
    var linkURL = $getItemValue(ctx, "Link URL");
    linkURL.overrideValueRenderer($urlHtmlEncode);
    ```

  - Get all the properties that will be displayed for the current item. line1 is derived from the Line 1 UI property, which is mapped to the SpecterPropertyType managed property

    ```
    var line1 = $getItemValue(ctx, "Line 1");
    var line2 = $getItemValue(ctx, "Line 2");
    ```

  - Get the URL of the picture that will be displayed for the item

    ```
    var pictureURL = $getItemValue(ctx, "Picture URL");
    var pictureId = encodedId + "picture";
    ```

- Create HTML markups for content to be displayed

  The pictureMarkup value is derived from the getPictureMarkup function, which retrieves the HTML markup of an image with the image's URL and ID

  ```
  var pictureMarkup = Srch.ContentBySearch.getPictureMarkup(pictureURL, 468, 220,
                              ctx.CurrentItem, "cbs-largePictureImg", line1, pictureId);
  ```

- Process the values of managed properties before we display them

  - Get the Specter Property Type values for the current item. specterPropertyType is derived from the SpecterPropertyType managed property

    ```
    var specterPropertyType = $getItemValue(ctx, "SpecterPropertyType");
    ```

  - Get lastModifiedTime for the item and translate the value into Month and Date

    ```
    var lastModifiedTime = $getItemValue(ctx, "LastModifiedTime");
    ```

  - Utility function used to created "date" and "month" from the LastModifiedTime managed property. It gets translated into short month names

    ```
    var m_names = new Array("Jan", "Feb", "Mar",
        "Apr", "May", "Jun", "Jul", "Aug", "Sep",
        "Oct", "Nov", "Dec");

    var d = new Date(lastModifiedTime);
    var date = d.getDate();
    var d_month = d.getMonth();
    var month = m_names[d_month];
    ```

Adding HTML Markup

Now we are ready to add some HTML markup to the custom item display template file to display data for each item. Scroll down the Item template HTML file to find the original HTML we want to remove (see Listing 9-10).

Listing 9-10. Out-of-the-Box HTML Markup in the Item_LargePicture HTML File

```
<div class="cbs-largePictureContainer" id="_#= containerId =#_"
        data-displaytemplate="ItemLargePicture">
            <div class="cbs-largePictureImageContainer" id="_#= pictureContainerId =#_">
                <a class="cbs-pictureImgLink" href="_#= linkURL =#_"
                    title="_#= $htmlEncode(line1) =#_" id="_#= pictureLinkId =#_">
                    _#= pictureMarkup =#_
                </a>
            </div>
            <div class="cbs-largePictureDataOverlay"  id="_#= dataContainerOverlayId =#_"></div>
            <div class="cbs-largePictureDataContainer" id="_#= dataContainerId =#_">
                <a class="cbs-largePictureLine1Link" href="_#= linkURL =#_"
                    title="_#= $htmlEncode(line1) =#_" id="_#= line1LinkId =#_">
                    <h2 class="cbs-largePictureLine1 ms-noWrap" id="_#= line1Id =#_">
                        _#= line1 =#_
                    </h2>
                </a>
                <div class="cbs-largePictureLine2 ms-noWrap" title="_#= $htmlEncode(line2) =#_"
                        id="_#= line2Id =#_" > _#= line2 =#_</div>
            </div>
        </div>
```

Before we remove it, however, let's review the out-of-the-box HTML. Note the out-of-the-box template uses the ID from the search result as unique identifiers for some of the HTML tags. It displays the Title and Description managed properties for each result. It also shows pictureMarkup, which is a variable that was created from inline JavaScript shown previously that gets the HTML markup of the image for each search result. The inline JavaScript lives right above this code as shown in the previous section.

Let's first replace this HTML markup with the HTML markup in Listing 9-11 to render each search result with the responsive design we implemented in the previous section. The HTML in Listing 9-11 generates the HTML markup for the Item display template while referencing the custom CSS for look and feel.

Listing 9-11. New HTML Markup for the New Item Display Template

```
<span class="_#= specterPropertyType=#_">
            <a href="_#= linkURL =#_" class="thumb">
                _#= pictureMarkup =#_
                <div class="date">
                        <div class="d">_#= date=#_</div>
                        <div class="m">_#= month=#_</div>
                </div>
            </a>
            <div class="caption">Property Type: _#= specterPropertyType=#_</div>
</span>
```

The end product of this HTML markup is Figure 9-56. As you can see, the display template displays an image, the last modified date, and the property type of a Floor Plan item.

Figure 9-56. End product of the HTML markup for the custom Item display template

Let's discuss each part of the HTML markup in detail.

- `<li>`

  Recall from earlier that we talked about each Item display template renders an empty `<li>` tag, and under the `<li>` tag is where the content for each item goes. Inside of the Item display template, you will not see the actual `<li>` tag because it is generated for each item by SharePoint during runtime. Hence we cannot add any style, ID, or CSS class to this `<li>`. Recall from the Style for Each Item section, we created the CSS style for an `<li>` tag under a `<ul>` tag that has a `feature` class. Because we have already added the `feature` class to the `<ul>` tag, the `<li>` generated by SharePoint will automatically pick up the style we have created under the `.feature li` CSS code block demonstrated in Listing 9-2. As a result, each item will now be displayed in a three-column table.

- `<a href="_#= lineURL =#_ class="thumb">`

- For each search result, we want the image to link to the URL of the search result. `lineURL` is a variable created from inline JavaScript, which is mapped to the Path managed property (as described in the previous section). The `thumb` class is added to style the display of each result item as specified by the CSS code block (Listing 9-3) in the `style.css` file we have in the Master Page Gallery.

- `_#= pictureMarkup =#_`

  For each search result, we want to display an image of the floor plan. `pictureMarkup` is a variable that was created from inline JavaScript that gets the HTML markup of the image for each search result (as described in the previous section).

- `<div class="date"><div class="d">_#= date =#_</div><div class="m">_#= month =#_</div></div>`

For each search result, we want to show the date the floor plan was modified. Both `"date"` and `"month"` are variables created from inline JavaScript that gets the date and month values from the `LastModified` managed property. The `date` and `month` class are added to style each result item with a circle for the date as specified in a CSS code block (Listing 9-5) in the `style.css` file we have in the Master Page Gallery.

- `<div class="caption">Property Type: _#= specterPropertyType=#_</div>`

  For each search result, we want to show the property type of each floor plan. `specterPropertyType` is a variable created from inline JavaScript that gets the value from the `SpecterPropertyType` managed property (as described in the previous section). The `caption` class is added to style each result item with a circle for the date as specified in a CSS code block (Listing 9-4) in the `style.css` file we have in the Master Page Gallery.

As you can see, we are displaying the values of many managed properties throughout the template. We have plugged these values using the `_#=` and `=#_` tags into the appropriate DIV or SPAN tags for formatting.

Integrating Search Results with the Custom Item Display Template

We have made all the necessary changes for the custom Item display template, `Item_LargePicture_Specter.html`, to render each result based on the Specter design. For other scenarios, if you have a different look and feel for each item, you would need to add specific CSS and HTML markup in the custom Item display template HTML file.

1. Continue with the `Item_LargePicture_Specter.html` file, save the file, and upload it to the same location as the rest of the display templates.

2. After uploading the file, note the Content Type is automatically selected as Item Display Template as a result of the file naming convention (see Figure 9-57). Also note that the title is automatically generated with the same text as the one we have indicated in the `<title>` tag in the HTML file. Under Target Control Type, make sure the Content Search Web Parts check box is selected, as this display template is specifically created for the Content Search web part. Click Save.

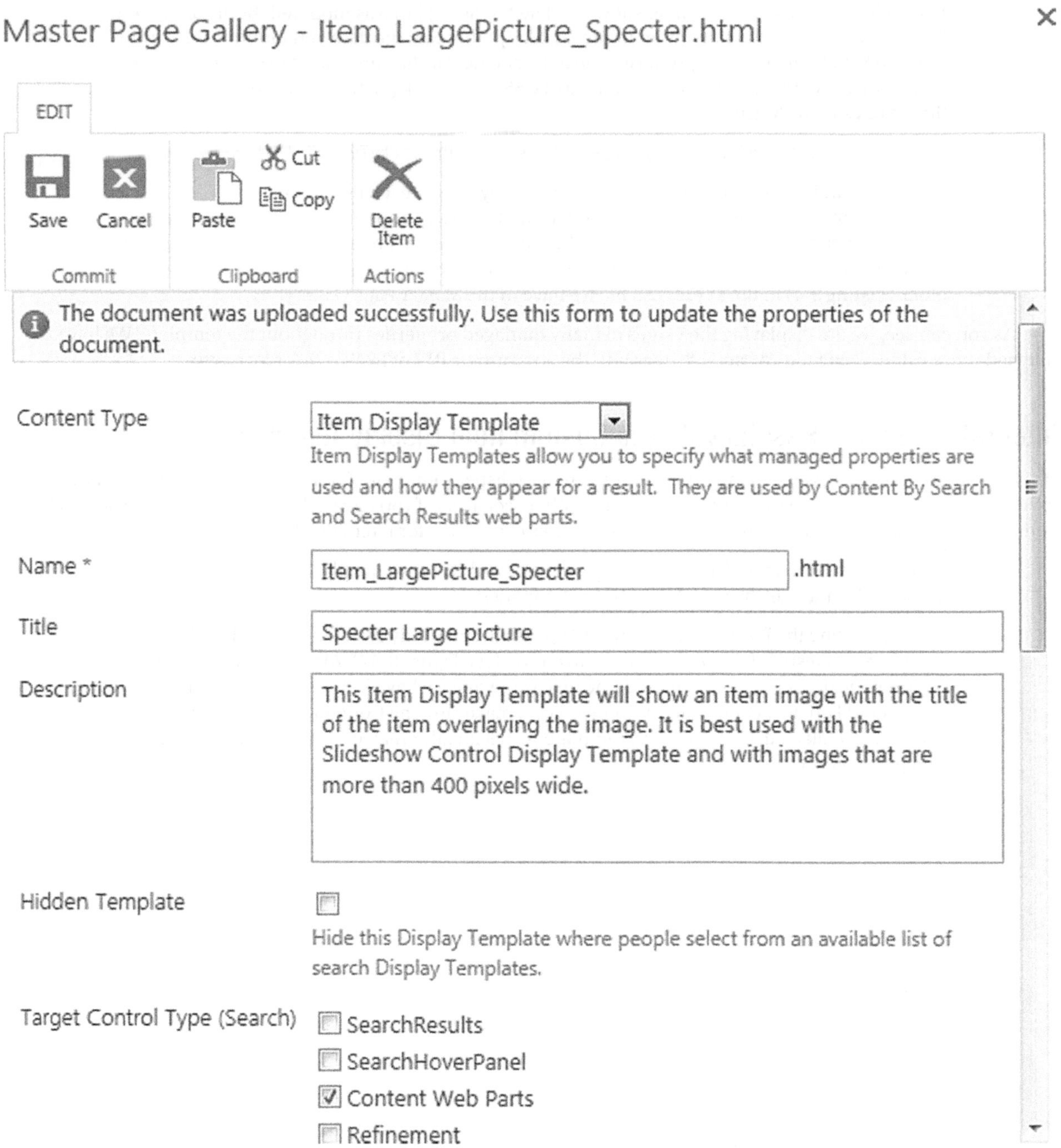

Master Page Gallery - Item_LargePicture_Specter.html ✕

EDIT

💾 Save	✖ Cancel	📋 Paste	✂ Cut / 📋 Copy	✖ Delete Item
Commit		Clipboard		Actions

ℹ The document was uploaded successfully. Use this form to update the properties of the document.

Content Type

> Item Display Template ▼
>
> Item Display Templates allow you to specify what managed properties are used and how they appear for a result. They are used by Content By Search and Search Results web parts.

Name *

> Item_LargePicture_Specter .html

Title

> Specter Large picture

Description

> This Item Display Template will show an item image with the title of the item overlaying the image. It is best used with the Slideshow Control Display Template and with images that are more than 400 pixels wide.

Hidden Template

> ☐
>
> Hide this Display Template where people select from an available list of search Display Templates.

Target Control Type (Search)
☐ SearchResults
☐ SearchHoverPanel
☑ Content Web Parts
☐ Refinement

Figure 9-57. Properties to set when uploading a custom Item display template file to the Master Page Gallery

3. After we have deployed both the Control and the Item display templates, we need to integrate them with our search solution. We can integrate by configuring the Content Search web part.

4. Navigate to the Floor Plans page and click Edit page.

5. Edit the Content Search web part. Once the web part configuration pane is opened on the right, in the Display Templates section, select List Specter in the Control drop-down list and select Specter Large Picture in the Item drop-down list (see Figure 9-58). Click Apply.

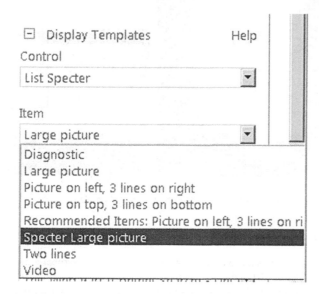

Figure 9-58. *Change Control display template to List Specter and Item display template to Specter Large Picture*

■ **Note** To get the same branding as the Specter design, make sure you are using the same Specter Group master page from Chapter 5 because we need to reference styles added to the `style.css` file, which is included in the Specter Group master page.

Once the page is saved, the result page should look like Figure 9-59.

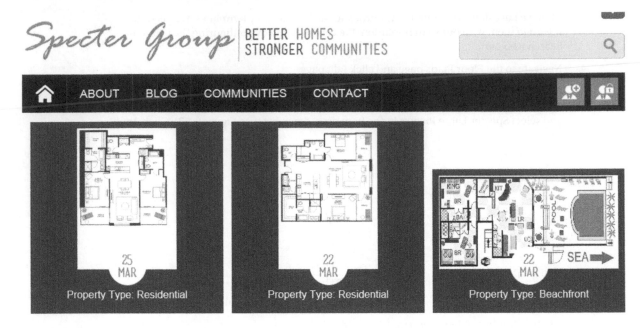

Figure 9-59. *Result Floor Plans page after adding custom Control and custom Item display templates*

Limitations of Display Templates

Earlier, we learned that each Item display template generates its own `<li>` tag during runtime. This means we cannot add ID, CSS class, or styles to the `<li>` tag because it does not exist in the display template at design time. When designing an HTML page, there are times when it requires us to add a CSS class to the `<li>` tag for each item; for example, when dealing with jQuery plug-ins, such as Isotope to provide dynamic filtering features to a list. In the case of Isotope, to make the filtering feature work, we need to add a CSS class to a `<ul>` tag and its immediate children `<li>` tags. Because we are working with display templates in SharePoint, when SharePoint renders each item with a given Item display template, an `<li>` tag will be automatically generated. Hence, when designing the display template, we cannot configure the `<li>` tag with any CSS class or ID, as required by the Isotope plug-in. As a result, the filtering feature provided by the Isotope jQuery plug-in does not work in display templates in SharePoint without changing the plug-in's code.

Query Rules, Result Types, and Display Templates

In the previous section, we looked at how to create a content rollup solution using custom display templates and the cross-site publishing feature. Now we are going to look at how floor plans are rendered in search. We look at how we can fine-tune search queries and customize the display of results when users search for floor plans. SharePoint 2013 provides new features like query rules, result types, and display templates to allow better tuning and better presentation of search results based on the intent of the user's query.

For the Specter Group Floor Plans scenario, we are going to create a query rule and a result type for floor plans, such that when users search for the keyword "floor plans," the following things happen:

- We create a condition for the query rule to match on the keyword "floor plans."

- Once the condition is matched, we promote a few beachfront properties to the top of the results if the current month is in the summer by configuring the publishing criteria of the query rule.

- We render the block of results for floor plans with its own user interface by creating a result type for floor plans.

For an example of how to configure query rules and result types, refer to the sections "Create a Query Rule to add a Summer Promotion for Beachfront Properties" and "Adding a Result Type for Floor Plans to Use Best Bet Item Display Templates," respectively.

Query Rules

In SharePoint 2010, one query has one set of results. In SharePoint 2013, we are able to fine-tune search results based on the intent of the user's query. When users enter a query, we help them find what they are really looking for by fine-tuning the query and adding additional information to offer results that we think the users are looking for. We can create query rules to trigger multiple queries and multiple results sets for a user's search requests. All matching query rules can generate results. The query orchestration engine retrieves all the different sets of results and renders them to the user. The results are then rendered in a specific user interface based on their result types and the display templates associated with it. For more information on result types and associated display templates, refer to the section "Result Types" later in this chapter.

When creating a new query rule, there are three components to configure:

1. Condition: Set of conditions to match for this rule to fire (example: no conditions means the rule will be fired every time).

2. Action: What to do when this rule is applied (when conditions are matched).

3. Publishing: When should the rule be active.

Query Rules Creation

Query rules can be created at various levels, in the Search Service application from Central Admin or at the site collection level. They are inherited by default, such that query rules created in the Search Service application are inherited by all the site collections and query rules created at the site collection level are inherited by all sites within the site collection. They can also be deactivated at a level to ensure the rule is never applied for queries submitted at that level.

■ **Note**   If multiple query rules are active and more than one rule can be matched for a given query, then the rules will be executed in no specific order because there is no prescribed order for execution. To ensure query rules are ranked for orders of execution, a custom group needs to be created to organize the query rules. Refer to `http://sprwd.com/4czkg54` for more information.

Query Rules Conditions

Conditions allow us to define the criterion under which the query rule should apply. Each query rule can have multiple conditions. If no condition is specified, the query rule is triggered every time. If multiple conditions are specified, as long as one of the conditions is matched, then the query rule will be invoked. There are six types of conditions to choose from when creating a query rule:

- Query Matches Keyword Exactly: Query contains a specific word or words.

- Query Matches Dictionary Exactly: Query contains a word in a specific dictionary.

- Query Contains Action Term: Query contains an action word that matches a specific phrase or term set.

- Query More Common in Source: Query is common in a different source (like Videos Results Source).

- Result Type Commonly Clicked: Results include a common result type (like file type).

- Advanced Query Text Match: Advanced rule to match across a set of terms, dictionary, regular expression, and so on.

■ **Note** For more information on all the query rule conditions, refer to http://sprwd.com/sqs8jgt.

For the Specter Group Floor Plans scenario, we are going to configure our query rule for Floor Plans with the condition to match keyword "Floor plans." Refer to the section "Creating a Query Rule to Add a Summer Promotion for Beachfront Properties" later in this chapter for more detail.

Query Rule Actions

Next, we need to configure actions to specify what happens when the query rule is applied. We can add multiple actions for each query rule. There are three options for actions:

- Assign promoted results: A promoted result is a result that appears at the top of the search results. This is similar to Best Bets in SharePoint 2010 or Visual Best Bets in FAST Search for SharePoint 2010. We can promote a result as a link or as a banner, which is a quick and easy way to visually present a certain result to users.

- Add result block: A result block is several search results displayed as a group. Similar to promoting a search result, we can promote a result block.

  - A result block specifies an additional query to run and how to display the results.

  - A result block uses a result source, which can be results from the local search index or results from outside of SharePoint, such as Exchange or OpenSearch. Both search scopes and federated locations features from SharePoint 2010 have evolved into result sources. An example of a result source using OpenSearch is federating search results from Bing by providing the OpenSearch URL for its search service. An example of an out-of-the-box result source, Documents, returns all files from the local SharePoint index.

  - While configuring a result block, this feature includes a full query designer for building and testing queries, similar to Query Builder in the Content Search web part.

  - A result block can be configured to use specific custom display templates.

- Change ranked results by changing the query: Change the way SharePoint handles a particular query by supplementing a query with additional keywords or managed property restrictions. This feature can be used to tune search results. The original query can be changed by modifying the query terms, adding additional terms, applying an XRANK formula to the query, and so on.

■ **Caution** Expanding the original query increases the time needed to execute the search query because additional queries are executed and additional result sets are returned. Be cautious when designing a query, as it might return too many search results, such that the query gets timed out or takes a really long time to finish.

■ **Note** When ranking a result block, the ranking applies to the entire block, not to individual items within the block. Every individual query made by every individual user is logged, as well as the user's click-through choices. As items in a result block are clicked, the entire result block shows up higher in the search results. In time, the entire result block can start to percolate up to the top of the search results if users continue to select items in it.

For the Specter Group Floor Plans scenario, we are going to configure our query rule for Floor Plans with an action to add promoted results for a few beachfront properties.

Query Rules Publishing

The publishing options for a query rule determine when the rule can be used. By default, a rule is active until it is deactivated. We can also configure a rule to be active during a certain time. A good application of this is when a rule is set up for commerce scenarios. For example, we can set up a rule to promote certain products to the top for sale during a particular period of time, such as the holiday period.

In the Specter Group's scenario, we want to show beachfront properties in the summer period. Refer to the section "Creating a Query Rule to Add a Summer Promotion for Beachfront Properties" later in this chapter for more detail.

Result Types

We have created query rules to help us get the results. Now let's see how we can display the results. SharePoint 2013 introduces a new framework, result types, for presenting search results to end users. Each result type has its own display template, making different types of results look distinct from each other and surfacing properties that are most relevant to that type of results. We can create result types to invoke display templates based on a set of rules. Each result type has the following elements.

- We need to create rules for the result type to determine when it should be applied. Each rule is based on a set of criteria such as content type, managed property, or result source. To create a result type, add a condition for ContentType that equals YourContentTypeValue. Depending on the complexity of the logic, result types can contain multiple conditions to match multiple values for multiple properties.

- Once we have defined the conditions for our result type, we need to configure the Action for the result type. For a given result type, we can choose our display template from the Action drop-down list, which includes all the available display templates. Display templates define the visual layout of a result type. For more information on display templates, refer to the section "Introduction to Display Templates" earlier in this chapter.

By default, SharePoint offers several out-of-the-box result types. For example:

- Documents result type: Rich document results for Word, Excel, and PowerPoint.

- Conversation result type: Rich conversation results for newsfeed, comments, replies, and community discussions.

- Video result type: Rich video results for video content.

For the Specter Group Floor Plans scenario, we create a custom result type for floor plans to point the Floor Plans result type to the Best Bet Item display template. Now when users issue a query, each result is evaluated against the result type rules. If the item is a result from the Floor Plan result source, the result item will be displayed using the Best Bet Item display template to distinguish it from all other results in the list. Otherwise, the result item will be displayed using another default template.

Creating a Query Rule to Add a Summer Promotion for Beachfront Properties

For the Specter Group search scenario, when users search for "floor plans," we want to create a query rule to promote beachfront properties during the summer season. Because our query rules are used to display results to site visitors of the Specter Group public-facing site, we create the query rule at the site level for the public-facing site. Figure 9-60 shows the default search results page when a user enters "floor plans." As you can see, results of all types from the search index are interleaved based on their ranking. Each result has a result type, which determines how the item is rendered in the Search Results web part.

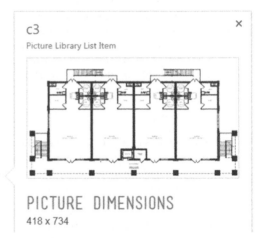

Figure 9-60. *Search results with out-of-the-box configurations*

Let's create a query rule to promote beachfront properties during the summer promotion season.

1. On the Specter Group public-facing site, click Site Settings.

2. Under the Search section, click Query Rules.

3. On the Manage Query Rules page, on the Select a Result Source menu, select the Floor Plan result source for the new query rule (see Figure 9-61).

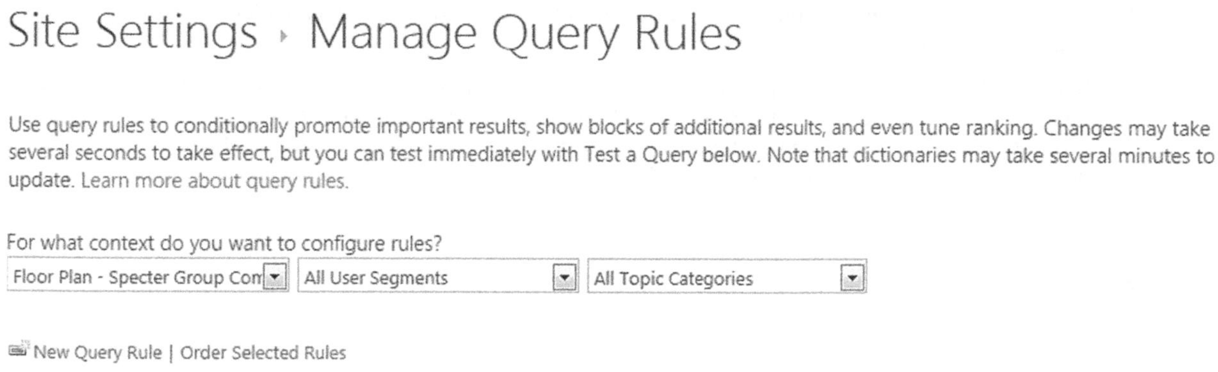

Site Settings ▸ Manage Query Rules

Use query rules to conditionally promote important results, show blocks of additional results, and even tune ranking. Changes may take several seconds to take effect, but you can test immediately with Test a Query below. Note that dictionaries may take several minutes to update. Learn more about query rules.

For what context do you want to configure rules?

| Floor Plan - Specter Group Com ▾ | All User Segments ▾ | All Topic Categories ▾ |

▨ New Query Rule | Order Selected Rules

Figure 9-61. *Create a new query rule for a result source*

4. Click New Query Rule.

5. On the Add Query Rule page, in the General Information section, in the Rule name field, type `Summer Promotion` as the name of the new query rule (see Figure 9-62).

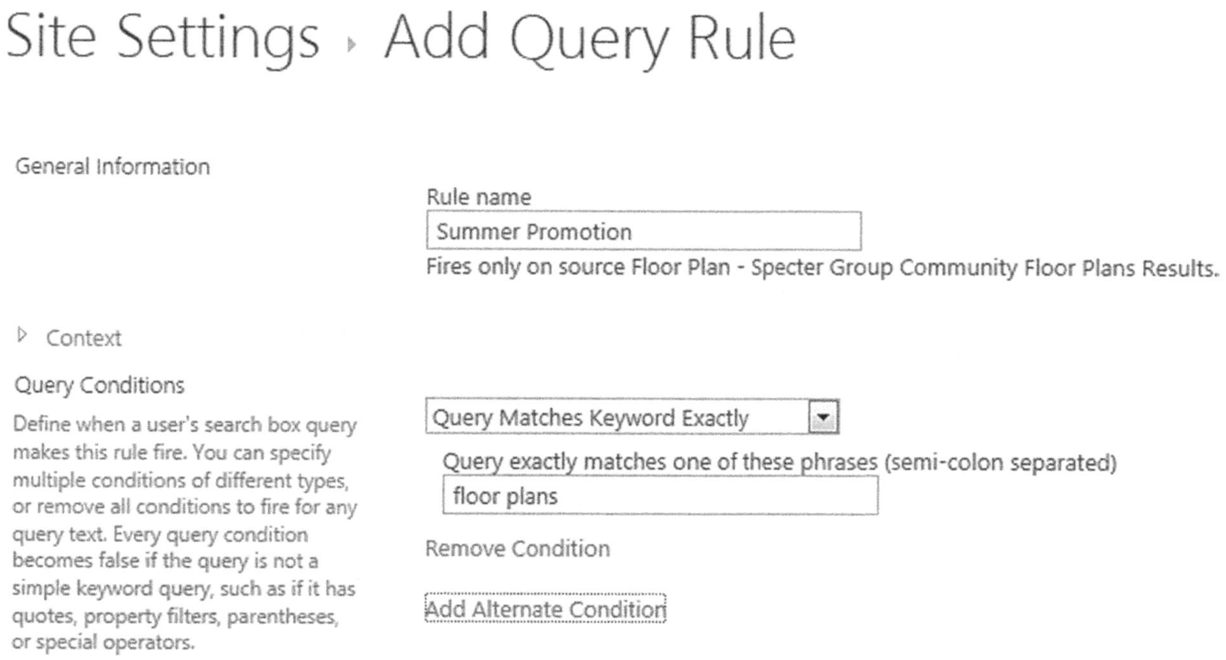

Site Settings ▸ Add Query Rule

General Information

Rule name

| Summer Promotion |

Fires only on source Floor Plan - Specter Group Community Floor Plans Results.

▷ Context

Query Conditions

Define when a user's search box query makes this rule fire. You can specify multiple conditions of different types, or remove all conditions to fire for any query text. Every query condition becomes false if the query is not a simple keyword query, such as if it has quotes, property filters, parentheses, or special operators.

| Query Matches Keyword Exactly ▾ |

Query exactly matches one of these phrases (semi-colon separated)

| floor plans |

Remove Condition

Add Alternate Condition

Figure 9-62. *Add a condition to a query rule*

6. Expand the Context section and note that the Floor Plan result source is selected by default.

7. Going down the page, in the Query Conditions section, ensure Query Matches Keyword Exactly is selected in the drop-down list. Enter `floor plans` in the text box as the query phrase to match (see Figure 9-62).

8.   In the Actions section, click the Add Promoted Result link to add promotion for a few beachfront properties.

9.   In the Add Promoted Result window, shown in Figure 9-63, select the Add new promoted result option. Enter `Beachfront property` in the Title field, then enter the URL for the promotion banner. Select the Render the URL as a banner instead of as a hyperlink check box to render the image as a banner. Click Save to continue.

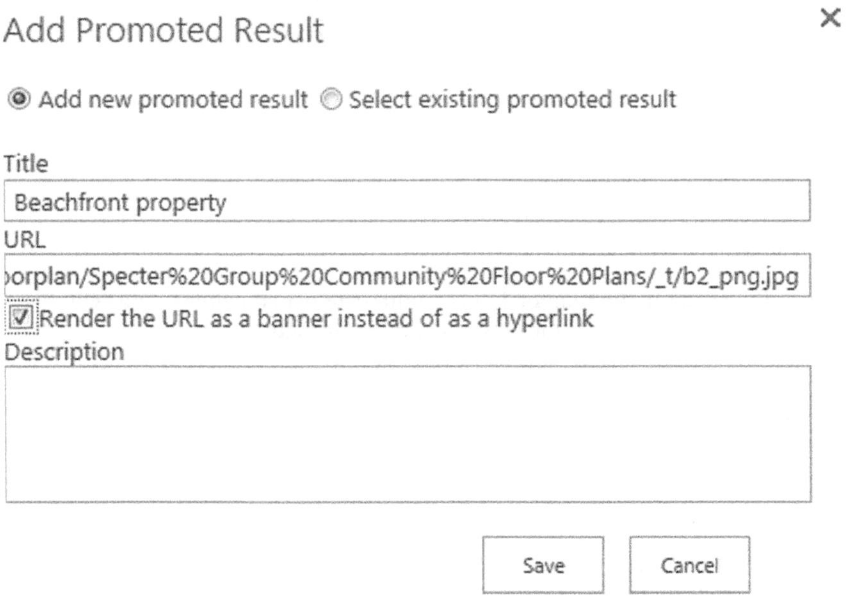

Add Promoted Result   ✕

◉ Add new promoted result ◯ Select existing promoted result

Title

| Beachfront property |

URL

| orplan/Specter%20Group%20Community%20Floor%20Plans/_t/b2_png.jpg |

☑ Render the URL as a banner instead of as a hyperlink

Description

| |

[Save]   [Cancel]

Figure 9-63. *Add a promoted result as the query rule's action*

10.   Perform the same steps for a few beachfront properties in the Actions setting of the new query rule. Once that is completed, the Actions setting should look like Figure 9-64.

Actions

When your rule fires, it can enhance search results in three ways. It can add promoted results above the ranked results. It can also add blocks of additional results. Like normal results, these blocks can be promoted to always appear above ranked results or ranked so they only appear if highly relevant. Finally, the rule can change ranked results, such as tuning their ordering.

Promoted Results

1 ▾ Beachfront property edit remove

2 ▾ Beachfront property edit remove

Add Promoted Result

Result Blocks

Add Result Block

Change ranked results by changing the query

Figure 9-64. *Configure Actions for a query rule*

11. Continue down the page and expand the Publishing section. Ensure the Is Active check box is selected and enter date values for Start Date and End Date to make sure this query rule is only active during certain dates (see Figure 9-65). Click Save to create the new query rule.

Figure 9-65. Configure Publishing for a query rule to specify when the rule is active

Once the query rule is created, we see a summary of the query rule from the Manage Query Rules page like that shown in Figure 9-66, when filtered by the Floor Plan result source. This is a quick way to view all query rules that can be invoked at this site.

Figure 9-66. Summary of the new query rule

12. To test the query rule, navigate to the search page to ensure the new query rule is applied. On the search page, enter floor plans in the search box. You should see the promoted results shown in Figure 9-67 appear at the top of the page.

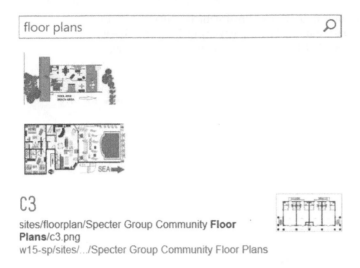

Figure 9-67. *Search results page with promoted results after the new query rule is triggered*

Adding a Result Type for Floor Plans to Use Best Bet Item Display Templates

Our next scenario is to create a result type for Floor Plans so that when users search for floor plans, they will be able to quickly spot the results in the Floor Plans result source from all other results in the list.

1. From the Specter Group public-facing site, click Site Settings.

2. Under the Search section, click Result Types.

3. On the Manage Result Types page, click New Result Type at the top. Enter Floor Plans as the name of the new result type. Next to Conditions, select the Floor Plan result source to match (see Figure 9-68). By configuring the result source as its only condition, any result item in the Floor Plan result source will use this result type for rendering.

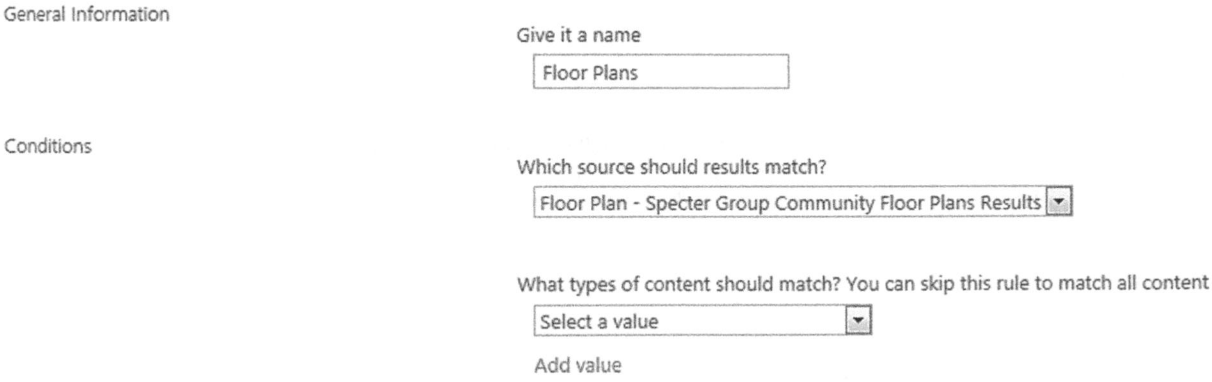

General Information

Give it a name

> Floor Plans

Conditions

Which source should results match?

> Floor Plan - Specter Group Community Floor Plans Results ▾

What types of content should match? You can skip this rule to match all content

> Select a value ▾

Add value

Figure 9-68. *Create a new result type for all items in a result source*

4. Next, for the Actions property, we need to select the Best Bet Item display template from the drop-down list to highlight the floor plan results the users are interested in (see Figure 9-69).

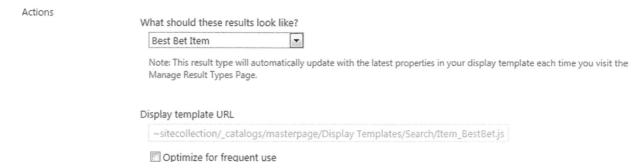

Actions

What should these results look like?

Best Bet Item ▾

Note: This result type will automatically update with the latest properties in your display template each time you visit the Manage Result Types Page.

Display template URL

~sitecollection/_catalogs/masterpage/Display Templates/Search/Item_BestBet.js

☐ Optimize for frequent use

Figure 9-69. *Configure the new result type to use the Best Bet Item display template*

5. Click Save to create the result type. On the Manage Result Types page, we can view a summary of the new result type (see Figure 9-70).

1 ▾   Floor Plans   4/7/2013

Match these types of content
SharePoint Picture Library List Item

Display results with this template
Best Bet Item

Figure 9-70. *Summary of the new result type*

6. To test the new Floor Plans result type, navigate to the search page and enter `Floor Plans` in the search box. You should see the results shown in Figure 9-71.

 C3

SPECTER GROUP - PAGES

CatalogItem-Property-Type   3/25/2013 7:18 AM System Account
System Account ... **Floor-Plans**   3/31/2013 7:06 PM System
Account System Account System Account Body only ...
w15-sp/Pages/Forms/AllItems.aspx

CATEGORY - PROPERTY - TYPE

Floor Plans ... Lorem ipsum dolor sit amet, consectetur adipiscing elit
... Maecenas massa arcu, posuere eget hendrerit at, venenatis sit
amet elit ...
w15-sp/Pages/Category-Property-Type.aspx

 2BD

Figure 9-71. *Search results page with promoted results at the top and best bet rendering of all floor plan items after the new query rule is triggered and the new result type is added*

Now we have the promoted results at the top of the page and each floor plan result is rendered using the Best Bet Item display template so that they are distinguished from the rest of the results in the list.

Summary

With the new publishing and search features in SharePoint 2013, we are able to use the power of search to surface dynamic web content on sites. In this chapter, we learned how to create beautiful search experiences using the new user experience framework in SharePoint 2013 by using the new Content Search web part combined with HTML, JavaScript, CSS, query rules, result types, and display templates. We created a content rollup solution by creating custom display templates for SharePoint's Content Search web part. Then, we look at how to fine-tune search queries and customize the display of results in a search by using query rules and result types to improve the search experience.

CHAPTER 10

Building Rich Interactive Forms

In the previous chapter we walked you through a step-by-step guide on how to use the new search-driven content capabilities. In this chapter we demonstrate how you can build feature-rich forms on SharePoint 2013 that leverage the new client-side enhanced APIs. We continue to make use of the Twitter Bootstrap framework; in this scenario we integrate with SharePoint 2013 some of Bootstrap's built in components such as the Typeahead, which provides autocomplete functionality, in addition to the built-in CSS styles that we apply to our form. We also make use of several open source jQuery plug-ins to handle validation and date formatting to enhance the user experience before data is posted to SharePoint.

Our Scenario

As with every other chapter in this book, we would like to provide you with a solution within the context of building the Specter Group public web site features. Specter Group would like to have an online Open House Registration system to allow potential buyers to attend any scheduled event. Users will fill out a short form that allows them to select the Open House and fill out basic information. This information will then be saved for Specter Group internal staff to review.

The New REST API

SharePoint 2013 offers a new App development model and also includes several client-side APIs. One of the most appealing ones is the REST API, which allows you to retrieve data such as list, web, and site information from custom applications or components, both inside and outside of your SharePoint site. We use this API throughout our exercise.

If you are familiar with REST, then it will be simple enough for you to call this API. For example, if you wanted to get all the publishing pages from your site and in particular only the Title field, you can do this either programmatically via JavaScript or typing the following URL in the web browser:

```
http://spectergroup.com/_api/web/lists/Pages/items/?$select=Title.
```

The response you get from the server is shown in Listing 10-1.

Listing 10-1. Server Response When Typing the URL in the Browser

```
<?xml version="1.0" encoding="utf-8"?>
<feed xml:base="http://spectergroup.com/_api/" xmlns="http://www.w3.org/2005/Atom"
    xmlns:d="http://schemas.microsoft.com/ado/2007/08/dataservices"
    xmlns:m="http://schemas.microsoft.com/ado/2007/08/dataservices/metadata"
    xmlns:georss="http://www.georss.org/georss" xmlns:gml="http://www.opengis.net/gml">
```

```
<id>ec6b06fe-6c82-4269-85dc-3a5c65746f4b</id>
<title />
<updated>2013-01-17T20:38:40Z</updated>
<entry m:etag="&quot;52&quot;">
  <id>11b04758-94bc-445c-9c95-16841ace8552</id>
  <category term="SP.Data.PagesItem"
      scheme="http://schemas.microsoft.com/ado/2007/08/dataservices/scheme" />
  <link rel="edit" href="Web/Lists(guid'0ba42e94-8f5c-444d-b7b1-14280729ed5b')/Items(2)" />
  <title />
  <updated>2013-01-17T20:38:40Z</updated>
  272103_1_En
    <name />
  </author>
  <content type="application/xml">
    <m:properties>
      <d:Title>Home</d:Title>
    </m:properties>
  </content>
</entry>
<entry m:etag="&quot;8&quot;">
  <id>f0adff88-b414-4148-b214-454c5fbd08ba</id>
  <category term="SP.Data.PagesItem"
      scheme="http://schemas.microsoft.com/ado/2007/08/dataservices/scheme" />
  <link rel="edit"
      href="Web/Lists(guid'0ba42e94-8f5c-444d-b7b1-14280729ed5b')/Items(13)" />
  <title />
  <updated>2013-01-17T20:38:40Z</updated>
  272103_1_En
    <name />
  </author>
  <content type="application/xml">
    <m:properties>
      <d:Title>ContactUs</d:Title>
    </m:properties>
  </content>
</entry>
</feed>
```

There are many complex API calls you can make with REST. You can select the response format by specifying this at the time of making the call using either 'application/json;odata=verbose' in the accept header to get a JSON response or 'application/atom+xml' in the accept header to get an Atom formatted response. The default format is Atom, however, and it is shown in Listing 10-1.

■ **Tip** To learn more about supported REST Services Architecture, URL syntax, and namespaces, visit http://sprwd.com/aakzgfp. JSON is a widely used lightweight data interchange format; you can learn more at JSON.org.

Creating a Registration Form

The sample form we will create in this walkthrough will be created using a page layout that includes all the necessary scripts and logic. We then create a new publishing content page from this layout and publish it on the web site for anonymous users to fill out. The form uses two SharePoint lists, "Open Houses," which is used to retrieve all Open House events, and "Open House Registrations," which is used to save user registrations, as shown in Figure 10-1.

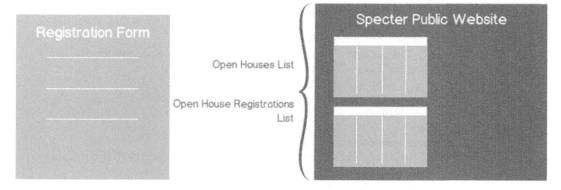

Figure 10-1. *The event registration system design*

▪ **Tip**   To learn how to create SharePoint Apps go to `http://sprwd.com/42etghp`. To learn about creating page layouts, see Chapter 7.

Creating the Page Layout

Our first task is to create a page layout, a topic we covered in Chapter 7. The following steps describe how to create a page layout for our rich form.

1.   Navigate to the Design Manager in a browser.

2.   Click Step 6 on Design Manager's left navigation pane, Edit Page Layouts.

3.   In the middle of the page, click the Create Page Layout link to open a dialog box.

4.   Provide a Name, select the Specter Group master page and the Welcome page content type.

5.   Click OK.

6.   Open the page layout via Dreamweaver. You will find this recently created layout in the root of the Master Pages and Page Layouts Location.

▪ **Tip**   A good place to move our recently created page layout is the design folder we originally created (SpecterGroup) where all other design artifacts reside and that also resides within the root of the Master Page Gallery.

---

7. Add the Form HTML markup inside PlaceHolderMain, which already has the Bootstrap CSS classes referenced as shown in Listing 10-2.

Listing 10-2. The HTML Form Using the Bootstrap Styles

```
<div class="container-fluid">
    <div class="row-fluid">
        <div class="span4 offset4 well">
            <form class="form-horizontal" id="openHouseRegistration" action="">
             <fieldset>
                <div class="control-group">
                    <label class="control-label" for="firstname">First Name</label>
                     <div class="controls">
                        <input type="text" id="firstname"
                                    name="firstname" placeholder="" />
                    </div>
                </div>
                <div class="control-group">
                    <label class="control-label" for="lastname">Last Name</label>
                     <div class="controls">
                        <input type="text" id="lastname"
                                    name="lastname" placeholder="" />
                    </div>
                </div>
                <div class="control-group">
                    <label class="control-label" for="email">E-mail</label>
                     <div class="controls">
                        <div class="input-prepend"><span class="add-on">
                            <i class="icon-envelope"></i></span>
                                <input type="text" id="email" name="email" />
                        </div>
                        </div>
                </div>
                <div class="control-group">
                    <label class="control-label" for="spectertypeahead">
                                    Select an Open House</label>
                        <div class="controls">
                            <div class="input-append">
                                <input type="text" id="spectertypeahead"
                                    name="spectertypeahead"/>
                                <span class="add-on"><i class="icon-calendar"></i></span></div>
                            </div>
                </div>
                <div class="control-group">
                    <div class="controls">
                        <button class="btn btn-success">Register me!</button>
                    </div>
                        </div>
                </fieldset>
            </form>
        </div>
    </div>
</div>
```

Because the Specter HTML master page references all the necessary Bootstrap JavaScript and CSS we included in Chapter 5, our form should display as shown in Figure 10-2 when previewed.

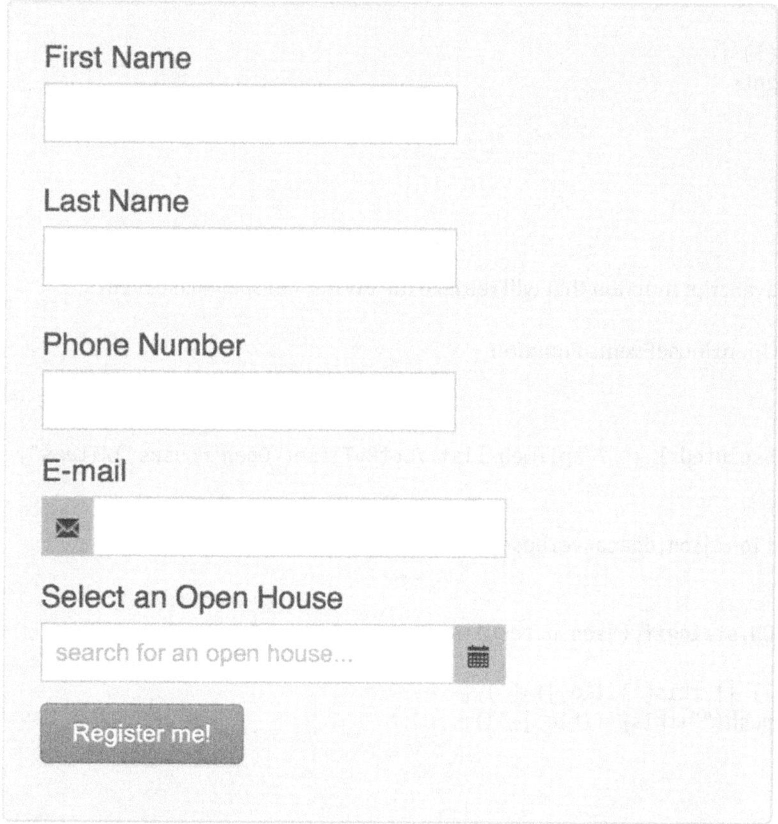

Figure 10-2. *The Open House Registration form using Bootstrap styles*

Adding JavaScript Code

Now that we have our HTML, we need to include JavaScript code to the <HEAD> section of our page layout as the open source JavaScript libraries we use throughout this exercise were not included in the general design and therefore are not included in the HTML master page created in Chapter 4. To ensure these libraries are added to the <HEAD> tag of your page, you must place your code within the content placeholder, PlaceHolderAdditionalPageHead. The JavaScript code starts by creating an array called openHouseEvents that will hold retrieved items. A shell for the function responsible for making the REST call to retrieve these items is added that we will call GetOpenHouseEvents, as shown on Listing 10-3.

Listing 10-3. The Initial Script Tag With Declared Array and Shell for our Function That Retrieves Open House Events via REST

```
<script type="text/javascript">
    var openHouseEvents=[];
     jQuery(document).ready(function($) {
        //retrieve all open house events
        GetOpenHouseEvents($);
    });
    function GetOpenHouseEvents($){
    }
</script>
```

In Listing 10-4, we present the entire JavaScript function that will retrieve the events, GetOpenHouseEvents.

Listing 10-4. The Full Contents of the GetOpenHouseEvents Function

```
function GetOpenHouseEvents($) {
    $.ajax({
        url: _spPageContextInfo.webAbsoluteUrl + "/_api/web/lists/GetByTitle('Open Houses')/items",
        type: 'GET',
        async:false,
        headers: {"accept": "application/json;odata=verbose",},
        dataType: 'JSON',
        success: function(json) {
            var obj = $.parseJSON(JSON.stringify(json.d.results));
            $.each(obj, function() {
                if(this['Title']!=null || this['Title']!='') {
                    openHouseEvents.push(""+this['Title']+"");
                }
            });
        },
        error: function (XMLHttpRequest, textStatus, errorThrown) {
            alert("error :"+XMLHttpRequest.responseText);
        }
    });
}
```

There are many things going on within this function. A standard jQuery-based Ajax call is used, but the URL parameter value is of special interest. Notice how the code uses the existing page client-side variable available to you _spPageContextInfo.webAbsoluteUrl and concatenate it with the actual REST query. In other words, you don't have to hard-code the base URL. The _spPageContextInfo variable is set by SharePoint for every page; it includes other useful properties such as WebTitle, webLogoUrl, and userId to name a few.

■ **Caution**   If you find that your REST calls are not working, always ensure you have the proper headers. The ACCEPT header value must be set to "application/json;odata=verbose".

Once you receive a successful response from the server, each items is stored in a variable. You then take each item's Title property and add it to the global array that was created, openHouseEvents. You do this because Bootstrap Typeahead (see the section "Using Bootstrap Typeahead" later in this chapter) expects a properly formatted JSON string. The response for this query actually returns a lot of metadata for each of the items, as shown in Figure 10-3.

```
▼ json: [object Object]
  ▼ d: [object Object]
    ▼ results: [object Array]
      ▼ 0: [object Object]
        ▶ AttachmentFiles: [object Object]
          Attachments: false
          AuthorId: 1073741823
        ▶ ContentType: [object Object]
          ContentTypeId: "0x01001D694E17219E6644A38DED24A39EBD03"
          Created: "2013-01-20T16:53:41Z"
          EditorId: 1073741823
          Event_x0020_Date: "2013-01-19T02:00:00Z"
        ▶ FieldValuesAsHtml: [object Object]
        ▶ FieldValuesAsText: [object Object]
        ▶ FieldValuesForEdit: [object Object]
        ▶ File: [object Object]
          FileSystemObjectType: 0
        ▶ FirstUniqueAncestorSecurableObject: [object Object]
        ▶ Folder: [object Object]
          GUID: "31dd728d-c2c7-464b-8054-f5d3704bae66"
          ID: 1
          Id: 1
          Modified: "2013-01-20T16:53:41Z"
          OData__UIVersionString: "1.0"
        ▶ ParentList: [object Object]
        ▶ RoleAssignments: [object Object]
        ▶ Specter_x0020_Community: [object Object]
          Title: "Otay Crossing Grand Opening"
        ▶ __metadata: [object Object]
        ▶ __proto__: [object Object] 🔒
      ▶ 1: [object Object]
```

Figure 10-3. *REST call response without selecting specific fields returns all metadata for each List item*

What if you wanted to only get specific List item fields? You can modify the url value in Listing 10-4 with the following URL:

```
"/_api/web/lists/GetByTitle('Open Houses')/items/?$select=Title,Event_x0020_Date"
```

This indeed returns only the fields we wish to retrieve, as shown in Figure 10-4.

```
Object { results=[2] }
[ Object { __metadata={…}, Title="Grand Opening", Event_x0020_Date="2013-02-20T16:00:00Z" }, Object { __metadata={…},
Title="10 Year Anniversary", Event_x0020_Date="2013-01-25T08:00:00Z" } ]
Object { __metadata={…}, Title="Grand Opening", Event_x0020_Date="2013-02-20T16:00:00Z" }
Object { id="f0f0f5c1-2e52-4560 8d42-b2ud951cc737", uri="http://192.168.3.120:45...844228992f68')/Items(3)",
etag=""1"", more… }
"Grand Opening"
"2013-02-20T16:00:00Z"
Object { __metadata={…}, Title="10 Year Anniversary", Event_x0020_Date="2013-01-25T08:00:00Z" }
Object { id="49acd7e3-bdbe-48a1-b73b-7dd98b14156a", uri="http://192.168.3.120:45...844228992f68')/Items(4)",
etag=""1"", more… }
"10 Year Anniversary"
"2013-01-25T08:00:00Z"
```

Figure 10-4. *Retrieving specific metadata yields this response, which contains only the Title and Event Date*

Using Bootstrap Typeahead

One of the features we'd like to implement on our registration form is the ability to autocomplete or suggest events available when a user starts typing. This is a common feature found in many custom apps and web sites. For example, when using Google search, as you start typing, autocomplete shows up to assist in finding what we need.

Typeahead is the perfect component to help us make this happen. Now that our JavaScript function GetOpenHouseEvents is working and storing data in our array, we use a single line of code to implement the Typeahead.

You only need to modify the previous function triggered on the document ready event, and add code to initialize the Typeahead component as shown in Listing 10-5.

Listing 10-5. The Modified Document Ready Function to Include Initializing Typeahead

```
jQuery(document).ready(function($) {
    //retrieve all open house events
    GetOpenHouseEvents($);

    //initialize the typeahead
    $('#spectertypeahead').typeahead({source: openHouseEvents });
});
```

In Listing 10-5, you are getting a handle of the input text field with the ID spectertypeahead. The code then initializes the typeahead plugin on that selector and passes the contents of your array as the data source. At this point your Typeahead functionality should be fully working on your form and should look similar to Figure 10-5.

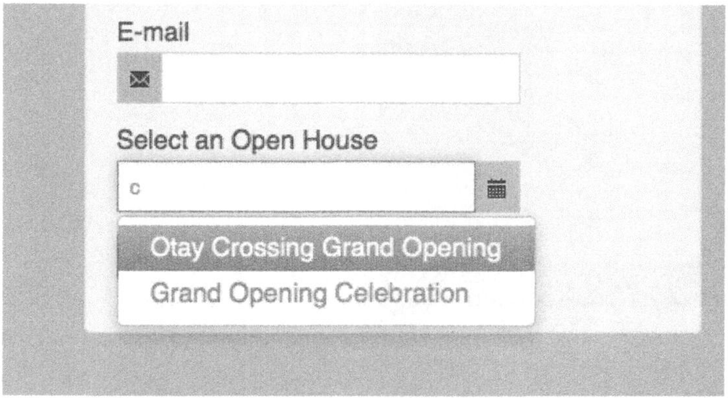

Figure 10-5. *fully working Typeahead showing open house events by title*

You may extend the previous example in many ways, including adding columns to what is displayed on autocomplete. To add a column such as the date you must modify your JavaScript function GetOpenHouseEvents, in particular the portion where each event is added to the array. The previous code currently only adds the Title property, but you are retrieving the Event Date as well. To use the Event Date column, refer to Listing 10-6.

Listing 10-6. Adding the Event Date to Each Array Item

```
function GetOpenHouseEvents() {
    $.ajax({
        url: _spPageContextInfo.webAbsoluteUrl + "/_api/web/lists/GetByTitle('Open Houses')/items",
        type: 'GET',
        async:false,
        headers: {"accept": "application/json;odata=verbose",},
        dataType: 'JSON',
        success: function(json) {
            var obj = $.parseJSON(JSON.stringify(json.d.results));
            $.each(obj, function() {
                if(this['Title']!=null || this['Title']!='') {
                    openHouseEvents.push(""+this['Title']+ " - "+ this["Event_x0020_Date"] +"");
                }
            });
        },
        error: function (XMLHttpRequest, textStatus, errorThrown) {
            alert("error :"+XMLHttpRequest.responseText);
        }
    });
}
```

Once you update the code shown in Listing 10-6, the date displays; however, it is not formatted correctly, as shown in Figure 10-6.

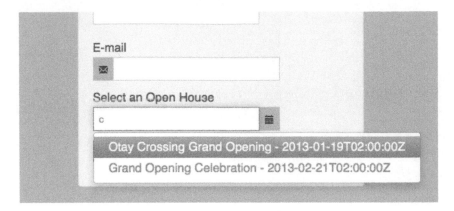

Figure 10-6. *Typeahead displays our open house event title and event date in ISO format*

It would be nice to display the date to the right of the title of every event in the friendly format of, for example, "01 Jan". There are many ways to format a date using JavaScript including open source frameworks, jQuery plug-ins, and even your own Date string processor. In the next example we leverage the Data.js framework, which is extremely powerful and can be used for more complex use cases.

■ **Tip** We use the open source Date.js library for our formatting. Download and learn more about this framework at http://sprwd.com/ddd9ztv.

After adding the Date.js library to your Specter HTML master page, you are ready to implement the formatting of your event date (see Listing 10-7).

Listing 10-7. The Success Function Portion of the GetOpenHouseEvents Function Applying Friendly Date Formatting

```
$.each(obj, function() {
    if(this['Title']!=null || this['Title']!='') {
        openHouseEvents.push(""+this['Title']+ " - "+
            new Date(this["Event_x0020_Date"]).toString("d MMM")+"");
    }
});
```

Once you make this modification to your function, the date is shown in the desired format, as shown in Figure 10-7.

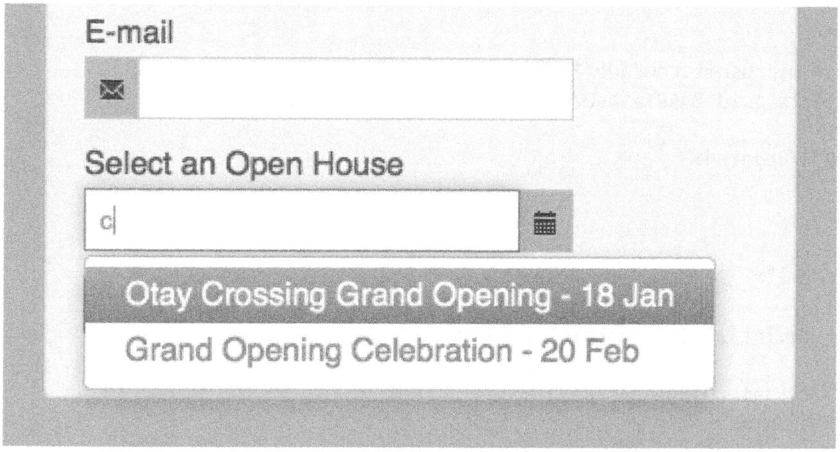

Figure 10-7. *Typeahead shows open house title and formatted date*

Once the date is included in the values shown on the Typeahead drop-down, users can search for an open house by date or any keyword.

Saving Form Data to SharePoint List

At this point we have seen how we can use SharePoint 2013's REST API to retrieve information from our SharePoint site, so we are now ready to see how we can save information to a SharePoint list.

The REST URL is similar, however we must add data in JSON format with the name and values of the fields that correspond to the List fields that we wish to save values for.

Determining the Entity Type of Our List Item

To successfully save a new SharePoint list item, we must specify the entity type of the object. You'll notice the type of item is set to SP.Data.Open_x0020_House_x0020_RegistrationsListItem and this certainly does not seem generic. So how do we obtain this?

We can determine the object type by going to the following URL on the web browser:

http://spectergroup.com/_api/web/lists?$select=Title,Id,Description,BaseTemplate,ListItemEntityTypeFullName

Querying for this metadata allows us to retrieve the information we need to be able to save new items, and the response is shown in Listing 10-8.

Listing 10-8. The Response We Get Shows the Entity Type Full Name for the List Item We Want to Save

```
<?xml version="1.0" encoding="utf-8" ?>
<feed xml:base="http://spectergroup.com/_api/" xmlns="http://www.w3.org/2005/Atom"
      xmlns:d="http://schemas.microsoft.com/ado/2007/08/dataservices"
      xmlns:m="http://schemas.microsoft.com/ado/2007/08/dataservices/metadata"
      xmlns:georss="http://www.georss.org/georss" xmlns:gml="http://www.opengis.net/gml">
  <id>17f84048-d7a5-4e31-b2d2-e492aec29dc7</id>
  <title />
  <updated>2013-01-17T01:20:22Z</updated>
  - <entry m:etag=""3="""">
    <id>http://spectergroup.com/_api/Web/Lists(guid'8b581a1a-0789-4b4c-8f23-58fcee487feb')
```

```
    </id>
    <category term="SP.List"
            scheme="http://schemas.microsoft.com/ado/2007/08/dataservices/scheme" />
    <link rel="edit" href="Web/Lists(guid'8b581a1a-0789-4b4c-8f23-58fcee487feb')" />
    <title />
    <updated>2013-01-17T01:20:22Z</updated>
  - 272103_1_En
    <name />
    </author>
  - <content type="application/xml">
    - <m:properties>
      <d:BaseTemplate m:type="Edm.Int32">100</d:BaseTemplate>
      <d:Description />
      <d:Id m:type="Edm.Guid">8b581a1a-0789-4b4c-8f23-58fcee487feb</d:Id>
        <d:ListItemEntityTypeFullName>
            SP.Data.Open_x0020_House_x0020_RegistrationsListItem
        </d:ListItemEntityTypeFullName>
      <d:Title>Open House Registrations</d:Title>
    </m:properties>
    </content>
  </entry>
</feed>
```

Now that we know the entity type of the list item we would like to save, we can create our JavaScript function, which we will name `RegisterUserForEvent` as shown in Listing 10-9.

Listing 10-9. The JavaScript Function to Save New User Registrations Uses the REST API

```
function RegisterUserForEvent(){
    $.ajax({
        url: _spPageContextInfo.webAbsoluteUrl +
            "/_api/web/lists/GetByTitle('Open House Registrations')/items",
        type: 'POST',
        dataType:"JSON",
        data: JSON.stringify({
            '__metadata': {
                'type': 'SP.Data.Open_x0020_House_x0020_RegistrationsListItem'
            },
            'Title': $('#firstname').val() +" "+ $('#lastname').val() + " registered!",
            'Last_x0020_Name': $('#firstname').val(),
            'First_x0020_Name': $('#lastname').val(),
            'Email': $('#email').val()
        }),
        headers: {
            'accept': "application/json;odata=verbose",
            'content-type': "application/json;odata=verbose",
            'X-RequestDigest': $('#__REQUESTDIGEST').val()
        },
        success: doSuccess,
        error: doError
    });
}
```

Taking a closer look at this function, you will see that we use jQuery to get a handle on each form text field by ID and map it to the appropriate List field. For the List Item Title field, we simply concatenate the first name and last name plus another string.

■ **Tip** You will also notice on our function shown in Listing 10-9, we include additional header information. Of special interest is the X-RequestDigest the value of which we obtain from the hidden form field. We include as it is a security measure related to Cross-Site Request Forgery (CSRF). You can learn more about security best practices for SharePoint at http://sprwd.com/56hfm9n.

Within our Ajax code snippet we have specified the success and error statuses to be handled by a function. Both functions are shown in Listing 10-10. Both functions are very straightforward. In the case of a successful save action, we simply output an alert message indicating this. In the case when we receive an error, we output the actual error in a friendly format.

Listing 10-10. The Success and Error Handling Functions

```
doSuccess= function () {
    alert('You are now registered, thank you!');
}
doError= function (err) {
    alert(JSON.stringify(err));
}
```

Using Twitter Bootstrap Modal to Show Success Message

We are only displaying a simple JavaScript alert for a successful save, but we can certainly make use of enticing Twitter Bootstrap features to make this look better! To do this, you can modify the doSuccess function, as shown in Listing 10-11 and add Bootstrap's Modal component.

Listing 10-11. Using Bootstrap Modal Component on Successful Registration

```
doSuccess= function () {
    $('.modal').modal('show');
}
```

In addition to modifying the doSuccess function, you must also add the HTML markup to the custom page layout you created earlier in this chapter to declare the Bootstrap styled modal as shown in Listing 10-12.

Listing 10-12. The Bootstrap Modal HTML Markup to Display on Successful Open House Registration

```
<div id="myModal" class="modal hide fade" tabindex="-1" role="dialog"
        aria-labelledby="myModalLabel" aria-hidden="true">
    <div class="modal-header">
        <h3 id="myModalLabel ">SUCCESS! - You are registered.</h3>
    </div>
    <div class="modal-body">
        <p>We have registered you for this Open House, you will receive an email confirmation shortly.
        <br/><br/>-Specter Group.
```

```
            </p>
        </div>
        <div class="modal-footer">
            <button class="btn" data-dismiss="modal" aria-hidden="true">Close</button>
        </div>
</div>
```

After a successful registration, users will now see the modal as shown in Figure 10-8.

SUCCESS! - YOU ARE REGISTERED.

We have registered you for this Open House, you will receive an email confirmation shortly.

-Specter Group.

Close

Figure 10-8. Bootstrap modal dialog box shown on successful open house registration

The data that is saved is shown in Figure 10-9.

Title	Jessica Specter registered!
First Name	Specter
Last Name	Jessica
Email	jessica@spectergroup.com

Created at 1/23/2013 9:55 PM by   System Account

Last modified at 1/23/2013 9:55 PM by   System Account

Close

Figure 10-9. The saved open house registration list item

Implementing Form Validation

Specter Group would like to ensure as much as possible that they receive valid information when a user submits a registration for an open house. Just as with Date formatting, there are multiple methods to provide client-side form validation, including plug-ins, frameworks, and even custom code. We will implement basic validation by leveraging a powerful, preexisting plug-in, an open source jQuery plug-in for Bootstrap, jqBootstrapValidation. You can download jqBootstrapValidation from http://sprwd.com/8qwfa32.

Once you have included the jqBootstrapValidation plugin JavaScript file on your HTML master page, you are ready to use the plugin. First, you will need to tell the validation plugin what type of fields you would like to validate, as shown in Listing 10-13. Add this code block to your page layout placeholder called PlaceHolderAdditionalPageHead as you did in previous examples.

Listing 10-13. Configuring the Validation Plug-In

```
<script>
    jQuery(document).ready(function ($) {
        $("input,select,textarea").not("[type=submit]").jqBootstrapValidation();
    });
</script>
```

You can then modify your HTML markup to perform the desired validation as shown in Listing 10-14. The code checks for a valid e-mail address and at least two characters for the first and last names.

Listing 10-14. HTML Markup Using Validation Plug-In

```
<form class="form-horizontal" id="openHouseRegistration" action="">
    <fieldset>
        <div class="control-group">
            <label class="control-label" for="firstname">First Name</label>
            <div class="controls">
                <input type="text" id="firstname" name="firstname" minlength="2"
                    data-validation-minlength-message="Please type your first name.No initials."/>
            </div>
        </div>
        <div class="control-group">
            <label class="control-label" for="lastname">Last Name</label>
            <div class="controls">
                <input type="text" id="lastname" name="lastname" minlength="2"
                        data-validation-minlength-message="Please type your last name. No initials."/>
            </div>
        </div>
        <div class="control-group">
            <label class="control-label" for="phone">Phone Number</label>
            <div class="controls">
                <div class="input-prepend">
                    <input type="text" id="phone" pattern="^\(?([0-9]{3})\)?[-. ]?([0-9]{3})
                        [-. ]?([0-9]{4})$" data-validation-pattern-message="How about a valid
                        phone number?"/>
                </div>
            </div>
        </div>
        <div class="control-group">
```

```
                <label class="control-label" for="email">E-mail</label>
                <div class="controls">
                    <div class="input-prepend">
                        <span class="add-on"><i class="icon-envelope"></i></span>
                        <input type="email" id="email"
                            data-validation-email-message="How about a valid email address?" />
                    </div>
                </div>
            </div>
            <div class="control-group">
                <label class="control-label" for="spectertypeahead">Select an Open House </label>
                <div class="controls">
                    <div class="input-append">
                        <input type="text" id="spectertypeahead"
                            name="spectertypeahead" placeholder="search for an open house..." />
                        <span class="add-on"><i class="icon-calendar"></i></span>
                    </div>
                </div>
            </div>
            <div class="control-group">
                <div class="controls">
                    <button class="btn btn-success"
                        onClick="javascript:RegisterUserForEvent();return false;">Register me!
                    </button>
                </div>
            </div>
        </div>
    </fieldset>
</form>
```

The validation plugin is very flexible. As an example, you can specify a RegEx pattern to validate the phone number. Entering incorrect information displays the error messages configured as shown in Figure 10-10.

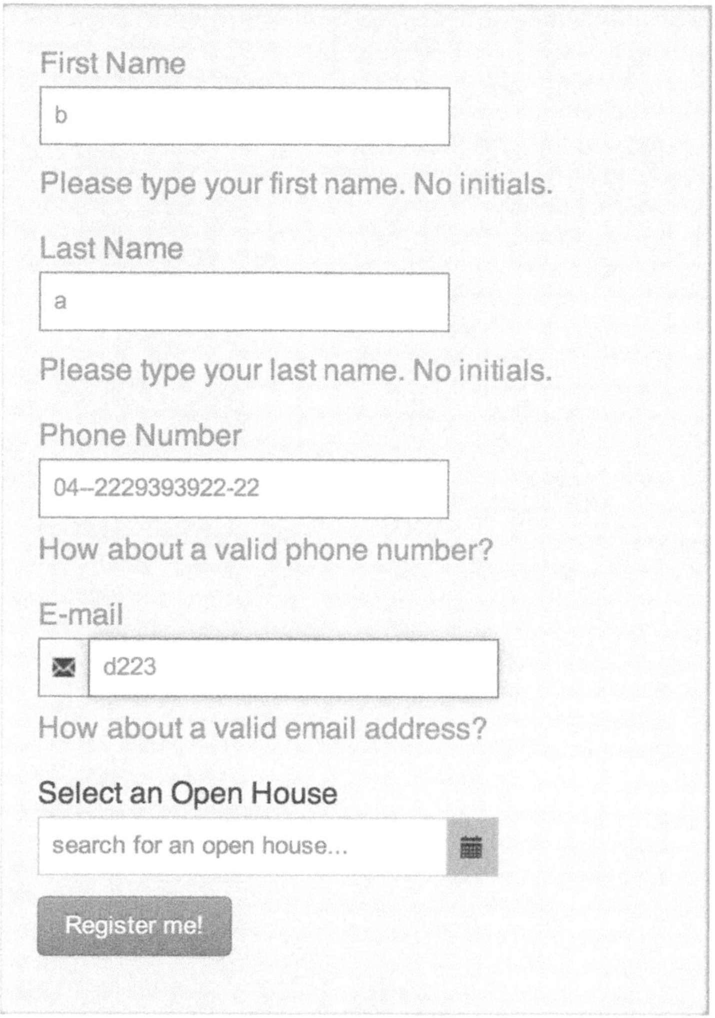

Figure 10-10. *The validation on the open house registration form fully working, displaying error messages instantaneously*

■ **Tip** For more complex validation, be sure to take a look at the documentation for the jqBoostrapValidation plugin at http://sprwd.com/8qwfa32

Summary

In this chapter we worked with the REST API in the context of building a rich open house registration form for the Specter web site. We showed how you can retrieve and save information and the specific syntax needed. In addition, to further enrich the form functionality, we implemented the Bootstrap Typeahead and used other open source frameworks to demonstrate instant form validation. In Chapter 11 you will learn how to use new client-side APIs and HTML5 to upload multiple files that are larger than 1.5 MB to SharePoint.

CHAPTER 11

Uploading and Working with Files

The ability to allow users to upload files is a very important feature in modern web design. SharePoint provides out-of-the-box file upload capability, but the out-of-the-box file upload control is embedded in a SharePoint page without providing any extensibility to this feature. There are times when business logic requires us to provide users with file upload capability without ever leaving the page (e.g., when filling out a form) or to provide a different user interface or file preview capability. In such advanced scenarios for working with files, we need to allow users to upload files to SharePoint from the client side.

Traditionally, HTTP and HTML have provided very limited support for accessing files on a client device. Even as the rest of the web has been evolving, the way we work with files has changed very little since it was first introduced with the <input type="file"> control. Now in HTML5 and related APIs, we now have far more options for working with files than ever before. Specifically, before SharePoint 2013, uploading files to SharePoint from a client application was a daunting undertaking. With the new client object model in SharePoint 2013, we can perform basic operations on files through JavaScript and we can now upload files that are up to 2 GB.

In this chapter, we first discuss the basics for working with files using the HTML5 File API and then we discuss the enhancements and usage scenarios of various client-side APIs in SharePoint 2013. For our Specter scenario, we first demonstrate how to access local file resources using the HTML5 File API and then how to upload files to SharePoint by leveraging the new client object model. We continue to use Twitter Bootstrap framework to enhance the user interface and user experience. In this chapter, we demonstrate how to combine the features of HTML5, Bootstrap plug-ins, and the SharePoint 2013 client object model to support advanced scenarios for working with files.

Our Scenario

As already mentioned, although SharePoint provides out-of-the-box file upload capability, it does not always satisfy all business requirements. Therefore, we need to build a solution that allows users to upload files to SharePoint from the client side. The public Specter Group Community web site needs a way to allow users to upload pictures of their communities to their sites. Because this is a community site shared by many users, Specter Group wants to provide a simple user interface that allows users to upload their pictures without leaving the user's Community home page. The user should see a file upload control on the home page (see Figure 11-1). The user first clicks the Select file button, which opens the File Select window to allow the user to select multiple local files to upload.

Figure 11-1. *Example of file upload control*

After the user selects a file, the page displays a preview of the image next to the file upload control (see Figure 11-2). The user now has the option to click the Change button to change the file selected, the Remove button to remove the file selected, or the Upload button to upload the file to SharePoint. After the image is uploaded, the image files are all stored in a document library on the community site.

Figure 11-2. *Example of a file upload control, and options to change, remove, and upload files. Once the file is selected from the file system, the file name should be visible in the text box and a preview of the selected file should be visible*

Basics for HTML5 File API

Before we dive into the specific solution, let's take a look at the basics of how to access local file resources using the HTML5 File API. Before HTML5, we had to create custom solutions that relied on browser plug-ins, Adobe Flash, or Microsoft Silverlight for file uploads. It's important to note that out of the box, SharePoint 2013 file upload control supports file upload feature as well as drag and drop for uploading multiple files. When working with Internet Explorer 8, 9, and 10, this feature depends on the UploadCtl ActiveX plug-in. When working with the latest versions of Chrome and Firefox, this feature depends on HTML5. Now when working with local file resources in our own file upload solution, we can use the HTML5 File API, which was introduced to the DOM in HTML5. To name a few commonly used interfaces, the File API includes a FileList interface for accessing selected files from the underlying system. It also includes a File interface to access read-only information about a file such as its name, data, and date last modified. In addition, it has an interface for FileReader, which provides methods to read a file and an event model to obtain the results of these reads. In later sections of this chapter, we look at the FileReader API in more detail.

■ **Note**   To use the File API, we need to make sure the browser supports it. Specifically, the FileReader API works for the following major browsers: Internet Explorer 10+, Firefox 3.6+, Chrome 6.0+, and Opera 11.1+. For a complete list of browsers, refer to http://sprwd.com/15WJfvm. For older browsers, we need to provide a fallback solution that typically requires the use of a browser plug-in, Adobe Flash, or Microsoft Silverlight. For the purpose of this book, we focus our solution on HTML5 and supported browsers.

Accessing a File

The File type is an abstract representation of a file. Each instance of File has several properties:

- Name: The file name.
- size: The size of the file in bytes.
- type: The MIME type of the file

A File object contains all the basic information about a file without providing direct access to the file content. It's important to assess the file's properties before reading the content because file content requires disk access, time, and resources.

Using the File API, we can ask the user to select local files to upload, and then we can read the content from the file before upload. The selection process can be done by either using an HTML `<input type="file" id="input">` element, or by dragging and dropping. HTML5 allows selection of multiple files in these input controls using the `multiple` attribute, as shown in Listing 11-1.

Listing 11-1. The multiple Attribute of the Input Tag Allows Users to Select More Than One File When Browsing for Files

```
<input type="file" multiple />
```

■ **Note**   The `multiple` attribute of the input tag is not supported in Internet Explorer 9 and earlier versions.

To access all the files selected by the user, get the `files` property from the file input control, as shown in Listing 11-2. HTML5 defines a `files` property for all `<input type="file" >` controls. This collection is a FileList, which is an array that contains File objects that represent the files selected by the user.

Listing 11-2. JavaScript Code to Access the First File Using Classical DOM Selector

```
var selected_file = document.getElementById('input').files[0];
```

To access a file, get the file from the `files` collection, as shown in Listing 11-3.

Listing 11-3. jQuery to Access a File Using a jQuery Selector

```
var selected_file = $('#input').get(0).files[0];
```

Change Event

We can access the selected file(s) from an onchange event or we can dynamically add a change listener, as shown in Listing 11-4.

Listing 11-4. Add Change Event to Detect File Upload

```
<input type = "file" id="input" onchange="getFiles(this.files)">
```

The `getFiles()` function in this case is an event handler function we are going to create in the next section, shown in Listing 11-5. Once the user selects a file, the `getFiles()` function gets called with a FileList object containing File objects.

Listing 11-5. Dynamically Add a Change Listener to a File Input Control with ID "Input"

```
var inputElement = document.getElementById("input");
inputElement.addEventListener("change", getFiles, false);
function getFiles() {
    var fileList = this.files;
    /* this file list contains all the selected files */
}
```

To access each file from the FileList array, enumerate through the array, as shown in Listing 11-6.

Listing 11-6. Get a File from the FileList Array

```
for (var i = 0, numFiles = filesList.length; i < numFiles; i++) {
   var file = fileList[i];
     ..
}
```

Getting File Content

Once we have the file, our next step is to read the content from the file. From the HTML5 File API, the FileReader object reads data from a file and stores it in a JavaScript variable. The read is done asynchronously so that the process does not block the browser from other activities.

There are various formats that a FileReader can create to get the content from the file:

- readAsText(): Returns the file content as plain text. It does not properly handle binary files.

- readAsArrayBuffer(): Returns the file content as an ArrayBuffer object (best for binary data such as images).

■ **Note**   If the solution requires the content parameter to be a Base64 encoded byte array, then this option requires a type conversion from the ArrayBuffer object to a Base64 encoded byte array, which might not be easy to implement. We want to use this method when the solution does not require any specific type for the content parameter. We will see a specific implementation for Specter Group that uses this method in the section "Uploading Files to a SharePoint Document Library Using the REST API" later in this chapter.

- readAsDataURL(): Returns the file content as a data URL (can be used in a web page to display the content as an image).

■ **Note**   If the solution requires the content parameter to be a Base64 encoded byte array, then this option requires a type conversion from the Base64 encoded string object to a Base64 encoded byte array. We will see a specific implementation for Specter Group that uses this method in the section "Showing Thumbnails for Images" later in this chapter.

To use these methods, we need to first call the method to initiate a file read, then wait for the load event before the actual read begins. We also need to implement a load event handler to get the result of the read as represented by event.target.result. As seen in Listing 11-7, the onload handler is called when the file is successfully read. The onerror handler is called if an error occurred while the file is being read and event.target.error contains the error information when failed. To get the actual content, the result property of event.target contains the file content on success.

Listing 11-7. When Reading a Plain Text File, We Can Use readAsText()Method to Get the Content in Plain Text Format

```
var reader = new FileReader();
reader.onload = function(event) {
   var contents = event.target.result;
   console.log("File contents: " + contents);
};
```

```
reader.onerror = function(event) {
   console.error("File could not be read! Code " + event.target.error.code);
};
```

```
reader.readAsText(file);
```

When reading an image file, we can use the readAsDataURL() method to get a data URL that contains all of the image data and can be passed directly to the "src" attribute of an image control on a web page, as shown in the example in Listing 11-8.

Listing 11-8. Using the readAsDataURL()Method to Get Content

```
var reader = new FileReader();
reader.onload = function(event) {
   var dataUri = event.target.result;
   img = document.createElement("img");

   img.src = dataUri;
   document.body.appendChild(img);
};

reader.onerror = function(event) {
   console.error("File could not be read! Code " + event.target.error.code);
};

reader.readAsDataURL(file);
```

When dealing with binary files (e.g., image files), we should use the readAsArrayBuffer() method to get the file content in raw bytes, as shown in Listing 11-9. An ArrayBuffer object represents a finite number of bytes.

Listing 11-9. Using the readAsArrayBuffer() Method to Get the File Content

```
var reader = new FileReader();
reader.onload = function(event) {
   var buffer = event.target.result;
   // buffer is an ArrayBuffer object that contains the file content In raw bytes
};

reader.onerror = function(event) {
   console.error("File could not be read! Code " + event.target.error.code);
};

reader.readAsArrayBuffer(file);
```

Client-Side API Enhancements in SharePoint 2013

Before we dive into our specific solution, let's review the basics of how to use SharePoint 2013 client-side APIs to upload files to SharePoint. Microsoft has made a lot of enhancements in the client-side APIs since SharePoint 2010. In SharePoint 2010, the Client-side Object Model was made accessible through Windows Communication Foundation (WCF) entry point client.svc. Developers were not allowed to directly access client.svc, but instead calls to client.svc must go through a supported entry point from the .NET Framework, JavaScript, or Silverlight.

Hence, developers had three different types of client object models to work with: .NET Framework, JavaScript, and Silverlight. It was much easier to access the .NET managed Client-side Object Model through C# or VB.NET by simply adding a reference to the Client-side Object Model proxy assemblies. With the .NET Framework managed Client-side Object Model, developers had Intellisense as well as compile time type checking. With the JavaScript-driven Client-side Object Model, it was much harder to use without compile time type checking and more limited in the operations SharePoint provides.

In SharePoint 2013, the client-side API entry point has been extended with REST capabilities. The old `client.svc` entry point is no longer visible, but instead it is now mapped to the new `/_api` entry point. The new entry point now supports direct access from REST-based calls, accepts HTTP GET, PUT, and POST requests, and it was implemented in accordance with the ODATA protocol. It is now much easier to make a REST-based call from JavaScript than it is to call into the JavaScript-driven Client-side Object Model that SharePoint provides. With all the capabilities of the client-side API now exposed as REST calls, developers can now work with SharePoint on other non-Microsoft platforms by creating HTTP requests using GETs, PUTs, and POSTs. In SharePoint 2010, to perform basic operations on a list, we relied on `ListData.svc`. Now we can use both the JavaScript-driven Client-side Object Model and the REST-based model to perform the same operations on a list.

In summary, SharePoint 2013 offers developers four different client-side APIs to work with:

- .NET Framework client object model

- JavaScript client object model

- Silverlight client object model

- REST/OData endpoints

With all the different types of APIs in SharePoint 2013, it is important to look at different factors to determine the right API to use for development. In the following tip, the reference URL provides additional guidance on which set of APIs to use for common scenarios in SharePoint. For example, the type of application to build can significantly affect the type of API to use. The developer's existing skills can help determine the right API for the application if the developer already has experience in the respective programming models. Finally, where the application runs (server, cloud, client, etc.) can also affect the decision because some environments only support a subset of the APIs.

■ **Tip**   For guidance on which set of APIs can be used for which set of common scenarios of SharePoint solutions, refer to `http://sprwd.com/z3ubdee`.

Uploading Files to a SharePoint Document Library Using the REST API

As mentioned earlier, although SharePoint provides out-of-the-box file upload capability, it does not always satisfy all business requirements. Therefore, we need to build a solution that allows users to upload files to SharePoint from the client side. In the previous section, we introduced various types of SharePoint 2013 client APIs to use to interact directly with SharePoint content from different client technologies. For the purpose of showing the complete upload file solution for Specter Group, we focus on using the REST interface because it supports upload file sizes up to 2 GB.

■ **Note**   Both the JavaScript client object model and the REST interface enable us to upload files to a SharePoint document library. However, when we need to upload a binary file that is larger than 1.5 MB, the REST interface is our only option. The maximum size of a binary file we can create with REST is 2 GB. The JavaScript client object model is limited with uploading files up to 1.5 MB.

SharePoint 2013 provides access to a REST web service that uses the OData protocol to perform Create, Read, Update, and Delete (CRUD) operations on SharePoint list data. Almost every API in the client object models has a corresponding REST endpoint. To use the REST capabilities in SharePoint 2013, we need to construct a RESTful HTTP request to an endpoint that corresponds to the desired operation.

To upload a file to a SharePoint document library, we need to do the following:

1. Before making an HTTP request for creating files in a document library against the REST endpoint of the document library, we must know the URL of the endpoint and the OData representation of the SharePoint entity.

2. To validate the URL of a REST endpoint, navigate to the URL in the browser and ensure the XML returned is correct, as shown in Figure 11-3.

3. Once we have verified the REST endpoint URL, we need to plug the URL into the code, as shown in Listing 11-10. In a later section, "jQuery for Specter Group File Upload," we look at how to integrate this jQuery script with the rest of the Specter upload file solution.

4. Make an HTTP request for creating files in a document library against the REST endpoint of the document library, as shown in Listing 11-10.

   a. Specify that it is a POST http request.

   b. Specify we want the OData representation of the result to be in JSON format.

   c. Specify form digest value for the request.

   d. Set the content length to the length of the file content.

   e. Set the `processData` property to false to ensure no conversion is done on the data property, which is the content of the file.

For example, before making the REST call to upload a file to a folder, let's navigate to the REST endpoint of the folder. To navigate to the REST endpoint of the `Communities` folder in a document library called `Documents` in the `fileuploadtest` site collection, enter the following URL in the browser:

```
http://{webapplicationURL}/sites/fileuploadtest/_api/web/GetFolderByServerRelativeUrl('/sites/
fileuploadtest/Documents/Communities')
```

The browser will return an OData representation of the folder, as shown in Figure 11-3. We use this REST endpoint in Listing 11-10 to add a document to the `Communities` folder in the `Documents` library. Note, if we are uploading a file into the root of the document library, the syntax will look similar to this:

```
http://{webapplicationURL}/sites/fileuploadtest/_api/web/GetFolderByServerRelativeUrl('/sites/
fileuploadtest/Documents')
```

```xml
- <content type="application/xml">
   - <m:properties>
        <d:ItemCount m:type="Edm.Int32">9</d:ItemCount>
        <d:Name>communities</d:Name>
        <d:ServerRelativeUrl>/sites/fileuploadtest/documents/communities</d:ServerRelativeUrl>
        <d:WelcomePage/>
     </m:properties>
  </content>
```

Figure 11-3. XML returned by the browser when navigating to a folder of a SharePoint document library via a REST URL

> ■ **Important** When using jQuery Ajax to make the REST request, we need to pass the file content as the "data" of the request. The data property represents the data to be sent to the server. It is of type `Object` or `string`. By default, the `data` property is always converted to a query string, if the object is not already a string. For our purpose, we need to send the data as a plain object, not a string. Use the `processData:false` option in jQuery Ajax to prevent the data object from being automatically converted into a string.

To create a file in SharePoint, make a POST http request against the REST endpoint of the document library. When making the request, specify whether to receive the OData representation of the result in XML or JSON, as shown in Listing 11-10.

Listing 11-10. Creating a File in SharePoint by Making a POST http Request Against the REST Endpoint of the Document Library

```
// Assume the file object represents the actual file to be uploaded
// Assume the buffer object represents the content of the file
// Make a jQuery ajax request against the REST endpoint URL

$.ajax({
    // Specify the REST endpoint URL that represents the folder for our file and the action to add a file
    url: _spPageContextInfo.webAbsoluteUrl + "/_api/web/" +

GetFolderByServerRelativeUrl('/sites/fileuploadtest/Documents/Communities)/Files/Add(url='"
        + file.name + "',overwrite=true)",

    // Specify this is a POST http request
    method: 'POST',

    // buffer is the content of the file
    data: buffer,

    // Specify the header information of the HTTP request
    headers: {
        // Specify we want the OData representation of the result to be in JSON format

        'content-type': "application/json;odata=verbose",

        // Specify form digest value for the request.
        // Because our solution resides in SharePoint (inline script and stand-alone .js files),
        we do not need
        // to make a separate HTTP request to retrieve the form digest value.
        // Instead, we can retrieve the value in JavaScript.

        'X-RequestDigest': $('#__REQUESTDIGEST').val(),

        // Set the content-length to the length of the file content

        'content-length': buffer.length
    },
```

```
// By default, the data property of an Ajax request is converted to a query string if not already
a string.
// When the processData property is set to false, it tells jQuery Ajax to ensure no conversion is
done on
// the data property. In this case, the data is the buffer object that represents the content of the file.
processData: false,

// Successful upload event handler
success: function (e) {
    alert('successfully done');
},

// Failure upload event handler
error: function (err) {
    alert("Error in JSON: " + JSON.stringify(err));
},
});
```

Implementing the Specter Group File Upload Solution

In the previous sections, we looked at the basics of working with files in HTML5 and how to upload files to SharePoint using the new SharePoint REST API. Now let's dive into our implementation of the Specter Group file upload solution.

Integrating with the Bootstrap File Upload Plug-In

Specter Group would like to provide end users with a file upload solution that is more visually appealing. To do this, we can integrate our solution with the open source jQuery Bootstrap file upload plug-in. For the purpose of demonstrating the file upload feature, we focus our discussion around the jQuery Bootstrap file upload plug-in, assuming the reader has prior knowledge of the Twitter Bootstrap framework.

In Chapter 5, we covered integrating the Bootstrap framework with SharePoint Master Page, but here's a quick recap of how to get started with the Bootstrap framework:

1. Download the Bootstrap artifacts from `http://twitter.github.com/bootstrap`.

2. After uploading the .css, .js, and .img files to their respective folders in the Master Page gallery, we register them in the master page (see an example in Listing 11-11).

   Listing 11-11. Register Reference to Bootstrap CSS Style Sheets in the Header Section of the Master Page

   ```
   <link href="css/bootstrap.css" rel="stylesheet">
   <link href="css/bootstrap-responsive.css" rel="stylesheet">
   ```

Now, let's get started with the Bootstrap file upload plug-in, by performing the following steps:

1. Download the Bootstrap file upload plug-in from `http://sprwd.com/asmsura`.

2. After uploading the .css and .js files to their respective folders in the Master Page gallery, we need to register them in the page layout (see Listings 11-12 and 11-13).

   Listing 11-12. Register Reference to Bootstrap File Upload Plug-In CSS Style Sheets in the Page Layout

   ```
   <link href="css/bootstrap-fileupload.css" rel="stylesheet">
   ```

Listing 11-13. Register Reference to Bootstrap File Upload .js Files in the Page Layout

```
<script src="js/bootstrap-fileupload.js"></script>
```

■ **Note**   For more detailed information about how to integrate the Bootstrap framework with SharePoint Master Page, please refer to Chapter 5.

HTML for Specter Group File Upload

Once the Bootstrap file upload styles and .js files are integrated in SharePoint, we can use the file upload plug-in to create visually appealing file or image upload widgets.

To add HTML5 controls to a SharePoint page, from a SharePoint page, click the gear icon at the top right corner, then click Edit page, as shown in Figure 11-4.

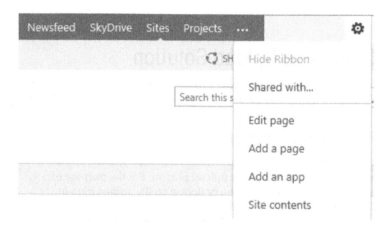

Figure 11-4. *To modify a SharePoint page, click Edit page from the gear in the top right corner*

Click inside of the page's content area, and then click Edit Source toward the right end of the top ribbon menu, as shown in Figure 11-5.

Figure 11-5. *Edit page content on a SharePoint page to add HTML5 controls to the page by clicking the Edit Source button on the ribbon*

To use the file upload plug-in, we need to add data attributes to the HTML controls to trigger functions in the Bootstrap-fileupload.js to handle file input events and control visibility of the HTML controls on the page. As Listing 11-14 shows, the main container should have the .fileupload-new class. The code in Listing 11-14 does the following:

1. If an existing file is present, the css .fileupload-exists class will toggle the visibility of controls.

2. Elements inside the main container with the css .fileupload-new and .fileupload-exists class will be shown or hidden based on the current state.

3. The content of .fileupload-path is replaced with a file name when a file is selected.

4. The Remove button clears the file with data-dismiss="fileupload".

5. The Upload button triggers Upload function with data-dismiss="fileuploadnow".

Listing 11-14. HTML Content Using the Bootstrap Styles as Well as Data Attributes to Trigger the File Upload Plug-In

```
<div data-provides="fileupload" class="fileupload fileupload-new">
    <div class="input-append">
        <div class="uneditable-input span3">
        <!-- If an existing file is present, the .fileupload-exists class will make the control
        visible. -->
            <i class="icon-file fileupload-exists"></i>
            <!-- The content of .fileupload-path is replaced with a filename when a file is selected. -->
            <span class="fileupload-path"></span>
        </div>
        <span class="btn btn-file">
            <span class="fileupload-new">Select file</span>
            <!-- If an existing file is present, the .fileupload-exists class will make the control
            visible. -->
            <span class="fileupload-exists">Change</span>

            <!-- Input file control -->
            <input type="file"/>
        </span>
        <!-- If an existing file is present, the .fileupload-exist class will make the control
        visible. -->
        <!-- The Remove button clears the file with data-dismiss="fileupload". -->

        <a href="#" class="btn fileupload-exists" data-dismiss="fileupload" >Remove</a>

        <!-- The Upload button triggers Upload function with data-dismiss="fileuploadnow" -->
        <a href="#" class="btn fileupload-exists" data-dismiss="fileuploadnow">Upload</a>
    </div>
</div>
```

After editing the HTML source, save the changes in the page. The new file upload control should appear as in Figure 11-6.

Figure 11-6. *File upload control after integrating Bootstrap file upload plug-in with SharePoint 2013*

jQuery for Specter Group File Upload

With the Bootstrap file upload .css and .js files integrated in SharePoint, we can use the file upload plug-in to trigger file upload events as well as change control behaviors on the page.

1. Listen on click event on the "fileupload" data-provide to trigger fileupload event handlers in the Bootstrap file upload plug-in (Listing 11-15).

2. Get current state of all the HTML controls (Listing 11-16).

3. Provide a Listen function that routes events to their respective event handler functions (Listing 11-17).

4. Provide a change function that handles user interface changes (Listing 11-18).

5. Provide an upload function that handles reading the file content and adding the file to the SharePoint document library using REST API (Listing 11-19).

6. Add e.preventDefault() to each event handler to prevent default action of the POST event from being triggered because the default action for the POST request will take the user to the site's home page.

Listing 11-15. To Trigger the fileupload data-api, We Listen on the Click Event on the "fileupload" data-provide

```
$(document).on('click.fileupload.data-api', '[data-provides="fileupload"]', function (e) {
    var $this = $(this);
    if ($this.data('fileupload')) return $this.fileupload($this.data());

    var $target = $(e.target).closest('[data-dismiss="fileupload"],[data-trigger="fileupload"]');
    if ($target.length > 0) {
        $target.trigger('click.fileupload');
        e.preventDefault();
    }
});
```

Listing 11-16. From the Fileupload Constructor, We Can Get Reference to the Controls and Their Current States on the Page

```
var Fileupload = function (element, options) {
    this.$element = $(element);

    // determine if the file uploaded is an image file
    this.type = this.$element.data('uploadtype') ||
        (this.$element.find('.thumbnail').length > 0 ? "image" : "file");

    // find the input file control in the DOM
    this.$input = this.$element.find(':file');
    if (this.$input.length === 0) return;

    this.name = this.$input.attr('name') || options.name;

    this.$hidden = this.$element.find('input[type=hidden][name="' + this.name + '"]');

    if (this.$hidden.length === 0) {
        this.$hidden = $('<input type="hidden" />');
        this.$element.prepend(this.$hidden);
    }

    // save current state of all controls on the page save state for if file exists,
    html for image preview,
    // file path, and hidden values
    this.original = {
        'exists': this.$element.hasClass('fileupload-exists'),

        //original for preview of image file (will cover this in later section,
        "Showing Thumbnails for Images")
        'preview': this.$preview.html(),
        'path': this.$path.html(),
        'hiddenVal': this.$hidden.val()
    }
    // find the remove button
    this.$remove = this.$element.find('[data-dismiss="fileupload"]');
    // find the upload button
    this.$uploadnow = this.$element.find('[data-dismiss="fileuploadnow"]');

    // register the click event on the fileupload data-provides <div> tag call an event handler
    method when
    // the section is clicked.
    this.$element.find('[data-trigger="fileupload"]').on('click.fileupload',
    $.proxy(this.trigger, this)) ;
    // listen for events to trigger event handlers in the js file
    this.listen();
}
```

Listing 11-17. The listen Function Detects When a Click Event Is Triggered; Based on the Control That Is Clicked, the Corresponding Function Is Called to Handle the Event

```
listen: function () {
    // when the file input control is changed, call the change function
    this.$input.on('change.fileupload', $.proxy(this.change, this));
    $(this.$input[0].form).on('reset.fileupload', $.proxy(this.reset, this));

    // when the remove button is clicked, call the clear function
    if (this.$remove) this.$remove.on('click.fileupload', $.proxy(this.clear, this));

    // when the upload button is clicked, call the upload function
    if (this.$uploadnow) this.$uploadnow.on('click.fileupload', $.proxy(this.upload, this));
},
```

Listing 11-18. The change Function Handles User Interface Changes, Such as Displaying the Name of the File, and Unhiding the "Remove" and "Upload" Buttons When the File Has Been Selected by the User

```
change: function (e, invoked) {
    // get the file from file input control
    file = e.target.files !== undefined ? e.target.files[0] :
        (e.target.value ? { name:
        e.target.value.replace(/^.+\\\/, '')} : null);

    if (!file) {
        // if file is invalid, we clear the controls and return from the function
        this.clear();
        return;
    }

    // Ensure the file is a valid file and it is an image file,
    // and the browser supports use of the HTML5 File API
    if ( (typeof file.type !== "undefined" ? file.type.match('image.*') :
        file.name.match('\\.(gif|png|jpe?g)$')) && typeof FileReader !== "undefined") {

        // creates a variable for the FileReader to get file content
        var urlReader = new FileReader();
        var element = this.$element;

        // callback function for readAsDataURL() FileReader onload event
        // This is used to provide users with image preview. (will cover this in later section)

        urlReader.onload = function (e)  {
            ...
            // (will cover this in the " Showing Thumbnails for Images" section of this chapter)
        }
        urlReader.onerror = function (e) {
            alert("File could not be read! Code " + e.target.error.code);
        };

        // trigger FileReader readAsDataURL to get file content as a data URL for image preview
        urlReader.readAsDataURL(file);
```

```
      // set the file path control in HTML to the name of the file
      this.$path.text(file.name);
   }
   else {
      alert("Unable to get a file.");
   }
},
```

Listing 11-19. The upload Function Handles Reading the File Content and Adding the File to the Document Library

```
upload: function (e) {
   if (!file) {
      alert("no file to upload");
      this.clear();
      return;
   }

   // create a variable for FileReader to get content from file
   var bufferReader = new FileReader();

   // callback function for the readAsArrayBuffer()
   // FileReader onload event
   bufferReader.onload = function (e) {
      // Get ArrayBuffer from FileReader
      var buffer = e.target.result;

      // Make a jQuery ajax request against the REST endpoint URL
      $.ajax({
         // Specify the REST endpoint URL that represents the folder for our file and the action to
         // add a file
         url: _spPageContextInfo.webAbsoluteUrl +
            "/_api/web/GetFolderByServerRelativeUrl('/sites/fileuploadtest/Documents" +
            "/Communities)/Files/Add(url='" + file.name + "',overwrite=true)",

         // Specify this is a POST http request
         method: 'POST',

         // buffer is the content of the file and it is the ArrayBuffer returned from the
         // FileReader read
         data: buffer,

         // Specify the header information of the request
         headers: {
            // Specify we want the OData representation of the result to be in JSON format
            'content-type': "application/json;odata=verbose",

            // Specify form digest value for the request. Since our solution resides in SharePoint
            // (inline script and stand-alone .js files), we do not need to make a separate HTTP request
            // to retrieve the form digest value. Instead, we can retrieve the value in JavaScript code.
            'X-RequestDigest': $('#__REQUESTDIGEST').val(),
```

```
                // Set the content-length to the length of the file content
                "content-length": buffer.length
            },

            // By default the data property is converted to a query string if not already a string,
            // This property tells jQuery Ajax to ensure no conversion is done on the data, in this case the
            // data is the buffer returned by the FileReader after getting the content from the image file
            processData: false,

            // Successful upload event handler
            success: function (e) {
                alert('successfully done');
            },

            // Failure upload event handler
            error: function (err) {
                alert("Error in JSON: " + JSON.stringify(err));
            },
        });
    }

    // when FileReader did not read successfully
    bufferReader.onerror = function (e) {
        alert("File could not be read! Code " +  e.target.error.code);
    };

    // trigger FileReader readAsArrayBuffer to get file content as an ArrayBuffer
    bufferReader.readAsArrayBuffer(file);

    // The default action for the POST request will take the user to the site's home page.
    If this is not the
    // desired behavior, use this jQuery method to prevent default action of the POST event from
    // being triggered.
    e.preventDefault();
},
```

After adding all the HTML and jQuery, the File Upload control should look similar to Figure 11-7.

Figure 11-7. *File upload control after adding more buttons to handle change, remove, and upload events and display of file name after a file has been selected*

After users added new image files using the Specter Group File Upload solution, check the `Communities` folder in the Documents library. It should be filled with new files, as shown in Figure 11-8.

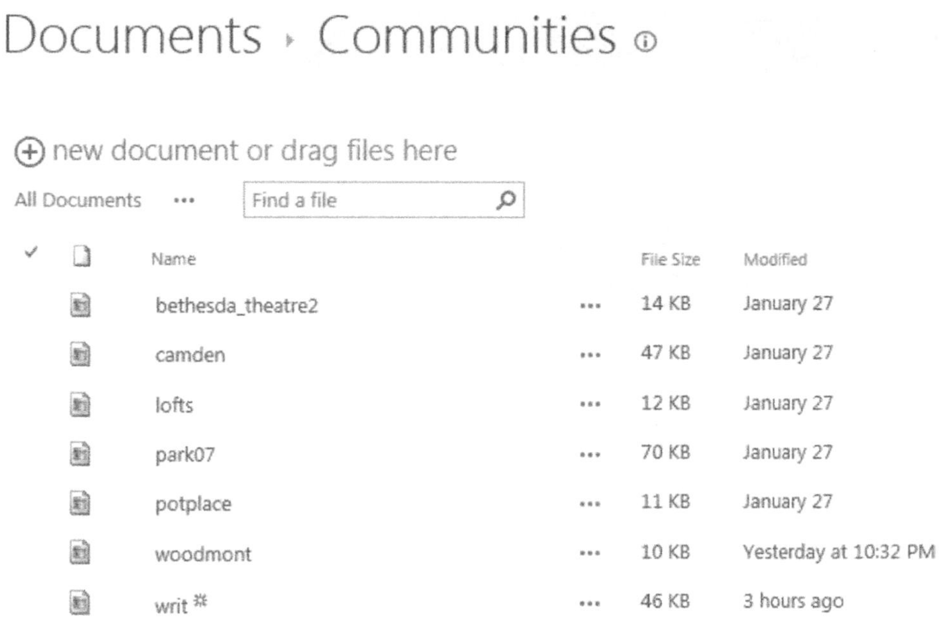

Documents › Communities ⓘ

⊕ new document or drag files here

All Documents   ⋯ | Find a file | 🔎 |

✓	🗋	Name		File Size	Modified
	🖹	bethesda_theatre2	⋯	14 KB	January 27
	🖹	camden	⋯	47 KB	January 27
	🖹	lofts	⋯	12 KB	January 27
	🖹	park07	⋯	70 KB	January 27
	🖹	potplace	⋯	11 KB	January 27
	🖹	woodmont	⋯	10 KB	Yesterday at 10:32 PM
	🖹	writ ✵	⋯	46 KB	3 hours ago

Figure 11-8. *After files are uploaded, we check the destination folder in the Documents library and see all the files have been uploaded for the user*

Advanced Specter Group File Upload Topics

Based on our requirements, we now proceed to design the solution to filter images file types when browsing files to upload, display Thumbnails for images once the files are selected, select files using drag and drop, as well as show file read progress capabilities.

Filtering File Types When Browsing Files to Upload

Based on our requirement, we want to filter out nonimage file types when users are browsing for files to upload, as shown in Figure 11-9. We do so by adding the accept attribute to the file upload input control, as shown in Listing 11-20.

▪ **Note**   Currently, only Opera and Google Chrome are filtering out the proper file types when the user is browsing the files.

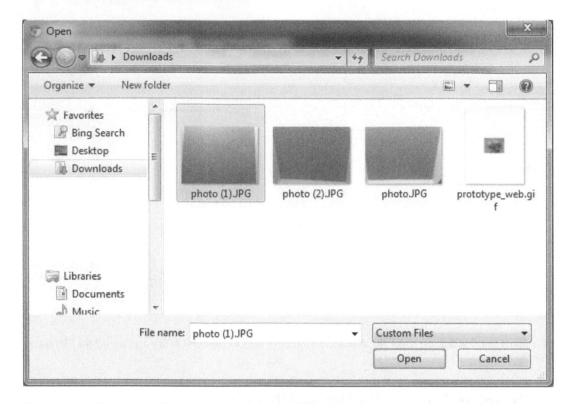

Figure 11-9. *File types are filtered when browsing local files for upload.*
Note: The file type drop-down list in the file browsing window is set to Custom Files instead of the default All Files

Listing 11-20. Add the accept Attribute to the File Upload Input Control to Filter Out Nonimage Files When Users Are Browsing for Local Files

```
<input type="file" accept="image/x-png, image/gif, image/jpeg" multiple />
```

Showing Thumbnails for Images

Now that we have the file upload control, our users can select any local image file for upload. Specter wants to enable the users to preview their selected images by displaying thumbnail previews of the image files before the user actually uploads the files.

1. Add an HTML section to allow preview images to be added to the page. The content of the class ".fileupload-preview" is replaced with an image <img> tag when a file is selected (Listing 11-21).

2. From jQuery Ajax, get the HTML section from DOM to add the image control. From the Fileupload constructor, get the reference of the preview HTML from the page (Listing 11-22). (To see the rest of the Fileupload constructor, refer to Listing 11-16.)

3. After the user selects an image file, in the change function, we need to display a preview of the image on the page. Get the file content by using the FileReader readAsDataURL() method. For more information on readAsDataURL(), refer to the section "Getting File Content" earlier in this chapter (Listing 11-23).

4. Add image control to HTML section for preview (Listing 11-23).

Listing 11-21. Add an HTML Section to Allow Preview Image to Be Added to the SharePoint Page

```
<span class="fileupload-preview"></span>
```

Listing 11-22. Add the Reference and Code for the Preview HTML Control in the jQuery Ajax Code

```
var Fileupload = function (element, options) {
   ...
   //find the preview section on the page for us to add image tag to and display it on the
   // page when it is not hidden
   this.$preview = this.$element.find('.fileupload-preview');
   var height = this.$preview.css('height');
   if (this.$preview.css('display') != 'inline' && height != '0px' && height != 'none')
      this.$preview.css('line-height', height);
   ...
}
```

Listing 11-23. Get Image Content from the File Using readAsDataURL() and Adding an Image Control to HTML

```
change: function (e, invoked) {
   ...
   // Get image preview html and make sure it is ready in the DOM
   if (this.$preview.length > 0 &&
       (typeof file.type !== "undefined" ? file.type.match('image.*') :
       file.name.match('\\.(gif|png|jpe?g)$')) &&
       typeof FileReader !== "undefined") {

      // create a variable for FileReader to get content from file
      var urlReader = new FileReader();

      //get the preview html from DOM
      var preview = this.$preview;
      var element = this.$element;

      // callback function for readAsDataURL() FileReader onload event
      urlReader.onload = function (e) {
         // set image control's source in preview html to the data URL returned by the file content
         preview.html('<img src="' + e.target.result + '" ' + (preview.css('max-height') != 'none' ?
            'style="max-height: ' + preview.css('max-height') + ';"' : '') + ' />');
      }
      // if FileReader failed to read the content
      urlReader.onerror = function (e) {
         alert("File could not be read! Code " + e.target.error.code);
      };
```

```
        // trigger FileReader readAsDataURL to get file content as a data URL
        urlReader.readAsDataURL(file);

    }
    else {
        alert("Unable to get a file.");
    }
},
```

After adding the HTML and jQuery for showing image preview, the File Upload control should look similar to Figure 11-10 and Figure 11-11.

Figure 11-10. *Example file upload after selecting an image of a community. We display the file name as well as a thumbnail preview of the image file*

Figure 11-11. *Example file upload after selecting an image of a community*

Selecting Files Using Drag and Drop

Using the new HTML5 drag and drop API and the new File API, we can now create a drag-and-drop experience for users to upload files in our own solution. It's important to note that out of the box, SharePoint 2013 file upload control supports drag and drop for uploading multiple files. When working with Internet Explorer 8, 9, and 10, this feature depends on the UploadCtl ActiveX plug-in. When working with the latest versions of Chrome and Firefox, this feature depends on HTML5. To learn more about the HTML5 drag and drop API, refer to http://sprwd.com/b4hkxhg.

With the HTML5 drag and drop API, we start with the drop event when the user releases the mouse and the mouse-up event occurs. The drop event then returns an evt.dataTransfer object. The dataTransfer object contains dataTransfer.files, which is a FileList object that represents a list of files that were dropped. Using the File API, we iterate through the individual File instances and use a FileReader object to read the file content.

1. Add an HTML section for drag and drop (Listing 11-24).

2. Register event handlers for drag and drop events. Register JavaScript event handlers on the drop area with all the different drag and drop events that can occur in that area (Listing 11-25).

3. For each event handler, add evt.preventDefault to stop an event from propagating
    further (Listing 11-26).

4. For drop event handler, get files that were dropped by the user (Listing 11-27).

Listing 11-24. Create HTML Section to Allow Drag and Drop

```
<div id="droparea"><span id="droplabel">Drop file here...</span></div>
```

Listing 11-25. Register Event Handlers for Drag and Drop Events

```
// get reference to the drop area in DOM
var droparea = document.getElementById("droparea");

// init event handlers
droparea.addEventListener("dragenter", dragEnter, false);
droparea.addEventListener("dragexit", dragExit, false);
droparea.addEventListener("dragover", dragOver, false);
droparea.addEventListener("drop", drop, false);
```

Listing 11-26. Implement Handlers to Stop Event from Propagating Further for dragEnter, dragExit, and dragOver Events

```
function dragEnter(evt) {
   evt.stopPropagation();
   evt.preventDefault();
}
```

Listing 11-27. Implement Handler for the Drop Event to Get the Files That Were Dropped by the User from the dataTransfer Object

```
function drop (evt) {
   // stop event from propagating further
   evt.stopPropagation();
   evt.preventDefault();

   // get the FileList object that represents a list of files the user dropped
   var files = evt.dataTransfer.files;
   var count = files.length;

   // Only call the handler if 1 or more files are dropped.
   if (count > 0) processFiles(files);
   // call function to get file content for each file
}
```

Showing Upload Progress Bar

We want to show users the progress of events on a web page. For our scenario, we want to show users progress of file upload. Because we are leveraging the SharePoint client object model, our data transfer requests to the server are processed asynchronously, which makes it hard for us to track progress of the server upload. Instead, we demonstrate how to request data from a disk and show the progress of reading the content with FileReader.

From the FileReader API, there are six different events during the process of file read. We have already looked at the load and the error events, as shown in Listing 11-7, when processing the content after a file read. For the purpose of showing progress, we focus on the progress event (Listings 11-28 and 11-29). The event object for the progress event contains three properties to monitor data read:

- loaded: The number of bytes the file reader has already read

- lengthComputable: A Boolean indicating if the browser can determine the complete size of the data

- total: Total number of bytes to be read

Listing 11-28. Add an HTML5 Progress Bar to the Page to Show User Progress

```
<progress id="readprogress" ></progress>
```

Listing 11-29. Tie the Progress Value of the HTML Control to the Actual Progress of Reading the File from the File System

```
var reader = new FileReader(),
   progressControl = document.getElementById("readprogress");

   reader.onprogress = function(event) {
      if (event.lengthComputable) {
         progressControl.max = event.total;
         progressControl.value = event.loaded;
      }
   };

reader.onloadend = function(event) {
   var contents = event.target.result,
       error    = event.target.error;

   if (error != null) {
      alert("File could not be read! Code " + error.code);
   }
   else {
      progressControl.max = 1;
      progressControl.value = 1;
   }
};

reader.readAsArrayBuffer(file);
```

After adding the HTML and jQuery for showing upload progress to our solution, the File Upload control should look similar to Figure 11-12 after the user selects a file to upload from the local file system.

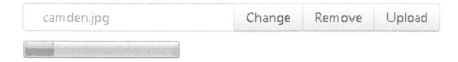

Figure 11-12. *Example of displaying progress bar after user selects a local file to upload*

Summary

Today, many web sites offer users the ability to upload files. Together with HTML5 and enhanced client object model APIs in SharePoint 2013, this allows us to add file upload functionalities to forms, SharePoint pages, and even solutions that sit outside of SharePoint. We looked at how we can get files from local file systems and how to read file content by using the new File API in HTML5. We then demonstrated adding files to the SharePoint document library by using the new REST API. Finally, to enhance the user experience, we integrated our solution with the Bootstrap file upload plug-in to leverage the look and feel.

■ ■ ■

CHAPTER 12

Integrating Location-Based Features

We have been looking at many new features and capabilities in SharePoint 2013 related to building responsive web sites. With the rapid adoption of smart phones and tablets, we have the opportunity to use GPS capabilities in mobile devices to support location-based features in our web sites. Knowing the user's location helps to boost the quality of the site. In this chapter, we demonstrate how to use the new geolocation metadata field in SharePoint 2013 and the HTML5 Geolocation API to integrate maps and location-based features into a site. First, we look at the basics of the HTML5 Geolocation API. Then we demonstrate the new geolocation features in SharePoint 2013. Finally, we explore how we can extend the new geolocation features in SharePoint 2013 and walk through an example by building our own SharePoint-hosted app to integrate SharePoint geolocation, HTML5 geolocation, and Bing Maps features into the Specter Group community site.

Our Scenario

In the public Specter Group site, we want to use geolocation features. Specter's objective is to enable existing property owners to engage with other community members. Specter Group wants to display geolocation information for each community site. Based on our business requirements, each community site's home page should display a map with a pin showing the location of this community on the map, as shown in Figure 12-1. The map displays the actual location of the community and the properties with pins. When a user clicks on the pin, a bubble displays the property owner's family name. When a user adds a property to the community, the user can either let the site automatically detect the geolocation data for the user or the user can enter the address of the property before the property is added to the community list.

Figure 12-1. Example of map control on community site home page based on Specter Group's business requirements

Geolocation Enhancement

Leveraging user location to deliver enhanced experience is an important aspect of modern web development. To ensure a site gives users an adaptive experience, often we want to utilize the user's location information. Today, geolocation is one of the best supported features across mobile browsers as well as desktop browsers. In the past, to know a user's location, they had to manually enter their location or click on a map. Today, with the HTML5 Geolocation API, we can locate our users to show more relevant content based on their location and we can reduce manual data entry related to geolocation. There are a few ways a mobile browser or a desktop browser can detect its location. If the device is GPS-enabled, it can use the GPS on the mobile device to accurately determine the location. Another method is to use assistive GPS that uses triangulation among mobile phone towers to determine location. If the device is using WiFi from hotspots, it can use the hotspots to determine the location. If it is not a mobile device, such as a desktop browser, it can obtain location information using known IP address ranges. As web developers, we need to be aware of all the different methods a browser uses to detect location, as the solution might require a certain level of accuracy of the location returned.

■ **Note** When it comes to sharing physical location of the user, privacy should be considered. Based on the Geolocation API, user agents must not send location information to web sites without the express permission of the user. For geolocation detection to work, the user must agree to share location information with the site.

HTML5 Geolocation

To incorporate geolocation into our site, let's first understand the HTML5 Geolocation API. The HTML5 Geolocation API is used to determine the geographical position of a user. Then we see how to display the result in a map using both Google Maps and Bing Maps service.

■ **Note**   For more information on how to use the HTML5 Geolocation API, refer to `http://sprwd.com/z6kwj8`.

Getting Current Position

We start with the HTML5 Navigator object and its attribute, geolocation object. We also have available to us the `getCurrentPosition()` JavaScript function that gets the user location. It takes two parameters in the form of callbacks, one for a successful location query and the other for a failed location query. The successful callback takes a `Position` object as a parameter. The failed callback takes the `Error` object.

Refer to Listing 12-1 for the following walkthrough. First, let's check if geolocation is supported by the browser. Internet Explorer 9+, Firefox 3.5+, Chrome 5+, Safari 5+, Opera 10.6+, iPhone 3+, Android 2+, and Windows Phone 7.5+ all support geolocation features. It is important to consider that even with all the supported browsers, location information might still not be available because the user might be running an older browser or have devices that do not support geolocation, or the user might have disabled share location. In such cases, we should always provide an alternative method for the users to manually enter their location in the failed location query callback function.

Listing 12-1. Basic getCurrentPosition() Example to Obtain Your Current Coordinates

```
<html>
<body>
    <p id="demo">Click the button to get your coordinates:</p>
    <button onclick="getUserLocation()">Get</button>
    <script>
        var x=document.getElementById("demo");
        function getUserLocation(){
            if (navigator.geolocation) {
                navigator.geolocation.getCurrentPosition(showUserPosition, showError);
            }
            else{x.innerHTML="Geolocation is not supported by this browser.";}
        }
        function showUserPosition(position) {
            x.innerHTML="Latitude: " + position.coords.latitude +
                                "<br>Longitude: " + position.coords.longitude;
        }
        function showError(error) {
            switch(error.code)  {
                case error.PERMISSION_DENIED:
                    x.innerHTML="User denied the request for Geolocation."
                    break;
                case error.POSITION_UNAVAILABLE:
                    x.innerHTML="Location information is unavailable."
                    break;
                case error.TIMEOUT:
                    x.innerHTML="The request to get user location timed out."
                    break;
```

```
                case error.UNKNOWN_ERROR:
                    x.innerHTML="An unknown error occurred."
                    break;
            }
        }
    </script>
</body>
</html
```

After checking that geolocation is supported, call the getCurrentPosition() method. If it is not supported, display a message to the user or allow the user to manually enter the information. After the getCurrentPosition function executes, if it queried the location successfully, it executes the successful callback function, showUserPosition(). The showUserPosition() function takes the Position object as its parameter, which contains the coordinates to be displayed. If the location query failed, it executes the showError function, and the code below displays an error message to the user based on the error code. If instead of displaying an error message, we want to allow users to enter an address, we can add the code for resolving an address into geolocation coordinates here as well. For information on how to implement this, refer to the section "Resolving Geolocation From an Address" later in this chapter.

After the user loads this page, the page will look like Figure 12-2.

Click the button to get your coordinates:

Figure 12-2. *HTML5 Geolocation API example site*

As previously mentioned, due to user privacy, the geolocation position is not available until the user approves sharing location information with the site. As soon as the user clicks Get, the browser prompts the user to request permission to track the user's physical location (see Figure 12-3).

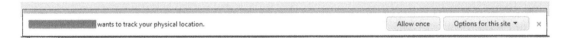

Figure 12-3. *The browser will request user permission to share location data with the site due to user privacy*

After the user clicks Allow once, the result coordinates are displayed, as shown in Figure 12-4.

Latitude: 37.584242
Longitude: -122.044201

Figure 12-4. *HTML5 Geolocation API example returns user's latitude and longitude values*

From the code in Listing 12-1, we can get the latitude and longitude values from the position object. There are additional properties we can use from the position object that can help the site. For instance, we can get the value of the accuracy property to evaluate if the location returned is acceptable. Using the speed property, we can determine if the user is moving. If the user is moving, we can use the `watchPosition()` function, which returns the current position of the user and continues to return updated positions as the user is moving. To stop the `watchPosition()` function , we can use the `clearWatch()` function. Refer to Table 12-1 for a list of properties returned by the HTML5 Geolocation API.

Table 12-1. *HTML5 Geolocation API Properties and Functions*

Property	Description	Value	Unit
`coords.latitude`	The latitude as a decimal number	Double	Degrees
`coords.longitude`	The longitude as a decimal number	Double	Degrees
`coords.altitude`	The accuracy of position	Double or null	Meters
`coords.accuracy`	The altitude in meters above the mean sea level	Double	Meters
`coords.altitudeAccuracy`	The altitude accuracy of position	Double or null	Meters
`coords.heading`	The heading as degrees clockwise from north	Double or null	Degrees clockwise
`coords.speed`	The speed in meters per second	Double or null	Meters/second
`timestamp`	The date/time of the response	DOMTimeStamp	The Date object

Displaying Results on a Map

With the location of the user available, we now have the option to display the location in a map. To display the result in a map, we need to use a map service that can use latitude and longitude values.

Using the Google Map service and the Google static maps API, we can update the HTML and JavaScript from Listing 12-1, providing an additional `<div>` container before the `<script>` block and replacing the `showUserPosition()` JavaScript function (see Listing 12-2).

Listing 12-2. Show a Map Using Coordinates Returned from HTML5 API and Google Maps API

```
<div id="mapholder"></div>
<script>
    function showUserPosition(position) {
        var latlon=position.coords.latitude+","+position.coords.longitude;
        var img_url="http://maps.googleapis.com/maps/api/staticmap?center="
            +latlon+"&zoom=14&size=400x300&sensor=false";
        document.getElementById("mapholder").innerHTML="<img src='"+img_url+"'>";
    }
</script>
```

After the page is loaded, the user sees a map like the one in Figure 12-5.

Click the button to get your position:

Figure 12-5. *HTML5 Geolocation API example uses Google Maps service to display an area map centered on the current geolocation position returned from the browser*

If we want to use Bing Maps, we can leverage the Bing Maps service and Bing Maps Interactive Software Development Kit (SDK) for AJAX version 6.3, as seen in Listing 12-3.

Listing 12-3. Show a Map Using Coordinates and the Bing Maps Service

```
<div id='myMap' style="position:relative; width:400px; height:400px;"></div>
<script type="text/javascript"
           src="http://ecn.dev.virtualearth.net/mapcontrol/mapcontrol.ashx?v=6.2">
</script>
<script>
    var map = null;
    function showUserPosition (position) {
        map = new VEMap('myMap');
        map.LoadMap(new VELatLong(position.coords.latitude, position.coords.longitude),
                           10 ,'h' ,false);
    }
</script>
```

■ Note To learn more about how to use Bing Maps Interactive SDK for AJAX version 6.3, refer to http://sprwd.com/dfsnvmc.

After the page is loaded, the user sees something like Figure 12-6.

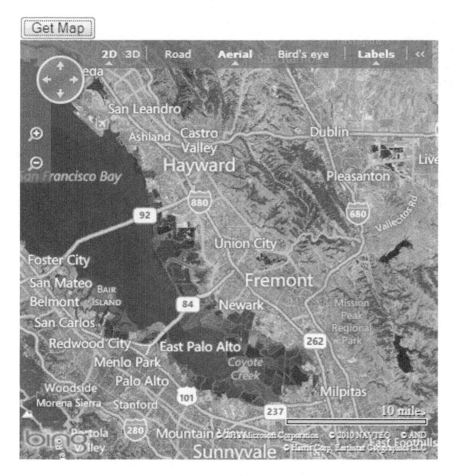

Figure 12-6. *HTML5 Geolocation API example uses Bing Maps service to display an area map centered on the current geolocation position returned from the browser*

Showing a Position Marker on the Map

Now that we have the map centered on our current location, we need to display a position marker on the map to show each location. In the following sections, we demonstrate two methods for showing a position marker by using the Google Maps JavaScript API and then the Bing Maps AJAX control 7.0 Interactive SDK.

Using Google Maps JavaScript API

To use Google Maps in the solution, we need to reference the Google Maps JavaScript API. First, we need to include the Google JavaScript API in the script header. Then, we need to create a Google Maps object and a Google Maps marker object for each position on the map, as shown in Listing 12-4.

427

Listing 12-4. Show a Pin on a Google Map Using Coordinates and Google Maps API (Based on Listing 12-2)

```
<div id="mapholder"></div>
<script src="http://maps.google.com/maps/api/js?sensor=false"></script>
<script>
    function showUserPosition(position) {
        lat=position.coords.latitude;
        lon=position.coords.longitude;
        latlon=new google.maps.LatLng(lat, lon)
        mapholder=document.getElementById('mapholder')
        mapholder.style.height='350px';
        mapholder.style.width='500px';

        var myOptions={
            center:latlon,zoom:14,
            mapTypeId:google.maps.MapTypeId.ROADMAP,
            mapTypeControl:false,
            navigationControlOptions:{style:google.maps.NavigationControlStyle.SMALL}
        };
        var map=new google.maps.Map(document.getElementById("mapholder"),myOptions);
        var marker=new google.maps.Marker({position:latlon,map:map,title:"Your location!"});
    }
```

After the page is loaded, the user sees a map like the one in Figure 12-7.

Click the button to get your position:

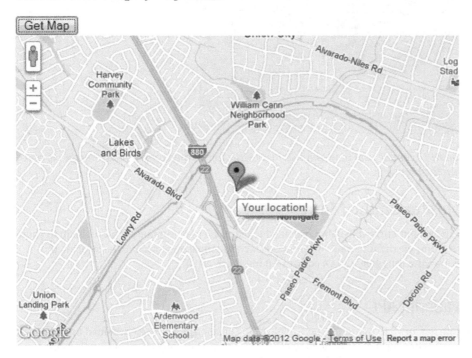

Figure 12-7. *HTML5 Geolocation API example uses Google Maps service to display a position marker on a map for the current geolocation position returned from the browser*

Using Bing Maps AJAX control 7.0 Interactive SDK

To use the Bing Maps service, to add pins to the map, we need to use Bing Maps AJAX control 7.0 Interactive SDK, which requires us to first create a Bing Maps key. Creating a Bing Maps account is quick and easy. Visit www.bingmapsportal.com to set up a Bing Maps key and to learn more about usage limits and options. Once logged in to www.bingmapsportal.com with a Microsoft account, click Create or view keys on the left menu (see Figure 12-8).

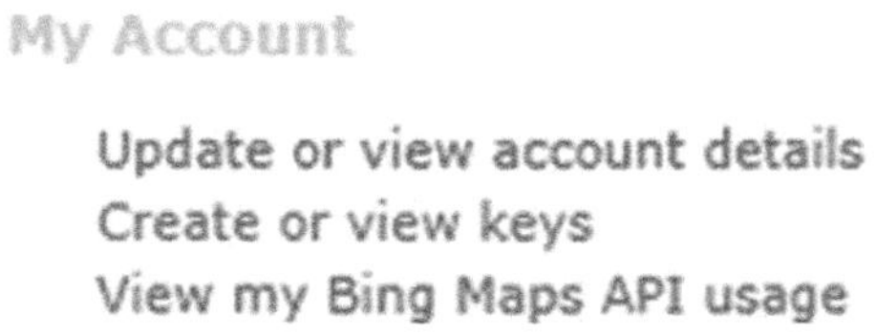

My Account

Update or view account details
Create or view keys
View my Bing Maps API usage

Figure 12-8. *Create a Bing Maps key to use the Bing Maps service and API*

We can now create a Bing Maps key for our site, in our example the Specter Group public web site. During the development cycle, we should create a trial key. A trial key is used for evaluation during a 90-day evaluation period and must not exceed 10,000 transactions of any type in any 30-day period. Once the site goes into production, depending on the size of the application, consider a basic key or an enterprise key. For the purpose of demonstration, we create a trial key (see Figure 12-9).

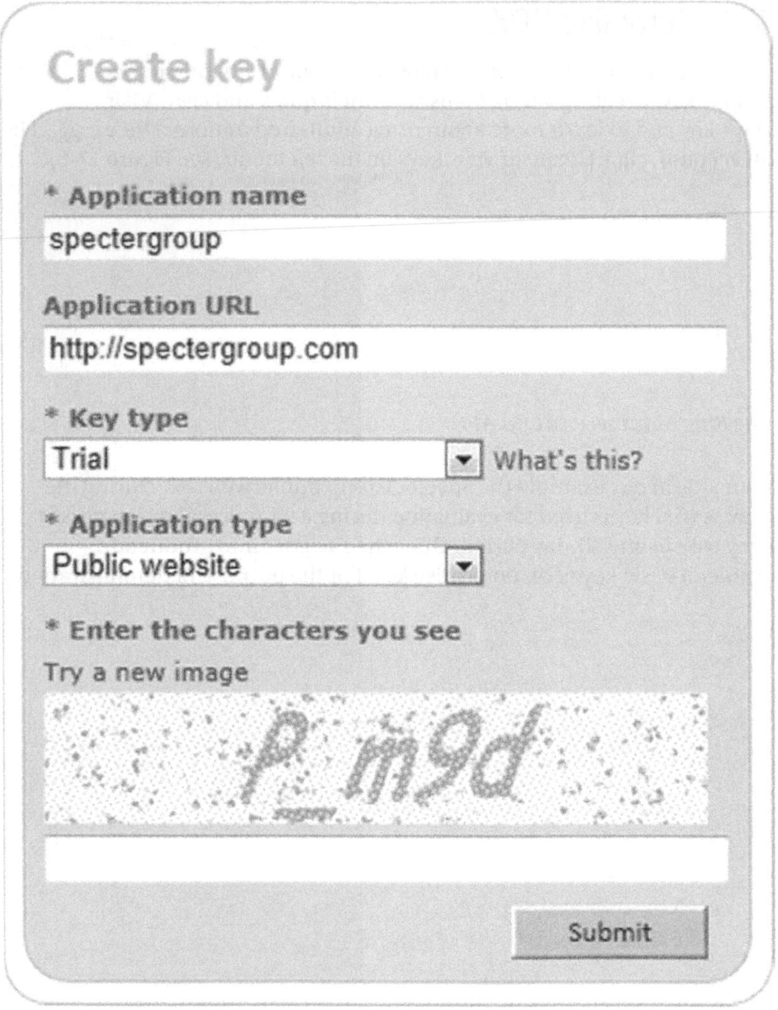

Figure 12-9. *Create a trial Bing Maps key for Specter Group sites*

Once the key is created, it is added to the list of keys and applications in the Bing Maps portal. We can then use the Bing Maps service and the Bing Maps AJAX control 7.0 Interactive SDK to create a map and add the user's locations as pins to the map (see Listing 12-5).

■ **Note**   To use the Bing Maps AJAX control 7.0 Interactive SDK and the Bing Maps service, we need to add the new Bing Maps key into our code.

Listing 12-5. Show a Pushpin on a Bing Map Using Coordinates and Bing Maps Service (Based on Listing 12-3)

```
<div id='myMap' style="position:relative; width:400px; height:400px;"></div>
<script type="text/javascript"
            src="http://ecn.dev.virtualearth.net/mapcontrol/mapcontrol.ashx?v=7.0">
</script>
<script>
    var map = null;
    function showUserPosition(position) {
        var lat = position.coords.latitude;
        var long = position.coords.longitude;
        map = new Microsoft.Maps.Map(document.getElementById('myMap'),
            {credentials: 'Your Bing Maps key'});
        map.setView({ zoom: 10, center: new Microsoft.Maps.Location(lat, long) });
        var pushpin= new Microsoft.Maps.Pushpin(map.getCenter(), null);
        map.entities.push(pushpin);
        pushpin.setLocation(new Microsoft.Maps.Location(lat, long));
    }
</script>
```

After the page is loaded, the user sees a map similar to the one in Figure 12-10.

Click the button to get your position:

Figure 12-10. *HTML5 Geolocation API example uses Bing Maps service to display a position marker on a map for the current geolocation position returned from the browser*

Using SharePoint 2013 Geolocation Features

We just looked at the HTML5 Geolocation API and how to use it for a general web site. Now let's look at what SharePoint has to offer by again visiting our scenario. For the public Specter Group site, we need to consider how to build the geolocation solution with SharePoint 2013. In the past with SharePoint 2010, we had to do a lot of work to build a geolocation solution using a combination of SharePoint lists, Silverlight 4, the SharePoint Silverlight client object model, and Bing Maps SDK. In SharePoint 2013, we can now build a geolocation solution with little effort and without outside objects such as Silverlight.

SharePoint 2013 introduces a new geolocation field type that enables us to create SharePoint lists with location information. With a column of type Geolocation, we can save location information as a paired value of latitude and longitude coordinates in decimal degrees (see Figure 12-11).

Figure 12-11. *SharePoint 2013 introduces a geolocation-typed column that allows us to keep track of geolocation data in a SharePoint list. The column expects latitude and longitude decimal values*

When a SharePoint list contains a geolocation-typed column, SharePoint automatically provides us with a map view that displays all the list items as pins on a Bing Maps Ajax v7.0 control as well as a list of the list items in the left pane. With both the Geolocation field and the Map view, we can now provide users with a map experience using the data we have stored in SharePoint (see Figure 12-12).

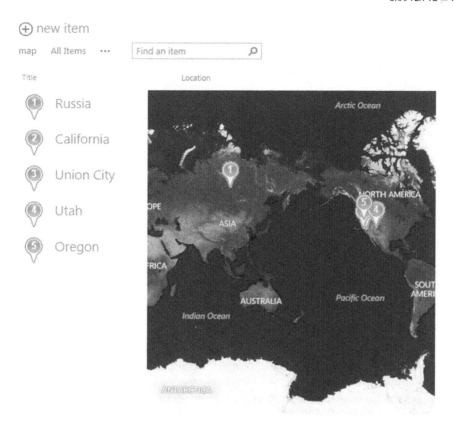

Figure 12-12. *SharePoint 2013 lists containing a geolocation column can provide a map view to view the list data in a map experience*

Enabling SharePoint Bing Maps Integration With PowerShell

Before we can use any of the new geolocation features in SharePoint 2013, we need to configure a Bing Maps key for the SharePoint environment. If a Bing Maps key is not available for the SharePoint environment, follow the creation process described earlier in this chapter. After a key has been obtained, we can set the Bing Maps key at the SharePoint farm level or at a web level. If a key is not set at the web level or at the farm level, the user sees an error similar to the one shown in Figure 12-13.

The specified credentials are invalid. You can sign up for a free developer account at http://www.bingmapsportal.com

Figure 12-13. A warning will appear on a map before Bing Maps key is set at the SharePoint 2013 web or farm level

To set the Bing Maps key at the farm level, log on to the SharePoint farm with administrative privileges. Register the Bing Maps key for the SharePoint farm using SharePoint 2013 Management Shell, as seen in Listing 12-6.

Listing 12-6. PowerShell to Enable SharePoint Bing Maps Integration for the Whole Farm

```
Set-SPBingMapsKey -BingKey "Your Bing Maps key"
```

We can set the Bing Maps key at the web level programmatically using either the SharePoint .NET client object model or the SharePoint JavaScript client object model. We will go through the steps for setting the Bing Maps key programmatically in the section "Setting Bing Maps Key Using JavaScript Client Object Model" later in this chapter. It is important to note that the Bing Maps key set at the web level takes precedence over the Bing Maps key set at the farm level.

Adding a Geolocation Site Column Using PowerShell

Once we have enabled Bing Maps and SharePoint integration, we need to create a geolocation site column to be added to our Master Community content type or to be added to a custom list.

■ **Note**   From the SharePoint user interface, we cannot create a new column based on the new geolocation type. It can be done with PowerShell or programmatically. We demonstrate how to do so programmatically using client-side object model in the section "Creating a Custom List Instance With a Geolocation Column" later in this chapter.

---

1. Using SharePoint 2013 Management Shell, create a geolocation site column with PowerShell. The PowerShell script in Listing 12-7 will create a geolocation site column for one of the Specter Group community sites.

   Listing 12-7. Example of PowerShell Script to Create a Geolocation Site Column for a Site Collection

   ```
   $weburl = "http://spectergroup.com/sites/EagleVista"
   $fieldXml = "<Field Type ='Geolocation' DisplayName='Location' />"
   $web = get-spweb $weburl
   $field = $web.Fields.AddFieldAsXml($fieldXml)
   $web.Update()
   ```

■ **Note**   For demonstration purposes, we are using PowerShell to create a site column for a site collection. For production use, to ensure this type of column is available throughout SharePoint, we recommend creating this type of column within the content type hub so that it can be reused without going through PowerShell every time. For more information on how to set up Content Type hubs, refer to Chapter 6.

---

2. Navigate to the site column collection of the community site. We should see the new Geolocation column under Custom columns (see Figure 12-14). We can also add this column to the Master Community content type.

   Custom Columns

Category Picture	Hyperlink or Picture	Eagle Vista
Description	Single line of text	Eagle Vista
Location	Geolocation	Eagle Vista

   Figure 12-14. *PowerShell created a geolocation-type site column*

3. With the new geolocation site column, we can now create a list for all the properties in a community. Create a new custom list called Houses.

4. Add two columns, one text column called Family and one geolocation column called Location. Navigate to List Settings.

5. To add a geolocation column to the custom list, click Add from existing site columns, then select Custom Columns from the drop-down list.

6. From the Available site columns, select Location and click Add to add the column. Click OK. The custom list should now have the columns shown in Figure 12-15.

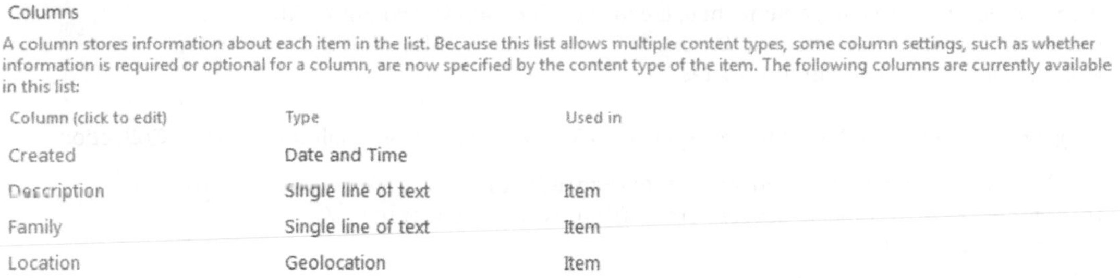

Columns

A column stores information about each item in the list. Because this list allows multiple content types, some column settings, such as whether information is required or optional for a column, are now specified by the content type of the item. The following columns are currently available in this list:

Column (click to edit)	Type	Used in
Created	Date and Time	
Description	Single line of text	Item
Family	Single line of text	Item
Location	Geolocation	Item

Figure 12-15. *Add geolocation site column to a custom list*

Based on Specter Group's business requirements, when a community user adds a property to the community, the site can automatically detect the geolocation data for the user before the property is added to the community list. The new custom list we just created allows the community users to add a new property to the community by automatically detecting the user's geolocation information. Users can also manually enter latitude and longitude values for their properties in the community (see Figure 12-16).

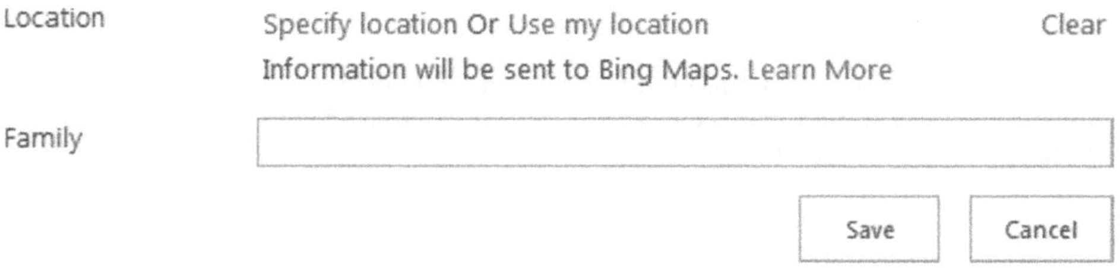

Location   Specify location Or Use my location   Clear
                  Information will be sent to Bing Maps. Learn More

Family   [   ]

                                              Save   Cancel

Figure 12-16. *Create new list item by autodetecting location or by specifying latitude and longitude values*

To specify the location, the user has two options. The user can click Use my location to allow the browser to detect his or her geolocation information. Note that after the user clicks the hyperlink, the browser requests the user's permission to track his or her location. The user needs to click Allow to enable geolocation detection in the browser. Once the location is determined, the user sees the location in a Bing Maps control, as shown in Figure 12-17.

Location   Specify location Or Use my location   Clear

Information will be sent to Bing Maps. Learn More

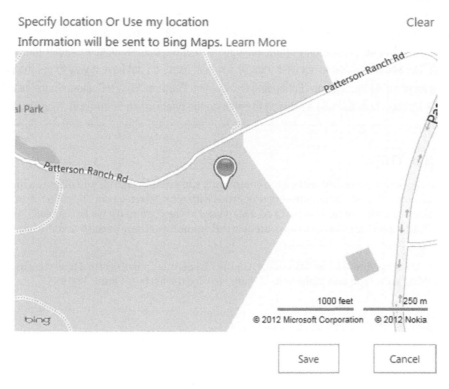

Figure 12-17. *Autodetection of user's location when creating a new list item (new property in the community)*

Alternately, the user can click Specify Location to manually enter a latitude value and a longitude value (see Figure 12-18).

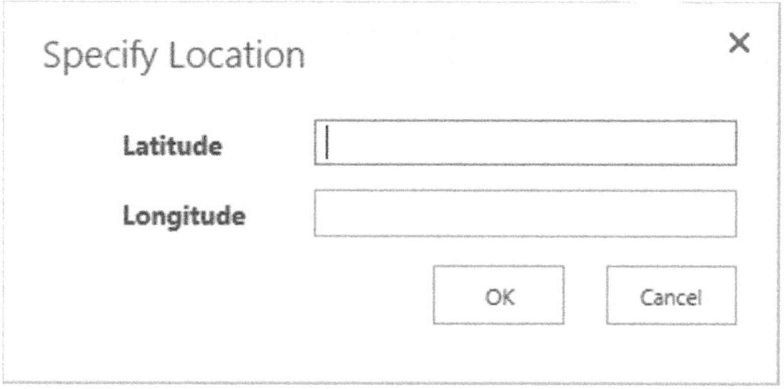

Figure 12-18. *A user can manually enter a latitude and longitude value*

■ **Limitation**   Although SharePoint offers users two options to create a location, both offer limited functionality and poor user experience. The first option only offers autodetection of the current location, rather than allowing the user to select a location. The second option is not user friendly, as most users do not have a way to get the latitude and longitude coordinates of a location. In the section "Enhancing Geolocation Features With a Custom SharePoint App" later in this chapter, we walk through how to build a solution to enhance the geolocation features in SharePoint.

Presenting a Map

As stated in Specter Group's requirements, each community site's home page should display a map that shows the location of the community and the community properties with pins. When a user clicks on the pin, a bubble displays the property address details. We need to first add a Map view to the custom list we have created in the previous step. Then, we need to add the House list as a web part on the Community Home page so that the houses will be shown on a map on the Home page.

1. Create a Map view for the custom list. On the List Settings page, create a new view using the Map View type and make it the default view for the list (see Figure 12-19).

Map View
View list data that includes a geographical location on a map.

Figure 12-19.   *Create a Map view for the custom list*

2. Navigate to the community site's home page.

3. Edit the page. Click anywhere within a content area. Select the Insert tab from the ribbon menu at the top of the page.

4. Under Categories, click Apps. Under Parts, click the name of the custom list (Houses) we just created (see Figure 12-20). Then click the Add button to the right.

Figure 12-20.   *Add the custom list as a web part to the home page to view all items in a map on the home page*

Once the list web part is added to the home page, it should look similar to the image in Figure 12-21. Note that values of all the non-geolocation-typed columns referenced by the view are displayed in the left pane next to the map control.

Figure 12-21. *Custom list on the Community home page to display all Community properties in a map*

Enhancing Geolocation Features With a Custom SharePoint App

In the previous sections, we have demonstrated how to accomplish all the Specter Group's business requirements with only out-of-the-box geolocation features in SharePoint 2013. But what if we need to implement and deploy the same solution to multiple community sites? What if the users do not know the latitude and longitude values of their houses? In the following sections, we will extend the geolocation features available in SharePoint 2013 to meet all of our requirements by building our own Geolocation SharePoint App.

Getting Started

Before we dive into the implementation of a custom SharePoint App, let's review the basics of SharePoint Apps and the prerequisites for creating a SharePoint-hosted App.

SharePoint Apps Overview

SharePoint 2013 introduces a new app model for creating applications in SharePoint. SharePoint Apps are self-contained pieces of functionalities that extend the capabilities of a SharePoint web site. Much like an app on a mobile device,

439

SharePoint Apps can be discovered by users and administrators from the SharePoint App Store or from their organization's private App Catalog and can be installed to their SharePoint sites. SharePoint Apps enable users to reuse the same content and functionalities across different sites. A SharePoint App is essentially an application that is registered with SharePoint to run in the scope in which it is installed. We can use SharePoint Apps to package data and functionalities to be reused by different sites while providing the same familiar user experience.

SharePoint Apps can be hosted on separate web servers, they can be hosted in Windows Azure, or they can be hosted within SharePoint. There are three hosting options for SharePoint Apps: SharePoint-hosted, provider-hosted, and autohosted. An app can be both SharePoint-hosted and remotely hosted. Each approach has its benefits. SharePoint-hosted apps only contain SharePoint components that are installed on the local SharePoint farm if on premises or on its own tenancy if on SharePoint online. Both provider-hosted and autohosted apps are meant for applications that include at least one remote component. Provider-hosted apps contain non-SharePoint components that are deployed and hosted on either a separate server on premises or on a cloud account. Autohosted apps are installed to a SharePoint host web with the remote components automatically installed into a Windows Azure web site account.

For the purposes of this chapter, we create a SharePoint-hosted app because all of the components are local SharePoint components. SharePoint-hosted apps are installed on a SharePoint site (referred to as the host web), and their resources are hosted on an isolated subsite of the host SharePoint site (referred to as the app web). This type of app is the best approach when we want to reuse common SharePoint artifacts, such as lists and web parts.

■ **Note**   SharePoint-hosted apps can use only client-side code and not any server-side code.

Configuring an Isolated App Domain in SharePoint

In our development environment, we need to start by making sure we have configured an isolated app domain in the SharePoint 2013 dev farm to create and deploy SharePoint-hosted apps. The app domain should be a URL namespace we reserve as a namespace for all Specter Group SharePoint Apps. We can configure an app domain for SharePoint in Central Administration or through PowerShell.

■ **Note**   To configure a SharePoint farm to host SharePoint Apps, we have to create a new name in DNS to host apps and a wildcard cname record for the new domain so that all requests for the app domain will be directed to this instance of SharePoint. Refer to the following link for steps to configure an app domain: http://sprwd.com/262kbat.

For demonstration purposes, we use PowerShell to configure an app domain for SharePoint. For Specter Group, we need to create an isolated app domain apps.spectergroup.com using SharePoint Management Shell as an administrator using the PowerShell command in Listing 12-8.

Listing 12-8. PowerShell to Configure App Domain for SharePoint

```
Set-SPAppDomain "apps.spectergroup.com"
```

In addition to creating the app domain, we also need to create a tenant name app using the PowerShell command in Listing 12-9.

Listing 12-9 PowerShell to Set app Tenant Name for SharePoint

```
Set-SPAppSiteSubscriptionName -Name "app"
```

Once this domain has been reserved, every time a SharePoint-hosted app is provisioned, the app will get a new URL that looks similar to http://app-898d05664cd685.apps.spectergroup.com.

Creating a New Active Directory Account for App Deployment

For developing and deploying SharePoint Apps, in SharePoint 2013, the system account is no longer supported to deploy or purchase any app from the market. It is now prohibited due to security reasons. We need to create a new Active Directory account for App deployment and log on to the development environment with the new account.

Create a new Active Directory account in the Specter group domain. Ensure that the account is a local admin as well as a farm admin in the SharePoint farm. Before creating and deploying any new apps, log on to the SharePoint development machine with the new account.

Installing Visual Studio 2012 and SharePoint Development Tools

Finally, in our development environment, we also need to install Visual Studio 2012 and SharePoint development tools for Visual Studio 2012. To read more about how to set up a SharePoint development environment, please refer to the section "On-Premises Development Environment" in the Appendix.

Creating a SharePoint-Hosted App

Using SharePoint development tools in Visual Studio 2012, we can create and deploy a SharePoint-hosted app.

1. Right-click to run Visual Studio 2012 as an administrator.

2. Click File ➤ New ➤ Project (see Figure 12-22).

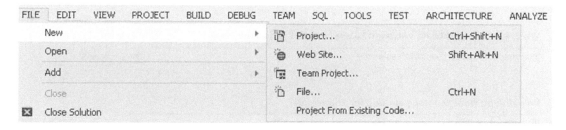

Figure 12-22. *Create a new project in Visual Studio 2012*

3. At the New Project prompt, expand Office/SharePoint ➤ Apps, and select App for SharePoint 2013 (see Figure 12-23).

Figure 12-23. Create a new App for SharePoint 2013 project in Visual Studio

4. Fill in the project name and file path information. Click OK.

5. At the New App for SharePoint prompt, do the following:

    a. Enter a name for the app.

    b. Enter a URL for the SharePoint site to deploy and test the app.

    c. Select SharePoint-hosted from the list of hosting options (see Figure 12-24).

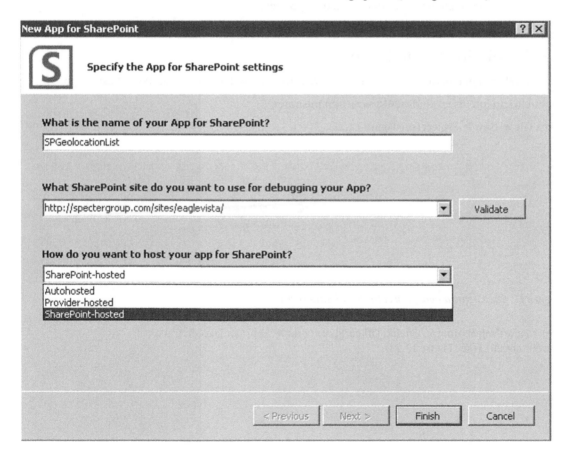

Figure 12-24. Specify settings for the new SharePoint App

    d. Click Finish.

Once the project is loaded in Visual Studio, select the name of the new project. In the Properties pane, enter a community site URL in the Site URL property. For our demonstration, it has been set to http://spectergroup.com/sites/eaglevista/ (see Figure 12-25). If we want to deploy the app to a different site, we need to update the Site URL property with the URL of the new site for deployment before we rebuild and redeploy the project.

Server Connection	Online
Site URL	http://spectergroup.com/sites/eaglevista/

Figure 12-25. *Specify the URL of a SharePoint site to be used for testing and deploying the new app*

Select the name of the new project, right-click the project, and select Build, then select Deploy. If the app did not install correctly, check to make sure the site URL is valid and administrative access has been granted for the developer to deploy the app on that site. If the following error is encountered, refer to the previous section, "Creating a New Active Directory Account for App Deployment" to create a new Active Directory user account specifically for deployment of apps. Then log into the development environment with the new Active Directory account.

```
Error occurred in deployment step 'Install app for SharePoint': The System Account cannot perform
this action.
```

If the app is deployed successfully, navigate to the URL of the test site in the Site URL project property and click View all site content. The new app is now installed (see Figure 12-26).

SPGeolocationList

new!

Figure 12-26. *New App installed in SharePoint site*

Click to launch the new app. If single sign-on has not been set up for the SharePoint domain or the app domain across the organization, you might be prompted for a credential, so enter a valid credential. The app shows the Default.aspx page by default, as shown in Figure 12-27.

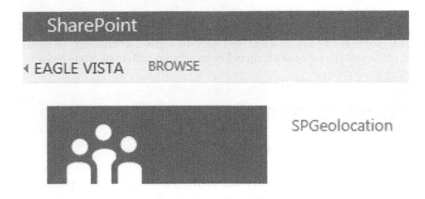

Figure 12-27. *App launches with the Default.aspx page*

Note, by default, an app's AppManifest.xml file in the project has set the Start page property to be the Default.aspx page (see Figure 12-28). Therefore, when the app launches, Default.aspx is the first page we see. You can change this to point to another page in the App if desired.

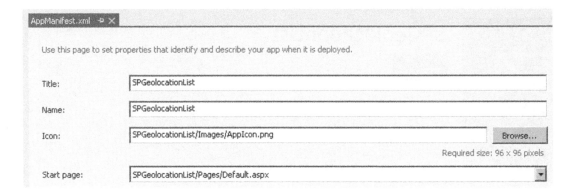

Figure 12-28. *App is set to launch the Default.aspx page first*

We now have successfully created and deployed a new SharePoint-hosted app. It does not do anything yet, but at least the shell is ready for our custom App. Before we add more content to the app, let's review the project structure of a SharePoint-hosted app. Expand the app project in Visual Studio. The files and folders displayed in Figure 12-29 are included by default.

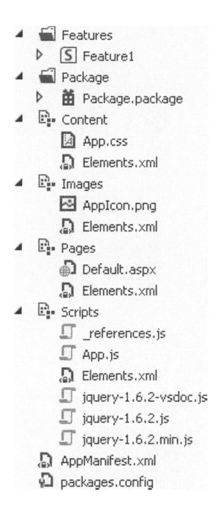

Figure 12-29. *SharePoint-hosted app Project file structure*

The Features folder is used to deploy features to SharePoint. By default, each app contains a feature called "[app name] Feature 1". The feature is scoped at the web level and deploys all the files under Pages, Scripts, Content, Images, and any other items created in the app to SharePoint (see Figure 12-30). These features are similar to the features you might have created for SharePoint 2010.

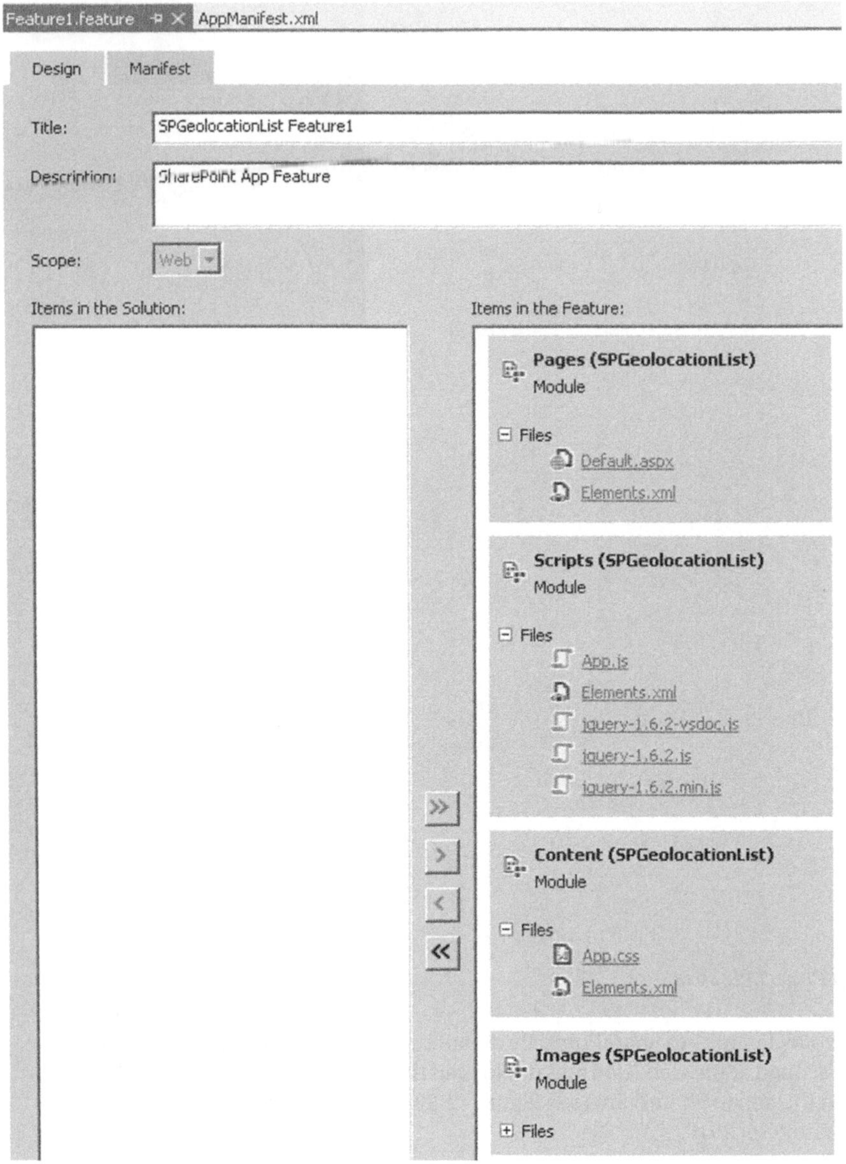

Figure 12-30. *Features XML structure to deploy files in App to SharePoint*

The Package folder in Figure 12-31 contains all the deployable files to the SharePoint server.

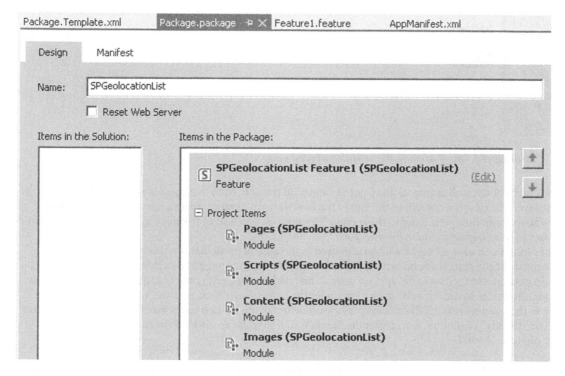

Figure 12-31. *Package XML structure to deploy files in App to SharePoint*

The Content folder in Figure 12-29 contains all CSS style sheets and any SharePoint components used in the app. For SharePoint components, we can add SharePoint lists, remote event receivers, content types, workflows, site columns, modules, SharePoint pages, Client web part for the host web, and user interface custom actions for the host web. For CSS files, we should keep our CSS inside of the App.css file because by default the Default.aspx page adds a reference to the App.css file. If we need to add new CSS files to the app, we need to first add the files under the Content folder, then we also need to add their references to the Default.aspx page under the page header section, as seen in Listing 12-10.

Listing 12-10. Add Referenced CSS and JavaScript Files to the PlaceHolderAdditionalPageHead Section in App's Default.aspx File

```
<asp:Content ContentPlaceHolderId="PlaceHolderAdditionalPageHead" runat="server">
        <!-- Add your CSS styles to the following file -->
        <link rel="Stylesheet" type="text/css" href="../Content/App.css" />
        <!--the rest of the content block-->
</asp:Content>
```

The Images folder contains all the icons and images used in the app. We can change the app icon for our Specter Group apps by renaming our own logo file AppIcon.png. Ensure the icon image has the dimension of 96 × 96. After we redeploy the App, the new logo is now using our own logo, as seen in Figure 12-32.

Figure 12-32. *New deployed App now using the modified AppIcon.png*

The Pages folder contains all .aspx and .html pages created in the app. Note these pages are relative to the app web, not the host web. To view the content in the app in the host web, we need to create a client web part to surface the content in a SharePoint host web. Refer to the section "Creating an App Part to Display Geolocation App Content in Host Web" later in this chapter for more information.

The Scripts folder contains all the JavaScript files used in the app. In particular, we should keep our app JavaScript code inside of the App.js file because by default the Default.aspx page adds a reference to the App.js file. If we need to add new JavaScript files to the app, we need to first add the files under the Scripts folder, then we also need to add their references to the Default.aspx page under the page header section. Note, we can also add inline JavaScript code to the header section. The inline JavaScript code in Listing 12-11 triggers functions, specifically in this case the sharePointReady() function, to run after the SharePoint JavaScript sp.js loads to ensure the SharePoint clientcontext object is loaded.

Listing 12-11. Add Inline JavaScript Code to the PlaceHolderAdditionalPageHead Section in App's Default.aspx File

```
<asp:Content ContentPlaceHolderId="PlaceHolderAdditionalPageHead" runat="server">
    <!-- Add your JavaScript to the following file -->
    <script type="text/javascript" src="../Scripts/App.js"></script>
    <script type="text/javascript" src="../Scripts/jquery-1.6.2.min.js"></script>
    <!-- The following script runs when the DOM is ready. The inline code uses a SharePoint feature
to ensure -->
    <!-- The SharePoint script file sp.js is loaded and will then execute the sharePointReady()
function in App.js -->
    <script type="text/javascript">
        $(document).ready(function () {
            SP.SOD.executeFunc('sp.js', 'SP.ClientContext', function () { sharePointReady(); });
        });
    </script>
    <!--the rest of the content block-->
</asp:Content>
```

The AppManifest.xml is the app definition file that defines the title, start page, permissions needed, feature prerequisites, and capability prerequisites for the app. When we open the XML file in an XML editor, we can also define Product ID, Version, SharePoint minimum version, and app permission requests (resources required by the app) for the app.

■ **Note**   When building Apps to access data from the host site or specific service applications, the App developer needs to make sure the App requests permissions it needs to run, through the app manifest file. The App installer must grant all the permissions the App requests before the App can run. To learn more about App permissions in SharePoint 2013, refer to http://sprwd.com/sbd5640.

Adding Geolocation Features to the SharePoint-Hosted App

Now that we have created a SharePoint-hosted app for our community site, let's go through the implementation of adding enhancements to the geolocation features to meet Specter Group's requirements.

Setting Bing Maps Key Using JavaScript Client Object Model

Earlier, we were able to set the Bing Maps key at the farm level using PowerShell. What if we do not have administrative access to the SharePoint servers to run PowerShell? What if we only want to set the Bing Maps key at the web level? We can do so by setting the Bing Maps key programmatically using either the SharePoint .NET client object model or the SharePoint JavaScript client object model. Because we are building a SharePoint-hosted app, we will need to use client-side API, such as the SharePoint JavaScript client object model to set the Bing Maps key.

1.   Open the App.js file to add the JavaScript in Listing 12-12 for setting the Bing Maps key.

Listing 12-12. Set the Bing Map Key Using the JavaScript Object Model

```
function sharePointReady() {
        context = new SP.ClientContext.get_current();
        web = context.get_web();
        var props = web.get_allProperties();
        props.set_item("BING_MAPS_KEY", "ApqzNRuOmn1Li2ngnD2x-
                ZCwalMBOm1IavSP5tcINeZRQ7feN1uppjEt-GpSPLiN");
        web.update();
        context.executeQueryAsync(onSetmapkeySuccess, onSetmapkeyFail);
}
function onSetmapkeySuccess() {
        alert("set map success");
}
function onSetmapkeyFail() {
        alert("set map failed");
}
```

2.   Recall that in Listing 12-11, the inline JavaScript code in the Default.aspx page triggers the sharePointReady() function to run after the SharePoint JavaScript's sp.js loads to ensure the SharePoint clientcontext object is loaded.

3.   In App.js, the sharePointReady() function first gets the current SharePoint context, then uses the JavaScript object model to update the SharePoint web Bing Maps key property with a valid Bing Maps key if it doesn't have one already.

4.   ExecuteQueryAsync takes in two parameters in the form of callback functions. Each callback will let us know if the execution completed successfully or failed.

After we rebuild and redeploy the app, we should see the alert success message shown in Figure 12-33 after loading the new app.

Figure 12-33. *Bing Maps key set successfully at the web level using the JavaScript object model*

Creating a Custom List Instance with a Geolocation Column

Once we have enabled Bing Maps and SharePoint integration using the JavaScript object model, we need to create a custom list instance within the App. Note that this custom list instance is not created for the host web; rather it will be part of the App web. The list instance will be available to users when they are in the App.

1. In Visual Studio, below the app project, right-click the Content folder.

2. Select Add ➤ New Item from the shortcut menu.

3. At the Add New Item prompt, select List (see Figure 12-34).

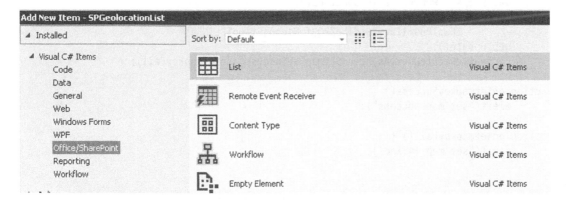

Figure 12-34. *Add a custom list to the App from Visual Studio*

4. Provide a name for the List: LocationList.

5. Click Add.

6. When prompted to choose list settings, select Default (Blank) from the customizable list drop-down (see Figure 12-35).

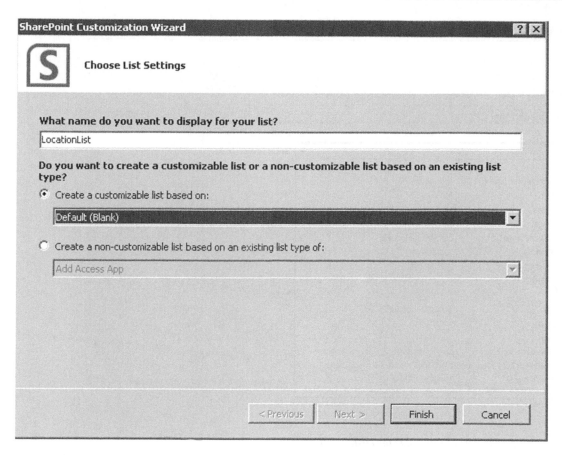

Figure 12-35. *Create a customizable list*

7. Click Finish.

8. After the list instance is created within the App, it will display the Columns view for us to add new columns to the custom list.

9. Click on a new row and select the Location column of type Geolocation from the drop-down list (see Figure 12-36). We see this geolocation column in this development environment because we have previously added a geolocation-type column in this community site via PowerShell.

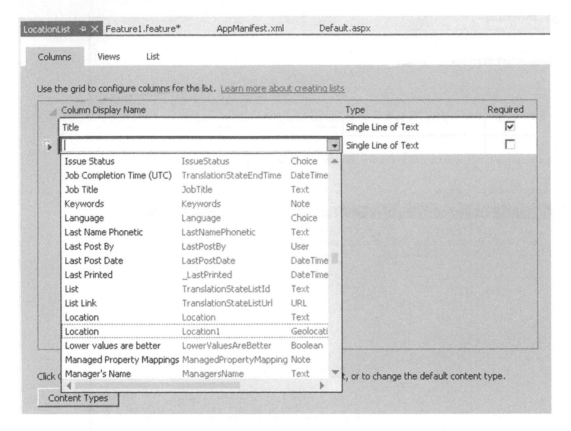

Figure 12-36. *Add a geolocation column to the custom list*

10. Expand the Content folder and find the Schemas.xml file for the LocationList.

11. Open Schemas.xml in the XML editor. Note the following column was added to the schema of the custom list. The specific GUIDs will be different in your environment.

```
<Field Type="Geolocation" DisplayName="Location" ID="{be075499-998a-4924-a69a-8fe11bcc612d}"
SourceID="{b9497bff-6e4c-4f72-89dd-80be589aebd0}" StaticName="Location1" Name="Location1" />
```

12. For users to interact with the new custom list instance in the App web, we can add a button on the Default.aspx page to allow users to navigate to the custom list (see Listing 12-13).

Listing 12-13. HTML Code Added to App's Default.aspx page to Display Link to the Custom List Instance

```
<asp:Content ContentPlaceHolderId="PlaceHolderMain" runat="server">
    <div>
        <input type="button" id="button" value="Location List" onclick="location.href =
'../Lists/LocationList'"/>
        <br /><br />
```

```
        <!-- ... rest of PlaceHolderMain ... -->
    </div>
</asp:Content>
```

After we deploy the app to the community site, the user can click the Location List button shown in Figure 12-37 to view the list.

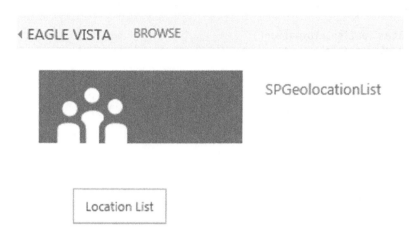

Figure 12-37. *Click the Location List button in the App to navigate to the custom list*

Then the user will see the custom list exactly like the out-of-the-box list we created earlier in the host web. The user can add a new item by clicking New item (see Figure 12-38) and then manually entering the latitude and longitude values or using the current location as detected by the browser.

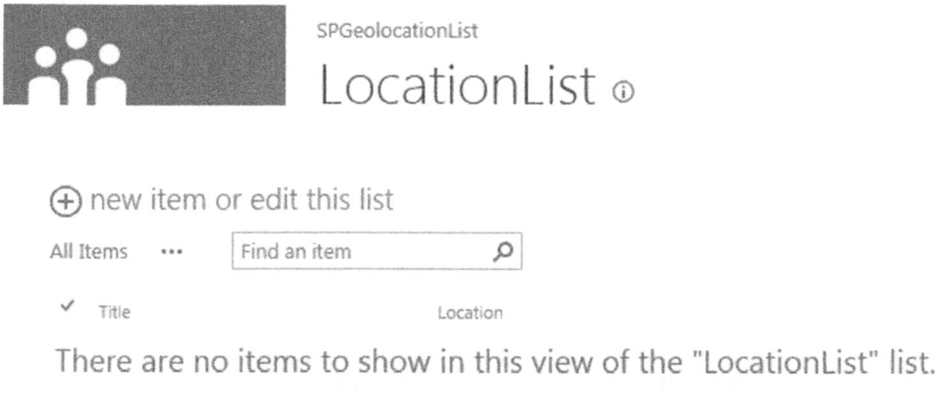

SPGeolocationList

LocationList ⓘ

⊕ new item or edit this list

All Items   ••• | Find an item   🔍 |

✓   Title   Location

There are no items to show in this view of the "LocationList" list.

Figure 12-38. *Custom list in the App has the same geolocation functionalities*

Using the JavaScript Client Object Model to Add a List Item

Now to allow users to enter an address or automatically detect location, we need to allow them to do so on the Default.aspx page without having to go to the actual SharePoint list (LocationList) to add a new item. Before we look at how to add HTML controls to the Default.aspx page to trigger the JavaScript function createListItem(), let's implement the JavaScript code for adding a new item to the list.

Open the App.js file in the Visual Studio project and add the JavaScript function in Listing 12-14 to the file. This function programmatically adds a new item to the LocationList custom list instance.

Listing 12-14. Using JavaScript CSOM to Add a List Item

```
//create an item in a list
function createListItem() {
    var oList = web.get_lists().getByTitle('LocationList');

    var itemCreateInfo = new SP.ListItemCreationInformation();
    this.oListItem = oList.addItem(itemCreateInfo);
    oListItem.set_item('Title', title);

    alert('Adding new location: (lat: ' + locationLat + ' long: ' + locationLong + ')');
    oListItem.set_item('Location1', 'POINT (' + locationLong + ' ' + locationLat + ')');
    oListItem.update();

    context.load(oListItem);
    context.executeQueryAsync(
        Function.createDelegate(this, this.onQuerySucceeded),
        Function.createDelegate(this, this.onQueryFailed)
    );
}

function onQuerySucceeded() {
    alert('Item created!');// + oListItem.get_id());
    window.location.reload();
}

function onQueryFailed(sender, args) {
    alert('Request failed. ' + args.get_message() +
        '\n' + args.get_stackTrace());
}
```

1. With the current SharePoint context, we can get the web object of the app web.

2. Get the LocationList by doing a title lookup from the list collection.

3. Create a new ListItemCreationInformation object to add a new item to the list.

4. Once the item has been added, we need to set the list item's fields one by one.

    a. First set the Title column value.

    b. Set the Location column value by constructing the value of the geolocation field with the actual latitude and longitude values in the "POINT (long, lat)" format.

5. After the columns are set, we need to update the new list item to save the values.

Using HTML5 Geolocation API to Autodetect Location

Before we enable the App to trigger the JavaScript function we created in the previous section to programmatically add a new list item to the list, we need to add a few controls on the Default.aspx page to get information from the user.

1. Open the Default.aspx page in the Visual Studio project.

2. Add a text field familytext for the Title (Family) column.

3. Add a button autodetectbutton for autodetecting the user's location by calling the getcurrentaddress() function, which uses the HTML5 API to get the geolocation from the browser (see Listing 12-15).

Listing 12-15. Default.aspx HTML to Allow Browser to Autodetect User's Location

```
<asp:Content ContentPlaceHolderId="PlaceHolderMain" runat="server">
    <div>
        *Family: <input id="familytext" type="text" style="width:400px"
                        value="Type family name here..." />
        <br /><br />
        <input type="button" id ="autodetectbutton" value="Use current location"
        onclick="getcurrentaddress();"/>
         <br /><br />
        <!-- ... rest of PlaceHolderMain ... -->
    </div>
</asp:Content>
```

In addition to getting information from the users, we also need to show users the actual list after the new items are created. Note that we are adding an XsltListViewWebPart control, which is the common web part for displaying any list in SharePoint.

4. On the Default.aspx page, we need to add the XsltListViewWebPart control shown in Listing 12-16 to the page below the autodetectbutton button.

Listing 12-16. Add an XsltListViewWebPart Control to the Default.aspx Page to Show the Geolocation List

```
<WebPartPages:WebPartZone runat="server" FrameType="TitleBarOnly" ID="full" Title="loc:full" >
    <WebPartPages:XsltListViewWebPart ID="XsltListViewWebPart2" runat="server"
        ListUrl="Lists/LocationList" IsIncluded="True"
        NoDefaultStyle="TRUE" Title="locationlist"
        PageType="PAGE_NORMALVIEW" Default="True" ViewContentTypeId="0x">
    </WebPartPages:XsltListViewWebPart>
</WebPartPages:WebPartZone>
```

At this point, the Default.aspx page should contain the controls shown in Figure 12-39.

SPGeolocationList

Location List

*Family: | Type family name here... |

Use current location

locationlist

⊕ new item or edit this list

Current View   ••• | Find an item   🔍 |

✓   Title   Location

There are no items to show in this view of the "LocationList" list.

Figure 12-39. *Default.aspx page to allow users to add information to the location list*

Next, we need to add JavaScript functions for autodetecting the user's location.

1. Open the App.js file and add the JavaScript in Listing 12-17 for detecting geolocation.

Listing 12-17. JavaScript Function to Autodetect User's Location Using HTML5 Geolocation API

```
function getcurrentaddress() {
    if (navigator.geolocation) {
        navigator.geolocation.getCurrentPosition(showPosition, showError);
    }
    else {
        alert("Geolocation is not supported by this browser.");
    }
}
function showPosition(position) {
    locationLat = position.coords.latitude;
    locationLong = position.coords.longitude;
    alert('Current lat: ' + locationLat + ' long: ' + locationLong);
    createListItem();
}
function showError(error) {
    switch (error.code) {
        case error.PERMISSION_DENIED:
            alert("User denied the request for Geolocation.");
            break;
        case error.POSITION_UNAVAILABLE:
            alert("Location information is unavailable.");
            break;
```

```
                case error.TIMEOUT:
                    alert("The request to get user location timed out.");
                    break;
                case error.UNKNOWN_ERROR:
                    alert("An unknown error occurred.");
                    break;
        }
}
```

2. The showPosition callback function resolves the latitude and longitude values and calls the createListItem() function in Listing 12-18 to create a new list item using the latitude and longitude values.

Listing 12-18. JavaScript Function to Create a New List Item Using the familytext Value as the Title of the New Item and the Latitude and Longitude Values as the Location

```
function createListItem() {
    var family = $('#familytext').val(); //get value for the Title column
    var oList = web.get_lists().getByTitle('LocationList');

    var itemCreateInfo = new SP.ListItemCreationInformation();
    this.oListItem = oList.addItem(itemCreateInfo);
    oListItem.set_item('Title', family);     //set Title column to the familytext field value

    alert('Adding new location: (lat: ' + locationLat + ' long: ' + locationLong + ')');
    //construct value for the geolocation column using the latitude and longitude
    //values we got from showPosition()
    oListItem.set_item('Location1', 'POINT (' + locationLong + ' ' + locationLat + ')');
    oListItem.update();

    context.load(oListItem);
    context.executeQueryAsync(
        Function.createDelegate(this, this.onQuerySucceeded),
        Function.createDelegate(this, this.onQueryFailed)
    );
}
function onQuerySucceeded() {
    alert('Item created!');// + oListItem.get_id());
    window.location.reload(); //reload the page to show new items
}
function onQueryFailed(sender, args) {
    alert('Request failed. ' + args.get_message() + '\n' + args.get_stackTrace());
}
```

3. The showError callback function displays error messages to users when autodetection fails.

4. With the geolocation values resolved in the showPosition() function and a valid value for the Title (family) column, we can now map the columns with these values to create a new list item in the createListItem() function (see Listing 12-18).

5. Once the item has been added, we notify the user the item has been created and reload the page to allow the XsltListViewWebPart to show the latest items in the list.

After we redeploy the app, the user can now create a new item. The user enters a value for the Family text field. Then the user clicks the Use current location button. The user is prompted to allow the site to track physical location. If the user clicks Allow, an alert window shows the latitude and longitude values, as shown in Figure 12-40.

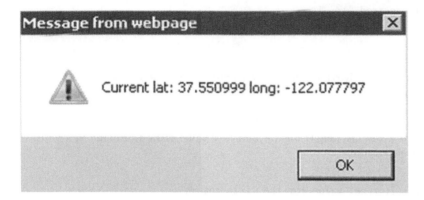

Figure 12-40. *Alert window showing the user's current geolocation coordinates using HTML5 Geolocation API*

The user then gets an alert confirming the item has been created. The page then refreshes to show the web part of the list with the newly created item (see Figure 12-41).

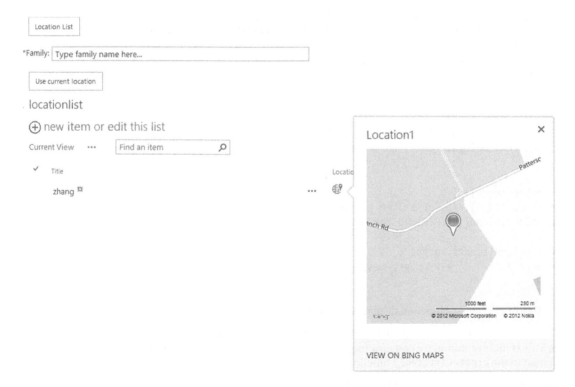

Figure 12-41. *After the item has been programmatically added to the list*

Resolving Geolocation from an Address

Autodetection of the location might not always be what the user is looking to do. Based on our requirements, community users would also like to enter the address of their properties regardless of where they are physically. We can support this by programmatically resolving geolocation information from a physical address entered by the user.

1. Open the `Default.aspx` page.

2. Under the header of the page, within the `PlaceHolderAdditionalPageHead` content placeholder, add a reference to the Bing Maps JavaScript as shown in Listing 12-19.

Listing 12-19. Add a Reference to the Bing Maps JavaScript API to the Default.aspx Page

```
<asp:Content ContentPlaceHolderId="PlaceHolderAdditionalPageHead" runat="server">
    <!-- Add reference to bing map -->
    <script src="http://ecn.dev.virtualearth.net/mapcontrol/mapcontrol.ashx?v=7.0"></script>
    <!-- ... rest of Content Placeholder Content ... -->
</asp:Content>
```

3. Below the `autodetectbutton`, add a text field `addresstext` for users to enter an address (see Listing 12-20).

Listing 12-20. New Controls to Add to the Default.aspx Page for Resolving Location From an Address

```
Type Address: <input id="addresstext" type="text" style="width:400px"
                        value="Type address here..." onclick ="clearaddressdefault();" />
<input type="button" id ="getaddressbutton" value="Get address" onclick="getaddress();"/><br />

<div id='mapDiv' style="position:relative; width:0px; height:0px;"></div>
```

4. Add a button `getaddressbutton` for users to trigger the `getaddress()` function, which uses Bing Maps JavaScript API to resolve latitude and longitude values from an address (see Listing 12-20).

5. Add a div `mapDiv` to be used by Bing Maps JavaScript. We can hide it in our solution because we do not need the Bing Maps API to show a separate map control (see Listing 12-20).

6. In the `App.js` file, at the top of the file, add a variable for the Bing Maps map object:

   ```
   var map;
   ```

7. At the end of the `SharePointReady()` function, add the code in Listing 12-21 to initiate the map object using the Bing Maps key.

Listing 12-21. JavaScript Code to Initiate the Bing Maps Map Object

```
map = new Microsoft.Maps.Map(
            document.getElementById("mapDiv"),
            { credentials: "Your Bing Maps key",
            mapTypeId: Microsoft.Maps.MapTypeId.road });
```

8. Add the `getaddress()` function in Listing 12-22 to the `App.js` file to get the address from the `addresstext` text field.

Listing 12-22. JavaScript Functions to Request Bing Maps Service to Resolve Locations From an Address

```javascript
function getaddress() {
    var address = $('#addresstext').val();
    ClickGeocode();
}

function ClickGeocode(credentials) {
    map.getCredentials(MakeGeocodeRequest);
}

function MakeGeocodeRequest(credentials) {
    var geocodeRequest = "http://dev.virtualearth.net/REST/v1/Locations?query=" +
        encodeURI(document.getElementById('addresstext').value) +
        "&output=json&jsonp=GeocodeCallback&key=" + credentials;
    CallRestService(geocodeRequest);
}

function GeocodeCallback(result) {
    alert("Found location: " + result.resourceSets[0].resources[0].name);

    if (result &&
        result.resourceSets &&
        result.resourceSets.length > 0 &&
        result.resourceSets[0].resources &&
        result.resourceSets[0].resources.length > 0) {

        //get lat and lon
        var lat = result.resourceSets[0].resources[0].point.coordinates[0];
        var long = result.resourceSets[0].resources[0].point.coordinates[1];
        locationLat = lat;
        locationLong = long;
        createListItem();
    }
}
```

9. Add the `ClickGeocode()` and the `MakeGeocodeRequest` function in Listing 12-22 to the `App.js` file. These functions make a request to the Bing Maps service to get an address resolved providing the Bing Maps key credential and the address entered by the user. Note, in the request, it also tells the service the name of the callback function: `GeocodeCallback`.

10. Add the `GeocodeCallback` function in Listing 12-22 to the `App.js` file. This function is called when the service returns the geolocation result in JSON. We use the result object to get the name of the returned location and the latitude and longitude coordinates. Then we call the `createListItem()` function in Listing 12-18 to create a new item based on the new coordinates.

After we redeploy the app, the user can enter an address in the address field and click the Get address button, as shown in Figure 12-42, to have the geolocation coordinates resolved all from the `Default.aspx` page.

Figure 12-42. *App now allows users to enter an address*

After the user clicks the Get address button, if the location is found, the user sees an alert like the one in Figure 12-43.

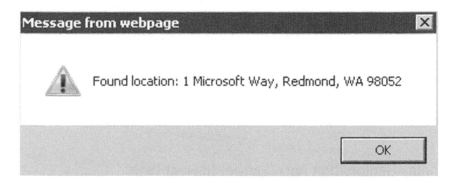

Figure 12-43. *Alert showing the user the location has been found and the proper address as resolved by the Bing Maps service*

After clicking OK, the user sees an alert confirming the item has been added to the list and the page refreshes with the latest item on the list, as shown in Figure 12-44.

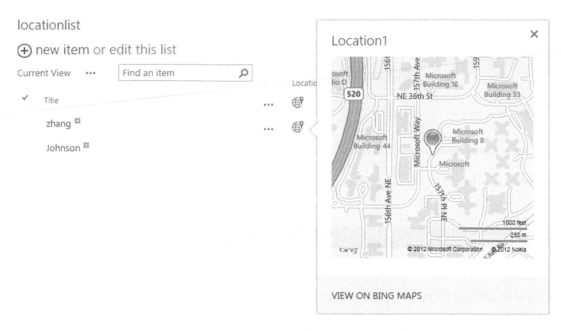

Figure 12-44. *New list item added after user enters an address to be resolved into geolocation coordinates*

Creating an App Part to Display Geolocation App Content in Host Web

As mentioned earlier in this chapter, SharePoint-hosted apps are installed on a SharePoint site (referred to as the host web), and their resources and content are hosted on an isolated subsite of the host SharePoint site (referred to as the app web). So far we have been performing all of our user actions in the app web instead of the host web (community site). Based on our requirements, we need to expose all the functionalities we have created to the host web (community's home page). We can do so by creating an app part. With app parts, we can display the content in our app right in the host web using an IFrame.

■ **Note**   To learn more about creating app parts with SharePoint Apps, refer to `http://sprwd.com/76uyrzd`.

---

1. Starting from Visual Studio, right-click the Content folder below the app project, and click Add ➤ New Item.

2. At the Add New Item prompt, select Office/SharePoint and click Client Web Part (Host Web) (see Figure 12-45).

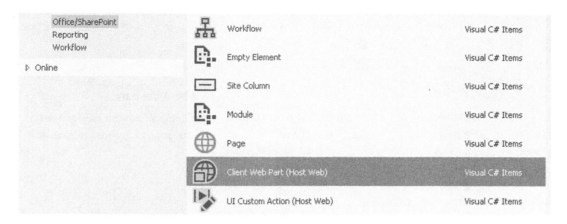

Figure 12-45. *Add a client web part component to the App to surface content from the app web*

3. Name the web part SPGeolocationListWebPart.

4. After the new client web part is added to the project, the Element.xml file (see Listing 12-23) for the web part will automatically open for editing. Within this file, we can edit the Title, Description, Default width, and Default height values. Make sure the name property of the web part is the same as the name of the web part file we just added to the project.

Listing 12-23. Client Web Part Contains an Element.xml File That Allows Configuration of Title, Description, Width, and Height

```
<ClientWebPart Name="SPGeolocationListWebPart"
                Title="SPGeolocationListWebPart"
                Description="This is the SPGeolocationListWebPart."
                DefaultWidth="500"
                DefaultHeight="600">
```

5. Within the same Element.xml file, we also need to ensure the following section (see Listing 12-24) is set to the app's Default.aspx page as the web part will render this page by default.

Listing 12-24. Use Element.xml File to Configure Page to Render Within the Client Web Part

```
<Content Type="html" Src="~appWebUrl/Pages/Default.aspx" />
```

6. For the client web part to surface content from the app, we need to add the AllowFraming tag in the Default.aspx page to allow it to render in an IFrame. Open the Default.aspx page and add the AllowFraming tag in Listing 12-25.

Listing 12-25. Add AllowFraming Tag to the Default.aspx Page to Ensure This Page Can Be Displayed in an IFrame

```
<WebPartPages:AllowFraming ID="AllowFraming1" runat="server" />
```

7. After we redeploy the app, edit the community's home page.

8. Click the Insert tab on the ribbon, and then select App Part.

9. From the list of App Parts, select the new Client web part we just deployed (see Figure 12-46) and add it to the page.

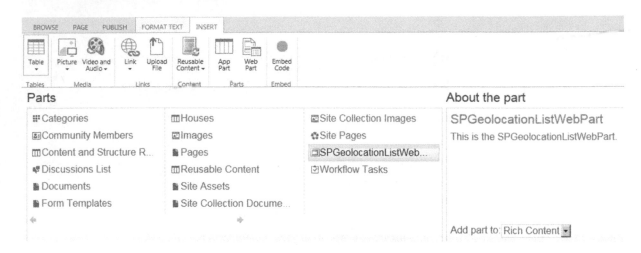

Figure 12-46. *Add client web part to the community site home page (host web)*

After the web part is added, users can perform all the functions they were doing in the app web in the host community site (see Figure 12-47).

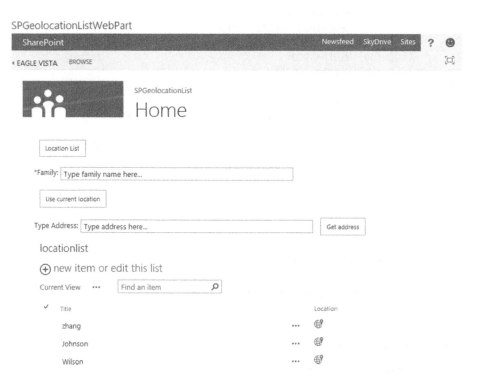

Figure 12-47. *Work with the App and its content from the host web after adding the App's client web part to the page*

Deploying the Geolocation App to an App Catalog

After we have implemented and tested the SharePoint-hosted app, we need to deploy it to an App Catalog in the Specter Group production site for more community sites to utilize the app.

If we do not have an App Catalog in our SharePoint environment, we need to create one.

1. Navigate to Central Administration.

2. On the Apps page, in the App Management section, click Manage App Catalog.

3. Select a web application we want to create an app catalog for if it is not already selected.

4. In the App Catalog site section, select Create a new app catalog site, then click OK.

After the App Catalog is created, we can navigate to the App Catalog site.

1. From the development environment, move the .app SharePoint app file from the solution bin directory to a location that is accessible from the App Catalog.

2. On the App Catalog site, find the Apps for SharePoint library, then click New app to add a new file with the .app extension (see Figure 12-48).

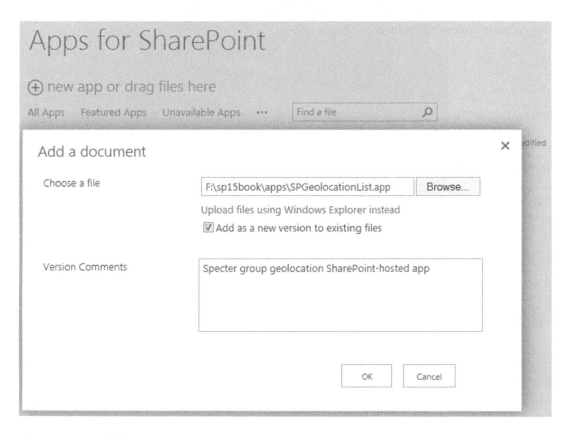

Figure 12-48. *Add the App's package .app file to the App Catalog to deploy the App*

3. After the App is added, we need to add a few pieces of metadata for the new App.

4. Under Category, select an existing value or provide a new value to group the apps in the App Catalog (see Figure 12-49).

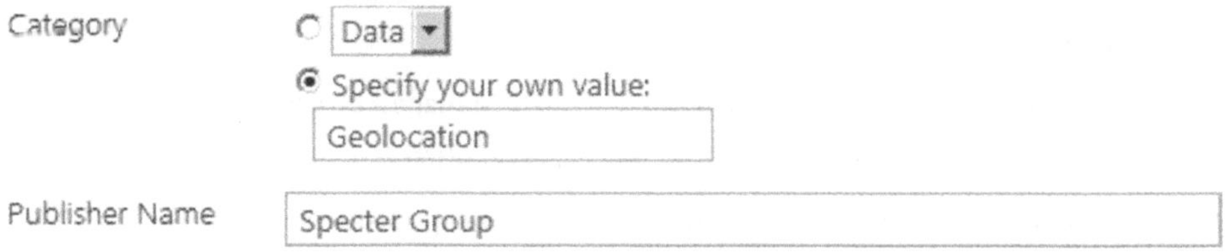

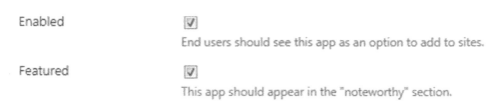

Figure 12-49. *Add metadata to the newly deployed App*

5. Under the Publisher Name, in our case we specify Specter Group as the App's publisher (see Figure 12-49).

6. We also need to ensure the app is enabled for end users to find and to add to their site. Because this App is going to be needed for all the community sites, we should set the app to appear in the Noteworthy section (see Figure 12-50).

Enabled   ☑
End users should see this app as an option to add to sites.

Featured   ☑
This app should appear in the "noteworthy" section.

Figure 12-50. *Enable the App to be searched and added to users' sites*

Now that the app is in the App Catalog, a user can click Settings ➤ Add an app to find the app in the App Catalog, as seen in Figure 12-51.

Apps you can add

SPGeolocationList
from Specter group
App Details

Figure 12-51. *App as seen by users after it's added to the company's App Catalog*

The user can double-click the app to add it. Before the app can be installed, the user must click Trust It to allow the app to be installed (see Figure 12-52).

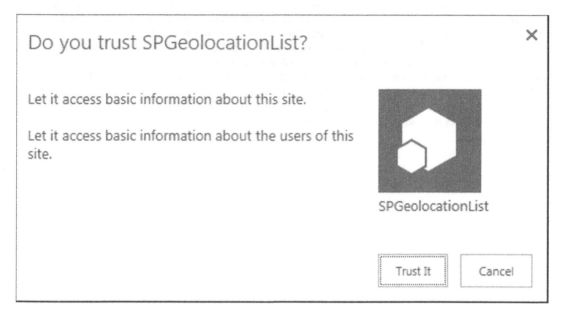

Figure 12-52. *Users need to trust the app before it can be installed to their sites*

After the app is added, the app looks like the following and is ready for use. Users can click to start the app and add and remove locations or they can add an App part (client web part) to any SharePoint page and use the app and its content within the host web.

Figure 12-53. *The new app is added to the user's site ready for use*

Summary

With the rapid adoption of smart phones and tablets, we have the opportunity to use GPS capabilities to support location-based features in our web site. In this chapter, we have demonstrated the basic features provided by HTML5 geolocation API and how we can utilize it in our own web site. We then learned how to configure and use the new geolocation column and the new map view in SharePoint 2013. Based on our business requirements, we needed to extend the SharePoint 2013 geolocation features by creating a geolocation SharePoint-hosted app. For the app, we used SharePoint JavaScript client object model to programmatically add a list item to a list. We also used the HTML5 Geolocation API to autodetect geolocation information from the user's browser. We then used Bing Maps JavaScript API to resolve geolocation coordinates from a user-provided address. Finally, we created an App part that allows users to add a Client web part to display the content from the app in the host web.

■ ■ ■

CHAPTER 13

Integrating Feeds and Social Media

Almost every company today leverages social media sites such as Facebook and Twitter to reach their relevant audience and keep a relationship with them. When building a web site, access to and integration with these networks is very important. This chapter looks at different methods to integrate your social feeds as well as sharing from within your SharePoint site. The presence of these networks on your site, however added, is crucial to increase the interaction between your visitors and your brand. If someone chooses to follow you on Twitter or to like your Facebook page, they are choosing to stay within your reach by getting regular updates through these networks. In this chapter, we take a look at the different popular social networks and how they are different from one another. We then look at some of the different ways to have a site interact with these networks, from feeds to sharing as well as other techniques. Finally, we go through the steps to integrate these types of social networks in a SharePoint site.

Our Scenario

Because the Specter Group is launching a brand new responsive site with SharePoint 2013, they want to make sure that the social networks used by the company are accessible from the site. One of the objectives is to make sure a visitor can come to this web site as a central hub using all social portals Specter Group is using. Access to their Facebook page, YouTube videos, Twitter account, and Google+ page, along with any other or future networks is important. The Specter Group is very active on Twitter and requested that a feed of their Twitter account be shown on all pages of the site as well. Finally, as part of our business requirement and overall goal to increase the brand's visibility online, sharing or recommending pages should be easily accessible to the user.

■ **Note** In the scenario in which Specter Group adds social integration to the web site, it is assumed that each relevant network that has already been set up is being kept alive with content.

As our work is to extend the web site to interact with a few of these social networks, it's important to understand how they each work at a high level.

- Facebook: Organizations create Facebook pages and use them to share news, announcements, pictures, videos, promotions, and any other marketing material. The objective of the web site should always be to facilitate the process of liking the organization's Facebook page.

- Twitter: Similarly, an organization will have a Twitter page with followers. Through our web site design, we want users to easily share pages on their own Twitter account, thus increasing our reach. Twitter can also be used to facilitate communication with our end users, so it's important to understand and plan what you need to accomplish with Twitter before starting the design.

- LinkedIn: LinkedIn is geared toward a professional network, where members enter their work-related profiles and companies create their pages. As with other services, users can share their feed and follow company pages, but it also allows for profile card summaries, a company's information and profile, and the ability to apply for a job. Of course there are other plug-ins such as "Jobs you may be interested in" and "Recommend with LinkedIn" available, but we use the more popular plug-ins for the Specter Group SharePoint site.

- Google+: Another social network available is Google's very own Google+. Again the same principle is applied: The organization will create a business page, share its news, and allow Google+ users to follow the organization's page. The distinctive Google+ feature is its +1 button, which allows users to recommend a page to their friends and followers.

Social

We could write an entire book on social networks and how to use them properly. Increasing search engine optimization (SEO) through the use of these tools on your site, building engagement models, targeting the right audience, and so much more fit under this broad title. Social networks have become very important when building a web site design and need more than a chapter to be explained. For the purposes of this book, we focus on basic integration of these networks on a site.

It goes without saying that there are many social media networks that can be relevant to an organization while being less relevant to others. When building the design of a site, even before thinking about the kind of integration that is required, you should know what social networks the organization is engaged in and define clear goals of what the web site should be using. Some organizations might be seeking an increase in Twitter followers, whereas others might seek to increase YouTube subscriptions and the sharing of videos. Once these goals are known, you can start identifying the types of integration you seek to add on your site.

■ **Note**   Social media in the heart of the enterprise has become a very broad and popular subject in the last years. We strongly recommend you learn about this and the different related topics from subject matter experts in the field before adding them in the site's design.

Levels of Social Media Integration

It's important to understand that there are different levels of social media integration. As part of the planning of our web site design, we must choose how we want to leverage these networks. No two organizations are the same: The target market is very different for each of them and so is the way each organization chooses to communicate or interact with its market. We use the Specter Group site design to provide an example of one of the many possible mobile strategies you can use. We must first look at different possible integrations and see which might work for this site.

Basic: Link to Social Pages

A basic but necessary way to integrate your organization's social media on your web site is by adding hyperlinks to the organization's pages on the respective social networks. A common practice is to add clickable icons that direct to your social pages (see Figure 13-1).

Figure 13-1. *Social networks listed on a site as hyperlinks*

■ **Note** We look at how to add this social toolbar on the Specter Group site later in this chapter.

Subscribing: Following or Liking Social Pages

Another way of adding social networks on your site is through the notion of liking, subscribing, or following a social page (see Figure 13-2). Each social network has its own way of doing this. Note that there are differences in each network, such as liking a page on Facebook is not the same as following a page on Facebook.

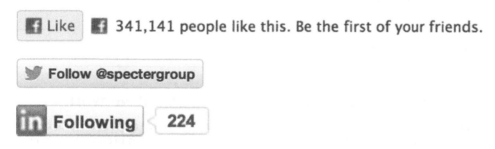

Figure 13-2. *The Like and Follow buttons of Facebook, Twitter, and LinkedIn*

Facebook is the social network most organizations get confused with. The popular comment is, "We need a Like button on our web site," when what is really desired is a Follow button. The issue comes with the terminology used in day-to-day activities in using Facebook. When managing a Facebook page, we are seeking more Likes, which translates into users automatically seeing our updates on their feed. However, when we are on a web site, the Like button no longer means the same thing. When clicked, it tells Facebook that the user wants to tell his or her network that he or she likes this specific online web page. It has nothing to do with the brand it represents. If the requirement is to increase the company's Facebook page's number of followers, we need a Follow button.

All the different social plug-ins are available on the developer pages of each social network, the most popular of which are shown in Table 13-1.

Table 13-1. *URLs for Social Network Plug-Ins*

Network	Developer Page
Facebook	`https://developers.facebook.com`
Twitter	`https://dev.twitter.com`
LinkedIn	`http://developer.linkedin.com`
Google+	`https://developers.google.com/+/`

Embedding a Feed on a Page

A common practice is to embed a Twitter feed of the organization's account or to follow specific mentions and hashtags. In the example of social media integration shown in Figure 13-3, we added the Twitter feed in the footer of our site.

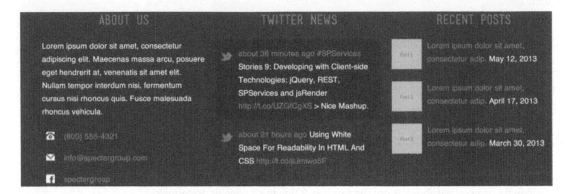

Figure 13-3. *Footer with Twitter News displayed*

■ **Note** We look at how to add this social toolbar on the Specter Group site later on in this chapter.

Sharing: Allowing Visitors to Share an Activity to Their Social Network

Also very popular, in this scenario the visitor can share what he or she is looking at, purchased or done to his or her social networks. This can be added in various contexts, from sharing the web site the visitor is on to announcements or blog posts inside the web site (see Figure 13-4). This aspect of integration has to be as quick and painless as possible to visitors, as otherwise they might just give up on their will to share.

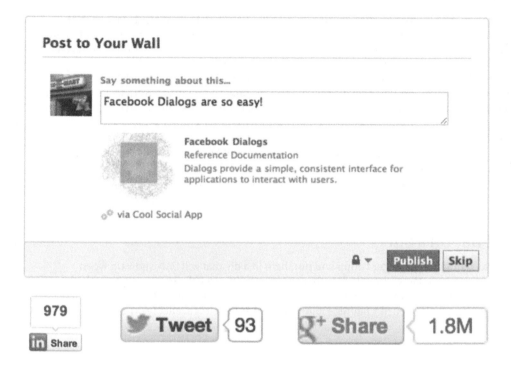

Figure 13-4. *Social networks' various share buttons*

Every social network comes with its own special interactions. More often than not, you will find many different social plug-ins available through each social network's developer page. For example, one might want to use the LinkedIn Recommend button for each of the team members on the web site.

Building the Basic Links to the Social Network Pages

Adding links to our social networks sounds like a trivial task. And as far as the integration part, in most cases it is fairly straightforward. What is often skipped is the actual planning that goes on before starting to write any code. Do you plan to add all your social networks? What is their expected behavior? Will they open in a separate window or tab? What is meant by the expected behavior is very important: We need to define how these links will be presented on our pages and how much real estate they will be given. This will be different for every organization.

Planning the Implementation

One of the requirements for Specter Group was for the web site to be the central hub for visitors. From there, anyone should be able to visit Specter Group's Facebook or Twitter page. However, the need for the links to the social networks was not so predominant that we would give them too much real estate on the page. We decided to go with a toggle menu that would show these networks if the visitor requested it.

Deciding where to put the links to the social networks can be challenging, especially in a responsive design. Obviously, the business requirements for the brand and the site have a large role to play in this. Are we trying to direct our audience to our Facebook and Twitter accounts where we have a strong established presence, or are we just providing links to them for those that are actively searching for them?

Having larger, more prominent links to the active social networks the company is using tends to lead the user away from our web site. This is done mostly when the type of service our site offers does not incite the user to visit often. Our company needs to keep a constant relationship with its audience and if there is no reason to come back to the site then the risk of losing that audience increases.

For these reasons, we decided that Specter Group did not need large accessible social network links because the audience will be coming back to visit the site often. For example, a clothing company will want users to visit and follow their Facebook page. The clothing company can then regularly update their site visitors and customers with new styles as seasons change.

Although we chose to limit the number of social networks shown on the social bar, we could not remove two very popular links, the RSS feed and a link to the YouTube channel. Although they are not necessarily considered social networks, they are often grouped with them and visitors have come to expect this presentation. The RSS feed allows visitors to subscribe to anything you have enabled an RSS feed for on your site. Most often this will be a blog or news section. YouTube, of course, is used to share videos.

Adding the Social Bar on a Site

We chose the social networks required for Specter Group and put them in a div that will only show up when requested. The best way to do this is to start without hiding them so that you can see the end result. In code shown in Listing 13-1 we add the HTML structure for our social bar, followed by the CSS in Listing 13-2 to style it. This social bar is added to the HTML master page we created in Chapter 4 and Chapter 5 so that it is available on all pages of the site.

Listing 13-1. Adding the HTML for the Social Bar

```
<div class="social cf down">
    <ul class="cf">
        <li>
            <a href="http://www.facebook.com/spectergroup">
                <img src="img/social/Facebook.png" alt="Facebook">
            </a>
        </li>
        <li>
            <a href="http://www.twitter.com/spectergroup">
                <img src="img/social/Twitter.png" alt="Twitter">
            </a>
        </li>
        <li>
            <a href="https://plus.google.com/u/0/b/123456789012345678 90/">
                <img src="img/social/Google+.png" alt="Google+">
            </a>
        </li>
        <li>
            <a href="http://ca.linkedin.com/in/spectergroup">
                <img src="img/social/LinkedIn.png" alt="Linked In">
            </a>
        </li>
        <li>
            <a href="http://www.spectergroup.com/feed">
                <img src="img/social/RSS.png" alt="Blog">
            </a>
        </li>
```

```
        <li>
            <a href="http://www.youtube.com/user/spectergroup">
                <img src="img/social/YouTube.png" alt="YouTube">
            </a>
        </li>
    </ul>
    <a class="social-toggle" title="Follow Us">
        Toggle
    </a>
</div>
```

Listing 13-2. Adding the CSS for the Social Bar

```css
/*social*/
header .social {
    position: absolute;
    top: -39px;
    right: 10px;
    height: 32px;
    padding: 0px 7px 7px;
    background: #993300 none;
    border-radius: 0px 0px 0px 5px;
    -moz-border-radius: 0px 0px 0px 5px;
    -webkit-border-radius: 0px 0px 0px 5px;
}
header .social ul {
    display: block;
}
header .social ul li {
    float: left;
    display: block;
    padding-left: 7px;
}
header .social ul li:first-child {
    padding-left: 0px;
}
header .social ul li a {
    display: block;
    width: 32px;
    height: 32px;
}
header .social a.social-toggle {
    position: absolute;
    bottom: -20px;
    right: 0px;
    display: block;
    padding: 0px 10px 8px 10px;
    height: 14px;
    width: 16px;
    background: #993300 url('../img/icon-arrows-vert.png') no-repeat 10px 0px;
    text-indent: -9999px;
    border-radius: 0px 0px 5px 5px;
```

```
    -moz-border-radius: 0px 0px 5px 5px;
    -webkit-border-radius: 0px 0px 5px 5px;
    -webkit-transition: all 0s ease;
    -moz-transition: all 0s ease;
    -o-transition: all 0s ease;
    transition: all 0s ease;
}
header .social a.social-toggle:hover {
    cursor: pointer;
}
header .social.down {
    top: 0px;
}
header .social.down a.social-toggle {
    background-position: 10px -25px;
}
.csstransforms.csstransitions header .social {
    -webkit-transition: top 500ms ease;
    -moz-transition: top 500ms ease;
    -o-transition: top 500ms ease;
    transition: top 500ms ease;
}
/*end social*/
```

Figure 13-5 shows the social bar that results from our code to this point.

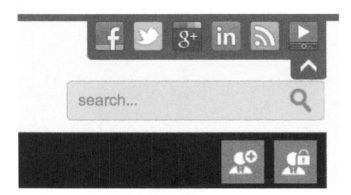

Figure 13-5. *The Social Networks bar expanded*

As you can see, all of Specter Group's networks were added in an unordered list inside a div. This div holds the list of icons as well as the toggle button we plan to use. To make the change as smooth as possible, add a class to your div called down that will simply change the top position of the div from off the screen to 0 from the top. With the help of the new CSS3 transition property and simple JavaScript with some jQuery to toggle the class down on or off, we have exactly what we need (see Listing 13-3).

Listing 13-3. Provide a Click Function to Display or Hide the Social Icon Bar

```
<script>
//social
jQuery(document).ready(function($) {
    $('header .social a.social-toggle').click(function() {
        if ($('header .social').hasClass('down')) $('header .social').removeClass('down');
        else $('header .social').addClass('down');
    });
});
</script>
```

The code in Listing 13-3 enables the social bar to be collapsed, as shown in Figure 13-6, or expanded as we saw previously in Figure 13-5.

Figure 13-6. *The Social Networks bar collapsed*

In this section, we built a simple social network bar that we added to the header of the Specter Group HTML master page. Now, in the next two sections let's add a Facebook Follow button and embed a Twitter feed on our site.

Adding a Facebook Follow Button

The first thought that might come to mind is "Why not use a Like button instead?" and that is a very good question. The Facebook Like button only allows visitors to tell everyone on their feed that they "like" this specific page; it has nothing to do with subscribing to Specter Group's Facebook page. If the goal is to increase the number of subscribers or followers, we need to choose the Facebook Follow social plug-in. Thankfully, you do not need to reinvent the wheel for this one: Facebook provides a lot of information, including a code builder. Simply take the code generated by Facebook and add it to your master page.

■ **Note**   All of the documentation and code generators are located on Facebook's developer page at
`https://developers.facebook.com`.

Once on the Facebook developer page, click the Social Plugins link in the Docs section. From there, you can choose the Follow button from a list of social plug-ins for Facebook.

First, enter the URL of the Facebook page for which you need to create a Follow button. Next, choose the layout, if you need to show the profile pictures and some of the color and font schemes (see Figure 13-7).

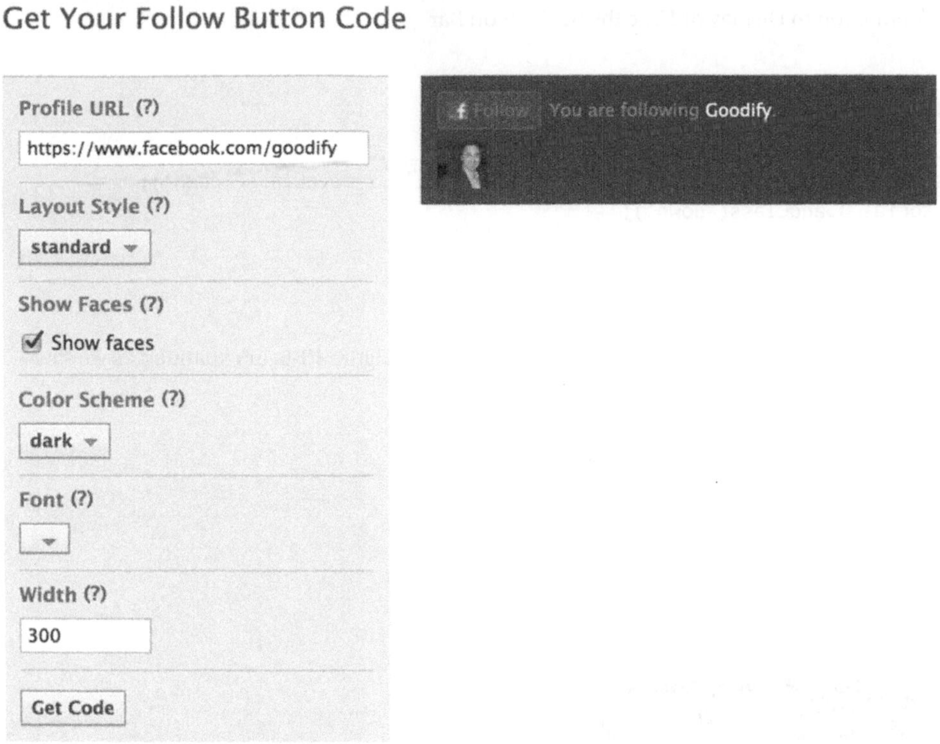

Get Your Follow Button Code

Figure 13-7. *Facebook Follow button properties*

Set the various properties for your Follow button:

- The Profile URL must have Follow enabled whether it's a user or a page. Facebook pages have this enabled by default.

- Layout Style allows you to pick what the button looks like.

- Show Faces displays the profile picture of the logged-in visitor's friends that follow this page.

- Color Scheme will make the widget with either a dark or light background.

- You may also set the font that should be used within the widget.

- We chose a width of 300 to make sure it always fits in our About Us column in the footer. Remember not to exceed a width of 320 pixels or otherwise this button might break on smaller viewports.

The code that Facebook generates uses a script that turns the social plug-ins into IFRAMES. Therefore we must be vigilant when implementing it to respect our responsive design.

Once you click Get Code, Facebook offers you the options to implement it in HTML5, XFBML, IFRAME, or URL (see Figure 13-8).

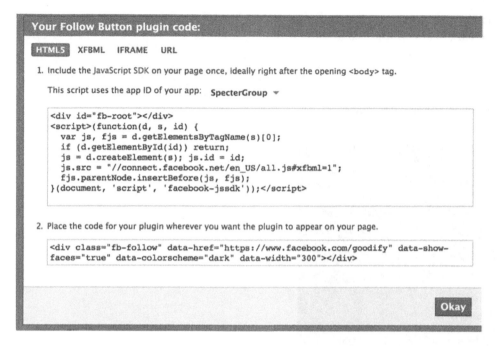

Figure 13-8. *Facebook button plug-in code*

■ **Note**   Facebook offers an extensive amount of documentation for each of these plug-in codes and languages at
`https://developers.facebook.com`.

Make sure you have no JavaScript errors on your page before testing this as they might stop the Facebook Social
plug-in from working. Also, Facebook suggests adding the div directly after the opening body tag. Although this is true
on most public HTML sites, SharePoint is a little different. Ideally, place this code in your HTML master page after
the opening div with an ID of s4-workspace. SharePoint adds a few tags of its own after the opening body tag that
interfere with the expected values for the fb-root div.

To make sure this works with our tailored responsive column design in the footer, we add the Follow button
HTML before the closing tag of the About Us fluid column (see Listing 13-4).

Listing 13-4. Follow Button div Added to Footer

```
<!—previous code of the footer not shown -->
<footer>
  ...
  <div class="span4">
    <h4>ABOUT US</h4>
    <p>Lorem ipsum dolor sit amet</p>
    <ul class="contact">
      <li class="phone">(800) 555-4321</li>
      <li class="email"><a href="mailto:info@spectergroup.com">info@spectergroup.com</a></li>
      <li class="fb"><a href="http://www.facebook.com">spectergroup</a></li>
    </ul>
```

```
    <div class="fb-follow" data-href="https://www.facebook.com/goodify" data-show-faces="true"
        data-colorscheme="dark" data-width="300">
    </div>
    ...
</footer>
```

Figure 13-9 shows the Follow button in the footer.

Figure 13-9. *Facebook Follow button*

Adding a Twitter Feed to the Site

Twitter has some of the easiest methods for developers to interact with when building a site. As mentioned earlier, Twitter also has a developer center, `https://dev.twitter.com`, where we can find all the information we need to start integrating feeds into our site. Feeds can show anything from an account's tweets, to a hashtag, as well as lists. Hashtags are words in a tweet that begin with a pound sign (#), telling Twitter that this word is used to categorize the tweet. They help users find others talking about the same topic. A Twitter list allows the user to choose specific accounts to receive tweets from in a group. Many consider it to be grouping multiple accounts to make a single custom feed.

Building the Basic Feed

When deciding to add a Twitter feed to a site, you must look at what kind of interaction or customization you are looking for. The Twitter developer site offers a "widget" generator that will be an embedded timeline based on your settings (see Figure 13-10). You can find the generator at `https://twitter.com/settings/widgets`.

Figure 13-10. *Tweet feed widget*

■ **Note**   To use an embedded Twitter feed, we must generate the code by specifying the domain on which it will be used. This is a Twitter security measure. It does support "localhost," which is not helpful for SharePoint.

There are a few reasons we might use the embedded Twitter feed. It's quick and easy to create with a widget generator. A major disadvantage is that like the Facebook Follow button we saw earlier, it adds itself through an IFRAME on our page. Not only does that make it almost impossible to brand, but it isn't friendly to our responsive design. Lucky for us there are other ways to add a Twitter feed on our site.

Use jQuery to Display a Twitter Feed

For the Specter Group site, it was important for us to incorporate our look and feel for the company Twitter feed. The default embedded timeline Twitter offers makes us work with an IFRAME, which is not exactly desired in this situation. Of course, we could create our own feeds with the documentation available on http://dev.twitter.com. We can run a search on Twitter and load the results as just plain HTML on our page. See Listing 13-5 for the script used to fetch the Twitter feed information.

Listing 13-5. Add Twitter Feed Using jQuery

```
<!--we must link to the jQuery library if we have not already-->
<script type="text/javascript" src="//ajax.googleapis.com/ajax/libs/jquery/1.9.1/jquery.min.js">
</script>
```

```
<div id="twitter_feed">
</div>
<script type="text/javascript">
   jQuery(document).ready(function($) {
      var script=document.createElement('script');
      script.type='text/javascript';
      script.src=
         'http://search.twitter.com/search.json?&q=%23SharePoint&callback=processTheseTweets&_='
         + new Date().getTime();
      // Loading it in Body
      $("body").append(script);
   });
   function processTheseTweets(jsonData) {
      var shtml = '';
      var results = jsonData.results;
      if(results) {
         $.each(results, function(index,value){shtml += "<p class='title'><span class='author'>"
            + value.from_user
            + "</span>: " + value.text + "<span class='date'>" + value.created_at +
               "</span></p>";});
         // Load the HTML in the #twitter_feed div
         $("#twitter_feed").html( shtml );
      }
   }
</script>
```

Another solution would be to use one of the many already available jQuery libraries for Twitter feeds. For Specter Group, we used the open source project from Github called seaofclouds. It is available in the form of a jQuery library and all it requires is a few settings to let it know what you want to display. The advantage of using a plug-in such as this for your web site is the immense capability to customize the way the information is presented.

1. Add the reference to the jQuery library in your master page or on the page to which you wish to add the Twitter feed. The code is shown in Listing 13-6.

    Listing 13-6. Reference the jQuery Library

    ```
    <script language="javascript" src="/tweet/jquery.tweet.js"
    type="text/javascript"></script>
    ```

2. Add the necessary settings in a script file or in a `script` tag in the head of your master page (see Listing 13-7).

    Listing 13-7. Add Twitter Feed Using jQuery Plug-In seeofclouds

    ```
    // Tweet feed
    $("#tweets").tweet({
      count: 3,
      username: "spectergroup"
    });
    ```

3. Then simply create a `div`, in this case with an ID of `tweets` and a class of `tweet` (see Listing 13-8).

Listing 13-8. HTML for seaofclouds

```
<div id="tweets" class="footer-col tweet">
    <h4>TWITTER NEWS</h4>
</div>
```

4. Finally edit the CSS to get the look and feel for your Twitter feed, as shown in Listing 13-9.

Listing 13-9. Custom Styles to Control the Look of the Twitter Feed

```
/* Tweet widget CSS */
.tweet, .query { }
.tweet .tweet_list, .query .tweet_list {
   -webkit-border-radius: .5em;
   list-style-type: none;
   margin: 0;
   padding: 0;
   overflow-y: hidden;
}
.tweet .tweet_list .awesome,.tweet .tweet_list .epic,.query .tweet_list .awesome,.query
    .tweet_list .epic {
   text-transform: uppercase;
}
.tweet .tweet_list li, .query .tweet_list li {
   overflow-y: auto;
   overflow-x: hidden;
   padding: 1em ;
   background-image: url(../img/icon-bird.png);
   background-repeat: no-repeat;
   background-position: 6px 19px;
   padding-left: 40px;
}
.tweet a,.query  a {
}
.tweet .tweet_list .tweet_odd,.query .tweet_list .tweet_odd {
   background-color: rgba(0,0,0,0.2);
}
.tweet .tweet_list .tweet_avatar,.query .tweet_list .tweet_avatar {
   padding-right: .5em;
   float: left;
}
.tweet .tweet_list .tweet_avatar img, .query .tweet_list .tweet_avatar img {
   vertical-align: middle;
}
/*end tweets*/
```

Figure 13-11 shows the resulting feed.

Figure 13-11. Styled Twitter feed using jQuery plug-in seaofclouds

---

■ **Note**   Find this library and all associated files at `http://sprwd.com/87jm3mc`.

Choosing Between Sharing Tools and Building Your Own

Social sharing has become very popular if not mandatory today. Over time, certain third parties decided to create tools to help site designers quickly and easily integrate all the social sharing widgets they needed instead of managing them all manually. In this section, we look at the differences between these tools and building our own customized widgets.

Sharing Tools

Planning to add sharing to social network options on a site rarely involves just one social network. We always want to make sure that whichever social network the visitor is using, we make it possible for them to share it easily. The problem is it can be quite time consuming to get each social network's code and add it to your site. To help developers integrate sharing to multiple social media sites at the same time, quickly and easily, a few solutions have surfaced on the market. Among them are two very popular ones today: ShareThis and AddThis.

■ **NOTE**   There are other sites that offer this service but these are the popular ones. See `http://sharethis.com/` and `http://www.addthis.com/`.

Using tools like ShareThis and AddThis can literally get social links up and running on your site, like the one in Figure 13-12, in under ten minutes.

Figure 13-12. *ShareThis used to add social feeds*

Most sharing tools allow some customizations as well. For the sharing tools to appear above, we simply copied and pasted the references to their JavaScript library in the head tag of our master page and added the JavaScript code the sharing tool provided at the desired location. However, we tend to lose control over the experience the visitor has with sharing to social networks. Something to point out is that social networking sites often redirect the user to the login page instead of showing a pop-up. This can result in a very bad experience for s site visitor. That's why we sometimes look at a more customized experience and create our own sharing buttons.

For example, after going through the first steps of building a custom ShareThis button, we received the `script` tags shown in Listing 13-10 and placed them in the head section of our master page.

Listing 13-10. ShareThis Script Tags

```
<script type="text/javascript">var switchTo5x=true;</script>
<script type="text/javascript" src="http://w.sharethis.com/button/buttons.js"></script>
<script type="text/javascript" src="http://s.sharethis.com/loader.js"></script>
```

And we put the code shown in Listing 13-11 right below the `footer` tags. Although you can add it anywhere, it is common to add it toward the closing `</body>` tag of your code.

Listing 13-11. ShareThis Script Tags

```
<script type="text/javascript">stLight.options({publisher: "8a70d7ad-79f0-4d6f-910c-
    619d9c964da2", doNotHash: false, doNotCopy: false, hashAddressBar: false});</script>

<script>
var options={ "publisher": "8a70d7ad-79f0-4d6f-910c-619d9c964da2", "position": "left", "ad": {
    "visible": false, "openDelay": 5, "closeDelay": 0}, "chicklets": { "items": ["facebook",
    "twitter", "linkedin", "yammer", "googleplus"]}};
var st_hover_widget = new sharethis.widgets.hoverbuttons(options);
</script>
```

Depending on the requirements of social networks and the importance of the design, this could be a very quick and viable option. Note that they do allow some customization through the use of their API, but that is outside the scope of this book.

Custom Sharing Experience

Building your own sharing buttons can greatly enhance the user's experience on your web site. From the image icon used to click to the pop-up window to write a custom message on their feed, everything can be reworked. If the design of the web site uses the new Microsoft Modern UI with tiles but the sharing buttons are traditional, your site design suddenly does not feel finished. The disadvantage to building your own sharing buttons is the time you invest in building and testing it to get the solution working exactly as defined in the design mockups. The end result is usually much more satisfying to the web site's visitor.

As updates are added to the sharing tools like AddThis, much more visual customizations are added for the designer to play with. However easy and quick it is to get up and running certain facts remain. You depend on these external services, so if they are down so are your site's sharing widgets, all at once. There is also a matter of performance as these tools are scripts loading more scripts. For the sake of the Specter Group site, we will look at adding a custom Share to Twitter button.

Adding a Custom Share to Twitter Button

To create a custom Share button, we'll have to first investigate how this can be done. As mentioned earlier, there are various ways to build these solutions. We're going to look straight at the source on the developer resource site that Twitter offers.

Building Your Own Twitter Button

Twitter offers different ways to communicate or share a message. We can easily add a Share button on a page, but the real value is in preparing the message for the user to post with the desired hashtags or mentions. A Twitter message's reach is greatly increased when using these in a tweet. For Specter Group's site, we want to allow visitors to contact the support team through Twitter in a quick and easy way.

First we look at the available Share buttons on the developer page of Twitter (see Figure 13-13).

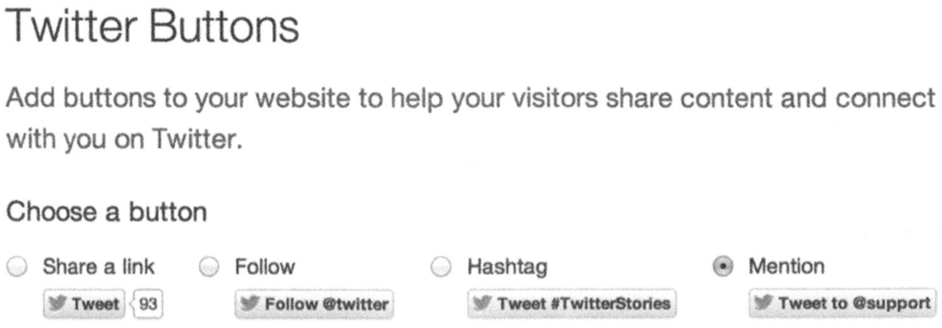

Twitter Buttons

Add buttons to your website to help your visitors share content and connect with you on Twitter.

Choose a button

○ Share a link	○ Follow	○ Hashtag	● Mention
🐦 Tweet · 93	🐦 Follow @twitter	🐦 Tweet #TwitterStories	🐦 Tweet to @support

Figure 13-13. *Available Twitter buttons*

If you are planning to use the available Twitter share buttons, integration will be a breeze. Simply set your configurations, as shown in Figure 13-14, and copy and paste the code where needed.

Button options

Tweet to   `@`   spectergroup

Tweet text   ○   No default text

          ◉   Some Custom Text

Recommend   `@`   spectergroup

            `@`   username

         ☑   Large button

Preview and code

Try out your button, then copy and paste the code below into the HTML for your site.

🐦 **Tweet to @spectergroup**

```
<a href="https://twitter.com/intent/tweet?s
<script>!function(d,s,id){var js,fjs=d.getElem
```

Figure 13-14. *Twitter Share button options*

In this example, we added the generated code before the closing tag of the About Us section in the footer. The result is shown in Figure 13-15.

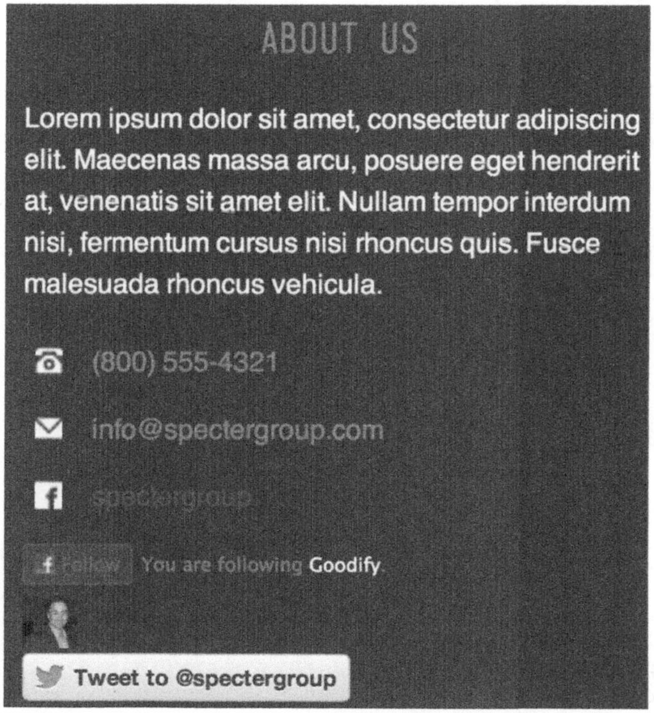

Figure 13-15. *Twitter Share button added to footer*

■ **Tip** Generate a Twitter button at `http://sprwd.com/57jvv3c`.

When this button is clicked, the user is prompted to log in to Twitter and a message is already generated contacting the Specter Group support team (see Figure 13-16).

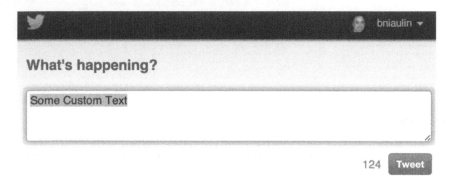

Figure 13-16. *Twitter dialog to send a tweet to launching site's Twitter feed*

■ **Note** All of the information on customizing the button for Twitter can be found at `http://sprwd.com/f9in5n7`.

Creating Your Own Twitter Button

What's fun with Twitter is that you have easy control over the button's look and feel. You do not need to be a social media integration expert to get things running. Almost everything can be done with a hyperlink and some CSS. Let's change the default Share button we added earlier to a custom one.

The CSS

Listing 13-12 shows the CSS we opted to use to style our custom Share button.

Listing 13-12. Style a Twitter Button

```
<style type="text/css" media="screen">
   #custom-tweet-button a {
      display: block;
      padding: 2px 5px 2px 40px;
      background: url('/_catalogs/masterpage/spectergroupbootstrap
         /img/icon-bird.png') 1px center no-repeat;
   }
</style>
```

This should give the custom feel we are looking for.

The HTML

A very simple div with a hyperlink will do the trick with Twitter (see Listing 13-13).

Listing 13-13. HTML for a Custom Twitter Button

```
<div id="custom-tweet-button">
   <a href="https://twitter.com/share?text=I%20made%20a%20custom%20Tweet%20Button!"
      target="_blank">Rock it!</a>
</div>
```

Figure 13-17 shows the result for the few lines of HTML and CSS we wrote.

Figure 13-17. *Custom Twitter button added to footer*

The Pop-Up Issue

There is one issue with the customized Twitter Share button for the user's experience. Right now, it's just a hyperlink with some CSS. This means that when users click on it, it will simply open a page and navigate to the login and share screen in full screen mode. We'll need to go the extra mile and add some JavaScript to turn it into a friendly pop-up menu.

There are many different ways to do this, and as an example we used jQuery to provide a pop-up on click in Listing 13-14.

Listing 13-14. Create a New Window for the Custom Twitter Button When Clicked

```
<script>
jQuery(document).ready(function($) {
   $('.popup').click(function(event) {
      var width = 575,
```

```
        height = 400,
        left   = ($(window).width()  - width) / 2,
        top    = ($(window).height() - height) / 2,
        url    = this.href,
        opts   = 'status=1' +
                   ',width-' + wldth +
                   ',height=' + height +
                   ',top='   + top   +
                   ',left='  + left;

    window.open(url, 'twitter', opts);

    return false;
  });
});
</script>
```

The script is saying to change the sizing of a window opened by a link that has the .popup CSS class. For the script to work, we need to go back and edit the HTML for the Share button we made earlier (see Listing 13-15).

Listing 13-15. Modified Listing 13-12 with Additional Class

```
<div id="custom-tweet-button">
  <a class="popup" href="https://twitter.com/share?text=
    I%20made%20a%20custom%20Tweet%20Button!&url=http%3A%2F%2Fspectergroup.com"
    target="_blank">Rock it!</a>
</div>
```

Now we have the expected behavior of a pop-up window when clicking on the custom Share button. Figure 13-18 shows the result of a traditional pop-up window.

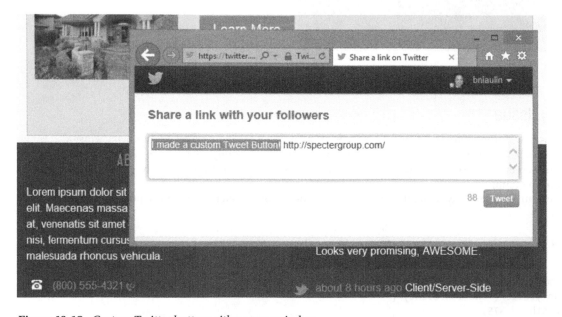

Figure 13-18. *Custom Twitter button with pop-up window*

Additionally we can find all the documentation necessary to build our own sharing buttons online for each social network:

Twitter: `https://dev.twitter.com/`

Facebook: `http://developers.facebook.com/`

LinkedIn: `https://developer.linkedin.com/`

Google+: `https://developers.google.com/+/`

Yammer: `https://developer.yammer.com/`

There is a lot more that can be done with social integration for a given site and we hope this chapter has provided a good primer.

A good way to start is by browsing the web for prebuilt projects like the one we used; they can save you a lot of time and often offer very solid solutions. Make sure to always start with a plan for what is needed in your organization and how it should be implemented or experienced on your site, though. This step is often forgotten and yet is very important to the success of your site's overall design

Summary

Social networking has become part of our everyday lives and companies know it. It has become part of marketing efforts to engage and reach the target audience. When building a new site it is important to consider which social network we are using and how we plan to integrate them into our site.

In this chapter, we started by understanding the business's need for sharing with social networks. We then continued by exploring the different levels of social media integration like basic links or sharing buttons. Then we built our very own social bar, Facebook Follow button, and Twitter feed, and even looked at building our own custom Twitter sharing button over the prebuilt widgets. All the while, we considered our responsive web design. It is common for easy solutions to use IFRAMES that can be difficult to work with in a responsive design. Because SharePoint 2013 supports the new HTML5 doctype and so do most of these social sharing widgets, we should leverage them as much as possible or create our own custom solutions. Thankfully there is a lot of documentation available on this on each of the social network's sites.

■ ■ ■

CHAPTER 14

Supporting Multilingual Web Sites

To compete in today's globalized marketplace for products and services, businesses need to ensure their web sites support multiple languages. The majority of the Internet's content is in English and as a result, it is also one of the most competitive languages to market in. There are other huge markets to be targeted that are much less saturated and provide more cost-effective marketing opportunities. Potential customers in different markets appreciate businesses that make the effort to provide them information about products and services in their native language. Many users become disengaged with sites that do not facilitate access through their local languages. A company's web site can demonstrate the company's maturity and show customers the company is capable of conducting business in multiple languages. The need for multilingual web sites is growing. More companies are making the investment to make their web sites multilingual, which has produced measurable improvements in company sales and customer satisfaction. In this chapter, we build our own multilingual sites using the Variations and Translation Services features in SharePoint 2013.

Multilingual Support

When we create an Internet site, it's important to note that the instant we publish a page onto the World Wide Web, it becomes global. We need to ensure the site is flexible and adaptable to international requirements. The process is less painful if we plan for multilingual support from the start, before the site first launches. Adapting the site content for international users requires a two-step process: localization and optimization.

The localization aspect requires a professionally qualified native-speaking translator for each of the target languages. The translation of the site is made easier if we use minimal rich media content, as it's difficult to edit, copy, and perform word counts, processes that are crucial to translation.

To optimize the site for international users, we shouldn't translate our keywords and phrases directly from our English language site. People might use abbreviations, acronyms, or synonyms to search for products and services locally. We should instead research key terms users use to search for items in their respective markets. We can then incorporate these keywords and phrases into our professionally translated site. We should always keep search engine optimization (SEO) in mind when building modern Internet sites. Having the site content in different languages allows for different versions of keyword targeting and a better chance of attracting more users through search engines.

Most browsers today detect localization of the user, which allows web sites to dynamically display content in the targeted language. In some cases, we might want to consider creating an entrance page or a menu to allow users to choose a navigation language for the site.

Our Scenario

The public Specter Group web site is targeted to showcase community properties to public visitors and potential buyers. Based on market research and census data, most of Specter Group's communities are located in areas that have a high percentage (40%) of German-speaking population. To attract more visitors, Specter Group plans to provide a multilingual experience on the public site. Specter Group's objective is to enable users to view content on the site and find the information they need in the language of their choice. Although the majority of the content published in the site will be in English, the most important content about the company and company news will be available in German and English. In addition, Specter Group wants the site to automatically detect the user's localization and display the content in the target language per the user's browser settings.

Multilingual Enhancements in SharePoint 2013

Microsoft has made several enhancements in multilingual functionality since SharePoint 2010. Things are much faster, repeatable, and manageable.

Before we dive into specific multilingual features in the following sections, let's compare the new features in SharePoint 2013 with how things worked in SharePoint 2010. Using features from its predecessors, SharePoint 2013 is still using the Labels and Variations features for translation. The Variations feature has been available since SharePoint 2007. Although variations underwent technical changes in the last few iterations of the product, the concept remains unchanged in SharePoint 2013. When we do translation exports from one site to another variation site, the export packages are much smaller compared to a single big job in SharePoint 2010. Unlike the exported CAB package generated by SharePoint 2010, SharePoint 2013 is now using the industry-standard XLIFF file format to export content for translation to a third-party translation service and to import the content back to SharePoint after it has been translated. SharePoint now relies on timer jobs that run a queue or a replication list. As the queue gets processed, items in the queue get marked as replicated. If we need to stop or pause the replication process for any reason, as soon as the process restarts again, it will go back to the queue or the replication list and continue to process where it left off. This process enables us to publish more than one label at a time.

New in SharePoint 2013, a publishing page's metadata emits the page's language for search engines at the time it performs the indexing. Another new feature is the machine-based translation via the Bing Translation service. This allows the content to be automatically translated in the cloud. Before SharePoint 2013, lists and libraries that did not have content pages did not automatically have the content replicated and we did not have the option to enable replication unless the content was referenced from within a page that was replicated. Now in SharePoint 2013, we can replicate a list or library and translate it from one label to another.

■ **Tip** The Variations feature is available in the Standard and Enterprise editions of SharePoint 2013. They are also available on Office365 for Midsize business and above. For more up to date information on feature availability on SharePoint online and license requirements, refer to Microsoft TechNet at `http://sprwd.com/dhmpvbk`.

Along with the cross-site publishing feature, host header site collections, and managed navigation features, we now have the ability to have multilingual-friendly URLs. We can export content for translation to a third-party translation service by using the industry-standard XLIFF file format and import the content back to SharePoint after it has been translated. This can be done on an entire label, one page, navigation, or selected items. Instead of pushing the updated content, label owners are notified of changes and can pull content on demand.

■ **Tip** For SharePoint apps, if the app specifies supported languages or locales, then the app will fail to install if the supported languages are not included in the server language packs installed on the SharePoint installations. Note that this is not an issue for Office 365 as all language packs have been installed there.

Planning for Multilingual Sites

Multilingual sites support users in different regions who speak different languages to access the content of the site. We can use SharePoint 2013 variations features to create multilingual sites to make it easy to track site content updates and changes. Before we start the implementation, we need to determine the languages and locales requirements of our site to plan for which language features and components to install and configure on our servers.

Language and Locale Requirements

It's important to determine all the languages and locales we have to support for the Specter Group site now and in the future. It is easier to install language support during initial deployment instead of waiting to install when the servers are running in a full production environment. The actual content of a site can be created in any language. We do not have to create a site in a specific language to view the content in that language. The locales are regional settings that specify how numbers, calendars, dates, and times are displayed. Locales are independent of the language of the site. Unlike language setting of a site, locales can be changed at any time. If there is a need to add additional languages to the site in the future, we need to first ensure the site supports multilingual when it was created. To design a site with multilingual support, refer to the section "Implementing Multilingual" later in this chapter. Then, we need to ensure the language pack for each additional language is deployed to the environment and a new variation label for each additional language is created for the site.

■ **Important**   After a site has been created for a specific language, the default language of the site cannot be changed. The user can use the multilingual user interface to select an alternative language in which to display the site.

For Specter Group, we need to support both the English and the German language today and maybe Spanish in the future. The locales we need to support are en-us for the English (United States) locale, de-de for the German (Germany) locale, and es-es for the Spanish (Spain) locale.

■ **Note**   For a list of supported languages and locales, refer to `http://sprwd.com/yrazwyy`.

Plan for Variations and Labels

The variation feature enables us to make the same content available to specific audiences across different sites in different languages depending on the language settings. Each site collection can have one variation hierarchy defined. We can create target sites for different languages and locales based on a source site with a language and locale within the same site collection. A variation consists of a set of labels, one for each language. Then the variation feature will create subsites, one for each label (language). We need to determine what labels we need to create based on the list of languages we need to support. Then we need to decide what language the source content should be. For more information on how to use Variations for multilingual sites, refer to the section "Creating Variation Hierarchy."

■ **Note** A variation can have only one source label and cannot be changed after it's created. Each variation hierarchy can have up to 50 labels for a site collection. Practically speaking, because the Variations feature is only applicable at the site collection level, when a site collection supports multilingual, it supports the creation of variation labels for one variation hierarchy within the site collection. With the limitation of 50 labels for each variation hierarchy, we can have no more than 50 languages for a given site collection.

Variation supports friendly URLs to help users navigate to the language of their choice. We can then export and import content for translation by a third party using the industry-standard XLIFF file format. Within an exported package, we can include labels, a page for translation and replication, a variety of list items, and navigation.

For Specter Group, we will have two labels, one as the source, en-us English (United States), and one as the target, de-de German (Germany). In the future, we might need to create another target label, es-es Spanish (Spain).

Language Pack Requirements

Every language has a language pack. A language pack is a set of files that when installed enables the user to interact with an application in a language other than the one in which the application was initially created, including other font characters if they are necessary. Based on the list of languages we want to support in the site, we need to install all the corresponding language packs on our web front end and application servers in our server farm. To learn how to install language packs, refer to the section "Deploying Language Packs" later in this chapter. Once the language packs are installed, language-specific site templates become available in SharePoint for creating new sites, as shown in Figure 14-1.

Template Selection

Select experience version:

2013 ▼

Select a language:

German ▼

English
German
Spanish

Se   ate:

arbeit   Ente

Figure 14-1. As soon as a language pack is installed in the farm, we can create a new site collection in that language

After a site is created with a specific language site template, many user interface elements will then be displayed in the language of the specified site template, such as ribbon elements, list and site column headers, site settings, lists, document libraries, site templates, and managed metadata tagging (see Figure 14-2).

Template Selection

Select experience version:

2013 ▾

Select a language:

German ▾

Select a template:

Zusammenarbeit   Enterprise   Veröffentlichen   Benutzerdefiniert

Veröffentlichungsportal
Unternehmenswiki
Produktkatalog

Eine Startwebsitehierarchie für eine im Internet veröffentlichte Website oder ein
großes Intranetportal. Diese Website kann problemlos mit einem unverkennbaren
Branding angepasst werden. Sie umfasst eine Homepage, eine Unterwebsite mit
Beispielpresseerklärungen, ein Suchcenter und eine Anmeldeseite. Normalerweise
verfügt diese Website über deutlich mehr Leser als Mitwirkende, und sie wird zum
Veröffentlichen von Webseiten mit Genehmigungsworkflows verwendet.

Figure 14-2. *Once a language is selected during the new site collection creation process, we will see all the language-specific site templates*

■ **Note**   Once language packs are installed, they provide translation only for the user interface elements, not for the content created in pages or web parts.

By default, sites and site collections are created in the base language in which the SharePoint product was installed. For instance, if we have a French version of SharePoint 2013, then the default language for creating new sites will be French. If we need to create sites, site collections, or web pages in a language other than the default SharePoint product language, we must first install the language pack for that other language on all the web front-end and application servers before we can select the language to create a new site.

■ **Note**   Each language has a specific language pack. We must install the language pack on all of the web front-end and application servers to ensure the servers can render the content in the specified language.

Content Translation

Translating content can be a time-consuming process. We need to determine what type of translation service we want to use for the site based on time, resource, cost, and quality requirements. We demonstrate both machine translation and manual translation in later sections of this chapter. To read more about how to set up machine translation, refer to the section "Machine Translation" later in this chapter. For our scenario, Specter Group not only wants to translate the content into the language, but also to ensure the meaning of the content is preserved. To ensure quality of the translation as well as to save time, we use a translation agency to translate the content. We need to export the content for translation to the third-party translation service by using the industry-standard XLIFF file format and import the content back to SharePoint after it has been translated.

Navigation Term Sets

When planning for multilingual sites, we need to determine how to provide multilingual support for site navigation. If we are creating a static site navigation, then we need to manually translate the navigation terms into each target language. If we are using the Managed Navigation feature to use term sets to create the site navigation in publishing site collections, then we need to copy the navigation term set from the authoring site and translate it into the same language that is used for variation labels.

■ **Note**   To learn more about how to set up terms and term sets using Managed Metadata Service and how to create managed navigation using these terms, refer to Chapter 6 as we walk through the process of creating dynamic navigation for our example site.

Optimize for Search

Most popular search engines today use the content of the page to determine its language. To ensure the language is obvious to the search engine, avoid having side-by-side translations and avoid content in one language with the navigation in another. Leverage the URL to provide guidance about the page's language and content.

To attract more visitors, we need to increase the discoverability of our site through popular search engines. To boost the rankings of our site, we need to ensure certain search keywords and translated keywords are included in our URLs. We can also use the URL to provide guidance to the search engine and to the visitors about the page's language and content. In SharePoint 2013, we can leverage term sets and labels to generate our site URLs to ensure keywords and localizations of a page are included in the friendly URL.

If the site is required to target content to a specific country, then using a country-code top-level domain (ccTLD) such as .es for Spain and .fr for France in the URL can be useful. This can have the added benefit of giving the localized site a more local feel, which can help engender trust. For such a scenario, we can use cross-site publishing together with the variations and translation features to create multiple sites that target different countries. Because our Specter Group site is for visitors in the United States and Germany, we need to create two site collections: Spectergroup.com for English and Spectergroup.de for German.

We need to translate not only the content itself, but also the URLs of our site. The URLs of a site are one of the most important page properties that determine the ranking and discoverability of a page in search results. We need to leverage the URLs to increase the visibility of our site in search engines. In the section "Manual Translation" later in this chapter, we look at how to translate the URLs of a page during the translation process.

Deploying Language Packs

Language packs are required to enable multilingual support in SharePoint without requiring separate installations. We must install language packs, which contain language-specific site templates, on all web and application servers.

■ **Note**   Once a site or site collection has been created with a language-specific site template, the site or site collection will always display the content in that particular language.

Each language has a unique language identifier (language ID), which is used by all SharePoint components to determine the language to display and how to interpret content that is put on the site.

■ **Caution** When uninstalling SharePoint, we must uninstall the language packs before we uninstall SharePoint.

Downloading Language Packs

To install language packs, we must first download the language packs for each language we want to support.

1. Navigate to the download link for SharePoint Server 2013 language packs.

■ **Note** To download the language pack for SharePoint Foundation 2013, go to http://sprwd.com/10ch7jB. As of this writing, the language pack for SharePoint Server 2013 is not publicly available. You must download the language pack through an MSDN subscription. If you have access to MSDN, go to http://sprwd.com/68tn7k6 and select the language from the menu on the left.

---

2. From the download page, click the Change language drop-down box to select the language.

3. Click Download to download the executable.

4. The page will present a dialog box. Click Save to download the executable file to the local computer.

5. In our case, we started with the English version of SharePoint 2013. To support German language, we select the German language package to download (see Figure 14-3).

Figure 14-3. *Select a language pack to download*

Installing Language Packs on the Web and Application Servers

In our server farm environment, we need to install the German language pack to all the SharePoint web front-end and application servers. We need to log in to each server with an account that is a server administrator on the servers as well as a security administrator in SQL. Then we run setup.exe for the language pack. When prompted with the Microsoft Software License Terms page, select the I accept the terms of this agreement check box. Then click Continue. The Setup Wizard installs the language pack.

After the installation is completed, run the SharePoint products configuration wizard to ensure the language pack is installed and configured successfully for SharePoint.

■ **Note** The SharePoint products Configuration Wizard can detect when a server in the farm does not have the language pack installed. It will stop the configuration process until all servers have the new language pack installed.

After running psconfig, make sure to deactivate and reactivate any language-specific features before using the new language pack.

After the language pack is installed, the language-specific site templates are added to the following directory:

%COMMONPROGRAMFILES%\Microsoft Shared\Web server extensions\15\TEMPLATE\LanguageID

In our case, after installing the German language pack, all site templates are in the following directory:

%COMMONPROGRAMFILES%\Microsoft Shared\Web server extensions\15\TEMPLATE\1031

The 1031 folder is the language ID for German (Germany). At this point, Specter Group site owners and SharePoint administrators can create sites and site collections based on the German-language site templates by selecting German from the Select a language drop-down list (see Figure 14-4).

Template Selection

Select experience version:

2013 ▼

Select a language:

German ▼
English
German
Spanish

Figure 14-4. Create a new site collection or site using all the available languages in the environment

Implementing Multilingual

Now that we have the language packs installed in our environment, let's proceed to implement the site to provide multilingual support with SharePoint 2013 multilingual features.

We start with the Specter Group News site collection as our authoring site collection with the Variation feature enabled, as shown in Figure 14-5. The content is created and maintained in the News site collection and is accessible to content authors only. Using the cross-site publishing feature, we then publish the news content from the News variation webs to the public Specter Group English and German site collections, as shown in Figure 14-5.

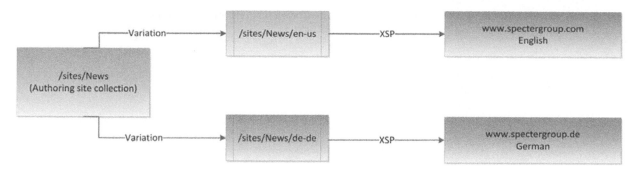

Figure 14-5. *Multilingual solution using variation and cross-site publishing features in SharePoint*

Creating Variation Hierarchy

To support multilingual, we need to first define a source language with its hierarchy and for every language (label) that we create to mirror the content. With this design, we have a single site collection with a hierarchy of webs for every language.

For the Specter Group News site, we need to create a publishing site collection, /sites/news, as our authoring site collection for all news content. First we need to configure Variation settings on our authoring site collection.

From /sites/news Site Settings, under Site Collection Administration, click Variations Settings to open the screen shown in Figure 14-6.

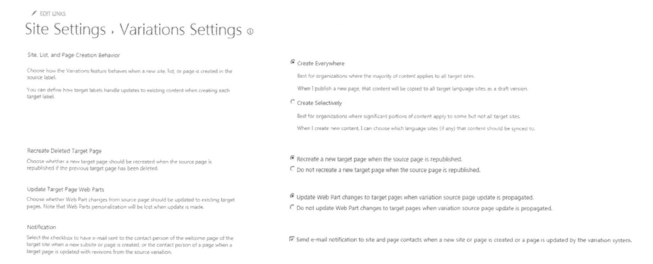

Figure 14-6. *Configure settings for Variations feature in a site collection*

For the Site, List, and Page Creation Behavior setting, selecting the Create Everywhere option will allow the content on the source variation site to be automatically created on all the target variation sites. If the Create Selectively option is selected, then the content author needs to manually select the target variation site to publish each time.

To create the variation hierarchy, we need to create variation labels. First, we create a root variation label (en-us) and then we create a target variation label (de-de).

1. Navigate to Site Settings and click Variation Labels, which opens the screen shown in Figure 14-7.

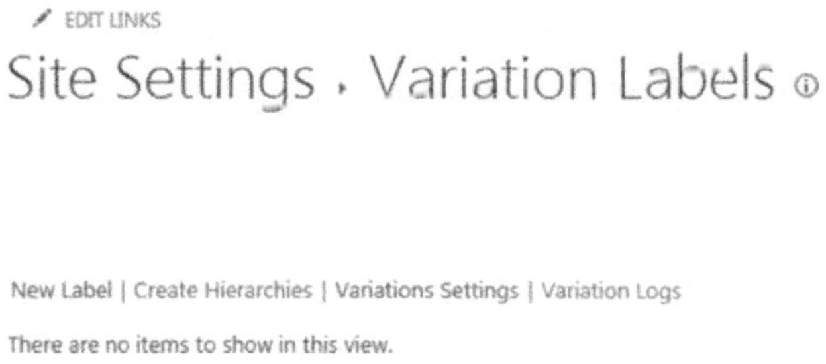

Site Settings › Variation Labels ⓘ

New Label | Create Hierarchies | Variations Settings | Variation Logs

There are no items to show in this view.

Figure 14-7. *From Site Settings, click Variation Labels to create variation labels and hierarchies*

2. Click the New Label link to create a label. For the first label, the Create Variation Label page will be presented to configure the root label (see Figure 14-8).

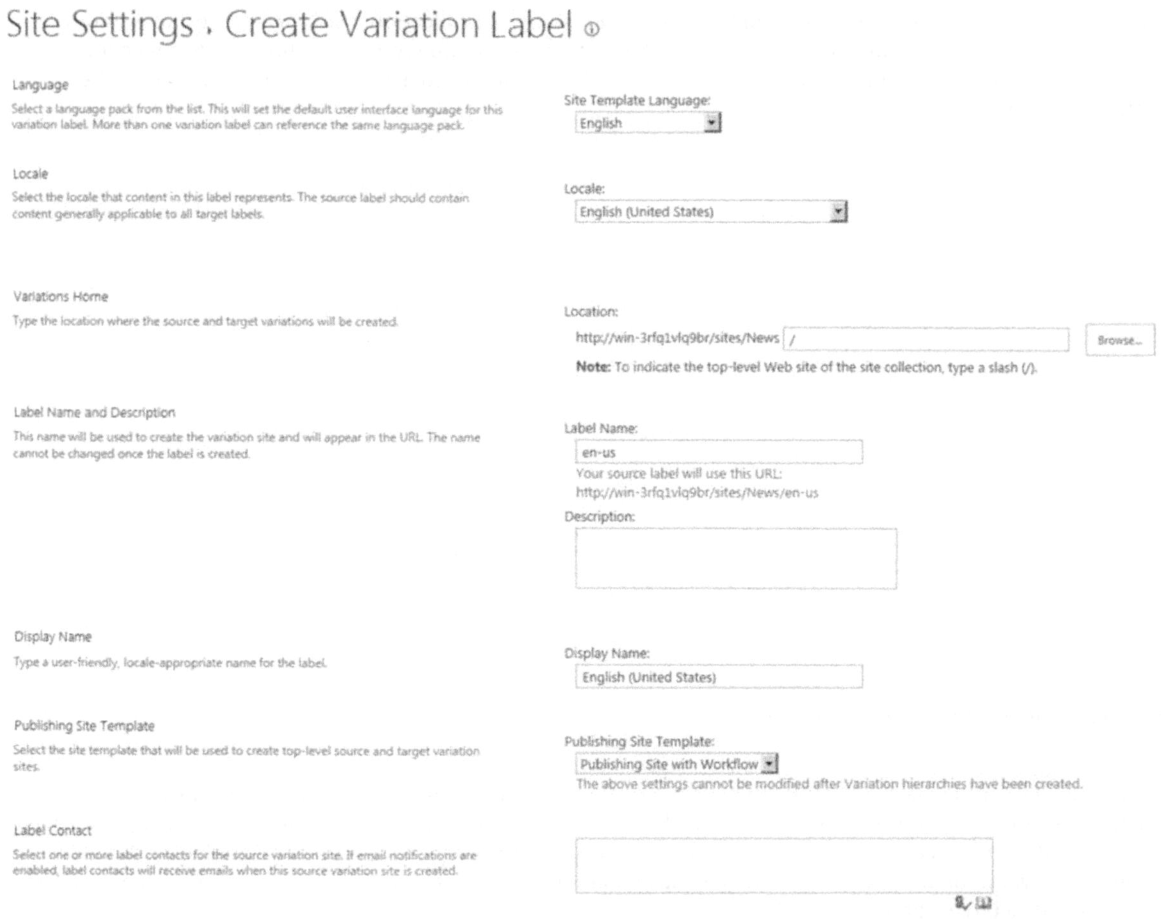

Site Settings › Create Variation Label ⓘ

Language

Select a language pack from the list. This will set the default user interface language for this variation label. More than one variation label can reference the same language pack.

Site Template Language:

English ▾

Locale

Select the locale that content in this label represents. The source label should contain content generally applicable to all target labels.

Locale:

English (United States) ▾

Variations Home

Type the location where the source and target variations will be created.

Location:

http://win-3rfq1vlq9br/sites/News | / | Browse...

Note: To indicate the top-level Web site of the site collection, type a slash (/).

Label Name and Description

This name will be used to create the variation site and will appear in the URL. The name cannot be changed once the label is created.

Label Name:

en-us

Your source label will use this URL:
http://win-3rfq1vlq9br/sites/News/en-us

Description:

Display Name

Type a user-friendly, locale-appropriate name for the label.

Display Name:

English (United States)

Publishing Site Template

Select the site template that will be used to create top-level source and target variation sites.

Publishing Site Template:

Publishing Site with Workflow ▾

The above settings cannot be modified after Variation hierarchies have been created.

Label Contact

Select one or more label contacts for the source variation site. If email notifications are enabled, label contacts will receive emails when this source variation site is created.

Figure 14-8. *Create source label first before creating all other target labels*

3. Because our root label is en-us, we need to select English from the Language drop-down list.

4. Select English (United States) for the Locale setting.

5. For the Variations Home setting, we want to enter / to make sure the root site, /sites/news/, is the home site for all variation features.

6. For Label Name and Description settings, ensure we have en-us as our root label. Leave all other settings as the defaults.

7. Click Create to complete. Navigate back to the Variation Labels page and you should see the new "en-us" label created (see Figure 14-9).

New Label | Create Hierarchies | Variations Settings | Variation Logs

Label	Display Name	Language	Locale
en-us	English (United States)	English (United States)	English (United States)

Figure 14-9. *From the Variation Labels page, view all the labels and hierarchies created*

8. To create the target German variation label, click the New Label link.

9. From the Configure Your Target Label page shown in Figure 14-10, choose German from the Language drop-down list.

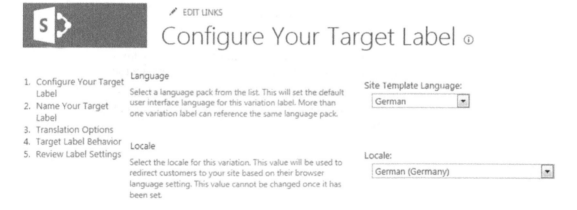

Figure 14-10. *Create a target label by specifying a language and locale*

10. Select German (Germany) from the Locale drop-down list.

11. On the Name Your Target Label page shown in Figure 14-11, ensure the label name is de-de.

✎ EDIT LINKS

Name Your Target Label ⓘ

1. Configure Your Target Label
2. Name Your Target Label
3. Translation Options
4. Target Label Behavior
5. Review Label Settings

Label and Description

Type the name and description for this variation label.

Label Name:

de-de

Your target label will use this URL:
http://w15-sp/sites/news/de-de

Description:

Display Name

Type a user-friendly, locale-appropriate name for the label.

Display Name:

German (Germany)

Hierarchy Creation

This label's structure will be built based on the source hierarchy during Hierarchy Creation. Select the portion of the source hierarchy you would like copied.

◉ Publishing Sites, Lists with Variations, and All Pages

◎ Publishing Sites Only

◎ Root Site Only

Figure 14-11. *Specify a name and what content to propagate for the new target label*

12. For Hierarchy Creation, select the type of content the target site wants to propagate from the source site. In our case, we want to propagate everything from source site to target site.

13. While creating these variation labels, we can configure how translation needs to happen. For the purpose of showing manual and machine translation, we allow both human and machine translation (see Figure 14-12).

✎ EDIT LINKS

Translation Options ⓘ

1. Configure Your Target Label
2. Name Your Target Label
3. Translation Options
4. Target Label Behavior
5. Review Label Settings

Create Translation Package

Enabling human translation on this target will allow users to export content to an XLIFF file. Users may then send the file to a translator for professional translation.

◎ Disable human translation on this target label

◉ Allow human translation on this target label

Translator Language

German (Germany) ▼

Machine Translation

Enabling machine translation on this target will allow users to send content online to Microsoft for translation. We may use content users send us to improve the quality of translations.
Learn more.

◎ Disable Machine Translation on this target label

◉ Allow Machine Translation on this target label

Machine Translation Language

German ▼

Figure 14-12. *For the new target label, specify the method of translation to enable*

14. We also need to configure target label behavior to ensure page changes are propagated from the source to the target sites. For Page Update Behavior, we need to specify whether we want to automatically push updates from the source page to the target site as a draft version or we need a target site contributor to review the change before syncing the current source version to the target as a draft version. In our case, we want to have SharePoint automatically push the update to the target (see Figure 14-13).

○ Users can manually sync updates from source variation pages
  Target page contributors can view the changes between the current, updated source version and the source version most recently synced to the target. Target page contributors can then sync the current source version to the target as a draft version at their discretion.

⦿ Automatically update target variation pages
  When an update to an existing source page is designated as actionable for this target variation label, propagate the actionable version from the source to this target as a draft version.

Figure 14-13. *Specify how updates should be propagated for the new target label*

15. Navigate back to the Variation Labels page. You should see both the new en-us label and the new de-de label created (see Figure 14-14). Notice in some cases, the new target label is not hyperlinked and the Hierarchy Is Created column has a value of No.

New Label | Create Hierarchies | Variations Settings | Variation Logs

Label	Display Name	Language	Locale	Human Translation	Machine Translation	Is Source	Description	Hierarchy Is Created
en-us	English (United States)	English (United States)	English (United States)	Disabled	Disabled	Yes		Yes
de-de	German (Germany)	German (Germany)	German (Germany)	German (Germany)	German	No		No

Figure 14-14. *View the new target label after it has been created*

■ **Note** At this point, if the target label is not hyperlinked and the Hierarchy Is Created column has a value of No, then we need to complete two steps to ensure the hierarchy and the label subsites are created successfully. First, to ensure a subsite is created for each target label, we need to click the Create Hierarchies link on the Variation Labels page. View all site content to make sure a subsite has been created for the new target label. Then, to ensure the Hierarchy is created, the Variations Create Hierarchies Job Definition timer job needs to run successfully.

16. To ensure the Variations Create Hierarchies timer job is running, go to Central Administration. Click Monitoring in the left navigation menu. Then click Check job status to find the Variations Create Hierarchies Job Definition timer job to ensure the job ran (see Figure 14-15).

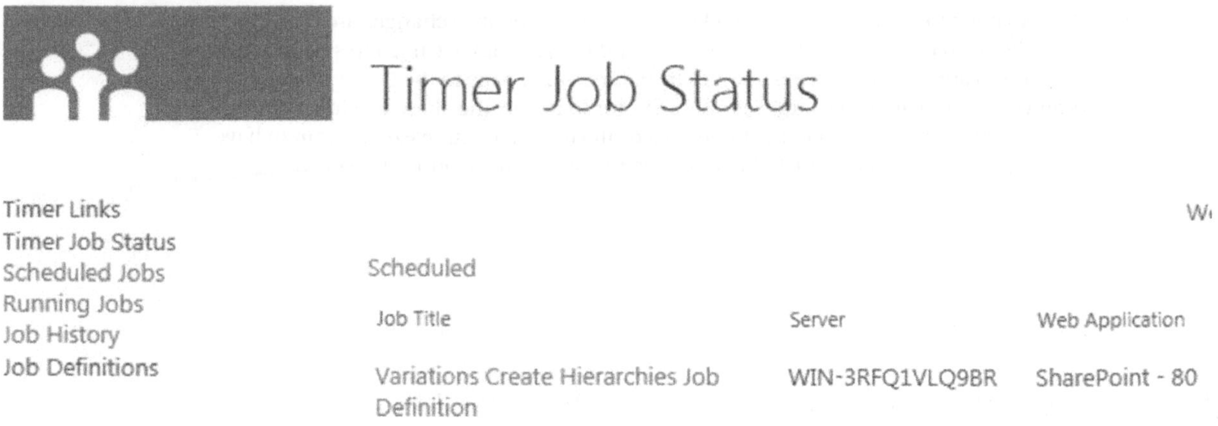

Timer Job Status

Timer Links

Timer Job Status

Scheduled Jobs   Scheduled

Running Jobs

Job History   Job Title   Server   Web Application

Job Definitions
                         Variations Create Hierarchies Job   WIN-3RFQ1VLQ9BR   SharePoint - 80
                         Definition

Figure 14-15. *View timer job status for all variation-related jobs*

17. If the job did not run, we can go to Central Admin to trigger the job manually to run now. Click Job Definitions on the left navigation menu. Find and click the Variations Create Hierarchies Job Definition timer job. From Edit Timer Job, click Run Now button to trigger the job to run immediately (see Figure 14-16).

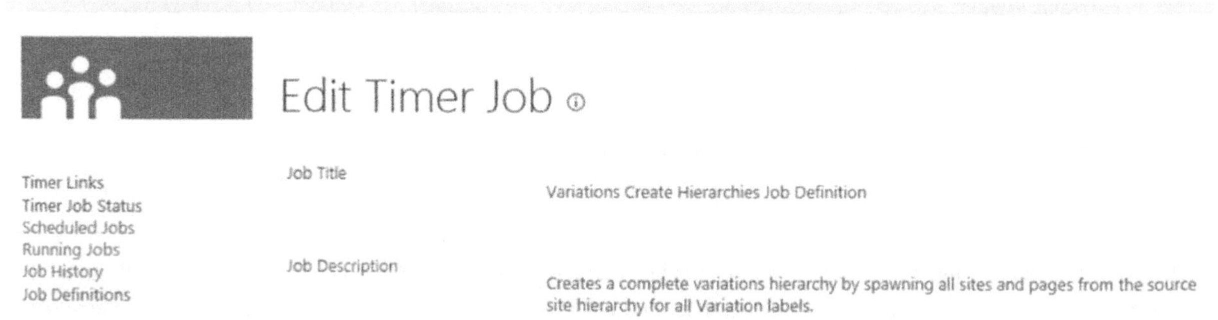

Edit Timer Job ⓘ

Timer Links   Job Title
Timer Job Status   Variations Create Hierarchies Job Definition
Scheduled Jobs
Running Jobs
Job History   Job Description
Job Definitions   Creates a complete variations hierarchy by spawning all sites and pages from the source
                                                    site hierarchy for all Variation labels.

Figure 14-16. *Edit a timer job to run the job immediately*

18. After the job is completed, navigate back to the Variation Labels page, as shown in Figure 14-17. You should see the new en-us label and the new de-de label created and the Hierarchy is Created column has the value of Yes for all the labels.

New Label | Create Hierarchies | Variations Settings | Variation Logs

Label	Display Name	Language	Locale	Human Translation	Machine Translation	Is Source	Description	Hierarchy Is Created
en-us	English (United States)	English (United States)	English (United States)	Disabled	Disabled	Yes		Yes
de-de	German (Germany)	German (Germany)	German (Germany)	German (Germany)	German	No		Yes

Figure 14-17. *View the new target label along with the navigation URL of the subsite and the status of the creation of the hierarchy*

19. To ensure each label has a subsite, click Site Contents on the left navigation menu, which opens the screen shown in Figure 14-18.

Figure 14-18. *View All site content to view subsites created for each label*

20. By default, when users navigate to the variation root site (/sites/news), they are redirected to the appropriate top site of a variation label based on the language setting of their web browser. As soon as variation is enabled for a site collection, a new redirect page, VariationRoot.aspx, is added to the root site's Pages library (see Figure 14-19).

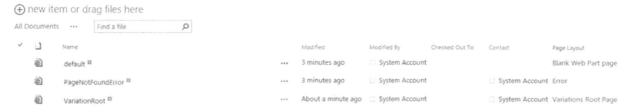

Figure 14-19. *After variation labels are created, the VariationRoot page is created for redirecting users to the top site of a variation label based on the language setting of the user's browser*

21. From the variation root site's Site Settings, click Welcome Page link. The Welcome page is set to the VariationRoot.aspx page, which redirects the user to the appropriate top site of a variation label based on the user's browser language setting.

22. It is possible to change this behavior by updating the VariationRoot redirection page with a custom page that redirects the user based on other criteria. To test the default behavior, change the browser setting to German language. For Internet Explorer, from Internet Options, click Languages.

23. At the Language Preference prompt, add the German (Germany) language we want to use. Once the language is added, promote the language to the top so that the browser will use German first, as shown in Figure 14-20.

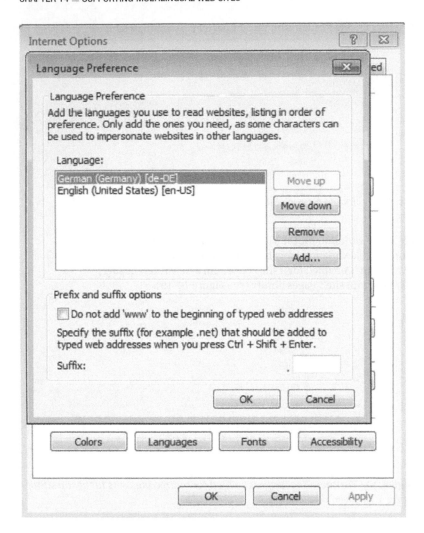

Figure 14-20. *Configure the language setting in Internet Explorer*

> **24.** Close all the browsers and relaunch the /sites/news site. You should be redirected to the /sites/news/de-de welcome page (see Figure 14-21).

Figure 14-21. *Users will be redirected to the home page of the variation site matching their language settings*

Setting Up Translation

SharePoint 2013 introduces Translation Services. Using Translation Services, we can choose to have the content translated automatically by machine translation or we can use manual translation using XLIFF translation packages to export the content from SharePoint and have the content translated by a translation agency. Machine translation is fast and reduces costs, but artificial intelligence today still lacks the ability to ensure the meaning of the content is preserved. To ensure the quality of the translation and to save time, it makes sense to use a translation agency to manually translate the content.

Creating Content

Before we set up translation, we need to create some content. We first create a new page in the English source site and add some content to the page (see Figure 14-22). Then we publish the page.

Figure 14-22. *Create a new page in source label site to be published and propagated to the target labels*

After a few minutes, navigate to the de-de target label site. We should see the new page in the target site (see Figure 14-23).

Figure 14-23. *New page is propagated to all target label sites*

If we don't see the new page in the target site or if we want to push the updates to the target site without waiting, we can navigate to the pages library in the English source site and click Update all targets on the Variations ribbon toolbar (see Figure 14-24).

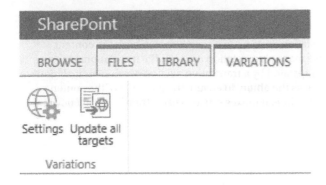

Figure 14-24. Manually push all updates to all target sites instead of waiting for SharePoint to automatically push updates

From the target /sites/news/de-de German site, you should see a new page in the Pages Library that was propagated from the source /sites/news/en-us English site. Navigate to the new test page. You should see the same English content on the target German page. To perform translation, we can choose from the options on the Varianten (Variations) ribbon toolbar shown in Figure 14-25.

Figure 14-25. Variation ribbon toolbar contains options for translation

For the purpose of demonstration, we use the English equivalent screen shot of the Variation ribbon toolbar (see Figure 14-26).

Figure 14-26. Variation ribbon toolbar (in English) contains options for translation

Machine Translation

In some situations, we might want to rely on machine translation to provide a quick way to translate certain content. New in SharePoint 2013, we can now integrate with Bing Translation to automatically translate the content.

Setting Up Machine Translation

To enable machine translation, we need to create a Machine Translation Service application and configure the Machine Translation Service from Central Administration or PowerShell.

■ **Note** For more detailed information on creating a Machine Translation Service application and configuring the Machine Translation Service, go to TechNet at `http://sprwd.com/34ceirg`. Because machine translation depends on access to the Bing Translation service, ensure the server running machine translations can connect to the Internet.

Performing Machine Translation

For machine translation, we can select a page to translate. Then choose the Machine Translate icon from the Variations ribbon toolbar (refer to Figure 14-26). We see a note for submitting the machine translation request and a message that the process will take a few minutes.

■ **Note** The first time we use machine translation in the environment after it's been set up will take a longer time (around 30 minutes) to complete the process because the process also includes time to initiate communication between the Bing Translation service and the server on which the machine translation service is running.

To view the status of the translation request, we can click the Translation Status icon on the Variation ribbon toolbar (refer to Figure 14-26). This action will take us to the Translation Status list in the root site to view the queue for translation requests and the status of each request (see Figure 14-27).

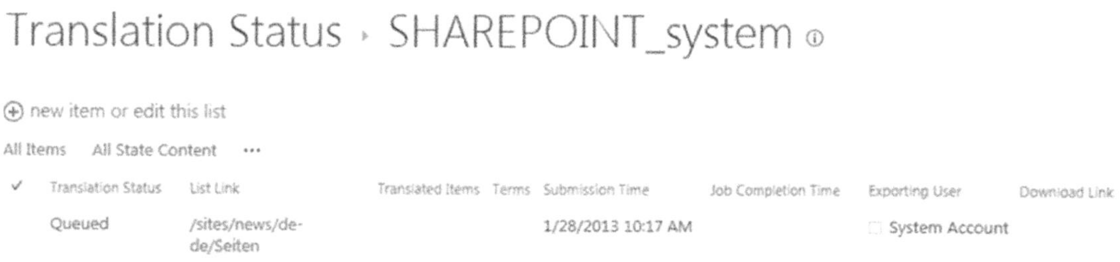

Translation Status › SHAREPOINT_system ⓘ

⊕ new item or edit this list

All Items   All State Content   ···

✓	Translation Status	List Link	Translated Items	Terms	Submission Time	Job Completion Time	Exporting User	Download Link
	Queued	/sites/news/de-de/Seiten			1/28/2013 10:17 AM		☐ System Account	

Figure 14-27. *View status of a new translation request. Initially, request is in Queued state*

Initially, the status of a request is Queued. After a few minutes, the queued request will change its Translation Status from Queued to In Progress (see Figure 14-28).

Figure 14-28. *Once the translation request is being processed, the status changes to In Progress*

During the machine translation process, there are a few timer jobs that will run. To view the status of these timer jobs, go to Central Administration. Click Monitoring in the left navigation menu. Then click Job Definitions to find timer jobs related to the Machine Translation Service (see Figure 14-29).

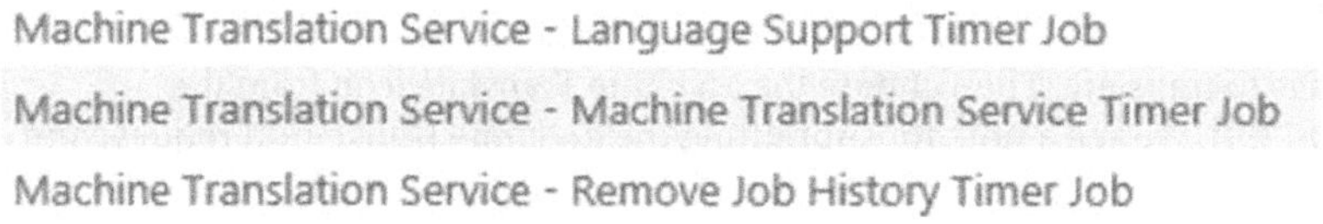

Machine Translation Service - Language Support Timer Job

Machine Translation Service - Machine Translation Service Timer Job

Machine Translation Service - Remove Job History Timer Job

Figure 14-29. *Machine translation related timer jobs*

To trigger these timer jobs to run immediately, we can click on the timer job, then click Run now. If we want these timer jobs to run more often, we can configure the recurring schedule of the job to run more often, from Hourly to Minutes (see Figure 14-30).

Edit Timer Job ⊙

Job Title

Machine Translation Service - Machine Translation Service Timer Job

Job Description

Initiates translation of documents which have been submitted to the Machine Translation Service.

Job Properties

This section lists the properties for this job.

Web application: N/A

Last run time: 1/27/2013 2:39 AM

Recurring Schedule

Use this section to modify the schedule specifying when the timer job will run. Daily, weekly, and monthly schedules also include a window of execution. The timer service will pick a random time within this interval to begin executing the job on each applicable server. This feature is appropriate for high-load jobs which run on multiple servers on the farm. Running this type of job on all the servers simultaneously might place an unreasonable load on the farm. To specify an exact starting time, set the beginning and ending times of the interval to the same value.

This timer job is scheduled to run:

   ⦿ Minutes   Every [1]   minute(s)

   ○ Hourly

   ○ Daily

   ○ Weekly

   ○ Monthly

Figure 14-30. *Edit a timer job to configure it to run more often by changing it to run in minutes*

To look at the translation jobs and status in detail, we can navigate to the Variation Logs list in the variation root site (/sites/news). In our case, the log indicates a translation package for the page we want to translate has been created and exported for machine translation (see Figure 14-31).

Variation Logs

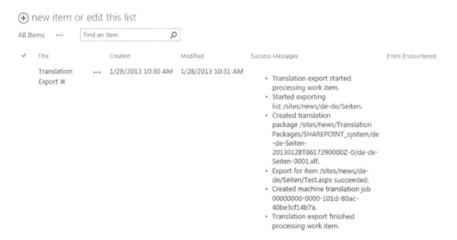

⊕ new item or edit this list

All Items   ···   [Find an item   🔍]

✓	Title	Created	Modified	Success Messages	Errors Encountered
	Translation Export ⌕ ···	1/28/2013 10:30 AM	1/28/2013 10:31 AM	• Translation export started processing work item. • Started exporting list /sites/news/de-de/Seiten. • Created translation package /sites/news/Translation Packages/SHAREPOINT_system/de-de-Seiten-20130128T0617290000Z-0/de-de-Seiten-0001.xlf. • Export for item /sites/news/de-de/Seiten/Test.aspx succeeded. • Created machine translation job 00000000-0000-101d-80ac-40be3cf14b7a. • Translation export finished processing work item.	

Figure 14-31. *View Variation Logs to see when a translation package is exported for machine translation*

After about five minutes (30 minutes if it is the first time we are making a machine translation request), the page is translated. From Variation Logs, note the machine translation job completes with importing the translation package with the translated content (see Figure 14-32).

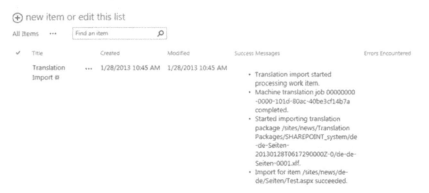

Figure 14-32. *Once machine translation has translated the content, a translation package is imported into SharePoint for the target label*

In the Translation Status list, the machine translation request has been completed and the status is shown as Translated (see Figure 14-33). Note the whole process took about 30 minutes from the first time a machine translation request is made.

Figure 14-33. *Once machine translation is completed, the translation request is in Translated status*

Navigate to the translated page on the target site (de-de subsite), and you should see translated content on the page, as shown in Figure 14-34.

Figure 14-34. *Content on target label site is now translated by machine translation (Bing Translation service)*

Going forward, we could use machine translation to translate the News content for Specter Group. For example, to create a new page for quarter earnings, we first create the page in the Pages library from the en-us source site, as shown in Figure 14-35.

/ EDIT LINKS   Search this site

SpecterGroup Fourth Quarter Earnings Sneak Peek

SpecterGroup, Inc. Earnings Preview Cheat Sheet

Wall St. Earnings Expectations: The average analyst estimate is for profit of 31 cents per share, a rise of more than twofold from the company's actual earnings for the year-ago quarter. During the past three months, the average estimate has moved up from 29 cents. Between one and three months ago, the average estimate moved up. It has risen from 30 cents during the last month. Analysts are projecting net income of 70 cents per share versus a loss of one cent last year.

Past Earnings Performance: The company is looking to top estimates for the third straight quarter. Last quarter, it reported profit of 27 cents per share against a mean estimate of net income of 20 cents, and the quarter before, the company exceeded forecasts by 8 cents with profit of 13 cents versus a mean estimate of net income of 5 cents.

Balance Sheet Analysis: The company's current ratio of assets to liabilities came in at 3.19 last quarter. Having a ratio above 2:1 is usually considered a good indicator of a company's liquidity and ability to meet creditor demands. The company improved this liquidity measure from 3.16 in the second quarter to the last quarter driven in part by an increase in current assets. Current assets increased 2.7% to $6.11 billion while liabilities rose by 1.7% to $1.92 billion.

Figure 14-35. *Example of a page created in source label site*

We then perform the steps outlined in this section to allow machine translation on the new page. The result page in the German site (`/sites/news/de-de`) looks like Figure 14-36.

Figure 14-36. *Example of a translated page in target label site*

Manual Translation

Machine translation is fast and reduces costs. However, for our scenario, Specter Group not only wants to translate the content into the language, but also to ensure that the meaning of the content is preserved. To ensure quality of the translation as well as to save time, we will be using a translation agency to translate the content. We need to export the content for translation to the third-party translation service by using the industry-standard XLIFF file format and import the content back to SharePoint after it has been translated.

To demonstrate this process, let's first create a new page, Manual translation page, and add some content to the page in the English source site (see Figure 14-37).

Figure 14-37. Create a page in source label site to be propagated to target label sites

After we have published the page, wait a few minutes for the updates to propagate to the target German site. Once the new page is added, select the page, then click the Create Translation Package icon in the Variations ribbon toolbar. Then we will be prompted by the browser to download the exported Translation package.

Figure 14-38. Translation package in XLIFF format is exported

Download the file and save it locally. This file contains all the information needed to get the content translated. At this point, we want to send this file to a translation agency to get the content translated. Then import the updated translation package back to SharePoint. From the Translation Status list, as soon as we request creation of a translation package, a new human translation request is queued (see Figure 14-39).

Figure 14-39. View translation status of a manual translation request

For the purpose of demonstration, let's take a look at the XLIFF file we just downloaded by opening the file in Notepad. The file contains source and target language information as well as the content to be translated in HTML format, as you can see in Figure 14-40.

```
de-de-Seiten-Manual-translation-page.aspx.xlf - Notepad

File  Edit  Format  View  Help
<?xml version="1.0" encoding="utf-8"?>
<xliff version="1.2" xmlns="urn:oasis:names:tc:xliff:document:1.2">
  <file original="73db2348-e0bc-40d2-89aa-71488c8bc695" source-language="en-US" target-
language="de-DE" datatype="html" tool-id="SharePoint Server 2013">
    <header>
      <note>type=ListItem</note>
      <note>translatorType=Vendor</note>
      <note>packageGroupId=b7bb04be-11dc-4064-b5ad-6655e61b55f5</note>
      <tool tool-id="SharePoint Server 2013" tool-name="Microsoft® SharePoint® Server 2013"
/>
      <note>webId=56757bb1-21aa-4800-b1d7-c1fc8b4c0705</note>
      <note>listId=b12f90bf-db9a-4ca6-a11f-15a7a18f021f</note>
      <note>url=Seiten/Manual-translation-page.aspx</note>
      <note>sourceVersion=1</note>
    </header>
    <body>
      <trans-unit id="fa564e0f-0c70-4ab9-b863-0177e6ddd247" datatype="plaintext">
        <source>Manual translation page</source>
        <note>fieldTitle=Titel</note>
      </trans-unit>
      <trans-unit id="f55c4d88-1f2e-4ad9-aaa8-819af4ee7ee8" datatype="html">
        <source>
          <bpt id="0">&lt;p&gt;</bpt>Welcome to SpecterGroup!<ept
id="0">&lt;/p&gt;</ept></source>
        <note>fieldTitle=Seiteninhalt</note>
      </trans-unit>
    </body>
  </file>
</xliff>
```

Figure 14-40. *Translation package exported to be translated*

Once we get the translated XLIFF file back from a translation agency, the file will be updated with the target (translated) content, as shown in Figure 14-41. Note, the page title element has a target property that contains a translated value and the page content element has a target property that contains a translated value.

```
de-de-Seiten-Manual-translation-page.aspx - translated - Notepad

File  Edit  Format  View  Help
<?xml version="1.0" encoding="utf-8"?>
<xliff version="1.2" xmlns="urn:oasis:names:tc:xliff:document:1.2">
  <file original="73db2348-e0bc-40d2-89aa-71488c8bc695" source-language="en-US" target-
language="de-DE" datatype="html" tool-id="SharePoint Server 2013">
    <header>
      <note>type=ListItem</note>
      <note>translatorType=Vendor</note>
      <note>packageGroupId=b7bb04be-11dc-4064-b5ad-6655e61b55f5</note>
      <tool tool-id="SharePoint Server 2013" tool-name="Microsoft® SharePoint® Server 2013"
/>
      <note>webId=56757bb1-21aa-4800-b1d7-c1fc8b4c0705</note>
      <note>listId=b12f90bf-db9a-4ca6-a11f-15a7a18f021f</note>
      <note>url=Seiten/Manual-translation-page.aspx</note>
      <note>sourceVersion=1</note>
    </header>
    <body>
      <trans-unit id="fa564e0f-0c70-4ab9-b863-0177e6ddd247" datatype="plaintext">
        <source>Manual translation page</source>
        <target>Manuelle Übersetzung Seite</target>
        <note>fieldTitle=Titel</note>
      </trans-unit>
      <trans-unit id="f55c4d88-1f2e-4ad9-aaa8-819af4ee7ee8" datatype="html">
        <source>
          <bpt id="0">&lt;p&gt;</bpt>willkommen SpecterGroup!<ept
id="0">&lt;/p&gt;</ept></source>
        <target>
          <bpt id="0">&lt;p&gt;</bpt>willkommen SpecterGroup!<ept
id="0">&lt;/p&gt;</ept></target>
        <note>fieldTitle=Seiteninhalt</note>
      </trans-unit>
    </body>
  </file>
</xliff>
```

Figure 14-41. *Translation package containing translated content and page title to be imported*

We can now import the translation package for the page by clicking the Upload Translation icon on the Variations ribbon toolbar. Then we are prompted to provide a file location to the XLIFF file (see Figure 14-42).

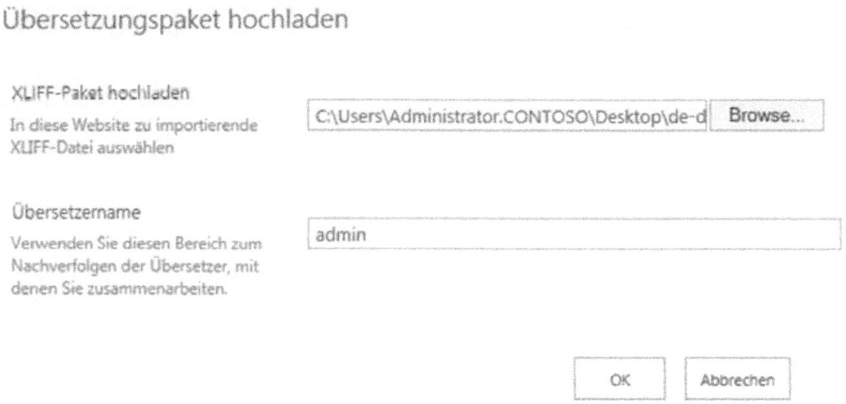

Übersetzungspaket hochladen
XLIFF-Paket hochladen
In diese Website zu importierende XLIFF-Datei auswählen
C:\Users\Administrator.CONTOSO\Desktop\de-d
Browse...
Übersetzername
Verwenden Sie diesen Bereich zum Nachverfolgen der Übersetzer, mit denen Sie zusammenarbeiten.
admin
OK
Abbrechen

Figure 14-42. *Import translation package into SharePoint*

Once importing the translation package is completed, navigate to the target page on the German site. Note in Figure 14-43 that both the content and the page title are now translated.

LINKS BEARBEITEN
Manuelle Übersetzung Seite
LINKS BEARBEITEN
Websiteinhalte
Noch nicht veröffentlicht. Besuchern wird diese Seite nicht angezeigt. Seite veröffentlichen.
Willkommen SpecterGroup!

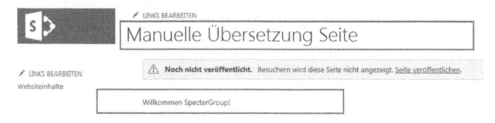

Figure 14-43. *Translated content with translated page title in target label site*

Often we might want to look at the method of translation or the name of the translator we used for a page. To do so, navigate to the target site's pages library, and next to each translated page, in the Translator Name column, you see the name of the translator if translated manually or Machine Translation Service if translated by machine (see Figure 14-44).

Seiten ⓘ

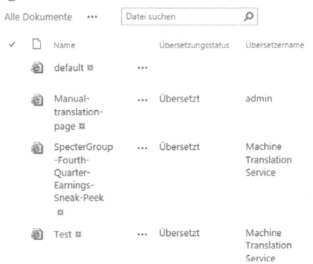

⊕ Neues Element oder Dateien hierhin ziehen

		Name	Übersetzungsstatus	Übersetzername
✓	📄			
	📄	default ✵ •••		
	📄	Manual-translation-page ✵ •••	Übersetzt	admin
	📄	SpecterGroup-Fourth-Quarter-Earnings-Sneak-Peek ✵ •••	Übersetzt	Machine Translation Service
	📄	Test ✵ •••	Übersetzt	Machine Translation Service

Figure 14-44. *For all translated pages, view pages in target the site to reference translator name*

Setting Up Cross-Site Publishing

We now have the Specter Group News site collection as our authoring site collection with Variations enabled. The content is created and maintained in the News site collection, specifically in the English source site, and is accessible to content authors only. Using the Cross-Site Collection Publishing feature, we publish the news content from the News variation webs to the public Specter Group English and German site collections.

We first need to create a publishing site collection with English language for the Specter Group English site, www.spectergroup.com. Then we need to create a publishing site collection with German language for the Specter Group German site, www.spectergroup.de.

1. From the Specter Group News site collection, navigate to Site Settings to enable the Cross-Site Collection Publishing feature, shown in Figure 14-45.

Cross-Site Collection Publishing

Enables site collection to designate lists and document libraries as catalog sources for Cross-Site Collection Publishing.

Figure 14-45. *To use cross-site publishing, enable the Cross-Site Collection Publishing feature*

2. Navigate to the Pages library in /sites/news/en-us and enable the library as a catalog.

3. Navigate to the Pages library in /sites/news/de-de and enable the library as a catalog.

4. From www.spectergroup.com, connect to the English catalog from /sites/News/en-us.

5. From www.spectergroup.de, connect to the German catalog from /sites/News/de-de.

6. Once cross-site publishing is set up, as soon as a page is published from its authoring site in /sites/news/en-us or /sites/news/de-de, it will appear on www.spectergroup.com and www.spectergroup.de, respectively.

■ **Note** You can learn more about the cross-site publishing feature in SharePoint 2013 in Chapter 8, where we demonstrate how to enable content in a list or library for reuse and how to consume the published content by a target site collection for our example site.

Summary

Today, many companies operate globally. Even when dealing with home markets, companies often need to appeal to customers who speak different languages. To attract visitors and potential customers, companies need to make the effort to provide users with information about products and services in their native language. More companies are making the investment to make their web sites multilingual, which has produced measurable improvements in company sales and customer satisfaction. Providing multilingual support for a public web site is one of the most important decisions when planning for a new web site. Using the new translation and publishing capabilities provided by SharePoint 2013, we were able to build a multilingual web site using the standard functionalities.

■ ■ ■

Configuring a Development Environment

Throughout this book you have been exposed to many aspects of working with SharePoint 2013, including how to brand SharePoint and how to build simple SharePoint Apps. Most SharePoint projects are developed not in a production environment, but rather in some type of development environment. If you do not have access to an existing development environment in your organization, this appendix is for you. If your organization already has a SharePoint 2013 development environment, or you are looking for additional options, you might find some useful alternatives in this appendix.

In this appendix we look at how you can quickly set up a SharePoint 2013 environment to work through the examples in this book. Many of the features outlined in this book are currently only available in on-premise environments, although often an Office 365 development site will be more than adequate. All of the examples provided in this book were built and tested in on-premise virtual machine environments as well as Cloudshare-based cloud environments.

This appendix also includes a detailed look at software tools first introduced in this book's Introduction as well as additional tools that you might find useful. We have found these tools can help your SharePoint branding projects, including popular web editors and image creation and manipulation tools.

Types of Development Environments

There are two primary types of SharePoint development environments: on-premise environments and cloud-based environments. Each of these types of environments can also be split into subcategories.

With on-premise development environments, you can have SharePoint farms installed on servers that you access via a LAN, a VPN, or other such network connection. You might also have a SharePoint environment installed and running in a local virtual machine on your workstation itself.

There are also different types of cloud-based environments. The most well-known cloud-based SharePoint environment is Microsoft Office 365. There are other cloud solutions offered by companies such as Cloudshare (www.cloudshare.com), Rackspace (www.rackspace.com), and Windows Azure (www.windowsazure.com). The cloud offerings differ by company and have unique pros and cons.

If you do not already have an on-premise development environment available to you, we recommend that you use a cloud-based environment to work through the examples in this book because creating an on-premise development environment for SharePoint 2013 development can be time consuming, resource intensive, and difficult to set up and configure properly. We want you to be able to start working through this book today.

On-Premise Development Environment

Using a local on-premise, virtual-machine-based development environment is a popular solution, although creating such an environment is beyond the scope of this book. The hardware and software requirements and the configuration options are much higher than with previous versions of SharePoint. There are many good resources available online if you decide you want to use an on-premise development environment. Get started with the MSDN article "Start: Set up the development environment for SharePoint 2013" at http://sprwd.com/f7idv3n.

If you are interested in learning more about installing SharePoint 2013 in a virtual machine, refer to "Install and configure a virtual environment for SharePoint 2013" at http://sprwd.com/g2ru7ez and "How to: Set up an on-premises development environment for apps for SharePoint" at http://sprwd.com/57vo6u2. All of the examples in this book can be built on an on-premise, virtual-machine-based environment.

Cloud-Based Development Environment

As we previously stated, a cloud-based development environment is our recommended development environment if you do not already have an existing SharePoint 2013 development site. We review the most popular cloud environments along with how to sign up and configure them so that you can work through the examples in this book. In the next section we review which cloud-based development environment would be best for you, depending on which aspects of this book you intend to focus.

Office 365 Developer Site

Office 365 provides an exciting new development environment for SharePoint 2013. You can now sign up for and use an Office 365 Developer Site, which gives you many of the benefits on an on-premise SharePoint installation without the hassle of configuring and maintaining a SharePoint development farm. With the introduction of SharePoint 2013, SharePoint Online, the SharePoint component of Office 365, now allows access to the full publishing infrastructure for both public-facing and intranet sites. An Office 365 Developer Site can be used to sharpen your branding skills, as all branding examples up through Chapter 7 will function in a development site. Later chapters might not work in an Office 365 Developer Site as mentioned in each chapter. For those examples, a different cloud solution will be necessary.

An Office 365 Developer Site can also be used to build SharePoint-hosted apps and even apps for Office documents and mail items. An Office 365 Developer Site comes preconfigured with OAuth and you also get an isolated app domain for your SharePoint-hosted apps. SharePoint-hosted apps include certain limitations to server-side code, but with the greatly enhanced Client Side Object Model you might find the ease of use and configuration of an Office 365 Developer Site reason enough to do away with server-side code in your apps.

With an Office 365 Developer Site you can also deploy the Napa Office 365 Development Tools to your preconfigured site. The Napa tools can help jumpstart your SharePoint development by providing a browser-based development environment, freeing you from having to install Visual Studio to your workstation. The Napa tools are useful but you will find the toolset is designed for more simple application development. We recommend a local installation of Visual Studio to follow along with the examples in this book, but again, the Napa tools are worth considering for simpler SharePoint App development.

There are a few drawbacks with an Office 365 Developer Site. First, as of this printing, cross-site publishing is not available in Office 365. Further, the content search web part is also not available. You can use the search results web part, which is similar to the content search web part, in an Office 365 Developer Site. Unfortunately our examples in Chapters 8 and 9 require a different development environment.

■ **Tip** For TechNet's overview of Office 365 Developer Sites, visit "Sign up for an Office 365 Developer Site" at http://sprwd.com/x8dwotx.

Signing Up for a Office 365 Developer Site

Before you can use an Office 365 Developer Site you must sign up for a Developer Site account.

1. Visit http://sprwd.com/x8dwotx for the most up-to-date up link to sign up for an Office 365 Developer Site account.

2. There are currently three ways to obtain an Office 365 Developer Site.

    a. If you have an MSDN subscription, Visual Studio Ultimate, and Visual Studio Premium with MSDN subscriptions, receive a 1-year Office 365 Developer Site.

    b. If you already have an Office 365 subscription at the E1 or E3 level you can provision a Developer Site from your Office 365 admin center.

    c. You can start a free 30-day free trial or purchase an Office 365 developer subscription.

■ **Note** Further information on all three paths to a Developer Site can be obtained from the sign-in link provided in step 1.

---

3. Once you have finished the sign-up process, you will be redirected to your Office 365 Admin Center page. Before you can begin building SharePoint Apps, you must wait for your SharePoint site to be provisioned, which may take a few additional minutes. Once SharePoint has been provisioned you can begin developing Apps, although you might first want to install the Napa Development Tools.

Installing Napa Development Tools

The Napa Development Tools App affords you the ability to build apps for both Office and SharePoint within a browser, without having to install any additional tools such as Visual Studio 2012. All you will need to do is add the Napa Development Tools App to your Office 365 SharePoint Online Development Site, launch the tool, and create an app for SharePoint all in the browser. An added plus is that once you are ready to leverage the power of Visual Studio, the Napa Developer Tools App provides a quick and easy method to download your project and resume your app development within Visual Studio itself.

1. Log in to your Office 365 account and on the Admin Center page, click the Build Apps link at the top of the page.

2. You are redirected to your SharePoint Online Developer Site home page. Click the Build an app tile to launch the App Development tool.

3. If you have not yet added the Napa Development Tools App to this site, you will be redirected to the App Store to add it. The app is free and you will be asked to log in to the App Store to add the app. After the app has been installed, you are asked if you trust the Napa Office 365 Development Tools, which you must trust to continue.

4. You will be redirected to your Developer Site. Return to your Developer Site home page and click the Build an app tile again. This time you are redirected to build a new app, using the power of the Napa Development Tools.

Additional Office 365 Developer Site Resources

TechNet provides an extensive array of additional resources for developing apps with Office 365 and SharePoint Online.

- Create apps for Office and SharePoint by using "Napa" Office 365 Development Tools

  http://sprwd.com/dvquuhs

- How to: Create a basic app for SharePoint by using "Napa" Office 365 Development Tools

  http://sprwd.com/zyzg5h

- How to: Create a basic SharePoint-hosted app

  http://sprwd.com/mgg4p46

- How to: Create a cloud-hosted app that includes a custom SharePoint list and content type

  http://sprwd.com/ukgfgzo

Third-Party Cloud-Based Development Environments

To be able to work through every example in this book, you are going to need access to a full installation of SharePoint 2013. Office 365 provides you almost everything you need but as we saw in the previous section, there are limitations. If you are looking for a development environment that comes preconfigured, maybe even with all of the tools you will need installed, third-party clouds are for you.

The third-party cloud solutions that we recommend are different than Office 365. With Office 365 you only have access to your site via a browser-based interface or with a tool such as SharePoint Designer. The third-party clouds we recommend provide you your own virtual machine that includes a full installation of SharePoint. Although you are using the cloud to store your development environment, you are getting full, on-premise-like functionality.

There are multiple companies that provide SharePoint hosting and development services. We introduce three of them.

Cloudshare

Cloudshare provides development virtual machines preinstalled with different flavors of SharePoint including SharePoint 2010 and SharePoint 2013. These offerings include different license levels as well as different preinstalled development tools, such as Visual Studio and SharePoint Designer. New environments can be provisioned in minutes and Cloudshare accounts can be paid for on a month-to-month basis. Cloudshare only charges a fixed monthly fee, and they handle all server and software installation and maintenance, as well as all software licensing.

Cloudshare services have become a popular developer tool because of the rapid nature of site deployment and the ability to not have to concern oneself with licensing.

■ **Tip** You can learn more about Cloudshare and their services at www.cloudshare.com. You can sign up for a free Cloudshare trial and be using many of the examples in this book in well under an hour.

All of the examples in this book were tested on Cloudshare environments, so if you are looking for a no-hassle development environment, this is the service for you.

As an added bonus of this book, we have provided a Cloudshare environment that has been preconfigured with Windows Server 2012, SharePoint 2013, Visual Studio 2012, and SharePoint Designer 2013. Not only that, but this environment also has a full and complete copy of the Specter Group site that we developed throughout this book. This provides you a hands-on site that you can dig into to see the entire site design in action. You can create a trial account at Cloudshare with a preloaded copy of our fully functional demo development server at http://sprwd.com/sprwd-cs-demo.

When you sign up for your trial account using the preceding link, you will be redirected to your Cloudshare account page. It will take a few minutes to create a new VM based on the snapshot of our demo environment. When the process is complete, you should see a page similar to Figure A-1. Two areas have been highlighted in the figure. The first is the minutes you have left until the VM turns itself off. Click Extend to extend your VM to 180 minutes. You can extend this time as often as you need. If the time expires, your VM will hibernate until you access it again. The second button highlighted is the button to click to open your VM directly in your browser.

Figure A-1. *Cloudshare demo environment account page*

After you click the View VM button shown in Figure A-1, your VM will launch in your browser (see Figure A-2). Notice the icons in the upper right corner that allow you to view the VM in full screen mode and other views. You can even use Remote Desktop Connection Manager to connect to this VM using a Remote Desktop Connection. We also highlighted the VM settings menu tab found on the left of your browser where you can find VM settings including VM account information.

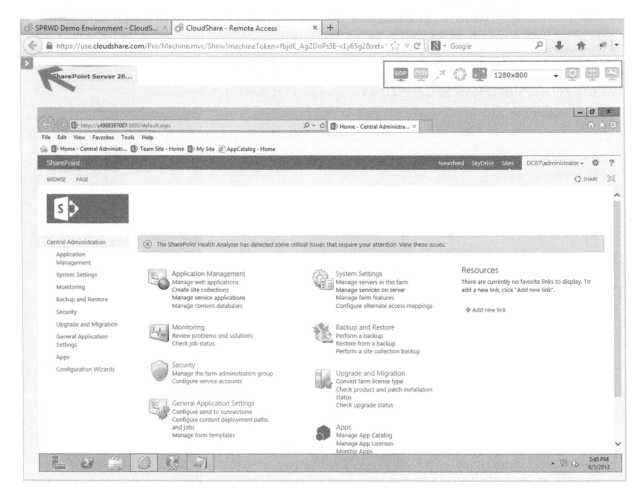

Figure A-2. *Demo Cloudshare VM*

There is much you can do with Cloudshare. We hope that even if you have your own on-premise or cloud-based development environment, you find that the demo VM helps you benefit from the material in this book. To learn more about how to use Cloudshare VMs, visit `http://support.cloudshare.com`.

Rackspace Services for SharePoint

If you are looking for a full installation of SharePoint in a cloud-based environment that is for development as well as ready for prime time, you will need an enterprise-level hosting service such as Rackspace. Rackspace has been providing site, server, and cloud hosting services for many years. They also provide tailored SharePoint hosting services.

The difference between a service such as Cloudshare and Rackspace is that Rackspace provides an always-on, enterprise-ready environment for full-fledged production sites as well as development servers. Rackspace does not offer all of the development tools preinstalled, nor will they handle all of the licensing for you. The server deployment process with Rackspace takes longer than with Cloudshare, but that is because you get to pick and choose what you want to install and how you want to install it.

■ **Tip**   You can learn more about Rackspace SharePoint services at
www.rackspace.com/enterprise_hosting/sharepoint/.

Windows Azure Infrastructure Services

Microsoft offers another cloud-based hosting solution that is more in line with the offerings of Rackspace Services for SharePoint. This service is a part of Windows Azure, Microsoft's general cloud computing initiative, and is called Windows Azure Infrastructure Services.

With this cloud solution, Windows Azure handles the servers, network, storage, and virtualization while providing you an open environment to easily provision your own virtual machines. Windows Azure Infrastructure Services' pricing model might be attractive to you when used for development as they offered metered usage. This means that you only pay by the hour while your virtual machines are active and when you are accessing your development environment.

Similar to Rackspace SharePoint services, with Windows Azure Infrastructure Services, you have to manage software licenses and software installation including account management. Essentially Windows Azure Infrastructure Services provides you almost all of the pros and cons of an on-premise development environment without having to manage the hardware.

■ **Tip**   You can learn how to create and set up an entire SharePoint 2013 Lab in the Cloud with Windows Azure Infrastructure Services at http://sprwd.com/cjqxzhg.

Choosing a Development Environment

Now that we have seen different types of development environments, we can determine which one is right for you. One method to determine the right environment to base your decision on your goals. Which examples in this book are most important to you? By looking at the tasks that you wish to accomplish, we can determine the best environment.

If you choose to use a cloud-based development environment, the best way to decide is to determine what your end needs are. Cloudshare provides a very inexpensive virtual machine development environment that you can create, remove, and replace in minutes. Cloudshare is best for those who want a development environment quickly but are willing to sacrifice some server configuration options. Rackspace, on the other hand, provides enterprise-level hosting services that are useful from development to full production on a large-scale farm. If you are looking for a more robust solution but are not as concerned about cost or the added time it might take to set up a development environment, Rackspace or Windows Azure is your best bet.

■ **Tip**   If you do not have a preexisting development environment available to you, and you wish to be able to work through all of the examples in this book, we recommend Cloudshare as the most cost-effective, hassle-free, feature-rich development environment.

Development Environment for Branding

To a great extent, the examples in this book relate around specific HTML and CSS design and UI tasks that might arise while branding a SharePoint 2013 site. As we have seen, most branding is accomplished with custom master pages, page layouts, CSS style sheets, images, and JavaScript files and libraries. None of these file types require a client-based .NET compiler such as Visual Studio 2012, nor do they require being built and deployed as an app. This being the case, your development environment can be much less complex than for developing apps. Your development environment could be any SharePoint installation that you have access to, including an off-site SharePoint development installation as well as a local virtual-machine-based SharePoint installation. Because you will access SharePoint using WebDAV with a client application such as Adobe Dreamweaver or SharePoint Designer 2013, you do not require direct access to the SharePoint hive the way you might for app development.

Therefore, if you are more interested in the branding aspects of this book, either an Office 365 Development Site or a cloud-based virtual machine from Cloudshare would work great. If, on the other hand, you intend to create and publish a branding app for SharePoint, you will likely need to consider an Office 365 Developer Site. This solution provides you the ability to create, package, and sell your branding App to the App Store much more quickly than with Cloudshare. Although this type of app development is outside of the scope of this book, in the case of a branding app, you would need a local installation of Visual Studio.

App Development Environment

App development, such as the Geolocation App developed in Chapter 12, might require a different type of development environment. This will depend on where you wish to host the app. As shown in Chapter 12, if you do not require access to server code (i.e., can use the JavaScript Object Model or the Client Side Object Model), a SharePoint hosted app will work. If this is the case, your development SharePoint installation need not be local, but does need to be configured with an isolated app domain. Office 365 is ideal in this situation.

If, on the other hand, your app requires full control permissions or access to server-side controls, your development environment must be a local, full SharePoint installation configured with an isolated app domain and Visual Studio 2012. In this case, without access to a local development environment provided by your organization, a third-party cloud provider such as Cloudshare is the way to go.

General Software Requirements

Successful SharePoint branding projects require certain types of software, many of which we describe and use throughout this book. We provided a list of software that you will need to have to work through the examples in this book in the Introduction. Next we introduce additional types of software that might help you with your project as well as specific software packages that we use ourselves and recommend.

Web Editor

Essentially every SharePoint 2013 branding project you encounter will require some sort of web site editing tool. With the power of WebDAV, any text editor will do, as you can map your SharePoint site's WebDAV directory in Windows Explorer. As we show in Chapter 4, we also can use WebDAV how to map to this directory on a Mac as well. Once your SharePoint site's WebDAV directory has been mapped, you can open .html, .css, and .js files, as well as copy images and other assets directly to your SharePoint site. Something as simple as Notepad might suffice. There are many more powerful tools that can help you write HTML and CSS code.

SharePoint Designer

If you have branded a SharePoint 2010 or SharePoint 2007 site before, you are probably familiar with SharePoint Designer (SPD). With the new release of SharePoint 2013, Microsoft again released a new version of SPD, SPD 2013. Most of the features available to us in SPD 2010 are also available to us in SPD 2013, except a few very important features, the most popular of which was the Design View in SPD 2010. The Design View has been removed from SPD 2013, so we can only work with .html, .master, and .aspx pages in Code View.

SPD 2013 is offered as a free download from Microsoft and can be found at www.microsoft.com/en-us/download.
Pros:

- Free.

- Connects quickly and natively with SharePoint 2013.

- Includes many additional tools such as the ability to insert web parts directly into your code.

- Provides additional functionality such as the ability to check in, check out, and publish files.

- Can set the default and custom master page without having to use the browser.

- Includes intelliSENSE for standard HTML and CSS tagging.

- A generally all-around web editor for SharePoint 2013 branding assets.

Cons:

- There is no Design View or WYSIWYG editor.

- Does not natively recognize HTML5 or CSS3 tags.

- Ongoing support from Microsoft might be limited. There is no guarantee that the next version of SharePoint will include an updated version of SPD.

Adobe Dreamweaver

Adobe Dreamweaver, currently a part of Adobe's Creative Suite, was just recently added as a valuable tool for directly branding SharePoint sites with the addition of Design Manager and general connectively with WebDAV now included with SharePoint 2013. Dreamweaver has been around for quite a while, and assuming you are using one of the more recent versions of Dreamweaver including CS6 or later, you can use many of the design features available in Dreamweaver for HTML5 and CSS3. Dreamweaver also includes a Design View like interface if you need to make simple design changes to a HTML master page or HTML page layout.

Using WebDAV, Dreamweaver can map itself to your SharePoint 2013 Master Page Gallery, thus allowing Dreamweaver to think it is working on a general site while SharePoint 2013 will handle the conversion of the .html files to .master and .aspx files.
Pros:

- A part of a very powerful suite of web site design tools, Adobe's Creative Suite.

- Recognizes HTML5 and CSS3.

- Includes autocomplete and tag assistance (i.e., intelliSENSE).

- Contains SPD 2010 Design View like features.

- Is generally one of the powerful HTML5/CSS3 web site design tools available.

Cons:

- Is not free.

- Does not natively connect to SharePoint 2013, meaning you must check out, check in, and publish files via the web interface or SPD 2013. Also does not provide access to set the default or custom master page. This too much be completed in the browser.

- The Design View is not perfect, as the HTML page layouts do not always include all of the necessary HTML for a perfect view of how a page layout might appear.

Notepad++

Another popular free tool for web site editing is Notepad++ (`http://notepad-plus-plus.org/`). Notepad++ is a very simple yet powerful source code editing tool for many languages, including HTML, CSS, and JavaScript. Be aware that this is a coder's tool; that is, it is for those of us who do not miss Design View in SharePoint 2013 because we never used it anyhow because it would mess up our HTML. If you are a coder and want an extremely lightweight tool to connect to your SharePoint 2013 branding assets, this is for you.

Pros:

- It's free.

- Excellent, simple coder's tool, providing a very lean program with little simple overhead so it loads fast and uses far fewer CPU cycles and memory than other design tools.

- Provides native recognition of most HTML, CSS, and JavaScript code, providing color coding and indentation.

Cons:

- Does not have any sort of Design View; this is a tool primarily for coders.

- Does not include autocomplete and tag assistance.

- Does not natively connect to SharePoint 2013, meaning you must check out, check in, and publish files via the web interface or SPD 2013. Also does not provide access to set the default or custom master page. This too much be completed in the browser.

Visual Studio

You will want to use Visual Studio 2012 (Ultimate, Premium, or Professional) if you intend to develop SharePoint Apps, especially those that will not be SharePoint hosted. As we saw previously in this Appendix, if you plan to develop simple apps for SharePoint, you might consider an Office 365 Developer Site using the Napa Development Tools App, as that way you can use a browser-based version of Visual Studio. For complex apps, a locally installed version of Visual Studio 2012 is the way to go.

Microsoft provides Visual Studio as its premier application development tool. This tool can do it all from C++ development to Visual Basic development and of course SharePoint 2013 branding and app development. As of December 2012, Expression Blend, Microsoft's primary competitor for Adobe Creative Suite, is being discontinued and bundled directly into Visual Studio. It appears as though Visual Studio might become the go-to tool for branding SharePoint 2013, although many developers already use Visual Studio for App development as well as for branding.

If you are building an app for SharePoint 2013 that utilizes the server-side object model, Visual Studio 2012 must be installed on the environment where SharePoint is hosted. With SharePoint 2010, we used to be able to install SharePoint directly in Windows 7 or Windows 8, but with SharePoint 2013, this is no longer the case. If you intend to use the client-side object model, you can connect a Visual Studio 2012 project to a SharePoint 2013 or Office 365 Developer Site for app development.

■ **Note** Learn how to create Office 365 and cloud-based development environments earlier in this Appendix.

When you install Visual Studio 2012 and Office Developer Tools for Visual Studio 2012, you get all of templates and tools to develop SharePoint 2013 on your local development machine.

Visual Studio Installation and Configuration

Installing Visual Studio and configuring it for SharePoint development is not difficult, but there are additional tools you will need to install.

1. Install a typical installation of Visual Studio 2012. Refer to MSDN for general instructions: http://sprwd.com/32nyugj.

2. After you have installed Visual Studio, you must download and install the Microsoft Office Developer Tools for Visual Studio 2012. Download this from MSDN at http://sprwd.com/ydnthq.

The Microsoft Office Developer Tools for Visual Studio 2012 will help you develop Apps for SharePoint-hosted, provider-hosted, and autohosted SharePoint Apps. If you intend to target x64-bit applications, you will need to install the x64-bit versions of the tool assemblies separately.

Image Editor

Although not directly required, it might be difficult to work with images needed throughout a site, including background images and textures and general site images without an image editor of some kind. We recommend any of the following.

Adobe Photoshop

Adobe Photoshop, also a part of Adobe's Creative Suite, is the go-to tool for image creation and manipulation. This is a powerful tool for creating site mockups as well as creating, editing, and manipulating specific site images. Learn more at www.adobe.com/products/photoshop.html.

Gimp

GNU Image Manipulation Program (GIMP; www.gimp.org) is an open source image manipulation program, very similar to Adobe Photoshop. Gimp is free, which is a huge plus, but if you are used to Photoshop then be ready for a shift in the development environment. The Gimp user interface is very different than the user interface for Photoshop. Once you get used to Gimp's interface, you will likely find that Gimp is just as powerful and feature rich as Photoshop.

Adobe Illustrator

Adobe Illustrator, again a part of Adobe's Creative Suite, provides a vector-based graphics tool. Illustrator was originally used for print projects such as banners, flyers, pamphlets, and so on, but for quite a while now it has also been used for web site mockup development as well as vector-based image creation. If you have not used a vector-based graphics program such as Illustrator you might be in for a shock. You will find that Illustrator has powerful mockup tools that can help you create images that can scale quickly and near perfectly because of the vector-based properties of graphics storage within Illustrator.

A big plus with Illustrator is that if you create image assets such as logos, background textures, and so on, in Illustrator, you can quickly copy these over to Photoshop or Gimp, even if you need to provide pixel placement of additional elements.

Xara Web Designer

Xara Web Designer (`www.xara.com/us/products/webdesigner/`) is a very simple yet powerful web site design tool, targeting web site builders. The tool is inexpensive, yet it provides a feature-rich, template-based solution that gives the designer complete control of page layouts. It is kind of like a mashup of a web site editing tool such as Dreamweaver and a graphics tool such as Photoshop. The end mockups can be saved as layered Photoshop files for additional editing in Photoshop or even Gimp. But as an added plus, as you are creating a mockup of your sites and page layouts, Xara Web Designer also creates the HTML, CSS, and JavaScript necessary to generate the look you design. Xara Web Designer is therefore not only a graphics tool, but a light web site editor tool as well. We list it here as an image editor tool because you will likely want to use another web editor tool such as SPD, Dreamweaver, or even Notepad++ to tweak the HTML published by Xara Web Designer before importing your code to SharePoint 2013 Design Manager.

Summary

In this appendix we reviewed the different development environments available to you, including on-premise development, development for Office 365, and development on a cloud service such as Cloudshare. We dove into each environment type and walked through the installation or setup process. We concluded with a look at the different software packages that will make working with and developing for SharePoint 2013 possible.

Index

■ J, K

■ L

■ M

■ N, O, P